THE WORLD'S CLASSICS

LEVIATHAN

THOMAS HOBBES was born near Malmesbury in Wiltshire in 1588. Well taught in local schools and, from his own reports, ill taught at Oxford, he was employed as tutor and secretary by the Cavendish family for much of his life. His three tours of the Continent before 1640 introduced him to the new learning of Galileo and others, and established the connections necessary for his sojourn in Paris, 1640–51, during the English Civil Wars.

His first substantial original work was *The Elements of Law* (1640). Its arguments concerning nature, man, and society were redeployed and extended in *De Cive* (1642), his masterpiece *Leviathan* (1651), and *De Corpore* (1655), as well as in numerous other fiercely controversial publications.

Popularly condemned for his political philosophy, his analysis of morality, and his 'atheism', his works were nevertheless widely read in England and Europe. After the Restoration in 1660 he survived his own notoriety under the protection of Charles II and the Earl of Devonshire. He died at Hardwick Hall in 1679, his character as a philosopher almost universally denigrated; his character as a man able to attract the kindness and friendship of almost all who knew him.

JOHN GASKIN is the Professor of Naturalistic Philosophy and Head of the Department of Philosophy in the University of Dublin. He is also a Fellow of Trinity College Dublin. A graduate of Oxford University, his publications include *The Quest for Eternity* (1984), *Hume's Philosophy of Religion* (1988 and 1993), and *Varieties of Unbelief* (1989). He has previously edited a volume of David Hume's works on religion and Hobbes's *The Elements of Law* for World's Classics. His latest publication is *The Epicurean Philosophers* (1995), which includes translations of the complete works of Epicurus and Lucretius.

THE WORLD'S CLASSICS

———

THOMAS HOBBES

Leviathan

———

Edited with an Introduction by
J. C. A. GASKIN
Fellow of Trinity College Dublin

Oxford New York

OXFORD UNIVERSITY PRESS

1996

Oxford University Press, Walton Street, Oxford OX2 6DP

Oxford New York
Athens Auckland Bangkok Bombay
Calcutta Cape Town Dar as Salaam Delhi
Florence Hong Kong Istanbul Karachi
Kuala Lumpur Madras Madrid Melbourne
Mexico City Nairobi Paris Singapore
Taipei Tokyo Toronto
and associated companies in
Berlin Ibadan

Oxford is a trade mark of Oxford University Press

Editorial matter © J. C. A. Gaskin 1996

First published as a World's Classics paperback 1996

British Library Cataloguing in Publication Data
Data available

Library of Congress Cataloging in Publication Data
Hobbes, Thomas, 1588–1679.
Leviathan/Thomas Hobbes; edited with an introduction by J.C.A. Gaskin.
(World's classics)
Includes bibliographical references and index.
1. Political science—Early works to 1800. 2. State, The. I. Gaskin, J.C.A.
(John Charles Addison) II. Title. III. Series.
JC153.H65 1996 320.1—dc20 95-40506
ISBN 0-19-282392-2 (pbk.)

1 3 5 7 9 10 8 6 4 2

Typeset by Best-set Typesetter Ltd., Hong Kong
Printed and bound in Great Britain by
Mackays of Chatham PLC,
Chatham, Kent

PREFACE

No one can pretend that editions of *Leviathan* are now few or hard to locate. But they often represent editorial extremes. One extreme retains antique spelling, every odd use of italics or capital letters, and even the curiosities of seventeenth-century typography. The other extreme changes italics, punctuation, paragraph lengths, and in short anything (except the order of the words themselves) which the editor thinks will make the text easier to read according to the fashion of the moment. The normal reader will surely look for something between these extremes: something which reproduces as faithfully as possible what Hobbes actually sanctioned for publication, but without the accidental impediments which play no part in what Hobbes meant or what he wished to be read. I have attempted to provide such a text. It is free from antique spellings and printing conventions which had no significance even in the seventeenth century. It is authentic and complete in all other respects.

The notes—philosophical, textual, historical, and biographical—offer information if it is wanted. They make a special effort to indicate where the thought and arguments of *Leviathan* may be followed in other of Hobbes's major philosophical works. The Introduction takes up some of the more obvious issues raised by *Leviathan* without attempting any grand assessment. A great philosophical text should be read with the new eyes of each generation, sharpened by relevant information, not directed by old judgements. The judgements and the overviews can be built into the picture later. The excitement of the ideas must come first.

To facilitate references to and within the text I have inserted a new run of paragraph numbers for each chapter, as Hobbes himself did in his other main philosophical works. For the same reason I have put the page numbers of the original 1651 edition in the margins: a mode of reference used by a number of commentators.

All the editorial material is new with the exception of two notes and parts of five paragraphs which are adapted from similar material in my World's Classics edition of *The Elements of Law* (*Human Nature* and *De Corpore Politico*). I am grateful to the work done by Richard Tuck in recording in his edition of *Leviathan* the variants in the large paper copies. As explained in the Note on the Text, these are incorporated into the present edition.

I would like to express my indebtedness to my editor, Judith Luna, for her patience and encouragement, and to William Lyons for his friendly advice and generous help. I would further like to express my gratitude to Trinity College Dublin, for awarding me a grant from the Arts and Social Sciences Benefactions Fund to enable me to undertake some of the work required, to Marsh's Library for allowing me access to their copies of the Head edition, and finally again to Trinity College for granting me sabbatical leave to bring this book to a conclusion.

JOHN GASKIN

CONTENTS

A Scheme of Reference   ix

Introduction   xi

A Note on the Text   xliv

Select Bibliography   l

Chronology   liii

LEVIATHAN   I

    The Epistle Dedicatory   3

    The Contents of the Chapters   5

    The Introduction   7

    Part 1. OF MAN   9

    Part 2. OF COMMONWEALTH   111

    Part 3. OF A CHRISTIAN COMMONWEALTH   247

    Part 4. OF THE KINGDOM OF DARKNESS   403

    A Review, and Conclusion   467

Explanatory Notes   477

Index of Subjects   501

A SCHEME OF REFERENCE

Elements of Law	*The Elements of Law Natural and Politic* (1640), Part I *Human Nature*, Part II *De Corpore Politico*, ed. J. C. A. Gaskin (World's Classics, 1994).
De Cive	*Philosophical Rudiments concerning Government and Society* (1651), the English version of the Latin *De Cive* (1642), ed. Howard Warrender (Oxford, 1983). Spelling has been modernized in quotations cited.
Leviathan	*Leviathan, or The Matter, Form, and Power of a Commonwealth Ecclesiastical and Civil* (1651).
De Corpore	*Elements of Philosophy, the First Section concerning Body* (1656), the English version of the Latin *De Corpore* (1655). Quotations are from the first volume of the *English Works of Thomas Hobbes*, ed. W. Molesworth (London, 1839).
White's De Mundo Examined	*Thomas White's De Mundo Examined* (written *c.*1641) translated from the Latin by H. W. Jones and first published 1976 (Bradford University Press).

In all the above editions Hobbes or his editors have numbered the chapters in a single run of numbers from start to finish ignoring the Parts. Except in the case of *Leviathan* (where they are supplied in the present text), Hobbes also numbered the paragraphs or 'articles' in each chapter. This provides a convenient and brief method of reference to the works. Thus, for example, *De Cive*, X. 6, means chapter X, paragraph 6. Until the *Clarendon Edition of the Works of Thomas Hobbes* is completed, other works of his must still be referred to in the *English Works of Thomas Hobbes*, ed. W. Molesworth, 11 vols. (London, 1839). For short reference, *English Works*, followed by volume and page.

INTRODUCTION

THE memorable vividness of language, the sustained interconnections of argument, the insistent logic, the vast scale of the structure, and the learning and mental power required to sustain it all: these never fail in *Leviathan*. The result is one of the most powerful, influential, and eagerly refuted books ever written, and the only work in English on political philosophy that ranks with Plato, Aristotle, Hegel, and Marx.

Education, Influences, and Outcomes

Thomas Hobbes was born on 5 April 1588 at Westport, adjoining Malmesbury in Wiltshire, where his father was parson—a man who 'disesteemed learning . . . as not knowing the sweetness of it'[1]—and who vanished early from the scene after assaulting one of his parishioners. His brother, Francis Hobbes, a wealthy glover without children of his own, thus assumed responsibility *in loco parentis* for the costs of young Thomas's education.

At the age of 4 Hobbes went to Westport Church School, and at 8 to a private school at Malmesbury, where, according to his biographer Aubrey, he became proficient in Greek and Latin under the instruction of 'a good Graecian . . . the first that came into our parts hereabout since the Reformation'. In early 1603 he matriculated at Magdalen Hall, Oxford (the buildings are now part of Magdalen College) and there acquired the life-long distaste for universities which surfaces not infrequently in *Leviathan* and in his polemical disputes with academics. Poised between the out-moded fashion for burning heretics, and the minor vindictiveness of refus-ing honorary degrees, Oxford belatedly vent its anger upon Hobbes in 1683 by ordering copies of *De Cive* and *Leviathan* to be burnt along with other 'Pernicious Books and Damnable Doctrines' on account of their being 'Heretical and Blasphemous, infamous to Christian Religion, and destructive of all Government in Church and State'.[2] But, academic ani-mosities apart, Oxford in the first decade of the seventeenth century

---

[1] This, and many other charming details about Hobbes's character and life, can be found in John Aubrey's 'Brief Life'. This life, together with translations of Hobbes's own 'Prose Life' and 'Verse Life' (both originally written in Latin) can be found in the World's Classics edition of *The Elements of Law* (*Human Nature* and *De Corpore Politico*), Oxford, 1994.

[2] *The Judgement and Decree of the University of Oxford Past in their Convocation* (Oxford, 1683). Quoted in S. I. Mintz, *The Hunting of Leviathan* (Cambridge, 1969).

indeed seems to have had little to commend it. Its intellectual enterprise was, according to Hobbes, jejune scholastic logic and useless Aristotelian physics. As usual, its students were prone to drunken brawling; less usually, its politics sheltered both Papal and Puritan sedition. Anthony Wood records that in 1608, just after Hobbes went down, 'a young forward bachelor' was disciplined for maintaining 'that it was lawful for a subject, in cause of religion, to forsake his prince, and take up arms against him';[3] a principle that was to cast a long and destructive shadow over seventeenth-century life and politics.

In early 1608 Hobbes graduated BA, having for no ascertainable reason spent one more than the then normal four years at the University. At the same time he was recommended by the Principal of Magdalen Hall to Sir William Cavendish (created Earl of Devonshire in 1618) as tutor and travelling companion to his eldest son. Although his employment was interrupted by force of circumstances on several occasions, Hobbes was eventually to sever his connections with the Cavendish family only under the force of final circumstances when he died at Hardwick Hall on 4 December 1679.

In the thirty years after 1608, Hobbes published nothing but a translation of Thucydides' *History of the Peloponnesian War*. It is strange to speak of the formative years of a man's life as being between the ages of 20 and 52, but so it was with Hobbes. Before 1640 he had probably written no original work.[4] Between 1640 and his death, his philosophical works in English fill seven massive volumes in the Molesworth edition, and these of course do not include original Latin works like *De Homine* and the unpublished *White's De Mundo Examined* (see Scheme of Reference, p. ix). But the grounds for this extraordinary late flowering were being prepared throughout what, for Hobbes, counted as his long youth. The biographical chronology is somewhat difficult to establish, and the personal details are fragmentary, but the preparation clearly included Hobbes's knowledge and experience of the forces and events which led to the outbreak of civil war in 1642, together with a number of intellectual stimuli encountered piecemeal in his reading and travels.

Throughout the period 1603 (when the United Kingdom of England

---

[3] Quoted in George Croom Robertson, *Hobbes* (Edinburgh and London, 1886), 5. Even in 1995, this is still the only reasonably extensive compilation of information about Hobbes's life.

[4] A possible exception is the semi-Aristotelian 'Short Tract on First Principles', maybe written by Hobbes about 1630 and first published in 1889 as an Appendix to F. Tönnies's edition of *The Elements of Law*.

and Scotland was established at the accession of James I) to 1642 (when civil war finally broke out between Charles I and the rebellious parliamentarians) civil society was increasingly threatened by claims that private consciences in matters of religion could absolve a man from his legal obligations to a sovereign, by Roman and Presbyterian claims to authority which could override the secular powers in a body politic, and by conflicts between king and parliament concerning the right to raise taxes, the government of the Church (and what sort of Church), the direction of foreign policy, and other constitutional matters.

The common consent of historians is that James did not have the political abilities and personal authority of his august predecessor, Elizabeth I, and almost from the beginning tensions developed between the high-handed episcopalian king and his ever more puritanical and commercially minded parliaments. But in the new conditions, as Davies observes,

it is very doubtful whether even Queen Elizabeth could have succeeded, for both these sovereigns regarded parliament as an unwelcome and intrusive body that had to be cajoled by occasional concessions into granting much-needed subsidies. Consequently they directed all their efforts to excluding the estates from any share in administration and listened to criticisms only when they either became unusually vehement or when the fiscal situation was especially serious.[5]

When this attitude was combined, as it was combined in both James I and Charles I (who succeeded his father in 1625), with a belief that a king had a divine right to govern and, moreover, to govern the established Church as a high Anglican in an increasingly puritanical country, the conditions for conflict with a parliament (whose constitutional lawyers were intent on returning to a supposed time in which Lords and Commons had more authority) were all in place.

In 1629 Charles dismissed his parliament and for eleven years ruled by royal prerogative with great care and economy. But in 1640 a need for money to raise an army to contain the rebellion of Presbyterian forces in Scotland obliged him to summon a parliament, the 'Short Parliament'. It sat in May 1640. The king could get nothing from it but unacceptable demands, and it was speedily dissolved. But the king's financial plight was now so serious that another parliament had to be called. In November 1640 the anti-Royalist Long Parliament met for the first time. The increasingly desperate move and counter-move of king and Commons over the next eighteen months precipitated the now virtually inevitable civil war.

[5] Godfrey Davies, *The Early Stuarts 1603–1660* (Oxford, 1959), 15.

Separated by religious, constitutional, social, and economic differences, Royalists and Parliamentarians fought it out over four years. The issue was defeat for the Royalists. The king surrendered to the Scots in May 1646. In 1649 he was executed in London. After what was in effect a second civil war, 1648–51, in which Cromwell's army suppressed rebellions in Scotland and Ireland and Royalist risings in Wales, Cromwell became Lord Protector. In 1660, after the death of Cromwell, Charles II was restored as king by general agreement.

It is virtually certain that Hobbes became aware of the acute political dangers inherent in combining constitutional problems with dogmatic and divisive religious convictions while he was still at Oxford. It is a fact indisputable that sixty years later, in *Behemoth* or *The History of the Causes of the Civil Wars of England*, he maintained that 'the core of rebellion . . . are the Universities'. The reasons he gives for this judgement are illuminating:

And as the Presbyterians brought with them into their churches their divinity [Calvinism] from the universities, so did many of the gentlemen bring their politics from thence into the Parliament; but neither of them did this very boldly in the time of Queen Elizabeth. And . . . certainly the chief leaders were ambitious ministers and ambitious gentlemen; the ministers envying the authority of bishops, whom they thought less learned; and the gentlemen envying the privy-council, whom they thought less wise than themselves. For it is a hard matter for men, who do all think highly of their own wits, when they have also acquired the learning of the university, to be persuaded that they want any ability requisite for the government of a commonwealth, especially having read the glorious histories . . . of the ancient popular governments of the Greeks and Romans, amongst whom . . . popular government . . . passed by the name of liberty. (*English Works*, vi. 192–3)

What is more, Hobbes's awareness of the dangers in the political situation between 1608 and 1640 was made more acute and immediate by his continuous association with men of considerable power in the state: the Cavendishes, Bacon (who was Lord Chancellor in 1618—Hobbes acted as amanuensis for him in the early 1620s), the Earl of Newcastle (another Cavendish), and Sir Gervase Clifton, among others.

The political fears and dangers that formed the background against which Hobbes began to write in 1640 are a matter of history. The intellectual background is less accessible, but at least five special influences can be identified. They are:

1. Particularly prior to 1628, when Hobbes's 'young master' died (by then the second Earl of Devonshire), Hobbes had the unusual advantage of free access to the libraries at the great houses of the Cavendishes, Chatsworth and Hardwick Hall. As Hobbes wrote in 1629 in the dedicat-

ory letter to his Thucydides, addressed to the third Earl, then only 10 years old, 'For by the experience of many years . . . I have this: there was not any, who more really . . . favoured those that studied the liberal arts more liberally, than my Lord your father did; nor in whose house, a man should less need the university than in his.'

2. When Hobbes went down from Oxford, he was competent in Latin and Greek. Within a few years, by his own admission, he had become rusty as a consequence of attending to the social affairs of his employers. Some time about 1616 he set about repairing his knowledge. As a result he became able to communicate accurately and with sophistication in the common language of European learning, Latin. His first work published on the Continent, *De Cive*, and much of his correspondence in the 1640s were in that language. His recovery of an expert command of Greek—then a rare accomplishment—shows itself in his distinguished translation of Thucydides published in 1629.

3. As his subsequent references show, Thucydides provided an enduring lesson for Hobbes. The lesson was that Athenian democracy was ultimately incapable of imposing the unity of organization and the continuity of purpose required for the successful prosecution of policies needed for the long-term preservation of the commonwealth; democracy was not a bad, but an inefficient species of sovereign power.

4. Hobbes enjoyed a belated but influential encounter (in about 1628 if Aubrey is correct) with the geometry of Euclid; an encounter which not only led him to a sometimes disastrously misguided practice of the skill, but much more importantly drew his attention to the use of definitions in rigorous argument. In *Leviathan* he was to call geometry 'the only science that it hath pleased God hitherto to bestow on mankind' (IV. 12; see also V. 7). Be that as it may, geometry was, and remained until the middle of the nineteenth century, the paradigm for deductive probity.

5. It is possible that Hobbes left Oxford with some unfocused awareness that traditional academic instruction was worthless in relation to the new ideas that were appearing on the Continent. It is certain that three extensive visits to Europe with his noble charges (1610–c.1615, 1629–30, and 1634–6) not only gave him a fluent knowledge of French and some ability in Italian, but also established his unbounded enthusiasm for optics and for the new science of motion. In his travels he met and talked with Galileo and Gassendi, and through friendship with Marin Mersenne established the intellectual connections that were to be so valuable during his long residence in Paris in the 1640s. His encounter with questions about the mechanical nature of sensation was particularly influential. According

to his own report, written in the third person in 'The Prose Life' (1676), this took place in Paris during his sojourn in 1636/7 when he was there as mentor to the third Earl of Devonshire:

When he became aware of the variety of movement contained in the natural world, he first inquired as to the nature of these motions, to determine the ways in which they might effect the senses, the intellect, the imagination, together with the other natural properties. He communicated his findings on a daily basis to the Reverend Father Marin Mersenne, of the Order of the Minim Brothers, a scholar who was venerated as an outstanding exponent of all branches of philosophy.

Out of this crucible of influences and skills—acute awareness of political dangers, access to learned men and great libraries, travel, skill in Latin and Greek, the warnings of Thucydides, addiction to geometry and fascination with optics, mechanics, and contemporary theories of sensation—emerged, in 1640, Hobbes's first original work, *The Elements of Law Natural and Politic*. It was initially circulated in a number of manuscript copies and eventually printed in 1650 as two separate volumes, *Human Nature* and *De Corpore Politico*.

At the end of 1640 Hobbes fled to Paris to avoid the impending civil strife in England, and in fear lest the *Elements of Law* might put him in danger from the warring parties. For although its immediate implication would have been support for the king, it gave final legitimacy to any *de facto* government. In Paris, and in the stimulating company of Mersenne, Gassendi, eventually Descartes, and others in Mersenne's salon, Hobbes's philosophical writings grew rapidly. In 1642 *De Cive* appeared in Paris (two further Latin editions were published in Amsterdam in 1647, and the English version in London in 1651).

In 1646 he was working on *De Corpore*, although it was not to be published until 1655. In the same year he became tutor in mathematics—politics were expressly excluded from his brief—to the future Charles II, then sheltering in Paris. The following summer he suffered a serious illness from which dates the palsy which eventually compelled him to make use of an amanuensis in all his writing. Despite this, *Leviathan* was written in Paris between about 1648 and 1651. The exact commencement and conclusion of the activity cannot be ascertained. But John Aubrey's account of a typical day's work in his later years could easily describe the way *Leviathan* was written:

He rose about seven, had his breakfast of bread and butter; and took his walk, meditating till ten; then he did put down the minute of his thoughts, which he penned in the afternoon ... He was never idle; his thoughts were always working . . . His dinner was provided for him exactly by eleven . . . After dinner he took a pipe of tobacco, and then threw himself immediately on his bed . . . and took a nap of about half an hour. In the afternoon he penned his morning thoughts.

Leviathan was published in London in 1651, probably in May, and Hobbes returned to his own country, this time to stay, early in the following year. The return was not entirely what he might have chosen in other circumstances despite being, as he said, minded to go home after so long a sojourn abroad. But *Leviathan* had offended the Royalists in Paris on account of its 'atheism' and the political ambiguity already noticed in *The Elements of Law*. It also antagonized the French clerical authorities because of its unsparing attack upon the political claims of the Roman Church. Hobbes felt unsafe. In London, after a wretched journey from France, he made his submission to the Council of State and resumed private life, mainly in the capital, pouring out vigorously controversial works on liberty and necessity, mathematics, Boyle's scientific method, physics (*De Corpore*), human nature (*De Homine*), histories, books on law, and latterly translations of Homer.

For all his reputed disputatiousness and refusal to admit himself wrong, even when manifestly in error, and despite the violent attacks provoked by the supposed irreligion, moral subversion, and ambiguous political allegiance of *Leviathan*, Hobbes was a man much befriended by the good and the great. Clarendon liked him despite attacking his ideas. Charles II treated him with a bemused and protective affection once he was king. Aubrey revered him. The Cavendish family befriended him almost throughout his long life.

In 1675 Hobbes was still mainly resident in London. But he was 87 years old, and while most of his critics thought it time he departed to a much hotter world, he himself chose merely to retire to a better one in Derbyshire. At Chatsworth he was cherished and sustained by the Cavendish family. In October 1679 he suffered a strangury—a retention of urine—'I shall be glad then to find a hole to creep out of the world at.' On about 28 November he suffered a stroke. He died on 4 December at the great age of 91. A broadsheet which circulated in London after his death concluded:

> Ninety years' eating and immortal Jobs
> Here MATTER lies, and there's an end of Hobbes!

But it was not. Despite the hostility of politicians, despite angry refutations by countless[6] books and pamphlets, and despite the Convocation of Oxford

---

[6] Not exactly countless. S. I. Mintz, in his outstanding monograph *The Hunting of Leviathan*, identifies 107 up to the end of the century.

University, neither ballad-makers, nor divines, nor academics, nor politicians could bury the ideas as nature had ultimately buried the man.

The Grand Design in Three Parts

At some time in the early 1640s, possibly as early as the writing of *The Elements of Law* (which reads like a first mapping of the ideas), Hobbes had conceived a vast design for a systematic account of science and philosophy: a basic or first philosophy (essentially materialism), a natural science (mainly the mechanics of moving bodies), and a human physiology and psychology (based on the mechanics) leading to a moral and political philosophy. In short it was to be an account of 'body natural' leading to an account of what in *The Elements* he calls 'body politic' or, more famously, to an account of the 'artificial man' which *is* Leviathan.[7]

The idea for such a comprehensive philosophy was first announced in *De Cive*, in the Latin 'Preface to the Reader' which Hobbes added in the Amsterdam edition of 1647. In the words of the English version of 1651:

I was studying Philosophy for my mind's sake, and I had gathered together its first Elements in all kinds, and having digested them into three Sections by degrees, I thought to have written them so as in the first I would have treated of a body, and its general properties; in the second of man and his special faculties, and affections; in the third, of civil government and the duties of Subjects: Wherefore the first Section would have contained the first Philosophy, and certain elements of Physics; in it we would have considered the reasons of Time, Place, Cause, Power, Relation, Proportion, Quantity, Figure and motion. In the second we would have been conversant about imagination, Memory, intellect, ratiocination, appetite, will, good and evil, honest and dishonest, and the like.

The third section is *De Cive* itself. Part of Hobbes's summary of it in the Preface is also a description of what had already been his main concerns in the chapters XIV–XXIX of *The Elements of Law* and what, with many additions, would be his central concern in *Leviathan*. In the words of the *De Cive* Preface:

I demonstrate in the first place, that the state of men without civil society (which state we may properly call the state of nature) is nothing else but a mere war of all against all; and in that war all men have equal right unto all things; Next, that all men as soon as they arrive to understanding of this hateful condition, do desire (even nature itself compelling them) to be freed from this misery. But that this

---

[7] *Leviathan* is the name of the text. 'Leviathan' is Hobbes's name for the organic structure which is the sovereign power and people together. The name is full of associations. See note to p. 7 of the text.

cannot be done except by compact, they all quit that right which they have unto all things. Furthermore I declare, and confirm what the nature of compacts is; how and by what means the right of one might be transferred unto another to make their compacts valid; also what rights, and to whom they must necessarily be granted for the establishing of Peace, I mean what those dictates of reason are, which may properly be termed the Laws of Nature.

In *De Corpore*, I. 9, a part of the work written about the same time as the Preface to *De Cive*, but not published until 1655, Hobbes describes a very similar progression of philosophy and science, but in different terms:

The principal parts of philosophy are two. For two chief kinds of bodies, and very different from one another, offer themselves to such as search after their generation and properties; one whereof being the work of nature, is called a *natural body*, the other is called a *commonwealth*, and is made by the wills and agreement of men. And from these spring the two parts of philosophy, called *natural* and *civil*. But seeing that, for the knowledge of the properties of a commonwealth, it is necessary first to know the dispositions, affections, and the manners of men, civil philosophy is again commonly divided into two parts, whereof one, which treats of men's dispositions and manners, is called *ethics*; and the other, which takes cognizance of their civil duties, is called *politics*, or simply *civil philosophy*. In the first place, therefore (after I have set down such premises as appertain to the nature of philosophy in general), I will discourse of *bodies natural*; in the second, of the *dispositions and manners of men*; and in the third, of the *civil duties of subjects*.

From this outline it will be evident that even if Hobbes had never written *Leviathan*, much of its content would have been conveyed in one way or another by his other works, particularly if *The Elements of Law* and *De Cive* are read as a whole. What Hobbes did in *Leviathan*, under the pressure of urgent concern about the civil and religious wars in England, was to produce a brilliant additional statement of his ideas, complete in itself, but sustained by the substructure of his philosophical system.[8] The focus of

[8] Hobbes did complete his systematic 'three sections' of philosophy, but not in their logical order. Taking the proposed logical order as a pattern, his publications, including *Leviathan*, complete it as follows:

FIRST PHILOSOPHY, (*a*) philosophy in general: *Elements of Law*, chs. I–VI; *De Corpore*, chs. I–VI; *White's De Mundo Examined*, chs. I and XXX (not published until 1976), *Leviathan*, I–V. (*b*) BODY or BODY NATURAL: *De Corpore*, chs. VII–XXX, with numerous sections concerning mathematics and geometry. (The account of body natural is largely taken for granted in *Leviathan*.)

MAN: *Elements of Law*, chs. VII–XIII; *De Homine* (which also includes much material on optics), *Leviathan*, VI–XI.

COMMONWEALTH or BODY POLITIC (including the thesis that 'man by nature is in a state of war' and the Laws of Nature): *Elements of Law*, chs. XIV–XXIX; *De Cive*, chs. I–XIV, *Leviathan*, XII–XXXI. Matters arising, (*a*) because woven into the fabric of the body politic,

attention of the new work was an analysis of the breakdown in civil society, and the construction of a political philosophy that would obviate the causes of such a breakdown.

The Structure of Leviathan

The main outline of Hobbes's thesis in *Leviathan* can be stated briefly. He states it himself at the end of Part 2 (XXXI. 1 and 5).[9] It is first argued that human nature is commonly concerned with self-preservation, and with the attaining of whatever each individual holds to be his or her personal and individual good. Given that human nature usually functions in this way, then its unrestrained outcome will be a miserable conflict of isolated individuals, each taking what he can get. Hobbes calls this the 'state of war'. However, human beings have the sagacity to discern what articles of peace (or 'laws of nature') have to be enforced in order to avoid the state of war of each against every man. But it is usually unsafe or disadvantageous for individuals to be bound by these articles unless everyone else is at the same time similarly bound. This binding of all to observe the laws of nature is achieved by a compact in which each gives up the right of nature (to do whatever he or she wants at any given moment) to a sovereign power in a civil society. The sovereign enforces the laws of nature, and all that follows from that. The rest of *Leviathan* is concerned with defining religious, legal, and constitutional structures which will sustain the sovereign power in a peaceful and secure body politic, rather than lead to the breakdowns Hobbes had experienced.

A similar thesis had earlier been set out by Hobbes in *The Elements of Law*. There is in both books a preliminary attempt to relate a basic mechanic of body and motion to sensation, and sensation to the push–pull of desires and aversions. There is in both a consequential analysis of what unconstrained human beings in fact are, and how they function. There is an account of the state of war: what life would be like if human beings acted in accordance with the natures they really have. There is in both books an account of the rational precepts (or 'laws of nature') we have to adopt if we

---

RELIGION (or BODY SPIRITUAL): *Elements of Law*, chs. XI, XXV, and XXVI; *De Cive*, chs. XV–XVIII, *Leviathan*, XII, XXXII–XLVII; (*b*) because a major philosophical dispute arising from the nature of man: LIBERTY and NECESSITY: touched upon in *Elements of Law* and *De Cive*, extensively examined in the controversy with Bishop Bramhall *Of Liberty and Necessity* (1654) and *Questions concerning Liberty, Necessity and Chance* (1656), touched upon in *Leviathan*.

[9] If a chapter and paragraph reference is given without the title of the work attached, the reference will be to the present text of *Leviathan*.

are to avoid the state of war. There is an account of how the end, peace, can be attained if each man yields some of his natural freedom to a common power, a sovereign. Finally, but much more extensively in *Leviathan*, there is an account of how the forces that destroy the body politic can be restrained: particularly the forces of religion.

Before examining some of the details in this structure, it should be noted that in *Leviathan* Hobbes virtually takes for granted both a fundamental ontological position, a form of materialism which I shall call 'one-world realism', and a philosophical method which might be called 'argument by definition'.

One-World Realism

Hobbes's fundamental ontology is that the constituents of the universe are '*imagined space*', that which may be filled, and which appears to be external to us (*De Corpore*, VII. 2), together with something, *body*, which is 'that, which having no dependence upon our thought, is coincident or coextended with some part of space', and so fills 'that which some call *real space*' (*De Corpore*, VIII. 1). Given this ontology, it is further taken as evident that bodies move,[10] and that they have other related features such as solidity which result in the mechanical communication of motion.

Although Hobbes has somewhat greater concern with problems about perception—how the 'external' world relates to each person's 'internal' experience—his fundamental position is essentially the same as the ancient archetype of unified materialism to be found in Democritus and Epicurus. Thus in the 'Letter to Herodotus' Epicurus maintained that:

The whole of being consists of bodies and space. For the existence of bodies is everywhere attested by sense itself, and it is upon sensation that reason must rely when it attempts to infer the unknown from the known. And if there were no space (which we call also void, and place, and intangible nature), bodies would have nothing in which to be and through which to move, as they are plainly seen to move. Beyond bodies and space there is nothing which by mental apprehension or on its analogy we can conceive to exist.[11]

Hobbes's own emphatic statement of an almost identical position is in *Leviathan*, XXXIV. 2, and again in XLVI. 15:

[10] The movement Hobbes (and of course Galileo) is concerned with is the reversal of the principle of Aristotle's that bodies are at rest unless something moves them. Hobbes is closer to the Epicurean premiss that everything moves unless something stops the motion. His account of the law of inertia is in *De Corpore*, VIII. 19. See also *Leviathan*, II. 2.

[11] See John Gaskin (ed.), *The Epicurean Philosophers* (London and Vermont, 1995), 14. For Lucretius' treatment of the same topic see *De Rerum Natura*, Book I, lines 329–35 and 430–48: ibid. 95 and 97.

the *universe*, that is, the whole mass of all things that are . . . is corporeal, that is to say, body; and hath the dimensions of magnitude, namely, length, breadth, and depth: also every part of body, is likewise body, and hath the like dimensions; and consequently every part of the universe, is body, and that which is not body, is no part of the universe: and because the universe is all, that which is no part of it, is *nothing*; and consequently *nowhere*.

Such an ontology was unproblematic for the Epicureans. For them the human soul is a mortal part of the human body, the gods (who anyway have no concern for us or awareness of us) exist as the most rarefied of bodies in inter-mundane space, and things move of themselves because of the inherent movement of their constituent particles. But Hobbes cannot reach *exactly* these conclusions in the context of the Christianity he was required to affirm, and which would certainly cause him to be punished here and now if he did not affirm it. Nevertheless his argument in *Leviathan* goes an astonishingly long way towards affirming a species of theistic materialism. Spirits are bodies of a sort. The soul is life. God is corporeal. I will call this meta-philosophy, whether Epicurean or Hobbesian, one-world realism. It is one-world because it explicitly excludes any other order of being: all that is has to be explained within *one* system. It is realism because it both minimizes philosophical problems concerning the relation between 'external' and 'internal' experience, and because it excludes as unreal all that is not of this, the natural, world. Hobbes does indeed retain and use the term 'supernatural', but it is in order to indicate an epistemological distinction between scientific knowledge and the way in which God 'speaks' or conveys a revelation to a few, and only a *very* few people. The supernatural is a rare source of extraordinary knowledge, not an order of being metaphysically distinct from this one. (See III. 7; VIII. 22; XII. 19, 22, 24; XV. 8; XXIX. 8; XXXIV. 20, *et al.*)

Why does Hobbes so comprehensively adhere to one-world realism? Because it does away with the 'insignificant speech' of the despised academic theologians, because it fits in with ordinary sense experience, because it is and was to remain the foundation of the explanatory success of the new post-Aristotelian sciences, and because it lends itself to the whole sweep of argument in *Leviathan* that connects body natural with body politic, and religion (matters concerning body spiritual) with both.

Argument by Definition

The process of definition is rooted in Hobbes's account of language, given briefly in *Leviathan*, IV, and also in *Elements of Law*, V. In simple terms he regards language as names added together by association. Each name 'is the voice of a man, arbitrarily imposed, for a mark to bring to his mind some conception [image, idea, or understanding] concerning the thing on which it is imposed' (*Elements*, V. 2). His later account in *De Corpore*, II. 4, makes it clear that the mark must somehow bring to *our* minds a *shared* conception. Language is between people, not distinct for each person. But, on occasions, it is necessary to be particularly clear about exactly what conception a compounded name brings to mind. (A compounded name is one which contains several conceptions, as 'bird' contains the conceptions 'bipedal', 'beaked', 'feathered', etc. On Hobbes's showing most names will be compounded and therefore capable of such analytical explication.) Or it may be necessary to introduce a new compounded name to unite conceptions previously separated (for example, 'endeavour' as introduced by Hobbes in *Leviathan*, VI. 1, and in *De Corpore*, XV. 2). Or it may be necessary, especially when teaching or communicating knowledge, to separate a compounded name into its component conceptions so that the compounded name is more clearly conceived than before. *Leviathan*, X, has a cluster of such compounded names unpacked into their components as part of Hobbes's explication of the passions. In such cases definitions of names are used for analysis, clarification, or the introduction of new names. Apart from certain technical requirements (for which see *De Corpore*, VI. 13–19), the primary requirements of a definition are that it should be clear and agreed.

To be clear and agreed, the definition must 'resolve' the word to be defined in such a way that the receiver of the definition has conceptions called to mind by the names used in the definition which are similar to, but clearer than, the conception he originally had of the compounded name being defined. The definition must also convey the same conception to the receiver of the definition as it does to the giver of the definition; a requirement which, we should note, cannot be known to be satisfied until later use shows agreement in the way in which the defined term is being employed.

In *Leviathan* Hobbes often, but not always, signals the definition of a term by means of capital letters for the word(s) defined. The first example is SENSE (I. 2), the next IMAGINATION (II. 2), and there are scores more in the text. He is inclined to claim that he is merely reporting common usage in his definitions, as when he says in the summary of his arguments in XXXII. 1 that he has drawn conclusions 'from definitions . . . universally agreed on'. But it is evident that he sometimes introduces new terms by means of them ('endeavour' is an obvious example) or, much more contentiously, subtly adjusts the conceptions a compounded name brings to mind (e.g. 'life' defined as motion) so that the adjusted conceptions can later be used in a surprising or reductionist way, or to subvert conventional conclusions. A further caveat about Hobbes's method of argument by definition is that it can produce apparently substantial and certainly alarming conclusions which are true in virtue of the meaning of the terms used and hence true without reference to new observation or experience. A critical example is the way in which he uses definitions of 'good' and 'voluntary' to produce the conclusion that one's own good is the object of all voluntary action (see below). So Hobbes uses definitions for clarity, for quasi-geometrical rigour, to introduce new terms, *and* to adjust our conceptions of familiar terms in ways which will make them consistent with the unified philosophical objective worked out in the details of *Leviathan* to apply to the body natural, the body politic, and the body spiritual.

Leviathan: *Some Problems in the Anatomy*

Leviathan argues with such sustained rigour, and with such a concentration of historical, political, scientific, legal, linguistic, theological, and biblical information, that book-length discussion is in some respects easier than the brief comments possible within an introduction. Nevertheless, certain items are too crucial, too obtrusive, or too controversial to be ignored in any treatment. Some of these are noted below in the sort of order in which they are likely to be encountered in the text. I say 'sort of order' because matter concerned directly or indirectly with God and religion occupies roughly half of the whole book, and my beginning with God and religious language, and ending with the religious conscience and religious power as it impinges upon the body politic, is to some extent arbitrary.

God, the Soul, and Insignificant Speech

Whether Hobbes within himself believed in God and personal immortality, and in what way, and with what qualifications, is not decisively ascertainable from his published or surviving private writing. But the problem for him was that if he did not believe (or only believed in a very unorthodox way), other people did believe, and the circumstances of his time—social pressures and specific laws against heresy and atheism—obliged him to maintain in public that he believed, and that his belief was orthodox. The trouble was that his commitment to what I have called one-world realism made the commonest verbal expressions of orthodox belief literally insignificant according to his view of significance.

According to Hobbes, we know that 'there must be . . . one first mover; that is, a first, and an eternal cause of all things; which is that which men mean by the name of God' (XII. 6), and again 'of necessity[12] he must come to this thought at last, that there is some cause, whereof there is no former cause, but is eternal; which is it men call God' (XI. 25). The same thought occurs elsewhere in Hobbes's works, for example in *Elements of Law*, XI. 2. But in the parallel passage in the *Elements* the negativity of Hobbes's account of deity could scarcely be more clearly stated:

Forasmuch as God Almighty is incomprehensible, it followeth that we can have no conception or image of the Deity; and consequently all his attributes signify our inability and defect of power to conceive any thing concerning his nature, and not any conception of the same, excepting only this: *that there is a God.*

The details of this negative theology are unpacked in *Leviathan*, XXXI. 14–28, but the conclusion appears earlier on: 'Whatsoever we imagine, is *finite*. Therefore there is no idea, or conception of any thing we call *infinite* . . . And therefore the name of God is used, not to make us conceive him . . . but that we may honour him' (III. 12). Such negative theology (often allied with versions of fideism) is a recognizable strand in Christian thinking, but in Hobbes it seems to go uncomfortably far, so far that many of the ways in which God is spoken to and about lose their normal significance. Thus in the *Elements*, XI. 3:

And whereas we attribute to God Almighty, seeing, hearing, speaking, knowing, loving, and the like; by which names we understand something in the men to whom we attribute them, we understand nothing by them in the nature of God. (Cf. *Leviathan*, XXXVI. 9.)

But this highly restrictive characterization of the language we can significantly use in talk about God is only part of the problem Hobbes creates for orthodox religion.

---

[12] In the work unpublished in his lifetime, *White's De Mundo Examined*, Hobbes somewhat qualifies his published view that the existence of God can be taken as 'necessary' or in some way *proved*. In the unpublished work he takes 'demonstrable truth' in the narrow sense of logically demonstrable, i.e. the formal consequences of proposition(s) in subject–predicate form. In that sense God's existence is not demonstrable. Thus in XXVI. 2 he remarks: 'For someone to prove that something exists, there is need of the senses, or experience . . . Under these circumstances there is no doubt that those who declare that they will show that God exists . . . act unphilosophically.' Hobbes further defends this failure of proof by appeal to a quasi-fideistic position long recognized by Christianity: 'When a demonstration persuades us of the truth of any proposition, that is no longer faith, but is natural knowledge', therefore the more philosophical proof progresses, the more religion is weakened (XXVI. 4).

Granted that Hobbes's appeal to the argument from a regress of causal explanations establishes the basic proposition *that God exists* (without allowing us to say any more than this about Him, Her, or It), one common and arguably orthodox answer to the question *in what way* God exists, is that God exists other than as composed of the material that in a gathered form makes up the bodies that exist in the universe. God is a universal bodiless spirit. In a more philosophical phrase, God is an 'immaterial substance', not identifiable with the world or any part of it. Now, while Hobbes clearly affirms that God and the world are not identical (e.g. *Leviathan*, XXXI. 15), he also affirms with equal clarity and greater frequency that 'immaterial substance' (and cognate phrases) are without any signification.[13] Such locutions, he maintains, are like trying to explain what something is by calling it a bodiless body, or describing the shape of something as a round square. A very similar problem of insignificant speech attaches to the way in which we often try to think (i.e. use words) about human souls:

But the opinion that such spirits were incorporeal, or immaterial, could never enter into the mind of any man by nature; because, though men may put together words of contradictory signification, as spirit, and incorporeal; yet they can never have the imagination of any thing answering to them. (XII. 7)

The solution, and Hobbes vigorously argues that it is consistent with the real meaning of all the relevant scriptural passages, is that both God and human souls are spirits corporeal: that is to say entities which are not accessible to the senses but *are* within the compass of one-world realism. Criticized concerning this matter in Bramhall's *The Catching of the Leviathan* (1658), Hobbes replied unequivocally in *An Answer to Bishop Bramhall* (written about 1668, but not published until 1682) that God is corporeal: 'To his Lordship's question here: *What I leave God to be?* I answer, I leave him to be a most pure, simple, invisible spirit corporeal. By corporeal I mean a substance that has magnitude . . .' (*English Works*, iv. 313), and 'Spirit is thin, fluid, transparent, invisible body' (ibid. 309). In another flourish Hobbes makes clear that his rejection of insignificant formulas does not carry with it a rejection of mystery in biblical religion:

When the nature of the thing is incomprehensible, I can acquiesce in the Scripture: but when the signification of words is incomprehensible, I cannot acquiesce in the authority of a Schoolman. (Ibid. 314)

Thus Hobbes asserts the minimum proposition *God exists*. He rejects as

---

[13] See *Leviathan*, IV. 24; VIII. 27; XII. 7; XLIV. 16; XLV. 2, *et al.*

insignificant speech the commonest notion of *how* God's existence can be characterized, and he affirms God's existence as something within the conceptual scope of one-world realism. He argues that this novel (but quasi-Epicurean) view is consistent with scriptural sources, is indeed their real meaning.

He asserts an analogous minimalism about human souls: 'The *soul* in scripture, signifieth always, either the life, or the living creature; and the body and soul jointly, the *body alive*' (XLIV. 15). But life is defined in his Introduction as 'but a motion of limbs', and again 'life itself is but motion' (VI. 58). Hence, if the soul is to be described at all, it must be described as a corporeal spirit because only what is corporeal can move. But in Ch. XXXVIII, when writing about resurrection and eternal life, Hobbes is even more restrictive about souls than he is about what we can significantly say concerning God:

> That the soul of man is in its own nature eternal, and a living creature independent on the body; or that any mere man is immortal, otherwise than by the resurrection in the last day . . . is a doctrine not apparent in Scripture.   (XXXVIII. 4)

And his account of resurrection, heavily emphasizing the credal and Pauline resurrection of the *body*, is not a rising upwards to the life of an empyrean heaven, but to a new life on earth, for as long as the earth lasts.

It could even be argued that if and when the fit between biblical religion and the one-world realism of the new sciences breaks down, Hobbes has in reserve a separation between philosophy and science on the one hand, and religion on the other. But it is a suspect separation. It is hinted at in the phrase quoted above: 'When the nature of the thing is incomprehensible . . .'. It is officially stated in *De Corpore*, I. 8, where Hobbes remarks: '[Philosophy] excludes *theology*, I mean the doctrine of God, eternal, ingenerable, incomprehensible, and in whom there is nothing neither to divide nor compound, nor any generation to be conceived.' But here what is identified as theology and excluded from philosophy and science is precisely the insignificant speech he attacks in *Leviathan*.

Although Hobbes may have been a sincere reformer in his proposals about how we should understand God and the soul, most of his contemporaries thought that he was not sincere, or if sincere was in serious error. Even now his account of the corporeal spirit which is God looks as if it would be more easily satisfied by whatever, for example, radio waves are, or whatever gravity is, than by the personal agent characterized in traditional Christianity. On the other hand his biblical exegesis now looks remarkably modern; partly, one suspects, because it is among the first attempts to do what so many would now try to do, namely read the Bible in a way which makes it compatible with the one-world realism of success-ful modern science.

Human Nature

In *Leviathan*, VI. 1, Hobbes employs a conventional distinction between 'vital' motions and 'animal' or 'voluntary' motions.[14] Vital motions are the involuntary movements of the body performed as part of the process of being alive—heartbeats, breathing, bowel movements, and so on. Animal motions are voluntary motions including speaking, eating, and most move-ments of our limbs. Now, Hobbes explains, 'sense, is motion in the organs and interior parts of man's body, caused by the action of the things we see, hear, etc.' This motion is conveyed as *endeavour*, via the nerves, to the brain. (Endeavour is motion too minute or too quick to be observable.) At the brain—and here the account in *Leviathan* has to be augmented—the motion does not stop, 'but proceeding to the heart, of necessity must there either help or hinder that motion which is called vital' (*Elements of Law*, VII. 1). If it assists the vital motions, a feeling of pleasure occurs. If it retards them, a feeling of pain occurs. Pleasure is provocation to move towards that which causes the pleasure; pain is provocation to move away. The internal beginning of such animal movement is endeavour, and is felt as appetite (desire or love) or as aversion (fear or hatred). Such endeavours show themselves in animal movements towards or away from the object, and:

whatsoever is the object of any man's appetite or desire; that is it, which he for his part calleth *good*: and the object of his hate, and aversion, *evil* . . . For these words of good, evil . . . are ever used with relation to the person that useth them: there being nothing simply and absolutely so; nor any common rule of good and evil; to be taken from the nature of the objects themselves; but from the person of the man (where there is no commonwealth;) or, (in a commonwealth,) from the person that representeth it . . .   (VI. 7)

Thus a mechanistic connection is established between the 'first philo-sophy' of body and motion, and human nature and behaviour. We are all, as a matter of fact, if Hobbes is right, physically wired up to respond in certain ways to the stimuli of certain movements, and we use our personal or egocentric language of good and evil according to the way the wires pull.

But because of the way in which Hobbes has defined 'voluntary' and

---

[14] The same distinction, for the same purposes, is deployed in *Elements of Law*, VII. 1–2, and *De Corpore*, XXV. 1–4.

'will' (VI. 53), *all* voluntary actions (which are not directed by fear) will by definition be directed towards what is desired, that is, towards what each person in isolation calls his or her internally perceived good. Thus Hobbes draws (and often draws) the conclusion that 'of the voluntary [i.e. willed] acts of every man, the object is some good to himself' (XIV. 8, see also XV. 4; XV. 16; XIX. 9; XXVII. 8). The same conclusion appears in *Elements of Law*, 'every man's end being some good to himself' (XXIV. 4), and again, emphatically, in *De Cive*:

for every man is desirous of what is good for him, and shuns what is evil, but chiefly the chiefest of natural evils, which is death; and this he doth, by a certain impulsion of nature, no less than that whereby a stone moves downward.   (I. 7)

But here, it will be noticed, there is more emphasis on the 'selfish hypotheses' (as Hume called it) or 'psychological egoism' (as it is sometimes now called) as a natural fact. We are subject to 'the impulsion of nature'. The peculiarity of treating this alleged natural fact as true by definition (the way in which Hobbes usually treats it) is that it actually weakens the force of the fact. This is because most people find that matter-of-fact generalizations (or scientific statements) are more convincing if they are supported by observational evidence than if they are merely asserted as the necessary consequence of previously given definitions. Nevertheless for Hobbes, by definition, 'I voluntarily do X' is necessarily equivalent to saying 'X is good for me' (whether, for example, X is satisfying my lust at someone else's cost, or helping the needy at my own cost). One outcome of this is that my desires (defined as identical with my egocentric good) can include, and undoubtedly sometimes will include, the good of others.[15]

I think Hobbes intends to admit this possibility. Thus at VI. 22 he writes: 'Desire of good to another, BENEVOLENCE, GOOD WILL, CHARITY. If to man generally, GOOD NATURE' (see also *De Cive*, III. 8 and IX. 18). But it is also true that much of his analysis of the passions is directed towards exposing the underlying reality and prevalence of ruthless self-seeking and self-presentation, of desires for power, success, acquisitions, and

[15] John Aubrey provides a personal anecdote about Hobbes which casts practical light on this point: 'One time, I remember, going in the Strand, a poor and infirm old man craved his alms. He, beholding him with eyes of pity and compassion, put his hand in his pocket, and gave him 6*d*. Said a divine (that Dr Jaspar Mayne) that stood by—"Would you have done this, if it had not been Christ's command?"—"Yea", said he.—"Why?" quoth the other.—"Because," said he, "I was in pain to consider this miserable condition of the old man; and now my alms, giving him some relief, doth also ease me." ' The anecdote does not show a direct desire for the good of another, but the good of oneself indirectly achieved by the good of another. Hobbes as a man is more complex than his philosophy would allow him to be.

satisfactions that are wholly selfish and which are, moreover, insatiable. The normal human being will not only be actively seeking his or her own ends, but the activity will never bring repose. 'Life itself is but motion, and can never be without desire' (VI. 58) and (from the parallel passage in *Elements of Law*, VII. 7) 'FELICITY, therefore (by which we mean continual delight), consisteth not in having prospered, but in prospering'. What is if anything worse, is that the endless quest to satisfy our separate desires will be competitive. The point is most explicitly brought out in *Elements*, VII. 4: 'because the power of one man resisteth and hindereth the effects of the power of another: power simply is no more, but the excess of the power of one above that of another'.

Nowhere in literature is such an analysis more perceptively deployed than in the prose poem which concludes *Elements of Law*, IX, a portrait (echoed in *Leviathan*, VI) of human nature as it commonly is, and as it would commonly show itself if the bonds of society broke or had never been formed. Life would be a 'race we must suppose to have no other goal, nor no other garland, but being foremost. And in it.' It will be a race in which 'Continually to out-go the next before is felicity. And to foresake the course is to die.' And it is a race we can all recognize.

It is possible to read Hobbes's analysis as a chilling foresight of the development of the culture of the rat race, or, in C. B. Macpherson's phrase, the 'possessive individualism' of bourgeois society. But Hobbes does not overtly present it in that way. The race is what would occur if there were *no* society in the sense of an organized body politic, although the existence of a body politic does not, of itself, preclude all tendencies to a competitive race. And the race would happen because of the normal prevalence of real selfishness among human beings, a selfishness too common, powerful, and restless, according to Hobbes, for political society to be possible as a spontaneous growth from the good will of men.[16]

[16] C. B. Macpherson's *The Political Theory of Possessive Individualism* (Oxford, 1962), together with other essays of his relating to Hobbes, presents a fascinating, challenging, but, I think, almost wholly misguided interpretation of Hobbes in terms of Marxist accounts of bourgeois man in a market economy. Thus he argues that 'Hobbes's state of nature or "natural condition of mankind" is not about "natural" man as opposed to civilized man but is about men whose desires are specifically civilized' (p. 18), and that what starts 'as an analysis of the nature of men in complete abstraction from society, soon becomes an analysis of men in established social relationships', i.e. those established by the market economy (p. 19). But even if—what is historically very dubious—seventeenth-century England was manifesting the characteristics of the bourgeois market economy which Marxists love to identify, Hobbes clearly draws his account of human nature not from it, but from a mechanistic physiology with universal application; and his empirical evidence is drawn from Thucydides and ancient or remote societies, not from the activities of London merchants. As Sir Isaiah Berlin remarks in his

The analysis of natural, unrestrained human behaviour is thus the hinge upon which the whole of Hobbes's political theory turns. In sum, his thesis is that it is a fact of nature that we are wired up to act according to our desires. Such action is 'voluntary', and the objects of our desire are what we egocentrically call 'good'. But egocentric good includes both our own selfish good *and* the altruistic good of others. But again it is a fact of nature that altruistic good is seldom what we desire (except, perhaps, in family or small local groups). Thus unless some power greater than our individual selves can be devised to control us, a horrible fragmented conflict will be the human norm: what Hobbes calls 'the state of war'.

The State of War

If human nature is as Hobbes finds it to be, and if that nature were given free rein in dealings between all people who have no close family relationships, and if, as he convincingly holds, each man has a right of nature[17] to do whatever is necessary to protect his life and person, then the outcome would be to make the lives of all of us utterly wretched. The wording of *Leviathan*, XIII. 9, is known wherever English is spoken. The description in the corresponding passage in *De Cive*, I. 13, is almost as vivid. Human societies would be 'few, fierce, short-lived, poor, nasty, and destroyed of all that pleasure, and beauty of life, which peace and society are wont to bring with them'. This is the 'calamity of a war with every other man, (which is the greatest evil that can happen in this life)' (*Leviathan*, XXX. 3).

The question which has always been asked—Hobbes asks it himself in both *De Cive* and *Leviathan*—is whether the supposed state of war was ever historically real. If not, is it 'realistic' in some significant way in which Disneyland or even William Morris's communist utopia in *News from Nowhere* is not realistic?

augustly polite criticism, the heart of Macpherson's belief 'will seem unplausible to anyone who reads Hobbes without Mr Macpherson's preconceptions' ('Hobbes, Locke and Professor Macpherson', in *Political Quarterly*, 1964; reprinted in P. King (ed.), *Thomas Hobbes: Critical Assessments* (London, 1993), i. 55–76). But of course no one will deny that human nature as Hobbes describes it is more readily manifested in some social conditions than in others: for example, in a Roman Senate or a modern multinational corporation rather than in a medieval village under the feudal system or a Russian labour camp under Stalin.

[17] A right to do Y is defined by Hobbes in terms which make it equivalent to a freedom to do or forbear from doing Y, i.e. no law forbids or obliges the doing of Y (XIV. 3). In the absence of civil society, there is no law at all. Hence, in such a condition each man has unrestricted freedom to do what he will. The right of nature is thus complete freedom: 'the liberty each man hath, to use his own power, as he will . . . for the preservation of his own nature' (*Leviathan*, XIV. 1).

Hobbes's answer to the historical question is a qualified affirmative. We have 'the experience of savage nations that live at this day' and 'the histories of our ancestors, the old inhabitants of Germany' (*Elements of Law*, XIV. 12; cf. *De Cive*, I. 13, and *Leviathan*, XIII. 11). What is more, whenever a political society degenerates into civil war, some approach to the state of war is achieved (the inhabitants of Beirut, Bosnia, Somalia, and the Sudan might well agree). So the historical reality of Hobbes's state of war is partly our knowledge of savage societies, and of ancient approximations to it, and partly our experience of civil wars. But it is also realistic in the sense that it would be the inevitable outcome of human nature if human nature is in fact the acquisitive, competitive, fearful, egocentric thing Hobbes identifies. The state of war is in this respect an apocalyptic myth: what would be the reality if human beings acted according to their nature in certain physically possible, easily imaginable, and almost experienced conditions. But it is not what normally holds. Why? Because the state of war is a state of perpetual fear of death and lesser evils. It is the greatest general calamity that can happen in this life, and 'reason suggesteth convenient articles of peace, upon which men may be drawn to agreement . . . otherwise . . . called laws of nature' (*Leviathan*, XIII. 14).

Laws of Nature

An 'article of peace', or 'law of nature', or, as Hobbes calls it in *De Cive*, II. 1, a 'dictate of right reason', is defined in *Leviathan*, XIV. 3, as 'a precept, or general rule, found out by reason, by which a man is forbidden to do, that, which is destructive of his life, or taketh away the means of preserving the same; and to omit, that, by which he thinketh it may be best preserved'.

Two features immediately differentiate Hobbes's 'laws of nature' from older uses of the term *lex naturalis*. One is that Hobbes's definition is totally man-centred. The forbidding and requiring of the general definition are no more than we anyway desire by nature, and the 'obligation' of precepts formulated according to such a definition will be no more than what we all seek without reference to 'law', namely the preservation of our own life. The problem, to be dealt with later, is that until other people are also obeying the precepts, it will usually *not* be in the best interests of my life and prosperity to observe them. In a simple instance, if everyone else is seizing and plundering what they can get, it is not usually in my interests to refrain from doing likewise. In what sense then, if any, do the laws of nature bind or oblige when there are no structures for enforcing the initial truce in which men can give up their right of nature (i.e. their complete freedom to do anything they please)?

The question is partly answered in the important and easily overlooked distinction Hobbes makes between obligation *in foro interno* (literally 'in the internal forum') and *in foro externo*. In *Elements of Law*, XVII. 10, he puts the matter thus: 'The force therefore of the law of nature is not *in foro externo*, till there be security for men to obey it; but it is always *in foro interno*, wherein the action of obedience being unsafe, the will and readiness to perform is taken for the performance.' In *Leviathan*, XV. 36, the distinction is given similarly as 'The laws of nature oblige *in foro interno*; that is to say, they bind to a desire they should take place: but *in foro externo*; that is, to the putting them in act, not always.' So Hobbes is saying that during the state of war the laws of nature only bind, only are 'laws',[18] in the very restricted sense that we can rationally discern that the preferable state of peace would be achieved by obeying them, and therefore within ourselves we wish to obey them, while not being able to do so in public practice.

The second feature which distinguishes Hobbes's laws of nature from the traditional laws of nature is that Hobbes's precepts are, at the start, independent of the will of God. They are the 'dictates of right reason' whether or not they also happen to have been confirmed in the thick darkness of Mount Sinai or anywhere else. Nevertheless, Hobbes is most concerned to show (e.g. *Elements of Law*, XVIII; *De Cive*, IV; *Leviathan*, XXVI. 24, 40, *et al.*) that the laws of nature are also the laws of God. This not only gives them an authority they might not have had as precepts of reason; it also makes them properly *laws*, since God 'by right commandeth all things' (XV. 41). What is more they are 'eternal' (XV. 38), if only for the reason that human nature is constant, and therefore the articles of peace that can be identified as necessary for the avoidance of the state of war at any one time, will be the same at any other time. And they are also moral laws (XXVI. 36, 40) because, as Hobbes puts it in *Elements of Law*, 'they concern men's manners [conduct] and conversation one towards another' (XVIII. 1; see also *Leviathan*, XL. 1, and especially *De Cive*, III. 31).

The fundamental law of nature—the principle which generates all the rest—is, according to Hobbes, seek peace and follow it where it may be found, and when it may not, by right of nature, defend yourself by all the means you can (*Leviathan*, XIV. 4; *De Cive*, II. 2).

---

[18] As he points out in XV. 41, until they are enforced by him that has a command over others, they are more properly conclusions concerning what is needed for self-defence than laws proper.

The second law, which Hobbes takes to be derivable from the first, but still fundamental enough to stand apart from the other seventeen he identifies in *Leviathan*, XV (a slightly different set is identified in *De Cive*, II), is that a man be willing, when others are too, for the sake of peace, to lay down his right of nature (i.e. his freedom) to do all things, and 'be contented with so much liberty against other men, as he would allow other men against himself' (XIV. 5). Hobbes adds that this is the law of the Gospels: 'Whatsoever you require that others should do to you, that do ye to them'; the worldly version of which is 'Do not that to others, you would not have done to yourself' (*De Cive*, III. 26; see also what Hobbes calls the 'law of all men' in *Leviathan*, XV. 35; XXVI. 13; XLII. 11, etc.). This is both the second fundamental law and, as Hobbes emphatically states in XV. 35, the test to which all others can be put, after which 'there is none of these laws of nature that will not appear unto him very reasonable'.

So the laws of nature are generated by the two fundamental articles of peace. They do not need to be justified by the external authority of God, although in fact they have such authority. They are the minimum conditions that must be observed if we are to avoid what we most dread—the state of war, and the constant fear of death and injury. They are discoverable by reason. They bind *in foro interno* because we wish them to be observed. They bind *in foro externo*, in as far as there is power to enforce them. That power is the sovereign to which, in a body politic, we give up our right of nature, our freedom to do whatever we desire. But the laws of nature 'of themselves, without the terror of some power, to cause them to be observed, are contrary to our natural passions' (XVII. 2) as these show themselves in each man seeking his own private good. So common consent to observe the laws of nature is not enough. Hobbes puts the point most clearly in *De Cive*, V. 4:

> somewhat else must be done, that those who have once consented for the *common good*, to peace and mutual help, may by fear be restrained, lest afterwards they again dissent, when their private *interest* shall appear discrepant from the *common good*.

The 'somewhat else' is the erection of a common power, some 'one man or assembly of men' which is sovereign (*Leviathan*, XVII. 13) and to which each man transfers by a form of contract some of the right of nature, and some of the power he previously exercised freely.

The Body Politic, Civil Society or Commonwealth

Once the sovereign power is in position (I shall return to a theoretical problem about this), the state, Leviathan, exists. Once it exists, all the items Hobbes has been anticipating in his theory begin to fall into place. Power is best concentrated in one person, natural or civil (i.e. *one* centre of sovereignty, not a divided and potentially conflicting power), which embodies the powers of the greatest number of separate men (X. 3). The *common* (not the private) rules of good and evil are enforced by the sovereign (VI. 7). These rules are the civil laws (XVIII. 16; XXVI. 3). The 'laws' of nature, which start as 'not property laws, but qualities that dispose men to peace', become laws when enforced as 'part of the civil law in all commonwealths of the world' (XXVI. 8, 22). Then they oblige *in foro externo*. No law can be technically unjust because 'unjust' *means* 'contrary to some law'; but a law can be bad if it is one that is not needful for the good of the people, or is ambiguous or unclear (XXX. 20–2). The sovereign is bound by the laws of nature, not by civil laws as such, and the sovereign has duties (XXX. 1).[19]

The theoretical problem about the emergence of Leviathan, the body politic, is how, given the state of war, our rational perception of what the articles of peace are could ever in practice result in us getting together to give up our natural liberty to a common coercive power. The condition of general fear would seem to subvert the process before it could start. I think Hobbes's response can only be in terms of the way he characterizes the state of war. It need not ever have been a total and all-pervasive reality— or only at some incalculably remote period in human history when family or tiny tribal groups substituted for the body politic and began, by their example, to give clues to the articles of peace later followed among tribes and peoples. What Hobbes is concerned with is that rational and intelligent human beings should be aware of the theoretically possible ultimate state of war to which we could degenerate; from which, as soon as we begin to experience it, we strive to escape; and which savage societies and civil wars to some degree show us. Indeed, our awareness of the real threat of the state of war is such that we always, eventually, do try to come to agreements about government. A particular case of the 'making of union', probably known to Hobbes, occurred during the voyage of the *Mayflower* in 1620. On that occasion the need for mutual co-operation and order, in a situation where no authority existed to enforce the King's writ, resulted in a written compact or constitution in which the Pilgrim Fathers bound themselves into 'a civil body politic' for the sake of order and the enforcement of law. And the example is always followed 'for the avoidance of war'

---

[19] A preliminary discussion of the possible 'incommodity' of power given to the sovereign is in XVIII. 20.

in every institution from super-states to merchant banks and socialist communes. Hobbes is addressing rational human beings aware of the potential for civil discord, not hypothetical savages unaware of the possibilities of civil peace.

The practical problem, which everyone who reads *Leviathan* notices, is that Hobbes is so concerned to avoid the calamities of confusion and civil war that he justifies the exercise of virtual dictatorship by the sovereign power. Only in the most extreme circumstance where one's life is threatened may one legitimately resist. In the three and a half centuries since Hobbes constructed his great justification of the absolute state, democracies have painstakingly put in place structures which are designed to limit the power of the sovereign in relation to citizens without facilitating disorder, conflict, and collapse into approximations to civil war. But when those structures fail, or even when a working dictatorship crumbles into anarchy, the apocalyptic judgement of Hobbes is regularly reported— '*anything* would be better than this'. Whether one accepts such a judgement is not, I think, a matter of absolute reasoning, but of where one has lived, and what one has experienced.

Among the factors which, in Hobbes's experience, most readily contributed to civil war and the tendency to regress into the state of war, were the private religious conscience and the power of Churches exerted as an alternative source of sovereignty on earth. About half of *Leviathan* is devoted to dismantling these threats. For most of the twentieth century they appeared to be irrelevant to political theory. The rise of Islamic and other fundamentalist religions has tragically reversed this complacency, and the least read section of Hobbes's argument becomes again sharply relevant: killing for the sake of religion is back in fashion.

Conscience, Religion, and the Dissolution of Commonwealth

In Ch. XXIX of *Leviathan* Hobbes identifies a number of factors which weaken the body politic and tend therefore to return it to the state of war. Conspicuous among these are (i) 'that every private man is judge of good and evil action', (ii) that what is done against conscience is sin, (iii) that faith and sanctity (or, as he later says, 'salvation') come from private supernatural revelation, and (iv) the setting up of a 'ghostly' authority against the civil, as if there were 'another kingdom, as it were a kingdom of fairies, in the dark' that 'moveth the members of a commonwealth, by the terror of punishments, and hope of rewards . . . otherwise than by the civil power' (§15, and compare with XXXVIII. 1).

Hobbes's arguments against (i) to (iv) are scattered throughout Parts 1 and 2 of *Leviathan* and then subjected to a sustained, sophisticated, and concentrated deployment in Parts 3 and 4. His exegesis of biblical texts and theological positions is learned, at times radically modernistic, and surprisingly[20] convincing. It all moves to the same conclusion, namely that, when properly understood, the claims of religion, and the 'consciences' to which they give rise, can be accommodated within this-world realism, and man-centred political structures, without in any way risking the precious salvation which depends upon the one essential belief *that Jesus is the Christ*.

The process of accommodation is once again driven by somewhat restrictive but not altogether strange definitions: thus (i) has already been dealt with in the distinction between the selfish and private good of my own desires, and the common and public good of the laws of nature codified and enforced in civil laws. In the case of (ii), Hobbes contrives to leave the proposition intact while divesting it of any danger that my private conscience could justify disobedience to the civil laws. Thus in VII. 4 he argues that conscience starts as con-science, or knowledge mutually with another or others of a certain fact:

Afterwards, men made use of the same word metaphorically, for the knowledge of their own secret facts . . . And last of all, men, vehemently in love with their own opinions . . . gave those their opinions also that reverenced name of conscience, as if they would have it seem unlawful to change or speak against them; and so pretend to know they are true, when they know at most, but that they think so.

More crisply, in *Elements of Law*, VI. 8, (private) conscience appears as simply a man's opinion of his own evidence. On the other hand, 'public conscience', as defined in *Leviathan*, is the civil law (XXIX. 6, 7). But since sin is 'nothing but the transgression of the law' (XXIX. 15), obeying the law must be both avoiding sin and acting according to conscience when one is a member of a civil society. When one is not, conscience can only mean obeying the laws of nature (XXX. 30): and nothing can stop you obeying those *in foro interno* (and in practice *in foro externo*, if you want to take the risks). So obeying one's conscience can only mean obeying the civil laws,

---

[20] Surprising, because Hobbes's attempts to cool down what is involved in being a Christian, and to interpret certain key theological conceptions within this-world realism, have to be conducted without the perspective of the historical criticism of the scriptures which began to appear in the eighteenth century. All Hobbes can do is take the texts as literally as is possible, and try to show that their actual meaning is closer, for example, to talking about resurrection of the body on earth, than to survival of a sort of ghost in some heavenly nowhere. The only permitted deviation from such literal interpretations is when an allegorical interpretation can be argued for. With these limited tools Hobbes accomplishes surprising things.

and the laws of nature, and no clash with the sovereign power in a well-informed body politic is possible.

The conscientious objector will immediately wish to ask what happens in a civil society when the positive law, which is supposed to be the laws of nature expressed and interpreted (for the avoidance of ambiguity and dispute) through the particular wisdom of the sovereign power, manifestly contravenes the natural law. For example, suppose that at some future time a legally constituted government of a certain state passed a law that all citizens of the state who were not genetically Celtic in origin should be given lethal injections. This would be clearly contrary to the second (fundamental) law of nature. Hobbes can only give a very limited reply. The intended victim may certainly resist: no man does or can give away in his compact with the state the right to defend himself if violent hands are laid upon him (XIV. 29); and certainly the sovereign is bound by the laws of nature (XXX. 15), although how this obligation is to be enforced other than by God is unclear. Similarly, the other citizens may obey conscience as the laws of nature *in foro interno*, by not wishing the genocide. But it is not clear what they should publicly *do*. Perhaps it could be said Hobbes does not consider the possibility of such depravity by the sovereign power. But he should have considered it. It was what had happened on religious principles in the Low Countries in the sixteenth century, and what would happen again, on political principles, in the twentieth century.

Hobbes's argument against (iii), that a man must act in accordance with his private religious beliefs and revelations, is more extensive and more effective. If they are in accord with the state religion there is no problem. If they are not in accord, then *in foro interno* they cannot be commanded since 'internal faith is in its own nature invisible' (XLII. 43; see also XLII. 11). If they are not in accord with what someone may by law be required to do or say as a citizen, then the offence to God 'is not his, but his sovereign's' if the citizen obey the law. The only acceptable martyrs therefore are those who were put to death as actual witnesses, with their own eyes, of the resurrection of Jesus, 'whereas they which were not so, can witness no more, but that their antecessors said it' (XLII. 12). And Hobbes adds a great deal more in Ch. XLIII to the effect that salvation requires only 'faith in Christ, and obedience to laws', not tenacious observation of private religious demands.

But quite apart from the legalistic bonds with which Hobbes confines and renders harmless private religious revelations, he makes it abundantly clear that such revelations are also particularly liable to error. None of us has any self-authenticating revelations; and even if we claim any, they are likely to be in conflict with the private revelations of others. Hence the great majority of human beings to whom God does not offer real or supposed supernatural revelations should, for the sake of peace and harmony, leave the sovereign power to decide which particular revelation will underpin the established religious procedures for the state. The whole argument is summed up in XLIII. 22–3:

Having thus shown what is necessary to salvation; it is not hard to reconcile our obedience to God, with our obedience to the civil sovereign; who is either Christian, or infidel. If he be a Christian, he alloweth the belief of this article, that *Jesus is the Christ* . . . which is all the faith necessary to salvation. And because he is a sovereign, he requireth obedience . . . to all the civil laws; in which are contained all the laws of nature, that is all the laws of God . . . And when the civil sovereign is an infidel, every one of his own subjects that resisteth him, sinneth against the laws of God (for such are the laws of nature). . . . And for their *faith*, it is internal, and invisible . . . and [they] need not put themselves into danger for it. But if they do, they ought to expect their reward in heaven, and not complain of their lawful sovereign; much less make war upon him.

It will be noticed that Hobbes also goes a remarkably long way in Ch. XXXVIII towards cooling down the fiery punishments and excessive rewards with which a man (or Church) might threaten himself or others for *not* acting according to religious beliefs, even if the beliefs are held to be essentials.

But Hobbes's most extensive concern is with (iv), the threat to the body politic from claims by Churches, particularly the Roman and Presbyterian Churches, to have powers over and above those of the civil sovereign.[21] The core of his argument is that scriptural sources simply do not justify such claims. In particular, obedience to a sovereign (be it man or council of men) cannot legitimately be abrogated on account of his, her, or their imposition of what is supposed to be a heresy, because 'heresy signifies no more than private opinion; but has only a greater tincture of choler' (XI. 19), whereas the religion that is lawful in a state *cannot* be heresy: heresy or private opinion can only exist in relation to it (XLII. 130), and heresy cannot matter to the official religion, or damage the state, so long as it is adhered to within a man's private being, *in foro interno* (which is all that can really affect the standing of a man with his god).

The overwhelming impression made by *Leviathan* is that although Hobbes consistently and carefully affirms that God exists (and nothing

---

[21] Hobbes is rather diffident about linking the Roman and Presbyterian Churches in this way, but he does in *Leviathan*, XLII. 4.

much more can be said) and that Jesus is the Christ (and nothing much more need be said), all the dangerous teeth of religion are being drawn or filed down. In the case of personal religion, a man may be taught what to believe, but if he believes something else then that is his business, provided he obeys the law. Anyway, the punishments at the day of general resurrection may well not be as bad as expected, particularly error about the mere details of belief. In the case of institutional religion, unless, as in the Vatican, the civil state is identical with the religious power, the institutional religion has no more power, and can justify no more power, than it is allowed under the laws of the civil state. If this is a fair view of Hobbes on religion, it is quite remarkably like the freedom of belief and the arrangements between Church and State which twentieth-century social democracies have in fact established, and which religious fundamentalists now seek to overthrow.

The Influence of Leviathan

Hobbes, as his critics were not slow to complain, was an infernally good writer. His epigrammatic definitions ('*Fear* of power invisible, feigned by the mind, or imagined from tales publicly allowed, RELIGION; not allowed, SUPERSTITION', VI. 36), his many and sometimes profound insights into the human condition ('To have done more hurt to a man, than he can, or is willing to expiate, inclineth the doer to hate the sufferer. For he must expect revenge, or forgiveness; both which are hateful', XI. 8), his ability to sustain a clear structure of argument over many subdivisions, his systematic presentation of points for or against a position, not to mention his delightful use of metaphors (note, for example, the extended use of the 'kingdom of fairies' in XLVII. 21–33), his vivid language and quotable aphorisms, and his sometimes mischievous wit, all these made *Leviathan* a popular, if not a popularly approved book. So the immediate and to a certain extent the lasting influence of *Leviathan* was to provoke refutations, or the affirmation of moral, religious, or political positions which were contrary to it.

In matters of religion Hobbes was for long held to be so much in error that his views amounted to atheism. Thus Joseph Glanville (among others) argued that his dismissal of any real supernatural power in witchcraft, and his refusal to speak to God as a supernatural spirit, amounted to a denial of the existence of God and the activity of spirits.

In morality, the unflattering but supposedly realistic self-interest Hobbes identified at the core of human nature provoked both an apparent cultural following, and a sophisticated philosophical reaction. The cultural following had of course other causes, particularly the sudden relaxation of the joyless repression of the Puritans that took place at the Restoration in 1660. But there are examples in Restoration drama of characters who justify their actions in a pseudo–Hobbesian way by reference to their own interests, and regard this as more 'natural', closer to the real nature of human beings, than the pretences of conventional morality could bring them. (Mirabell in Congreve's *The Way of the World* of 1700 and Horner in Wycherley's *The Country Wife* are of this type.) Indeed, it could, I think, be argued that the motivation of self-interest, derivable in part from some understandings and many misunderstandings of Hobbes, forms as significant a feature of literature in the period 1660–1760 as the motivation of subconscious sexuality does in the literature of the first half of the twentieth century.

The philosophical reaction to Hobbes's account of human nature and morality is evident in the greatest writers of the period: Shaftesbury, Butler, Hutcheson, and Hume among others. They all, in different ways, seek to show that human nature is more complex than Hobbes allowed and that self-interest has many facets. It includes the 'original joy' (as Shaftesbury calls it) of doing good to others. It can be short-term and impetuous (and as such is often self-destructive), or cool, considered, and long-term (in which form it is often consistent with the public good). It need not exclude motives of benevolence and sympathy, and so on.[22] Another aspect of Hobbes's morality to which philosophers and theologians took strong exception was his supposed moral relativism. Thus Samuel Clarke and William Wollaston at the beginning of the eighteenth century are much concerned to emphasize the absolute nature of moral rules: morality is not a matter of fashion or subjective decision. But properly understood Hobbes had never said that it was, only that the natural man outside a body politic would act relative to his own decisions about what was good for him. In civil society on the other hand moral laws would be particular formulations of the laws of nature, and the laws of nature are not subjective. They are the articles of peace which are universally applicable because human nature is everywhere the same. As so often with Hobbes, he is criticized (on this occasion as a moral relativist) on account of an incomplete understanding of what he says.

In political theory Hobbes once again provoked an adverse reaction, not

---

[22] Useful guides to this area are provided by any of the following selections from the original material: D. H. Monro, *A Guide to the British Moralists* (London, 1972); D. D. Raphael, *British Moralists*, 2 vols. (Oxford, 1969); L. A. Selby-Bigge, *British Moralists*, 2 vols. (Oxford, 1897 and reprints).

merely from Royalists who could find no unambiguous endorsement of their views about monarchy in his pages, but from almost all writers in what might loosely be called the democratic tradition. Thus Hegel, who thought well of Hobbes, writing over 150 years later in his *Lectures on the History of Philosophy*, observes that 'Society, the state, is to Hobbes absolutely pre-eminent, it is the determining power without appeal as regards law and positive religion and their external relations; and because he placed these in subjection to the state, his doctrines were of course regarded with the utmost horror.' Locke's *Two Treatises of Civil Government* (1690), although not directly aimed at Hobbes, ably illustrate one anti-Hobbesian thesis in the democratic tradition, namely that bad but constitutionally immovable government may be changed (it had been changed in 1689) and society remain intact: 'There remains still in the People a supreme power to remove or alter the Legislative, when they find the Legislative act contrary to the trust reposed in them.' (The whole of the last chapter of the *Second Treatise* argues this thesis.) There is no *necessary* connection, Locke would argue, between the onset of the state of war as Hobbes defined it and a legal change of government (for example by an election or referendum) or even, in very carefully defined circumstances, an illegal change of government.

In the middle of the eighteenth century Hume could report that Hobbes was 'much neglected', but his mechanistic psychology, the push–pull of desires and aversions, fitted so well with the ideas of Benthamite utilitarianism that in John Austin's utilitarian account of law as command, *The Province of Jurisprudence Determined* (1832), Hobbes's account of sovereignty is central to the argument.

In the prolix literature of the twentieth century Hobbes has been much fought over by different interpreters. Some idea of the scale of the discussion can be gathered from William Sacksteder's *Hobbes Studies (1879–1979): A Bibliography* (Bowling Green, Ohio, 1982) and a short cut to some of its main components can be read in D. D. Raphael's *Hobbes: Morals and Politics* (London, 1977). But it is since 1945 that Hobbes's account of the state of war has acquired a new and unexpected relevance. As Howard Warrender pointed out in his article on Hobbes in the *Encyclopedia Americana*, sovereign states now have a relation to each other similar to that which Hobbes attributed to individual men: there is the potential for the war of each against every one, with fear and the balance of power (in precisely Hobbes's sense: 'power simply is no more, but the excess of the power of one above that of another') keeping such peace as there is. As Warrender remarks, 'on Hobbes's assumptions, it would thus be rational to form a World State' (or, one might add, at the very least a United Nations with sovereign and coercive powers).

More recently still, as I have indicated elsewhere in this Introduction, Hobbes's concern with confining and emasculating the political claims of religion, and the public damage that private religious beliefs can inflict, has acquired a new and horribly unwelcome relevance in the world. For us, as for him, it is simply not acceptable that fanatics and self-appointed prophets should enjoy unchallenged claims to philosophical or conscientious grounds for their attempts to subvert by violence the established structures of the body politic.

The Memorable Result

No more comprehensive, tightly structured, and closely argued political philosophy exists than Hobbes set out in *Leviathan*. It shocks our conventional assumptions, and it is disquieting. For the sake of peace and order, religion cannot be allowed the political power and conscientious authority it has often claimed. To cure our political ills and contain the state of war we may have to submit to governments we thoroughly dislike. The most prevalent and powerful traits of human nature are unpleasant and socially destructive. It is this insight which touches a raw nerve of truth with so many readers. Modern man, if not all mankind, is ominously close to Hobbes's account of us—competitive, acquisitive, possessive, restless, individualistic, self-concerned, and insatiable in our demands for whatever we see in isolation as our own good. It is this point of realism which almost all other political philosophies underestimate, and which Hobbes gets memorably right in his great endeavour to deliver us from a life consistent with our own natures, and of our own making; a life which would be solitary, poor, nasty, brutish, and short.

A NOTE ON THE TEXT

A RECENT editor of *Leviathan* commented that 'there has never been an accurate edition of the work'. If by 'accurate' is meant a text devoid of errata, with every word and mark of punctuation exactly as Hobbes would have chosen it to be at the last possible moment before first publication, or with every variation recorded and resolved in the text as Hobbes would have wished it resolved, then indeed there never has been and never will be an accurate edition. But some editions have been and will be more accurate than others, and some editions will be more easy to read and use than others. The present text is intended to be as faithful as possible to Hobbes's usually clear intentions without noting explicitly every minute stylistic or typographical variation, and without retaining accidental impediments such as the antique spelling and the italicization of proper names which form no part of what Hobbes intended us to read and think about.

The Obstacles to an Accurate Text

According to appearances, *Leviathan* was published in English only once in Hobbes's lifetime, namely in London in 1651 (probably in early May) with the imprint 'London, Printed for Andrew Crooke, at the Green Dragon in St Pauls Church-yard, 1651'. But in fact three separate editions bear this imprint, two of them considerably later than the first. The three are readily distinguished by the ornaments which appear on their title-pages. As suggested by H. MacDonald and M. Hargreaves in their *Thomas Hobbes: A Bibliography* (London, 1952), the editions may be designated the 'Head', the 'Bear', and the 'Ornaments' respectively. Only the Head (see reproduced title-page, p. 1 in this volume) was in fact printed and published in London in 1651 under Hobbes's somewhat distant supervision from Paris. The Bear may well have been printed in Holland towards the end of the 1660s, presumably to circumvent the current prohibition of its further printing in London, and the Ornaments was printed later still, although possibly in London. The later printing of the Bear and the Ornaments is established, among other things, by a different set of printer's errors supervening on the Head text, by signs of wear on the famous frontispiece engraving, and by their somewhat more modern spelling. There is, however, no substantial reason to suppose that Hobbes was responsible for the minute textual variations which distinguish the

Bear and the Ornaments from each other and from the Head, or even that he knew about their printing. It is thus accepted practice that all good editions are reproductions of copies of the Head, or based on such copies.

But even when attention is confined to the Head edition, it is virtually impossible to find any two copies that are absolutely identical, or to be able to claim that any particular copy is definitive. The variations between copies probably result from two factors: the technology of seventeenth-century printing, and the peculiar circumstances under which Hobbes corrected the proof sheets.

Very few if any seventeenth-century printers would have had a sufficient store of movable type to set up a whole book—especially one as long as *Leviathan*. The normal practice was thus to set up a few formes of type (each forme containing two, four, or eight pages depending on the intended size of the finished book). The formes were corrected and printed on to large sheets which were laid aside to be folded and cut in due course to make the pages of the final volume. The type was then distributed to be reused in later pages, and so on until the book was completed. Corrections were made by the in-house proof-reader and sometimes also (as in the case of *Leviathan*) by the author.

The difficulty was that Hobbes was in Paris throughout the printing of *Leviathan*, and we know from Edward Hyde, Earl of Clarendon, who was visited by him in April 1651, that the book 'was then printing in England, and that he received every week a sheet to correct of which he shewed me one or two sheets' (*A Brief View and Survey* [of *Leviathan*], Oxford, 1676, pp. 7–8): a slow, cumbersome, and expensive process. What appears to have happened, at least what would readily account for the small variations between copies of the Head edition, is that a number of sheets were printed with in-house proof-reader's corrections while the printers were waiting for Hobbes's corrections to be returned. (There is evidence that Parts I and II were printed by one firm, and Parts III and IV by another.) When his corrections were received and incorporated into the text, the sheets were then printed again to make up the number of copies required for the completed publication, and then laid aside, as explained, with those already printed. But when the final folding and sewing was being done, the sheets were combined without regard to the way they had been corrected. The outcome is that it is unusual to find two Head copies which are absolutely identical.

It must, however, be emphasized that the vast majority of the variations are minute. They usually amount to no more than grammatical corrections, the resolution of ambiguities, variations in punctuation, or making the wording consistent with something written elsewhere in the same paragraph. In effect this means that any copy of the Head edition would make a respectable text for ordinary reading, or for the study of Hobbes's philosophy. But it is possible to do better than simply reprinting a copy of the Head with errata and other obvious errors corrected. Two further sources exist against which any given copy of the Head can be checked.

The first is a scribal manuscript, with some emendations in Hobbes's own hand, now in the British Library. It is claimed to be, and very probably is the copy Hobbes caused to be made and which he presented to the future Charles II in November or December 1651. It consists of 248 sheets of vellum, written on both sides in a fine but very small hand, in ink which has partly rubbed off or faded except for the few sheets where the vellum has been of poor quality and consequently absorbed the ink. Perversely, these remain sharp and clear, while the rest of the text is miserably difficult to read and sometimes all but impossible. The relation between this manuscript (which I shall refer to as the written copy) and the printed text is complicated. For example, some of Hobbes's emendations serve to bring the written copy into line with the printed copies. Other differences may relate to its particular and rather special reader. I have not used it in the preparation of the present text except to draw attention in my notes to some occasions when a variation seems significant and interesting.

The second, and for practical purposes the more helpful check on the Head text, is provided by the large-paper copies. These were the 'de luxe' or presentation copies of the book, and they alone, as Richard Tuck suggests (and I would agree with him), seem to have been made up from gatherings of the fully corrected sheets. Tuck has identified the variations against a normal copy of the Head edition. They are silently incorporated into the present text except in the few cases when they might be construed as substantial. These substantial variations are noted. But a full record of alternative readings and an assessment of their significance must await Noel Malcolm's critical edition in the *Clarendon Edition of the Works of Thomas Hobbes*.

The Principles of this Edition

From what I have said it will be clear that a minutely and definitively correct edition of *Leviathan* is not possible. Nevertheless, an entirely satisfactory philosophical text (and certainly one as good as or better than most of Hobbes's contemporaries could have read) is achievable by incorporating into a Head copy the errata which it lists, by correcting the obvious minor printer's errors, and by adopting the alternative readings from the large-paper text. In the present edition these things have been done, and the following principles followed:

1. Seventeenth-century punctuation in the Head edition is retained on the grounds that 'modernization' is a non-standard operation which interposes an editor's opinion between what Hobbes intended and what the reader can see. Exceptions (if they so count) are: putting in the apostrophe in the possessive case wherever it is needed by modern convention, and, in a tiny handful of instances towards the end of *Leviathan*, replacing a colon with a full stop, where this is sanctioned by both the Bear and Ornaments editions.

2. Spelling is modernized throughout. It cannot, for example, alter what Hobbes meant us to understand if we print 'near' rather than 'neer'. To keep mid-seventeenth-century spelling (already being modernized by the time the Ornaments edition was printed) simply hinders the reader without getting one whit closer to understanding Hobbes's work.

3. Hobbes's use of italics is somewhat excessive by modern standards. Nevertheless, I have felt bound to retain them in most cases. He employs them for quotations (or close paraphrases), for emphasis (particularly for contrasting pairs of words in juxtaposition), for foreign words, for titles of books, and sometimes for proper names. Only the last seems to be a mere uninformative typographical convention, and it is the only one I have modified to roman type.

4. When giving particular attention to a concept, often for the purposes of introducing a definition, Hobbes commonly prints the word in running capitals, presumably to help catch the eye. This convention is retained.

5. In accordance with modern practice I have replaced with lower-case letters the initial capital letters Hobbes usually gives to substantives in his text, and to the first word following a colon. Again there seems to be no intrusion into what he means if we now read, for example, 'the ground of courage is always strength or skill' rather than 'the ground of Courage is always Strength or Skill'. Nevertheless, in any doubtful case (e.g. 'Schools'), where Hobbes might wish to give a special dignity or quasi proper-name status to a noun, I have let his capitals stand.

6. In keeping with what will be done in the Clarendon Press edition, and what has already been done in Edwin Curley's American text of *Leviathan*, each Head paragraph has been numbered with a new run of arabic numerals for each chapter. Hobbes had already done this in *The Elements of Law* and in *De Cive*, and was to revert to the practice in *De Corpore*. The device is extremely useful for quick reference. Thus XLII. 54 means Chapter XLII, paragraph 54. To further facilitate cross-refer-

ence with other editions, the page number of the original Head pages is given in square brackets in the margin: a device adopted by a number of modern editors.

7. Hobbes usually gives biblical references in the text enclosed by round brackets, but he sometimes uses commas, and occasionally puts references in the margin. In the present text all such references are given in the text in round brackets except where they form part of the grammatical structure of a clause or sentence.

8. With one category excepted, all the present editor's notes—sources, philosophical notes, biographies, translations, textual comments, etc.—are signalled in the text with an asterisk. The exception is where a curious or obsolete word can be explained by at most two familiar words. In order to save the reader turning to extremely brief endnotes, such explanations are given in square brackets in the text immediately following the word they explain.

The Latin Leviathan

The *Leviathan* which provoked the furious rage of divines and politicians in the first fifty years after its publication, which survived the neglect of the mid-eighteenth century to become the subject of so many reprints and so much comment from the 1880s onwards, and which in 1946 elicited Oakeshott's famous judgement that 'The *Leviathan* is the greatest, perhaps the sole, masterpiece of political philosophy written in the English language. And the history of our civilization can provide only a few works of similar scope and achievement to set beside it', is the English *Leviathan*. But there is another *Leviathan*. A Latin version appeared in Amsterdam in 1668 and again in 1670, and the same version appeared in London in 1678, with a possible earlier printing there in 1676 (although this may be a false attribution for another issue of the Amsterdam sheets).

The Latin version differs significantly from the English. It is thus misleading to think of it as a translation, despite a general (but only a general) paragraph-by-paragraph parallel. Very briefly, the differences are: (*a*) that much of the Latin reads like a close paraphrase in which particular details filled out by the English text have been ignored; (*b*) that, despite this, numerous substantial adjustments and additions to the English text have been made, most of them seemingly to rebut charges of atheism and heresy, or to correct what Hobbes came to regard as errors (in a reply to Bishop Bramhall he explicitly says that an error of argument is being corrected in the edition being printed in Holland); and (*c*) that the Latin text, apart from a near reworking of the material in Chapters XLVI and

XLVII, also has a three-chapter Appendix which never had any English equivalent. The additional chapters are: 'On the Nicene Creed', 'On Heresy', and 'On certain Objections to *Leviathan*' (the last being again mainly concerned with charges of atheism and heresy).

In preparing the present text of the English *Leviathan* I have made no attempt to indicate where it differs from the Latin version. There are two reasons for this. One is that the task has already been done, for example by Julius Lips in ch. VII of *Die Stellung des Thomas Hobbes zu den politischen Parteien der grossen Englischen Revolution* (Leipzig, 1927) and in François Tricaud's French translation of *Leviathan* (Paris, 1971). A translation by George Wright of the Appendix can be found in the journal *Interpretation* (1991), 323–412. Wright also provides a substantial commentary.

The other reason for ignoring the Latin *Leviathan* in the present edition is that it is the English text which is, and, with the exception of a short period on the continent of Europe in the late seventeenth century, always has been the *Leviathan* which the world has argued over and discussed. Hobbes specialists, particularly those concerned with later adjustments to Hobbes's views about religion, cannot disregard the Latin version. The student of moral and political philosophy, and the ordinary reader concerned to grasp Hobbes's ideas and their influence, can disregard it; and almost always has. The Latin version is a relatively obscure work for scholars. The English version is the book which has challenged, and continues to challenge, the moral, political, and religious ideas of the world. This is the text which is 'the greatest, perhaps the sole, masterpiece of political philosophy written in the English language'.

SELECT BIBLIOGRAPHY

THE literature spawned by Hobbes's publications in general and *Leviathan* in particular, both in his own century and again in the second half of the twentieth century, is so vast that any select bibliography that is to be useful has to be very select indeed. Between 1651 and about 1700 the reason for the attention was the huge opposition provoked by what were taken to be his ideas about politics, religion, and morality. This is fascinatingly documented in S. I. Mintz, *The Hunting of Leviathan* (Cambridge, 1969). More recently, the literature reflects the extraordinary scale and variety of the subjects to which Hobbes contributed, their capacity to interest philosophers and scholars with diverse views, their continuing ability to provoke controversy and divergent interpretations, and their sheer excitement as ideas.

A general, easy account of his life and works can be found in *Hobbes* by G. Croom Robertson (Edinburgh, 1886) and in Leslie Stephen's *Hobbes* (London, 1904). Some of the details of his private life and activities can be found in the edition of his collected letters, *The Correspondence of Thomas Hobbes*, ed. Noel Malcolm (2 vols., Clarendon Press, Oxford, 1994). The three main contemporary biographical documents, Aubrey's 'Brief Life' and Hobbes's own 'Prose Life' and 'Verse Life' (in English translations), are included in the World's Classics edition of *The Elements of Law* (*Human Nature* and *De Corpore Politico*).

Three general accounts of Hobbes's ideas are notably useful: *Hobbes* by Richard Peters (Harmondsworth, 1956), *Hobbes* by Tom Sorell (London and New York, 1986), and *Hobbes* by Richard Tuck (Oxford and New York, 1989).

His general philosophy and philosophy of science is well dealt with in J. W. N. Watkin's *Hobbes's System of Ideas* (London, 1965, revised edition 1989) as well as by Peters and Sorell. The most exhaustive (some might say exhausting) account of Hobbes's philosophy of science is still F. Brandt's *Thomas Hobbes's Mechanical Conception of Nature* (Copenhagen, 1928, and English translation, London, same year).

A useful introduction to Hobbes's moral and political philosophy—for long treated as almost the only concern of *Leviathan*—is in D. D. Raphael's lucid *Hobbes: Morals and Politics* (London, 1977); particularly valuable is his survey of major book-length interpretations of Hobbes. Among such interpretations the following stand out: Leo Strauss, *The*

1

Political Philosophy of Thomas Hobbes (Oxford, 1936); Howard Warrender, *The Political Philosophy of Hobbes: His Theory of Obligation* (Oxford, 1957); C. B. Macpherson, *The Political Theory of Possessive Individualism* (Oxford, 1962); and Michael Oakeshott, *Hobbes on Civil Association* (Oxford, 1975). Their views are summarized and developed, together with other important essays, in the collection *Hobbes Studies*, ed. K. Brown (Oxford, 1965).

Other important books on *Leviathan* include F. S. McNeilly, *The Anatomy of Leviathan* (London, 1968); D. Gauthier, *The Logic of Leviathan* (Oxford, 1969); D. Johnson, *The Rhetoric of Leviathan* (Princeton, NJ, 1986); S. A. Lloyd, *Ideals as Interests in Hobbes's Leviathan: The Power of Mind over Matter* (Cambridge, 1992).

Hobbes's account of, and views about, religion as a social and political phenomenon (and to a lesser extent his philosophy of religion and personal beliefs) should be studied in F. C. Hood, *The Divine Politics of Thomas Hobbes* (Clarendon Press, Oxford, 1964), and in A. P. Martinich's *The Two Gods of Leviathan* (Cambridge, 1992) as well as in Lloyd (see above). But much of the best material is in articles. A massive collection of these—on religion and other Hobbes topics—has been edited by P. King and published as *Thomas Hobbes: Critical Assessments* (4 vols., London, 1993).

Other useful collections of articles are: *Hobbes and Rousseau*, ed. M. Cranston and R. Peters (New York, 1972); *Hobbes's Science of Natural Justice*, ed. C. Walton and P. J. Johnson (Dordrecht, 1987); and *Perspectives on Thomas Hobbes*, ed. G. A. J. Rogers and A. Ryan (Oxford, 1988).

Hobbes's own works are still only available as a whole in *The English Works of Thomas Hobbes*, ed. Sir William Molesworth (11 vols., London, 1839) together with his edition of the Latin works (5 vols., London, 1845), although a complete edition of the philosophical works is in preparation for Oxford University Press. But the two works most closely relevant to *Leviathan* are easily available. They are *The Elements of Law* (*Human Nature* and *De Corpore Politico*), ed. J. C. A. Gaskin, World's Classics (Oxford, 1994), and *De Cive*, ed. H. Warrender (Clarendon Press, Oxford, 1983). Also relevant to some of the earlier chapters of *Leviathan* is Hobbes's *Thomas White's De Mundo Examined*, translated by H. W. Jones (first published Bradford and London, 1976). Hobbes returns to the history and politics that form the background to *Leviathan* in two later works now available in modern editions: *A Dialogue between a Philosopher and a Student of the Common Laws of England* (Chicago, 1971), and *Behemoth* (London, 1969).

A facsimile of a Head copy of *Leviathan* was published by The Scolar

Press Ltd., Menston, England, in 1969. A more readily available and remarkably accurate printing of the Head text was done at the Clarendon Press, Oxford, 1909, with numerous reprints. The Latin *Leviathan* was published in Amsterdam in 1668. The differences between it and the English version are discussed by François Tricaud, *Leviathan* (Paris, 1971).

The point of departure for those interested in the editions of Hobbes's works, their order, and printing histories in his lifetime, is *Thomas Hobbes: A Bibliography*, by H. MacDonald and M. Hargreaves (London, 1952).

CHRONOLOGY

1588   Birth of Thomas Hobbes at Westport near Malmesbury, Wiltshire, on Good Friday, 5 April: 'His mother fell in labour with him upon the fright of the invasion of the Spaniards' (Aubrey). Spanish Armada dispersed and defeated.

1592–1602   Hobbes educated to high standards in Greek and Latin at local schools, initially in Westport (1592–6) then in Malmesbury (1596–1602).

1603   Death of Elizabeth I. Kingdoms of England and Scotland united under the first Stuart king, James I of England and VI of Scotland.

1603–8   Hobbes at Magdalen Hall, Oxford. Awarded BA in February 1608. Dislikes Oxford's Aristotelianism etc.

1608–26   Employed by Sir William Cavendish (created first Earl of Devonshire 1618) as tutor to his son and later as the first Earl's own secretary.

1610–15[?]   Hobbes's *first* visit to Continent with Cavendish's son.

1621–6   Conversations with Francis Bacon (forerunner of British empiricist tradition in philosophy).

1625   Death of James I, accession of Charles I.

1626   Death of first Earl of Devonshire. Hobbes's former pupil becomes second Earl. Hobbes retained as his secretary.

1629–40   Charles I governs without an English Parliament.

1629   Hobbes's translation of Thucydides' *History of the Peloponnesian War* published. Leaves the Cavendish family's employment as a result of economies made after the untimely death of second Earl in 1628.

1629–30   Hobbes's *second* visit to Continent (as travelling tutor to the son of Sir Gervase Clifton). Possibly in this period Hobbes became vividly aware both of methods of proof and deduction in Euclidian geometry and of the significance of the question 'What is sensation?'

1630   Re-employed by Cavendish family, with whom he retained connections until the end of his life. Earliest assignable date for composition of a short Latin thesis (attributed to Hobbes) relating sensation to varieties of movement (latest possible date: 1637).

1634–6   Hobbes's *third* visit to Continent travelling as mentor to the young third Earl of Devonshire: meets Marin Mersenne (clerical patron of new learning in France; via Mersenne he later offered objections to Descartes's *Meditations* before its publication in 1641); met and admired Galileo and others.

1640-2   Acute constitutional crisis between king and the Long Parliament (first met November 1640) establishes conditions for civil war.

1640   'My little Treatise in English', namely *Elements of Law, Natural and Politic* (containing *Human Nature* and *De Corpore Politico*), written and widely circulated among friends in MS copies.

1640-51   Sojourn in France, to which Hobbes fled at the end of 1640 in anticipation of civil war in England, and in apprehension of the dangers to himself inherent in his doctrines as expressed in the 'little Treatise'. Became friend of Mersenne, Gassendi, and other adventurous intellectuals.

1642-6   First civil war, between Royalists and Parliamentary forces, mainly in England.

1642   *De Cive* (an expanded version of *De Corpore Politico*) published in Latin in Paris.

1645/6   First conversations with Bramhall, Bishop of Derry, concerning liberty and necessity.

1646   Charles surrenders to Scots (May) and is handed over to English Parliamentary forces (Jan. 1647). Hobbes appointed tutor (Oct.) to future Charles II, who was by then taking refuge in Paris.

1647   Severe illness begins in August: receives sacrament according to rite of Church of England from future Bishop of Durham.

1647-50   *Leviathan* written in France.

1648   Meets Descartes in Paris. Mersenne dies and Hobbes begins to feel unsafe in Paris because of his hostility to Roman Catholicism.

1648-51   Second civil war: Cromwell, in command of Parliamentary army, suppresses rebellion in Ireland, Presbyterian and Royalist forces in Scotland, and Royalist uprisings in Wales.

1649   Charles I executed in London.

1650   *Human Nature* and *De Corpore Politico* published separately in London, probably without Hobbes's authority.

1651   The English version of *De Cive* published in London (Mar.?). *Leviathan* published in London (May?). The written copy of *Leviathan* presented to Charles II (Nov/Dec?).

1652   Hobbes returns to England (Feb.).

1653   Cromwell declared Lord Protector.

1654   *De Cive* placed on the Index at Rome. Controversy with Bishop Bramhall concerning liberty and free will receives unauthorized publication in *Of Liberty and Necessity*.

1655   *De Corpore* published in Latin.

1656   *Questions concerning Liberty, Necessity and Chance*, a further debate between Hobbes and Bramhall, given authorized publication. *De Corpore* published in English (do not confuse with *De Corpore Politico*, the second Part of *The Elements of Law*).

1656–78   Published controversy with Oxford mathematicians Seth Ward and John Wallis concerning Hobbes's claim in ch. XX of *De Corpore* to have 'squared the circle'. Hobbes manifestly worsted.

1658   *De Homine* published in Latin (an original work repeating some of the ideas in, but not a version of, *Human Nature*, and including much new material on optics). Death of Cromwell.

1660   Charles II returns to London as king (29 May). Hobbes befriended by Charles after Restoration, welcomed at Court, and given a pension (sometimes paid).

1661–2   Controversy with Boyle concerning scientific method.

1665–6   Plague in London.

1666   Fire of London (Sept.).

1666   House of Commons seeks information about 'Mr Hobbes's *Leviathan*' in relation to its bill against atheism (Oct.). Aubrey reports that about this time 'some of the bishops made a motion to have the good old gentleman burnt for a heretic'. *A Dialogue between a Philosopher and a Student of the Common Laws of England* written at instigation of Aubrey. (Published 1681.)

1668   *Behemoth* (a history of the Civil Wars, 1640–60) written but, at wish of the king, not published. Latin version of *Leviathan* published in Amsterdam.

1673   Translation into English of *Odyssey* published: 'I had nothing else to do.'

1675–9   At Chatsworth and Hardwick Hall in semi-retirement under protection of Cavendish family.

1676   Translation of *Iliad* added to new edition of *Odyssey*.

1679   Thomas Hobbes dies at Hardwick Hall on 4 Dec. and is buried at parish church of Ault Hucknall.

1682   *An Answer to Bishop Bramhall* published (a reply written about 1668 to Bramhall's objections to *Leviathan*). Authorized edition of *Behemoth* published. (A probably unauthorized edition had been published in London in 1679.)

1683   Oxford University condemns and burns copies of *Leviathan* and *De Cive*.

1685   Death of Charles II, James II becomes king.

1688   James deposed in bloodless revolution.

1689   Bill of Rights. William and Mary become joint sovereigns.

LEVIATHAN,

OR

The Matter, Forme, & Power

OF A

COMMON-WEALTH

ECCLESIASTICALL

AND

CIVILL.

By THOMAS HOBBES *of* Malmesbury.

LONDON,

Printed for ANDREW CROOKE, at the Green Dragon
in St. *Pauls* Church-yard, 1 6 5 1.

The engraved title-page of the Head Edition

TO MY MOST HONOURED FRIEND
MR. FRANCIS GODOLPHIN
OF *Godolphin*

HONOURED SIR,

YOUR most worthy brother Mr Sidney Godolphin,* when he lived, was pleased to think my studies something, and otherwise to oblige me, as you know, with real testimonies of his good opinion, great in themselves, and the greater for the worthiness of his person. For there is not any virtue that disposeth a man, either to the service of God, or to the service of his country, to civil society, or private friendship, that did not manifestly appear in his conversation, not as acquired by necessity, or affected upon occasion, but inherent, and shining in a generous constitution of his nature. Therefore, in honour and gratitude to him, and with devotion to yourself, I humbly dedicate unto you this my discourse of Commonwealth. I know not how the world will receive it, nor how it may reflect on those that shall seem to favour it. For in a way beset with those that contend, on one side for too great liberty, and on the other side for too much authority, 'tis hard to pass between the points of both unwounded. But yet, methinks, the endeavour to advance the civil power, should not be by the civil power condemned; nor private men, by reprehending it, declare they think that power too great. Besides, I speak not of the men, but (in the abstract) of the seat of power, (like to those simple and unpartial creatures in the Roman Capitol, that with their noise defended those within it, not because they were they, but there,) offending none, I think, but those without, or such within (if there be any such) as favour them. That which perhaps may most offend, are certain texts of Holy Scripture, alleged by me to other purpose than ordinarily they use to be by others. But I have done it with due submission, and also (in order to my subject) necessarily; for they are the outworks of the enemy, from whence they impugn the civil power. If notwithstanding this, you find my labour generally decried, you may be pleased to excuse yourself, and say I am a man that love my own opinions, and think all true I say, that I honoured your brother, and honour you, and have presumed on that, to assume the title (without your knowledge) of being, as I am,

SIR,

Your most humble,

and most obedient Servant,

Paris, April $\frac{15}{25}$, 1651.　　　　　　　　　　THOMAS HOBBES.

3

THE CONTENTS OF THE CHAPTERS

THE FIRST PART: OF MAN

Introduction 7

1. Of Sense 9
2. Of Imagination 10
3. Of the Consequence or Train of Imaginations 15
4. Of Speech 20
5. Of Reason and Science 27
6. Of the Interior Beginnings of Voluntary Motions, commonly called the Passions; and the Speeches by which they are expressed 33
7. Of the Ends or Resolutions of Discourse 42
8. Of the Virtues, commonly called Intellectual, and their contrary Defects 45
9. Of the Several Subjects of Knowledge 54
10. Of Power, Worth, Dignity, Honour, and Worthiness 58
11. Of the Difference of Manners 65
12. Of Religion 71
13. Of the Natural Condition of Mankind as concerning their Felicity and Misery 82
14. Of the First and Second Natural Laws, and of Contract 86
15. Of other Laws of Nature 95
16. Of Persons, Authors, and Things Personated 106

THE SECOND PART: OF COMMONWEALTH

17. Of the Causes, Generation, and Definition of a Commonwealth 111
18. Of the Rights of Sovereigns by Institution 115
19. Of several Kinds of Commonwealth by Institution; and of Succession to the Sovereign Power 123
20. Of Dominion Paternal, and Despotical 132
21. Of the Liberty of Subjects 139
22. Of Systems Subject, Political, and Private 148
23. Of the Public Ministers of Sovereign Power 159
24. Of the Nutrition, and Procreation of a Commonwealth 163

25. Of Counsel   168
26. Of Civil Laws   175
27. Of Crimes, Excuses, and Extenuations   192
28. Of Punishments, and Rewards   205
29. Of those things that Weaken, or tend to the Dissolution
    of a Commonwealth   212
30. Of the Office of the Sovereign Representative   222
31. Of the Kingdom of God by Nature   235

THE THIRD PART: OF A CHRISTIAN COMMONWEALTH

32. Of the Principles of Christian Politics   247
33. Of the Number, Antiquity, Scope, Authority, and
    Interpreters of the Books of Holy Scripture   251
34. Of the Signification, of Spirit, Angel, and Inspiration, in the
    Books of Holy Scripture   260
35. Of the Signification in Scripture of the Kingdom of God,
    of Holy, Sacred, and Sacrament   271
36. Of the Word of God, and of Prophets   277
37. Of Miracles, and their Use   290
38. Of the Signification in Scripture of Eternal Life, Hell,
    Salvation, the World to Come, and Redemption   297
39. Of the Signification in Scripture of the word Church   310
40. Of the Rights of the Kingdom of God, in Abraham, Moses,
    the High Priests, and the Kings of Judah   312
41. Of the Office of Our Blessed Saviour   321
42. Of Power Ecclesiastical   327
43. Of what is Necessary for a Man's Reception into the Kingdom
    of Heaven   390

THE FOURTH PART: OF THE KINGDOM OF DARKNESS

44. Of Spiritual Darkness from Misinterpretation of Scripture   403
45. Of Demonology, and other Relics of the Religion of
    the Gentiles   424
46. Of Darkness from Vain Philosophy; and Fabulous
    Traditions   441
47. Of the Benefit proceeding from such Darkness; and to
    whom it accrueth   457

    A Review and Conclusion   467

THE INTRODUCTION

1. NATURE (the art whereby God hath made and governs the [1]
world) is by the *art* of man, as in many other things, so in this also
imitated, that it can make an artificial animal. For seeing life is but
a motion of limbs,* the beginning whereof is in some principal part
within; why may we not say, that all *automata* (engines that move
themselves by springs and wheels as doth a watch) have an artificial
life? For what is the *heart*, but a *spring*; and the *nerves*, but so many
strings; and the *joints*, but so many *wheels*, giving motion to the whole
body, such as was intended by the artificer? *Art* goes yet further,
imitating that rational and most excellent work of nature, *man*. For
by art is created that great LEVIATHAN* called a COMMONWEALTH, or
STATE, (in Latin CIVITAS) which is but an artificial man; though of
greater stature and strength than the natural, for whose protection
and defence it was intended; and in which, the *sovereignty* is an
artificial *soul*, as giving life and motion to the whole body; the
magistrates, and other *officers* of judicature and execution, artificial
joints; *reward* and *punishment* (by which fastened to the seat of the
sovereignty, every joint and member is moved to perform his duty)
are the *nerves*, that do the same in the body natural; the *wealth* and
riches of all the particular members, are the *strength*; *salus populi* (the
people's safety) its *business*; *counsellors*, by whom all things needful for
it to know, are suggested unto it, are the *memory*; *equity* and *laws*, an
artificial *reason* and *will*; *concord*, *health*; *sedition*, *sickness*; and *civil
war*, *death*. Lastly, the *pacts* and *covenants*, by which the parts of this
body politic were at first made, set together, and united, resemble
that *fiat*, or the *let us make man*, pronounced by God in the creation.

2. To describe the nature of this artificial man, I will consider [2]
First, the *matter* thereof, and the *artificer*; both which is *Man*.

Secondly, *how*, and by what *covenants* it is made; what are the
rights and just *power* or *authority* of a *sovereign*; and what it is that
preserveth and *dissolveth* it.

Thirdly, what is a *Christian Commonwealth*.

Lastly, what is the *Kingdom of Darkness*.

3. Concerning the first, there is a saying much usurped of late,
that *wisdom* is acquired, not by reading of *books*,* but of *men*. Consequently whereunto, those persons, that for the most part can give

no other proof of being wise, take great delight to show what they think they have read in men, by uncharitable censures of one another behind their backs. But there is another saying not of late understood, by which they might learn truly to read one another, if they would take the pains; and that is, *nosce teipsum, read thyself*: which was not meant, as it is now used, to countenance, either the barbarous state of men in power, towards their inferiors; or to encourage men of low degree, to a saucy behaviour towards their betters; but to teach us, that for the similitude of the thoughts, and passions of one man, to the thoughts, and passions of another, whosoever looketh into himself, and considereth what he doth, when he does *think*, *opine*, *reason*, *hope*, *fear*, &c, and upon what grounds; he shall thereby read and know, what are the thoughts, and passions of all other men, upon the like occasions. I say the similitude of *passions*, which are the same in all men, *desire*, *fear*, *hope*, &c; not the similitude of the *objects* of the passions, which are the things *desired*, *feared*, *hoped*, &c: for these the constitution individual, and particular education do so vary, and they are so easy to be kept from our knowledge, that the characters of man's heart, blotted and confounded as they are, with dissembling, lying, counterfeiting, and erroneous doctrines, are legible only to him that searcheth hearts. And though by men's actions we do discover their design sometimes; yet to do it without comparing them with our own, and distinguishing all circumstances, by which the case may come to be altered, is to decipher without a key, and be for the most part deceived, by too much trust, or by too much diffidence; as he that reads, is himself a good or evil man.

4. But let one man read another by his actions never so perfectly, it serves him only with his acquaintance, which are but few. He that is to govern a whole nation, must read in himself, not this, or that particular man; but mankind: which though it be hard to do, harder than to learn any language, or science; yet, when I shall have set down my own reading orderly, and perspicuously, the pains left another, will be only to consider, if he also find not the same in himself. For this kind of doctrine admitteth no other demonstration.

PART 1

OF MAN

CHAPTER I

OF SENSE*

1. CONCERNING the thoughts of man, I will consider them first [3]
singly, and afterwards in train, or dependence upon one another.
Singly, they are every one a *representation* or *appearance*, of some
quality, or other accident of a body without us; which is commonly
called an *object*. Which object worketh on the eyes, ears, and other
parts of a man's body; and by diversity of working, produceth
diversity of appearances.

2. The original of them all, is that which we call SENSE, for there
is no conception in a man's mind, which hath not at first, totally, or
by parts, been begotten upon the organs of sense. The rest are
derived from that original.

3. To know the natural cause of sense, is not very necessary to
the business now in hand; and I have elsewhere written* of the same
at large. Nevertheless, to fill each part of my present method, I will
briefly deliver the same in this place.

4. The cause of sense, is the external body, or object, which
presseth the organ proper to each sense, either immediately,
as in the taste and touch; or mediately, as in seeing, hearing, and
smelling: which pressure, by the mediation of the nerves, and other
strings, and membranes of the body, continued inwards to the
brain and heart, causeth there a resistance, or counter-pressure, or
endeavour* of the heart, to deliver itself: which endeavour because
outward, seemeth to be some matter without. And this *seeming*, or
fancy,* is that which men call *sense*; and consisteth, as to the eye, in
a *light*, or *colour figured*; to the ear, in a *sound*; to the nostril, in an
odour; to the tongue and palate, in a *savour*; and to the rest of the
body, in *heat*, *cold*, *hardness*, *softness*, and such other qualities, as we
discern by *feeling*. All which qualities called *sensible*, are in the object
that causeth them, but so many several motions of the matter, by
which it presseth our organs diversely. Neither in us that are

pressed, are they any thing else, but divers motions; (for motion produceth nothing but motion.) But their appearance to us is fancy, the same waking, that dreaming. And as pressing, rubbing, or striking the eye, makes us fancy a light; and pressing the ear, produceth a din; so do the bodies also we see, or hear, produce the same by their strong, though unobserved action. For if those colours, and sounds, were in the bodies, or objects that cause them, [4] they could not be severed from them, as by glasses, and in echoes by reflection, we see they are; where we know the thing we see, is in one place; the appearance, in another. And though at some certain distance, the real and very object seem invested with the fancy it begets in us; yet still the object is one thing, the image or fancy is another. So that sense in all cases, is nothing else but original fancy, caused (as I have said) by the pressure, that is, by the motion, of external things upon our eyes, ears, and other organs thereunto ordained.

5. But the philosophy-schools, through all the universities of Christendom, grounded upon certain texts of Aristotle, teach another doctrine; and say, for the cause of *vision*, that the thing seen, sendeth forth on every side a *visible species* (in English) a *visible show*, *apparition*, or *aspect*, or *a being seen*; the receiving whereof into the eye, is *seeing*. And for the cause of *hearing*, that the thing heard, sendeth forth an *audible species*, that is, an *audible aspect*, or *audible being seen*; which entering at the ear, maketh *hearing*. Nay for the cause of *understanding* also, they say the thing understood sendeth forth an *intelligible species*, that is, an *intelligible being seen*; which coming into the understanding, makes us understand. I say not this, as disproving the use of universities: but because I am to speak hereafter of their office in a commonwealth, I must let you see on all occasions by the way, what things would be amended in them; amongst which the frequency of insignificant speech is one.

CHAPTER II

OF IMAGINATION

1. THAT when a thing lies still, unless somewhat else stir it, it will lie still for ever, is a truth that no man doubts of. But that when a thing is in motion, it will eternally be in motion, unless somewhat

else stay it, though the reason be the same, (namely, that nothing can change itself,) is not so easily assented to.* For men measure, not only other men, but all other things, by themselves: and because they find themselves subject after motion to pain, and lassitude, think every thing else grows weary of motion, and seeks repose of its own accord; little considering, whether it be not some other motion, wherein that desire of rest they find in themselves, consisteth. From hence it is, that the schools say, heavy bodies fall downwards, out of an appetite to rest, and to conserve their nature in that place which is most proper for them; ascribing appetite, and knowledge of what is good for their conservation, (which is more than man has) to things inanimate, absurdly.

2. When a body is once in motion, it moveth (unless something else hinder it) eternally; and whatsoever hindreth it, cannot in an instant, but in time, and by degrees quite extinguish it; and as we see in the water, though the wind cease, the waves give not over rolling for a long time after; so also it happeneth in that motion, which is [5] made in the internal parts of a man, then, when he sees, dreams, &c. For after the object is removed, or the eye shut, we still retain an image of the thing seen, though more obscure than when we see it. And this is it, the Latins call *imagination*, from the image made in seeing; and apply the same, though improperly, to all the other senses. But the Greeks call it *fancy*; which signifies *appearance*, and is as proper to one sense, as to another. IMAGINATION therefore is nothing but *decaying sense*; and is found in men, and many other living creatures, as well sleeping, as waking.

3. The decay of sense in men waking, is not the decay of the motion made in sense; but an obscuring of it, in such manner, as the light of the sun obscureth the light of the stars; which stars do no less exercise their virtue by which they are visible, in the day, than in the night. But because amongst many strokes, which our eyes, ears, and other organs receive from external bodies, the predominant only is sensible; therefore the light of the sun being predominant, we are not affected with the action of the stars. And any object being removed from our eyes, though the impression it made in us remain; yet other objects more present succeeding, and working on us, the imagination of the past is obscured, and made weak; as the voice of a man is in the noise of the day. From whence it followeth, that the longer the time is, after the sight, or sense of any object, the weaker is the imagination. For the continual change

of man's body, destroys in time the parts which in sense were moved: so that distance of time, and of place, hath one and the same effect in us. For as at a great distance of place, that which we look at, appears dim, and without distinction of the smaller parts; and as voices grow weak, and inarticulate: so also after great distance of time, our imagination of the past is weak; and we lose (for example) of cities we have seen, many particular streets; and of actions, many particular circumstances. This *decaying sense*, when we would express the thing itself, (I mean *fancy* itself) we call *imagination*, as I said before: but when we would express the decay, and signify that the sense is fading, old, and past, it is called *memory*. So that imagination and memory, are but one thing, which for divers considerations hath divers names.

Memory.

4. Much memory, or memory of many things, is called *experience*. Again, imagination being only of those things which have been formerly perceived by sense, either all at once, or by parts at several times; the former, (which is the imagining the whole object, as it was presented to the sense) is *simple* imagination; as when one imagineth a man, or horse, which he hath seen before. The other is *compounded*; as when from the sight of a man at one time, and of a horse at another, we conceive in our mind a Centaur. So when a man compoundeth the image of his own person, with the image of the actions of another man; as when a man imagines himself a Hercules or an Alexander, (which happeneth often to them that are much taken with reading of romances) it is a compound imagination, and

[6] properly but a fiction of the mind. There be also other imaginations that rise in men, (though waking) from the great impression made in sense: as from gazing upon the sun, the impression leaves an image of the sun before our eyes a long time after; and from being long and vehemently attent upon geometrical figures, a man shall in the dark (though awake) have the images of lines, and angles before his eyes: which kind of fancy hath no particular name; as being a thing that doth not commonly fall into men's discourse.

Dreams.

5. The imaginations of them that sleep, are those we call *dreams*. And these also (as all other imaginations) have been before, either totally, or by parcels in the sense. And because in sense, the brain, and nerves, which are the necessary organs of sense, are so benumbed in sleep, as not easily to be moved by the action of external objects, there can happen in sleep, no imagination; and therefore no dream, but what proceeds from the agitation of

the inward parts of man's body; which inward parts, for the connexion they have with the brain, and other organs, when they be distempered, do keep the same in motion; whereby the imaginations there formerly made, appear as if a man were waking; saving that the organs of sense being now benumbed, so as there is no new object, which can master and obscure them with a more vigorous impression, a dream must needs be more clear, in this silence of sense, than are our waking thoughts. And hence it cometh to pass, that it is a hard matter, and by many thought impossible to distinguish exactly between sense and dreaming. For my part, when I consider, that in dreams, I do not often, nor constantly think of the same persons, places, objects, and actions that I do waking; nor remember so long a train of coherent thoughts, dreaming, as at other times; and because waking I often observe the absurdity of dreams, but never dream of the absurdities of my waking thoughts; I am well satisfied, that being awake, I know I dream not; though when I dream, I think myself awake.*

6. And seeing dreams are caused by the distemper of some of the inward parts of the body; divers distempers must needs cause different dreams. And hence it is, that lying cold breedeth dreams of fear, and raiseth the thought and image of some fearful object (the motion from the brain to the inner parts, and from the inner parts to the brain being reciprocal:) and that as anger causeth heat in some parts of the body, when we are awake; so when we sleep, the overheating of the same parts causeth anger, and raiseth up in the brain the imagination of an enemy. In the same manner; as natural kindness, when we are awake causeth desire; and desire makes heat in certain other parts of the body; so also, too much heat in those parts, while we sleep, raiseth in the brain an imagination of some kindness shown. In sum, our dreams are the reverse of our waking imaginations; the motion when we are awake, beginning at one end; and when we dream, at another.

7. The most difficult discerning of a man's dream, from his waking thoughts, is then, when by some accident we observe not that we have slept: which is easy to happen to a man full of fearful thoughts; and whose conscience is much troubled; and that sleepeth, without the circumstances, of going to bed, or putting off his clothes, as one that noddeth in a chair. For he that taketh pains, and industriously lays himself to sleep, in case any uncouth and exorbitant fancy come unto him, cannot easily think it other than a

Apparitions or visions.

[7]

dream. We read of Marcus Brutus, (one that had his life given him by Julius Caesar, and was also his favourite, and notwithstanding murdered him,) how at Philippi, the night before he gave battle to Augustus Caesar, he saw a fearful apparition, which is commonly related by historians* as a vision: but considering the circumstances, one may easily judge to have been but a short dream. For sitting in his tent, pensive and troubled with the horror of his rash act, it was not hard for him, slumbering in the cold, to dream of that which most affrighted him; which fear, as by degrees it made him wake; so also it must needs make the apparition by degrees to vanish: and having no assurance that he slept, he could have no cause to think it a dream, or any thing but a vision. And this is no very rare accident: for even they that be perfectly awake, if they be timorous, and superstitious, possessed with fearful tales, and alone in the dark, are subject to the like fancies; and believe they see spirits and dead men's ghosts walking in churchyards; whereas it is either their fancy only, or else the knavery of such persons, as make use of such superstitious fear, to pass disguised in the night, to places they would not be known to haunt.

8. From this ignorance of how to distinguish dreams, and other strong fancies, from vision and sense, did arise the greatest part of the religion of the Gentiles* in time past, that worshipped satyrs, fawns, nymphs, and the like; and now-a-days the opinion that rude [common] people have of fairies, ghosts, and goblins, and of the power of witches. For as for witches, I think not that their witchcraft is any real power; but yet that they are justly punished, for the false belief they have, that they can do such mischief, joined with their purpose to do it if they can: their trade being nearer to a new religion, than to a craft or science. And for fairies, and walking ghosts, the opinion of them has I think been on purpose, either taught, or not confuted, to keep in credit the use of exorcism, of crosses, of holy water, and other such inventions of ghostly* men. Nevertheless, there is no doubt, but God can make unnatural apparitions: but that he does it so often, as men need to fear such things, more than they fear the stay, or change, of the course of nature, which he also can stay, and change, is no point of Christian faith. But evil men under pretext that God can do any thing, are so bold as to say any thing when it serves their turn, though they think it untrue; it is the part of a wise man, to believe them no further, than right reason makes that

which they say, appear credible. If this superstitious fear of spirits were taken away, and with it, prognostics from dreams, false prophecies, and many other things depending thereon, by which, crafty ambitious persons abuse the simple people, men would be much [8] more fitted than they are for civil obedience.

9. And this ought to be the work of the schools: but they rather nourish such doctrine. For (not knowing what imagination, or the senses are), what they receive, they teach: some saying, that imaginations rise of themselves, and have no cause: others that they rise most commonly from the will; and that good thoughts are blown (inspired) into a man, by God; and evil thoughts by the Devil: or that good thoughts are poured (infused) into a man, by God, and evil ones by the Devil. Some say the senses receive the species of things, and deliver them to the common sense; and the common sense delivers them over to the fancy, and the fancy to the memory, and the memory to the judgment, like handing of things from one to another, with many words making nothing understood.

10. The imagination that is raised in man (or any other creature *Understanding.* endued with the faculty of imagining) by words, or other voluntary signs, is that we generally call *understanding*; and is common to man and beast. For a dog by custom will understand the call, or the rating of his master; and so will many other beasts. That understanding which is peculiar to man, is the understanding not only his will; but his conceptions and thoughts, by the sequel and contexture of the names of things into affirmations, negations, and other forms of speech: and of this kind of understanding I shall speak hereafter.

CHAPTER III

OF THE CONSEQUENCE OR TRAIN OF IMAGINATIONS*

1. BY *Consequence*, or TRAIN of thoughts, I understand that succession of one thought to another, which is called (to distinguish it from discourse in words) *mental discourse*.

2. When a man thinketh on any thing whatsoever, his next thought after, is not altogether so casual as it seems to be. Not every thought to every thought succeeds indifferently.* But as we have no

imagination, whereof we have not formerly had sense, in whole, or in parts; so we have no transition from one imagination to another, whereof we never had the like before in our senses. The reason whereof is this. All fancies are motions within us, relics of those made in the sense: and those motions that immediately succeeded one another in the sense, continue also together after sense: insomuch as the former coming again to take place, and be predominant, the latter followeth, by coherence of the matter moved, in such manner, as water upon a plane table is drawn which way any one part of it is guided by the finger. But because in sense, to one and the same thing perceived, sometimes one thing, sometimes another succeedeth, it comes to pass in time, that in the imagining of any thing, there is no certainty what we shall imagine [9] next; only this is certain, it shall be something that succeeded the same before, at one time or another.

Train of thoughts unguided.

3. This train of thoughts, or mental discourse, is of two sorts. The first is *unguided, without design*, and inconstant; wherein there is no passionate thought, to govern and direct those that follow, to itself, as the end and scope of some desire, or other passion: in which case the thoughts are said to wander, and seem impertinent [unrelated] one to another, as in a dream. Such are commonly the thoughts of men, that are not only without company, but also without care of any thing; though even then their thoughts are as busy as at other times, but without harmony; as the sound which a lute out of tune would yield to any man; or in tune, to one that could not play. And yet in this wild ranging of the mind, a man may oft-times perceive the way of it, and the dependence of one thought upon another. For in a discourse of our present civil war, what could seem more impertinent, than to ask (as one did) what was the value of a Roman penny? Yet the coherence to me was manifest enough. For the thought of the war, introduced the thought of the delivering up the king to his enemies; the thought of that, brought in the thought of the delivering up of Christ; and that again the thought of the 30 pence, which was the price of that treason: and thence easily followed that malicious question; and all this in a moment of time; for thought is quick.

Train of thoughts regulated.

4. The second is more constant; as being *regulated* by some desire, and design. For the impression made by such things as we desire, or fear, is strong, and permanent, or, (if it cease for a time,) of quick return: so strong it is sometimes, as to hinder and break our

sleep. From desire, ariseth the thought of some means we have seen produce the like of that which we aim at; and from the thought of that, the thought of means to that mean; and so continually, till we come to some beginning within our own power. And because the end, by the greatness of the impression, comes often to mind, in case our thoughts begin to wander, they are quickly again reduced into the way: which observed by one of the seven wise men,* made him give men this precept, which is now worn out, *Respice finem*; that is to say, in all your actions, look often upon what you would have, as the thing that directs all your thoughts in the way to attain it.

5. The train of regulated thoughts is of two kinds; one, when of an effect imagined, we seek the causes, or means that produce it; and this is common to man and beast. The other is, when imagining any thing whatsoever, we seek all the possible effects, that can by it be produced; that is to say, we imagine what we can do with it, when we have it. Of which I have not at any time seen any sign, but in man only; for this is a curiosity hardly incident to the nature of any living creature that has no other passion but sensual, such as are hunger, thirst, lust, and anger. In sum, the discourse of the mind, when it is governed by design, is nothing but *seeking*, or the faculty of invention, which the Latins called *sagacitas*, and *solertia*; a [10] hunting out of the causes, of some effect, present or past; or of the effects, of some present or past cause. Sometimes a man seeks what he hath lost; and from that place, and time, wherein he misses it, his mind runs back, from place to place, and time to time, to find where, and when he had it; that is to say, to find some certain, and limited time and place, in which to begin a method of seeking. Again, from thence, his thoughts run over the same places and times, to find what action, or other occasion might make him lose it. This we call *remembrance*, or calling to mind: the Latins call it *reminiscentia*, as it   *Remembrance.* were a *re-conning* of our former actions.

6. Sometimes a man knows a place determinate, within the compass whereof he is to seek; and then his thoughts run over all the parts thereof, in the same manner, as one would sweep a room, to find a jewel; or as a spaniel ranges the field,* till he find a scent; or as a man should run over the alphabet, to start a rhyme.

7. Sometimes a man desires to know the event of an action; and   *Prudence.* then he thinketh of some like action past, and the events thereof one after another; supposing like events will follow like actions. As he

that foresees what will become of a criminal, re-cons what he has seen follow on the like crime before; having this order of thoughts, the crime, the officer, the prison, the judge, and the gallows. Which kind of thoughts, is called *foresight*, and *prudence*, or *providence*; and sometimes *wisdom*; though such conjecture, through the difficulty of observing all circumstances, be very fallacious. But this is certain; by how much one man has more experience of things past, than another; by so much also he is more prudent, and his expectations the seldomer fail him. The *present* only has a being in nature; things *past* have a being in the memory only, but things *to come* have no being at all; the *future* being but a fiction of the mind, applying the sequels of actions past, to the actions that are present; which with most certainty is done by him that has most experience; but not with certainty enough. And though it be called prudence, when the event answereth our expectation; yet in its own nature, it is but presumption. For the foresight of things to come, which is providence, belongs only to him by whose will they are to come. From him only, and supernaturally, proceeds prophecy. The best prophet naturally is the best guesser; and the best guesser, he that is most versed and studied in the matters he guesses at: for he hath most *signs* to guess by.

Signs.   8. A *sign* is the evident antecedent, of the consequent; and contrarily, the consequent of the antecedent, when the like consequences have been observed, before: and the oftener they have been observed, the less uncertain is the sign. And therefore he that has most experience in any kind of business, has most signs, whereby to guess at the future time; and consequently is the most prudent: and so much more prudent than he that is new in that kind of business, as not to be equalled by any advantage of natural and extemporary wit: though perhaps many young men think the contrary.

9. Nevertheless it is not prudence that distinguisheth man from
[11]   beast. There be beasts, that at a year old observe more, and pursue that which is for their good, more prudently, than a child can do at ten.

Conjecture of   10. As prudence is a *presumption* of the *future*, contracted from
the time past.   the *experience* of time *past*: so there is a presumption of things past taken from other things (not future but) past also. For he that hath seen by what courses and degrees, a flourishing state hath first come into civil war, and then to ruin; upon the sight of the ruins of any

other state, will guess, the like war, and the like courses have been there also. But this conjecture, has the same uncertainty almost with the conjecture of the future; both being grounded only upon experience.

11. There is no other act of man's mind, that I can remember, naturally planted in him, so, as to need no other thing, to the exercise of it, but to be born a man, and live with the use of his five senses. Those other faculties, of which I shall speak by and by, and which seem proper to man only, are acquired, and increased by study and industry; and of most men learned by instruction, and discipline; and proceed all from the invention of words, and speech. For besides sense, and thoughts, and the train of thoughts, the mind of man has no other motion; though by the help of speech, and method, the same faculties may be improved to such a height, as to distinguish men from all other living creatures.

12. Whatsoever we imagine is *finite*.* Therefore there is no idea, or conception of any thing we call *infinite*. No man can have in his mind an image of infinite magnitude; nor conceive infinite swiftness, infinite time, or infinite force, or infinite power. When we say any thing is infinite, we signify only, that we are not able to conceive the ends, and bounds of the things named; having no conception of the thing, but of our own inability. And therefore the name of God is used, not to make us conceive him; (for he is incomprehensible; and his greatness, and power are unconceivable;) but that we may honour him. Also because whatsoever (as I said before,) we conceive, has been perceived first by sense, either all at once, or by parts; a man can have no thought, representing any thing, not subject to sense. No man therefore can conceive any thing, but he must conceive it in some place; and endued with some determinate magnitude; and which may be divided into parts; nor that any thing is all in this place, and all in another place at the same time; nor that two, or more things can be in one, and the same place at once:* for none of these things ever have, or can be incident to sense; but are absurd speeches, taken upon credit (without any signification at all,) from deceived philosophers, and deceived, or deceiving Schoolmen.

[12]

CHAPTER IV

OF SPEECH

Original of speech.

1. THE invention of *printing*, though ingenious, compared with the invention of *letters*, is no great matter. But who was the first that found the use of letters, is not known. He that first brought them into Greece, men say was Cadmus, the son of Agenor, king of Phoenicia. A profitable invention for continuing the memory of time past, and the conjunction of mankind, dispersed into so many, and distant regions of the earth; and withal difficult, as proceeding from a watchful observation of the divers motions of the tongue, palate, lips, and other organs of speech; whereby to make as many differences of characters, to remember them. But the most noble and profitable invention of all other, was that of SPEECH, consisting of *names* or *appellations*, and their connexion; whereby men register their thoughts; recall them when they are past; and also declare them one to another for mutual utility and conversation; without which, there had been amongst men, neither commonwealth, nor society, nor contract, nor peace, no more than amongst lions, bears, and wolves. The first author of speech was God himself, that instructed Adam how to name such creatures as he presented to his sight; for the Scripture goeth no further in this matter. But this was sufficient to direct him to add more names, as the experience and use of the creatures should give him occasion; and to join them in such manner by degrees, as to make himself understood; and so by succession of time, so much language might be gotten, as he had found use for; though not so copious, as an orator or philosopher has need of. For I do not find any thing in the Scripture, out of which, directly or by consequence can be gathered, that Adam was taught the names of all figures, numbers, measures, colours, sounds, fancies, relations; much less the names of words and speech, as *general, special, affirmative, negative, interrogative, optative, infinitive,* all which are useful; and least of all, of *entity, intentionality, quiddity,* and other insignificant words of the School.

2. But all this language gotten, and augmented by Adam and his posterity, was again lost at the Tower of Babel, when by the hand of God, every man was stricken for his rebellion, with an oblivion of his former language. And being hereby forced to

disperse themselves into several parts of the world, it must needs be, that the diversity of tongues that now is, proceeded by degrees from them, in such manner, as need (the mother of all inventions) taught them; and in tract of time grew everywhere more copious.

3. The general use of speech, is to transfer our mental discourse, into verbal; or the train of our thoughts, into a train of words; and that for two commodities; whereof one is, the registering of the consequences of our thoughts; which being apt to slip out of our memory, and put us to a new labour, may again be recalled, by such words as they were marked by. So that the first use of names, is to serve for *marks*, or *notes* of remembrance. Another is, when many use the same words, to signify (by their connexion and order,) one to another, what they conceive, or think of each matter; and also what they desire, fear, or have any other passion for. And for this use they are called *signs*. Special uses of speech are these; first, to register, what by cogitation, we find to be the cause of any thing, present or past; and what we find things present or past may produce, or effect: which in sum, is acquiring of arts. Secondly, to show to others that knowledge which we have attained; which is, to counsel, and teach one another. Thirdly, to make known to others our wills, and purposes, that we may have the mutual help of one another. Fourthly, to please and delight ourselves, and others, by playing with our words, for pleasure or ornament, innocently.

The use of speech. [13]

4. To these uses, there are also four correspondent abuses. First, when men register their thoughts wrong, by the inconstancy of the signification of their words; by which they register for their conceptions, that which they never conceived; and so deceive themselves. Secondly, when they use words metaphorically; that is, in other sense than that they are ordained for; and thereby deceive others. Thirdly, when by words they declare that to be their will, which is not. Fourthly, when they use them to grieve one another: for seeing nature hath armed living creatures, some with teeth, some with horns, and some with hands, to grieve an enemy, it is but an abuse of speech, to grieve him with the tongue, unless it be one whom we are obliged to govern; and then it is not to grieve, but to correct and amend.

Abuses of speech.

5. The manner how speech serveth to the remembrance of the consequence of causes and effects, consisteth in the imposing of *names*, and the *connexion* of them.

6. Of names, some are *proper*, and singular to one only thing; as *Peter, John, this man, this tree*: and some are *common* to many things; as *man, horse, tree*; every of which though but one name, is nevertheless the name of divers particular things; in respect of all

which together, it is called an *universal*; there being nothing in the world universal but names;* for the things named are every one of them individual and singular.

7. One universal name is imposed on many things, for their similitude in some quality, or other accident: and whereas a proper name bringeth to mind one thing only; universals recall any one of those many.

8. And of names universal, some are of more, and some of less extent; the larger comprehending the less large: and some again of equal extent, comprehending each other reciprocally. As for example, the name *body* is of larger signification than the word *man*, and comprehendeth it; and the names *man* and *rational*, are of

[14] equal extent, comprehending mutually one another. But here we must take notice, that by a name is not always understood, as in grammar, one only word; but sometimes by circumlocution many words together. For all these words, *he that in his actions observeth the laws of his country*, make but one name, equivalent to this one word, *just*.

9. By this imposition of names, some of larger, some of stricter signification, we turn the reckoning of the consequences of things imagined in the mind, into a reckoning of the consequences of appellations. For example, a man that hath no use of speech at all, (such, as is born and remains perfectly deaf and dumb,) if he set before his eyes a triangle, and by it two right angles, (such as are the corners of a square figure,) he may by meditation compare and find, that the three angles of that triangle, are equal to those two right angles that stand by it. But if another triangle be shown him different in shape from the former, he cannot know without a new labour, whether the three angles of that also be equal to the same. But he that hath the use of words, when he observes, that such equality was consequent, not to the length of the sides, nor to any other particular thing in his triangle; but only to this, that the sides were straight, and the angles three; and that that was all, for which he named it a triangle; will boldly conclude universally, that such equality of angles is in all triangles whatsoever; and register his invention in these general terms, *every triangle hath its three angles*

22

equal to two right angles. And thus the consequence found in one particular, comes to be registered and remembered, as an universal rule; and discharges our mental reckoning, of time and place; and delivers us from all labour of the mind, saving the first; and makes that which was found true *here*, and *now*, to be true in *all times* and *places*.

10. But the use of words in registering our thoughts, is in nothing so evident as in numbering. A natural fool that could never learn by heart the order of numeral words, as *one*, *two*, and *three*, may observe every stroke of the clock, and nod to it, or say *one, one, one*; but can never know what hour it strikes. And it seems, there was a time when those names of number were not in use; and men were fain to apply their fingers of one or both hands, to those things they desired to keep account of; and that thence it proceeded, that now our numeral words are but ten, in any nation, and in some but five, and then they begin again. And he that can tell ten, if he recite them out of order, will lose himself, and not know when he has done: much less will he be able to add, and subtract, and perform all other operations of arithmetic. So that without words, there is no possibility of reckoning of numbers; much less of magnitudes, of swiftness, of force, and other things, the reckonings whereof are necessary to the being, or well-being of mankind.

11. When two names are joined together into a consequence, or affirmation; as thus, *a man is a living creature*; or thus, *if he be a man, he is a living creature*, if the latter name *living creature*, signify all that the former name *man* signifieth, then the affirmation, or consequence, is *true*; otherwise *false*. For *true* and *false* are attributes [15] of speech, not of things. And where speech is not, there is neither *truth* nor *falsehood*. *Error* there may be, as when we expect that which shall not be; or suspect what has not been: but in neither case can a man be charged with untruth.

12. Seeing then that *truth* consisteth in the right ordering of *Necessity of* names in our affirmations, a man that seeketh precise truth, had *definitions.* need to remember what every name he uses stands for; and to place it accordingly; or else he will find himself entangled in words, as a bird in lime twigs;* the more he struggles, the more belimed. And therefore in geometry, (which is the only science that it hath pleased God hitherto to bestow on mankind,) men begin at settling the significations of their words; which settling of significations, they call *definitions*;* and place them in the beginning of their reckoning.

13. By this it appears how necessary it is for any man that aspires to true knowledge, to examine the definitions of former authors; and either to correct them, where they are negligently set down; or to make them himself. For the errors of definitions multiply themselves, according as the reckoning proceeds; and lead men into absurdities, which at last they see, but cannot avoid, without reckoning anew from the beginning; in which lies the foundation of their errors. From whence it happens, that they which trust to books, do as they that cast up many little sums into a greater, without considering whether those little sums were rightly cast up or not; and at last finding the error visible, and not mistrusting their first grounds, know not which way to clear themselves, but spend time in fluttering over their books; as birds that entering by the chimney, and finding themselves enclosed in a chamber, flutter at the false light of a glass window, for want of wit to consider which way they came in. So that in the right definition of names, lies the first use of speech; which is the acquisition of science:* and in wrong, or no definitions, lies the first abuse; from which proceed all false and senseless tenets; which make those men that take their instruction from the authority of books, and not from their own meditation, to be as much below the condition of ignorant men, as men endued with true science are above it. For between true science, and erroneous doctrines, ignorance is in the middle. Natural sense and imagination, are not subject to absurdity. Nature itself cannot err: and as men abound in copiousness of language; so they become more wise, or more mad than ordinary. Nor is it possible without letters for any man to become either excellently wise, or (unless his memory be hurt by disease, or ill constitution of organs) excellently foolish. For words are wise men's counters, they do but reckon by them: but they are the money of fools, that value them by the authority of an Aristotle, a Cicero, or a Thomas, or any other doctor whatsoever, if but a man.*

Subject to names.

14. *Subject to names*, is whatsoever can enter into, or be considered in an account; and be added one to another to make a sum; or subtracted one from another and leave a remainder. The Latins [16] called accounts of money *rationes*, and accounting, *ratiocinatio*: and that which we in bills or books of account call *items*, they called *nomina*; that is, *names*: and thence it seems to proceed, that they extended the word *ratio*, to the faculty of reckoning in all other things. The Greeks have but one word λόγος, for both *speech* and

24

reason; not that they thought there was no speech without reason; but no reasoning without speech: and the act of reasoning they called *syllogism*; which signifieth summing up of the consequences of one saying to another. And because the same things may enter into account for divers accidents; their names are (to show that diversity) diversely wrested, and diversified. This diversity of names may be reduced to four general heads.

15. First, a thing may enter into account for *matter*, or *body*; as *living, sensible, rational, hot, cold, moved, quiet*; with all which names the word *matter*, or *body*, is understood; all such, being names of matter.

16. Secondly, it may enter into account, or be considered, for some accident or quality, which we conceive to be in it; as for *being moved*, for *being so long*, for *being hot*, &c; and then, of the name of the thing itself, by a little change or wresting, we make a name for that accident, which we consider; and for *living* put into the account *life*; for *moved, motion*; for *hot, heat*; for *long, length*, and the like: and all such names, are the names of the accidents and properties, by which one matter, and body is distinguished from another. These are called *names abstract*; because severed (not from matter, but) from the account of matter.

17. Thirdly, we bring into account, the properties of our own bodies, whereby we make such distinction: as when anything is *seen* by us, we reckon not the thing itself; but the *sight*, the *colour*, the *idea* of it in the fancy: and when anything is *heard*, we reckon it not; but the *hearing*, or *sound* only, which is our fancy or conception of it by the ear: and such are names of fancies.

18. Fourthly, we bring into account, consider, and give names to, *names* themselves, and to *speeches*: for *general, universal, special, equivocal*, are names of names. And *affirmation, interrogation, commandment, narration, syllogism, sermon, oration*, and many other such, are names of speeches. And this is all the variety of names *positive*; which are put to mark somewhat which is in nature, or may be feigned by the mind of man, as bodies that are, or may be conceived to be; or of bodies, the properties that are, or may be feigned to be; or words and speech. *Use of names positive.*

19. There be also other names, called *negative*; which are notes to signify that a word is not the name of the thing in question; as these words *nothing, no man, infinite, indocible* [unteachable], *three want four*, and the like; which are nevertheless of use in reckoning, or in *Negative names with their uses.*

correcting of reckoning; and call to mind our past cogitations, though they be not names of any thing; because they make us refuse to admit of names not rightly used.

Words insignificant.

[17]

20. All other names are but insignificant sounds; and those of two sorts. One, when they are new, and yet their meaning not explained by definition; whereof there have been abundance coined by Schoolmen, and puzzled philosophers.

21. Another, when men make a name of two names, whose significations are contradictory and inconsistent; as this name, an *incorporeal body*, or (which is all one) an *incorporeal substance*, and a great number more. For whensoever any affirmation is false, the two names of which it is composed, put together and made one, signify nothing at all. For example, if it be a false affirmation to say *a quadrangle is round*, the word *round quadrangle* signifies nothing; but is a mere sound. So likewise, if it be false, to say that virtue can be poured, or blown up and down, the words *inpoured virtue, inblown virtue*, are as absurd and insignificant, as a *round quadrangle*. And therefore you shall hardly meet with a senseless and insignificant word, that is not made up of some Latin or Greek names. A Frenchman seldom hears our Saviour called by the name of *parole*, but by the name of *verbe* often; yet *verbe* and *parole* differ no more, but that one is Latin, the other French.

Understanding.

22. When a man upon the hearing of any speech, hath those thoughts which the words of that speech, and their connexion, were ordained and constituted to signify; then he is said to understand it; *understanding* being nothing else but conception* caused by speech. And therefore if speech be peculiar to man (as for aught I know it is,) then is understanding peculiar to him also. And therefore of absurd and false affirmations, in case they be universal, there can be no understanding; though many think they understand, then, when they do but repeat the words softly, or con them in their mind.

23. What kinds of speeches signify the appetites, aversions, and passions of man's mind; and of their use and abuse, I shall speak when I have spoken of the passions.

Inconstant names.

24. The names of such things as affect us, that is, which please, and displease us, because all men be not alike affected with the same thing, nor the same man at all times, are in the common discourses of men, of *inconstant* signification. For seeing all names are imposed to signify our conceptions; and all our affections are but

conceptions; when we conceive the same things differently, we can hardly avoid different naming of them. For though the nature of that we conceive, be the same; yet the diversity of our reception of it, in respect of different constitutions of body, and prejudices of opinion, gives every thing a tincture of our different passions. And therefore in reasoning, a man must take heed of words; which besides the signification of what we imagine of their nature, have a signification also of the nature, disposition, and interest of the speaker; such as are the names of virtues, and vices; for one man calleth *wisdom*, what another called *fear*; and one *cruelty*, what another *justice*; one *prodigality*, what another *magnanimity*; and one *gravity*, what another *stupidity*, &c.* And therefore such names can never be true grounds of any ratiocination. No more can metaphors, and tropes [figures] of speech: but these are less dangerous, because they profess their inconstancy; which the other do not.

CHAPTER V

OF REASON AND SCIENCE

1. WHEN a man *reasoneth*, he does nothing else but conceive a sum total, from *addition* of parcels; or conceive a remainder, from *subtraction* of one sum from another: which (if it be done by words,) is conceiving of the consequence from the names of all the parts, to the name of the whole; or from the names of the whole and one part, to the name of the other part. And though in some things, (as in numbers,) besides adding and subtracting, men name other operations, as *multiplying* and *dividing*; yet they are the same; for multiplication, is but adding together of things equal; and division, but subtracting of one thing, as often as we can. These operations are not incident to numbers only, but to all manner of things that can be added together, and taken one out of another. For as arithmeticians teach to add and subtract in *numbers*; so the geometricians teach the same in *lines*, *figures* (solid and superficial,) *angles*, *proportions*, *times*, degrees of *swiftness*, *force*, *power*, and the like; the logicians teach the same in *consequences of words*; adding together two *names*, to make an *affirmation*; and two *affirmations*, to make a *syllogism*; and *many syllogisms* to make a *demonstration*;

Reason what it is.
[18]

and from the *sum*, or *conclusion* of a *syllogism*, they subtract one *proposition*, to find the other. Writers of politics, add together *pactions* [contracts] to find men's *duties*; and lawyers, *laws*, and *facts*, to find what is *right* and *wrong* in the actions of private men. In sum, in what matter soever there is place for *addition* and *subtraction*, there also is place for *reason*; and where these have no place, there *reason* has nothing at all to do.

Reason defined.

2. Out of all which we may define, (that is to say determine,) what that is, which is meant by this word *reason*, when we reckon it amongst the faculties of the mind. For REASON, in this sense, is nothing but *reckoning* (that is, adding and subtracting) of the consequences of general names agreed upon, for the *marking* and *signifying* of our thoughts; I say *marking* them, when we reckon by ourselves; and *signifying*, when we demonstrate, or approve our reckonings to other men.

Right reason where.

3. And as in arithmetic, unpractised men must, and professors themselves may often err, and cast up false; so also in any other subject of reasoning, the ablest, most attentive, and most practised men, may deceive themselves, and infer false conclusions; not but that reason itself is always right reason, as well as arithmetic is a certain and infallible art: but no one man's reason, nor the reason of any one number of men, makes the certainty; no more than an account is therefore well cast up, because a great many men have unanimously approved it. And therefore, as when there is a [19] controversy in an account, the parties must by their own accord, set up for right reason, the reason of some arbitrator, or judge, to whose sentence they will both stand, or their controversy must either come to blows, or be undecided, for want of a right reason constituted by nature; so is it also in all debates of what kind soever: and when men that think themselves wiser than all others, clamour and demand right reason for judge; yet seek no more, but that things should be determined, by no other men's reason but their own, it is as intolerable in the society of men, as it is in play after trump is turned, to use for trump on every occasion, that suite whereof they have most in their hand. For they do nothing else, that will have every of their passions, as it comes to bear sway in them, to be taken for right reason, and that in their own controversies: bewraying [revealing] their want of right reason, by the claim they lay to it.

4. The use and end of reason, is not the finding of the sum, *The use of* and truth of one, or a few consequences, remote from the first *reason.* definitions, and settled significations of names; but to begin at these; and proceed from one consequence to another. For there can be no certainty of the last conclusion, without a certainty of all those affirmations and negations, on which it was grounded, and inferred. As when a master of a family, in taking an account, casteth up the sums of all the bills of expense, into one sum; and not regarding how each bill is summed up, by those that give them in account; nor what it is he pays for; he advantages himself no more, than if he allowed the account in gross, trusting to every of the accountants' skill and honesty: so also in reasoning of all other things, he that takes up conclusions on the trust of authors, and doth not fetch them from the first items in every reckoning, (which are the significations of names settled by definitions), loses his labour; and does not know any thing; but only believeth.

5. When a man reckons without the use of words, which may be *Of error and* done in particular things (as when upon the sight of any one thing, *absurdity.* we conjecture what was likely to have preceded, or is likely to follow upon it;) if that which he thought likely to follow, follows not; or that which he thought likely to have preceded it, hath not preceded it, this is called ERROR; to which even the most prudent men are subject. But when we reason in words of general signification, and fall upon a general inference which is false, though it be commonly called *error*, it is indeed an ABSURDITY, or senseless speech. For error is but a deception, in presuming that somewhat is past, or to come; of which, though it were not past, or not to come; yet there was no impossibility discoverable. But when we make a general assertion, unless it be a true one, the possibility of it is inconceivable. And words whereby we conceive nothing but the sound, are those we call *absurd, insignificant*, and *nonsense*. And therefore if a man should talk to me of a *round quadrangle*; or *accidents of bread in cheese*; or, *immaterial substances*; or of *a free subject*; *a free will*; or any *free*, but free from being hindered by opposition,* I should not say he were in an error, but that his words were without meaning; that is to say, absurd.

6. I have said before, (in the second chapter,) that a man did [20] excel all other animals in this faculty, that when he conceived any thing whatsoever, he was apt to inquire the consequences of it, and what effects he could do with it. And now I add this other degree of the same excellence, that he can by words reduce the consequences he finds to general rules, called *theorems*, or *aphorisms*; that is, he can reason, or reckon, not only in number, but in all other things, whereof one may be added unto, or subtracted from another.

7. But this privilege, is allayed by another; and that is, by the privilege of absurdity; to which no living creature is subject, but man only. And of men, those are of all most subject to it, that profess philosophy. For it is most true that Cicero saith of them somewhere; that there can be nothing so absurd, but may be found in the books of philosophers.* And the reason is manifest. For there is not one of them that begins his ratiocination from the definitions, or explications of the names they are to use; which is a method that hath been used only in geometry; whose conclusions have thereby been made indisputable.

Causes of absurdity.

8. The first cause of absurd conclusions I ascribe to the want of method; in that they begin not their ratiocination from definitions;

1. that is, from settled significations of their words: as if they could cast account, without knowing the value of the numeral words, *one, two*, and *three*.

9. And whereas all bodies enter into account upon divers considerations, (which I have mentioned in the precedent chapter;) these considerations being diversely named, divers absurdities proceed from the confusion, and unfit connexion of their names into assertions. And therefore

2.   10. The second cause of absurd assertions, I ascribe to the giving of names of *bodies*, to *accidents*; or of *accidents* to *bodies*; as they do, that say, *faith is infused*, or *inspired*; when nothing can be *poured*, or *breathed* into anything, but body; and that, *extension* is *body*; that *phantasms* are *spirits*, &c.

3.   11. The third I ascribe to the giving of the names of the *accidents* of *bodies without us*, to the *accidents* of our *own bodies*; as they do that say the *colour is in the body*; *the sound is in the air*, &c.

4.   12. The fourth, to the giving of the names of *bodies*, to *names*, or *speeches*; as they do that say, that *there be things universal*; that *a living creature is genus*, or *a general thing*, &c.

5.   13. The fifth, to the giving of the names of *accidents*, to *names* and *speeches*; as they do that say, *the nature of a thing is its definition*; *a man's command is his will*; and the like.

30

14. The sixth, to the use of metaphors, tropes, and other 6.
rhetorical figures, instead of words proper. For though it be lawful
to say (for example) in common speech, *the way goeth, or leadeth
hither, or thither; the proverb says this or that* (whereas ways cannot go,
nor proverbs speak;) yet in reckoning, and seeking of truth,
such speeches are not to be admitted.

15. The seventh, to names that signify nothing;* but are 7.
taken up, and learned by rote from the schools, as *hypostatical,* [21]
transubstantiate, consubstantiate, eternal-now, and the like canting of
Schoolmen.

16. To him that can avoid these things, it is not easy to fall into
any absurdity, unless it be by the length of an account; wherein he
may perhaps forget what went before. For all men by nature reason
alike, and well, when they have good principles. For who is so
stupid, as both to mistake in geometry, and also to persist in it, when
another detects his error to him?

17. By this it appears that reason is not as sense, and memory,   *Science.*
born with us; nor gotten by experience only, as prudence is; but
attained by industry; first in apt imposing of names; and secondly by
getting a good and orderly method in proceeding from the elements,
which are names, to assertions made by connexion of one of them
to another; and so to syllogisms, which are the connexions of
one assertion to another, till we come to a knowledge of all the
consequences of names appertaining to the subject in hand; and that
is it, men call SCIENCE. And whereas sense and memory are but
knowledge of fact, which is a thing past, and irrevocable; *Science* is
the knowledge of consequences, and dependence of one fact upon
another: by which, out of that we can presently do, we know how to
do something else when we will, or the like, another time: because
when we see how any thing comes about, upon what causes, and by
what manner; when the like causes come into our power, we see how
to make it produce the like effects.

18. Children therefore are not endued with reason at all, till they
have attained the use of speech; but are called reasonable creatures,
for the possibility apparent of having the use of reason in time
to come. And the most part of men, though they have the use
of reasoning a little way, as in numbering to some degree; yet it
serves them to little use in common life; in which they govern
themselves, some better, some worse, according to their differences
of experience, quickness of memory, and inclinations to several

ends; but specially according to good or evil fortune, and the errors of one another. For as for *science*, or certain rules of their actions, they are so far from it, that they know not what it is. Geometry they have thought conjuring: but for other sciences, they who have not been taught the beginnings, and some progress in them, that they may see how they be acquired and generated, are in this point like children, that having no thought of generation, are made believe by the women, that their brothers and sisters are not born, but found in the garden.

19. But yet they that have no *science*, are in better, and nobler condition, with their natural prudence; than men, that by mis-reasoning, or by trusting them that reason wrong, fall upon false and absurd general rules. For ignorance of causes, and of rules, does not set men so far out of their way, as relying on false rules, and taking for causes of what they aspire to, those that are not so, but rather causes of the contrary.

20. To conclude, the light of human minds is perspicuous words, but by exact definitions first snuffed, and purged from ambiguity; *reason* is the *pace*; increase of *science*, the *way*; and the benefit of mankind, the *end*. And on the contrary, metaphors, and senseless and ambiguous words, are like *ignes fatui*;* and reasoning upon them, is wandering amongst innumerable absurdities; and their end, contention, and sedition, or contempt [indifference].

[22]

Prudence & sapience, with their difference.

21. As, much experience, is *prudence*; so, is much science, *sapience*. For though we usually have one name of wisdom for them both; yet the Latins did always distinguish between *prudentia* and *sapientia*; ascribing the former to experience, the latter to science. But to make their difference appear more clearly, let us suppose one man endued with an excellent natural use, and dexterity in handling his arms; and another to have added to that dexterity, an acquired science, of where he can offend, or be offended by his adversary, in every possible posture, or guard: the ability of the former, would be to the ability of the latter, as prudence to sapience; both useful; but the latter infallible. But they that trusting only to the authority of books, follow the blind blindly, are like him that, trusting to the false rules of a master of fence, ventures presumptuously upon an adversary, that either kills or disgraces him.

Signs of science.

22. The signs of science, are some, certain and infallible; some, uncertain. Certain, when he that pretendeth the science of any thing, can teach the same; that is to say, demonstrate the truth

thereof perspicuously to another; uncertain, when only some particular events answer to his pretence, and upon many occasions prove so as he says they must. Signs of prudence are all uncertain; because to observe by experience, and remember all circumstances that may alter the success, is impossible. But in any business, whereof a man has not infallible science to proceed by; to forsake his own natural judgment, and be guided by general sentences read in authors, and subject to many exceptions, is a sign of folly, and generally scorned by the name of pedantry. And even of those men themselves, that in councils of the commonwealth, love to show their reading of politics and history, very few do it in their domestic affairs, where their particular interest is concerned; having prudence enough for their private affairs: but in public they study more the reputation of their own wit, than the success of another's business.

CHAPTER VI   [23]

OF THE INTERIOR BEGINNINGS OF VOLUNTARY MOTIONS; COMMONLY CALLED THE PASSIONS. AND THE SPEECHES BY WHICH THEY ARE EXPRESSED

1.* THERE be in animals, two sorts of *motions* peculiar to them: one called *vital*; begun in generation, and continued without interruption through their whole life; such as are the *course* of the *blood*, the *pulse*, the *breathing*, the *concoction* [digestion], *nutrition*, *excretion*, &c; to which motions there needs no help of imagination: the other is *animal motion*, otherwise called *voluntary motion*; as to *go*, to *speak*, to *move* any of our limbs, in such manner as is first fancied in our minds. That sense, is motion in the organs and interior parts of man's body, caused by the action of the things we see, hear, &c; and that fancy is but the relics of the same motion, remaining after sense, has been already said in the first and second chapters. And because *going, speaking*, and the like voluntary motions, depend always upon a precedent thought of *whither*, *which way*, and *what*; it is evident, that the imagination is the first internal beginning of all voluntary motion. And although unstudied men, do not conceive any motion at all to be there, where the thing moved is

Motion vital and animal.

33

invisible; or the space it is moved in, is (for the shortness of it) insensible; yet that doth not hinder, but that such motions are. For let a space be never so little, that which is moved over a greater space, whereof that little one is part, must first be moved over that. These small beginnings of motion, within the body of man, before they appear in walking, speaking, striking, and other visible actions,

Endeavour.   are commonly called ENDEAVOUR.*

2. This endeavour, when it is toward something which causes it,

Appetite.   is called APPETITE, or DESIRE; the latter, being the general name; and
Desire.   the other oftentimes restrained to signify the desire of food, namely
Hunger.   *hunger* and *thirst*. And when the endeavour is fromward something,
Thirst.   it is generally called AVERSION. These words *appetite*, and *aversion* we
Aversion.   have from the Latins; and they both of them signify the motions, one of approaching, the other of retiring. So also do the Greek words for the same, which are ὁρμὴ and ἀφορμὴ. For nature itself does often press upon men those truths, which afterwards, when they look for somewhat beyond nature, they stumble at. For the Schools find in mere appetite to go, or move, no actual motion at all: but because some motion they must acknowledge, they call it metaphorical motion; which is but an absurd speech: for though words may be called metaphorical; bodies, and motions can not.

Love. Hate.   3. That which men desire, they are also said to LOVE: and to HATE those things, for which they have aversion. So that desire, and love,
[24]   are the same thing; save that by desire, we always signify the absence of the object; by love, most commonly the presence of the same. So also by aversion, we signify the absence; and by hate, the presence of the object.

4. Of appetites and aversions, some are born with men; as appetite of food, appetite of excretion, and exoneration,* (which may also and more properly be called aversions, from somewhat they feel in their bodies;) and some other appetites, not many. The rest, which are appetites of particular things, proceed from experience, and trial of their effects upon themselves, or other men. For of things we know not at all, or believe not to be, we can have no further desire, than to taste and try. But aversion we have for things, not only which we know have hurt us; but also that we do not know whether they will hurt us, or not.

Contempt.   5. Those things which we neither desire, nor hate, we are said to *contemn*: CONTEMPT being nothing else but an immobility, or contumacy [obstinacy] of the heart, in resisting the action of certain things; and proceeding from that the heart is already moved otherwise, by other more potent objects; or from want of experience of them.

6.* And because the constitution of a man's body is in continual mutation; it is impossible that all the same things should always cause in him the same appetites, and aversions: much less can all men consent, in the desire of almost any one and the same object.

7. But whatsoever is the object of any man's appetite or desire; that is it, which he for his part calleth *good*: and the object of his *Good.* hate, and aversion, *evil*; and of his contempt, *vile* and *inconsiderable*. *Evil.* For these words of good, evil, and contemptible, are ever used with relation to the person that useth them: there being nothing simply and absolutely so; nor any common rule of good and evil, to be taken from the nature of the objects themselves; but from the person of the man (where there is no commonwealth;) or, (in a commonwealth,) from the person that representeth it; or from an arbitrator or judge, whom men disagreeing shall by consent set up, and make his sentence the rule thereof.

8. The Latin tongue has two words, whose significations approach to those of good and evil; but are not precisely the same; and those are *pulchrum* and *turpe*. Whereof the former signifies that, *Pulchrum.* which by some apparent signs promiseth good; and the latter, that, *Turpe.* which promiseth evil. But in our tongue we have not so general names to express them by. But for *pulchrum*, we say in some things, *fair*; in others, *beautiful*, or *handsome*, or *gallant*, or *honourable*, or *comely*, or *amiable*; and for *turpe*, *foul*, *deformed*, *ugly*, *base*, *nauseous*, and the like, as the subject shall require; all which words, in their proper places, signify nothing else, but the mien or countenance, that promiseth good and evil. So that of good there be three kinds; good in the promise, that is *pulchrum*; good in effect, as the end desired, which is called *jucundum*, *delightful*; and good as the means, *Delightful.* which is called *utile*, *profitable*; and as many of evil: for *evil*, in *Profitable.* promise, is that they call *turpe*; evil in effect, and end, is *molestum*, *Unpleasant.* unpleasant, troublesome; and evil in the means, *inutile*, *unprofitable*, *Unprofitable.* hurtful.

9. As, in sense, that which is really within us, is (as I have said [25] before*) only motion, caused by the action of external objects, but in appearance; to the sight, light and colour; to the ear, sound; to the nostril, odour, &c: so, when the action of the same object is continued from the eyes, ears, and other organs to the heart; the real

effect there is nothing but motion, or endeavour; which consisteth in appetite, or aversion, to, or from the object moving. But the *Delight.* appearance, or sense of that motion, is that we either call *delight*, or *Displeasure.* *trouble of mind.*

10. This motion, which is called appetite, and for the appearance *Pleasure.* of it *delight*, and *pleasure*, seemeth to be, a corroboration of vital motion, and a help thereunto; and therefore such things as caused delight, were not improperly called *jucunda*, *(à juvando,)* from *Offence.* helping or fortifying; and the contrary, *molesta*, *offensive*, from hindering, and troubling the motion vital.

11. *Pleasure* therefore, (or *delight*,) is the appearance, or sense of good; and *molestation* or *displeasure*, the appearence, or sense of evil. And consequently all appetite, desire, and love, is accompanied with some delight more or less; and all hatred, and aversion, with more or less displeasure and offence.

12. Of pleasures, or delights, some arise from the sense of an *Pleasures of* object present; and those may be called *pleasures of sense*; (the word *sense.* *sensual*, as it is used by those only that condemn them, having no place till there be laws.) Of this kind are all onerations and exonerations* of the body; as also all that is pleasant, in the *sight*, *hearing, smell, taste*, or *touch*; others arise from the expectation, that proceeds from foresight of the end, or consequence of things; *Pleasures of* whether those things in the sense please or displease: and these are *the mind.* *pleasures of the mind* of him that draweth those consequences; *Joy.* and are generally called JOY. In the like manner, displeasures, are *Pain.* some in the sense, and called PAIN; others, in the expectation of *Grief.* consequences, and are called GRIEF.

13. These simple passions called *appetite, desire, love, aversion, hate, joy,* and *grief,* have their names for divers considerations diversified. As first, when they one succeed another, they are diversely called from the opinion men have of the likelihood of attaining what they desire. Secondly, from the object loved or hated. Thirdly, from the consideration of many of them together. Fourthly, from the alteration or succession itself.

Hope. 14.* For *appetite* with an opinion of attaining, is called HOPE.

Despair. 15. The same, without such opinion, DESPAIR.

Fear. 16. *Aversion*, with opinion of HURT from the object, FEAR.

17. The same, with hope of avoiding that hurt by resistance, *Courage.* COURAGE.

Anger. 18. Sudden *courage*, ANGER.

19. Constant *hope*, CONFIDENCE of ourselves.   *Confidence.*

20. Constant *despair*, DIFFIDENCE of ourselves.   *Diffidence.*

21. *Anger* for great hurt done to another, when we conceive the [26]
same to be done by injury, INDIGNATION.   *Indignation.*

22. *Desire* of good to another, BENEVOLENCE, GOOD WILL, *Benevolence.*
CHARITY. If to man generally, GOOD NATURE.   *Good nature.*

23. *Desire* of riches, COVETOUSNESS: a name used always in *Covetousness.*
signification of blame; because men contending for them, are
displeased with one another's attaining them; though the desire in
itself, be to be blamed, or allowed, according to the means by which
these riches are sought.

24. *Desire* of office, or precedence, AMBITION: a name used also in *Ambition.*
the worse sense, for the reason before mentioned.

25. *Desire* of things that conduce but a little to our ends; and fear *Pusillanimity.*
of things that are but of little hindrance, PUSILLANIMITY.

26. *Contempt* of little helps, and hindrances, MAGNANIMITY. *Magnanimity.*

27. *Magnanimity*, in danger of death, or wounds, VALOUR, FORTI- *Valour.*
TUDE.

28. *Magnanimity*, in the use of riches, LIBERALITY.   *Liberality.*

29. *Pusillanimity*, in the same WRETCHEDNESS, MISERABLENESS; or *Miserableness.*
PARSIMONY; as it is liked, or disliked.

30. *Love* of persons for society, KINDNESS.   *Kindness.*

31. *Love* of persons for pleasing the sense only, NATURAL LUST. *Natural lust.*

32. *Love* of the same, acquired from rumination, that is, *Luxury.*
imagination of pleasure past, LUXURY.

33. *Love* of one singularly, with desire to be singularly beloved, *The passion*
THE PASSION OF LOVE. The same, with fear that the love is not *of love.*
mutual, JEALOUSY.   *Jealousy.*

34. *Desire*, by doing hurt to another, to make him condemn some *Revengefulness.*
fact of his own, REVENGEFULNESS.

35. *Desire*, to know why, and how, CURIOSITY; such as is in no *Curiosity.*
living creature but *man*: so that man is distinguished, not only by his
reason; but also by this singular passion from other *animals*; in
whom the appetite of food, and other pleasures of sense, by
predominance, take away the care of knowing causes; which is a lust
of the mind, that by a perseverance of delight in the continual
and indefatigable generation of knowledge, exceedeth the short
vehemence of any carnal pleasure.

36. *Fear* of power invisible, feigned by the mind, or imagined *Religion.*
from tales publicly allowed, RELIGION; not allowed, SUPERSTITION.* *Superstition.*

True religion. And when the power imagined, is truly such as we imagine, TRUE RELIGION.

Panic terror. 37. *Fear*, without the apprehension of why, or what, PANIC TERROR, called so from the fables, that make Pan the author of them; whereas, in truth, there is always in him that so feareth, first, some apprehension of the cause, though the rest run away by example; every one supposing his fellow to know why. And therefore this passion happens to none but in a throng, or multitude of people.

Admiration. 38. *Joy*, from apprehension of novelty, ADMIRATION; proper to man, because it excites the appetite of knowing the cause.

39. *Joy*, arising from imagination of a man's own power and *Glory.* ability, is that exultation of the mind which is called GLORYING: [27] which if grounded upon the experience of his own former actions, is the same with *confidence*: but if grounded on the flattery of others; or only supposed by himself, for delight in the consequences of it, is *Vain-glory.* called VAIN-GLORY: which name is properly given; because a well grounded *confidence* begetteth attempt; whereas the supposing of power does not, and is therefore rightly called *vain*.

Dejection. 40. *Grief*, from opinion of want of power, is called DEJECTION of mind.

41. The *vain-glory* which consisteth in the feigning or supposing of abilities in ourselves, which we know are not, is most incident to young men, and nourished by the histories, or fictions of gallant persons; and is corrected oftentimes by age, and employment.

Sudden glory. 42. *Sudden glory*, is the passion which maketh those *grimaces*
Laughter. called LAUGHTER; and is caused either by some sudden act of their own, that pleaseth them; or by the apprehension of some deformed thing in another, by comparison whereof they suddenly applaud themselves. And it is incident most to them, that are conscious of the fewest abilities in themselves; who are forced to keep themselves in their own favour, by observing the imperfections of other men. And therefore much laughter at the defects of others, is a sign of pusillanimity. For of great minds, one of the proper works is, to help and free others from scorn; and compare themselves only with the most able.

Sudden 43. On the contrary, *sudden dejection*, is the passion that causeth
dejection. WEEPING; and is caused by such accidents, as suddenly take away
Weeping. some vehement hope, or some prop of their power: and they are most subject to it, that rely principally on helps external, such as are

women, and children. Therefore some weep for the loss of friends; others for their unkindness; others for the sudden stop made to their thoughts of revenge, by reconciliation. But in all cases, both laughter, and weeping, are sudden motions; custom taking them both away. For no man laughs at old jests; or weeps for an old calamity.

44. *Grief*, for the discovery of some defect of ability, is SHAME, or the passion that discovereth itself in BLUSHING; and consisteth in the apprehension of some thing dishonourable; and in young men, is a sign of the love of good reputation, and commendable: in old men it is a sign of the same; but because it comes too late, not commendable. *Shame.* *Blushing.*

45. The *contempt* of good reputation is called IMPUDENCE. *Impudence.*

46. *Grief*, for the calamity of another, is PITY; and ariseth from the imagination that the like calamity may befall himself; and therefore is called also COMPASSION, and in the phrase of this present time a FELLOW-FEELING: and therefore for calamity arriving from great wickedness, the best men have the least pity; and for the same calamity, those hate pity, that think themselves least obnoxious to the same. *Pity.*

47. *Contempt*, or little sense of the calamity of others, is that which men call CRUELTY; proceeding from security of their own fortune. For, that any man should take pleasure in other men's great harms, without other end of his own, I do not conceive it possible. *Cruelty.* [28]

48. *Grief*, for the success of a competitor in wealth, honour, or other good, if it be joined with endeavour to enforce [exert] our own abilities to equal or exceed him, is called EMULATION: but joined with endeavour to supplant, or hinder a competitor, ENVY. *Emulation.* *Envy.*

49. When in the mind of man, appetites, and aversions, hopes, and fears, concerning one and the same thing, arise alternately; and divers good and evil consequences of the doing, or omitting the thing propounded, come successively into our thoughts; so that sometimes we have an appetite to it; sometimes an aversion from it; sometimes hope to be able to do it; sometimes despair, or fear to attempt it; the whole sum of desires, aversions, hopes and fears, continued till the thing be either done, or thought impossible, is that we call DELIBERATION. *Deliberation.*

50. Therefore of things past, there is no *deliberation*; because manifestly impossible to be changed: nor of things known to be impossible, or thought so; because men know, or think such

deliberation vain. But of things impossible, which we think possible, we may deliberate; not knowing it is in vain. And it is called *deliberation*; because it is a putting an end to the *liberty* we had of doing, or omitting, according to our own appetite, or aversion.

51. This alternate succession of appetites, aversions, hopes and fears, is no less in other living creatures than in man: and therefore beasts also deliberate.

52. Every *deliberation* is then said to *end*, when that whereof they deliberate, is either done, or thought impossible; because till then we retain the liberty of doing, or omitting, according to our appetite, or aversion.

53. In *deliberation*, the last appetite, or aversion, immediately adhering to the action, or to the omission thereof, is that we call the WILL; the act, (not the faculty,) of *willing*. And beasts that have *deliberation*, must necessarily also have *will*. The definition of the *will*, given commonly by the Schools,* that it is a *rational appetite*, is not good. For if it were, then could there be no voluntary act against reason. For a *voluntary act* is that, which proceedeth from the *will*, and no other. But if instead of a rational appetite, we shall say an appetite resulting from a precedent deliberation, then the definition is the same that I have given here. *Will* therefore *is the last appetite in deliberating.* And though we say in common discourse, a man had a will once to do a thing, that nevertheless he forbore to do; yet that is properly but an inclination, which makes no action voluntary; because the action depends not of it, but of the last inclination, or appetite. For if the intervenient appetites, make any action voluntary; then by the same reason all intervenient aversions, should make the same action involuntary; and so one and the same action, should be both voluntary and involuntary.

The will.

[29]

54. By this it is manifest, that not only actions that have their beginning from covetousness, ambition, lust, or other appetites to the thing propounded; but also those that have their beginning from aversion, or fear of those consequences that follow the omission, are *voluntary actions*.

Forms of speech, in passion.

55. The forms of speech by which the passions are expressed, are partly the same, and partly different from those, by which we express our thoughts. And first, generally all passions may be expressed *indicatively*; as *I love, I fear, I joy, I deliberate, I will, I command*: but some of them have particular expressions by

themselves, which nevertheless are not affirmations, unless it be when they serve to make other inferences, besides that of the passion they proceed from. Deliberation is expressed *subjunctively*; which is a speech proper to signify suppositions, with their consequences; as, *if this be done, then this will follow*; and differs not from the language of reasoning, save that reasoning is in general words; but deliberation for the most part is of particulars. The language of desire, and aversion, is *imperative*; as *do this, forbear that*; which when the party is obliged to do, or forbear, is *command*; otherwise *prayer*; or else *counsel*. The language of vain-glory, of indignation, pity and revengefulness, *optative*: but of the desire to know, there is a peculiar expression, called *interrogative*; as, *what is it, when shall it, how is it done*, and *why so?* Other language of the passions I find none: for cursing, swearing, reviling, and the like, do not signify as speech; but as the actions of a tongue accustomed.

56. These forms of speech, I say, are expressions, or voluntary significations of our passions: but certain signs they be not; because they may be used arbitrarily, whether they that use them, have such passions or not. The best signs of passions present, are either in the countenance, motions of the body, actions, and ends, or aims, which we otherwise know the man to have.

57. And because in deliberation, the appetites, and aversions are raised by foresight of the good and evil consequences, and sequels of the action whereof we deliberate; the good or evil effect thereof dependeth on the foresight of a long chain of consequences, of which very seldom any man is able to see to the end. But for so far as a man seeth, if the good in those consequences, be greater than the evil, the whole chain is that which writers call *apparent*, or *seeming good*. And contrarily, when the evil exceedeth the good, the whole is *apparent*, or *seeming evil*: so that he who hath by experience, or reason, the greatest and surest prospect of consequences, deliberates best himself; and is able when he will, to give the best counsel unto others. *Good and evil apparent*

58. *Continual success* in obtaining those things which a man from time to time desireth, that is to say, continual prospering, is that men call FELICITY; I mean the felicity of this life. For there is no such thing as perpetual tranquillity of mind, while we live here; because life itself is but motion, and can never be without desire, nor without fear, no more than without sense. What kind of felicity God hath ordained to them that devoutly honour Him, a man shall no sooner *Felicity.* [30]

know, than enjoy; being joys, that now are as incomprehensible, as the word of Schoolmen *beatifical vision* is unintelligible.

Praise.
Magnification.

μακαρισμός.

59. The form of speech whereby men signify their opinion of the goodness of any thing, is PRAISE. That whereby they signify the power and greatness of any thing, is MAGNIFYING. And that whereby they signify the opinion they have of a man's felicity, is by the Greeks called *μακαρισμός*,* for which we have no name in our tongue. And thus much is sufficient for the present purpose, to have been said of the PASSIONS.

CHAPTER VII

OF THE ENDS, OR RESOLUTIONS OF DISCOURSE

1. OF all *discourse*, governed by desire of knowledge, there is at last an *end*, either by attaining, or by giving over. And in the chain of discourse, wheresoever it be interrupted, there is an end for that time.

2. If the discourse be merely mental, it consisteth of thoughts that the thing will be, and will not be; or that it has been, and has not been, alternately. So that wheresoever you break off the chain of a man's discourse, you leave him in a presumption of *it will be*, or, *it will not be*; or, *it has been*, or, *has not been*. All which is *opinion*. And that which is alternate appetite, in deliberating concerning good and evil; the same is alternate opinion, in the enquiry of the truth of *past*, and *future*. And as the last appetite in deliberation, is called the *will*; so the last opinion in search of the truth of past, and future, is called

Judgment or
sentence final.

the JUDGMENT, or *resolute* and *final sentence* of him that *discourseth*. And as the whole chain of appetites alternate, in the question of good, or bad, is called *deliberation*; so the whole chain of opinions

Doubt.

alternate, in the question of true, or false, is called DOUBT.

3. No discourse whatsoever, can end in absolute knowledge of fact, past, or to come. For, as for the knowledge of fact, it is originally, sense; and ever after, memory. And for the knowledge of consequence, which I have said before is called science, it is not absolute, but conditional. No man can know by discourse, that this, or that, is, has been, or will be; which is to know absolutely: but only, that if this be, that is; if this has been, that has been; if this shall be,

that shall be: which is to know conditionally; and that not the consequence of one thing to another; but of one name of a thing, to another name of the same thing.

4. And therefore, when the discourse is put into speech, and begins with the definitions of words, and proceeds by connexion of the same into general affirmations, and of these again into syllogisms; the end or last sum is called the conclusion; and the thought of the mind by it signified, is that conditional knowledge, or [31] knowledge of the consequence of words, which is commonly called SCIENCE. But if the first ground of such discourse, be not definitions; *Science.* or if the definitions be not rightly joined together into syllogisms, then the end or conclusion, is again OPINION, namely of the truth of *Opinion.* somewhat said, though sometimes in absurd and senseless words, without possibility of being understood. When two, or more men, know of one and the same fact, they are said to be CONSCIOUS of it *Conscious.* one to another; which is as much as to know it together. And because such are fittest witnesses of the facts of one another, or of a third; it was, and ever will be reputed a very evil act, for any man to speak against his *conscience;** or to corrupt or force another so to do: insomuch that the plea of conscience, has been always hearkened unto very diligently in all times. Afterwards, men made use of the same word metaphorically, for the knowledge of their own secret facts, and secret thoughts; and therefore it is rhetorically said, that the conscience is a thousand witnesses. And last of all, men, vehemently in love with their own new opinions, (though never so absurd,) and obstinately bent to maintain them, gave those their opinions also that reverenced name of conscience, as if they would have it seem unlawful, to change or speak against them; and so pretend to know they are true, when they know at most, but that they think so.

5. When a man's discourse beginneth not at definitions, it beginneth either at some other contemplation of his own, and then it is still called opinion; or it beginneth at some saying of another, of whose ability to know the truth, and of whose honesty in not deceiving, he doubteth not; and then the discourse is not so much concerning the thing, as the person; and the resolution is called BELIEF, and FAITH: *faith, in* the man; *belief,* both *of* the man, and *of* *Belief. Faith.* the truth of what he says. So that in belief are two opinions; one of the saying of the man; the other of his virtue. To *have faith in*, or *trust to*, or *believe a man*, signify the same thing; namely, an opinion

of the veracity of the man: but to *believe what is said*, signifieth only an opinion of the truth of the saying. But we are to observe that this phrase, *I believe in*; as also the Latin, *credo in*; and the Greek, ιστένω ἔις, are never used but in the writings of divines. Instead of them, in other writings are put, *I believe him*; *I trust him*; *I have faith in him*; *I rely on him*: and in Latin, *credo illi*: *fido illi*: and in Greek, ιστένω αὐτὼ: and that this singularity of the ecclesiastic use of the word hath raised many disputes about the right object of the Christian faith.

6. But by *believing in*, as it is in the creed, is meant, not trust in the person; but confession and acknowledgment of the doctrine. For not only Christians, but all manner of men do so believe in God, as to hold all for truth they hear him say, whether they understand it, or not; which is all the faith and trust can possibly be had in any person whatsoever: but they do not all believe the doctrine of the creed.

[32]

7. From whence we may infer, that when we believe any saying whatsoever it be, to be true, from arguments taken, not from the thing itself, or from the principles of natural reason, but from the authority, and good opinion we have, of him that hath said it; then is the speaker, or person we believe in, or trust in, and whose word we take, the object of our faith; and the honour done in believing, is done to him only. And consequently, when we believe that the Scriptures are the word of God, having no immediate revelation from God himself, our belief, faith, and trust is in the church; whose word we take, and acquiesce therein. And they that believe that which a prophet relates unto them in the name of God, take the word of the prophet, do honour to him, and in him trust, and believe, touching the truth of what he relateth, whether he be a true, or a false prophet. And so it is also with all other history. For if I should not believe all that is written by historians, of the glorious acts of *Alexander*, or *Caesar*; I do not think the ghost of *Alexander*, or *Caesar*, had any just cause to be offended; or any body else, but the historian. If *Livy* say the Gods made once a cow speak, and we believe it not; we distrust not God therein, but *Livy*.* So that it is evident, that whatsoever we believe, upon no other reason, than what is drawn from authority of men only, and their writings; whether they be sent from God or not, is faith in men only.*

CHAPTER VIII

OF THE VIRTUES COMMONLY CALLED INTELLECTUAL;
AND THEIR CONTRARY DEFECTS

1. VIRTUE generally, in all sorts of subjects, is somewhat that is *Intellectual* valued for eminence; and consisteth in comparison. For if all things *virtue* were equal in all men, nothing would be prized. And by *virtues* *defined.* INTELLECTUAL, are always understood such abilities of the mind, as men praise, value, and desire should be in themselves; and go commonly under the name of a *good wit*; though the same word *wit*, be used also, to distinguish one certain ability from the rest.

2. These *virtues* are of two sorts; *natural*, and *acquired*. By natu- *Wit, natural,* ral, I mean not, that which a man hath from his birth: for that is *or acquired.* nothing else but sense; wherein men differ so little one from another, and from brute beasts, as it is not to be reckoned amongst virtues. But I mean, that *wit*, which is gotten by use only, and experience; without method, culture, or instruction. This NATURAL *Natural wit.* WIT, consisteth principally in two things; *celerity of imagining* (that is, swift succession of one thought to another;) and *steady direction* to some approved end. On the contrary a slow imagination, maketh that defect, or fault of the mind, which is commonly called DULL-NESS, *stupidity*, and sometimes by other names that signify slowness of motion, or difficulty to be moved.

3. And this difference of quickness, is caused by the difference of [33] men's passions; that love and dislike, some one thing, some another: and therefore some men's thoughts run one way, some another; and are held to, and observe differently the things that pass through their imagination. And whereas in this succession of men's thoughts, there is nothing to observe in the things they think on, but either in what they be *like one another*, or in what they be *unlike*, or *what they serve for*, or *how they serve to such a purpose*; those that observe their similitudes, in case they be such as are but rarely observed by others, are said to have a *good wit*; by which, in this *Good wit,* occasion, is meant a *good fancy*. But they that observe their differ- *or fancy.* ences, and dissimilitudes; which is called *distinguishing*, and *discerning*, and *judging* between thing and thing; in case, such discerning be not easy, are said to have a *good judgment*: and particularly in matter *Good* of conversation and business; wherein, times, places, and persons *judgment.*

45

Discretion. are to be discerned, this virtue is called DISCRETION. The former, that is, fancy, without the help of judgment, is not commended as a virtue: but the latter which is judgment, and discretion, is commended for itself, without the help of fancy. Besides the discretion of times, places, and persons, necessary to a good fancy, there is required also an often application of his thoughts to their end; that is to say, to some use to be made of them. This done; he that hath this virtue, will be easily fitted with similitudes, that will please, not only by illustration of his discourse, and adorning it with new and apt metaphors; but also, by the rarity of their invention. But without steadiness, and direction to some end, a great fancy is one kind of madness; such as they have, that entering into any discourse, are snatched from their purpose, by every thing that comes in their thought, into so many, and so long digressions, and parentheses, that they utterly lose themselves: which kind of folly, I know no particular name for: but the cause of it is, sometimes want of experience; whereby that seemeth to a man new and rare, which doth not so to others: sometimes pusillanimity; by which that seems great to him, which other men think a trifle: and whatsoever is new, or great, and therefore thought fit to be told, withdraws a man by degrees from the intended way of his discourse.

4. In a good poem, whether it be *epic*, or *dramatic*; as also in *sonnets*, *epigrams*, and other pieces, both judgment and fancy are required: but the fancy must be more eminent; because they please for the extravagancy; but ought not to displease by indiscretion.

5. In a good history, the judgment must be eminent; because the goodness consisteth, in the method, in the truth, and in the choice of the actions that are most profitable to be known. Fancy has no place, but only in adorning the style.

6. In orations of praise, and in invectives, the fancy is predominant; because the design is not truth, but to honour or dishonour; which is done by noble, or by vile comparisons. The judgment does but suggest what circumstances make an action laudable, or culpable.

[34] 7. In hortatives [exhortations], and pleadings, as truth, or disguise serveth best to the design in hand; so is the judgment, or the fancy most required.

8. In demonstration, in counsel, and all rigorous search of truth, judgment does all, except sometimes the understanding have need to be opened by some apt similitude; and then there is so much use

of fancy. But for metaphors, they are in this case utterly excluded. For seeing they openly profess deceit; to admit them into counsel, or reasoning, were manifest folly.

9. And in any discourse whatsoever, if the defect of discretion be apparent, how extravagant soever the fancy be, the whole discourse will be taken for a sign of want of wit; and so will it never when the discretion is manifest, though the fancy be never so ordinary.

10. The secret thoughts of a man run over all things, holy, profane, clean, obscene, grave, and light, without shame, or blame; which verbal discourse cannot do, farther than the judgment shall approve of the time, place, and persons. An anatomist, or a physician may speak, or write his judgment of unclean things; because it is not to please, but profit: but for another man to write his extravagant, and pleasant fancies of the same, is as if a man, from being tumbled into the dirt, should come and present himself before good company. And 'tis the want of discretion that makes the difference. Again, in professed remissness of mind, and familiar company, a man may play with the sounds, and equivocal significations of words; and that many times with encounters of extraordinary fancy: but in a sermon, or in public, or before persons unknown, or whom we ought to reverence, there is no jingling of words that will not be accounted folly: and the difference is only in the want of discretion. So that where wit is wanting, it is not fancy that is wanting, but discretion. Judgment therefore without fancy is wit, but fancy without judgment, not.

11. When the thoughts of a man, that has a design in hand, running over a multitude of things, observes how they conduce to that design; or what design they may conduce unto; if his observations be such as are not easy, or usual, this wit of his is called PRUDENCE; and dependeth on much experience, and memory of the *Prudence.* like things, and their consequences heretofore. In which there is not so much difference of men, as there is in their fancies and judgments; because the experience of men equal in age, is not much unequal, as to the quantity; but lies in different occasions; every one having his private designs. To govern well a family, and a kingdom, are not different degrees of prudence; but different sorts of business; no more than to draw a picture in little, or as great, or greater than the life, are different degrees of art. A plain husbandman is more prudent in affairs of his own house, than a privy-councillor in the affairs of another man.

12. To prudence, if you add the use of unjust, or dishonest means, such as usually are prompted to men by fear, or want; you have that crooked wisdom, which is called CRAFT; which is a sign of pusillanimity. For magnanimity is contempt of unjust, or dishonest helps. And that which the Latins call *versutia*, (translated into English, *shifting*,) and is a putting off of a present danger or incommodity, by engaging into a greater, as when a man robs one to pay another, is but a shorter-sighted craft, called *versutia*, from *versura*, which signifies taking money at usury, for the present payment of interest.

Craft.

[35]

13. As for *acquired wit*, (I mean acquired by method and instruction,) there is none but reason; which is grounded on the right use of speech; and produceth the sciences. But of reason and science, I have already spoken in the fifth and sixth chapters.

Acquired wit.

14. The causes of this difference of wits, are in the passions: and the difference of passions, proceedeth partly from the different constitution of the body, and partly from different education. For if the difference proceeded from the temper of the brain, and the organs of sense, either exterior or interior, there would be no less difference of men in their sight, hearing, or other senses, than in their fancies, and discretions. It proceeds therefore from the passions; which are different, not only from the difference of men's complexions; but also from their difference of customs, and education.

15. The passions that most of all cause the difference of wit, are principally, the more or less desire of power, of riches, of knowledge, and of honour. All which may be reduced to the first, that is, desire of power. For riches, knowledge and honour are but several sorts of power.

16. And therefore, a man who has no great passion for any of these things; but is as men term it indifferent; though he may be so far a good man, as to be free from giving offence; yet he cannot possibly have either a great fancy, or much judgment. For the thoughts, are to the desires, as scouts, and spies, to range abroad, and find the way to the things desired: all steadiness of the mind's motion, and all quickness of the same, proceeding from thence. For as to have no desire, is to be dead: so to have weak passions, is dullness; and to have passions indifferently for every thing, GIDDINESS, and *distraction*; and to have stronger and more vehement

Giddiness.

48

passions for any thing, than is ordinarily seen in others, is that which
men call MADNESS.   *Madness.*

17. Whereof there be almost as many kinds, as of the passions
themselves. Sometimes the extraordinary and extravagant passion,
proceedeth from the evil constitution of the organs of the body, or
harm done them; and sometimes the hurt, and indisposition of the
organs, is caused by the vehemence, or long continuance of the
passion. But in both cases the madness is of one and the same
nature.

18. The passion, whose violence, or continuance, maketh madness, is either great *vain-glory*; which is commonly called *pride*, and
self-conceit; or great *dejection* of mind.

19. Pride, subjecteth a man to anger, the excess whereof, is the   *Rage.*
madness called RAGE, and FURY. And thus it comes to pass that
excessive desire of revenge, when it becomes habitual, hurteth the   [36]
organs, and becomes rage: that excessive love, with jealousy, becomes also rage: excessive opinion of a man's own self, for divine
inspiration, for wisdom, learning, form, and the like, becomes
distraction, and giddiness: the same, joined with envy, rage:
vehement opinion of the truth of any thing, contradicted by others,
rage.

20. Dejection, subjects a man to causeless fears; which is a   *Melancholy.*
madness commonly called MELANCHOLY, apparent also in divers
manners; as in haunting of solitudes, and graves; in superstitious
behaviour; and in fearing some one, some another particular thing.
In sum, all passions that produce strange and unusual behaviour, are
called by the general name of madness. But of the several kinds   *Madness.*
of madness, he that would take the pains, might enrol a legion. And
if the excesses be madness, there is no doubt but the passions
themselves, when they tend to evil, are degrees of the same.

21. (For example,) though the effect of folly, in them that are
possessed of an opinion of being inspired, be not visible always in
one man, by any very extravagant action, that proceedeth from such
passion; yet, when many of them conspire together, the rage of the
whole multitude is visible enough. For what argument of madness
can there be greater, than to clamour, strike, and throw stones at our
best friends? Yet this is somewhat less than such a multitude will do.
For they will clamour, fight against, and destroy those, by whom all
their lifetime before, they have been protected, and secured from

injury. And if this be madness in the multitude, it is the same in every particular man. For as in the midst of the sea, though a man perceive no sound of that part of the water next him; yet he is well assured, that part contributes as much, to the roaring of the sea, as any other part, of the same quantity: so also, though we perceive no great unquietness, in one, or two men; yet we may be well assured, that their singular passions, are parts of the seditious roaring of a troubled nation. And if there were nothing else that bewrayed [revealed] their madness; yet that very arrogating such inspiration to themselves, is argument enough. If some man in Bedlam should entertain you with sober discourse; and you desire in taking leave, to know what he were, that you might another time requite his civility; and he should tell you, he were God the Father; I think you need expect no extravagant action for argument of his madness.

22. This opinion of inspiration, called commonly, private spirit, begins very often, from some lucky finding of an error generally held by others; and not knowing, or not remembering, by what conduct of reason, they came to so singular a truth, (as they think it, though it be many times an untruth they light on,) they presently admire themselves; as being in the special grace of God Almighty, who hath revealed the same to them supernaturally, by his Spirit.

23. Again, that madness is nothing else, but too much appearing passion, may be gathered out of the effects of wine, which are the same with those of the evil disposition of the organs. For the variety [37] of behaviour in men that have drunk too much, is the same with that of madmen: some of them raging, others loving, others laughing, all extravagantly, but according to their several domineering passions: for the effect of the wine, does but remove dissimulation, and take from them the sight of the deformity of their passions. For, (I believe) the most sober men, when they walk alone without care and employment of the mind, would be unwilling the vanity and extravagance of their thoughts at that time should be publicly seen: which is a confession, that passions unguided, are for the most part mere madness.

24. The opinions of the world, both in ancient and later ages, concerning the cause of madness, have been two. Some, deriving them from the passions; some, from demons, or spirits, either good or bad, which they thought might enter into a man, possess him, and move his organs in such strange, and uncouth manner, as madmen use to do. The former sort therefore, called such men, madmen: but

the latter, called them sometimes *demoniacs*, (that is, possessed with spirits;) sometimes *energumeni*, (that is, agitated, or moved with spirits;) and now in Italy they are called, not only *pazzi*, madmen; but also *spiritati*, men possessed.

25. There was once a great conflux of people in Abdera, a city of the Greeks, at the acting of the tragedy of *Andromeda*, upon an extreme hot day: whereupon, a great many of the spectators falling into fevers, had this accident from the heat, and from the tragedy together, that they did nothing but pronounce iambics, with the names of Perseus and Andromeda; which together with the fever, was cured by the coming on of winter: and this madness was thought to proceed from the passion imprinted by the tragedy.* Likewise there reigned a fit of madness in another Grecian city, which seized only the young maidens; and caused many of them to hang themselves. This was by most then thought an act of the Devil. But one that suspected, that contempt of life in them, might proceed from some passion of the mind, and supposing that they did not contemn also their honour, gave counsel to the magistrates, to strip such as so hanged themselves, and let them hang out naked. This, the story* says, cured that madness. But on the other side, the same Grecians, did often ascribe madness, to the operation of Eumenides, or Furies; and sometimes of Ceres, Phoebus, and other gods: so much did men attribute to phantasms, as to think them aërial living bodies; and generally to call them spirits. And as the Romans in this, held the same opinion with the Greeks: so also did the Jews; for they called madmen prophets, or (according as they thought the spirits good or bad) demoniacs; and some of them called both prophets, and demoniacs, madmen; and some called the same man both demoniac, and madman. But for the Gentiles, 'tis no wonder; because diseases, and health; vices and virtues; and many natural accidents, were with them termed, and worshipped as demons. So that a man was to understand by demon,* as well (sometimes) an ague, as a devil. But for the Jews to have such [38] opinion, is somewhat strange. For neither Moses, nor Abraham pretended to prophecy by possession of a spirit; but from the voice of God; or by a vision or dream: nor is there anything in his Law, moral, or ceremonial, by which they were taught, there was any such enthusiasm; or any possession. When God is said, (*Numb.* 11. 25) to take from the spirit that was in Moses, and give to the seventy elders, the Spirit of God (taking it for the substance of God) is not

divided. The Scriptures by the Spirit of God in man, mean a man's spirit, inclined to godliness. And where it is said,* (*Exod.* 28. 3) *Whom I have filled with the spirit of wisdom to make garments for Aaron*, is not meant a spirit put into them, that can make garments; but the wisdom of their own spirits in that kind of work. In the like sense, the spirit of man, when it produceth unclean actions, is ordinarily called an unclean spirit; and so other spirits, though not always, yet as often as the virtue or vice so styled, is extraordinary, and eminent. Neither did the other prophets of the old Testament pretend enthusiasm; or, that God spake in them; but to them, by voice, vision, or dream; and the *burthen of the Lord*, was not possession, but command. How then could the Jews fall into this opinion of possession? I can imagine no reason, but that which is common to all men; namely, the want of curiosity to search natural causes; and their placing felicity, in the acquisition of the gross pleasures of the senses, and the things that most immediately conduce thereto. For they that see any strange, and unusual ability, or defect, in a man's mind; unless they see withal, from what cause it may probably proceed, can hardly think it natural; and if not natural, they must needs think it supernatural; and then what can it be, but that either God, or the Devil is in him? And hence it came to pass, when our Saviour (*Mark* 3. 21) was compassed about with the multitude, those of the house doubted he was mad, and went out to hold him: but the Scribes said he had Beelzebub, and that was it, by which he cast out devils; as if the greater madman had awed the lesser. And that (*John* 10. 20) some said, *He hath a devil, and is mad*; whereas others holding him for a prophet, said, *These are not the words of one that hath a devil*. So in the old Testament he that came to anoint Jehu, (2 *Kings* 9. 11) was a prophet; but some of the company asked Jehu, *what came that madman for?* So that in sum, it is manifest, that whosoever behaved himself in extraordinary manner, was thought by the Jews to be possessed either with a good, or evil spirit; except by the Sadducees, who erred so far on the other hand, as not to believe there were at all any spirits, (which is very near to direct atheism;*) and thereby perhaps the more provoked others, to term such men demoniacs, rather than madmen.

26. But why then does our Saviour proceed in the curing of them, as if they were possessed; and not as if they were mad? To which I can give no other kind of answer, but that which is given to those that urge the Scripture in like manner against the opinion of

the motion of the earth. The Scripture was written to shew unto men the kingdom of God, and to prepare their minds to become his obedient subjects; leaving the world, and the philosophy thereof, to [39] the disputation of men, for the exercising of their natural reason.* Whether the earth's, or sun's motion make the day, and night; or whether the exorbitant actions of men, proceed from passion, or from the devil, (so we worship him not) it is all one, as to our obedience, and subjection to God Almighty; which is the thing for which the Scripture was written. As for that our Saviour speaketh to the disease, as to a person; it is the usual phrase of all that cure by words only, as Christ did, (and enchanters pretend to do, whether they speak to a devil or not.) For is not Christ also said (*Matt.* 8. 26) to have rebuked the winds? Is not he said also (*Luke* 4. 39) to rebuke a fever? Yet this does not argue that a fever is a devil. And whereas many of the devils are said to confess Christ; it is not necessary to interpret those places otherwise, than that those madmen confessed him. And whereas our Saviour (*Matt.* 12. 43) speaketh of an unclean spirit, that having gone out of a man, wandereth through dry places, seeking rest, and finding none; and returning into the same man, with seven other spirits worse than himself; it is manifestly a parable, alluding to a man, that after a little endeavour to quit his lusts, is vanquished by the strength of them; and becomes seven times worse than he was. So that I see nothing at all in the Scripture, that requireth a belief, that demoniacs were any other thing but madmen.

27. There is yet another fault in the discourses of some men; *Insignificant* which may also be numbered amongst the sorts of madness; namely, *speech.* that abuse of words, whereof I have spoken before in the fifth chapter, by the name of absurdity. And that is, when men speak such words, as put together, have in them no signification at all; but are fallen upon by some, through misunderstanding of the words they have received, and repeat by rote; by others, from intention to deceive by obscurity. And this is incident to none but those, that converse in questions of matters incomprehensible, as the Schoolmen; or in questions of abstruse philosophy. The common sort of men seldom speak insignificantly, and are therefore, by those other egregious persons counted idiots. But to be assured their words are without any thing correspondent to them in the mind, there would need some examples; which if any man require, let him take a Schoolman in his hands, and see if he can translate any one

chapter concerning any difficult point, as the Trinity; the Deity; the nature of Christ; transubstantiation; free-will, &c into any of the modern tongues, so as to make the same intelligible; or into any tolerable Latin, such as they were acquainted withal, that lived when the Latin tongue was vulgar. What is the meaning of these words. *The first cause does not necessarily inflow any thing into the second, by force of the essential subordination of the second causes, by which it may help it to work?* They are the translation of the title of the sixth chapter of *Suarez'* first book, *Of the concourse, motion, and help of God.** When men write whole volumes of such stuff, are they not [40] mad, or intend to make others so? And particularly, in the question of transubstantiation; where after certain words spoken; they that say, the white*ness*, round*ness*, magni*tude*, quali*ty*, corruptibili*ty*, all which are incorporeal, &c. go out of the wafer, into the body of our blessed Saviour, do they not make those *nesses, tudes,* and *ties,* to be so many spirits possessing his body? For by spirits, they mean always things, that being incorporeal, are nevertheless moveable from one place to another. So that this kind of absurdity, may rightly be numbered amongst the many sorts of madness; and all the time that guided by clear thoughts of their worldly lust, they forbear disputing, or writing thus, but lucid intervals. And thus much of the virtues and defects intellectual.

CHAPTER IX

OF THE SEVERAL SUBJECTS OF KNOWLEDGE*

1. THERE are of KNOWLEDGE two kinds; whereof one is *knowledge of fact*: the other *knowledge of the consequence of one affirmation to another.* The former is nothing else, but sense and memory, and is *absolute knowledge*; as when we see a fact doing, or remember it done: and this is the knowledge required in a witness. The latter is called *science*; and is *conditional*; as when we know, that, *if the figure shown be a circle, then any straight line through the centre shall divide it into two equal parts.* And this is the knowledge required in a philosopher; that is to say, of him that pretends to reasoning.

2. The register of *knowledge of fact* is called *history*. Whereof there be two sorts: one called *natural history*; which is the history of

such facts, or effects of nature, as have no dependence on man's *will*; such as are the histories of *metals*, *plants*, *animals*, *regions*, and the like. The other, is *civil history*; which is the history of the voluntary actions of men in commonwealths.

3. The registers of science, are such *books* as contain the *demonstrations* of consequences of one affirmation, to another; and are commonly called *books of philosophy*; whereof the sorts are many, according to the diversity of the matter; and may be divided in such manner as I have divided them in the following table.

SCIENCE, that is, knowledge of consequences; which is called also PHILOSOPHY.

Consequences from the accidents of bodies natural; which is called NATURAL PHILOSOPHY

Consequences from the accidents common to all bodies natural; which are *quantity*, and *motion*. . . . .

PHYSICS or consequences from *qualities*.

Consequences from the qualities of bodies *transient*, such as sometimes appear, sometimes vanish, *Meteorology*. . . . .

Consequences from the qualities of bodies *permanent*.

Consequences from the qualities of the *stars* . .

Consequences of the qualities from *liquid* bodies, that fill the space between the stars; such as are the *air*, or substances ethereal.

Consequences from the qualities of *bodies terrestrial*.

Consequences from the accidents of *politic* bodies; which is called POLITICS, and CIVIL PHILOSOPHY.

1. Of consequences from the *institution* of COMMON-WEALTHS, to the *rights*, and *duties* of the *body politic* or *sovereign*.
2. Of consequences from the same, to the *duty* and *right* of the *subjects*.

Consequences from quantity, and motion *indeterminate*; which being the principles or first foundation of philosophy, is called *Philosophia Prima*. . . . . . . — PHILOSOPHIA PRIMA. *Physics*

Consequences from motion and quantity *determined*.	Consequences from quantity, and motion determined.	By Figure . . .	*Mathematics.* — GEOMETRY.
		By Number . . .	ARITHMETIC.
	Consequences from the motion, and quantity of bodies in *special*.	Consequences from the motion and quantity of the greater parts of the world, as the *earth* and *stars*.	*Cosmography.* — ASTRONOMY. / GEOGRAPHY.
		Consequences from the motions of special kinds, and figures of body.	*Mechanics.* Doctrine of *weight.* — *Science* of ENGINEERS. ARCHITECTURE NAVIGATION.

. . . . METEOROLOGY

Consequences from the *light* of the stars. Out of this, and the motion of the sun, is made the science of . . . . } SCIOGRAPHY.

Consequences from the *influences* of the stars . . . . ASTROLOGY.

Consequences from the parts of the earth, that are *without sense*.	Consequences from the qualities of *minerals*, as *stones*, *metals*, &c.		
	Consequences from the qualities of *vegetables*.		
Consequences from the qualities of *animals*.	Consequences from the qualities of *animals in general*.	Consequences from *vision* . . . . — OPTICS.	
		Consequences from *sounds* . . . . — MUSIC.	
		Consequences from the rest of the *senses*.	
	Consequences from the qualities of *men in special*.	Consequences from the *passions* of men . . . . } ETHICS.	
		Consequences from *speech*.	In *magnifying, vilifying, &c.* } POETRY.
			In *persuading*, RHETORIC.
			In *reasoning*, LOGIC.
			In *contracting*, The *Science* of JUST and UNJUST.

57

CHAPTER X

OF POWER, WORTH, DIGNITY, HONOUR, AND
WORTHINESS

Power [41] 1. The POWER *of a man*, (to take it universally,) is his present means, to obtain some future apparent good. And is either *original* or *instrumental*.

2. *Natural power*, is the eminence of the faculties of body, or mind: as extraordinary strength, form, prudence, arts, eloquence, liberality, nobility. *Instrumental* are those powers, which acquired by these, or by fortune, are means and instruments to acquire more: as riches, reputation, friends, and the secret working of God, which men call good luck. For the nature of power, is in this point, like to fame, increasing as it proceeds; or like the motion of heavy bodies, which the further they go, make still the more haste.

3. The greatest of human powers, is that which is compounded of the powers of most men, united by consent, in one person, natural, or civil, that has the use of all their powers depending on his will; such as is the power of a commonwealth: or depending on the wills of each particular; such as is the power of a faction or of divers factions leagued. Therefore to have servants, is power; to have friends, is power: for they are strengths united.

4. Also riches joined with liberality, is power; because it procureth friends, and servants: without liberality, not so; because in this case they defend not; but expose men to envy, as a prey.

5. Reputation of power, is power; because it draweth with it the adherence of those that need protection.

6. So is reputation of love of a man's country, (called popularity,) for the same reason.

7. Also, what quality soever maketh a man beloved, or feared of many; or the reputation of such quality, is power; because it is a means to have the assistance, and service of many.

8. Good success is power; because it maketh reputation of wisdom, or good fortune; which makes men either fear him, or rely on him.

9. Affability of men already in power, is increase of power; because it gaineth love.

10. Reputation of prudence in the conduct of peace or war, is

power; because to prudent men, we commit the government of ourselves, more willingly than to others.

11. Nobility is power, not in all places, but only in those commonwealths, where it has privileges: for in such privileges consisteth their power.

12. Eloquence is power; because it is seeming prudence.

13. Form is power; because being a promise of good, it recommendeth men to the favour of women and strangers.   [42]

14. The sciences, are small power; because not eminent; and therefore, not acknowledged in any man; nor are at all, but in a few; and in them, but of a few things. For science is of that nature, as none can understand it to be, but such as in a good measure have attained it.

15. Arts of public use, as fortification, making of engines, and other instruments of war; because they confer to defence, and victory, are power: and though the true mother of them, be science, namely the mathematics; yet, because they are brought into the light, by the hand of the artificer, they be esteemed (the midwife passing with the vulgar for the mother,) as his issue.

16. The *value*, or WORTH of a man, is as of all other things, his *Worth.* price; that is to say, so much as would be given for the use of his power: and therefore is not absolute; but a thing dependent on the need and judgment of another. An able conductor of soldiers, is of great price in time of war present, or imminent; but in peace not so. A learned and uncorrupt judge, is much worth in time of peace; but not so much in war. And as in other things, so in men, not the seller, but the buyer determines the price. For let a man (as most men do,) rate themselves at the highest value they can; yet their true value is no more than it is esteemed by others.

17. The manifestation of the value we set on one another, is that which is commonly called honouring, and dishonouring. To value a man at a high rate, is to *honour* him; at a low rate, is to *dishonour* him. But high, and low, in this case, is to be understood by comparison to the rate that each man setteth on himself.

18. The public worth of a man, which is the value set on him by the commonwealth, is that which men commonly call DIGNITY. And *Dignity.* this value of him by the commonwealth, is understood, by offices of command, judicature, public employment; or by names and titles, introduced for distinction of such value.

19. To pray to another, for aid of any kind, is *to* HONOUR; because

a sign we have an opinion he has power to help; and the more difficult the aid is, the more is the honour.

20. To obey, is to honour, because no man obeys them, whom they think have no power to help, or hurt them. And consequently to disobey, is to *dishonour*.

21. To give great gifts to a man, is to honour him; because 'tis buying of protection, and acknowledging of power. To give little gifts, is to dishonour; because it is but alms, and signifies an opinion of the need of small helps.

22. To be sedulous in promoting another's good; also to flatter, is to honour; as a sign we seek his protection or aid. To neglect, is to dishonour.

23. To give way, or place to another, in any commodity, is to honour; being a confession of greater power. To arrogate, is to dishonour.

24. To show any sign of love, or fear of another, is to honour; for
[43] both to love, and to fear, is to value. To contemn [belittle], or less to love or fear, than he expects, is to dishonour; for it is undervaluing.

25. To praise, magnify, or call happy, is to honour; because nothing but goodness, power, and felicity is valued. To revile, mock, or pity, is to dishonour.

26. To speak to another with consideration, to appear before him with decency, and humility, is to honour him; as signs of fear to offend. To speak to him rashly, to do any thing before him obscenely, slovenly, impudently, is to dishonour.

27. To believe, to trust, to rely on another, is to honour him; sign of opinion of his virtue and power. To distrust, or not believe, is to dishonour.

28. To hearken to a man's counsel, or discourse of what kind soever, is to honour; as a sign we think him wise, or eloquent, or witty. To sleep, or go forth, or talk the while, is to dishonour.

29. To do those things to another, which he takes for signs of honour, or which the law or custom makes so, is to honour; because in approving the honour done by others, he acknowledgeth the power which others acknowledge. To refuse to do them, is to dishonour.

30. To agree with in opinion, is to honour; as being a sign of approving his judgment, and wisdom. To dissent, is dishonour, and an upbraiding of error; and (if the dissent be in many things) of folly.

31. To imitate, is to honour; for it is vehemently to approve. To imitate one's enemy, is to dishonour.

32. To honour those another honours, is to honour him; as a sign of approbation of his judgment. To honour his enemies, is to dishonour him.

33. To employ in counsel, or in actions of difficulty, is to honour; as a sign of opinion of his wisdom, or other power. To deny employment in the same cases, to those that seek it, is to dishonour.

34. All these ways of honouring, are natural; and as well within, as without commonwealths. But in commonwealths, where he, or they that have the supreme authority, can make whatsoever they please, to stand for signs of honour, there be other honours.

35. A sovereign doth honour a subject, with whatsoever title, or office, or employment, or action, that he himself will have taken for a sign of his will to honour him.

36. The king of Persia, honoured Mordecai,* when he appointed he should be conducted through the streets in the king's garment, upon one of the king's horses, with a crown on his head, and a prince before him, proclaiming, *thus shall it be done to him that the king will honour.* And yet another king of Persia, or the same another time, to one that demanded for some great service, to wear one of the king's robes, gave him leave so to do; but with this addition, that he should wear it as the king's fool; and then it was dishonour. So that of civil honour, the fountain is in the person of the commonwealth, and dependeth on the will of the sovereign; and is therefore temporary, and called *civil honour*; such as magistracy, offices, titles; and in [44] some places coats and scutcheons painted: and men honour such as have them, as having so many signs of favour in the commonwealth; which favour is power.

37. *Honourable* is whatsoever possession, action, or quality, is an argument and sign of power. *Honourable.*

38. And therefore to be honoured, loved, or feared of many, is honourable; as arguments of power. To be honoured of few or none, *dishonourable*. *Dishonourable.*

39. Dominion, and victory is honourable; because acquired by power; and servitude, for need, or fear, is dishonourable.

40. Good fortune (if lasting,) honourable; as a sign of the favour of God. Ill fortune, and losses, dishonourable. Riches, are honourable; for they are power. Poverty, dishonourable. Magnanimity, liberality, hope, courage, confidence, are honourable; for they pro-

ceed from the conscience of power. Pusillanimity, parsimony, fear, diffidence, are dishonourable.

41. Timely resolution, or determination of what a man is to do, is honourable; as being the contempt of small difficulties, and dangers. And irresolution, dishonourable; as a sign of too much valuing of little impediments, and little advantages: for when a man has weighed things as long as the time permits, and resolves not, the difference of weight is but little; and therefore if he resolve not, he overvalues little things, which is pusillanimity.

42. All actions, and speeches, that proceed, or seem to proceed, from much experience, science, discretion, or wit, are honourable; for all these are powers. Actions, or words that proceed from error, ignorance, or folly, dishonourable.

43. Gravity, as far forth as it seems to proceed from a mind employed on something else, is honourable; because employment is a sign of power. But if it seem to proceed from a purpose to appear grave, it is dishonourable. For the gravity of the former, is like the steadiness of a ship laden with merchandise; but of the latter, like the steadiness of a ship ballasted with sand, and other trash.

44. To be conspicuous, that is to say, to be known, for wealth, office, great actions, or any eminent good, is honourable; as a sign of the power for which he is conspicuous. On the contrary, obscurity, is dishonourable.

45. To be descended from conspicuous parents, is honourable; because they the more easily attain the aids, and friends of their ancestors. On the contrary, to be descended from obscure parentage, is dishonourable.*

46. Actions proceeding from equity, joined with loss, are honourable; as signs of magnanimity: for magnanimity is a sign of power. On the contrary, craft, shifting, neglect of equity, is dishonourable.

47. Covetousness of great riches, and ambition of great honours, are honourable; as signs of power to obtain them. Covetousness, and ambition, of little gains, or preferments, is dishonourable.

48. Nor does it alter the case of honour, whether an action (so it [45] be great and difficult, and consequently a sign of much power,) be just or unjust: for honour consisteth only in the opinion of power. Therefore the ancient heathen did not think they dishonoured, but greatly honoured the Gods, when they introduced them in their poems, committing rapes, thefts, and other great, but unjust, or

unclean acts: insomuch as nothing is so much celebrated in Jupiter, as his adulteries; nor in Mercury, as his frauds, and thefts: of whose praises, in a hymn of Homer,* the greatest is this, that being born in the morning, he had invented music at noon, and before night, stolen away the cattle of Apollo, from his herdsmen.

49. Also amongst men, till there were constituted great commonwealths, it was thought no dishonour to be a pirate, or a highway thief; but rather a lawful trade, not only amongst the Greeks, but also amongst all other nations; as is manifest by the histories* of ancient time. And at this day, in this part of the world, private duels are, and always will be honourable, though unlawful, till such time as there shall be honour ordained for them that refuse, and ignominy for them that make the challenge. For duels also are many times effects of courage; and the ground of courage is always strength or skill, which are power; though for the most part they be effects of rash speaking, and of the fear of dishonour, in one, or both the combatants; who engaged by rashness, are driven into the lists to avoid disgrace.

50. Scutcheons, and coats of arms hereditary, where they have any eminent privileges, are honourable; otherwise not: for their power consisteth either in such privileges, or in riches, or some such thing as is equally honoured in other men. This kind of honour, commonly called gentry, hath been derived from the ancient Germans. For there never was any such thing known, where the German customs were unknown. Nor is it now anywhere in use, where the Germans have not inhabited. The ancient Greek commanders, when they went to war, had their shields painted with such devices as they pleased; insomuch as an unpainted buckler was a sign of poverty, and of a common soldier: but they transmitted not the inheritance of them. The Romans transmitted the marks of their families: but they were the images, not the devices of their ancestors. Amongst the people of Asia, Africa, and America, there is not, nor was ever, any such thing. The Germans only had that custom; from whom it has been derived into England, France, Spain, and Italy, when in great numbers they either aided the Romans, or made their own conquests in these western parts of the world. *Coats of arms.*

51. For Germany, being anciently, as all other countries, in their beginnings, divided amongst an infinite number of little lords, or masters of families, that continually had wars one with another; those masters, or lords, principally to the end they might, when they

were covered with arms, be known by their followers; and partly for ornament, both painted their armour, or their scutcheon, or coat, with the picture of some beast, or other thing; and also put some [46] eminent and visible mark upon the crest of their helmets. And this ornament both of the arms, and crest, descended by inheritance to their children; to the eldest pure, and to the rest with some note of diversity, such as the old master, that is to say in Dutch, the *Here-alt* thought fit. But when many such families, joined together, made a greater monarchy, this duty of the Herealt, to distinguish scutcheons, was made a private office apart. And the issue of these lords, is the great and ancient gentry; which for the most part bear living creatures, noted for courage, and rapine; or castles, battlements, belts, weapons, bars, palisadoes, and other notes of war; nothing being then in honour, but virtue military. Afterwards, not only kings, but popular commonwealths, gave divers manners of scutcheons, to such as went forth to the war, or returned from it, for encouragement, or recompense to their service. All which, by an observing reader, may be found in such ancient histories, Greek and Latin, as make mention of the German nation, and manners, in their times.

Titles of honour.

52. Titles of *honour*, such as are duke, count, marquis, and baron, are honourable; as signifying the value set upon them by the sovereign power of the commonwealth: which titles, were in old time titles of office, and command, derived some from the Romans, some from the Germans and French. Dukes, in Latin *duces*, being generals in war: counts, *comites*, such as bear the general company out of friendship, and were left to govern and defend places conquered, and pacified: marquises, *marchiones*, were counts that governed the marches, or bounds of the empire. Which titles of duke, count, and marquis, came into the empire, about the time of Constantine the Great,* from the customs of the German *militia*. But baron, seems to have been a title of the Gauls, and signifies a great man; such as were the king's, or prince's men, whom they employed in war about their persons; and seems to be derived from *vir*, to *ber*, and *bar*, that signified the same in the language of the Gauls, that *vir* in Latin; and thence to *bero*, and *baro*: so that such men were called *berones*, and after *barones*; and (in Spanish) *varones*. But he that would know more particularly the original of titles of honour, may find it, as I have done this, in Mr Selden's most excellent treatise* of that subject. In process of time these offices of

honour, by occasion of trouble, and for reasons of good and peaceable government, were turned into mere titles; serving for the most part, to distinguish the precedence, place, and order of subjects in the commonwealth: and men were made dukes, counts, marquises, and barons of places, wherein they had neither possession, nor command: and other titles also, were devised to the same end.

53. WORTHINESS, is a thing different from the worth, or value of a man; and also from his merit, or desert, and consisteth in a particular power, or ability for that, whereof he is said to be worthy: which particular ability, is usually named FITNESS, or *aptitude*. *Worthiness.*

Fitness.

54. For he is worthiest to be a commander, to be a judge, or to have any other charge, that is best fitted, with the qualities required to the well discharging of it; and worthiest of riches, that has the qualities most requisite for the well using of them: any of which qualities being absent, one may nevertheless be a worthy man, and valuable for something else. Again, a man may be worthy of riches, office, and employment, that nevertheless, can plead no right to have it before another; and therefore cannot be said to merit or deserve it. For merit, presupposeth a right, and that the thing deserved is due by promise: of which I shall say more hereafter, when I shall speak of contracts. [47]

CHAPTER XI

OF THE DIFFERENCE OF MANNERS

1. BY MANNERS, I mean not here, decency of behaviour; as how one should salute another, or how a man should wash his mouth, or pick his teeth before company, and such other points of the *small morals*; but those qualities of mankind, that concern their living together in peace, and unity. To which end we are to consider, that the felicity of this life, consisteth not in the repose of a mind satisfied. For there is no such *finis ultimus*, (utmost aim,) nor *summum bonum*, (greatest good,) as is spoken of in the books of the old moral philosophers. Nor can a man any more live,* whose desires are at an end, than he, whose senses and imaginations are at a stand. Felicity is a continual progress of the desire, from one object to another; the attaining of *What is here meant by manners.*

the former, being still but the way to the latter. The cause whereof is, that the object of man's desire, is not to enjoy once only, and for one instant of time; but to assure for ever, the way of his future desire. And therefore the voluntary actions, and inclinations of all men, tend, not only to the procuring, but also to the assuring of a contented life; and differ only in the way: which ariseth partly from the diversity of passions, in divers men; and partly from the difference of the knowledge, or opinion each one has of the causes, which produce the effect desired.

A restless desire of power, in all men.

2. So that in the first place, I put for a general inclination of all mankind, a perpetual and restless desire of power after power, that ceaseth only in death. And the cause of this, is not always that a man hopes for a more intensive delight, than he has already attained to; or that he cannot be content with a moderate power: but because he cannot assure the power and means to live well, which he hath present, without the acquisition of more. And from hence it is, that kings, whose power is greatest, turn their endeavours to the assuring it at home by laws, or abroad by wars: and when that is done, there succeedeth a new desire; in some, of fame from new conquest; in others, of ease and sensual pleasure; in others, of admiration, or being flattered for excellence in some art, or other ability of the mind.

Love of contention from competition.

[48]

3. Competition of riches, honour, command, or other power, inclineth to contention, enmity, and war: because the way of one competitor, to the attaining of his desire, is to kill, subdue, supplant, or repel the other. Particularly, competition of praise, inclineth to a reverence of antiquity. For men contend with the living, not with the dead; to these ascribing more than due, that they may obscure the glory of the other.

Civil obedience from love of ease.

From fear of death, or wounds.

4. Desire of ease, and sensual delight, disposeth men to obey a common power: because by such desires, a man doth abandon the protection that might be hoped for from his own industry, and labour. Fear of death, and wounds, disposeth to the same; and for the same reason. On the contrary, needy men, and hardy, not contented with their present condition; as also, all men that are ambitious of military command, are inclined to continue the causes of war; and to stir up trouble and sedition: for there is no honour military but by war; nor any such hope to mend an ill game, as by causing a new shuffle.

5. Desire of knowledge, and arts of peace, inclineth men to obey

a common power: for such desire, containeth a desire of leisure; and *And from* consequently protection from some other power than their own. *love of arts.*

6. Desire of praise, disposeth to laudable actions, such as please *Love of* them whose judgment they value; for of those men whom we con- *virtue from* temn, we contemn also the praises. Desire of fame after death does *love of praise.* the same. And though after death, there be no sense of the praise given us on earth, as being joys, that are either swallowed up in the unspeakable joys of Heaven, or extinguished in the extreme torments of hell: yet is not such fame vain; because men have a present delight therein, from the foresight of it, and of the benefit that may redound thereby to their posterity: which though they now see not, yet they imagine; and any thing that is pleasure to the sense, the same also is pleasure in the imagination.*

7. To have received from one, to whom we think ourselves equal, *Hate, from* greater benefits than there is hope to requite, disposeth to counter- *difficulty of* feit love; but really secret hatred; and puts a man into the estate of *requiting* a desperate debtor, that in declining the sight of his creditor, tacitly *great benefits.* wishes him there, where he might never see him more. For benefits oblige; and obligation is thraldom; and unrequitable obligation, perpetual thraldom; which is to one's equal, hateful. But to have received benefits from one, whom we acknowledge for superior, inclines to love; because the obligation is no new depression: and cheerful acceptation, (which men call *gratitude*,) is such an honour done to the obliger, as is taken generally for retribution. Also to receive benefits, though from an equal, or inferior, as long as there is hope of requital, disposeth to love: for in the intention of the receiver, the obligation is of aid, and service mutual; from whence proceedeth an emulation of who shall exceed in benefiting; the most noble and profitable contention possible; wherein the victor is *And from* pleased with his victory, and the other revenged by confessing it. *conscience of*

8. To have done more hurt to a man, than he can, or is willing to *deserving to* expiate, inclineth the doer to hate the sufferer. For he must expect *be hated.* revenge, or forgiveness; both which are hateful. [49]

9. Fear of oppression, disposeth a man to anticipate, or to seek *Promptness to* aid by society: for there is no other way by which a man can secure *hurt, from* his life and liberty. *fear.*

10. Men that distrust their own subtlety, are in tumult, and *And from* sedition, better disposed for victory, than they that suppose *distrust of* themselves wise, or crafty. For these love to consult, the other *their own wit.* (fearing to be circumvented,) to strike first. And in sedition, men

67

being always in the precincts of battle, to hold together, and use all advantages of force, is a better stratagem, than any that can proceed from subtlety of wit.

Vain undertaking from vain-glory.

11. Vain-glorious men, such as without being conscious to themselves of great sufficiency, delight in supposing themselves gallant men, are inclined only to ostentation; but not to attempt: because when danger or difficulty appears, they look for nothing but to have their insufficiency discovered.

12. Vain-glorious men, such as estimate their sufficiency by the flattery of other men, or the fortune of some precedent action, without assured ground of hope from the true knowledge of themselves, are inclined to rash engaging; and in the approach of danger, or difficulty, to retire if they can: because not seeing the way of safety, they will rather hazard their honour, which may be salved with an excuse; than their lives, for which no salve is sufficient.

Ambition, from opinion of sufficiency.

13. Men that have a strong opinion of their own wisdom in matter of government, are disposed to ambition. Because without public employment in council or magistracy, the honour of their wisdom is lost. And therefore eloquent speakers are inclined to ambition; for eloquence seemeth wisdom, both to themselves and others.

Irresolution, from too great valuing of small matters.

14. Pusillanimity disposeth men to irresolution, and consequently to lose the occasions, and fittest opportunities of action. For after men have been in deliberation till the time of action approach, if it be not then manifest what is best to be done, 'tis a sign, the difference of motives, the one way and the other, are not great: therefore not to resolve then, is to lose the occasion by weighing of trifles; which is pusillanimity.

15. Frugality, (though in poor men a virtue,) maketh a man unapt to achieve such actions, as require the strength of many men at once: for it weakeneth their endeavour, which is to be nourished and kept in vigour by reward.

Confidence in others, from ignorance of the marks of wisdom and kindness.

16. Eloquence, with flattery, disposeth men to confide in them that have it; because the former is seeming wisdom, the latter seeming kindness. Add to them military reputation, and it disposeth men to adhere, and subject themselves to those men that have them. The two former, having given them caution against danger from him; the latter gives them caution against danger from others.

68

17. Want of science, that is, ignorance of causes, disposeth, or rather constraineth a man to rely on the advice, and authority of others. For all men whom the truth concerns, if they rely not on their own, must rely on the opinion of some other, whom they think wiser than themselves, and see not why he should deceive them. *And from ignorance of natural causes.*

18. Ignorance of the signification of words; which is, want of understanding, disposeth men to take on trust, not only the truth they know not; but also the errors; and which is more, the nonsense of them they trust: for neither error, nor nonsense, can without a perfect understanding of words, be detected. [50] *And from want of understanding.*

19. From the same it proceedeth, that men give different names, to one and the same thing, from the difference of their own passions: as they that approve a private opinion, call it opinion; but they that mislike it, heresy: and yet heresy signifies no more than private opinion; but has only a greater tincture of choler [anger].

20. From the same also it proceedeth, that men cannot distinguish, without study and great understanding, between one action of many men, and many actions of one multitude; as for example, between one action of all the senators of Rome in killing Cataline, and the many actions of a number of senators in killing Caesar; and therefore are disposed to take for the action of the people, that which is a multitude of actions done by a multitude of men, led perhaps by the persuasion of one.

21. Ignorance of the causes, and original constitution of right, equity, law, and justice, disposeth a man to make custom and example the rule of his actions; in such manner, as to think that unjust which it hath been the custom to punish; and that just, of the impunity and approbation whereof they can produce an example, or (as the lawyers which only use this false measure of justice barbarously call it) a precedent; like little children, that have no other rule of good and evil manners, but the correction they receive from their parents, and masters; save that children are constant to their rule, whereas, men are not so; because grown strong,* and stubborn, they appeal from custom to reason, and from reason to custom, as it serves their turn; receding from custom when their interest requires it, and setting themselves against reason, as oft as reason is against them: which is the cause, that the doctrine of right and wrong, is perpetually disputed, both by the pen and the sword: whereas the doctrine of lines, and figures, is not so; because *Adherence to custom, from ignorance of the nature of right and wrong.*

men care not, in that subject what be truth, as a thing that crosses no man's ambition, profit or lust. For I doubt not, but if it had been a thing contrary to any man's right of dominion, or to the interest of men that have dominion, *that the three angles of a triangle, should be equal to two angles of a square*; that doctrine should have been, if not disputed, yet by the burning of all books of geometry, suppressed, as far as he whom it concerned was able.

Adherence to private men, from ignorance of the causes of peace.

22. Ignorance of remote causes, disposeth men to attribute all events, to the causes immediate, and instrumental: for these are all the causes they perceive. And hence it comes to pass, that in all places, men that are grieved with payments to the public, discharge their anger upon the publicans, that is to say, farmers,* collectors, and other officers of the public revenue; and adhere to such as find fault with the public government; and thereby, when they have engaged themselves beyond hope of justification, fall also upon the [51] supreme authority, for fear of punishment, or shame of receiving pardon.

Credulity, from ignorance of nature.

23.* Ignorance of natural causes disposeth a man to credulity, so as to believe many times impossibilities: for such know nothing to the contrary, but that they may be true; being unable to detect the impossibility. And credulity, because men like to be hearkened unto in company, disposeth them to lying: so that ignorance itself without malice, is able to make a man both to believe lies, and tell them; and sometimes also to invent them.

Curiosity to know, from care of future time.

24. Anxiety for the future time, disposeth men to inquire into the causes of things: because the knowledge of them, maketh men the better able to order the present to their best advantage.

Natural religion from the same.

25. Curiosity, or love of the knowledge of causes, draws a man from the consideration of the effect, to seek the cause; and again, the cause of that cause; till of necessity he must come to this thought at last, that there is some cause, whereof there is no former cause, but is eternal; which is it men call God. So that it is impossible to make any profound inquiry into natural causes, without being inclined thereby to believe there is one God eternal; though they cannot have any idea of him in their mind, answerable to his nature. For as a man that is born blind, hearing men talk of warming themselves by the fire, and being brought to warm himself by the same, may easily conceive, and assure himself, there is somewhat there, which men call *fire*, and is the cause of the heat he feels; but cannot imagine what it is like; nor have an idea of it in his mind, such as they have that see it; so also, by the visible things in this world, and their admirable order, a man may conceive there is a cause of them, which men call God; and yet not have an idea,* or image of him in his mind.

26. And they that make little, or no inquiry into the natural causes of things, yet from the fear that proceeds from the ignorance itself, of what it is that hath the power to do them much good or harm, are inclined to suppose, and feign unto themselves, several kinds of powers invisible; and to stand in awe of their own imaginations; and in time of distress to invoke them; as also in the time of expected good success, to give them thanks; making the creatures of their own fancy, their gods. By which means it hath come to pass, that from the innumerable variety of fancy, men have created in the world innumerable sorts of gods. And this fear of things invisible, is the natural seed of that, which every one in himself calleth religion; and in them that worship, or fear that power otherwise than they do, superstition.

27. And this seed of religion, having been observed by many; some of those that have observed it, have been inclined thereby to nourish, dress, and form it into laws; and to add to it of their own invention, any opinion of the causes of future events, by which they thought they should be best able to govern others, and make unto themselves the greatest use of their powers.

CHAPTER XII   [52]

OF RELIGION

1. SEEING there are no signs, nor fruit of *religion*, but in man only; there is no cause to doubt, but that the seed of *religion*, is also only in man; and consisteth in some peculiar quality, or at least in some eminent degree thereof, not to be found in any other living creatures.

Religion, in man only.

2. And first, it is peculiar to the nature of man, to be inquisitive into the causes of the events they see, some more, some less; but all men so much, as to be curious in the search of the causes of their own good and evil fortune.

First, from his desire of knowing causes.

71

*From the con-
sideration of
the beginning
of things.*

3. Secondly, upon the sight of any thing that hath a beginning, to think also it had a cause, which determined the same to begin, then when it did, rather than sooner or later.

*From his
observation of
the sequel of
things.*

4. Thirdly, whereas there is no other felicity of beasts, but the enjoying of their quotidian [daily] food, ease, and lusts; as having little, or no foresight of the time to come, for want of observation, and memory of the order, consequence, and dependence of the things they see; man observeth how one event hath been produced by another; and remembereth in them antecedence and consequence; and when he cannot assure himself of the true causes of things, (for the causes of good and evil fortune for the most part are invisible,) he supposes causes of them, either such as his own fancy suggesteth; or trusteth to the authority of other men, such as he thinks to be his friends, and wiser than himself.

*The natural
cause of
religion, the
anxiety of the
time to come.*

5. The two first, make anxiety. For being assured that there be causes of all things that have arrived hitherto, or shall arrive hereafter; it is impossible for a man, who continually endeavoureth to secure himself against the evil he fears, and procure the good he desireth, not to be in a perpetual solicitude of the time to come; so that every man, especially those that are over provident, are in a state like to that of Prometheus. For as Prometheus, (which interpreted, is, *the prudent man*,) was bound to the hill Caucasus, a place of large prospect, where, an eagle feeding on his liver, devoured in the day, as much as was repaired in the night: so that man, which looks too far before him, in the care of future time, hath his heart all the day long, gnawed on by fear of death, poverty, or other calamity; and has no repose, nor pause of his anxiety, but in sleep.

*Which makes
them fear the
power of
invisible
things.*

6. This perpetual fear, always accompanying mankind in the ignorance of causes, as it were in the dark, must needs have for object something. And therefore when there is nothing to be seen, there is nothing to accuse, either of their good, or evil fortune, but some *power*, or agent *invisible*: in which sense perhaps it was, that some of the old poets said,* that the gods were at first created by human fear: which spoken of the gods, (that is to say, of the many gods of the Gentiles) is very true. But the acknowledging of one God, eternal, infinite, and omnipotent, may more easily be derived, from the desire men have to know the causes of natural bodies, and their several virtues, and operations; than from the fear of what was to befall them in time to come. For he that from any effect he seeth come to pass, should reason to the next and immediate cause

[53]

thereof, and from thence to the cause of that cause, and plunge himself profoundly in the pursuit of causes; shall at last come to this, that there must be (as even the heathen philosophers confessed) one first mover; that is, a first, and an eternal cause of all things; which is that which men mean by the name of God: and all this without thought of their fortune; the solicitude whereof, both inclines to fear, and hinders them from the search of the causes of other things; and thereby gives occasion of feigning of as many gods, as there be men that feign them.

7. And for the matter, or substance of the invisible agents, so fancied; they could not by natural cogitation, fall upon any other conceit, but that it was the same with that of the soul of man; and that the soul of man, was of the same substance, with that which appeareth in a dream, to one that sleepeth; or in a looking-glass, to one that is awake; which, men not knowing that such apparitions are nothing else but creatures of the fancy, think to be real, and external substances; and therefore call them ghosts; as the Latins called them *imagines*, and *umbrae*; and thought them spirits, that is, thin aërial bodies; and those invisible agents, which they feared, to be like them; save that they appear, and vanish when they please. But the opinion that such spirits were incorporeal, or immaterial, could never enter into the mind of any man by nature; because, though men may put together words of contradictory signification, as *spirit*, and *incorporeal*; yet they can never have the imagination of any thing answering to them: and therefore, men that by their own meditation, arrive to the acknowledgment of one infinite, omnipotent, and eternal God, chose rather to confess he is incomprehensible, and above their understanding, than to define his nature by *spirit incorporeal*, and then confess their definition to be unintelligible: or if they give him such a title, it is not *dogmatically*, with intention to make the divine nature understood; but *piously*, to honour him with attributes, of significations, as remote as they can from the grossness of bodies visible.

And suppose them incorporeal.

8. Then, for the way by which they think these invisible agents wrought their effects; that is to say, what immediate causes they used, in bringing things to pass, men that know not what it is that we call *causing*, (that is, almost all men) have no other rule to guess by, but by observing, and remembering what they have seen to precede the like effect at some other time, or times before, without seeing between the antecedent and subsequent event, any dependence or

But know not the way how they effect any thing.

connexion at all: and therefore from the like things past, they expect the like things to come; and hope for good or evil luck, superstitiously, from things that have no part at all in the causing of it: as the Athenians did for their war at Lepanto, demand another Phormio; the Pompeian faction for their war in Africa, another

[54]   Scipio;* and others have done in divers other occasions since. In like manner they attribute their fortune to a stander by, to a lucky or unlucky place, to words spoken, especially if the name of God be amongst them; as charming and conjuring (the liturgy of witches;) insomuch as to believe, they have power to turn a stone into bread, bread into a man, or any thing, into any thing.

But honour them as they honour men.

9. Thirdly, for the worship which naturally men exhibit to powers invisible, it can be no other, but such expressions of their reverence, as they would use towards men; gifts, petitions, thanks, submission of body, considerate addresses, sober behaviour, premeditated words, swearing (that is, assuring one another of their promises,) by invoking them. Beyond that reason suggesteth nothing; but leaves them either to rest there; or for further ceremonies, to rely on those they believe to be wiser than themselves.

And attribute to them all extraordinary events.

10. Lastly, concerning how these invisible powers declare to men the things which shall hereafter come to pass, especially concerning their good or evil fortune in general, or good or ill success in any particular undertaking, men are naturally at a stand; save that using to conjecture of the time to come, by the time past, they are very apt, not only to take casual things, after one or two encounters, for prognostics of the like encounter ever after, but also to believe the like prognostics from other men, of whom they have once conceived a good opinion.

Four things, natural seeds of religion.

11. And in these four things, opinion of ghosts, ignorance of second causes, devotion towards what men fear, and taking of things casual for prognostics, consisteth the natural seed of *religion*; which by reason of the different fancies, judgments, and passions of several men, hath grown up into ceremonies so different, that those which are used by one man, are for the most part ridiculous to another.

Made different by culture.

12. For these seeds have received culture from two sorts of men. One sort have been they, that have nourished, and ordered them, according to their own invention. The other have done it, by God's commandment, and direction: but both sorts have done it, with a purpose to make those men that relied on them, the more apt to

74

obedience, laws, peace, charity, and civil society. So that the religion of the former sort, is a part of human politics; and teacheth part of the duty which earthly kings require of their subjects. And the religion of the latter sort is divine politics; and containeth precepts to those that have yielded themselves subjects in the kingdom of God. Of the former sort, were all the founders of commonwealths, and the law-givers of the Gentiles: of the latter sort, were Abraham, Moses, and our blessed Saviour; by whom have been derived unto us the laws of the kingdom of God.

13. And for that part of religion, which consisteth in opinions concerning the nature of powers invisible, there is almost nothing that has a name, that has not been esteemed amongst the Gentiles, in one place or another, a god, or devil; or by their poets feigned to be inanimated, inhabited, or possessed by some spirit or other. *The absurd opinion of Gentilism.* [55]

14. The unformed matter of the world, was a god, by the name of Chaos.

15. The heaven, the ocean, the planets, the fire, the earth, the winds, were so many gods.

16. Men, women, a bird, a crocodile, a calf, a dog, a snake, an onion, a leek, were deified. Besides, that they filled almost all places, with spirits called *demons*: the plains, with Pan, and Panises, or Satyrs; the woods, with Fawns, and Nymphs; the sea, with Tritons, and other Nymphs; every river, and fountain, with a ghost of his name, and with Nymphs; every house with its *Lares*, or familiars; every man, with his *Genius*; hell, with ghosts, and spiritual officers, as Charon, Cerberus, and the Furies; and in the night time, all places with *larvae*, *lemures*, ghosts of men deceased, and a whole kingdom of fairies, and bugbears. They have also ascribed divinity, and built temples to mere accidents,* and qualities; such as are time, night, day, peace, concord, love, contention, virtue, honour, health, rust, fever, and the like; which when they prayed for, or against, they prayed to, as if there were ghosts of those names hanging over their heads, and letting fall, or withholding that good, or evil, for, or against which they prayed. They invoked also their own wit, by the name of Muses; their own ignorance, by the name of Fortune; their own lusts by the name of Cupid; their own rage, by the name of Furies; their own privy members, by the name of Priapus; and attributed their pollutions, to Incubi, and Succubae: insomuch as there was nothing, which a poet could introduce as a person in his poem, which they did not make either a *god*, or a *devil*.

17. The same authors of the religion of the Gentiles, observing the second ground for religion, which is men's ignorance of causes; and thereby their aptness to attribute their fortune to causes, on which there was no dependence at all apparent, took occasion to obtrude on their ignorance, instead of second causes, a kind of second and ministerial gods; ascribing the cause of fecundity, to Venus; the cause of arts, to Apollo; of subtlety and craft, to Mercury; of tempests and storms, to Aeolus; and of other effects, to other gods; insomuch as there was amongst the heathen almost as great variety of gods, as of business.

18. And to the worship, which naturally men conceived fit to be used towards their gods, namely, oblations, prayers, thanks, and the rest formerly named; the same legislators of the Gentiles have added their images, both in picture, and sculpture; that the more ignorant sort, (that is to say, the most part or generality of the people,) thinking the gods for whose representation they were made, were really included, and as it were housed within them, might so much the more stand in fear of them: and endowed them with lands, and houses, and officers, and revenues, set apart from all other human uses; that is, consecrated,* and made holy to those their idols; as caverns, groves, woods, mountains, and whole islands; and have [56] attributed to them, not only the shapes, some of men, some of beasts, some of monsters; but also the faculties, and passions of men and beasts; as sense, speech, sex, lust, generation, (and this not only by mixing one with another, to propagate the kind of gods; but also by mixing with men, and women, to beget mongrel gods, and but inmates of heaven, as Bacchus, Hercules, and others;) besides anger, revenge, and other passions of living creatures, and the actions proceeding from them, as fraud, theft, adultery, sodomy, and any vice that may be taken for an effect of power, or a cause of pleasure; and all such vices, as amongst men are taken to be against law, rather than against honour.

19. Lastly, to the prognostics of time to come; which are naturally, but conjectures upon experience of time past; and supernaturally, divine revelation; the same authors of the religion of the Gentiles, partly upon pretended experience, partly upon pretended revelation, have added innumerable other superstitious ways of divination; and made men believe they should find their fortunes, sometimes in the ambiguous or senseless answers of the priests at Delphi, Delos, Ammon, and other famous oracles; which answers,

were made ambiguous by design, to own the event both ways; or absurd, by the intoxicating vapour of the place, which is very frequent in sulphurous caverns: sometimes in the leaves of the Sybils; of whose prophecies (like those perhaps of Nostradamus* for the fragments now extant seem to be the invention of later times), there were some books in reputation in the time of the Roman republic: sometimes in the insignificant speeches of madmen, supposed to be possessed with a divine spirit, which possession they called enthusiasm; and these kinds of foretelling events, were accounted theomancy, or prophecy: sometimes in the aspect of the stars at their nativity; which was called horoscopy, and esteemed a part of judiciary astrology: sometimes in their own hopes and fears, called thumomancy, or presage: sometimes in the prediction of witches, that pretended conference with the dead; which is called necromancy, conjuring, and witchcraft; and is but juggling and confederate knavery: sometimes in the casual flight, or feeding of birds; called augury: sometimes in the entrails of a sacrificed beast; which was *aruspicina*: sometimes in dreams: sometimes in croaking of ravens, or chattering of birds: sometimes in the lineaments of the face; which was called metoposcopy; or by palmistry in the lines of the hand; in casual words, called *omina*: sometimes in monsters, or unusual accidents; as eclipses, comets, rare meteors, earthquakes, inundations, uncouth births, and the like, which they called *portenta*, and *ostenta*, because they thought them to portend, or foreshow some great calamity to come; sometimes, in mere lottery, as cross and pile; counting holes in a sieve; dipping of verses in Homer, and Virgil; and innumerable other such vain conceits. So easy are men to be drawn to believe any thing, from such men as have gotten credit with them; and can with gentleness, and dexterity, take hold of their fear, and ignorance.

20. And therefore the first founders, and legislators of commonwealths among the Gentiles, whose ends were only to keep the people in obedience, and peace, have in all places taken care; first, to imprint in their minds a belief, that those precepts which they gave concerning religion, might not be thought to proceed from their own device, but from the dictates of some god, or other spirit; or else that they themselves were of a higher nature than mere mortals, that their laws might the more easily be received: so Numa Pompilius* pretended to receive the ceremonies he instituted amongst the Romans, from the nymph Egeria: and the first king and founder of

[57]
The designs of the authors of the religion of the heathen.

the kingdom of Peru, pretended himself and his wife to be the children of the Sun; and Mahomet, to set up his new religion, pretended to have conferences with the Holy Ghost, in form of a dove.* Secondly, they have had a care, to make it believed, that the same things were displeasing to the gods, which were forbidden by the laws.* Thirdly, to prescribe ceremonies, supplications, sacrifices, and festivals, by which they were to believe, the anger of the gods might be appeased; and that ill success in war, great contagions of sickness, earthquakes, and each man's private misery, came from the anger of the gods;* and their anger from the neglect of their worship, or the forgetting, or mistaking some point of the ceremonies required. And though amongst the ancient Romans, men were not forbidden to deny, that which in the poets is written of the pains, and pleasures after this life; which divers of great authority, and gravity in that state have in their harangues openly derided; yet that belief was always more cherished, than the contrary.

21. And by these, and such other institutions, they obtained in order to their end, (which was the peace of the commonwealth,) that the common people in their misfortunes, laying the fault on neglect, or error in their ceremonies, or on their own disobedience to the laws, were the less apt to mutiny against their governors. And being entertained with the pomp, and pastime of festivals, and public games, made in honour of the gods, needed nothing else but bread, to keep them from discontent, murmuring, and commotion against the state. And therefore the Romans, that had conquered the greatest part of the then known world, made no scruple of tolerating any religion whatsoever in the city of Rome itself; unless it had something in it, that could not consist with their civil government; nor do we read, that any religion was there forbidden, but that of the Jews;* who (being the peculiar kingdom of God) thought it unlawful to acknowledge subjection to any mortal king or state whatsoever. And thus you see how the religion of the Gentiles was a part of their policy.

The true religion, and the laws of God's kingdom the same.

22. But where God himself, by supernatural revelation, planted religion; there he also made to himself a peculiar kingdom; and gave laws, not only of behaviour towards himself; but also towards one another; and thereby in the kingdom of God, the policy, and laws civil, are a part of religion; and therefore the distinction of temporal, and spiritual domination, hath there no place. It is true, that God is

king of all the earth: yet may he be king of a peculiar, and chosen [58]
nation. For there is no more incongruity therein, than that he that
hath the general command of the whole army, should have withal a
peculiar regiment, or company of his own. God is king of all the
earth by his power: but of his chosen people, he is king by covenant.
But to speak more largely of the kingdom of God, both by nature,
and covenant, I have in the following discourse assigned another
place (chapter 35).

23. From the propagation of religion, it is not hard to understand *The causes of*
the causes of the resolution of the same into its first seeds, or *change in*
principles; which are only an opinion of a deity, and of powers *religion.*
invisible, and supernatural; that can never be so abolished out of
human nature, but that new religions may again be made to spring
out of them, by the culture of such men, as for such purpose are in
reputation.

24. For seeing all formed religion, is founded at first, upon the
faith which a multitude hath in some one person, whom they believe
not only to be a wise man, and to labour to procure their happiness,
but also to be a holy man, to whom God himself vouchsafeth to
declare his will supernaturally; it followeth necessarily, when they
that have the government of religion, shall come to have either the
wisdom of those men, their sincerity, or their love suspected; or
when they shall be unable to show any probable token of divine
revelation; that the religion which they desire to uphold, must be
suspected likewise; and (without the fear of the civil sword) contradicted and rejected.

25. That which taketh away the reputation of wisdom, in him *Enjoining*
that formeth a religion, or addeth to it when it is already formed, *belief of*
is the enjoining of a belief of contradictories: for both parts of a *impossibilities.*
contradiction cannot possibly be true: and therefore to enjoin the
belief of them, is an argument of ignorance; which detects the
author in that; and discredits him in all things else he shall propound
as from revelation supernatural: which revelation a man may indeed
have of many things above, but of nothing against natural reason.

26. That which taketh away the reputation of sincerity, is the *Doing*
doing or saying of such things, as appear to be signs, that what they *contrary to*
require other men to believe, is not believed by themselves; all *the religion*
which doings, or sayings are therefore called scandalous, because *they establish.*
they be stumbling blocks, that make men to fall in the way of
religion: as injustice, cruelty, profaneness, avarice, and luxury. For

who can believe, that he that doth ordinarily such actions, as proceed from any of these roots, believeth there is any such invisible power to be feared, as he affrighteth other men withal, for lesser faults?

27. That which taketh away the reputation of love, is the being detected of private ends: as when the belief they require of others, conduceth or seemeth to conduce to the acquiring of dominion, [59] riches, dignity, or secure pleasure, to themselves only, or specially. For that which men reap benefit by to themselves, they are thought to do for their own sakes, and not for love of others.

Want of the testimony of miracles.

28. Lastly, the testimony that men can render of divine calling, can be no other, than the operation of miracles; or true prophecy (which also is a miracle;) or extraordinary felicity. And therefore, to those points of religion, which have been received from them that did such miracles; those that are added by such, as approve not their calling by some miracle, obtain no greater belief, than what the custom, and laws of the places, in which they be educated, have wrought into them. For as in natural things, men of judgment require natural signs, and arguments; so in supernatural things, they require signs supernatural, (which are miracles,) before they consent inwardly, and from their hearts.

29. All which causes of the weakening of men's faith, do manifestly appear in the examples following. First, we have the example of the children of Israel; who when Moses, that had approved his calling to them by miracles, and by the happy conduct of them out of Egypt, was absent but forty days, revolted from the worship of the true God, recommended to them by him; and setting up (*Exod.* 32. 1, 2) a golden calf for their god, relapsed into the idolatry of the Egyptians; from whom they had been so lately delivered. And again, after Moses, Aaron, Joshua, and that generation which had seen the great works of God in Israel, (*Judges* 2. 11) were dead; another generation arose, and served Baal. So that miracles failing, faith also failed.

30. Again, when the sons of Samuel, (1 *Sam.* 8. 3) being constituted by their father judges in Bersabee, received bribes, and judged unjustly, the people of Israel refused any more to have God to be their king, in other manner than he was king of other people; and therefore cried out to Samuel, to choose them a king after the manner of the nations. So that justice failing, faith also failed; insomuch, as they deposed their God, from reigning over them.

31. And whereas in the planting of Christian religion, the oracles
ceased in all parts of the Roman empire, and the number of
Christians increased wonderfully every day, and in every place, by
the preaching of the Apostles, and Evangelists; a great part of that
success, may reasonably be attributed, to the contempt, into which
the priests of the Gentiles of that time, had brought themselves, by
their uncleanness, avarice, and juggling between princes. Also the
religion of the church of Rome, was partly, for the same cause
abolished in England, and many other parts of Christendom; insomuch, as the failing of virtue in the pastors, maketh faith fail in the
people: and partly from bringing of the philosophy, and doctrine of
Aristotle into religion, by the Schoolmen; from whence there arose
so many contradictions, and absurdities, as brought the clergy into
a reputation both of ignorance, and of fraudulent intention; and
inclined people to revolt from them, either against the will of their
own princes, as in France, and Holland; or with their will, as in
England.

32. Lastly, amongst the points by the church of Rome declared [60]
necessary for salvation, there be so many, manifestly to the advantage of the Pope, and of his spiritual subjects, residing in the territories of other Christian princes, that were it not for the mutual
emulation of those princes, they might without war, or trouble,
exclude all foreign authority, as easily as it has been excluded in
England. For who is there that does not see, to whose benefit it
conduceth, to have it believed, that a king hath not his authority
from Christ, unless a bishop crown him? That a king, if he be a
priest, cannot marry? That whether a prince be born in lawful
marriage, or not, must be judged by authority from Rome? That
subjects may be freed from their allegiance, if by the court of Rome,
the king be judged an heretic? That a king (as Childeric of France)
may be deposed by a pope (as Pope Zachary,) for no cause; and his
kingdom given to one of his subjects? That the clergy, and regulars,
in what country soever, shall be exempt from the jurisdiction
of their king, in cases criminal? Or who does not see, to whose profit
redound the fees of private masses, and vales of purgatory;
with other signs of private interest, enough to mortify the most
lively faith, if (as I said) the civil magistrate, and custom did not
more sustain it, than any opinion they have of the sanctity, wisdom,
or probity of their teachers? So that I may attribute all the
changes of religion in the world, to one and the same cause;

and that is, unpleasing priests; and those not only amongst Catholics, but even in that church that hath presumed most of reformation.*

CHAPTER XIII

OF THE NATURAL CONDITION OF MANKIND AS CONCERNING THEIR FELICITY, AND MISERY

Men by nature equal.

1. NATURE hath made men so equal, in the faculties of the body, and mind; as that though there be found one man sometimes manifestly stronger in body, or of quicker mind than another; yet when all is reckoned together, the difference between man, and man, is not so considerable, as that one man can thereupon claim to himself any benefit, to which another may not pretend, as well as he. For as to the strength of body, the weakest has strength enough to kill the strongest, either by secret machination, or by confederacy with others, that are in the same danger with himself.

2. And as to the faculties of the mind, (setting aside the arts grounded upon words, and especially that skill of proceeding upon general, and infallible rules, called science; which very few have, and but in few things; as being not a native faculty, born with us; nor attained (as prudence,) while we look after somewhat else,) I find yet a greater equality amongst men, than that of strength. For prudence, is but experience; which equal time, equally bestows on all

[61] men, in those things they equally apply themselves unto. That which may perhaps make such equality incredible, is but a vain conceit of one's own wisdom, which almost all men think they have in a greater degree, than the vulgar; that is, than all men but themselves, and a few others, whom by fame, or for concurring with themselves, they approve. For such is the nature of men, that howsoever they may acknowledge many others to be more witty, or more eloquent, or more learned; yet they will hardly believe there be many so wise as themselves; for they see their own wit at hand, and other men's at a distance. But this proveth rather that men are in that point equal, than unequal. For there is not ordinarily a greater sign of the equal distribution of any thing, than that every man is contented with his share.

3. From this equality of ability, ariseth equality of hope in the *From* attaining of our ends. And therefore if any two men desire the same *equality* thing, which nevertheless they cannot both enjoy, they become *proceeds* enemies; and in the way to their end, (which is principally their own *diffidence.* conservation, and sometimes their delectation only,) endeavour to destroy, or subdue one another. And from hence it comes to pass, that where an invader hath no more to fear, than another man's single power; if one plant, sow, build, or possess a convenient seat, others may probably be expected to come prepared with forces united, to dispossess, and deprive him, not only of the fruit of his labour, but also of his life, or liberty. And the invader again is in the like danger of another.

4. And from this diffidence of one another, there is no way for *From* any man to secure himself, so reasonable, as anticipation; that is, by *diffidence* force, or wiles, to master the persons of all men he can, so long, till *war.* he see no other power great enough to endanger him: and this is no more than his own conservation requireth, and is generally allowed. Also because there be some, that taking pleasure in contemplating their own power in the acts of conquest, which they pursue farther than their security requires; if others, that otherwise would be glad to be at ease within modest bounds, should not by invasion increase their power, they would not be able, long time, by standing only on their defence, to subsist. And by consequence, such augmentation of dominion over men, being necessary to a man's conservation, it ought to be allowed him.

5. Again, men have no pleasure, (but on the contrary a great deal of grief) in keeping company, where there is no power able to over-awe them all. For every man looketh that his companion should value him, at the same rate he sets upon himself: and upon all signs of contempt, or undervaluing, naturally endeavours, as far as he dares (which amongst them that have no common power to keep them in quiet, is far enough to make them destroy each other,) to extort a greater value from his contemners, by damage; and from others, by the example.

6. So that in the nature of man, we find three principal causes of quarrel. First, competition; secondly, diffidence; thirdly, glory.

7. The first, maketh men invade for gain; the second, for safety; [62] and the third, for reputation. The first use violence, to make themselves masters of other men's persons, wives, children, and cattle; the second, to defend them; the third, for trifles, as a word, a smile,

a different opinion, and any other sign of undervalue, either direct in their persons, or by reflection in their kindred, their friends, their nation, their profession, or their name.

Out of civil states, there is always war of every one against every one.

8.* Hereby it is manifest, that during the time men live without a common power to keep them all in awe, they are in that condition which is called war; and such a war, as is of every man, against every man. For WAR, consisteth not in battle only, or the act of fighting; but in a tract of time, wherein the will to contend by battle is sufficiently known: and therefore the notion of *time*, is to be considered in the nature of war; as it is in the nature of weather. For as the nature of foul weather, lieth not in a shower or two of rain; but in an inclination thereto of many days together: so the nature of war, consisteth not in actual fighting; but in the known disposition thereto, during all the time there is no assurance to the contrary. All other time is PEACE.

The incommodities of such a war.

9. Whatsoever therefore is consequent to a time of war, where every man is enemy to every man; the same is consequent to the time, wherein men live without other security, than what their own strength, and their own invention shall furnish them withal. In such condition, there is no place for industry; because the fruit thereof is uncertain: and consequently no culture of the earth; no navigation, nor use of the commodities that may be imported by sea; no commodious building; no instruments of moving, and removing such things as require much force; no knowledge of the face of the earth; no account of time; no arts; no letters; no society; and which is worst of all, continual fear, and danger of violent death; and the life of man, solitary, poor, nasty, brutish, and short.

10. It may seem strange to some man, that has not well weighed these things; that nature should thus dissociate, and render men apt to invade, and destroy one another: and he may therefore, not trusting to this inference, made from the passions, desire perhaps to have the same confirmed by experience. Let him therefore consider* with himself, when taking a journey, he arms himself, and seeks to go well accompanied; when going to sleep, he locks his doors; when even in his house he locks his chests; and this when he knows there be laws, and public officers, armed, to revenge all injuries shall be done him; what opinion he has of his fellow-subjects, when he rides armed; of his fellow citizens, when he locks his doors; and of his children, and servants, when he locks his chests. Does he not there as much accuse mankind by his actions, as I do by

my words? But neither of us accuse man's nature in it. The desires, and other passions of man, are in themselves no sin. No more are the actions, that proceed from those passions, till they know a law that forbids them: which till laws be made they cannot know: nor can any law be made, till they have agreed upon the person that shall make it.

11. It may peradventure be thought, there was never such a time, [63] nor condition of war as this;* and I believe it was never generally so, over all the world: but there are many places, where they live so now. For the savage people in many places of America, except the government of small families, the concord whereof dependeth on natural lust, have no government at all; and live at this day in that brutish manner, as I said before. Howsoever, it may be perceived what manner of life there would be, where there were no common power to fear; by the manner of life, which men that have formerly lived under a peaceful government, use to degenerate into, in a civil war.

12. But though there had never been any time, wherein particular men were in a condition of war one against another; yet in all times, kings, and persons of sovereign authority, because of their independency, are in continual jealousies, and in the state and posture of gladiators; having their weapons pointing, and their eyes fixed on one another; that is, their forts, garrisons, and guns upon the frontiers of their kingdoms; and continual spies upon their neighbours; which is a posture of war. But because they uphold thereby, the industry of their subjects; there does not follow from it, that misery, which accompanies the liberty of particular men.

13. To this war of every man against every man, this also is consequent; that nothing can be unjust. The notions of right and wrong, justice and injustice have there no place. Where there is no common power, there is no law: where no law, no injustice. Force, and fraud, are in war the two cardinal virtues. Justice, and injustice are none of the faculties neither of the body, nor mind. If they were, they might be in a man that were alone in the world, as well as his senses, and passions. They are qualities, that relate to men in society, not in solitude. It is consequent also to the same condition, that there be no propriety, no dominion, no *mine* and *thine* distinct; but only that to be every man's, that he can get; and for so long, as he can keep it. And thus much for the ill condition, which man by

In such a war nothing is unjust.

mere nature is actually placed in; though with a possibility to come out of it, consisting partly in the passions, partly in his reason.

The passions that incline men to peace. 14. The passions that incline men to peace, are fear of death; desire of such things as are necessary to commodious living; and a hope by their industry to obtain them. And reason suggesteth convenient articles of peace, upon which men may be drawn to agreement. These articles, are they, which otherwise are called the Laws of Nature: whereof I shall speak more particularly, in the two following chapters.

[64]

CHAPTER XIV

OF THE FIRST AND SECOND NATURAL LAWS, AND OF CONTRACTS

Right of nature what. 1. THE RIGHT OF NATURE, which writers commonly call *jus naturale*, is the liberty each man hath, to use his own power, as he will himself, for the preservation of his own nature; that is to say, of his own life; and consequently, of doing any thing, which in his own judgment, and reason, he shall conceive to be the aptest means thereunto.

Liberty what. 2. By LIBERTY, is understood, according to the proper signification of the word, the absence of external impediments: which impediments, may oft take away part of a man's power to do what he would; but cannot hinder him from using the power left him, according as his judgment, and reason shall dictate to him.

A law of nature what. 3. A LAW OF NATURE, (*lex naturalis*,) is a precept, or general rule, found out by reason, by which a man is forbidden to do, that, which is destructive of his life, or taketh away the means of preserving the same; and to omit, that, by which he thinketh it may be best preserved. For though they that speak of this subject, use to confound *Difference of right and law.* *jus*, and *lex, right* and *law*; yet they ought to be distinguished; because RIGHT, consisteth in liberty to do, or to forbear: whereas LAW, determineth, and bindeth to one of them: so that law, and right, differ as much, as obligation, and liberty; which in one and the same matter are inconsistent.

Naturally every man has right to every thing. 4. And because the condition of man, (as hath been declared in the precedent chapter) is a condition of war of every one against every one; in which case every one is governed by his own reason;

and there is nothing he can make use of, that may not be a help unto him, in preserving his life against his enemies; it followeth, that in such a condition, every man has a right to every thing; even to one another's body. And therefore, as long as this natural right of every man to every thing endureth, there can be no security to any man, (how strong or wise soever he be,) of living out the time, which nature ordinarily alloweth men to live. And consequently it is a precept, or general rule of reason,* *that every man, ought to endeavour peace, as far as he has hope of obtaining it; and when he cannot obtain it, that he may seek, and use, all helps, and advantages of war.* The first branch of which rule, containeth the first, and fundamental law of nature; which is, *to seek peace, and follow it.* The second, the sum of the right of nature; which is, *by all means we can, to defend ourselves.* *The fundamental law of nature.*

5. From this fundamental law of nature, by which men are commanded to endeavour peace, is derived this second law; *that a man be willing, when others are so too, as far-forth, as for peace, and defence of himself he shall think it necessary, to lay down this right to all things; and be contented with so much liberty against other men, as he would allow other men against himself.* For as long as every man holdeth this right, of doing any thing he liketh; so long are all men in the condition of war. But if other men will not lay down their right, as well as he; then there is no reason for any one, to divest himself of his: for that were to expose himself to prey, (which no man is bound to) rather than to dipose himself to peace. This is that law of the Gospel; *whatsoever you require that others should do to you, that do ye to them.* And that law of all men, *quod tibi fieri non vis, alteri ne feceris.** *The second law of nature.* [65]

6. To *lay down* a man's *right* to any thing, is to *divest* himself of the *liberty*, of hindering another of the benefit of his own right to the same. For he that renounceth, or passeth away his right, giveth not to any other man a right which he had not before; because there is nothing to which every man had not right by nature: but only standeth out of his way, that he may enjoy his own original right, without hindrance from him; not without hindrance from another. So that the effect which redoundeth to one man, by another man's defect of right, is but so much diminution of impediments to the use of his own right original. *What it is to lay down a right.*

7. Right is laid aside, either by simply renouncing it; or by transferring it to another. By *simply* RENOUNCING; when he cares not to *Renouncing a right what it is.*

whom the benefit thereof redoundeth. By TRANSFERRING; when he intendeth the benefit thereof to some certain person, or persons. And when a man hath in either manner abandoned, or granted away his right; then he is said to be OBLIGED, or BOUND, not to hinder those, to whom such right is granted, or abandoned, from the benefit of it: and that he *ought*, and it is his DUTY, not to make void that voluntary act of his own: and that such hindrance is INJUSTICE, and INJURY, as being *sine jure*; the right being before renounced, or transferred. So that *injury*, or *injustice*, in the controversies of the world, is somewhat like to that, which in the disputations of scholars is called *absurdity*. For as it is there called an absurdity, to contradict what one maintained in the beginning: so in the world, it is called injustice, and injury, voluntarily to undo that, which from the beginning he had voluntarily done. The way by which a man either simply renounceth, or transferreth his right, is a declaration, or signification, by some voluntary and sufficient sign, or signs, that he doth so renounce, or transfer; or hath so renounced, or transferred the same, to him that accepteth it. And these signs are either words only, or actions only; or (as it happeneth most often) both words, and actions. And the same are the BONDS, by which men are bound, and obliged: bonds, that have their strength, not from their own nature, (for nothing is more easily broken than a man's word,) but from fear of some evil consequence upon the rupture.

8. Whensoever a man transferreth his right, or renounceth it; it is either in consideration of some right reciprocally transferred to himself; or for some other good he hopeth for thereby. For it is a voluntary act:* and of the voluntary acts of every man, the object is some *good to himself.* And therefore there be some rights, which no man can be understood by any words, or other signs, to have abandoned, or transferred. As first a man cannot lay down the right of resisting them, that assault him by force, to take away his life; because he cannot be understood to aim thereby, at any good to himself. The same may be said of wounds, and chains, and imprisonment; both because there is no benefit consequent to such patience; as there is to the patience of suffering another to be wounded, or imprisoned: as also because a man cannot tell, when he seeth men proceed against him by violence, whether they intend his death or not. And lastly the motive, and end for which this renouncing, and transferring of right is introduced, is nothing else but the security of a man's person, in his life, and in the means of so

88

preserving life, as not to be weary of it. And therefore if a man by words, or other signs, seem to despoil himself of the end, for which those signs were intended; he is not to be understood as if he meant it, or that it was his will; but that he was ignorant of how such words and actions were to be interpreted.

9. The mutual transferring of right, is that which men call CONTRACT. *Contract what.*

10. There is difference, between transferring of right to the thing; and transferring, or tradition, that is, delivery of the thing itself. For the thing may be delivered together with the translation of the right; as in buying and selling with ready-money; or exchange of goods, or lands: and it may be delivered some time after.

11. Again, one of the contractors, may deliver the thing contracted for on his part, and leave the other to perform his part at some determinate time after, and in the mean time be trusted; and then the contract on his part, is called PACT, or COVENANT: or both parts may contract now, to perform hereafter: in which cases, he that is to perform in time to come, being trusted, his performance is called *keeping of promise*, or faith; and the failing of performance (if it be voluntary) *violation of faith*. *Covenant what.*

12. When the transferring of right, is not mutual; but one of the parties transferreth, in hope to gain thereby friendship, or service from another, or from his friends; or in hope to gain the reputation of charity, or magnanimity; or to deliver his mind from the pain of compassion; or in hope of reward in heaven; this is not contract, but GIFT, FREE-GIFT, GRACE: which words signify one and the same thing. *Free-gift.*

13. Signs of contract, are either *express*, or *by inference*. Express, are words spoken with understanding of what they signify: and such words are either of the time *present*, or *past*; as, *I give, I grant, I have given, I have granted, I will that this be yours*: or of the future; as, *I will give, I will grant*: which words of the future are called PROMISE. *Signs of contract express.* *Promise.*

14. Signs by inference, are sometimes the consequence of words; sometimes the consequence of silence; sometimes the consequence of actions; sometimes the consequence of forbearing an action: and generally a sign by inference, of any contract, is whatsoever sufficiently argues the will of the contractor. [67] *Signs of contract by inference.*

15. Words alone, if they be of the time to come, and contain a bare promise, are an insufficient sign of a free-gift, and therefore not obligatory. For if they be of the time to come, as, *to-morrow I will* *Free gift passeth by words of the present or past.*

give, they are a sign I have not given yet, and consequently that my right is not transferred, but remaineth till I transfer it by some other act. But if the words be of the time present, or past, as, *I have given*, or *do give to be delivered to-morrow*, then is my morrow's right given away to-day; and that by the virtue of the words, though there were no other argument of my will. And there is a great difference in the signification of these words, *volo hoc tuum esse cras*, and *cras dabo*; that is, between *I will that this be thine to-morrow*, and, *I will give it thee to-morrow*: for the word *I will*, in the former manner of speech, signifies an act of the will present; but in the latter, it signifies a promise of an act of the will to come: and therefore the former words, being of the present, transfer a future right; the latter, that be of the future, transfer nothing. But if there be other signs of the will to transfer a right, besides words; then, though the gift be free, yet may the right be understood to pass by words of the future: as if a man propound a prize to him that comes first to the end of a race, the gift is free; and though the words be of the future, yet the right passeth: for if he would not have his words so be understood, he should not have let them run.

Signs of contract are words both of the past, present, and future.

16. In contracts, the right passeth, not only where the words are of the time present, or past; but also where they are of the future: because all contract is mutual translation, or change of right; and therefore he that promiseth only, because he hath already received the benefit for which he promiseth, is to be understood as if he intended the right should pass: for unless he had been content to have his words so understood, the other would not have performed his part first. And for that cause, in buying, and selling, and other acts of contract, a promise is equivalent to a covenant; and therefore obligatory.

Merit what.

17. He that performeth first in the case of a contract, is said to MERIT that which he is to receive by the performance of the other; and he hath it as *due*. Also when a prize is propounded to many, which is to be given to him only that winneth; or money is thrown amongst many, to be enjoyed by them that catch it; though this be a free gift; yet so to win, or so to catch, is to *merit*, and to have it as DUE. For the right is transferred in the propounding of the prize, and in throwing down the money; though it be not determined to whom, but by the event of the contention. But there is between these two sorts of merit, this difference, that in contract, I merit by virtue of my own power, and the contractor's need; but in this case of free

gift, I am enabled to merit only by the benignity of the giver: in contract, I merit at the contractor's hand that he should depart with his right; in this case of gift, I merit not that the giver should part [68] with his right; but that when he has parted with it, it should be mine, rather than another's. And this I think to be the meaning of that distinction of the Schools, between *meritum congrui*, and *meritum condigni*.* For God Almighty, having promised Paradise to those men (hoodwinked with carnal desires,) that can walk through this world according to the precepts, and limits prescribed by him; they say, he that shall so walk, shall merit Paradise *ex congruo*. But because no man can demand a right to it, by his own righteousness, or any other power in himself, but by the free grace of God only; they say, no man can merit Paradise *ex condigno*. This I say, I think is the meaning of that distinction; but because disputers do not agree upon the signification of their own terms of art, longer than it serves their turn; I will not affirm any thing of their meaning: only this I say; when a gift is given indefinitely, as a prize to be contended for, he that winneth meriteth, and may claim the prize as due.

18. If a covenant be made, wherein neither of the parties perform presently, but trust one another; in the condition of mere nature, (which is a condition of war of every man against every man,) upon any reasonable suspicion, it is void: but if there be a common power set over them both, with right and force sufficient to compel performance, it is not void. For he that performeth first, has no assurance the other will perform after; because the bonds of words are too weak to bridle men's ambition, avarice, anger, and other passions, without the fear of some coercive power; which in the condition of mere nature, where all men are equal, and judges of the justness of their own fears, cannot possibly be supposed. And therefore he which performeth first, does but betray himself to his enemy; contrary to the right (he can never abandon) of defending his life, and means of living.

Covenants of mutual trust, when invalid.

19. But in a civil estate, where there is a power set up to constrain those that would otherwise violate their faith, that fear is no more reasonable; and for that cause, he which by the covenant is to perform first, is obliged so to do.

20. The cause of fear, which maketh such a covenant invalid, must be always something arising after the covenant made; as some new fact, or other sign of the will not to perform: else it cannot make the covenant void. For that which could not hinder a man

from promising, ought not to be admitted as a hindrance of performing.

Right to the end, containeth right to the means.

21. He that transferreth any right, transferreth the means of enjoying it, as far as lieth in his power. As he that selleth land, is understood to transfer the herbage, and whatsoever grows upon it; nor can he that sells a mill turn away the stream that drives it. And they that give to a man the right of government in sovereignty, are understood to give him the right of levying money to maintain soldiers; and of appointing magistrates for the administration of justice.

No covenant with beasts.

[69]

22. To make covenants with brute beasts, is impossible; because not understanding our speech, they understand not, nor accept of any translation of right; nor can translate any right to another: and without mutual acceptation, there is no covenant.

Nor with God without special revelation.

23. To make covenant with God,* is impossible, but by mediation of such as God speaketh to, either by revelation supernatural, or by his lieutenants that govern under him, and in his name: for otherwise we know not whether our covenants be accepted, or not. And therefore they that vow anything contrary to any law of nature, vow in vain; as being a thing unjust to pay such vow. And if it be a thing commanded by the law of nature, it is not the vow, but the law that binds them.

No covenant, but of possible and future.

24. The matter, or subject of a covenant, is always something that falleth under deliberation; (for to covenant, is an act of the will; that is to say an act, and the last act, of deliberation;) and is therefore always understood to be something to come; and which is judged possible for him that covenanteth, to perform.

25. And therefore, to promise that which is known to be impossible, is no covenant. But if that prove impossible afterwards, which before was thought possible, the covenant is valid, and bindeth, (though not to the thing itself,) yet to the value; or, if that also be impossible, to the unfeigned endeavour of performing as much as is possible: for to more no man can be obliged.

Covenants how made void.

26. Men are freed of their covenants two ways; by performing; or by being forgiven. For performance, is the natural end of obligation; and forgiveness, the restitution of liberty; as being a retransferring of that right, in which the obligation consisted.

Covenants extorted by fear are valid.

27. Covenants entered into by fear, in the condition of mere nature, are obligatory. For example, if I covenant to pay a ransom, or service for my life, to an enemy; I am bound by it. For it is a

contract, wherein one receiveth the benefit of life; the other is to receive money, or service for it; and consequently, where no other law (as in the condition, of mere nature) forbiddeth the performance, the covenant is valid. Therefore prisoners of war, if trusted with the payment of their ransom, are obliged to pay it: and if a weaker prince, make a disadvantageous peace with a stronger, for fear; he is bound to keep it; unless (as hath been said before) there ariseth some new, and just cause of fear, to renew the war. And even in commonwealths, if I be forced to redeem myself from a thief by promising him money, I am bound to pay it, till the civil law discharge me. For whatsoever I may lawfully do without obligation, the same I may lawfully covenant to do through fear: and what I lawfully covenant, I cannot lawfully break.

28. A former covenant, makes void a later. For a man that hath passed away his right to one man to-day, hath it not to pass to-morrow to another: and therefore the later promise passeth no right, but is null.

The former covenant to one, makes void the later to another.

29.* A covenant not to defend myself from force, by force, is always void. For (as I have showed before) no man can transfer, or lay down his right to save himself from death, wounds, and imprisonment, (the avoiding whereof is the only end of laying down any right;) and therefore the promise of not resisting force, in no covenant transferreth any right; nor is obliging. For though a man may covenant thus, *unless I do so, or so, kill me*; he cannot covenant thus, *unless I do so, or so, I will not resist you, when you come to kill me*. For man by nature chooseth the lesser evil, which is danger of death in resisting; rather than the greater, which is certain and present death in not resisting. And this is granted to be true by all men, in that they lead criminals to execution, and prison, with armed men, notwithstanding that such criminals have consented to the law, by which they are condemned.

A man's covenant not to defend himself, is void.

[70]

30. A covenant to accuse oneself, without assurance of pardon, is likewise invalid. For in the condition of nature, where every man is judge, there is no place for accusation: and in the civil state, the accusation is followed with punishment; which being force, a man is not obliged not to resist. The same is also true, of the accusation of those, by whose condemnation a man falls into misery; as of a father, wife, or benefactor. For the testimony of such an accuser, if it be not willingly given, is presumed to be corrupted by nature: and therefore not to be received: and where a man's testimony is not to

No man obliged to accuse himself.

be credited, he is not bound to give it. Also accusations upon torture, are not to be reputed as testimonies. For torture is to be used but as means of conjecture, and light, in the further examination, and search of truth: and what is in that case confessed, tendeth to the ease of him that is tortured; not to the informing of the torturers: and therefore ought not to have the credit of a sufficient testimony: for whether he deliver himself by true, or false accusation, he does it by the right of preserving his own life.

The end of an oath.

31. The force of words, being (as I have formerly noted) too weak to hold men to the performance of their covenants; there are in man's nature, but two imaginable helps to strengthen it. And those are either a fear of the consequence of breaking their word; or a glory, or pride in appearing not to need to break it. This latter is a generosity too rarely found to be presumed on, especially in the pursuers of wealth, command, or sensual pleasure; which are the greatest part of mankind. The passion to be reckoned upon, is fear; whereof there be two very general objects: one, the power of spirits invisible; the other, the power of those men they shall therein offend. Of these two, though the former be the greater power, yet the fear of the latter is commonly the greater fear. The fear of the former is in every man, his own religion: which hath place in the nature of man before civil society. The latter hath not so; at least not place enough, to keep men to their promises; because in the condition of mere nature, the inequality of power is not discerned, but by the event of battle. So that before the time of civil society, or in the interruption thereof by war, there is nothing can strengthen a covenant of peace agreed on, against the temptations of avarice, ambition, lust, or other strong desire, but the fear of that invisible power, which they every one worship as God; and fear as a revenger of their perfidy. All therefore that can be done between two men not subject to civil power, is to put one another to swear by the God he feareth: which *swearing*, or OATH, is a *form of speech, added to a promise; by which he that promiseth, signifieth, that unless he perform, he renounceth the mercy of his God, or calleth to him for vengeance on himself.* Such was the heathen form, *Let* Jupiter *kill me else, as I kill this beast.* So is our form, *I shall do thus, and thus, so help me God.* And this, with the rites and ceremonies, which every one useth in his own religion, that the fear of breaking faith might be the greater.

The form of an oath.

32. By this it appears, that an oath taken according to any other form, or rite, than his, that sweareth, is in vain; and no oath: and that

there is no swearing by any thing which the swearer thinks not God. For though men have sometimes used to swear by their kings, for fear, or flattery; yet they would have it thereby understood, they attributed to them divine honour. And that swearing unnecessarily by God, is but profaning of his name: and swearing by other things, as men do in common discourse, is not swearing, but an impious custom, gotten by too much vehemence of talking.

No oath but by God.

33. It appears also, that the oath adds nothing to the obligation. For a covenant, if lawful, binds in the sight of God, without the oath, as much as with it: if unlawful, bindeth not at all; though it be confirmed with an oath.

An oath adds nothing to the obligation.

CHAPTER XV

OF OTHER LAWS OF NATURE

1. FROM that law of nature, by which we are obliged to transfer to another, such rights, as being retained, hinder the peace of mankind, there followeth a third; which is this, *that men perform their covenants made*: without which, covenants are in vain, and but empty words; and the right of all men to all things remaining, we are still in the condition of war.

The third law of nature, justice.

2. And in this law of nature, consisteth the fountain and original of JUSTICE. For where no covenant hath preceded, there hath no right been transferred, and every man has right to every thing; and consequently, no action can be unjust. But when a covenant is made, then to break it is *unjust*: and the definition of INJUSTICE, is no other than *the not performance of covenant*. And whatsoever is not unjust, is *just*.

Justice and injustice what.

3. But because covenants of mutual trust, where there is a fear of not performance on either part, (as hath been said in the former chapter,) are invalid; though the original of justice be the making of covenants; yet injustice actually there can be none, till the cause of such fear be taken away; which while men are in the natural condition of war, cannot be done. Therefore before the names of just, and unjust can have place, there must be some coercive power, to compel men equally to the performance of their covenants, by the terror of some punishment, greater than the benefit they expect by

Justice and propriety begin with the constitution of commonwealth

[72] the breach of their covenant; and to make good that propriety, which by mutual contract men acquire, in recompense of the universal right they abandon: and such power there is none before the erection of a commonwealth. And this is also to be gathered out of the ordinary definition of justice in the Schools: for they say, that *justice is the constant will of giving to every man his own.** And therefore where there is no *own*, that is, no propriety, there is no injustice; and where there is no coercive power erected, that is, where there is no commonwealth, there is no propriety; all men having right to all things: therefore where there is no commonwealth, there nothing is unjust. So that the nature of justice, consisteth in keeping of valid covenants: but the validity of covenants begins not but with the constitution of a civil power, sufficient to compel men to keep them: and then it is also that propriety begins.

Justice not contrary to reason.

4. The fool hath said in his heart, there is no such thing as justice;* and sometimes also with his tongue; seriously alleging, that every man's conservation, and contentment, being committed to his own care, there could be no reason, why every man might not do what he thought conduced thereunto: and therefore also to make, or not make; keep, or not keep covenants, was not against reason, when it conduced to one's benefit. He does not therein deny, that there be covenants; and that they are sometimes broken, sometimes kept; and that such breach of them may be called injustice, and the observance of them justice: but he questioneth, whether injustice, taking away the fear of God, (for the same fool hath said in his heart there is no God,) may not sometimes stand with that reason, which dictateth to every man his own good; and particularly then, when it conduceth to such a benefit, as shall put a man in a condition, to neglect not only the dispraise, and revilings, but also the power of other men. The kingdom of God is gotten by violence:* but what if it could be gotten by unjust violence? were it against reason so to get it, when it is impossible to receive hurt by it? and if it be not against reason, it is not against justice: or else justice is not to be approved for good. From such reasoning as this, successful wickedness hath obtained the name of virtue: and some that in all other things have disallowed the violation of faith; yet have allowed it, when it is for the getting of a kingdom. And the heathen that believed, that Saturn was deposed by his son Jupiter, believed nevertheless the same Jupiter to be the avenger of injustice: somewhat like to a piece of law in Coke's* *Commentaries on Littleton*; where he says, if the right heir of

the crown be attainted of treason; yet the crown shall descend to him, and *eo instante* the attainder be void: from which instances a man will be very prone to infer; that when the heir apparent of a kingdom, shall kill him that is in possession, though his father; you may call it injustice, or by what other name you will; yet it can never be against reason, seeing all the voluntary actions of men tend to the benefit of themselves; and those actions are most reasonable, that conduce most to their ends. This specious reasoning is nevertheless false.

[73]

5. For the question is not of promises mutual, where there is no security of performance on either side; as when there is no civil power erected over the parties promising; for such promises are no covenants: but either where one of the parties has performed already; or where there is a power to make him perform; there is the question whether it be against reason, that is, against the benefit of the other to perform, or not. And I say it is not against reason. For the manifestation whereof, we are to consider; first, that when a man doth a thing, which notwithstanding any thing can be foreseen, and reckoned on, tendeth to his own destruction, howsoever some accident which he could not expect, arriving may turn it to his benefit; yet such events do not make it reasonably or wisely done. Secondly, that in a condition of war, wherein every man to every man, for want of a common power to keep them all in awe, is an enemy, there is no man can hope by his own strength, or wit, to defend himself from destruction, without the help of confederates; where every one expects the same defence by the confederation, that any one else does: and therefore he which declares he thinks it reason to deceive those that help him, can in reason expect no other means of safety, than what can be had from his own single power. He therefore that breaketh his covenant, and consequently declareth that he thinks he may with reason do so, cannot be received into any society, that unite themselves for peace and defence, but by the error of them that receive him; nor when he is received, be retained in it, without seeing the danger of their error; which errors a man cannot reasonably reckon upon as the means of his security: and therefore if he be left, or cast out of society, he perisheth; and if he live in society, it is by the errors of other men, which he could not foresee, nor reckon upon; and consequently against the reason of his preservation; and so, as all men that contribute not to his destruction, forbear him only out of ignorance of what is good for themselves.

6.* As for the instance of gaining the secure and perpetual felicity of heaven, by any way; it is frivolous: there being but one way imaginable; and that is not breaking, but keeping of covenant.

7. And for the other instance of attaining sovereignty by rebellion; it is manifest, that though the event follow, yet because it cannot reasonably be expected, but rather the contrary; and because by gaining it so, others are taught to gain the same in like manner, the attempt thereof is against reason. Justice therefore, that is to say, keeping of covenant, is a rule of reason, by which we are forbidden to do any thing destructive to our life; and consequently a law of nature.

8. There be some that proceed further; and will not have the law of nature, to be those rules which conduce to the preservation of man's life on earth; but to the attaining of an eternal felicity after death; to which they think the breach of covenant may conduce; and consequently be just and reasonable; (such are they that think it a [74] work of merit to kill, or depose, or rebel against, the sovereign power constituted over them by their own consent.) But because there is no natural knowledge of man's estate after death; much less of the reward that is then to be given to breach of faith; but only a belief grounded upon other men's saying that they know it supernaturally, or that they know those, that knew them, that knew others, that knew it supernaturally; breach of faith cannot be called a precept of reason, or nature.

Covenants not discharged by the vice of the person to whom they are made.

9. Others, that allow for a law of nature, the keeping of faith, do nevertheless make exception of certain persons; as heretics, and such as use not to perform their covenant to others: and this also is against reason. For if any fault of a man, be sufficient to discharge our covenant made; the same ought in reason to have been sufficient to have hindered the making of it.

Justice of men and justice of actions what.

10. The names of just, and unjust, when they are attributed to men, signify one thing; and when they are attributed to actions, another. When they are attributed to men, they signify conformity, or inconformity of manners, to reason. But when they are attributed to actions, they signify the conformity, or inconformity to reason, not of manners, or manner of life, but of particular actions. A just man therefore, is he that taketh all the care he can, that his actions may be all just: and an unjust man, is he that neglecteth it. And such men are more often in our language styled by the names of righteous, and unrighteous; than just, and unjust; though the

meaning be the same. Therefore a righteous man, does not lose that title, by one, or a few unjust actions, that proceed from sudden passion, or mistake of things, or persons: nor does an unrighteous man, lose his character, for such actions, as he does, or forbears to do, for fear: because his will is not framed by the justice, but by the apparent benefit of what he is to do. That which gives to human actions the relish of justice, is a certain nobleness or gallantness of courage, (rarely found,) by which a man scorns to be beholding for the contentment of his life, to fraud, or breach of promise. This justice of the manners,* is that which is meant, where justice is called a virtue; and injustice a vice.

11. But the justice of actions denominates men, not just, but *guiltless*: and the injustice of the same, (which is also called injury,) gives them but the name of *guilty*.

12. Again, the injustice of manners, is the disposition, or aptitude to do injury; and is injustice before it proceed to act; and without supposing any individual person injured. But the injustice of an action, (that is to say injury,) supposeth an individual person injured; namely him, to whom the covenant was made: and therefore many times the injury is received by one man, when the damage redoundeth to another. As when the master commandeth his servant to give money to a stranger; if it be not done, the injury is done to the master, whom he had before covenanted to obey; but the damage redoundeth to the stranger, to whom he had no obligation; and therefore could not injure him. And so also in commonwealths, private men may remit to one another their debts; but not robberies or other violences, whereby they are endamaged; because the detaining of debt, is an injury to themselves; but robbery and violence, are injuries to the person of the commonwealth. *[75]*

Justice of manners, and justice of actions.

13. Whatsoever is done to a man, conformable to his own will signified to the doer, is no injury to him. For if he that doeth it, hath not passed away his original right to do what he please, by some antecedent covenant, there is no breach of covenant; and therefore no injury done him. And if he have; then his will to have it done being signified, is a release of that covenant: and so again there is no injury done him.

Nothing done to a man by his own consent can be injury.

14. Justice of actions, is by writers* divided into *commutative*, and *distributive*: and the former they say consisteth in proportion arithmetical; the latter in proportion geometrical. Commutative therefore, they place in the equality of value of the things contracted

Justice commutative and distributive.

for; and distributive, in the distribution of equal benefit, to men of equal merit. As if it were injustice to sell dearer than we buy; or to give more to a man than he merits. The value of all things contracted for, is measured by the appetite of the contractors: and therefore the just value, is that which they be contented to give. And merit (besides that which is by covenant, where the performance on one part, meriteth the performance of the other part, and falls under justice commutative, not distributive,) is not due by justice; but is rewarded of grace only. And therefore this distinction, in the sense wherein it useth to be expounded, is not right. To speak properly, commutative justice, is the justice of a contractor; that is, a performance of covenant, in buying, and selling; hiring, and letting to hire; lending, and borrowing; exchanging, bartering, and other acts of contract.

15. And distributive justice, the justice of an arbitrator; that is to say, the act of defining what is just. Wherein, (being trusted by them that make him arbitrator,) if he perform his trust, he is said to distribute to every man his own: and this is indeed just distribution, and may be called (though improperly) distributive justice; but more properly equity; which also is a law of nature, as shall be shown in due place.

The fourth law of nature, gratitude.

16. As justice dependeth on antecedent covenant; so does GRATITUDE depend on antecedent grace; that is to say, antecedent free gift: and is the fourth law of nature; which may be conceived in this form, *that a man which receiveth benefit from another of mere grace, endeavour that he which giveth it, have no reasonable cause to repent him of his good will.* For no man giveth, but with intention of good to himself; because gift is voluntary; and of all voluntary acts, the object is to every man his own good; of which if men see they shall be frustrated, there will be no beginning of benevolence, or trust; nor consequently of mutual help; nor of reconciliation of one man to another; and therefore they are to remain still in the condition of *war*; which is contrary to the first and fundamental law of nature, which commandeth men to *seek peace.* The breach of this law, is [76] called *ingratitude*; and hath the same relation to grace, that injustice hath to obligation by covenant.

The fifth, mutual accommodation, or complaisance.

17. A fifth law of nature, is COMPLAISANCE; that is to say, *that every man strive to accommodate himself to the rest.* For the understanding whereof, we may consider, that there is in men's aptness to society, a diversity of nature, rising from their diversity of affec-

tions; not unlike to that we see in stones brought together for building of an edifice. For as that stone which by the asperity, and irregularity of figure, takes more room from others, than itself fills; and for the hardness, cannot be easily made plain, and thereby hindereth the building, is by the builders cast away as unprofitable, and troublesome: so also, a man that by asperity of nature, will strive to retain those things which to himself are superfluous, and to others necessary; and for the stubbornness of his passions, cannot be corrected, is to be left, or cast out of society, as cumbersome thereunto. For seeing every man, not only by right, but also by necessity of nature, is supposed to endeavour all he can, to obtain that which is necessary for his conservation; he that shall oppose himself against it, for things superfluous, is guilty of the war that thereupon is to follow; and therefore doth that, which is contrary to the fundamental law of nature, which commandeth *to seek peace*. The observers of this law, may be called SOCIABLE, (the Latins call them *commodi*;) the contrary, *stubborn, insociable, froward* [perverse], *intractable*.

18. A sixth law of nature, is this, *that upon caution of the future time, a man ought to pardon the offences past of them that repenting, desire it*. For PARDON, is nothing but granting of peace; which though granted to them that persevere in their hostility, be not peace, but fear; yet not granted to them that give caution of the future time, is sign of an aversion to peace; and therefore contrary to the law of nature. *The sixth, facility to pardon.*

19. A seventh is, *that in revenges*, (that is, retribution of evil for evil,) *men look not at the greatness of the evil past, but the greatness of the good to follow*. Whereby we are forbidden to inflict punishment with any other design, than for correction of the offender, or direction of others. For this law is consequent to the next before it, that commandeth pardon, upon security of the future time. Besides, revenge without respect to the example, and profit to come, is a triumph, or glorying in the hurt of another, tending to no end; (for the end is always somewhat to come;) and glorying to no end, is vain-glory, and contrary to reason; and to hurt without reason, tendeth to the introduction of war; which is against the law of nature; and is commonly styled by the name of *cruelty*. *The seventh, that in revenges, men respect only the future good.*

20. And because all signs of hatred, or contempt, provoke to fight; insomuch as most men choose rather to hazard their life, than not to be revenged; we may in the eighth place, for a law of nature, *The eighth, against contumely.*

set down this precept, *that no man by deed, word, countenance, or gesture, declare hatred, or contempt of another*. The breach of which law, is commonly called *contumely*.

The ninth, against pride.

[77]

21. The question who is the better man, has no place in the condition of mere nature; where, (as has been shewn before,) all men are equal. The inequality that now is, has been introduced by the laws civil. I know that Aristotle in the first book of his *Politics*, for a foundation of his doctrine, maketh men by nature, some more worthy to command, meaning the wiser sort (such as he thought himself to be for his philosophy;) others to serve, (meaning those that had strong bodies, but were not philosophers as he;) as if master and servant were not introduced by consent of men, but by difference of wit: which is not only against reason; but also against experience. For there are very few so foolish, that had not rather govern themselves, than be governed by others: nor when the wise in their own conceit, contend by force, with them who distrust their own wisdom, do they always, or often, or almost at any time, get the victory. If nature therefore have made men equal, that equality is to be acknowledged: or if nature have made men unequal; yet because men that think themselves equal, will not enter into conditions of peace, but upon equal terms, such equality must be admitted. And therefore for the ninth law of nature, I put this, *that every man acknowledge another for his equal by nature*. The breach of this precept is *pride*.

The tenth, against arrogance.

22. On this law, dependeth another, *that at the entrance into conditions of peace, no man require to reserve to himself any right, which he is not content should be reserved to every one of the rest*. As it is necessary for all men that seek peace, to lay down certain rights of nature; that is to say, not to have liberty to do all they list: so is it necessary for man's life, to retain some; as right to govern their own bodies; enjoy air, water, motion, ways to go from place to place; and all things else, without which a man cannot live, or not live well. If in this case, at the making of peace, men require for themselves, that which they would not have to be granted to others, they do contrary to the precedent law, that commandeth the acknowledgment of natural equality, and therefore also against the law of nature. The observers of this law, are those we call *modest*, and the breakers *arrogant* men. The Greeks call the violation of this law λεονεξία; that is, a desire of more than their share.

23. Also if *a man be trusted to judge between man and man*, it is a precept of the law of nature, *that he deal equally between them.* For without that, the controversies of men cannot be determined but by war. He therefore that is partial in judgment, doth what in him lies, to deter men from the use of judges, and arbitrators; and consequently, (against the fundamental law of nature) is the cause of war.

The eleventh, equity.

24. The observance of this law, from the equal distribution to each man, of that which in reason belongeth to him, is called EQUITY, and (as I have said before) distributive justice: the violation, *acception* [favouritism] *of persons*, ροσω ολημψία.

25. And from this followeth another law, *that such things as cannot be divided, be enjoyed in common, if it can be; and if the quantity of the thing permit, without stint; otherwise proportionably to the number of them that have right.* For otherwise the distribution is unequal, and contrary to equity.

The twelfth, equal use of things common.

26. But some things there be, that can neither be divided, nor enjoyed in common. Then, the law of nature, which prescribeth equity, requireth, *that the entire right; or else, (making the use alternate,) the first possession, be determined by lot.* For equal distribution, is of the law of nature; and other means of equal distribution cannot be imagined.

[78]
The thirteenth, of lot.

27. Of *lots* there be two sorts, *arbitrary*, and *natural*. Arbitrary, is that which is agreed on by the competitors: natural, is either *primogeniture*, (which the Greek calls κληρονομία, which signifies, *given by lot*;) or *first seizure*.

The fourteenth, of primogeniture, and first seizing.

28. And therefore those things which cannot be enjoyed in common, nor divided, ought to be adjudged to the first possessor; and in some cases to the first born, as acquired by lot.*

29. It is also a law of nature, *that all men that mediate peace, be allowed safe conduct.* For the law that commandeth peace, as the *end*, commandeth intercession, as the *means*; and to intercession the means is safe conduct.

The fifteenth, of mediators.

30. And because, though men be never so willing to observe these laws, there may nevertheless arise questions concerning a man's action; first, whether it were done, or not done; secondly (if done) whether against the law, or not against the law; the former whereof, is called a question *of fact*; the latter a question *of right*, therefore unless the parties to the question, covenant mutually to stand to the sentence of another, they are as far from peace as ever.

The sixteenth, of submission to arbitrement.

This other, to whose sentence they submit is called an ARBITRATOR. And therefore it is of the law of nature, *that they that are at controversy, submit their right to the judgment of an arbitrator.*

The seventeenth, no man is his own judge.

31. And seeing every man is presumed to do all things in order to his own benefit, no man is a fit arbitrator in his own cause: and if he were never so fit; yet equity allowing to each party equal benefit, if one be admitted to be judge, the other is to be admitted also; and so the controversy, that is, the cause of war, remains, against the law of nature.

The eighteenth, no man to be judge, that has in him a natural cause of partiality.

32. For the same reason no man in any cause ought to be received for arbitrator, to whom greater profit, or honour, or pleasure apparently ariseth out of the victory of one party, than of the other: for he hath taken (though an unavoidable bribe, yet) a bribe; and no man can be obliged to trust him. And thus also the controversy, and the condition of war remaineth, contrary to the law of nature.

The nineteenth, of witnesses.

33. And in a controversy of *fact*, the judge being to give no more credit to one, than to the other, (if there be no other arguments) must give credit to a third; or to a third and fourth; or more: for else the question is undecided, and left to force, contrary to the law of nature.

34. These are the laws of nature, dictating peace, for a means of the conservation of men in multitudes; and which only concern the doctrine of civil society. There be other things tending to the destruction of particular men; as drunkenness, and all other parts of intemperance; which may therefore also be reckoned amongst those things which the law of nature hath forbidden; but are not necessary to be mentioned, nor are pertinent enough to this place.

[79]

A rule, by which the laws of nature may easily be examined.

35. And though this may seem too subtle a deduction of the laws of nature, to be taken notice of by all men; whereof the most part are too busy in getting food, and the rest too negligent to understand; yet to leave all men inexcusable, they have been contracted into one easy sum, intelligible even to the meanest capacity; and that is, *Do not that to another, which thou wouldest not have done to thyself*; which sheweth him, that he has no more to do in learning the laws of nature, but, when weighing the actions of other men with his own, they seem too heavy, to put them into the other part of the balance, and his own into their place, that his own passions, and self-love, may add nothing to the weight; and then there is none of these laws of nature that will not appear unto him very reasonable.

36. The laws of nature oblige *in foro interno*;* that is to say, they bind to a desire they should take place: but *in foro externo*; that is, to the putting them in act, not always. For he that should be modest, and tractable, and perform all he promises, in such time, and place, where no man else should do so, should but make himself a prey to others, and procure his own certain ruin, contrary to the ground of all laws of nature, which tend to nature's preservation. And again, he that having sufficient security, that others shall observe the same laws towards him, observes them not himself, seeketh not peace, but war; and consequently the destruction of his nature by violence.

The laws of nature oblige in conscience always, but in effect then only when there is security.

37. And whatsoever laws bind *in foro interno*, may be broken, not only by a fact contrary to the law, but also by a fact according to it, in case a man think it contrary. For though his action in this case, be according to the law; yet his purpose was against the law; which where the obligation is *in foro interno*, is a breach.

38. The laws of nature are immutable and eternal; for injustice, ingratitude, arrogance, pride, iniquity, acception of persons, and the rest, can never be made lawful. For it can never be that war shall preserve life, and peace destroy it.

The laws of nature are eternal;

39. The same laws, because they oblige only to a desire, and endeavour, I mean an unfeigned and constant endeavour, are easy to be observed. For in that they require nothing but endeavour; he that endeavoureth their performance, fulfilleth them; and he that fulfilleth the law, is just.

And yet easy.

40. And the science of them, is the true and only moral philosophy. For moral philosophy is nothing else but the science of what is *good*, and *evil*, in the conversation, and society of mankind. *Good*, and *evil*, are names that signify our appetites, and aversions; which in different tempers, customs, and doctrines of men, are different: and divers men, differ not only in their judgment, on the senses of what is pleasant, and unpleasant to the taste, smell, hearing, touch, and sight; but also of what is conformable, or disagreeable to reason, in the actions of common life. Nay, the same man, in divers times, differs from himself; and one time praiseth, that is, calleth good, what another time he dispraiseth, and calleth evil: from whence arise [80] disputes, controversies, and at last war. And therefore so long as a man is in the condition of mere nature, (which is a condition of war,) as private appetite is the measure of good, and evil: and consequently all men agree on this, that peace is good, and therefore also

The science of these laws, is the true moral philosophy.

the way, or means of peace, which (as I have shewed before) are *justice, gratitude, modesty, equity, mercy,* and the rest of the laws of nature, are good; that is to say; *moral virtues*; and their contrary *vices*, evil. Now the science of virtue and vice, is moral philosophy; and therefore the true doctrine of the laws of nature, is the true moral philosophy. But the writers of moral philosophy, though they acknowledge the same virtues and vices; yet not seeing wherein consisted their goodness; nor that they come to be praised, as the means of peaceable, sociable, and comfortable living; place them in a mediocrity of passions: as if not the cause, but the degree of daring, made fortitude; or not the cause, but the quantity of a gift, made liberality.

41. These dictates of reason, men used to call by the name of laws; but improperly: for they are but conclusions, or theorems concerning what conduceth to the conservation and defence of themselves; whereas law, properly is the word of him, that by right hath command over others. But yet if we consider the same theorems, as delivered in the word of God, that by right commandeth all things; then are they properly called laws.

CHAPTER XVI

OF PERSONS, AUTHORS, AND THINGS PERSONATED*

A person what.

1. A PERSON, is he, *whose words or actions are considered, either as his own, or as representing the words or actions of another man, or of any other thing to whom they are attributed, whether truly or by fiction.*

Person natural, and artificial.

2. When they are considered as his own, then is he called a *natural person*: and when they are considered as representing the words and actions of another, then is he a *feigned* or *artificial person*.

The word person, whence.

3. The word person is Latin: instead whereof the Greeks have ϱόσω ον, which signifies the *face*, as *persona* in Latin signifies the *disguise*, or *outward appearance* of a man, counterfeited on the stage; and sometimes more particularly that part of it, which disguiseth the face, as a mask or vizard [visor]: and from the stage, hath been translated to any representer of speech and action, as well in tribunals, as theatres. So that a *person*, is the same that an *actor* is, both on the stage and in common conversation; and to *personate*, is to *act*, or *represent* himself, or another; and he that acteth another, is said to bear his person, or act in his name; (in which sense Cicero useth it* where he says, *Unus sustineo tres personas; mei, adversarii, et judicis,* I bear three persons; my own, my adversary's, and the judge's;) and is called in divers occasions, diversely; as a *representer,* or *representa-* [81] *tive,* a *lieutenant,* a *vicar,* an *attorney,* a *deputy,* a *procurator,* an *actor,* and the like.

4. Of persons artificial, some have their words and actions *owned* by those whom they represent. And then the person is the *actor*; and *Actor.* he that owneth his words and actions, is the AUTHOR: in which case *Author.* the actor acteth by authority. For that which in speaking of goods and possessions, is called an *owner,* and in Latin *dominus,* in Greek κύριος; speaking of actions, is called author. And as the right of possession, is called dominion; so the right of doing any action, is called AUTHORITY and sometimes warrant.* So that by authority, is *Authority.* always understood a right of doing any act: and *done by authority,* done by commission, or licence from him whose right it is.

5. From hence it followeth, that when the actor maketh a cov- *Covenants by* enant by authority, he bindeth thereby the author, no less than if he *authority,* had made it himself; and no less subjecteth him to all the conse- *bind the* quences of the same. And therefore all that hath been said formerly, *author.* (chap. XIV) of the nature of covenants between man and man in their natural capacity, is true also when they are made by their actors, representers, or procurators, that have authority from them, so far forth as is in their commission, but no further.

6. And therefore he that maketh a covenant with the actor, or representer, not knowing the authority he hath, doth it at his own peril. For no man is obliged by a covenant, whereof he is not author; nor consequently by a covenant made against, or beside the authority he gave.

7. When the actor doth any thing against the law of nature by *But not the* command of the author, if he be obliged by former covenant to obey *actor.* him, not he, but the author breaketh the law of nature: for though the action be against the law of nature; yet it is not his: but contrarily, to refuse to do it, is against the law of nature, that forbiddeth breach of covenant.

8. And he that maketh a covenant with the author, by mediation *The authority* of the actor, not knowing what authority he hath, but only takes his *is to be* word; in case such authority be not made manifest unto him upon *shown.* demand, is no longer obliged: for the covenant made with the

author, is not valid, without his counter-assurance. But if he that so covenanteth, knew beforehand he was to expect no other assurance, than the actor's word; then is the covenant valid; because the actor in this case maketh himself the author. And therefore, as when the authority is evident, the covenant obligeth the author, not the actor; so when the authority is feigned, it obligeth the actor only; there being no author but himself.

Things personated, inanimate.

9. There are few things, that are incapable of being represented by fiction. Inanimate things, as a church, an hospital, a bridge, may be personated by a rector, master, or overseer. But things inanimate, cannot be authors, nor therefore give authority to their actors: yet the actors may have authority to procure their maintenance, given [82] them by those that are owners, or governors of those things. And therefore, such things cannot be personated, before there be some state of civil government.

Irrational.

10. Likewise children, fools, and madmen that have no use of reason, may be personated by guardians, or curators; but can be no authors (during that time) of any action done by them, longer than (when they shall recover the use of reason) they shall judge the same reasonable. Yet during the folly, he that hath right of governing them, may give authority to the guardian. But this again has no place but in a state civil, because before such estate, there is no dominion of persons.

False gods.

11. An idol, or mere figment of the brain, may be personated; as were the gods of the heathen; which by such officers as the state appointed, were personated, and held possessions, and other goods, and rights, which men from time to time dedicated, and consecrated unto them. But idols cannot be authors: for an idol is nothing. The authority proceeded from the state: and therefore before introduction of civil government, the gods of the heathen could not be personated.

The true God.

12. The true God may be personated. As he was; first, by Moses; who governed the Israelites (that were not his, but God's people,) not in his own name, with *hoc dicit Moses*; but in God's name, with *hoc dicit Dominus*.* Secondly, by the Son of man, his own Son, our blessed Saviour Jesus Christ, that came to reduce [recall] the Jews, and induce all nations into the kingdom of his father; not as of himself, but as sent from his father. And thirdly, by the Holy Ghost, or Comforter, speaking, and working in the Apostles: which Holy

Ghost, was a Comforter that came not of himself; but was sent, and proceeded from them both on the day of Pentecost.*

13. A multitude of men, are made *one* person, when they are by one man, or one person, represented; so that it be done with the consent of every one of that multitude in particular. For it is the *unity* of the representer, not the *unity* of the represented, that maketh the person *one*. And it is the representer that beareth the person, and but one person: and *unity*, cannot otherwise be understood in multitude.

A multitude of men, how one person.

14. And because the multitude naturally is not *one*, but *many*; they cannot be understood for one; but many authors, of every thing their representative saith, or doth in their name; every man giving their common representer, authority from himself in particular; and owning all the actions the representer doth, in case they give him authority without stint: otherwise, when they limit him in what, and how far he shall represent them, none of them owneth more, than they gave him commission to act.

Every one is author.

15. And if the representative consist of many men, the voice of the greater number, must be considered as the voice of them all. For if the lesser number pronounce (for example) in the affirmative, and the greater in the negative, there will be negatives more than enough to destroy the affirmatives; and thereby the excess of negatives, standing uncontradicted, are the only voice the representative hath.

An actor may be many men made one by plurality of voices. [83]

16. And a representative of even number, especially when the number is not great, whereby the contradictory voices are oftentimes equal, is therefore oftentimes mute, and incapable of action. Yet in some cases contradictory voices equal in number, may determine a question; as in condemning, or absolving, equality of votes, even in that they condemn not, do absolve; but not on the contrary condemn, in that they absolve not. For when a cause is heard; not to condemn, is to absolve: but on the contrary, to say that not absolving, is condemning, is not true. The like it is in a deliberation of executing presently, or deferring till another time: for when the voices are equal, the not decreeing execution, is a decree of dilation.

Representatives, when the number is even, unprofitable.

17. Or if the number be odd, as three, or more, (men or assemblies;) whereof every one has by a negative voice, authority to take away the effect of all the affirmative voices of the rest, this number

Negative voice.

is no representative; because by the diversity of opinions, and interests of men, it becomes oftentimes, and in cases of the greatest consequence, a mute person, and unapt, as for many things else, so for the government of a multitude, especially in time of war.

18. Of authors there be two sorts. The first simply so called; which I have before defined to be him, that owneth the action of another simply. The second is he, that owneth an action, or covenant of another conditionally; that is to say, he undertaketh to do it, if the other doth it not, at, or before a certain time. And these authors conditional, are generally called SURETIES, in Latin, *fidejussores*, and *sponsores*; and particularly for debt, *praedes*; and for appearance before a judge, or magistrate, *vades*.

OF COMMONWEALTH

CHAPTER XVII

OF THE CAUSES, GENERATION, AND DEFINITION OF A COMMONWEALTH*

1. THE final cause, end, or design of men, (who naturally love liberty, and dominion over others,) in the introduction of that restraint upon themselves, (in which we see them live in commonwealths,) is the foresight of their own preservation, and of a more contented life thereby; that is to say, of getting themselves out from that miserable condition of war, which is necessarily consequent (as hath been shown, chapter XIII) to the natural passions of men, when there is no visible power to keep them in awe, and tie them by fear of punishment to the performance of their covenants, and observation of those laws of nature set down in the fourteenth and fifteenth chapters. *The end of commonwealth, particular security:*

2. For the laws of nature (as *justice*, *equity*, *modesty*, *mercy*, and (in sum) *doing to others, as we would be done to*,) of themselves, without the terror of some power, to cause them to be observed, are contrary to our natural passions, that carry us to partiality, pride, revenge, and the like. And covenants, without the sword, are but words, and of no strength to secure a man at all. Therefore notwithstanding the laws of nature (which every one hath then kept, when he has the will to keep them, when he can do it safely) if there be no power erected, or not great enough for our security; every man will, and may lawfully rely on his own strength and art, for caution against all other men. And in all places, where men have lived by small families, to rob and spoil one another, has been a trade, and so far from being reputed against the law of nature, that the greater spoils they gained, the greater was their honour;* and men observed no other laws therein, but the laws of honour; that is, to abstain from cruelty, leaving to men their lives, and instruments of husbandry. And as small families did then; so now do cities and kingdoms which are but greater families (for their own security) enlarge their dominions, *Which is not to be had from the law of nature:*

upon all pretences of danger, and fear of invasion, or assistance that may be given to invaders, and endeavour as much as they can, to subdue, or weaken their neighbours, by open force, and secret arts, for want of other caution, justly; and are remembered for it in after ages with honour.

Nor from the conjunction of a few men or families:

[86]

3. Nor is it the joining together of a small number of men, that gives them this security; because in small numbers, small additions on the one side or the other, make the advantage of strength so great, as is sufficient to carry the victory; and therefore gives encouragement to an invasion. The multitude sufficient to confide in for our security, is not determined by any certain number, but by comparison with the enemy we fear; and is then sufficient, when the odds of the enemy is not of so visible and conspicuous moment, to determine the event of war, as to move him to attempt.

Nor from a great multitude, unless directed by one judgment.

4. And be there never so great a multitude; yet if their actions be directed according to their particular judgments, and particular appetites, they can expect thereby no defence, nor protection, neither against a common enemy, nor against the injuries of one another. For being distracted in opinions concerning the best use and application of their strength, they do not help, but hinder one another; and reduce their strength by mutual opposition to nothing: whereby they are easily, not only subdued by a very few that agree together; but also when there is no common enemy, they make war upon each other, for their particular interests. For if we could suppose a great multitude of men to consent in the observation of justice, and other laws of nature, without a common power to keep them all in awe; we might as well suppose all mankind to do the same; and then there neither would be, nor need to be any civil government, or commonwealth at all; because there would be peace without subjection.

And that continually.

5. Nor is it enough for the security, which men desire should last all the time of their life, that they be governed, and directed by one judgment, for a limited time; as in one battle, or one war. For though they obtain a victory by their unanimous endeavour against a foreign enemy; yet afterwards, when either they have no common enemy, or he that by one part is held for an enemy, is by another part held for a friend, they must needs by the difference of their interests dissolve, and fall again into a war amongst themselves.

6. It is true, that certain living creatures, as bees, and ants, live sociably one with another, (which are therefore by Aristotle numbered* amongst political creatures;) and yet have no other direction, than their particular judgments and appetites; nor speech, whereby one of them can signify to another, what he thinks expedient for the common benefit: and therefore some man may perhaps desire to know, why mankind cannot do the same. To which I answer,

7. First, that men are continually in competition for honour and dignity, which these creatures are not; and consequently amongst men there ariseth on that ground, envy and hatred, and finally war; but amongst these not so.

8. Secondly, that amongst these creatures, the common good differeth not from the private; and being by nature inclined to their private, they procure thereby the common benefit. But man, whose joy consisteth in comparing himself with other men, can relish nothing but what is eminent.

9. Thirdly, that these creatures, having not (as man) the use of reason, do not see, nor think they see any fault, in the administration of their common business: whereas amongst men, there are very [87] many, that think themselves wiser, and abler to govern the public, better than the rest; and these strive to reform and innovate, one this way, another that way; and thereby bring it into distraction and civil war.

10. Fourthly, that these creatures, though they have some use of voice, in making known to one another their desires, and other affections; yet they want that art of words, by which some men can represent to others, that which is good, in the likeness of evil; and evil, in the likeness of good; and augment, or diminish the apparent greatness of good and evil; discontenting men, and troubling their peace at their pleasure.

11. Fifthly, irrational creatures cannot distinguish between *injury*, and *damage*; and therefore as long as they be at ease, they are not offended with their fellows: whereas man is then most troublesome, when he is most at ease: for then it is that he loves to shew his wisdom, and control the actions of them that govern the commonwealth.

12. Lastly, the agreement of these creatures is natural; that of men, is by covenant only, which is artificial: and therefore it is no wonder if there be somewhat else required (besides covenant) to

Why certain creatures without reason, or speech, do nevertheless live in society, without any coercive power.

make their agreement constant and lasting; which is a common power, to keep them in awe, and to direct their actions to the common benefit.

The generation of a commonwealth.

13. The only way to erect such a common power, as may be able to defend them from the invasion of foreigners, and the injuries of one another, and thereby to secure them in such sort, as that by their own industry, and by the fruits of the earth, they may nourish themselves and live contentedly; is, to confer all their power and strength upon one man, or upon one assembly of men, that may reduce all their wills, by plurality of voices, unto one will: which is as much as to say, to appoint one man, or assembly of men, to bear their person; and every one to own, and acknowledge himself to be author of whatsoever he that so beareth their person, shall act, or cause to be acted, in those things which concern the common peace and safety; and therein to submit their wills, every one to his will, and their judgments, to his judgment. This is more than consent, or concord; it is a real unity of them all, in one and the same person, made by covenant of every man with every man, in such manner, as if every man should say to every man, *I authorize and give up my right of governing myself, to this man, or to this assembly of men, on this condition, that thou give up thy right to him, and authorize all his actions in like manner.* This done, the multitude so united in one person, is called a COMMONWEALTH, in Latin CIVITAS. This is the generation of that great LEVIATHAN, or rather (to speak more reverently) of that *Mortal God*, to which we owe under the *Immortal God*, our peace and defence. For by this authority, given him by every

[88] particular man in the commonwealth, he hath the use of so much power and strength conferred on him, that by terror thereof, he is enabled to conform* the wills of them all, to peace at home, and mutual aid against their enemies abroad. And in him consisteth the

The definition of a commonwealth.

essence of the commonwealth; which (to define it,) is *one person, of whose acts a great multitude, by mutual covenants one with another, have made themselves every one the author, to the end he may use the strength and means of them all, as he shall think expedient, for their peace and common defence.*

Sovereign, and subject, what.

14. And he that carrieth this person, is called SOVEREIGN, and said to have *sovereign power*; and every one besides, his SUBJECT.

15. The attaining to this sovereign power, is by two ways. One, by natural force; as when a man maketh his children, to submit themselves, and their children to his government, as being able to

destroy them if they refuse; or by war subdueth his enemies to his will, giving them their lives on that condition. The other, is when men agree amongst themselves, to submit to some man, or assembly of men, voluntarily, on confidence to be protected by him against all others. This latter, may be called a political commonwealth, or commonwealth by *institution*; and the former, a commonwealth by *acquisition*. And first, I shall speak of a commonwealth by institution.

CHAPTER XVIII

OF THE RIGHTS OF SOVEREIGNS BY INSTITUTION*

1. A *commonwealth* is said to be *instituted*, when a *multitude* of men do agree, and *covenant, every one, with every one*, that to whatsoever *man*, or *assembly of men*, shall be given by the major part, the *right* to *present* the person of them all (that is to say, to be their *representative*;) every one, as well he that *voted for it*, as he that *voted against it*, shall *authorize* all the actions and judgments, of that man, or assembly of men, in the same manner, as if they were his own, to the end, to live peaceably amongst themselves, and be protected against other men.

The act of instituting a commonwealth, what.

2. From this institution of a commonwealth are derived all the *rights*, and *faculties* of him, or them, on whom the sovereign power is conferred by the consent of the people assembled.

The consequences to such institutions, are

3. First, because they covenant, it is to be understood, they are not obliged by former covenant to any thing repugnant hereunto. And consequently they that have already instituted a commonwealth, being thereby bound by covenant, to own the actions, and judgments of one, cannot lawfully make a new covenant, amongst themselves, to be obedient to any other, in any thing whatsoever, without his permission. And therefore, they that are subjects to a monarch, cannot without his leave cast off monarchy, and return to the confusion of a disunited multitude; nor transfer their person from him that beareth it, to another man, or other assembly of men: for they are bound, every man to every man, to own, and be reputed author of all, that he that already is their sovereign, shall do, and judge fit to be done: so that any one man dissenting, all the rest

1. The subjects cannot change the form of government.

[89]

should break their covenant made to that man, which is injustice: and they have also every man given the sovereignty to him that beareth their person; and therefore if they depose him, they take from him that which is his own, and so again it is injustice. Besides, if he that attempteth to depose his sovereign, be killed, or punished by him for such attempt, he is author of his own punishment, as being by the institution, author of all his sovereign shall do: and because it is injustice for a man to do any thing, for which he may be punished by his own authority, he is also upon that title, unjust. And whereas some men have pretended for their disobedience to their sovereign, a new covenant, made, not with men, but with God; this also is unjust: for there is no covenant with God,* but by mediation of somebody that representeth God's person; which none doth but God's lieutenant, who hath the sovereignty under God. But this pretence of covenant with God, is so evident a lie, even in the pretenders' own consciences, that it is not only an act of an unjust, but also of a vile, and unmanly disposition.

2. Sovereign power cannot be forfeited.

4. Secondly, because the right of bearing the person of them all, is given to him they make sovereign, by covenant only of one to another, and not of him to any of them; there can happen no breach of covenant on the part of the sovereign; and consequently none of his subjects, by any pretence of forfeiture, can be freed from his subjection. That he which is made sovereign maketh no covenant with his subjects beforehand, is manifest; because either he must make it with the whole multitude, as one party to the covenant; or he must make a several covenant with every man. With the whole, as one party, it is impossible; because as yet they are not one person: and if he make so many several covenants as there be men, those covenants after he hath the sovereignty are void; because what act soever can be pretended by any one of them for breach thereof, is the act both of himself, and of all the rest, because done in the person, and by the right of every one of them in particular. Besides, if any one, or more of them, pretend a breach of the covenant made by the sovereign at his institution; and others, or one other of his subjects, or himself alone, pretend there was no such breach, there is in this case, no judge to decide the controversy; it returns therefore to the sword again; and every man recovereth the right of protecting himself by his own strength, contrary to the design they had in the institution. It is therefore in vain to grant sovereignty by way of precedent covenant. The opinion that any monarch receiveth his

power by covenant, that is to say on condition, proceedeth from want of understanding this easy truth, that covenants being but words, and breath, have no force to oblige, contain, constrain, or protect any man, but what it has from the public sword; that is, from the untied hands of that man, or assembly of men that hath the sovereignty, and whose actions are avouched by them all, and performed by the strength of them all, in him united. But when an [90] assembly of men is made sovereign; then no man imagineth any such covenant to have passed in the institution; for no man is so dull as to say, for example, the people of Rome, made a covenant with the Romans, to hold the sovereignty on such or such conditions; which not performed, the Romans might lawfully depose the Roman people. That men see not the reason to be alike in a monarchy, and in a popular government, proceedeth from the ambition of some, that are kinder to the government of an assembly, whereof they may hope to participate, than of monarchy, which they despair to enjoy.

5. Thirdly, because the major part hath by consenting voices declared a sovereign; he that dissented must now consent with the rest; that is, be contented to avow all the actions he shall do, or else justly be destroyed by the rest. For if he voluntarily entered into the congregation of them that were assembled, he sufficiently declared thereby his will (and therefore tacitly covenanted) to stand to what the major part should ordain: and therefore if he refuse to stand thereto, or make protestation against any of their decrees, he does contrary to his covenant, and therefore unjustly. And whether he be of the congregation, or not; and whether his consent be asked, or not, he must either submit to their decrees, or be left in the condition of war he was in before; wherein he might without injustice be destroyed by any man whatsoever.

3. No man can without injustice protest against the institution of the sovereign declared by the major part.

6. Fourthly, because every subject is by this institution author of all the actions, and judgments of the sovereign instituted; it follows, that whatsoever he doth, it can be no injury to any of his subjects; nor ought he to be by any of them accused of injustice. For he that doth anything by authority from another, doth therein no injury to him by whose authority he acteth: but by this institution of a commonwealth, every particular man is author of all the sovereign doth: and consequently he that complaineth of injury from his sovereign, complaineth of that whereof he himself is author; and therefore

4. The sovereign's actions cannot be justly accused by the subject.

ought not to accuse any man but himself; no nor himself of injury; because to do injury to one's self, is impossible. It is true that they that have sovereign power, may commit iniquity; but not injustice, or injury in the proper signification.

7. Fifthly, and consequently to that which was said last, no man that hath sovereign power can justly be put to death, or otherwise in any manner by his subjects punished. For seeing every subject is author of the actions of his sovereign; he punisheth another, for the actions committed by himself.

8. And because the end of this institution, is the peace and defence of them all; and whosoever has right to the end, has right to the means; it belongeth of right, to whatsoever man, or assembly that hath the sovereignty, to be judge both of the means of peace and defence; and also of the hindrances, and disturbances of the same; and to do whatsoever he shall think necessary to be done, both beforehand, for the preserving of peace and security, by prevention of discord at home, and hostility from abroad; and, when peace and security are lost, for the recovery of the same. And therefore,

9. Sixthly, it is annexed to the sovereignty, to be judge of what opinions and doctrines are averse, and what conducing to peace; and consequently, on what occasions, how far, and what, men are to be trusted withal, in speaking to multitudes of people; and who shall examine the doctrines of all books before they be published.* For the actions of men proceed from their opinions; and in the well-governing of opinions, consisteth the well-governing of men's actions, in order to their peace, and concord. And though in matter of doctrine, nothing ought to be regarded but the truth; yet this is not repugnant to regulating the same by peace. For doctrine repugnant to peace, can no more be true, than peace and concord can be against the law of nature. It is true, that in a commonwealth, where by the negligence, or unskilfulness of governors, and teachers, false doctrines are by time generally received; the contrary truths may be generally offensive: Yet the most sudden, and rough bustling in of a new truth, that can be, does never break the peace, but only sometimes awake the war. For those men that are so remissly governed, that they dare take up arms, to defend, or introduce an opinion, are still in war; and their condition not peace, but only a cessation of arms for fear of one another; and they live as it were, in the precincts of battle continually. It belongeth therefore to him that hath the

5. Whatsoever the sovereign doth is unpunishable by the subject.

6. The sovereign is judge of what is necessary for the peace and defence of his subjects.

[91]

And judge of what doctrines are fit to be taught them.

sovereign power, to be judge, or constitute all judges of opinions and doctrines, as a thing necessary to peace; thereby to prevent discord and civil war.

10. Seventhly, is annexed to the sovereignty, the whole power of prescribing the rules, whereby every man may know, what goods he may enjoy, and what actions he may do, without being molested by any of his fellow-subjects: and this is it men call *propriety*. For before constitution of sovereign power (as hath already been shown) all men had right to all things; which necessarily causeth war: and therefore this propriety, being necessary to peace, and depending on sovereign power, is the act of that power, in order to the public peace. These rules of propriety (or *meum* and *tuum*) and of *good*, *evil*, *lawful*, and *unlawful* in the actions of subjects, are the civil laws;* that is to say, the laws of each commonwealth in particular; though the name of civil law be now restrained to the ancient civil laws of the city of Rome; which being the head of a great part of the world, her laws at that time were in these parts the civil law.

7. The right of making rules; whereby the subjects may every man know what is so his own, as no other subject can without injustice take it from him.

11. Eighthly, is annexed to the sovereignty, the right of judicature; that is to say, of hearing and deciding all controversies, which may arise concerning law, either civil, or natural; or concerning fact. For without the decision of controversies, there is no protection of one subject, against the injuries of another; the laws concerning *meum* and *tuum* are in vain; and to every man remaineth, from the natural and necessary appetite of his own conservation, the right of protecting himself by his private strength, which is the condition of war, and contrary to the end for which every commonwealth is instituted.

8. To him also belongeth the right of judicature and decision of controversy.

[92]

12. Ninthly, is annexed to the sovereignty, the right of making war, and peace with other nations, and commonwealths; that is to say, of judging when it is for the public good, and how great forces are to be assembled, armed, and paid for that end; and to levy money upon the subjects, to defray the expenses thereof. For the power by which the people are to be defended, consisteth in their armies; and the strength of an army, in the union of their strength under one command; which command the sovereign instituted, therefore hath; because the command of the *militia*, without other institution, maketh him that hath it sovereign. And therefore whosoever is made general of an army, he that hath the sovereign power is always generalissimo [commander-in-chief].

9. And of making war, and peace, as he shall think best.

10. *And of choosing all counsellors and ministers, both of peace and war.*

13. Tenthly, is annexed to the sovereignty, the choosing of all counsellors, ministers, magistrates, and officers, both in peace, and war. For seeing the sovereign is charged with the end, which is the common peace and defence; he is understood to have power to use such means, as he shall think most fit for his discharge.

11. *And of rewarding and punishing, and that (where no former law hath determined the measure of it) arbitrarily.*

14. Eleventhly, to the sovereign is committed the power of rewarding with riches, or honour; and of punishing with corporal, or pecuniary punishment, or with ignominy every subject according to the law he hath formerly made; or if there be no law made, according as he shall judge most to conduce to the encouraging of men to serve the commonwealth, or deterring of them from doing disservice to the same.

12. *And of honour and order.*

15. Lastly, considering what value men are naturally apt to set upon themselves; what respect they look for from others; and how little they value other men; from whence continually arise amongst them, emulation, quarrels, factions, and at last war, to the destroying of one another, and diminution of their strength against a common enemy; it is necessary that there be laws of honour, and a public rate of the worth of such men as have deserved, or are able to deserve well of the commonwealth; and that there be force in the hands of some or other, to put those laws in execution. But it hath already been shown, that not only the whole militia, or forces of the commonwealth; but also the judicature of all controversies, is annexed to the sovereignty. To the sovereign therefore it belongeth also to give titles of honour; and to appoint what order of place, and dignity, each man shall hold; and what signs of respect, in public or private meetings, they shall give to one another.

These rights are indivisible.

16. These are the rights, which make the essence of sovereignty;* and which are the marks, whereby a man may discern in what man, or assembly of men, the sovereign power is placed, and resideth. For these are incommunicable, and inseparable. The power to coin money; to dispose of the estate and persons of infant heirs; to have praeemption in markets; and all other statute prerogatives, may be transferred by the sovereign; any yet the power to protect his subjects be retained. But if he transfer the militia, he [93] retains the judicature in vain, for want of execution of the laws: or if he grant away the power of raising money; the militia is in vain: or if he give away the government of doctrines, men will be frighted into rebellion with the fear of spirits. And so if we consider any one of the said rights, we shall presently see, that the holding of all the rest, will produce no effect, in the conservation of peace and justice, the end for which all commonwealths are instituted. And this division is it, whereof it is said, *a kingdom divided in itself cannot stand*:* for unless this division precede, division into opposite armies can never happen. If there had not first been an opinion received of the greatest part of England, that these powers were divided between the King, and the Lords, and the House of Commons, the people had never been divided and fallen into this civil war;* first between those that disagreed in politics; and after between the dissenters about the liberty of religion; which have so instructed men in this point of sovereign right, that there be few now (in England,) that do not see, that these rights are inseparable, and will be so generally acknowledged at the next return of peace; and so continue, till their miseries are forgotten; and no longer, except the vulgar be better taught than they have hitherto been.

17. And because they are essential and inseparable rights, it follows necessarily, that in whatsoever words any of them seem to be granted away, yet if the sovereign power itself be not in direct terms renounced, and the name of sovereign no more given by the grantees to him that grants them, the grant is void: for when he has granted all he can, if we grant back the sovereignty, all is restored, as inseparably annexed thereunto. *And can by no grant pass away without direct renouncing of the sovereign power.*

18. This great authority being indivisible, and inseparably annexed to the sovereignty, there is little ground for the opinion of them, that say of sovereign kings, though they be *singulis majores*, of greater power than every one of their subjects, yet they be *universis minores*, of less power than them all together. For if by *all together*, they mean not the collective body as one person, then *all together*, and *every one*, signify the same; and the speech is absurd. But if by *all together*, they understand them as one person (which person the sovereign bears,) then the power of all together, is the same with the sovereign's power; and so again the speech is absurd: which absurdity they see well enough, when the sovereignty is in an assembly of the people; but in a monarch they see it not; and yet the power of sovereignty is the same in whomsoever it be placed. *The power and honour of subjects vanisheth in the presence of the power sovereign.*

19. And as the power, so also the honour of the sovereign, ought to be greater, than that of any, or all the subjects. For in the sovereignty is the fountain of honour. The dignities of lord, earl, duke, and prince are his creatures. As in the presence of the master, the

servants are equal, and without any honour at all; so are the subjects, in the presence of the sovereign. And though they shine some more, some less, when they are out of his sight; yet in his presence, they shine no more than the stars in the presence of the sun.

[94]

Sovereign power not so hurtful as the want of it, and the hurt proceeds for the greatest part from not submitting readily to a less.

20. But a man may here object, that the condition of subjects is very miserable; as being obnoxious to the lusts, and other irregular passions of him, or them that have so unlimited a power in their hands. And commonly they that live under a monarch, think it the fault of monarchy; and they that live under the government of democracy, or other sovereign assembly, attribute all the inconvenience to that form of commonwealth; whereas the power in all forms, if they be perfect enough to protect them, is the same; not considering that the state of man can never be without some incommodity or other; and that the greatest, that in any form of government can possibly happen to the people in general, is scarce sensible, in respect of the miseries, and horrible calamities, that accompany a civil war; or that dissolute condition of masterless men, without subjection to laws, and a coercive power to tie their hands from rapine and revenge: nor considering that the greatest pressure of sovereign governors, proceedeth not from any delight, or profit they can expect in the damage, or weakening of their subjects, in whose vigour, consisteth their own strength and glory; but in the restiveness of themselves, that unwillingly contributing to their own defence, make it necessary for their governors to draw from them what they can in time of peace, that they may have means on any emergent occasion, or sudden need, to resist, or take advantage on their enemies. For all men are by nature provided of notable multiplying glasses (that is their passions and self-love,) through which, every little payment appeareth a great grievance; but are destitute of those prospective glasses, (namely moral and civil science,) to see afar off the miseries that hang over them, and cannot without such payments be avoided.

CHAPTER XIX

OF THE SEVERAL KINDS OF COMMONWEALTH BY INSTITUTION, AND OF SUCCESSION TO THE SOVEREIGN POWER*

1. THE difference of commonwealths, consisteth in the difference of the sovereign, or the person representative of all and every one of the multitude. And because the sovereignty is either in one man, or in an assembly of more than one; and into that assembly either every man hath right to enter, or not every one, but certain men distinguished from the rest; it is manifest, there can be but three kinds of commonwealth. For the representative must needs be one man, or more: and if more, then it is the assembly of all, or but of a part. When the representative is one man, then is the commonwealth a MONARCHY: when an assembly of all that will come together, then it is a DEMOCRACY, or popular commonwealth: when an assembly of a part only, then it is called an ARISTOCRACY.* Other kind of commonwealth there can be none: for either one, or more, or all, must have the sovereign power (which I have shown to be indivisible) entire.

The different forms of commonwealths but three.

2. There be other names of government, in the histories, and books of policy; as *tyranny*, and *oligarchy*: but they are not the names of other forms of government, but of the same forms misliked. For they that are discontented under *monarchy*, call it *tyranny*; and they that are displeased with *aristocracy*, call it *oligarchy*: so also, they which find themselves grieved under a *democracy*, call it *anarchy*, (which signifies want of government;) and yet I think no man believes, that want of government, is any new kind of government: nor by the same reason ought they to believe, that the government is of one kind, when they like it, and another, when they mislike it, or are oppressed by the governors.

[95]

Tyranny and oligarchy, but different names of monarchy, and aristocracy.

3. It is manifest, that men who are in absolute liberty, may, if they please, give authority to one man, to represent them every one; as well as give such authority to any assembly of men whatsoever; and consequently may subject themselves, if they think good, to a monarch, as absolutely, as to any other representative. Therefore, where there is already erected a sovereign power, there can be no other representative of the same people, but only to certain particu-

Subordinate representatives dangerous.

lar ends, by the sovereign limited. For that were to erect two sovereigns; and every man to have his person represented by two actors, that by opposing one another, must needs divide that power, which (if men will live in peace) is indivisible; and thereby reduce the multitude into the condition of war, contrary to the end for which all sovereignty is instituted. And therefore as it is absurd, to think that a sovereign assembly, inviting the people of their dominion, to send up their deputies, with power to make known their advice, or desires, should therefore hold such deputies, rather than themselves, for the absolute representatives of the people: so it is absurd also, to think the same in a monarchy. And I know not how this so manifest a truth, should of late be so little observed; that in a monarchy, he that had the sovereignty from a descent of six hundred years, was alone called sovereign, had the title of Majesty from every one of his subjects, and was unquestionably taken by them for their king, was notwithstanding never considered as their representative; that name without contradiction passing for the title of those men, which at his command were sent up by the people to carry their petitions, and give him (if he permitted it) their advice. Which may serve as an admonition, for those that are the true, and absolute representative of a people, to instruct men in the nature of that office, and to take heed how they admit of any other general representation upon any occasion whatsoever, if they mean to discharge the trust committed to them.

Comparison of monarchy, with sovereign assemblies.

4. The difference between these three kinds of commonwealth, consisteth not in the difference of power; but in the difference of convenience, or aptitude to produce the peace, and security of the people; for which end they were instituted. And to compare monarchy with the other two, we may observe; first, that whosoever beareth the person of the people, or is one of that assembly that bears it, beareth also his own natural person. And though he be [96] careful in his politic person to procure the common interest; yet he is more, or no less careful to procure the private good of himself, his family, kindred, and friends; and for the most part, if the public interest chance to cross the private, he prefers the private: for the passions of men, are commonly more potent than their reason. From whence it follows, that where the public and private interest are most closely united, there is the public most advanced. Now in monarchy, the private interest is the same with the public. The riches, power, and honour of a monarch arise only from the riches,

strength, and reputation of his subjects. For no king can be rich, nor glorious, nor secure; whose subjects are either poor, or contemptible, or too weak through want, or dissension, to maintain a war against their enemies: whereas in a democracy, or aristocracy, the public prosperity confers not so much to the private fortune of one that is corrupt, or ambitious, as doth many times a perfidious advice, a treacherous action, or a civil war.

5. Secondly, that a monarch receiveth counsel of whom, when, and where he pleaseth; and consequently may hear the opinion of men versed in the matter about which he deliberates, of what rank or quality soever, and as long before the time of action, and with as much secrecy, as he will. But when a sovereign assembly has need of counsel, none are admitted but such as have a right thereto from the beginning; which for the most part are of those who have been versed more in the acquisition of wealth than of knowledge; and are to give their advice in long discourses, which may, and do commonly excite men to action, but not govern them in it. For the *understanding* is by the flame of the passions, never enlightened, but dazzled. Nor is there any place, or time, wherein an assembly can receive counsel with secrecy, because of their own multitude.

6. Thirdly, that the resolutions of a monarch, are subject to no other inconstancy, than that of human nature; but in assemblies, besides that of nature, there ariseth an inconstancy from the number. For the absence of a few, that would have the resolution once taken, continue firm, (which may happen by security, negligence, or private impediments,) or the diligent appearance of a few of the contrary opinion, undoes to-day, all that was concluded yesterday.

7. Fourthly, that a monarch cannot disagree with himself, out of envy, or interest; but an assembly may; and that to such a height, as may produce a civil war.

8. Fifthly, that in monarchy there is this inconvenience; that any subject, by the power of one man, for the enriching of a favourite or flatterer, may be deprived of all he possesseth; which I confess is a great and inevitable inconvenience. But the same may as well happen, where the sovereign power is in an assembly: for their power is the same; and they are as subject to evil counsel, and to be seduced by orators, as a monarch by flatterers; and becoming one another's flatterers, serve one another's covetousness and ambition by turns.

And whereas the favourites of monarchs, are few, and they have none else to advance but their own kindred; the favourites of an [97] assembly, are many; and the kindred much more numerous, than of any monarch. Besides, there is no favourite of a monarch, which cannot as well succour his friends, as hurt his enemies: but orators, that is to say, favourites of sovereign assemblies, though they have great power to hurt, have little to save. For to accuse, requires less eloquence (such is man's nature) than to excuse; and condemnation, than absolution more resembles justice.

9. Sixthly, that it is an inconvenience in monarchy, that the sovereignty may descend upon an infant, or one that cannot discern between good and evil: and consisteth in this, that the use of his power, must be in the hand of another man, or of some assembly of men, which are to govern by his right, and in his name; as curators, and protectors of his person, and authority. But to say there is inconvenience, in putting the use of the sovereign power, into the hand of a man, or an assembly of men; is to say that all government is more inconvenient, than confusion, and civil war. And therefore all the danger that can be pretended, must arise from the contention of those, that for an office of so great honour, and profit, may become competitors. To make it appear, that this inconvenience, proceedeth not from that form of government we call monarchy, we are to consider, that the precedent monarch, hath appointed who shall have the tuition of his infant successor, either expressly by testament, or tacitly, by not controlling the custom in that case received: and then such inconvenience (if it happen) is to be attributed, not to the monarchy, but to the ambition, and injustice of the subjects; which in all kinds of government, where the people are not well instructed in their duty, and the rights of sovereignty, is the same. Or else the precedent monarch hath not at all taken order for such tuition; and then the law of nature hath provided this sufficient rule, that the tuition shall be in him, that hath by nature most interest in the preservation of the authority of the infant, and to whom least benefit can accrue by his death, or diminution. For seeing every man by nature seeketh his own benefit, and promotion; to put an infant into the power of those, that can promote themselves by his destruction, or damage, is not tuition, but treachery. So that sufficient provision being taken, against all just quarrel, about the government under a child, if any contention arise to the disturbance of the public peace, it is not to be attributed to the form of

monarchy, but to the ambition of subjects, and ignorance of their duty. On the other side, there is no great commonwealth, the sovereignty whereof is in a great assembly, which is not, as to consultations of peace, and war, and making of laws, in the same condition, as if the government were in a child. For as a child wants the judgment to dissent from counsel given him, and is thereby necessitated to take the advice of them, or him, to whom he is committed: so an assembly wanteth the liberty, to dissent from the counsel of the major part, be it good, or bad. And as a child has need of a tutor, or protector, to preserve his person, and authority: so also (in great commonwealths,) the sovereign assembly, in all great dangers and troubles, have need of *custodes libertatis*; that is of dictators, [98] or protectors of their authority; which are as much as temporary monarchs; to whom for a time, they may commit the entire exercise of their power; and have (at the end of that time) been oftener deprived thereof, than infant kings, by their protectors, regents, or any other tutors.

10. Though the kinds of sovereignty be, as I have now shown, but three; that is to say, monarchy, where one man has it; or democracy, where the general assembly of subjects hath it; or aristocracy, where it is in an assembly of certain persons nominated, or otherwise distinguished from the rest: yet he that shall consider the particular commonwealths that have been, and are in the world, will not perhaps easily reduce them to three, and may thereby be inclined to think there be other forms, arising from these mingled together. As for example, elective kingdoms; where kings have the sovereign power put into their hands for a time; or kingdoms, wherein the king hath a power limited: which governments, are nevertheless by most writers called monarchy. Likewise if a popular, or aristocratical commonwealth, subdue an enemy's country, and govern the same, by a president, procurator, or other magistrate; this may seem perhaps at first sight, to be a democratical, or aristocratical government. But it is not so. For elective kings, are not sovereigns, but ministers of the sovereign; nor limited kings sovereigns, but ministers of them that have the sovereign power: nor are those provinces which are in subjection to a democracy, or aristocracy of another commonwealth, democratically or aristocratically governed, but monarchically.

11. And first, concerning an elective king, whose power is limited to his life, as it is in many places of Christendom at this day; or to

certain years or months, as the dictator's power amongst the Romans; if he have right to appoint his successor, he is no more elective but hereditary. But if he have no power to elect his successor, then there is some other man, or assembly known, which after his decease may elect anew, or else the commonwealth dieth, and dissolveth with him, and returneth to the condition of war. If it be known who have the power to give the sovereignty after his death, it is known also that the sovereignty was in them before: for none have right to give that which they have not right to possess, and keep to themselves, if they think good. But if there be none that can give the sovereignty, after the decease of him that was first elected; then has he power, nay he is obliged by the law of nature, to provide, by establishing his successor, to keep those that had trusted him with the government, from relapsing into the miserable condition of civil war. And consequently he was, when elected, a sovereign absolute.

12. Secondly, that king whose power is limited, is not superior to him, or them that have the power to limit it; and he that is not [99] superior, is not supreme; that is to say not sovereign. The sovereignty therefore was always in that assembly which had the right to limit him; and by consequence the government not monarchy, but either democracy, or aristocracy; as of old time in Sparta; where the kings had a privilege to lead their armies; but the sovereignty was in the Ephori.*

13. Thirdly, whereas heretofore the Roman people, governed the land of Judea (for example) by a president; yet was not Judea therefore a democracy; because they were not governed by any assembly, into the which, any of them, had right to enter; nor an aristocracy; because they were not governed by any assembly, into which, any man could enter by their election: but they were governed by one person, which though as to the people of Rome was an assembly of the people, or democracy; yet as to the people of Judea, which had no right at all of participating in the government, was a monarch. For though where the people are governed by an assembly, chosen by themselves out of their own number, the government is called a democracy, or aristocracy; yet when they are governed by an assembly, not of their own choosing, 'tis a monarchy; not of *one* man, over another man; but of one people, over another people.

Of the right of succession.   14. Of all these forms of government, the matter being mortal, so that not only monarchs, but also whole assemblies die, it is necessary for the conservation of the peace of men, that as there was order taken for an artificial man, so there be order also taken, for an artificial eternity of life; without which, men that are governed by an assembly, should return into the condition of war in every age; and they that are governed by one man, as soon as their governor dieth. This artificial eternity, is that which men call the right of *succession*.

15. There is no perfect form of government, where the disposing of the succession is not in the present sovereign. For if it be in any other particular man, or private assembly, it is in a person subject, and may be assumed by the sovereign at his pleasure; and consequently the right is in himself. And if it be in no particular man, but left to a new choice; then is the commonwealth dissolved; and the right is in him that can get it; contrary to the intention of them that did institute the commonwealth, for their perpetual, and not temporary security.

16. In a democracy, the whole assembly cannot fail, unless the multitude that are to be governed fail. And therefore questions of the right of succession, have in that form of government no place at all.

17. In an aristocracy, when any of the assembly dieth, the election of another into his room belongeth to the assembly, as the sovereign, to whom belongeth the choosing of all counsellors, and officers. For that which the representative doth, as actor, every one of the subjects doth, as author. And though the sovereign assembly, may give power to others, to elect new men, for supply of their court; yet it is still by their authority, that the election is made; and by the same it may (when the public shall require it) be recalled.

18. The greatest difficulty about the right of succession, is in monarchy: and the difficulty ariseth from this, that at first sight, it is not manifest who is to appoint the successor; nor many times, who it is whom he hath appointed. For in both these cases, there is required a more exact ratiocination, than every man is accustomed to use. As to the question, who shall appoint the successor, of a monarch that hath the sovereign authority; that is to say, who shall determine of the right of inheritance, (for elective kings and princes have not the sovereign power in propriety, but in use only,) we are to consider, that either he that is in possession, has right to dispose of the succession, or else that right is again in

[100]

The present monarch hath right to dispose of the succession.

the dissolved multitude. For the death of him that hath the sovereign power in propriety, leaves the multitude without any sovereign at all; that is, without any representative in whom they should be united, and be capable of doing any one action at all: and therefore they are incapable of election of any new monarch; every man having equal right to submit himself to such as he thinks best able to protect him; or if he can, protect himself by his own sword; which is a return to confusion, and to the condition of a war of every man against every man, contrary to the end for which monarchy had its first institution. Therefore it is manifest, that by the institution of monarchy, the disposing of the successor, is always left to the judgment and will of the present possessor.

19. And for the question (which may arise sometimes) who it is that the monarch in possession, hath designed to the succession and inheritance of his power; it is determined by his express words, and testament; or by other tacit signs sufficient.

Succession passeth by express words;

20. By express words, or testament, when it is declared by him in his lifetime, *viva voce*, or by writing; as the first emperors of Rome declared who should be their heirs. For the word heir does not of itself imply the children, or nearest kindred of a man; but whomsoever a man shall any way declare, he would have to succeed him in his estate. If therefore a monarch declare expressly, that such a man shall be his heir, either by word or writing, then is that man immediately after the decease of his predecessor, invested in the right of being monarch.

Or, by not controlling a custom;

21. But where testament, and express words are wanting, other natural signs of the will are to be followed: whereof the one is custom. And therefore where the custom is, that the next of kindred absolutely succeedeth, there also the next of kindred hath right to the succession; for that, if the will of him that was in possession had been otherwise, he might easily have declared the same in his life-time. And likewise where the custom is, that the next of the male kindred succeedeth, there also the right of succession is in the next of the kindred male, for the same reason. And so it is if the custom were to advance the female. For whatsoever custom a man may by a word control, and does not, it is a natural sign he would have that custom stand.

22. But where neither custom, nor testament hath preceded, there it is to be understood, first, that a monarch's will is, that the government remain monarchical; because he hath approved that government in himself. Secondly, that a child of his own, male, or female, be preferred before any other; because men are presumed to be more inclined by nature, to advance their own children, than the children of other men; and of their own, rather a male than a female; because men, are naturally fitter than women, for actions of labour and danger. Thirdly, where his own issue faileth, rather a brother than a stranger; and so still the nearer in blood, rather than the more remote; because it is always presumed that the nearer of kin, is the nearer in affection; and 'tis evident that a man receives always, by reflection, the most honour from the greatness of his nearest kindred.

[101]
Or, by presumption of natural affection.

23. But if it be lawful for a monarch to dispose of the succession by words of contract, or testament, men may perhaps object a great inconvenience: for he may sell, or give his right of governing to a stranger; which, because strangers (that is, men not used to live under the same government, nor speaking the same language) do commonly undervalue one another, may turn to the oppression of his subjects; which is indeed a great inconvenience: but it proceedeth not necessarily from the subjection to a stranger's government, but from the unskilfulness of the governors, ignorant of the true rules of politics. And therefore the Romans when they had subdued many nations, to make their government digestible, were wont to take away that grievance, as much as they thought necessary, by giving sometimes to whole nations, and sometimes to principal men of every nation they conquered, not only the privileges, but also the name of Romans; and took many of them into the senate, and offices of charge, even in the Roman city. And this was it our most wise king James, aimed at, in endeavouring the union of his two realms of England and Scotland. Which if he could have obtained, had in all likelihood prevented the civil wars, which make both those kingdoms, at this present, miserable. It is not therefore any injury to the people, for a monarch to dispose of the succession by will; though by the fault of many princes, it hath been sometimes found inconvenient. Of the lawfulness of it, this also is an argument, that whatsoever inconvenience can arrive by giving a kingdom to a stranger, may arrive also by so marrying with strangers, as the right

To dispose of the succession, though to a king of another nation, not unlawful.

of succession may descend upon them: yet this by all men is accounted lawful.

CHAPTER XX

OF DOMINION PATERNAL, AND DESPOTICAL

A commonwealth by acquisition.

1. A COMMONWEALTH *by acquisition*, is that, where the sovereign power is acquired by force; and it is acquired by force, when men singly, or many together by plurality of voices, for fear of death, or bonds, do authorize all the actions of that man, or assembly, that hath their lives and liberty in his power.

[102]

Wherein different from a commonwealth by institution.

2. And this kind of dominion, or sovereignty, differeth from sovereignty by institution, only in this, that men who choose their sovereign, do it for fear of one another, and not of him whom they institute: but in this case, they subject themselves, to him they are afraid of. In both cases they do it for fear: which is to be noted by them, that hold all such covenants, as proceed from fear of death, or violence, void: which if it were true, no man, in any kind of commonwealth, could be obliged to obedience. It is true, that in a commonwealth once instituted, or acquired, promises proceeding from fear of death, or violence, are no convenants, nor obliging, when the thing promised is contrary to the laws; but the reason is not, because it was made upon fear, but because he that promiseth, hath no right in the thing promised. Also, when he may lawfully perform, and doth not, it is not the invalidity of the covenant, that absolveth him, but the sentence of the sovereign. Otherwise, whensoever a man lawfully promiseth, he unlawfully breaketh: but when the sovereign, who is the actor, acquitteth him, then he is acquitted by him that extorted the promise, as by the author of such absolution.

The rights of sovereignty the same in both.

3. But the rights, and consequences of sovereignty, are the same in both. His power cannot, without his consent, be transferred to another: he cannot forfeit it: he cannot be accused by any of his subjects, of injury: he cannot be punished by them: he is judge of what is necessary for peace; and judge of doctrines: he is sole legislator; and supreme judge of controversies; and of the times, and occasions of war, and peace: to him it belongeth to choose magis-

trates, counsellors, commanders, and all other officers, and ministers; and to determine of rewards, and punishments, honour, and
order. The reasons whereof, are the same which are alleged in the
precedent chapter, for the same rights, and consequences of sovereignty by institution.

4. Dominion is acquired two ways; by generation, and by con- *Dominion*
quest. The right of dominion by generation, is that, which the *paternal how*
parent hath over his children; and is called PATERNAL.* And is not *attained.*
so derived from the generation, as if therefore the parent had *Not by*
dominion over his child because he begat him; but from the *generation,*
child's consent, either express, or by other sufficient arguments *but by*
declared. For as to the generation, God hath ordained to man a *contract;*
helper; and there be always two that are equally parents: the
dominion therefore over the child, should belong equally to both;
and he be equally subject to both, which is impossible; for no man
can obey two masters. And whereas some have attributed the dominion to the man only, as being of the more excellent sex; they
misreckon in it. For there is not always that difference of strength,
or prudence between the man and the woman, as that the right can
be determined without war. In commonwealths, this controversy is
decided by the civil law: and for the most part, (but not always) the
sentence is in favour of the father; because for the most part commonwealths have been erected by the fathers, not by the mothers of [103]
families. But the question lieth now in the state of mere nature;
where there are supposed no laws of matrimony; no laws for the
education of children; but the law of nature, and the natural inclination of the sexes, one to another, and to their children. In this
condition of mere nature, either the parents between themselves
dispose of the dominion over the child by contract; or do not dispose
thereof at all. If they dispose thereof, the right passeth according to
the contract. We find in history* that the Amazons contracted with
the men of the neighbouring countries, to whom they had recourse
for issue, that the issue male should be sent back, but the female
remain with themselves: so that the dominion of the females was in
the mother.

5. If there be no contract, the dominion is in the mother. For in *Or education;*
the condition of mere nature, where there are no matrimonial laws,
it cannot be known who is the father, unless it be declared by the
mother: and therefore the right of dominion over the child
dependeth on her will, and is consequently hers. Again, seeing the

infant is first in the power of the mother, so as she may either nourish, or expose it; if she nourish it, it oweth its life to the mother; and is therefore obliged to obey her, rather than any other; and by consequence the dominion over it is hers. But if she expose it, and another find, and nourish it, the dominion is in him that nourisheth it. For it ought to obey him by whom it is preserved; because preservation of life being the end, for which one man becomes subject to another, every man is supposed to promise obedience, to him, in whose power it is to save, or destroy him.

Or precedent subjection of one of the parents to the other.

6. If the mother be the father's subject, the child, is in the father's power: and if the father be the mother's subject, (as when a sovereign queen marrieth one of her subjects,*) the child is subject to the mother; because the father also is her subject.

7. If a man and woman, monarchs of two several kingdoms, have a child, and contract concerning who shall have the dominion of him, the right of the dominion passeth by the contract. If they contract not, the dominion followeth the dominion of the place of his residence. For the sovereign of each country hath dominion over all that reside therein.

8. He that hath the dominion over the child, hath dominion also over the children of the child; and over their children's children. For he that hath dominion over the person of a man, hath dominion over all that is his; without which, dominion were but a title, without the effect.

The right of succession followeth the rules of the right of possession.
Despotical dominion how attained.

9. The right of succession to paternal dominion, proceedeth in the same manner, as doth the right of succession of monarchy; of which I have already sufficiently spoken in the precedent chapter.

[104]

10. Dominion acquired by conquest, or victory in war, is that which some writers call DESPOTICAL, from δεσ ότης, which signifieth a *lord*, or *master*; and is the dominion of the master over his servant. And this dominion is then acquired to the victor, when the vanquished, to avoid the present stroke of death, covenanteth either in express words, or by other sufficient signs of the will, that so long as his life, and the liberty of his body is allowed him, the victor shall have the use thereof, at his pleasure. And after such covenant made, the vanquished is a SERVANT, and not before: for by the word *servant* (whether it be derived from *servire*, to serve, or from *servare*, to save, which I leave to grammarians to dispute) is not meant a captive, which is kept in prison, or bonds, till the owner of him that took

him, or bought him of one that did, shall consider what to do with him: (for such men, (commonly called slaves,) have no obligation at all; but may break their bonds, or the prison; and kill, or carry away captive their master, justly:) but one, that being taken, hath corporal liberty allowed him; and upon promise not to run away, nor to do violence to his master, is trusted by him.

11. It is not therefore the victory, that giveth the right of dominion over the vanquished, but his own covenant. Nor is he obliged because he is conquered; that is to say, beaten, and taken, or put to flight; but because he cometh in, and submitteth to the victor; nor is the victor obliged by an enemy's rendering himself, (without promise of life,) to spare him for this his yielding to discretion; which obliges not the victor longer, than in his own discretion he shall think fit.

Not by the victory, but by the consent of the vanquished.

12. And that which men do, when they demand (as it is now called) *quarter*, (which the Greeks called ζωγρία, *taking alive*,) is to evade the present fury of the victor, by submission, and to compound for their life, with ransom, or service: and therefore he that hath quarter, hath not his life given, but deferred till farther deliberation; for it is not a yielding on condition of life, but to discretion. And then only is his life in security, and his service due, when the victor hath trusted him with his corporal liberty. For slaves that work in prisons; or fetters, do it not of duty, but to avoid the cruelty of their task-masters.

13. The master of the servant, is master also of all he hath; and may exact the use thereof; that is to say, of his goods, of his labour, of his servants, and of his children, as often as he shall think fit. For he holdeth his life of his master, by the covenant of obedience; that is, of owning, and authorizing whatsoever the master shall do. And in case the master, if he refuse, kill him, or cast him into bonds, or otherwise punish him for his disobedience, he is himself the author of the same; and cannot accuse him of injury.

14. In sum, the rights and consequences of both *paternal* and *despotical* dominion, are the very same with those of a sovereign by institution; and for the same reasons: which reasons are set down in the precedent chapter. So that for a man that is monarch of divers nations, whereof he hath, in one the sovereignty by institution of the people assembled, and in another by conquest, that is by the submission of each particular, to avoid death or bonds; to demand of one nation more than of the other, from the title of

conquest, as being a conquered nation, is an act of ignorance of the
[105] rights of sovereignty; for the sovereign is absolute over both alike; or
else there is no sovereignty at all; and so every man may lawfully
protect himself, if he can, with his own sword, which is the condition of war.

*Difference
between a
family and a
kingdom.*

15. By this it appears, that a great family if it be not part of some
commonwealth, is of itself, as to the rights of sovereignty, a little
monarchy; whether that family consist of a man and his children; or
of a man and his servants; or of a man, and his children, and servants
together: wherein the father or master is the sovereign. But yet a
family is not properly a commonwealth; unless it be of that power by
its own number, or by other opportunities, as not to be subdued
without the hazard of war. For where a number of men are manifestly too weak to defend themselves united, every one may use his
own reason in time of danger, to save his own life, either by flight,
or by submission to the enemy, as he shall think best; in the same
manner as a very small company of soldiers, surprised by an army,
may cast down their arms, and demand quarter, or run away, rather
than be put to the sword. And thus much shall suffice, concerning
what I find by speculation, and deduction, of sovereign rights, from
the nature, need, and designs of men, in erecting of commonwealths, and putting themselves under monarchs, or assemblies,
entrusted with power enough for their protection.

*The rights of
monarchy
from
Scripture.*

16. Let us now consider what the Scripture teacheth in the same
point. To Moses, the children of Israel say thus: *Speak thou to us,
and we will hear thee; but let not God speak to us, lest we die.* (*Exod.* 20.
19.) This is absolute obedience to Moses. Concerning the right of
kings, God himself by the mouth of Samuel, saith, (1 *Sam.* 8. 11, 12,
&c.) *This shall be the right of the king you will have to reign over you.
He shall take your sons, and set them to drive his chariots, and to be his
horsemen, and to run before his chariots; and gather in his harvest; and
to make his engines of war, and instruments of his chariots; and shall take
your daughters to make perfumes, to be his cooks, and bakers. He shall
take your fields, your vine-yards, and your olive-yards, and give them to
his servants. He shall take the tithe of your corn and wine, and give it to
the men of his chamber, and to his other servants. He shall take your
man-servants, and your maid-servants, and the choice of your youth,
and employ them in his business. He shall take the tithe of your flocks;
and you shall be his servants.** This is absolute power, and summed

up in the last words, *you shall be his servants*. Again, when the people heard what power their king was to have, yet they consented thereto, and say thus, (*verse* 19) *we will be as all other nations, and our king shall judge our causes, and go before us, to conduct our wars*. Here is confirmed the right that sovereigns have, both to the *militia*, and to all *judicature*; in which is contained as absolute power, as one man can possibly transfer to another. Again, the prayer of king Solomon to God, was this (1 *Kings* 3. 9): *Give to thy servant understanding, to judge thy people, and to discern between good and evil*. It belongeth therefore to the sovereign to be *judge*, and to prescribe the [106] rules of *discerning good* and *evil*: which rules are laws; and therefore in him is the legislative power. Saul sought the life of David; yet when it was in his power to slay Saul, and his servants would have done it, David forbad them, saying, (1 *Sam.* 24. 9) *God forbid I should do such an act against my Lord, the anointed of God*. For obedience of servants St. Paul saith: (*Col.* 3. 22) *Servants obey your masters in all things*; and, (*Col.* 3. 20) *children obey your parents in all things*. There is simple obedience in those that are subject to paternal, or despotical dominion. Again, (*Matt.* 23. 2, 3) *The Scribes and Pharisees sit in Moses' chair, and therefore all that they shall bid you observe, that observe and do*. There again is simple obedience. And St. Paul, (*Titus* 3. 2) *Warn them that they subject themselves to princes, and to those that are in authority, and obey them*. This obedience is also simple. Lastly, our Saviour himself acknowledges, that men ought to pay such taxes as are by kings imposed, where he says, *give to Caesar that which is Caesar's*; and paid such taxes himself. And that the king's word, is sufficient to take any thing from any subject, when there is need; and that the king is judge of that need: for he himself, as king of the Jews, commanded his disciples to take the ass, and ass's colt to carry him into Jerusalem, saying, (*Matt.* 21. 2, 3) *Go into the village over against you, and you shall find a she ass tied, and her colt with her, untie them, and bring them to me. And if any man ask you, what you mean by it, say the Lord hath need of them: and they will let them go*. They will not ask whether his necessity be a sufficient title; nor whether he be judge of that necessity; but acquiesce in the will of the Lord.

17. To these places may be added also that of *Genesis*, (3. 5) *Ye shall be as gods, knowing good and evil*. And verse 11. *Who told thee that thou wast naked? hast thou eaten of the tree, of which I commanded*

thee thou shouldest not eat? For the cognizance or judicature of *good* and *evil*, being forbidden by the name of the fruit of the tree of knowledge, as a trial of Adam's obedience; the devil to inflame the ambition of the woman, to whom that fruit already seemed beautiful, told her that by tasting it, they should be as gods, knowing *good* and *evil*. Whereupon having both eaten, they did indeed take upon them God's office, which is judicature of good and evil; but acquired no new ability to distinguish between them aright. And whereas it is said, that having eaten, they saw they were naked; no man hath so interpreted that place, as if they had been formerly blind, and saw not their own skins: the meaning is plain, that it was then they first judged their nakedness (wherein it was God's will to create them) to be uncomely; and by being ashamed, did tacitly censure God himself. And thereupon God saith, *Hast thou eaten, &c.* as if he should say, doest thou that owest me obedience, take upon thee to judge of my commandments? Whereby it is clearly, (though allegorically,) signified, that the commands of them that have the right to command, are not by their subjects to be censured, nor disputed.

[107]

Sovereign power ought in all commonwealths to be absolute.

18. So that it appeareth plainly, to my understanding, both from reason, and Scripture, that the sovereign power, whether placed in one man, as in monarchy, or in one assembly of men, as in popular, and aristocratical commonwealths, is as great, as possibly men can be imagined to make it. And though of so unlimited a power, men may fancy many evil consequences, yet the consequences of the want of it, which is perpetual war of every man against his neighbour, are much worse. The condition of man in this life shall never be without inconveniences; but there happeneth in no commonwealth any great inconvenience, but what proceeds from the subject's disobedience, and breach of those covenants, from which the commonwealth hath its being. And whosoever thinking sovereign power too great, will seek to make it less, must subject himself, to the power, that can limit it; that is to say, to a greater.

19. The greatest objection is, that of the practice; when men ask, where, and when, such power has by subjects been acknowledged. But one may ask them again, when, or where has there been a kingdom long free from sedition and civil war. In those nations, whose commonwealths have been long-lived, and not been destroyed but by foreign war, the subjects never did dispute of the

sovereign power. But howsoever, an argument from the practice of men, that have not sifted to the bottom, and with exact reason weighed the causes, and nature of commonwealths, and suffer daily those miseries, that proceed from the ignorance thereof, is invalid. For though in all places of the world, men should lay the foundation of their houses on the sand, it could not thence be inferred, that so it ought to be. The skill of making, and maintaining commonwealths, consisteth in certain rules, as doth arithmetic and geometry; not (as tennis-play) on practice only: which rules, neither poor men have the leisure, nor men that have had the leisure, have hitherto had the curiosity, or the method to find out.

CHAPTER XXI

OF THE LIBERTY OF SUBJECTS

1. LIBERTY,* or FREEDOM, signifieth (properly) the absence of opposition; (by opposition, I mean external impediments of motion;) and may be applied no less to irrational, and inanimate creatures, than to rational. For whatsoever is so tied, or environed, as it cannot move, but within a certain space, which space is determined by the opposition of some external body, we say it hath not liberty to go further. And so of all living creatures, whilst they are imprisoned, or restrained, with walls, or chains; and of the water whilst it is kept in by banks, or vessels, that otherwise would spread itself into a larger space, we use to say, they are not at liberty, to move in such manner, as without those external impediments they would. But when the impediment of motion, is in the constitution of the thing itself, we use not to say, it wants the liberty; but the power to move; as when a stone lieth still, or a man is fastened to his bed by sickness. *Liberty, what.*

2. And according to this proper, and generally received meaning of the word, a FREEMAN, *is he, that in those things, which by his strength and wit he is able to do, is not hindered to do what he has a will to.* But when the words *free*, and *liberty*, are applied to any thing but *bodies*, they are abused; for that which is not subject to motion, is not subject to impediment: and therefore, when 'tis said (for example) the way is free, no liberty of the way is signified, but of those that [108] *What it is to be free.*

walk in it without stop. And when we say a gift is free, there is not meant any liberty of the gift, but of the giver, that was not bound by any law, or covenant to give it. So when we *speak freely*, it is not the liberty of voice, or pronunciation, but of the man, whom no law hath obliged to speak otherwise than he did. Lastly, from the use of the word *free-will*, no liberty can be inferred of the will, desire, or inclination, but the liberty of the man; which consisteth in this, that he finds no stop, in doing what he has the will, desire, or inclination to do.*

Fear and liberty consistent.

3. Fear and liberty are consistent; as when a man throweth his goods into the sea for *fear* the ship should sink,* he doth it nevertheless very willingly, and may refuse to do it if he will: it is therefore the action, of one that was *free*: so a man sometimes pays his debt, only for *fear* of imprisonment, which because nobody hindered him from detaining, was the action of a man at *liberty*. And generally all actions which men do in commonwealths, for *fear* of the law, are actions, which the doers had *liberty* to omit.

Liberty and necessity consistent.

4. *Liberty*, and *necessity* are consistent: as in the water, that hath not only *liberty*, but a *necessity* of descending by the channel; so likewise in the actions which men voluntarily do: which, because they proceed from their will, proceed from *liberty*; and yet, because every act of man's will, and every desire, and inclination proceedeth from some cause, and that from another cause, in a continual chain, (whose first link is in the hand of God the first of all causes,) they proceed from *necessity*. So that to him that could see the connexion of those causes, the *necessity* of all men's voluntary actions, would appear manifest. And therefore God, that seeth, and disposeth all things, seeth also that the *liberty* of man in doing what he will, is accompanied with the *necessity* of doing that which God will, and no more, nor less.* For though men may do many things, which God does not command, nor is therefore author of them; yet they can have no passion, nor appetite to any thing, of which appetite God's will is not the cause. And did not his will assure the *necessity* of man's will, and consequently of all that on man's will dependeth, the *liberty* of men would be a contradiction, and impediment to the omnipotence and *liberty* of God. And this shall suffice, (as to the matter in hand) of that natural *liberty*, which only is properly called *liberty*.

5. But as men, for the attaining of peace, and conservation of themselves thereby, have made an artificial man, which we call a commonwealth; so also have they made artificial chains, called *civil laws*, which they themselves, by mutual covenants, have fastened at one end, to the lips of that man, or assembly, to whom they have given the sovereign power; and at the other end to their own ears. These bonds in their own nature but weak, may nevertheless be made to hold, by the danger, though not by the difficulty of breaking them.

Artificial bonds, or covenants.

[109]

6. In relation to these bonds only it is, that I am to speak now, of the *liberty of subjects*. For seeing there is no commonwealth in the world, wherein there be rules enough set down, for the regulating of all the actions, and words of men; (as being a thing impossible:) it followeth necessarily, that in all kinds of actions, by the laws praetermitted [passed over], men have the liberty, of doing what their own reasons shall suggest, for the most profitable to themselves. For if we take liberty in the proper sense, for corporal liberty; that is to say, freedom from chains, and prison, it were very absurd for men to clamour as they do, for the liberty they so manifestly enjoy. Again, if we take liberty, for an exemption from laws, it is no less absurd, for men to demand as they do, that liberty, by which all other men may be masters of their lives. And yet as absurd as it is, this is it they demand; not knowing that the laws are of no power to protect them, without a sword in the hands of a man, or men, to cause those laws to be put in execution. The liberty of a subject, lieth therefore only in those things, which in regulating their actions, the sovereign hath praetermitted: such as is the liberty to buy, and sell, and otherwise contract with one another; to choose their own abode, their own diet, their own trade of life, and institute their children as they themselves think fit; and the like.

Liberty of subjects consisteth in liberty from covenants.

7. Nevertheless we are not to understand, that by such liberty, the sovereign power of life, and death, is either abolished, or limited. For it has been already shown, that nothing the sovereign representative can do to a subject, on what pretence soever, can properly be called injustice, or injury; because every subject is author of every act the sovereign doth; so that he never wanteth right to any thing, otherwise, than as he himself is the subject of God, and bound thereby to observe the laws of nature. And therefore it may, and doth often happen in commonwealths, that a subject may be put to

Liberty of the subject consistent with the unlimited power of the sovereign.

death, by the command of the sovereign power; and yet neither do the other wrong: as when Jeptha* caused his daughter to be sacrificed: in which, and the like cases, he that so dieth, had liberty to do the action, for which he is nevertheless, without injury put to death. And the same holdeth also in a sovereign prince, that putteth to death an innocent subject. For though the action be against the law of nature, as being contrary to equity, (as was the killing of Uriah, by David;*) yet it was not an injury to Uriah, but to God. Not to Uriah, because the right to do what he pleased, was given him by Uriah himself: and yet to God, because David was God's subject; and prohibited all iniquity by the law of nature. Which distinction, David himself, when he repented the fact, evidently confirmed, saying, *To thee only have I sinned*. In the same manner, the people of

[110] Athens, when they banished the most potent of their commonwealth for ten years, thought they committed no injustice; and yet they never questioned what crime he had done; but what hurt he would do: nay they commanded the banishment of they knew not whom; and every citizen bringing his oystershell into the market place, written with the name of him he desired should be banished, without actually accusing him, sometimes banished an Aristides, for his reputation of justice; and sometimes a scurrilous jester, as Hyperbolus,* to make a jest of it. And yet a man cannot say, the sovereign people of Athens wanted right to banish them; or an Athenian the liberty to jest, or to be just.

The liberty which writers praise, is the liberty of sovereigns; not of private men.

8. The liberty, whereof there is so frequent, and honourable mention, in the histories, and philosophy of the ancient Greeks, and Romans, and in the writings, and discourse of those that from them have received all their learning in the politics, is not the liberty of particular men; but the liberty of the commonwealth: which is the same with that, which every man then should have, if there were no civil laws, nor commonwealth at all. And the effects of it also be the same. For as amongst masterless men, there is perpetual war, of every man against his neighbour; no inheritance, to transmit to the son, nor to expect from the father; no propriety of goods, or lands; no security; but a full and absolute liberty in every particular man: so in states, and commonwealths not dependent on one another, every commonwealth, (not every man) has an absolute liberty, to do what it shall judge (that is to say, what that man, or assembly that representeth it, shall judge) most conducing to their benefit. But withal, they live in the condition of a perpetual war, and upon the

confines of battle, with their frontiers armed, and cannons planted against their neighbours round about. The Athenians, and Romans were free; that is, free commonwealths: not that any particular men had the liberty to resist their own representative; but that their representative had the liberty to resist, or invade other people. There is written on the turrets of the city of Lucca in great characters at this day, the word LIBERTAS; yet no man can thence infer, that a particular man has more liberty, or immunity from the service of the commonwealth there, than in Constantinople. Whether a commonwealth be monarchical, or popular, the freedom is still the same.

9. But it is an easy thing, for men to be deceived, by the specious name of liberty; and for want of judgment to distinguish, mistake that for their private inheritance, and birth-right, which is the right of the public only. And when the same error is confirmed by the authority of men in reputation for their writings on this subject, it is no wonder if it produce sedition, and change of government. In these western parts of the world, we are made to receive our opinions concerning the institution, and rights of commonwealths, from Aristotle, Cicero, and other men, Greeks and Romans, that living under popular states, derived those rights, not from the principles of nature, but transcribed them into their books, out of the practice of their own commonwealths, which were popular; as the [111] grammarians describe the rules of language, out of the practice of the time; or the rules of poetry, out of the poems of Homer and Virgil. And because the Athenians were taught, (to keep them from desire of changing their government,) that they were freemen, and all that lived under monarchy were slaves; therefore Aristotle puts it down in his *Politics*, (*lib.* 6. *cap.* 2.) *In democracy*, LIBERTY *is to be supposed: for it is commonly held, that no man is* FREE *in any other government*. And as Aristotle; so Cicero, and other writers have grounded their civil doctrine, on the opinions of the Romans, who were taught to hate monarchy, at first, by them that having deposed their sovereign, shared amongst them the sovereignty of Rome; and afterwards by their successors. And by reading of these Greek, and Latin authors, men from their childhood have gotten a habit (under a false show of liberty,) of favouring tumults, and of licentious controlling the actions of their sovereigns; and again of controlling those controllers; with the effusion of so much blood; as I think I may truly say, there was never any thing so dearly bought, as these

western parts have bought the learning of the Greek and Latin tongues.

10. To come now to the particulars of the true liberty of a subject; that is to say, what are the things, which though commanded by the sovereign, he may nevertheless, without injustice, refuse to do; we are to consider, what rights we pass away, when we make a commonwealth; or (which is all one) what liberty we deny ourselves, by owning all the actions (without exception) of the man, or assembly we make our sovereign. For in the act of our *submission*, consisteth both our *obligation*, and our *liberty*; which must therefore be inferred by arguments taken from thence; there being no obligation on any man, which ariseth not from some act of his own; for all men equally, are by nature free. And because such arguments, must either be drawn from the express words, *I authorize all his actions*, or from the intention of him that submitteth himself to his power, (which intention is to be understood by the end for which he so submitteth;) the obligation, and liberty of the subject, is to be derived, either from those words, (or others equivalent;) or else from the end of the institution of sovereignty; namely, the peace of the subjects within themselves, and their defence against a common enemy.

11. First therefore, seeing sovereignty by institution, is by covenant of every one to every one; and sovereignty by acquisition, by covenants of the vanquished to the victor, or child to the parent; it is manifest, that every subject has liberty in all those things, the right whereof cannot by covenant be transferred. I have shewn before in the 14th chapter, that covenants, not to defend a man's own body, are void. Therefore,

12. If the sovereign command a man (though justly condemned,) to kill, wound, or maim himself; or not to resist those that assault him; or to abstain from the use of food, air, medicine, or any other thing, without which he cannot live; yet hath that man the liberty to disobey.

13. If a man be interrogated by the sovereign, or his authority, concerning a crime done by himself, he is not bound (without assurance of pardon) to confess it; because no man (as I have shown in the same chapter) can be obliged by covenant to accuse himself.

14. Again, the consent of a subject to sovereign power, is contained in these words, *I authorize, or take upon me, all his actions*; in

which there is no restriction at all, of his own former natural liberty: for by allowing him to *kill me*, I am not bound to kill myself when he commands me. It is one thing to say, *kill me, or my fellow, if you please*; another thing to say, *I will kill myself, or my fellow*. It followeth therefore, that

15. No man is bound by the words themselves, either to kill himself, or any other man; and consequently, that the obligation a man may sometimes have, upon the command of the sovereign to execute any dangerous, or dishonourable office, dependeth not on the words of our submission; but on the intention, which is to be understood by the end thereof. When therefore our refusal to obey, frustrates the end for which the sovereignty was ordained; then there is no liberty to refuse: otherwise there is.*

16. Upon this ground, a man that is commanded as a soldier to fight against the enemy, though his sovereign have right enough to punish his refusal with death, may nevertheless in many cases refuse, without injustice; as when he substituteth a sufficient solider in his place: for in this case he deserteth not the service of the commonwealth. And there is allowance to be made for natural timorousness; not only to women, (of whom no such dangerous duty is expected,) but also to men of feminine courage. When armies fight, there is on one side, or both, a running away; yet when they do it not out of treachery, but fear, they are not esteemed to do it unjustly, but dishonourably. For the same reason, to avoid battle, is not injustice, but cowardice. But he that enrolleth himself a soldier, or taketh imprest money [advance payment], taketh away the excuse of a timorous nature; and is obliged, not only to go to the battle, but also not to run from it, without his captain's leave. And when the defence of the commonwealth, requireth at once the help of all that are able to bear arms, every one is obliged; because otherwise the institution of the commonwealth, which they have not the purpose, or courage to preserve, was in vain.

Nor to warfare, unless they voluntarily undertake it.

17. To resist the sword of the commonwealth, in defence of another man, guilty, or innocent, no man hath liberty; because such liberty, takes away from the sovereign, the means of protecting us; and is therefore destructive of the very essence of government. But in case a great many men together, have already resisted the sovereign power unjustly, or committed some capital crime, for which every one of them expecteth death, whether have they not the liberty then to join together, and assist, and defend one another?

[113] Certainly they have: for they but defend their lives, which the guilty man may as well do, as the innocent. There was indeed injustice in the first breach of their duty; their bearing of arms subsequent to it, though it be to maintain what they have done, is no new unjust act. And if it be only to defend their persons, it is not unjust at all. But the offer of pardon taketh from them, to whom it is offered, the plea of self-defence, and maketh their perseverance in assisting, or defending the rest, unlawful.

The greatest liberty of subjects, dependeth on the silence of the law.

18. As for other liberties, they depend on the silence of the law. In cases where the sovereign has prescribed no rule, there the subject hath the liberty to do, or forbear, according to his own discretion. And therefore such liberty is in some places more, and in some less; and in some times more, in other times less, according as they that have the sovereignty shall think most convenient. As for example, there was a time, when in England a man might enter into his own land, (and dispossess such as wrongfully possessed it,) by force. But in aftertimes, that liberty of forcible entry, was taken away by a statute made (by the king) in parliament. And in some places of the world, men have the liberty of many wives: in other places, such liberty is not allowed.

19. If a subject have a controversy with his sovereign, of debt, or of right of possession of lands or goods, or concerning any service required at his hands, or concerning any penalty, corporal, or pecuniary, grounded on a precedent law; he hath the same liberty to sue for his right, as if it were against a subject; and before such judges, as are appointed by the sovereign. For seeing the sovereign demandeth by force of a former law, and not by virtue of his power; he declareth thereby, that he requireth no more, than shall appear to be due by that law. The suit therefore is not contrary to the will of the sovereign; and consequently the subject hath the liberty to demand the hearing of his cause; and sentence, according to that law. But if he demand, or take any thing by pretence of his power; there lieth, in that case, no action of law; for all that is done by him in virtue of his power, is done by the authority of every subject, and consequently he that brings an action against the sovereign, brings it against himself.

20. If a monarch, or sovereign assembly, grant a liberty to all, or any of his subjects, which grant standing, he is disabled to provide for their safety, the grant is void; unless he directly renounce, or transfer the sovereignty to another. For in that he might openly, (if

it had been his will,) and in plain terms, have renounced, or transferred it, and did not; it is to be understood it was not his will; but that the grant proceeded from ignorance of the repugnancy between such a liberty and the sovereign power: and therefore the sovereignty is still retained; and consequently all those powers, which are necessary to the exercising thereof; such as are the power of war, and peace, of judicature, of appointing officers, and councillors, of levying money, and the rest named in the eighteenth chapter.

21. The obligation of subjects to the sovereign, is understood to last as long, and no longer, than the power lasteth, by which he is able to protect them. For the right men have by nature to protect themselves, when none else can protect them, can by no covenant be relinquished. The sovereignty is the soul of the commonwealth; which once departed from the body, the members do no more receive their motion from it. The end of obedience is protection; which, wheresoever a man seeth it, either in his own, or in another's sword, nature applieth his obedience to it, and his endeavour to maintain it. And though sovereignty, in the intention of them that make it, be immortal; yet is it in its own nature, not only subject to violent death, by foreign war; but also through the ignorance, and passions of men, it hath in it, from the very institution, many seeds of a natural mortality, by intestine discord.

[114]
In what cases subjects are absolved of their obedience to their sovereign.

22. If a subject be taken prisoner in war; or his person, or his means of life be within the guards of the enemy, and hath his life and corporal liberty given him, on condition to be subject to the victor, he hath liberty to accept the condition; and having accepted it, is the subject of him that took him; because he had no other way to preserve himself. The case is the same, if he be detained on the same terms, in a foreign country. But if a man be held in prison, or bonds, or is not trusted with the liberty of his body; he cannot be understood to be bound by covenant to subjection; and therefore may, if he can, make his escape by any means whatsoever.

In case of captivity.

23. If a monarch shall relinquish the sovereignty, both for himself, and his heirs; his subjects return to the absolute liberty of nature; because, though nature may declare who are his sons, and who are the nearest of his kin; yet it dependeth on his own will, (as hath been said in the precedent chapter,) who shall be his heir. If therefore he will have no heir, there is no sovereignty, nor subjection. The case is the same, if he die without known kindred, and

In case the sovereign cast off the government from himself and his heirs.

without declaration of his heir. For then there can no heir be known, and consequently no subjection be due.

In case of banishment.

24. If the sovereign banish his subject; during the banishment, he is not subject. But he that is sent on a message, or hath leave to travel, is still subject; but it is, by contract between sovereigns, not by virtue of the covenant of subjection. For whosoever entereth into another's dominion, is subject to all the laws thereof; unless he have a privilege by the amity of the sovereigns, or by special licence.

In case the sovereign render himself subject to another.

25. If a monarch subdued by war, render himself subject to the victor; his subjects are delivered from their former obligation, and become obliged to the victor. But if he be held prisoner, or have not the liberty of his own body; he is not understood to have given away the right of sovereignty; and therefore his subjects are obliged to yield obedience to the magistrates formerly placed, governing not in their own name, but in his. For, his right remain-

[115] ing, the question is only of the administration; that is to say, of the magistrates and officers; which, if he have not means to name, he is supposed to approve those, which he himself had formerly appointed.

CHAPTER XXII

OF SYSTEMS SUBJECT, POLITICAL, AND PRIVATE

The divers sorts of systems of people.

1. HAVING spoken of the generation, form, and power of a commonwealth, I am in order to speak next of the parts thereof. And first of systems, which resemble the similar parts, or muscles of a body natural. By SYSTEMS; I understand any numbers of men joined in one interest, or one business. Of which, some are *regular*, and some *irregular*. *Regular* are those, where one man, or assembly of men, is constituted representative of the whole number. All other are *irregular*.

2. Of regular, some are *absolute*, and *independent*, subject to none but their own representative: such are only commonwealths; of which I have spoken already in the five last precedent

chapters. Others are dependent; that is to say, subordinate to some sovereign power, to which every one, as also their representative is *subject*.

3. Of systems subordinate, some are *political*, and some *private*. *Political* (otherwise called *bodies politic*, and *persons in law*,) are those, which are made by authority from the sovereign power of the commonwealth. *Private*, are those, which are constituted by subjects amongst themselves, or by authority from a stranger. For no authority derived from foreign power, within the dominion of another, is public there, but private.

4. And of private systems, some are *lawful*; some *unlawful*. *Lawful*, are those which are allowed by the commonwealth: all other are *unlawful*. *Irregular* systems, are those which having no representative, consist only in concourse of people; which if not forbidden by the commonwealth, nor made on evil design, (such as are conflux of people to markets, or shows, or any other harmless end,) are lawful. But when the intention is evil, or (if the number be considerable) unknown, they are unlawful.

5. In bodies politic, the power of the representative is always limited: and that which prescribeth the limits thereof, is the power sovereign. For power unlimited, is absolute sovereignty. And the sovereign in every commonwealth, is the absolute representative of all the subjects; and therefore no other, can be representative of any part of them, but so far forth, as he shall give leave. And to give leave to a body politic of subjects, to have an absolute representative to all intents and purposes, were to abandon the government of so much of the commonwealth, and to divide the dominion, contrary to their peace and defence; which the sovereign cannot be understood to do, by any grant, that does not plainly, and directly discharge them of [116] their subjection. For consequences of words, are not the signs of his will, when other consequences are signs of the contrary; but rather signs of error, and misreckoning; to which all mankind is too prone. *In all bodies politic the power of the representative is limited.*

6. The bounds of that power, which is given to the representative of a body politic, are to be taken notice of, from two things. One is their writ, or letters from the sovereign: the other is the law of the commonwealth.

7. For though in the institution or acquisition of a commonwealth, which is independent, there needs no writing, because the *By letters patents.*

power of the representative has there no other bounds, but such as are set out by the unwritten law of nature; yet in subordinate bodies, there are such diversities of limitation necessary, concerning their businesses, times, and places, as can neither be remembered without letters, nor taken notice of, unless such letters be patent,* that they may be read to them, and withal sealed, or testified, with the seals, or other permanent signs of the authority sovereign.

And the laws.

8. And because such limitation is not always easy, or perhaps possible to be described in writing; the ordinary laws, common to all subjects, must determine what the representative may lawfully do, in all cases, where the letters themselves are silent. And therefore,

When the representative is one man, his unwarranted acts are his own only.

9.* In a body politic, if the representative be one man, whatsoever he does in the person of the body, which is not warranted in his letters, nor by the laws, is his own act, and not the act of the body, nor of any other member thereof besides himself: because further than his letters, or the laws limit, he representeth no man's person, but his own. But what he does according to these, is the act of every one: for of the act of the sovereign every one is author, because he is their representative unlimited; and the act of him that recedes not from the letters of the sovereign, is the act of the sovereign, and therefore every member of the body is author of it.

When it is an assembly, it is the act of them that assented only.

10. But if the representative be an assembly; whatsoever that assembly shall decree, not warranted by their letters, or the laws, is the act of the assembly, or body politic, and the act of every one by whose vote the decree was made; but not the act of any man that being present voted to the contrary; nor of any man absent, unless he voted it by procuration [proxy]. It is the act of the assembly, because voted by the major part; and if it be a crime, the assembly may be punished, as far forth as it is capable, as by dissolution, or forfeiture of their letters, (which is to such artificial, and fictitious bodies, capital,) or (if the assembly have a common stock, wherein none of the innocent members have propriety,) by pecuniary mulct [fine]. For from corporal penalties nature hath exempted all bodies politic. But they that gave not their vote, are therefore innocent, because the assembly cannot represent any man in things unwarranted by their letters, and consequently are not involved in their votes.

11. If the person of the body politic being in one man, borrow money of a stranger, that is, of one that is not of the same body, (for no letters need limit borrowing, seeing it is left to men's own inclinations to limit lending), the debt is the representative's. For if he should have authority from his letters, to make the members pay what he borroweth, he should have by consequence the sovereignty of them; and therefore the grant were either void, as proceeding from error, commonly incident to human nature, and an insufficient sign of the will of the granter; or if it be avowed by him, then is the representer sovereign, and falleth not under the present question, which is only of bodies subordinate. No member therefore is obliged to pay the debt so borrowed, but the representative himself: because he that lendeth it, being a stranger to the letters, and to the qualification of the body, understandeth those only for his debtors, that are engaged: and seeing the representer can engage himself, and none else, has him only for debtor; who must therefore pay him, out of the common stock (if there be any,) or, (if there be none) out of his own estate.

12. If he come into debt by contract, or mulct, the case is the same.

13. But when the representative is an assembly, and the debt to a stranger; all they, and only they are responsible for the debt, that gave their votes to the borrowing of it, or to the contract that made it due, or to the fact for which the mulct was imposed; because every one of those in voting did engage himself for the payment: for he that is author of the borrowing, is obliged to the payment, even of the whole debt, though when paid by any one, he be discharged.

14. But if the debt be to one of the assembly, the assembly only is obliged to the payment, out of their common stock (if they have any:) for having liberty of vote, if he vote the money shall be borrowed, he votes it shall be paid; if he vote it shall not be borrowed, or be absent, yet because in lending, he voteth the borrowing, he contradicteth his former vote, and is obliged by the latter, and becomes both borrower and lender, and consequently cannot demand payment from any particular man, but from the common treasure only; which failing he hath no remedy, nor complaint, but against himself, that being privy to the acts of the assembly, and to their means to pay, and not being enforced, did nevertheless through his own folly lend his money.

Protestation against the decrees of bodies politic sometimes lawful; but against sovereign power never.

15. It is manifest by this, that in bodies politic subordinate, and subject to a sovereign power, it is sometimes not only lawful, but expedient, for a particular man to make open protestation against the decrees of the representative assembly, and cause their dissent to be registered, or to take witness of it; because otherwise they may be obliged to pay debts contracted, and be responsible for crimes committed by other men. But in a sovereign assembly, that liberty is taken away, both because he that protesteth there, denies their sovereignty; and also because whatsoever is commanded by the sovereign power, is as to the subject (though not so always in the sight of God) justified by the command; for of such command every subject is the author.

Bodies politic for government of a province,

[118]

colony, or town.

16. The variety of bodies politic, is almost infinite: for they are not only distinguished by the several affairs, for which they are constituted, wherein there is an unspeakable diversity; but also by the times, places, and numbers, subject to many limitations. And as to their affairs, some are ordained for government; as first, the government of a province may be committed to an assembly of men, wherein all resolutions shall depend on the votes of the major part; and then this assembly is a body politic, and their power limited by commission. This word province signifies a charge, or care of business, which he whose business it is, committeth to another man, to be administered for, and under him; and therefore when in one commonwealth there be divers countries, that have their laws distinct one from another, or are far distant in place, the administration of the government being committed to divers persons, those countries where the sovereign is not resident, but governs by commission, are called provinces. But of the government of a province, by an assembly residing in the province itself, there be few examples. The Romans who had the sovereignty of many provinces; yet governed them always by presidents, and praetors; and not by assemblies, as they governed the city of Rome, and territories adjacent. In like manner, when there were colonies sent from England, to plant Virginia, and Sommer-islands [the Bermudas]; though the governments of them here, were committed to assemblies in London, yet did those assemblies never commit the government under them to any assembly there, but did to each plantation send one governor. For though every man, where he can be present by nature, desires to participate of government; yet where they cannot be present, they are by nature also inclined, to commit the government of their common interest rather to a monarchical, than a popular form of government: which is also evident in those men that have great private estates; who when they are unwilling to take the pains of administering the business that belongs to them, choose rather to trust one servant, than an assembly either of their friends or servants. But howsoever it be in fact, yet we may suppose the government of a province, or colony committed to an assembly: and when it is, that which in this place I have to say, is this; that whatsoever debt is by that assembly contracted; or whatsoever unlawful act is decreed, is the act only of those that assented, and not of any that dissented, or were absent, for the reasons before alleged. Also that an assembly residing out of the bounds of that colony whereof they have the government, cannot execute any power over the persons, or goods of any of the colony, to seize on them for debt, or other duty, in any place without the colony itself, as having no jurisdiction, nor authority elsewhere, but are left to the remedy, which the law of the place alloweth them. And though the assembly have right, to impose a mulct upon any of their members, that shall break the laws they make; yet out of the colony itself, they have no right to execute the same. And that which is said here, of the rights of an assembly, for the government of a province, or a colony, is applicable also to an assembly for the government of a town, an university, or a college, or a church, or for any other government over the persons of men.

17. And generally, in all bodies politic, if any particular member [119] conceive himself injured by the body itself, the cognizance of his cause belongeth to the sovereign, and those the sovereign hath ordained for judges in such causes, or shall ordain for that particular cause; and not to the body itself. For the whole body is in this case his fellow-subject, which in a sovereign assembly, is otherwise: for there, if the sovereign be not judge, though in his own cause, there can be no judge at all.

18. In a body politic, for the well ordering of foreign traffic, the most commodious representative is an assembly of all the members; that is to say, such a one, as every one that adventureth his money, may be present at all the deliberations, and resolutions of the body, if they will themselves. For proof whereof, we are to consider the end, for which men that are merchants, and may buy and sell, *Bodies politic for ordering of trade.*

export, and import their merchandise, according to their own discretions, do nevertheless bind themselves up in one corporation. It is true, there be few merchants, that with the merchandise they buy at home, can freight a ship, to export it; or with that they buy abroad, to bring it home; and have therefore need to join together in one society; where every man may either participate of the gain, according to the proportion of his adventure; or take his own, and sell what he transports, or imports, at such prices as he thinks fit. But this is no body politic, there being no common representative to oblige them to any other law, than that which is common to all other subjects. The end of their incorporating, is to make their gain the greater; which is done two ways; by sole buying, and sole selling, both at home, and abroad. So that to grant to a company of merchants to be a corporation, or body politic, is to grant them a double monopoly, whereof one is to be sole buyers; another to be sole sellers. For when there is a company incorporate for any particular foreign country, they only export the commodities vendible in that country; which is sole buying at home, and sole selling abroad. For at home there is but one buyer, and abroad but one that selleth: both which is gainful to the merchant, because thereby they buy at home at lower, and sell abroad at higher rates: and abroad there is but one buyer of foreign merchandise, and but one that sells them at home; both which again are gainful to the adventurers.

19. Of this double monopoly one part is disadvantageous to the people at home, the other to foreigners. For at home by their sole exportation they set what price they please on the husbandry, and handy-works of the people; and by the sole importation, what price they please on all foreign commodities the people have need of; both which are ill for the people. On the contrary, by the sole selling of the native commodities abroad, and sole buying the foreign commodities upon the place, they raise the price of those, and abate the price of these, to the disadvantage of the foreigner: for where but one selleth, the merchandise is the dearer; and where but one [120] buyeth, the cheaper. Such corporations therefore are no other than monopolies; though they would be very profitable for a commonwealth, if being bound up into one body in foreign markets they were at liberty at home, every man to buy, and sell at what price he could.

20. The end then of these bodies of merchants, being not a common benefit to the whole body, (which have in this case no

common stock, but what is deducted out of the particular adventures, for building, buying, victualling and manning of ships,) but the particular gain of every adventurer, it is reason that every one be acquainted with the employment of his own; that is, that every one be of the assembly, that shall have the power to order the same; and be acquainted with their accounts. And therefore the representative of such a body must be an assembly, where every member of the body may be present at the consultations, if he will.

21. If a body politic of merchants, contract a debt to a stranger by the act of their representative assembly, every member is liable by himself for the whole. For a stranger can take no notice of their private laws, but considereth them as so many particular men, obliged every one to the whole payment, till payment made by one dischargeth all the rest: but if the debt be to one of the company, the creditor is debtor for the whole to himself, and cannot therefore demand his debt, but only from the common stock, if there be any.

22. If the commonwealth impose a tax upon the body, it is understood to be laid upon every member proportionably to his particular adventure in the company. For there is in this case no other common stock, but what is made of their particular adventures.

23. If a mulct be laid upon the body for some unlawful act, they only are liable by whose votes the act was decreed, or by whose assistance it was executed; for in none of the rest is there any other crime but being of the body; which if a crime, (because the body was ordained by the authority of the commonwealth,) is not his.

24. If one of the members be indebted to the body, he may be sued by the body; but his goods cannot be taken, nor his person imprisoned by the authority of the body; but only by authority of the commonwealth: for if they can do it by their own authority, they can by their own authority give judgment that the debt is due; which is as much as to be judge in their own cause.

25. These bodies made for the government of men, or of traffic, be either perpetual, or for a time prescribed by writing. But there be bodies also whose times are limited, and that only by the nature of their business. For example, if a sovereign monarch, or a sovereign assembly, shall think fit to give command to the towns, and other several parts of their territory, to send to him their deputies, to inform him of the condition, and necessities of the subjects, or to

A body politic for counsel to be given to the sovereign.

[121] advise with him for the making of good laws, or for any other cause, as with one person representing the whole country, such deputies, having a place and time of meeting assigned them, are there, and at that time, a body politic, representing every subject of that dominion; but it is only for such matters as shall be propounded unto them by that man, or assembly, that by the sovereign authority sent for them; and when it shall be declared that nothing more shall be propounded, nor debated by them, the body is dissolved. For if they were the absolute representatives of the people, then were it the sovereign assembly; and so there would be two sovereign assemblies, or two sovereigns, over the same people; which cannot consist with their peace. And therefore where there is once a sovereignty, there can be no absolute representation of the people, but by it. And for the limits of how far such a body shall represent the whole people, they are set forth in the writing by which they were sent for. For the people cannot choose their deputies to other intent, than is in the writing directed to them from their sovereign expressed.

A regular private body, lawful, as a family. 26. Private bodies regular, and lawful, are those that are constituted without letters, or other written authority, saving the laws common to all other subjects. And because they be united in one person representative, they are held for regular; such as are all families, in which the father, or master ordereth the whole family. For he obligeth his children, and servants, as far as the law permitteth, though not further, because none of them are bound to obedience in those actions, which the law hath forbidden to be done. In all other actions, during the time they are under domestic government, they are subject to their fathers, and masters, as to their immediate sovereigns. For the father, and master, being before the institution of commonwealth, absolute sovereigns in their own families, they lose afterward no more of their authority, than the law of the commonwealth taketh from them.

Private bodies regular, but unlawful. 27. Private bodies regular, but unlawful, are those that unite themselves into one person representative, without any public authority at all; such as are the corporations of beggars, thieves, and gipsies, the better to order their trade of begging and stealing; and the corporations of men, that by authority from any foreign person, unite themselves in another's dominion, for the easier propagation of doctrines, and for making a party, against the power of the commonwealth.

28. Irregular systems, in their nature but leagues, or sometimes *Systems*
mere concourse of people, without union to any particular design, *irregular,*
by obligation* of one to another, but proceeding only from a *such as are*
similitude of wills and inclinations, become lawful, or unlawful, *private*
according to the lawfulness, or unlawfulness of every particular *leagues.*
man's design therein: and his design is to be understood by the
occasion.

29. The leagues of subjects, (because leagues are commonly
made for mutual defence,) are in a commonwealth (which is no more
than a league of all the subjects together) for the most part unnecessary, and savour of unlawful design; and are for that cause unlawful,
and go commonly by the name of factions, or conspiracies. For a [122]
league being a connexion of men by covenants, if there be no power
given to any one man or assembly (as in the condition of mere
nature) to compel them to performance, is so long only valid, as
there ariseth no just cause of distrust: and therefore leagues between
commonwealths, over whom there is no human power established,
to keep them all in awe, are not only lawful, but also profitable for
the time they last. But leagues of the subjects of one and the same
commonwealth, where every one may obtain his right by means of
the sovereign power, are unnecessary to the maintaining of peace
and justice, and (in case the design of them be evil or unknown to
the commonwealth) unlawful. For all uniting of strength by private
men, is, if for evil intent, unjust; if for intent unknown, dangerous
to the public, and unjustly concealed.

30. If the sovereign power be in a great assembly, and a number *Secret cabals.*
of men, part of the assembly, without authority, consult apart, to
contrive the guidance of the rest; this is a faction, or conspiracy
unlawful, as being a fraudulent seducing of the assembly for their
particular interest. But if he, whose private interest is to be debated
and judged in the assembly, make as many friends as he can; in him
it is no injustice; because in this case he is no part of the assembly.
And though he hire such friends with money, (unless there be an
express law against it,) yet it is not injustice. For sometimes,
(as men's manners are,) justice cannot be had without money;*
and every man may think his own cause just, till it be heard, and
judged.

31. In all commonwealths, if private men entertain more ser- *Feuds of*
vants, than the government of his estate, and lawful employment he *private*
has for them requires, it is faction, and unlawful. For having the *families.*

protection of the commonwealth, he needeth not the defence of private force. And whereas in nations not thoroughly civilized, several numerous families have lived in continual hostility, and invaded one another with private force; yet it is evident enough, that they have done unjustly; or else they had no commonwealth.

Factions for government.

32. And as factions for kindred, so also factions for government of religion, as of Papists, Protestants, &c.* or of state, as patricians, and plebeians of old time in Rome, and of aristocraticals and democraticals of old time in Greece, are unjust, as being contrary to the peace and safety of the people, and a taking of the sword out of the hand of the sovereign.

Concourse of people.

33. Concourse of people is an irregular system, the lawfulness, or unlawfulness, whereof dependeth on the occasion, and on the number of them that are assembled. If the occasion be lawful, and manifest, the concourse is lawful; as the usual meeting of men at church, or at a public show, in usual numbers: for if the numbers be extraordinarily great, the occasion is not evident; and consequently he that cannot render a particular and good account of his being amongst them, is to be judged conscious of an unlawful, and tumultuous design. It may be lawful for a thousand men, to join to a petition to be delivered to a judge, or magistrate; yet if a thousand [123] men come to present it, it is a tumultuous assembly; because there needs but one or two for that purpose. But in such cases as these, it is not a set number that makes the assembly unlawful, but such a number, as the present officers are not able to suppress, and bring to justice.

34. When an unusual number of men, assemble against a man whom they accuse; the assembly is an unlawful tumult; because they may deliver their accusation to the magistrate by a few, or by one man. Such was the case of St. Paul at Ephesus; where Demetrius and a great number of other men, brought two of Paul's companions before the magistrate, saying with one voice, *Great is Diana of the Ephesians*; which was their way of demanding justice against them for teaching the people such doctrine, as was against their religion, and trade. The occasion here, considering the laws of that people, was just; yet was their assembly judged unlawful, and the magistrate reprehended them for it in these words (*Acts* 19. 40), *If Demetrius and the other workmen can accuse any man, of any thing, there be pleas, and deputies, let them accuse one another. And if you have any other thing to demand, your case may be judged in an assembly lawfully called.*

For we are in danger to be accused for this day's sedition, because, there is no cause by which any man can render any reason of this concourse of people. Where he calleth an assembly, whereof men can give no just account, a sedition, and such as they could not answer for. And this is all I shall say concerning *systems*, and assemblies of people, which may be compared (as I said,) to the similar parts of man's body; such as be lawful, to the muscles; such as are unlawful, to wens [warts], biles, and apostems [abscesses], engendered by the unnatural conflux of evil humours.

CHAPTER XXIII

OF THE PUBLIC MINISTERS OF SOVEREIGN POWER

1. IN the last chapter I have spoken of the similar parts of a commonwealth: in this I shall speak of the parts organical, which are public ministers.

2. A PUBLIC MINISTER, is he, that by the sovereign, (whether a monarch or an assembly,) is employed in any affairs, with authority to represent in that employment, the person of the commonwealth. And whereas every man, or assembly that hath sovereignty, representeth two persons, or (as the more common phrase is) has two capacities, one natural, and another politic, (as a monarch, hath the person not only of the commonwealth, but also of a man; and a sovereign assembly hath the person not only of the commonwealth, but also of the assembly); they that be servants to them in their natural capacity, are not public ministers; but those only that serve them in the administration of the public business. And therefore [124] neither ushers, nor sergeants, nor other officers that wait on the assembly, for no other purpose, but for the commodity of the men assembled, in an aristocracy, or democracy; nor stewards, chamberlains, cofferers, or any other officers of the household of a monarch, are public ministers in a monarchy. *Public minister who.*

3. Of public ministers, some have charge committed to them of a general administration, either of the whole dominion, or of a part thereof. Of the whole, as to a protector, or regent, may be committed by the predecessor of an infant king, during his minority, the whole administration of his kingdom. In which case, every subject is so far *Ministers for the general administration.*

obliged to obedience, as the ordinances he shall make, and the commands he shall give be in the king's name, and not inconsistent with his sovereign power. Of a part, or province; as when either a monarch, or a sovereign assembly, shall give the general charge thereof to a governor, lieutenant, praefect, or viceroy: and in this case also, every one of that province is obliged to all he shall do in the name of the sovereign, and that is not incompatible with the sovereign's right. For such protectors, viceroys, and governors, have no other right, but what depends on the sovereign's will; and no commission that can be given them, can be interpreted for a declaration of the will to transfer the sovereignty, without express and perspicuous words to that purpose. And this kind of public ministers resembleth the nerves, and tendons that move the several limbs of a body natural.

For special administration, as for economy.   4. Others have special administration; that is to say, charges of some special business, either at home, or abroad: as at home, first, for the economy of a commonwealth, they that have authority concerning the *treasure*, as tributes, impositions, rents, fines, or whatsoever public revenue, to collect, receive, issue, or take the accounts thereof, are public ministers: ministers, because they serve the person representative, and can do nothing against his command, nor without his authority: public, because they serve him in his political capacity.

5. Secondly, they that have authority concerning the *militia*; to have the custody of arms, forts, ports; to levy, pay, or conduct soliders; or to provide for any necessary thing for the use of war, either by land or sea, are public ministers. But a soldier without command, though he fight for the commonwealth, does not therefore represent the person of it; because there is none to represent it to. For every one that hath command, represents it to them only whom he commandeth.

For instruction of the people.   6. They also that have authority to teach, or to enable others to teach the people their duty to the sovereign power, and instruct them in the knowledge of what is just, and unjust, thereby to render them more apt to live in godliness, and in peace amongst themselves, and resist the public enemy, are public ministers: ministers, in that they do it not by their own authority, but by another's; and public, because they do it (or should do it) by no authority but that [125] of the sovereign. The monarch, or the sovereign assembly only hath immediate authority from God, to teach and instruct the people;

160

and no man but the sovereign, receiveth his power *Dei gratia* simply; that is to say, from the favour of none but God: all other, receive theirs from the favour and providence of God, and their sovereigns; as in a monarchy *Dei gratia et regis*; or *Dei providentia et voluntate regis.**

7. They also to whom jurisdiction is given, are public ministers. For in their seats of justice they represent the person of the sovereign; and their sentence, is his sentence; for (as hath been before declared) all judicature is essentially annexed to the sovereignty; and therefore all other judges are but ministers of him, or them that have the sovereign power. And as controversies are of two sorts, namely of *fact* and of *law*; so are judgments, some of fact, some of law: and consequently in the same controversy, there may be two judges, one of fact, another of law. *For judicature.*

8. And in both these controversies, there may arise a controversy between the party judged, and the judge; which because they be both subjects to the sovereign, ought in equity to be judged by men agreed on by consent of both; for no man can be judge in his own cause. But the sovereign is already agreed on for judge by them both, and is therefore either to hear the cause, and determine it himself, or appoint for judge such as they shall both agree on. And this agreement is then understood to be made between them divers ways; as first, if the defendant be allowed to except against such of his judges, whose interest maketh him suspect them, (for as to the complainant he hath already chosen his own judge,) those which he excepteth not against, are judges he himself agrees on. Secondly, if he appeal to any other judge, he can appeal no further; for his appeal is his choice. Thirdly, if he appeal to the sovereign himself, and he by himself, or by delegates which the parties shall agree on, give sentence; that sentence is final: for the defendant is judged by his own judges, that is to say, by himself.

9. These properties of just and rational judicature considered, I cannot forbear to observe the excellent constitution of the courts of justice, established both for Common, and also for Public Pleas in England. By Common Pleas, I mean those, where both the complainant and defendant are subjects: and by public, (which are also called Pleas of the Crown) those, where the complainant is the sovereign. For whereas there were two orders of men, whereof one was Lords, the other Commons; the Lords had this privilege, to have for judges if the plea were public* in all capital crimes, none

but Lords; and of them, as many as would be present; which being ever acknowledged as a privilege of favour, their judges were none but such as they had themselves desired. And in all controversies, every subject (as also in civil controversies the Lords) had for judges, men of the country where the matter in controversy lay; against which he might make his exceptions, till at last twelve men [126] without exception being agreed on, they were judged by those twelve. So that having his own judges, there could be nothing alleged by the party, why the sentence should not be final. These public persons, with authority from the sovereign power, either to instruct, or judge the people, are such members of the commonwealth, as may fitly be compared to the organs of voice in a body natural.

For execution.   10. Public ministers are also all those, that have authority from the sovereign, to procure the execution of judgments given; to publish the sovereign's commands; to suppress tumults; to apprehend, and imprison malefactors; and other acts tending to the conservation of the peace. For every act they do by such authority, is the act of the commonwealth; and their service, answerable to that of the hands, in a body natural.

11. Public ministers abroad, are those that represent the person of their own sovereign, to foreign states. Such are ambassadors, messengers, agents, and heralds, sent by public authority, and on public business.

12. But such as are sent by authority only of some private party of a troubled state, though they be received, are neither public, nor private ministers of the commonwealth; because none of their actions have the commonwealth for author. Likewise, an ambassador sent from a prince, to congratulate, condole, or to assist at a solemnity; though the authority be public; yet because the business is private, and belonging to him in his natural capacity; is a private person. Also if a man be sent into another country, secretly to explore their counsels, and strength; though both the authority, and the business be public; yet because there is none to take notice of any person in him, but his own; he is but a private minister; but yet a minister of the commonwealth; and may be compared to an eye in the body natural. And those that are appointed to receive the petitions or other informations of the people, and are as it were the public ear, are public ministers, and represent their sovereign in that office.

13. Neither a councillor (nor a council of state, if we consider it with no authority of judicature or command, but only of giving advice to the sovereign when it is required, or of offering it when it is not required,) is a public person. For the advice is addressed to the sovereign only, whose person cannot in his own presence, be represented to him, by another. But a body of councillors, are never without some other authority, either of judicature, or of immediate administration: as in a monarchy, they represent the monarch, in delivering his commands to the public ministers: in a democracy, the council, or senate propounds the result of their deliberations to the people, as a council; but when they appoint judges, or hear causes, or give audience to ambassadors, it is in the quality of a minister of the people: and in an aristocracy the council of state is the sovereign assembly itself; and gives counsel to none but themselves.

Councillors without other employment than to advise are not public ministers.

CHAPTER XXIV   [127]

OF THE NUTRITION, AND PROCREATION OF A COMMONWEALTH

1. THE NUTRITION of a commonwealth consisteth, in the *plenty*, and *distribution* of *materials* conducing to life: in *concoction*, or *preparation*; and (when concocted) in the *conveyance* of it, by convenient conduits, to the public use.

The nourishment of a commonwealth consisteth in the commodities of sea and land:

2. As for the plenty of matter, it is a thing limited by nature, to those commodities, which from (the two breasts of our common mother) land, and sea, God usually either freely giveth, or for labour selleth to mankind.

3. For the matter of this nutriment, consisting in animals, vegetals, and minerals, God hath freely laid them before us, in or near to the face of the earth; so as there needeth no more but the labour, and industry of receiving them. Insomuch as plenty dependeth (next to God's favour) merely on the labour and industry of men.

4. This matter, commonly called commodities, is partly *native*, and partly *foreign*: *native*, that which is to be had within the territory of the commonwealth: *foreign*, that which is imported from without.

And because there is no territory under the dominion of one commonwealth, (except it be of very vast extent,) that produceth all things needful for the maintenance, and motion of the whole body; and few that produce not some thing more than necessary; the superfluous commodities to be had within, become no more superfluous, but supply these wants at home, by importation of that which may be had abroad, either by exchange, or by just war, or by labour: for a man's labour also, is a commodity exchangeable for benefit, as well as any other thing: and there have been commonwealths that having no more territory, than hath served them for habitation, have nevertheless, not only maintained, but also increased their power, partly by the labour of trading from one place to another, and partly by selling the manufactures, whereof the materials were brought in from other places.

And the right distribution of them.

5. The distribution of the materials of this nourishment, is the constitution of *mine*, and *thine*, and *his*; that is to say, in one word *propriety*; and belongeth in all kinds of commonwealth to the sovereign power. For where there is no commonwealth, there is (as hath been already shown) a perpetual war of every man against his neighbour; and therefore every thing is his that getteth it, and keepeth it by force; which is neither *propriety*, nor *community*; but *uncertainty*. Which is so evident, that even Cicero, (a passionate defender of liberty,) in a public pleading, attributeth all propriety to the law civil, *Let the civil law*, saith he, *be once abandoned, or but negligently guarded, (not to say oppressed,) and there is nothing, that any man can* [128] *be sure to receive from his ancestor, or leave to his children.* And again; *Take away the civil law, and no man knows what is his own, and what another man's.** Seeing therefore the introduction of *propriety* is an effect of commonwealth; which can do nothing but by the person that represents it, it is the act only of the sovereign; and consisteth in the laws, which none can make that have not the sovereign power. And this they well knew of old, who called that νόμος, (that is to say, *distribution*,) which we call law; and defined justice, by *distributing* to every man *his own*.

All private estates of land proceed originally from the arbitrary distribution of the sovereign.

6. In this distribution, the first law, is for division of the land itself: wherein the sovereign assigneth to every man a portion, according as he, and not according as any subject, or any number of them, shall judge agreeable to equity, and the common good. The children of Israel, were a commonwealth in the wilderness; but wanted the commodities of the earth, till they were masters of the

Land of Promise; which afterward was divided amongst them, not by their own discretion, but by the discretion of Eleazar the Priest, and Joshua their General: who when there were twelve tribes, making them thirteen by subdivision of the tribe of Joseph; made nevertheless but twelve portions of the land; and ordained for the tribe of Levi no land; but assigned them the tenth part of the whole fruits; which division was therefore arbitrary. And though a people coming into possession of a land by war, do not always exterminate the ancient inhabitants, (as did the Jews,) but leave to many, or most, or all of them their estates; yet it is manifest they hold them afterwards, as of the victors' distribution; as the people of England held all theirs of William the Conqueror.

7. From whence we may collect, that the propriety which a subject hath in his lands, consisteth in a right to exclude all other subjects from the use of them; and not to exclude their sovereign, be it an assembly, or a monarch. For seeing the sovereign, that is to say, the commonwealth (whose person he representeth,) is understood to do nothing but in order to the common peace and security, this distribution of lands, is to be understood as done in order to the same: and consequently, whatsoever distribution another shall make in prejudice thereof, is contrary to the will of every subject, that committed his peace, and safety to his discretion, and conscience; and therefore by the will of every one of them, is to be reputed void. It is true, that a sovereign monarch, or the greater part of a sovereign assembly, may ordain the doing of many things in pursuit of their passions, contrary to their own consciences, which is a breach of trust, and of the law of nature; but this is not enough to authorize any subject, either to make war upon, or so much as to accuse of injustice, or any way to speak evil of their sovereign; because they have authorized all his actions, and in bestowing the sovereign power, made them their own. But in what cases the commands of sovereigns are contrary to equity, and the law of nature, is to be considered hereafter in another place.*

Propriety of a subject excludes not the dominion of the sovereign, but only of another subject.

8. In the distribution of land, the commonwealth itself, may be conceived to have a portion, and possess, and improve the same by their representative; and that such portion may be made sufficient, to sustain the whole expense to the common peace, and defence necessarily required: which were very true, if there could be any representative conceived free from human passions, and infirmities. But the nature of men being as it is, the setting forth of public land,

[129]
The public is not to be dieted.

165

or of any certain revenue for the commonwealth, is in vain; and tendeth to the dissolution of government, and to the condition of mere nature, and war, as soon as ever the sovereign power falleth into the hands of a monarch, or of an assembly, that are either too negligent of money, or too hazardous in engaging the public stock into a long or costly war. Commonwealths can endure no diet: for seeing their expense is not limited by their own appetite, but by external accidents, and the appetites of their neighbours, the public riches cannot be limited by other limits, than those which the emergent occasions shall require. And whereas in England, there were by the Conqueror, divers lands reserved to his own use, (besides forests, and chases, either for his recreation, or preservation of woods,) and divers services reserved on the land he gave his subjects; yet it seems they were not reserved for his maintenance in his public, but in his natural capacity: for he, and his successors did for all that, lay arbitrary taxes on all subjects' land, when they judged it necessary. Or if those public lands, and services, were ordained as a sufficient maintenance of the commonwealth, it was contrary to the scope of the institution; being (as it appeared by those ensuing taxes) insufficient, and (as it appears by the late small revenue of the crown) subject to alienation, and diminution. It is therefore in vain, to assign a portion to the commonwealth; which may sell, or give it away; and does sell, and give it away, when 'tis done by their representative.

The places and matter of traffic depend, as their distribution, on the sovereign.

9. As the distribution of lands at home; so also to assign in what places, and for what commodities, the subject shall traffic abroad, belongeth to the sovereign. For if it did belong to private persons to use their own discretion therein, some of them would be drawn for gain, both to furnish the enemy with means to hurt the commonwealth, and hurt it themselves, by importing such things, as pleasing men's appetites, be nevertheless noxious, or at least unprofitable to them. And therefore it belongeth to the commonwealth (that is, to the sovereign only,) to approve, or disapprove both of the places, and matter of foreign traffic.

The laws of transferring propriety belong also to the sovereign.

10. Further, seeing it is not enough to the sustentation [upkeep] of a commonwealth, that every man have a propriety in a portion of land, or in some few commodities, or a natural property in some useful art, and that there is no art in the world, but is necessary either for the being, or well-being almost of every particular man; it is necessary, that men distribute that which they can spare, and

transfer their propriety therein, mutually one to another, by exchange, and mutual contract. And therefore it belongeth to the [130] commonwealth, (that is to say, to the sovereign,) to appoint in what manner, all kinds of contract between subjects, (as buying, selling, exchanging, borrowing, lending, letting, and taking to hire,) are to be made; and by what words and signs they shall be understood for valid. And for the matter, and distribution of the nourishment, to the several members of the commonwealth, thus much (considering the model of the whole work) is sufficient.

11. By concoction, I understand the reducing of all commodities, which are not presently consumed, but reserved for nourishment in time to come, to something of equal value, and withal so portable, as not to hinder the motion of men from place to place; to the end a man may have in what place soever, such nourishment as the place affordeth. And this is nothing else but gold, and silver, and money. For gold and silver, being (as it happens) almost in all countries of the world highly valued, is a commodious measure of the value of all things else between nations; and money (of what matter soever coined by the sovereign of a commonwealth,) is a sufficient measure of the value of all things else, between the subjects of that commonwealth. By the means of which measures, all commodities, movable and immovable, are made to accompany a man to all places of his resort, within and without the place of his ordinary residence; and the same passeth from man to man, within the commonwealth; and goes round about, nourishing (as it passeth) every part thereof; in so much as this concoction, is as it were the sanguification of the commonwealth: for natural blood is in like manner made of the fruits of the earth; and circulating, nourisheth by the way every member of the body of man. *Money the blood of a commonwealth.*

12. And because silver and gold, have their value from the matter itself; they have first this privilege, that the value of them cannot be altered by the power of one, nor of a few commonwealths; as being a common measure of the commodities of all places. But base money, may easily be enhanced, or abased. Secondly, they have the privilege to make commonwealths move, and stretch out their arms, when need is, into foreign countries; and supply, not only private subjects that travel, but also whole armies with provision. But that coin, which is not considerable for the matter, but for the stamp of the place, being unable to endure change of air, hath its effect at home only; where also it is subject to the change of laws, and thereby

to have the value diminished, to the prejudice many times of those that have it.

The conduits and way of money to the public use.

13. The conduits, and ways by which it is conveyed to the public use, are of two sorts; one, that conveyeth it to the public coffers; the other, that issueth the same out again for public payments. Of the first sort, are collectors, receivers, and treasurers; of the second are the treasurers again, and the officers appointed for payment of several public or private ministers. And in this also, the artificial man maintains his resemblance with the natural; whose veins receiving the blood from the several parts of the body, carry it to the [131] heart; where being made vital, the heart by the arteries sends it out again, to enliven, and enable for motion all the members of the same.*

The children of a commonwealth colonies.

14. The procreation, or children of a commonwealth, are those we call *plantations*, or *colonies*; which are numbers of men sent out from the commonwealth, under a conductor, or governor, to inhabit a foreign country, either formerly void of inhabitants, or made void then by war. And when a colony is settled, they are either a commonwealth of themselves, discharged of their subjection to their sovereign that sent them, (as hath been done by many commonwealths, of ancient time,) in which case the commonwealth from which they went, was called their metropolis, or mother, and requires no more of them, than fathers require of the children, whom they emancipate, and make free from their domestic government, which is honour, and friendship; or else they remain united to their metropolis, as were the colonies of the people of Rome; and then they are no commonwealths themselves, but provinces, and parts of the commonwealth that sent them. So that the right of colonies (saving honour, and league with their metropolis,) dependeth wholly on their licence, or letters, by which their sovereign authorised them to plant.

CHAPTER XXV

OF COUNSEL

Counsel what.

1. How fallacious it is to judge of the nature of things, by the ordinary and inconstant use of words, appeareth in nothing more, than in the confusion of counsels, and commands,* arising from the

imperative manner of speaking in them both, and in many other occasions besides. For the words *do this*, are the words not only of him that commandeth; but also of him that giveth counsel; and of him that exhorteth; and yet there are but few, that see not that these are very different things; or that cannot distinguish between them, when they perceive who it is that speaketh, and to whom the speech is directed, and upon what occasion. But finding those phrases in men's writings, and being not able, or not willing to enter into a consideration of the circumstances, they mistake sometimes the precepts of counsellors, for the precepts of them that command; and sometimes the contrary; according as it best agreeth with the conclusions they would infer, or the actions they approve. To avoid which mistakes, and render to those terms of commanding, counselling, and exhorting, their proper and distinct significations, I define them thus.

2. COMMAND is, where a man saith, *do this*, or *do not this*, without expecting other reason than the will of him that says it. From this it followeth manifestly, that he that commandeth, pretendeth thereby his own benefit: for the reason of his command is his own will only, and the proper object of every man's will, is some good to himself.

Differences between command and counsel. [132]

3. COUNSEL, is where a man saith, *do*, or *do not this*, and deduceth his reasons from the benefit that arriveth by it to him to whom he saith it. And from this it is evident, that he that giveth counsel, pretendeth only (whatsoever he intendeth) the good of him, to whom he giveth it.

4. Therefore between counsel and command, one great difference is, that command is directed to a man's own benefit; and counsel to the benefit of another man. And from this ariseth another difference, that a man may be obliged to do what he is commanded; as when he hath covenanted to obey: but he cannot be obliged to do as he is counselled, because the hurt of not following it, is his own; or if he should covenant to follow it, then is the counsel turned into the nature of a command. A third difference between them is, that no man can pretend a right to be of another man's counsel; because he is not to pretend benefit by it to himself: but to demand right to counsel another, argues a will to know his designs, or to gain some other good to himself; which (as I said before) is of every man's will the proper object.

5. This also is incident to the nature of counsel; that whatsoever

it be, he that asketh it, cannot in equity accuse, or punish it: for to ask counsel of another, is to permit him to give such counsel as he shall think best; and consequently, he that giveth counsel to his sovereign, (whether a monarch, or an assembly) when he asketh it, cannot in equity be punished for it, whether the same be conformable to the opinion of the most, or not, so it be to the proposition in debate. For if the sense of the assembly can be taken notice of, before the debate be ended, they should neither ask, nor take any further counsel; for the sense of the assembly, is the resolution of the debate, and end of all deliberation. And generally he that demandeth counsel, is author of it; and therefore cannot punish it; and what the sovereign cannot, no man else can. But if one subject giveth counsel to another, to do anything contrary to the laws, whether that counsel proceed from evil intention, or from ignorance only, it is punishable by the commonwealth; because ignorance of the law, is no good excuse, where every man is bound to take notice of the laws to which he is subject.

Exhortation and dehortation, what.

6. EXHORTATION and DEHORTATION is counsel, accompanied with signs in him that giveth it, of vehement desire to have it followed: or to say it more briefly, *counsel vehemently pressed*. For he that exhorteth, doth not deduce the consequences of what he adviseth to be done, and tie himself therein to the rigour of true reasoning; but encourages him he counselleth, to action: as he that dehorteth, deterreth him from it. And, therefore, they have in their speeches, a regard to the common passions, and opinions of men, in deducing their reasons; and make use of similitudes, metaphors, examples, and other tools of oratory, to persuade their hearers of the utility, honour, or justice of following their advice.

[133]   7. From whence may be inferred, first, that exhortation and dehortation is directed to the good of him that giveth the counsel, not of him that asketh it, which is contrary to the duty of a counsellor; who (by the definition of counsel) ought to regard, not his own benefit, but his whom he adviseth. And that he directeth his counsel to his own benefit, is manifest enough, by the long and vehement urging, or by the artificial giving thereof; which being not required of him, and consequently proceeding from his own occasions, is directed principally to his own benefit, and but accidentally to the good of him that is counselled, or not at all.

8. Secondly, that the use of exhortation and dehortation lieth only where a man is to speak to a multitude; because when the

speech is addressed to one, he may interrupt him, and examine his reasons more rigorously, than can be done in a multitude; which are too many to enter into dispute, and dialogue with him that speaketh indifferently to them all at once.

9. Thirdly, that they that exhort and dehort, where they are required to give counsel, are corrupt counsellors, and as it were bribed by their own interest. For though the counsel they give be never so good; yet he that gives it, is no more a good counsellor, than he that giveth a just sentence for a reward, is a just judge. But where a man may lawfully command, as a father in his family, or a leader in an army, his exhortations and dehortations, are not only lawful, but also necessary, and laudable: but then they are no more counsels, but commands; which when they are for execution of sour labour, sometimes necessity, and always humanity requireth to be sweetened in the delivery, by encouragement, and in the tune and phrase of counsel, rather than in harsher language of command.

10.* Examples of the difference between command and counsel, we may take from the forms of speech that express them in Holy Scripture. *Have no other Gods but me; make to thyself no graven image; take not God's name in vain; sanctify the sabbath; honour thy parents; kill not; steal not, &c.* are commands; because the reason for which we are to obey them, is drawn from the will of God our king, whom we are obliged to obey. But these words, *Sell all thou hast; give it to the poor; and follow me*, are counsel; because the reason for which we are to do so, is drawn from our own benefit; which is this, that we shall have *treasure in Heaven*. These words, *Go into the village over against you, and you shall find an ass tied, and her colt; loose her, and bring her to me*, are a command: for the reason of their fact is drawn from the will of their Master: but these words, *Repent and be baptized in the name of Jesus*, are counsel; because the reason why we should so do, tendeth not to any benefit of God Almighty, who shall still be king in what manner soever we rebel; but of ourselves, who have no other means of avoiding the punishment hanging over us for our sins past.

11. As the difference of counsel from command, hath been now deduced from the nature of counsel, consisting in a deducing of the benefit, or hurt that may arise to him that is to be counselled, by the necessary or probable consequences of the action he propoundeth; so may also the differences between *apt*, and *inept* counsellors be

Differences of fit and unfit counsellors.

[134]

derived from the same. For experience,* being but memory of the consequences of like actions formerly observed, and counsel but the speech whereby that experience is made known to another; the virtues, and defects of counsel, are the same with the virtues, and defects intellectual: and to the person of a commonwealth, his counsellors serve him in the place of memory, and mental discourse. But with this resemblance of the commonwealth, to a natural man, there is one dissimilitude joined, of great importance; which is, that a natural man receiveth his experience, from the natural objects of sense, which work upon him without passion, or interest of their own; whereas they that give counsel to the representative person of a commonwealth, may have, and have often their particular ends, and passions, that render their counsels always suspected, and many times unfaithful. And therefore we may set down for the first condition of a good counsellor, *that his ends, and interests, be not inconsistent with the ends and interests of him he counselleth.*

12. Secondly, because the office of a counsellor, when an action comes into deliberation, is to make manifest the consequences of it, in such manner, as he that is counselled may be truly and evidently informed; he ought to propound his advice, in such form of speech, as may make the truth most evidently appear; that is to say, with as firm ratiocination, as significant and proper language, and as briefly, as the evidence will permit. And therefore *rash, and unevident inferences*; (such as are fetched only from examples, or authority of books, and are not arguments of what is good, or evil but witnesses of fact, or of opinion;) *obscure, confused, and ambiguous expressions, also all metaphorical speeches, tending to the stirring up of passion*, (because such reasoning, and such expressions, are useful only to deceive, or to lead him we counsel towards other ends than his own) *are repugnant to the office of a counsellor.*

13. Thirdly, because the ability of counselling proceedeth from experience, and long study; and no man is presumed to have experience in all those things that to the administration of a great commonwealth are necessary to be known, *no man is presumed to be a good counsellor, but in such business, as he hath not only been much versed in, but hath also much meditated on, and considered*. For seeing the business of a commonwealth is this, to preserve the people in peace at home, and defend them against foreign invasion, we shall find, it requires great knowledge of the disposition of mankind, of

the rights of government, and of the nature of equity, law, justice, and honour, not to be attained without study; and of the strength, commodities, places, both of their own country, and their neighbours; as also of the inclinations, and designs of all nations that may any way annoy them. And this is not attained to, without much experience. Of which things, not only the whole sum, but every one of the particulars requires the age, and observation of a man in years, [135] and of more than ordinary study. The wit required for counsel, as I have said before (chap. 8) is judgment. And the differences of men in that point come from different education, of some to one kind of study, or business, and of others to another. When for the doing of any thing, there be infallible rules, (as in engines, and edifices, the rules of geometry,) all the experience of the world cannot equal his counsel, that has learnt, or found out the rule. And when there is no such rule, he that hath most experience in that particular kind of business, has therein the best judgment, and is the best counsellor.

14. Fourthly, to be able to give counsel to a commonwealth, in a business that hath reference to another commonwealth, *it is necessary to be acquainted with the intelligences, and letters* that come from thence, *and with all the records of treaties, and other transactions of state* between them; which none can do, but such as the representative shall think fit. By which we may see, that they who are not called to counsel, can have no good counsel in such cases to obtrude.

15. Fifthly, supposing the number of counsellors equal, a man is better counselled by hearing them apart, than in an assembly; and that for many causes. First, in hearing them apart, you have the advice of every man; but in an assembly many of them deliver their advice with *aye*, or *no*, or with their hands, or feet, not moved by their own sense, but by the eloquence of another, or for fear of displeasing some that have spoken, or the whole assembly, by contradiction; or for fear of appearing duller in apprehension, than those that have applauded the contrary opinion. Secondly, in an assembly of many, there cannot choose but be some whose interests are contrary to that of the public; and these their interests make passionate, and passion eloquent, and eloquence draws others into the same advice. For the passions of men, which asunder are moderate, as the heat of one brand; in an assembly are like many brands,

that inflame one another (especially when they blow one another with orations) to the setting of the commonwealth on fire, under pretence of counselling it. Thirdly, in hearing every man apart, one may examine (when there is need) the truth, or probability of his reasons, and of the grounds of the advice he gives, by frequent interruptions, and objections; which cannot be done in an assembly, where (in every difficult question) a man is rather astonied [bewildered], and dazzled with the variety of discourse upon it, than informed of the course he ought to take. Besides, there cannot be an assembly of many, called together for advice, wherein there be not some, that have the ambition to be thought eloquent, and also learned in the politics; and give not their advice with care of the business propounded, but of the applause of their motley orations made of the divers coloured threads, or shreds of authors; which is an impertinence at least, that takes away the time of serious consul-

[136] tation, and in the secret way of counselling apart, is easily avoided. Fourthly, in deliberations that ought to be kept secret, (whereof there be many occasions in public business,) the counsels of many, and especially in assemblies, are dangerous; and therefore great assemblies are necessitated to commit such affairs to lesser numbers, and of such persons as are most versed in them, and in whose fidelity they have most confidence.

16. To conclude, who is there that so far approves the taking of counsel from a great assembly of counsellors, that wisheth for, or would accept of their pains, when there is a question of marrying his children, disposing of his lands, governing his household, or managing his private estate, especially if there be amongst them such as wish not his prosperity? A man that doth his business by the help of many and prudent counsellors, with every one consulting apart in his proper element, does it best, as he that useth able seconds at tennis play, placed in their proper stations. He does next best, that useth his own judgment only; as he that has no second at all. But he that is carried up and down to his business in a framed counsel, which cannot move but by the plurality of consenting opinions, the execution whereof is commonly (out of envy, or interest) retarded by the part dissenting, does it worst of all, and is like one that is carried to the ball, though by good players, yet in a wheel-barrow, or other frame, heavy of itself, and retarded also by the inconcurrent judgments, and endeavours of them that drive it; and so much the more, as they be more that set their hands to it; and most of all, when

there is one, or more amongst them, that desire to have him lose. And though it be true, that many eyes see more than one; yet it is not to be understood of many counsellors; but then only, when the final resolution is in one man. Otherwise, because many eyes see the same thing in divers lines, and are apt to look asquint towards their private benefit; they that desire not to miss their mark, though they look about with two eyes, yet they never aim but with one; and therefore no great popular commonwealth was ever kept up, but either by a foreign enemy that united them; or by the reputation of some eminent man amongst them; or by the secret counsel of a few; or by the mutual fear of equal factions; and not by the open consultations of the assembly. And as for very little common-wealths, be they popular, or monarchical, there is no human wisdom can uphold them, longer than the jealousy lasteth of their potent neighbours.

CHAPTER XXVI

OF CIVIL LAWS*

1. BY CIVIL LAWS, I understand the laws, that men are therefore bound to observe, because they are members, not of this, or that commonwealth in particular, but of a commonwealth. For the knowledge of particular laws belongeth to them, that profess the study of the laws of their several countries; but the knowledge of civil law in general, to any man. The ancient law of Rome was called their *civil law*, from the word *civitas*, which signifies a common-wealth: and those countries, which having been under the Roman empire, and governed by that law, retain still such part thereof as they think fit, and call that part the civil law, to distinguish it from the rest of their own civil laws. But that is not it I intend to speak of here; my design being not to show what is law here, and there; but what is law; as Plato, Aristotle, Cicero, and divers others have done, without taking upon them the profession of the study of the law.

Civil law what.

[137]

2. And first it is manifest, that law in general, is not counsel, but command; nor a command of any man to any man; but only of him, whose command is addressed to one formerly obliged to obey him.

And as for civil law, it addeth only the name of the person commanding, which is *persona civitatis*, the person of the commonwealth.

3. Which considered, I define civil law in this manner. CIVIL LAW, *is to every subject, those rules, which the commonwealth hath commanded him, by word, writing, or other sufficient sign of the will, to make use of, for the distinction of right, and wrong; that is to say, of what is contrary, and what is not contrary to the rule.*

4. In which definition, there is nothing that is not at first sight evident. For every man seeth, that some laws are addressed to all the subjects in general; some to particular provinces; some to particular vocations; and some to particular men; and are therefore laws, to every of those to whom the command is directed; and to none else. As also, that laws are the rules of just, and unjust; nothing being reputed unjust, that is not contrary to some law. Likewise, that none can make laws but the commonwealth; because our subjection is to the commonwealth only: and that commands, are to be signified by sufficient signs; because a man knows not otherwise how to obey them. And therefore, whatsoever can from this definition by necessary consequence be deduced, ought to be acknowledged for truth. Now I deduce from it this that followeth.

1.
The sovereign is legislator.

5. The legislator in all commonwealths, is only the sovereign, be he one man, as in a monarchy, or one assembly of men, as in a democracy, or aristocracy. For the legislator, is he that maketh the law. And the commonwealth only, prescribes, and commandeth the observation of those rules, which we call law: therefore the commonwealth is the legislator. But the commonwealth is no person, nor has capacity to do any thing, but by the representative, (that is, the sovereign;) and therefore the sovereign is the sole legislator. For the same reason, none can abrogate a law made, but the sovereign; because a law is not abrogated, but by another law, that forbiddeth it to be put in execution.

[138]
2.
And not subject to civil law.

6. The sovereign of a commonwealth, be it an assembly, or one man, is not subject to the civil laws. For having power to make, and repeal laws, he may when he pleaseth, free himself from that subjection, by repealing those laws that trouble him, and making of new; and consequently he was free before. For he is free, that can be free when he will: nor is it possible for any person to be bound to himself; because he that can bind, can release; and therefore he that is bound to himself only, is not bound.

7. When long use obtaineth the authority of a law, it is not the
length of time that maketh the authority, but the will of the sovereign signified by his silence, (for silence is sometimes an argument of
consent;) and it is no longer law, than the sovereign shall be silent
therein. And therefore if the sovereign shall have a question of right
grounded, not upon his present will, but upon the laws formerly
made; the length of time shall bring no prejudice to his right; but the
question shall be judged by equity. For many unjust actions, and
unjust sentences, go uncontrolled a longer time, than any man can
remember. And our lawyers account no customs law, but such as are
reasonable, and that evil customs are to be abolished: but the judgment of what is reasonable, and of what is to be abolished, belongeth
to him that maketh the law, which is the sovereign assembly, or
monarch.

*3.
Use, a law
not by virtue
of time, but
of the
sovereign's
consent.*

8. The law of nature, and the civil law, contain each other, and
are of equal extent. For the laws of nature, which consist in equity,
justice, gratitude, and other moral virtues on these depending, in
the condition of mere nature (as I have said before in the end of the
fifteenth chapter,) are not properly laws, but qualities that dispose
men to peace, and obedience. When a commonwealth is once settled, then are they actually laws, and not before; as being then the
commands of the commonwealth; and therefore also civil laws: for it
is the sovereign power that obliges men to obey them. For in the
differences of private men, to declare, what is equity, what is justice,
and what is moral virtue, and to make them binding, there is need of
the ordinances of sovereign power, and punishments to be ordained
for such as shall break them; which ordinances are therefore part of
the civil law. The law of nature therefore is a part of the civil law in
all commonwealths of the world. Reciprocally also, the civil law is a
part of the dictates of nature. For justice, that is to say, performance
of covenant, and giving to every man his own, is a dictate of the law
of nature. But every subject in a commonwealth, hath covenanted to
obey the civil law; (either one with another, as when they assemble
to make a common representative, or with the representative itself
one by one, when subdued by the sword they promise obedience,
that they may receive life;) and therefore obedience to the civil law
is part also of the law of nature. Civil, and natural law are not
different kinds, but different parts of law; whereof one part being
written, is called civil, the other unwritten, natural. But the right of
nature, that is, the natural liberty of man, may by the civil law be

*4.
The law of
nature, and
the civil law
contain each
other.*

abridged, and restrained: nay, the end of making laws, is no other, but such restraint; without the which there cannot possibly be any

peace. And law was brought into the world for nothing else, but to limit the natural liberty of particular men, in such manner, as they might not hurt, but assist one another, and join together against a common enemy.

5.

Provincial laws are not made by custom, but by the sovereign power.

9. If the sovereign of one commonwealth, subdue a people that have lived under other written laws, and afterwards govern them by the same laws, by which they were governed before; yet those laws are the civil laws of the victor, and not of the vanquished commonwealth. For the legislator is he, not by whose authority the laws were first made, but by whose authority they now continue to be laws. And therefore where there be divers provinces, within the dominion of a commonwealth, and in those provinces diversity of laws, which commonly are called the customs of each several province, we are not to understand that such customs have their force, only from length of time; but that they were anciently laws written, or otherwise made known, for the constitutions, and statutes of their sovereigns; and are now laws, not by virtue of the prescription of time, but by the constitutions of their present sovereigns. But if an unwritten law, in all the provinces of a dominion, shall be generally observed, and no iniquity appear in the use thereof; that law can be no other but a law of nature, equally obliging all mankind.

6.

Some foolish opinions of lawyers concerning the making of laws.

10. Seeing then all laws, written, and unwritten, have their authority, and force, from the will of the commonwealth; that is to say, from the will of the representative; which in a monarchy is the monarch, and in other commonwealths the sovereign assembly; a man may wonder from whence proceed such opinions, as are found in the books of lawyers of eminence in several commonwealths, directly, or by consequence making the legislative power depend on private men, or subordinate judges. As for example, *that the common law, hath no controller but the parliament*; which is true only where a parliament has the sovereign power, and cannot be assembled, nor dissolved, but by their own discretion. For if there be a right in any else to dissolve them, there is a right also to control them, and consequently to control their controllings. And if there be no such right, then the controller of laws is not *parliamentum*, but *rex in parliamento*. And where a parliament is sovereign, if it should assemble never so many, or so wise men, from the countries subject to

them, for whatsoever cause; yet there is no man will believe, that such an assembly hath thereby acquired to themselves a legislative power. *Item*, that the two arms of a commonwealth, are *force and justice; the first whereof is in the king; the other deposited in the hands of the parliament*. As if a commonwealth could consist, where the force were in any hand, which justice had not the authority to command and govern.

11. That law can never be against reason, our lawyers are agreed; and that not the letter, (that is every construction of it,) but that which is according to the intention of the legislator, is the law. And it is true: but the doubt is, of whose reason it is, that shall be received for law. It is not meant of any private reason; for then there would be as much contradiction in the laws, as there is in the Schools; nor yet, (as Sir Edward Coke* makes it,) an *artificial perfection of reason, gotten by long study, observation, and experience*, (as his was.) For it is possible long study may increase, and confirm erroneous sentences: and where men build on false grounds, the more they build, the greater is the ruin: and of those that study, and observe with equal time, and diligence, the reasons and resolutions are, and must remain discordant: and therefore it is not that *juris prudentia*, or wisdom of subordinate judges; but the reason of this our artificial man the commonwealth, and his command, that maketh law: and the commonwealth being in their representative but one person, there cannot easily arise any contradiction in the laws; and when there doth, the same reason is able, by interpretation, or alteration, to take it away. In all courts of justice, the sovereign (which is the person of the commonwealth,) is he that judgeth: the subordinate judge, ought to have regard to the reason, which moved his sovereign to make such law, that his sentence may be according thereunto; which then is his sovereign's sentence; otherwise it is his own, and an unjust one.

12. From this, that the law is a command, and a command consisteth in declaration, or manifestation of the will of him that commandeth, by voice, writing, or some other sufficient argument of the same, we may understand, that the command of the commonwealth, is law only to those, that have means to take notice of it. Over natural fools, children, or madmen there is no law, no more than over brute beasts; nor are they capable of the title of just, or unjust; because they had never power to make any covenant, or to understand the consequences thereof; and consequently never took upon

7.

[140]

Sir Edw. Coke upon Littleton, lib. 2, ch. 6, fol. 97, b.

8.

Law made, if not also made known, is no law.

them to authorize the actions of any sovereign, as they must do that make to themselves a commonwealth. And as those from whom nature, or accident hath taken away the notice of all laws in general; so also every man, from whom any accident, not proceeding from his own default, hath taken away the means to take notice of any particular law, is excused, if he observe it not; and to speak properly, that law is no law to him. It is therefore necessary, to consider in this place, what arguments, and signs be sufficient for the knowledge of what is the law; that is to say, what is the will of the sovereign, as well in monarchies, as in other forms of government.

Unwritten laws are all of them laws of nature. 13. And first, if it be a law that obliges all the subjects without exception, and is not written, nor otherwise published in such places as they may take notice thereof, it is a law of nature. For whatsoever men are to take knowledge of for law, not upon other men's words, but every one from his own reason, must be such as is agreeable to the reason of all men; which no law can be, but the law of nature. The laws of nature therefore need not any publishing, nor proclamation; as being contained in this one sentence, approved by all the world, *Do not that to another, which thou thinkest unreasonable to be done by another to thyself.*

[141] 14. Secondly, if it be a law that obliges only some condition of men, or one particular man, and be not written, nor published by word, then also it is a law of nature; and known by the same arguments, and signs, that distinguish those in such a condition, from other subjects. For whatsoever law is not written, or some way published by him that makes it law, can be known no way, but by the reason of him that is to obey it; and is therefore also a law not only civil, but natural. For example, if the sovereign employ a public minister, without written instructions what to do; he is obliged to take for instructions the dictates of reason; as if he make a judge, the judge is to take notice, that his sentence ought to be according to the reason of his sovereign, which being always understood to be equity, he is bound to it by the law of nature: or if an ambassador, he is (in all things not contained in his written instructions) to take for instruction that which reason dictates to be most conducing to his sovereign's interests; and so of all other ministers of the sovereignty, public and private. All which instructions of natural reason may be comprehended under one name of *fidelity*; which is a branch of natural justice.

15. The law of nature excepted, it belongeth to the essence of all other laws, to be made known, to every man that shall be obliged to obey them, either by word, or writing, or some other act, known to proceed from the sovereign authority. For the will of another, cannot be understood, but by his own word, or act, or by conjecture taken from his scope and purpose; which in the person of the commonwealth, is to be supposed always consonant to equity and reason. And in ancient time, before letters were in common use, the laws were many times put into verse; that the rude people taking pleasure in singing, or reciting them, might the more easily retain them in memory. And for the same reason Solomon (*Prov.* 7. 3) adviseth a man, to bind the ten commandments upon his ten fingers. And for the law which Moses gave to the people of Israel at the renewing of the covenant (*Deut.* 11. 19), he biddeth them to teach it their children, by discoursing of it both at home, and upon the way; at going to bed, and at rising from bed; and to write it upon the posts, and doors of their houses; and (*Deut.* 31. 12) to assemble the people, man, woman, and child, to hear it read.

16. Nor is it enough the law be written, and published; but also that there be manifest signs, that it proceedeth from the will of the sovereign. For private men, when they have, or think they have force enough to secure their unjust designs, and convoy them safely to their ambitious ends, may publish for laws what they please, without, or against the legislative authority. There is therefore requisite, not only a declaration of the law, but also sufficient signs of the author, and authority. The author, or legislator is supposed in every commonwealth to be evident, because he is the sovereign, who having been constituted by the consent of every one, is supposed by every one to be sufficiently known. And though the ignorance, and security of men be such, for the most part, as that when the memory of the first constitution of their commonwealth is worn out, they do not consider, by whose power they used to be defended against their enemies, and to have their industry protected, and to be righted when injury is done them; yet because no man that considers, can make question of it, no excuse can be derived from the ignorance of where the sovereignty is placed. And it is a dictate of natural reason, and consequently an evident law of nature, that no man ought to weaken that power, the protection whereof he hath himself demanded, or wittingly received against others. Therefore of who is

Nothing is law where the legislator cannot be known.

[142]

sovereign, no man, but by his own fault, (whatsoever evil men suggest,) can make any doubt. The difficulty consisteth in the evidence of the authority derived from him; the removing whereof, dependeth on the knowledge of the public registers, public counsels, public ministers, and public seals; by which all laws are sufficiently verified; verified, I say, not authorized: for the verification, is but the testimony and record, not the authority of the law; which consisteth in the command of the sovereign only.

Difference between verifying and authorizing.

The law verified by the subordinate judge.

17. If therefore a man have a question of injury, depending on the law of nature; that is to say, on common equity; the sentence of the judge, that by commission hath authority to take cognizance of such causes, is a sufficient verification of the law of nature in that individual case. For though the advice of one that professeth the study of the law, be useful for the avoiding of contention; yet it is but advice: 'tis the judge must tell men what is law, upon the hearing of the controversy.

By the public registers.

18. But when the question is of injury, or crime, upon a written law; every man by recourse to the registers, by himself, or others, may (if he will) be sufficiently informed, before he do such injury, or commit the crime, whether it be an injury, or not: nay he ought to do so: for when a man doubts whether the act he goeth about, be just, or unjust; and may inform himself, if he will; the doing is unlawful. In like manner, he that supposeth himself injured, in a case determined by the written law, which he may by himself, or others see and consider; if he complain before he consults with the law, he does unjustly, and bewrayeth a disposition rather to vex other men, than to demand his own right.

By letters patent, and public seal.

19. If the question be of obedience to a public officer; to have seen his commission, with the public seal, and heard it read; or to have had the means to be informed of it, if a man would, is a sufficient verification of his authority. For every man is obliged to do his best endeavour, to inform himself of all written laws, that may concern his own future actions.

The interpretation of the law dependeth on the sovereign power.

20. The legislator known; and the laws, either by writing, or by the light of nature, sufficiently published; there wanteth yet another very material circumstance to make them obligatory. For it is not the letter, but the intendment, or meaning; that is to say, the authentic interpretation of the law (which is the sense of the legislator,) in which the nature of the law consisteth; and therefore the interpretation of all laws dependeth on the authority sovereign; and the

[143]

interpreters can be none but those, which the sovereign, (to whom only the subject oweth obedience) shall appoint. For else, by the craft of an interpreter, the law may be made to bear a sense, contrary to that of the sovereign; by which means the interpreter becomes the legislator.

21. All laws, written, and unwritten, have need of interpretation. *All laws need* The unwritten law of nature, though it be easy to such, as without *interpretation.* partiality, and passion, make use of their natural reason, and therefore leaves the violators thereof without excuse; yet considering there be very few, perhaps none, that in some cases are not blinded by self-love, or some other passion, it is now become of all laws the most obscure; and has consequently the greatest need of able interpreters. The written laws, if they be short, are easily misinterpreted, from the divers significations of a word, or two: if long, they be more obscure by the divers significations of many words: insomuch as no written law, delivered in few, or many words, can be well understood, without a perfect understanding of the final causes [purposes], for which the law was made; the knowledge of which final causes is in the legislator. To him therefore there cannot be any knot in the law, insoluble; either by finding out the ends, to undo it by; or else by making what ends he will, (as Alexander did with his sword in the Gordian knot,) by the legislative power; which no other interpreter can do.

22. The interpretation of the laws of nature, in a commonwealth, *The* dependeth not on the books of moral philosophy. The authority of *authentical* writers, without the authority of the commonwealth, maketh not *interpretation* their opinions law, be they never so true. That which I have written *of law is not* in this treatise, concerning the moral virtues, and of their necessity, *writers.* for the procuring, and maintaining peace, though it be evident truth, is not therefore presently law; but because in all commonwealths in the world, it is part of the civil law. For though it be naturally reasonable; yet it is by the sovereign power that it is law: otherwise, it were a great error, to call the laws of nature unwritten law; whereof we see so many volumes published by divers authors, and in them so many contradictions of one another, and of themselves.

23. The interpretation of the law of nature, is the sentence of the *The interpreter of* judge constituted by the sovereign authority, to hear and determine *the law is the judge* such controversies, as depend thereon; and consisteth in the appli- *giving sentence* viva cation of the law to the present case. For in the act of judicature, the *voce in every particular case.*

judge doth no more but consider, whether the demand of the party, be consonant to natural reason, and equity; and the sentence he giveth, is therefore the interpretation of the law of nature; which interpretation is authentic; not because it is his private sentence; but because he giveth it by authority of the sovereign, whereby it becomes the sovereign's sentence; which is law for that time, to the parties pleading.

[144]

The sentence of a judge does not bind him, or another judge to give like sentence in like cases ever after.

24. But because there is no judge subordinate, nor sovereign, but may err in a judgment of equity; if afterward in another like case he find it more consonant to equity to give a contrary sentence, he is obliged to do it. No man's error becomes his own law; nor obliges him to persist in it. Neither (for the same reason) becomes it a law to other judges, though sworn to follow it. For though a wrong sentence given by authority of the sovereign, if he know and allow it, in such laws as are mutable, be a constitution of a new law, in cases, in which every little circumstance is the same; yet in laws immutable, such as are the laws of nature, they are no laws to the same, or other judges, in the like cases for ever after. Princes succeed one another; and one judge passeth, another cometh; nay, heaven and earth shall pass; but not one tittle of the law of nature shall pass; for it is the eternal law of God. Therefore all the sentences of precedent judges that have ever been, cannot altogether make a law contrary to natural equity: nor any examples of former judges, can warrant an unreasonable sentence, or discharge the present judge of the trouble of studying what is equity (in the case he is to judge,) from the principles of his own natural reason. For example sake, 'tis against the law of nature, *to punish the innocent*; and innocent is he that acquitteth himself judicially, and is acknowledged for innocent by the judge. Put the case now, that a man is accused of a capital crime, and seeing the power and malice of some enemy, and the frequent corruption and partiality of judges, runneth away for fear of the event, and afterwards is taken, and brought to a legal trial, and maketh it sufficiently appear, he was not guilty of the crime, and being thereof acquitted, is nevertheless condemned to lose his goods; this is a manifest condemnation of the innocent. I say therefore, that there is no place in the world, where this can be an interpretation of a law of nature, or be made a law by the sentences of precedent judges, that had done the same. For he that judged it first, judged unjustly; and no injustice can be a pattern of judgment to succeeding judges. A

written law may forbid innocent men to fly, and they may be punished for flying: but that flying for fear of injury, should be taken for
a presumption of guilt, after a man is already absolved of the crime
judicially, is contrary to the nature of a presumption, which hath no
place after judgment given. Yet this is set down by a great lawyer*
for the common law of England. *If a man* (saith he) *that is innocent,
be accused of felony, and for fear flyeth for the same; albeit he judicially
acquitteth himself of the felony; yet if it be found that he fled for the
felony, he shall notwithstanding his innocency, forfeit all his goods,
chattels, debts, and duties. For as to the forfeiture of them, the law will
admit no proof against the presumption in law, grounded upon his flight.*
Here you see, *an innocent man, judicially acquitted, notwithstanding
his innocency*, (when no written law forbad him to fly) after his
acquittal, *upon a presumption in law*, condemned to lose all the goods
he hath. If the law ground upon his flight a presumption of the fact,
(which was capital,) the sentence ought to have been capital: if the   [145]
presumption were not of the fact, for what then ought he to lose his
goods? This therefore is no law of England; nor is the condemnation
grounded upon a presumption of law, but upon the presumption of
the judges. It is also against law, to say that no proof shall be
admitted against a presumption of law. For all judges, sovereign and
subordinate, if they refuse to hear proof, refuse to do justice: for
though the sentence be just, yet the judges that condemn without
hearing the proofs offered, are unjust judges; and their presumption
is but prejudice; which no man ought to bring with him to the seat
of justice, whatsoever precedent judgments, or examples he shall
pretend to follow. There be other things of this nature, wherein
men's judgments have been perverted, by trusting to precedents:
but this is enough to show, that though the sentence of the judge, be
a law to the party pleading, yet it is no law to any judge, that shall
succeed him in that office.

25. In like manner, when question is of the meaning of written
laws, he is not the interpreter of them, that writeth a commentary
upon them. For commentaries are commonly more subject to cavil,
than the text; and therefore need other commentaries; and so there
will be no end of such interpretation. And therefore unless there be
an interpreter authorized by the sovereign, from which the subordinate judges are not to recede, the interpreter can be no other than
the ordinary judges, in the same manner, as they are in cases of the

unwritten law; and their sentences are to be taken by them that plead, for laws in that particular case; but not to bind other judges, in like cases to give like judgments. For a judge may err in the interpretation even of written laws; but no error of a subordinate judge, can change the law, which is the general sentence of the sovereign.

The difference between the letter and sentence of the law.

26. In written laws, men use to make a difference between the letter, and the sentence of the law: and when by the letter, is meant whatsoever can be gathered from the bare words, 'tis well distinguished. For the significations of almost all words, are either in themselves, or in the metaphorical use of them, ambiguous; and may be drawn in argument, to make many senses; but there is only one sense of the law. But if by the letter, be meant the literal sense, then the letter, and the sentence or intention of the law, is all one. For the literal sense is that, which the legislator intended, should by the letter of the law be signified. Now the intention of the legislator is always supposed to be equity: for it were a great contumely for a judge to think otherwise of the sovereign. He ought therefore, if the words of the law do not fully authorize a reasonable sentence, to supply it with the law of nature; or if the case be difficult, to respite [postpone] judgment till he have received more ample authority. For example, a written law ordaineth, that he which is thrust out of his house by force, shall be restored by force: it happens that a man by negligence leaves his house empty, and returning is kept out by force, in which case there is no special law ordained. It is evident,

[146] that this case is contained in the same law: for else there is no remedy for him at all; which is to be supposed against the intention of the legislator. Again, the word of the law, commandeth to judge according to the evidence: a man is accused falsely of a fact, which the judge himself saw done by another; and not by him that is accused. In this case neither shall the letter of the law be followed to the condemnation of the innocent, nor shall the judge give sentence against the evidence of the witnesses; because the letter of the law is to the contrary: but procure of the sovereign that another be made judge, and himself witness. So that the incommodity that follows the bare words of a written law, may lead him to the intention of the law, whereby to interpret the same the better; though no incommodity can warrant a sentence against the law. For every judge of right, and wrong, is not judge of what is commodious, or incommodious to the commonwealth.

27. The abilities required in a good interpreter of the law, that is *The abilities* to say, in a good judge, are not the same with those of an advocate; *required in a* namely the study of the laws. For a judge, as he ought to take notice *judge.* of the fact, from none but the witnesses; so also he ought to take notice of the law from nothing but the statutes, and constitutions of the sovereign, alleged in the pleading, or declared to him by some that have authority from the sovereign power to declare them; and need not take care beforehand, what he shall judge; for it shall be given him what he shall say concerning the fact, by witnesses; and what he shall say in point of law, from those that shall in their pleadings show it, and by authority interpret it upon the place. The Lords of Parliament in England were judges, and most difficult causes have been heard and determined by them; yet few of them were much versed in the study of the laws, and fewer had made profession of them: and though they consulted with lawyers, that were appointed to be present there for that purpose; yet they alone had the authority of giving sentence. In like manner, in the ordinary trials of right, twelve men of the common people, are the judges, and give sentence, not only of the fact, but of the right; and pronounce simply for the complainant, or for the defendant; that is to say, are judges, not only of the fact, but also of the right: and in a question of crime, not only determine whether done, or not done; but also whether it be *murder, homicide, felony, assault*, and the like, which are determinations of law: but because they are not supposed to know the law of themselves, there is one that hath authority to inform them of it, in the particular case they are to judge of. But yet if they judge not according to that he tells them, they are not subject thereby to any penalty; unless it be made appear, that they did it against their consciences, or had been corrupted by reward.

28. The things that make a good judge, or good interpreter of the laws, are, first, *a right understanding* of that principal law of nature called *equity*; which depending not on the reading of other men's writings, but on the goodness of a man's own natural reason, and meditation, is presumed to be in those most, that have had most [147] leisure, and had the most inclination to meditate thereon. Secondly, *contempt of unnecessary riches, and preferments*. Thirdly, *to be able in judgment to divest himself of all fear, anger, hatred, love, and compassion*. Fourthly, and lastly, *patience to hear; diligent attention in hearing; and memory to retain, digest, and apply what he hath heard*.

29. The difference and division of the laws, has been made in divers manners, according to the different methods, of those men that have written of them. For it is a thing that dependeth not on nature, but on the scope of the writer; and is subservient to every man's proper method. In the *Institutions* of Justinian,* we find

1.

seven sorts of civil laws. The *edicts, constitutions,* and *epistles of the prince,* that is, of the emperor; because the whole power of the people was in him. Like these, are the proclamations of the kings of England.

2.

30. *The decrees of the whole people of Rome* (comprehending the senate,) when they were put to the question by the *senate.* These were laws, at first, by the virtue of the sovereign power residing in the people; and such of them as by the emperors were not abrogated, remained laws by the authority imperial. For all laws that bind, are understood to be laws by his authority that has power to repeal them. Somewhat like to these laws, are the Acts of Parliament in England.

3.

31. *The decrees of the common people* (excluding the senate,) when they were put to the question by the *tribune* of the people. For such of them as were not abrogated by the emperors, remained laws by the authority imperial. Like to these, were the orders of the House of Commons in England.

4.

32. *Senatus consulta,* the *orders of the senate*; because when the people of Rome grew so numerous, as it was inconvenient to assemble them; it was thought fit by the emperor, that men should consult the senate, instead of the people; and these have some resemblance with the Acts of Council.

5.

33. *The edicts of praetors,* and (in some cases) of *aediles*: such as are the chief justices in the courts of England.

6.

34. *Responsa prudentum*; which were the sentences, and opinion of those lawyers, to whom the emperor gave authority to interpret the law, and to give answer to such as in matter of law demanded their advice; which answers, the judges in giving judgment were obliged by the constitutions of the emperor to observe: and should be like the reports of cases judged, if other judges be by the law of England bound to observe them. For the judges of the common law of England, are not properly judges, but *juris consulti*; of whom the judges, who are either the lords, or twelve men of the country, are in point of law to ask advice.

7.

35. Also, *unwritten customs,* (which in their own nature are an imitation of law,) by the tacit consent of the emperor, in case they be not contrary to the law of nature, are very laws.

36. Another division of laws, is into *natural* and *positive*. *Natural* are those which have been laws from all eternity; and are called not only *natural*, but also *moral* laws; consisting in the moral virtues, as justice, equity, and all habits of the mind that conduce to peace, and charity; of which I have already spoken in the fourteenth and fifteenth chapters.

Another division of law. [148]

37. *Positive*, are those which have not been from eternity; but have been made laws by the will of those that have had the sovereign power over others; and are either written, or made known to men, by some other argument of the will of their legislator.

38. Again, of positive laws some are *human*, some *divine*; and of human positive laws, some are *distributive*, some *penal*. *Distributive* are those that determine the rights of the subjects, declaring to every man what it is, by which he acquireth and holdeth a propriety in lands, or goods, and a right or liberty of action: and these speak to all the subjects. *Penal* are those, which declare, what penalty shall be inflicted on those that violate the law; and speak to the ministers and officers ordained for execution. For though every one ought to be informed of the punishments ordained beforehand for their transgression; nevertheless the command is not addressed to the delinquent, (who cannot be supposed will faithfully punish himself,) but to public ministers appointed to see the penalty executed. And these penal laws are for the most part written together with the laws distributive; and are sometimes called judgments. For all laws are general judgments, or sentences of the legislator; as also every particular judgment, is a law to him, whose case is judged.

39. *Divine positive laws* (for natural laws being eternal, and universal, are all divine,) are those, which being the commandments of God, (not from all eternity, nor universally addressed to all men, but only to a certain people, or to certain persons,) are declared for such, by those whom God hath authorized to declare them. But this authority of man to declare what be these positive laws of God, how can it be known? God may command a man by a supernatural way, to deliver laws to other men. But because it is of the essence of law, that he who is to be obliged, be assured of the authority of him that declareth it, which we cannot naturally take notice to be from God, *how can a man without supernatural revelation be assured of the revelation received by the declarer?** and *how can he be bound to obey them?*

Divine positive law how made known to be law.

For the first question, how a man can be assured of the revelation of another, without a revelation particularly to himself, it is evidently impossible. For though a man may be induced to believe such revelation, from the miracles they see him do, or from seeing the extraordinary sanctity of his life, or from seeing the extraordinary wisdom, or extraordinary felicity of his actions, all which are marks of God's extraordinary favour; yet they are not assured evidences of special revelation. Miracles are marvellous works: but that which is marvellous to one, may not be so to another. Sanctity may be feigned; and the visible felicities of this world, are most often the [149] work of God by natural, and ordinary causes. And therefore no man can infallibly know by natural reason, that another has had a supernatural revelation of God's will; but only a belief; every one (as the signs thereof shall appear greater, or lesser) a firmer or a weaker belief.

40. But for the second, how can he be bound to obey them; it is not so hard. For if the law declared, be not against the law of nature (which is undoubtedly God's law) and he undertake to obey it, he is bound by his own act; bound I say to obey it, but not bound to believe it: for men's belief, and interior cogitations, are not subject to the commands, but only to the operation of God, ordinary, or extraordinary. Faith of supernatural law, is not a fulfilling, but only an assenting to the same; and not a duty that we exhibit to God, but a gift which God freely giveth to whom he pleaseth; as also unbelief is not a breach of any of his laws; but a rejection of them all, except the laws natural. But this that I say, will be made yet clearer, by the examples and testimonies concerning this point in holy Scripture. The covenant God made with Abraham (in a supernatural manner) was thus, (*Gen.* 17. 10) *This is the covenant which thou shalt observe between me and thee and thy seed after thee.* Abraham's seed had not this revelation, nor were yet in being; yet they are a party to the covenant, and bound to obey what Abraham should declare to them for God's law; which they could not be, but in virtue of the obedience they owed to their parents; who (if they be subject to no other earthly power, as here in the case of Abraham) have sovereign power over their children, and servants. Again, where God saith to Abraham, *In thee shall all nations of the earth be blessed: for I know thou wilt command thy children, and thy house after thee to keep the way of the Lord, and to observe righteousness and judgment*, it is manifest, the obedience of his family, who had no revelation, depended on their former obligation to obey their sovereign. At Mount Sinai Moses only went up to God; the people were forbidden to approach on pain of death; yet they were bound to obey all that Moses declared to them for God's law. Upon what ground, but on this submission of their own, *Speak thou to us, and we will hear thee; but let not God speak to us, lest we die?* By which two places it sufficiently appeareth, that in a commonwealth, a subject that has no certain and assured revelation particularly to himself concerning the will of God, is to obey for such, the command of the commonwealth: for if men were at liberty, to take for God's commandments, their own dreams and fancies, or the dreams and fancies of private men; scarce two men would agree upon what are God's commandments; and yet in respect of them, every man would despise the commandments of the commonwealth. I conclude therefore, that in all things not contrary to the moral law, (that is to say, to the law of nature,) all subjects are bound to obey that for divine law, which is declared to be so, by the laws of the commonwealth. Which also is evident to any man's reason; for whatsoever is not against the law of nature, may be made law in the name of them that have the sovereign [150] power; and there is no reason men should be the less obliged by it, when it is propounded in the name of God. Besides, there is no place in the world where men are permitted to pretend other commandments of God, than are declared for such by the commonwealth. Christian states punish those that revolt from Christian religion, and all other states, those that set up any religion by them forbidden. For in whatsoever is not regulated by the commonwealth, 'tis equity (which is the law of nature, and therefore an eternal law of God) that every man equally enjoy his liberty.

41. There is also another distinction of laws, into *fundamental*, and *not fundamental*: but I could never see in any author, what a fundamental law signifieth. Nevertheless one may very reasonably distinguish laws in that manner.

Another division of laws.

42. For a fundamental law in every commonwealth is that, which being taken away, the commonwealth faileth, and is utterly dissolved; as a building whose foundation is destroyed. And therefore a fundamental law is that, by which subjects are bound to uphold whatsoever power is given to the sovereign, whether a monarch, or a sovereign assembly, without which the commonwealth cannot stand; such as is the power of war and peace, of judicature, of election of officers, and of doing whatsoever he shall think necessary

A fundamental law, what.

for the public good. Not fundamental is that, the abrogating whereof, draweth not with it the dissolution of the commonwealth; such as are the laws concerning controversies between subject and subject. Thus much of the division of laws.

Difference between law and right.

43. I find the words *lex civilis*, and *jus civile*, that is to say *law* and *right civil*, promiscuously used for the same thing, even in the most learned authors; which nevertheless ought not to be so. For *right* is *liberty*, namely that liberty which the civil law leaves us: but *civil law* is an *obligation*; and takes from us the liberty which the law of nature gave us. Nature gave a right to every man to secure himself by his own strength, and to invade a suspected neighbour, by way of prevention: but the civil law takes away that liberty, in all cases where the protection of the law may be safely stayed for. Insomuch as *lex* and *jus*, are as different as *obligation* and *liberty*.

And between a law and a charter.

44. Likewise *laws* and *charters* are taken promiscuously for the same thing. Yet charters are donations of the sovereign; and not laws, but exemptions from law. The phrase of a law is, *jubeo, injungo, I command* and *enjoin*: the phrase of a charter is, *dedi, concessi, I have given, I have granted*: but what is given or granted, to a man, is not forced upon him, by a law. A law may be made to bind all the subjects of a commonwealth: a liberty, or charter is only to one man, or some one part of the people. For to say all the people of a commonwealth, have liberty in any case whatsoever, is to say, that in such case, there hath been no law made; or else having been made, is now abrogated.

CHAPTER XXVII

OF CRIMES, EXCUSES, AND EXTENUATIONS

Sin what.

1. A SIN, is not only a transgression of a law, but also any contempt of the legislator. For such contempt, is a breach of all his laws at once. And therefore may consist, not only in the *commission* of a fact, or in speaking of words by the laws forbidden, or in the *omission* of what the law commandeth, but also in the *intention*, or purpose to transgress. For the purpose to break the law, is some degree of contempt of him, to whom it belongeth to see it executed. To be delighted in the imagination only, of being possessed of another

man's goods, servants, or wife, without any intention to take them from him by force or fraud, is no breach of the law, that saith, *Thou shalt not covet*: nor is the pleasure a man may have in imagining, or dreaming of the death of him, from whose life he expecteth nothing but damage, and displeasure, a sin; but the resolving to put some act in execution, that tendeth thereto. For to be pleased in the fiction of that, which would please a man if it were real, is a passion so adherent to the nature both of man, and every other living creature, as to make it a sin, were to make sin of being a man. The consideration of this, has made me think them too severe, both to themselves, and others, that maintain, that the first motions of the mind, (though checked with the fear of God) be sins.* But I confess it is safer to err on that hand, than on the other.

2. A CRIME, is a sin, consisting in the committing (by deed, or word) of that which the law forbiddeth, or the omission of what it hath commanded. So that every crime is a sin; but not every sin a crime. To intend to steal, or kill, is a sin, though it never appear in word, or fact: for God that seeth the thoughts of man, can lay it to his charge: but till it appear by something done, or said, by which the intention may be argued by a human judge, it hath not the name of crime: which distinction the Greeks observed, in the word ἁμάρτημα, and ἔγκλημα or αἰτία; whereof the former, (which is translated *sin*,) signifieth any swerving from the law whatsoever; but the two latter, (which are translated *crime*,) signify that sin only, whereof one man may accuse another. But of intentions, which never appear by any outward act, there is no place for human accusation. In like manner the Latins by *peccatum*, which is *sin*, signify all manner of deviation from the law; but by *crimen*, (which word they derive from *cerno*, which signifies *to perceive*,) they mean only such sins, as may be made appear before a judge; and therefore are not mere intentions.

A crime, what.

3. From this relation of sin to the law, and of crime to the civil law, may be inferred, first, that where law ceaseth, sin ceaseth. But because the law of nature is eternal, violation of covenants, ingratitude, arrogance, and all facts contrary to any moral virtue, can never cease to be sin. Secondly, that the civil law ceasing, crimes cease: for there being no other law remaining, but that of nature, there is no place for accusation; every man being his own judge, and accused only by his own conscience, and cleared by the uprightness of his own intention. When therefore his intention is right, his fact is no

Where no civil law is, there is no crime.

[152]

193

sin: if otherwise, his fact is sin; but not crime. Thirdly, that when the sovereign power ceaseth, crime also ceaseth: for where there is no such power, there is no protection to be had from the law; and therefore every one may protect himself by his own power: for no man in the institution of sovereign power can be supposed to give away the right of preserving his own body; for the safety whereof all sovereignty was ordained. But this is to be understood only of those, that have not themselves contributed to the taking away of the power that protected them: for that was a crime from the beginning.

Ignorance of the law of nature excuseth no man.

4. The source of every crime, is some defect of the understanding; or some error in reasoning; or some sudden force of the passions. Defect in the understanding, is *ignorance*; in reasoning, *erroneous opinion*. Again, ignorance is of three sorts; of the *law*, and of the *sovereign*, and of the *penalty*. Ignorance of the law of nature excuseth no man; because every man that hath attained to the use of reason, is supposed to know, he ought not to do to another, what he would not have done to himself. Therefore into what place soever a man shall come, if he do any thing contrary to that law, it is a crime. If a man come from the Indies hither, and persuade men here to receive a new religion, or teach them any thing that tendeth to disobedience of the laws of this country, though he be never so well persuaded of the truth of what he teacheth, he commits a crime, and may be justly punished for the same, not only because his doctrine is false, but also because he does that which he would not approve in another, namely, that coming from hence, he should endeavour to alter the religion there.* But ignorance of the civil law, shall excuse a man in a strange country, till it be declared to him; because, till then no civil law is binding.

Ignorance of the civil law excuseth sometimes.

5. In the like manner, if the civil law of a man's own country, be not so sufficiently declared, as he may know it if he will; nor the action against the law of nature; the ignorance is a good excuse: in other cases ignorance of the civil law, excuseth not.

Ignorance of the sovereign excuseth not.

6. Ignorance of the sovereign power, in the place of a man's ordinary residence, excuseth him not; because he ought to take notice of the power, by which he hath been protected there.

Ignorance of the penalty excuseth not.

7. Ignorance of the penalty, where the law is declared, excuseth no man: for in breaking the law, which without a fear of penalty to follow, were not a law, but vain words, he undergoeth the penalty, though he know not what it is; because, whosoever voluntarily doth

any action, accepteth all the known consequences of it; but punishment is a known consequence of the violation of the laws, in every commonwealth; which punishment, if it be determined already by [153] the law, he is subject to that; if not, then he is subject to arbitrary punishment. For it is reason, that he which does injury, without other limitation than that of his own will, should suffer punishment without other limitation, than that of his will whose law is thereby violated.

8. But when a penalty, is either annexed to the crime in the law itself, or hath been usually inflicted in the like cases; there the delinquent is excused from a greater penalty. For the punishment foreknown, if it be not great enough to deter men from the action, is an invitement to it: because when men compare the benefit of their injustice, with the harm of their punishment, by necessity of nature they choose that which appeareth best for themselves: and therefore when they are punished more than the law had formerly determined, or more than others were punished for the same crime; it is the law that tempted, and deceiveth them. *Punishments declared before the fact, excuse from greater punishments after it.*

9. No law, made after a fact done, can make it a crime: because if the fact be against the law of nature, the law was before the fact; and a positive law cannot be taken notice of, before it be made; and therefore cannot be obligatory. But when the law that forbiddeth a fact, is made before the fact be done; yet he that doth the fact, is liable to the penalty ordained after, in case no lesser penalty were made known before, neither by writing, nor by example, for the reason immediately before alleged. *Nothing can be made a crime by a law made after the fact.*

10. From defect in reasoning, (that is to say, from error,) men are prone to violate the laws, three ways. First, by presumption of false principles: as when men, from having observed how in all places, and in all ages, unjust actions have been authorized, by the force, and victories of those who have committed them; and that potent men, breaking through the cobweb laws of their country, the weaker sort, and those that have failed in their enterprises, have been esteemed the only criminals; have thereupon taken for principles, and grounds of their reasoning, *that justice is but a vain word: that whatsoever a man can get by his own industry, and hazard, is his own: that the practice of all nations cannot be unjust: that examples of former times are good arguments of doing the like again*; and many more of that kind: which being granted, no act in itself can be a crime, but must be made so (not by the law, but) by the success of them *False principles of right and wrong causes of crime.*

that commit it; and the same fact be virtuous, or vicious, as fortune pleaseth; so that what Marius makes a crime, Sylla shall make meritorious, and Caesar (the same laws standing) turn again into a crime, to the perpetual disturbance of the peace of the commonwealth.

False teachers misinterpreting the law of nature,

11. Secondly, by false teachers, that either misinterpret the law of nature, making it thereby repugnant to the law civil; or by teaching for laws, such doctrines of their own, or traditions of former times, as are inconsistent with the duty of a subject.

[154]

And false inferences from true principles by teachers.

12. Thirdly, by erroneous inferences from true principles; which happens commonly to men that are hasty, and precipitate in concluding, and resolving what to do; such as are they, that have both a great opinion of their own understanding, and believe that things of this nature require not time and study, but only common experience, and a good natural wit; whereof no man thinks himself unprovided: whereas the knowledge, of right and wrong, which is no less difficult, there is no man will pretend to, without great and long study. And of those defects in reasoning, there is none that can excuse (though some of them may extenuate) a crime, in any man, that pretendeth to the administration of his own private business; much less in them that undertake a public charge; because they pretend to the reason, upon the want whereof they would ground their excuse.

By their passions;

13. Of the passions that most frequently are the causes of crime, one, is vain glory, or a foolish overrating of their own worth; as if difference of worth, were an effect of their wit, or riches, or blood, or some other natural quality, not depending on the will of those that have the sovereign authority. From whence proceedeth a presumption that the punishments ordained by the laws, and extended generally to all subjects, ought not to be inflicted on them, with the same rigour they are inflicted on poor, obscure, and simple men, comprehended under the name of the *vulgar*.

Presumption of riches,

14. Therefore it happeneth commonly, that such as value themselves by the greatness of their wealth, adventure on crimes, upon hope of escaping punishment, by corrupting public justice, or obtaining pardon by money, or other rewards.

And friends;

15. And that such as have multitude of potent kindred; and popular men, that have gained reputation amongst the multitude, take courage to violate the laws, from a hope of oppressing the power, to whom it belongeth to put them in execution.

16. And that such as have a great, and false opinion of their own *Wisdom.*
wisdom, take upon them to reprehend the actions, and call in question the authority of them that govern, and so to unsettle the laws
with their public discourse, as that nothing shall be a crime, but
what their own designs require should be so. It happeneth also to the
same men, to be prone to all such crimes, as consist in craft, and in
deceiving of their neighbours; because they think their designs are
too subtle to be perceived. These I say are effects of a false presumption of their own wisdom. For of them that are the first movers in
the disturbance of commonwealth, (which can never happen without a civil war) very few are left alive long enough, to see their new
designs established: so that the benefit of their crimes, redoundeth
to posterity, and such as would least have wished it: which argues
they were not so wise, as they thought they were. And those that
deceive upon hope of not being observed, do commonly deceive
themselves, (the darkness in which they believe they lie hidden,
being nothing else but their own blindness;) and are no wiser than
children, that think all hid, by hiding their own eyes.

17. And generally all vain-glorious men, (unless they be withal
timorous), are subject to anger; as being more prone than others to   [155]
interpret for contempt, the ordinary liberty of conversation: and
there are few crimes that may not be produced by anger.

18. As for the passions, of hate, lust, ambition, and covetousness,   *Hatred, lust,*
what crimes they are apt to produce, is so obvious to every   *ambition,*
man's experience and understanding, as there needeth nothing to be   *covetousness,*
said of them, saving that they are infirmities, so annexed to the   *causes of*
nature, both of man, and all other living creatures, as that their   *crime.*
effects cannot be hindered, but by extraordinary use of reason, or a
constant severity in punishing them. For in those things men
hate, they find a continual, and unavoidable molestation; whereby
either a man's patience must be everlasting, or he must be eased by
removing the power of that which molesteth him: the former is
difficult; the latter is many times impossible, without some violation
of the law. Ambition, and covetousness are passions also that
are perpetually incumbent, and pressing; whereas reason is not
perpetually present, to resist them: and therefore whensoever
the hope of impunity appears, their effects proceed. And for lust,
what it wants in the lasting, it hath in the vehemence, which
sufficeth to weigh down the apprehension of all easy, or uncertain
punishments.

Fear sometimes cause of crime, as when the danger is neither present, nor corporeal.

19. Of all passions, that which inclineth men least to break the laws, is fear. Nay, (excepting some generous natures,) it is the only thing, (when there is appearance of profit, or pleasure by breaking the laws,) that makes men keep them. And yet in many cases a crime may be committed through fear.

20. For not every fear justifies the action it produceth, but the fear only of corporeal hurt, which we call *bodily fear*, and from which a man cannot see how to be delivered, but by the action. A man is assaulted, fears present death, from which he sees not how to escape, but by wounding him that assaulteth him: if he wound him to death, this is no crime; because no man is supposed at the making of a commonwealth, to have abandoned the defence of his life, or limbs, where the law cannot arrive time enough to his assistance. But to kill a man, because from his actions, or his threatenings, I may argue he will kill me when he can, (seeing I have time, and means to demand protection, from the sovereign power,) is a crime. Again, a man receives words of disgrace or some little injuries (for which they that made the laws, had assigned no punishment, nor thought it worthy of a man that hath the use of reason, to take notice of,) and is afraid, unless he revenge it, he shall fall into contempt, and consequently be obnoxious to the like injuries from others; and to avoid this, breaks the law, and protects himself for the future, by the terror of his private revenge. This is a crime: for the hurt is not corporeal, but phantastical, and (though in this corner of the world, made sensible by a custom not many years since begun, amongst young and vain men,) so light, as a gallant man, and one that is assured of his own courage, cannot take notice of. Also a man may stand in fear of spirits, either through his own superstition, or through too much credit given to other men, that tell him of strange dreams and

[156] visions; and thereby be made believe they will hurt him, for doing, or omitting divers things, which nevertheless, to do, or omit, is contrary to the laws; and that which is so done, or omitted, is not to be excused by this fear; but is a crime. For (as I have shown before in the second chapter) dreams be naturally but the fancies remaining in sleep, after the impressions our senses had formerly received waking; and when men are by any accident unassured they have slept, seem to be real visions; and therefore he that presumes to break the law upon his own, or another's dream, or pretended vision, or upon other fancy of the power of invisible spirits, than is permitted by the commonwealth, leaveth the law of nature, which is

a certain offence, and followeth the imagery of his own, or another private man's brain, which he can never know whether it signifieth any thing, or nothing, nor whether he that tells his dream, say true, or lie; which if every private man should have leave to do, (as they must by the law of nature, if any one have it) there could no law be made to hold, and so all commonwealth would be dissolved.

21. From these different sources of crimes, it appears already, that all crimes are not (as the Stoics of old time maintained*) of the same alloy. There is place, not only for EXCUSE, by which that which seemed a crime, is proved to be none at all; but also for EXTENUA-TION, by which the crime, that seemed great, is made less. For though all crimes do equally deserve the name of injustice, as all deviation from a straight line is equally crookedness, which the Stoics rightly observed: yet it does not follow that all crimes are equally unjust, no more than that all crooked lines are equally crooked; which the Stoics not observing, held it as great a crime, to kill a hen, against the law, as to kill one's father. *Crimes not equal.*

22. That which totally excuseth a fact, and takes away from it the nature of a crime, can be none but that, which at the same time, taketh away the obligation of the law. For the fact committed once against the law, if he that committed it be obliged to the law, can be no other than a crime. *Total excuses.*

23. The want of means to know the law, totally excuseth: for the law whereof a man has no means to inform himself, is not obligatory. But the want of diligence to inquire, shall not be considered as a want of means; nor shall any man, that pretendeth to reason enough for the government of his own affairs, be supposed to want means to know the laws of nature; because they are known by the reason he pretends to: only children, and madmen are excused from offences against the law natural.

24. Where a man is captive, or in the power of the enemy, (and he is then in the power of the enemy, when his person, or his means of living, is so,) if it be without his own fault, the obligation of the law ceaseth; because he must obey the enemy, or die; and consequently such obedience is no crime: for no man is obliged (when the protection of the law faileth,) not to protect himself, by the best means he can.

25. If a man by the terror of present death, be compelled to do a fact against the law, he is totally excused; because no law can oblige [157]

a man to abandon his own preservation. And supposing such a law were obligatory; yet a man would reason thus, *If I do it not, I die presently; if I do it, I die afterwards; therefore by doing it, there is time of life gained*; nature therefore compels him to the fact.

26. When a man is destitute of food, or other thing necessary for his life, and cannot preserve himself any other way, but by some fact against the law; as if in a great famine he take the food by force, or stealth, which he cannot obtain for money, nor charity; or in defence of his life, snatch away another man's sword; he is totally excused, for the reason next before alleged.

Excuses against the author. 27. Again, facts done against the law, by the authority of another, are by that authority excused against the author; because no man ought to accuse his own fact in another, that is but his instrument: but it is not excused against a third person thereby injured; because in the violation of the law, both the author, and actor are criminals. From hence it followeth that when that man, or assembly, that hath the sovereign power, commandeth a man to do that which is contrary to a former law, the doing of it is totally excused: for he ought not to condemn it himself, because he is the author; and what cannot justly be condemned by the sovereign, cannot justly be punished by any other. Besides, when the sovereign commandeth any thing to be done against his own former law, the command, as to that particular fact, is an abrogation of the law.

28. If that man, or assembly, that hath the sovereign power, disclaim any right essential to the sovereignty, whereby there accrueth to the subject, any liberty inconsistent with the sovereign power, that is to say, with the very being of a commonwealth, if the subject shall refuse to obey the command in any thing, contrary to the liberty granted, this is nevertheless a sin, and contrary to the duty of the subject: for he ought to take notice of what is inconsistent with the sovereignty, because it was erected by his own consent, and for his own defence; and that such liberty as is inconsistent with it, was granted through ignorance of the evil consequence thereof. But if he not only disobey, but also resist a public minister in the execution of it, then it is a crime; because he might have been righted, (without any breach of the peace,) upon complaint.

29. The degrees of crime are taken on divers scales, and measured, first, by the malignity of the source, or cause; secondly, by the contagion of the example; thirdly, by the mischief of the effect; and fourthly, by the concurrence of times, places, and persons.

30. The same fact done against the law, if it proceed from presumption of strength, riches, or friends to resist those that are to execute the law, is a greater crime, than if it proceed from hope of not being discovered, or of escape by flight: for presumption of impunity by force, is a root, from whence springeth, at all times, and upon all temptations, a contempt of all laws; whereas in the latter case, the apprehension of danger, that makes a man fly, renders him more obedient for the future. A crime which we know to be so, is greater than the same crime proceeding from a false persuasion that it is lawful; for he that committeth it against his own conscience, presumeth on his force, or other power, which encourages him to commit the same again: but he that doth it by error, after the error is shewn him, is conformable to the law.

Presumption of power aggravateth.

[158]

31. He, whose error proceeds from the authority of a teacher, or an interpreter of the law publicly authorized, is not so faulty, as he whose error proceedeth from a peremptory pursuit of his own principles and reasoning: for what is taught by one that teacheth by public authority, the commonwealth teacheth, and hath a resemblance of law, till the same authority controlleth it; and in all crimes that contain not in them a denial of the sovereign power, nor are against an evident law or authorized doctrine, excuseth totally: whereas he that groundeth his actions on his private judgment, ought according to the rectitude, or error thereof, to stand, or fall.

Evil teachers extenuate.

32. The same fact, if it have been constantly punished in other men, is a greater crime, than if there have been many precedent examples of impunity. For those examples, are so many hopes of impunity, given by the sovereign himself: and because he which furnishes a man with such a hope, and presumption of mercy, as encourageth him to offend, hath his part in the offence; he cannot reasonably charge the offender with the whole.

Examples of impunity, extenuate.

33. A crime arising from a sudden passion, is not so great, as when the same ariseth from long meditation: for in the former case there is a place for extenuation, in the common infirmity of human nature: but he that doth it with premeditation, has used circumspection, and cast his eye, on the law, on the punishment, and on the consequence thereof to human society; all which, in committing the crime, he hath contemned and postposed to his own appetite. But there is no suddenness of passion sufficient for a total excuse: for all the time between the first knowing of the law, and the commission

Premeditation aggravateth.

of the fact, shall be taken for a time of deliberation; because he ought by meditation of the law, to rectify the irregularity of his passions continually.

34. Where the law is publicly, and with assiduity, before all the people read, and interpreted; a fact done against it, is a greater crime, than where men are left without such instruction, to enquire of it with difficulty, uncertainty, and interruption of their callings, and be informed by private men: for in this case, part of the fault is discharged upon common infirmity; but, in the former, there is apparent negligence, which is not without some contempt of the sovereign power.

Tacit approbation of the sovereign extenuates.

[159]

35. Those facts which the law expressly condemneth, but the law-maker by other manifest signs of his will tacitly approveth, are less crimes, than the same facts, condemned both by the law, and law-maker. For seeing the will of the law-maker is a law, there appear in this case two contradictory laws; which would totally excuse, if men were bound to take notice of the sovereign's approbation, by other arguments, than are expressed by his command. But because there are punishments consequent, not only to the transgression of his law, but also to the observing of it, he is in part a cause of the transgression, and therefore cannot reasonably impute the whole crime to the delinquent. For example, the law condemneth duels; the punishment is made capital: on the contrary part, he that refuseth duel, is subject to contempt and scorn, without remedy; and sometimes by the sovereign himself thought unworthy to have any charge, or preferment in war: if thereupon he accept duel, considering all men lawfully endeavour to obtain the good opinion of them that have the sovereign power, he ought not in reason to be rigorously punished; seeing part of the fault may be discharged on the punisher: which I say, not as wishing liberty of private revenges, or any other kind of disobedience; but a care in governors, not to countenance any thing obliquely, which directly they forbid. The examples of princes, to those that see them, are, and ever have been, more potent to govern their actions, than the laws themselves. And though it be our duty to do, not what they do, but what they say; yet will that duty never be performed, till it please God to give man an extraordinary, and supernatural grace to follow that precept.

36. Again, if we compare crimes by the mischief of their effects, *Comparison* first, the same fact, when it redounds to the damage of many, is *of crimes* greater, than when it redounds to the hurt of few. And therefore, *from their effects.* when a fact hurteth, not only in the present, but also, (by example,) in the future, it is a greater crime, than if it hurt only in the present: for the former, is a fertile crime, and multiplies to the hurt of many; the latter is barren. To maintain doctrines contrary to the religion established in the commonwealth, is a greater fault, in an authorized preacher, than in a private person: so also is it, to live profanely, incontinently, or do any irreligious act whatsoever. Likewise in a professor of the law, to maintain any point, or do any act, that tendeth to the weakening of the sovereign power, is a greater crime, than in another man: also in a man that hath such reputation for wisdom, as that his counsels are followed, or his actions imitated by many, his fact against the law, is a greater crime, than the same fact in another: for such men not only commit crime, but teach it for law to all other men. And generally all crimes are the greater, by the scandal they give; that is to say, by becoming stumbling-blocks to the weak, that look not so much upon the way they go in, as upon the light that other man carry before them.

37. Also facts of hostility against the present state of the com- *Laesa* monwealth, are greater crimes, than the same acts done to private *Majestas.* men: for the damage extends itself to all: such are the betraying of the strengths, or revealing of the secrets of the commonwealth to an enemy; also all attempts upon the representative of the common- wealth, be it a monarch, or an assembly; and all endeavours by word, [160] or deed, to diminish the authority of the same, either in the present time, or in succession: which crimes the Latins understand by *crimina laesae majestatis,* and consist in design, or act, contrary to a fundamental law.

38. Likewise those crimes, which render judgments of no effect, *Bribery and* are greater crimes, than injuries done to one, or a few persons; as to *false* receive money to give false judgment, or testimony, is a greater *testimony.* crime, than otherwise to deceive a man of the like, or a greater sum; because not only he has wrong, that falls by such judgments; but all judgments are rendered useless, and occasion ministered to force, and private revenges.

39. Also robbery, and depeculation [embezzlement] of the public *Depeculation.* treasure, or revenues, is a greater crime, than the robbing, or defrauding of a private man; because to rob the public, is to rob many at once.

Counterfeiting authority.

40. Also the counterfeit usurpation of public ministry, the counterfeiting of public seals, or public coin, than counterfeiting of a private man's person, or his seal; because the fraud thereof, extendeth to the damage of many.

Crimes against private men compared.

41. Of facts against the law, done to private men, the greater crime, is that, where the damage in the common opinion of men, is most sensible. And therefore

42. To kill against the law, is a greater crime, than any other injury, life preserved.

43. And to kill with torment, greater, than simply to kill.

44. And mutilation of a limb, greater, than the spoiling a man of his goods.

45. And the spoiling a man of his goods, by terror of death, or wounds, than by clandestine surreption.

46. And by clandestine surreption, than by consent fraudulently obtained.

47. And the violation of chastity by force, greater, than by flattery.

48. And of a woman married, than of a woman not married.

49. For all these things are commonly so valued; though some men are more, and some less sensible of the same offence. But the law regardeth not the particular, but the general inclination of mankind.

50. And therefore the offence men take, from contumely, in words, or gesture, when they produce no other harm, than the present grief of him that is reproached, hath been neglected in the laws of the Greeks, Romans, and other both ancient, and modern commonwealths; supposing the true cause of such grief to consist, not in the contumely, (which takes no hold upon men conscious of their own virtue,) but in the pusillanimity of him that is offended by it.

51. Also a crime against a private man, is much aggravated by the person, time, and place. For to kill one's parent, is a greater crime, than to kill another: for the parent ought to have the honour of a sovereign, (though he surrendered his power to the civil law,) because he had it originally by nature. And to rob a poor man, is a [161] greater crime, than to rob a rich man; because it is to the poor a more sensible damage.

52. And a crime committed in the time, or place appointed for devotion, is greater, than if committed at another time or place: for it proceeds from a greater contempt of the law.

53. Many other cases of aggravation, and extenuation might be added: but by these I have set down, it is obvious to every man, to take the altitude of any other crime proposed.

54. Lastly, because in almost all crimes there is an injury done, *Public crimes* not only to some private men, but also to the commonwealth; the *what.* same crime, when the accusation is in the name of the commonwealth, is called a public crime: and when in the name of a private man, a private crime; and the pleas according thereunto called public, *judicia publica,* Pleas of the Crown; or Private Pleas. As in an accusation of murder, if the accuser be a private man, the plea is a Private Plea; if the accuser be the sovereign, the plea is a Public Plea.

CHAPTER XXVIII

OF PUNISHMENTS, AND REWARDS

1. A PUNISHMENT, *is an evil inflicted by public authority, on him that* The definition *hath done, or omitted that which is judged by the same authority to be a* of *transgression of the law; to the end that the will of men may thereby the* punishment. *better be disposed to obedience.*

2. Before I infer any thing from this definition, there is a question *Right to* to be answered, of much importance; which is, by what door the *punish* right, or authority of punishing in any case, came in. For by that *whence derived.* which has been said before, no man is supposed bound by covenant, not to resist violence; and consequently it cannot be intended, that he gave any right to another to lay violent hands upon his person. In the making of a commonwealth, every man giveth away the right of defending another; but not of defending himself. Also he obligeth himself, to assist him that hath the sovereignty, in the punishing of another; but of himself not. But to covenant to assist the sovereign, in doing hurt to another, unless he that so covenanteth have a right to do it himself, is not to give him a right to punish. It is manifest therefore that the right which the commonwealth (that is, he, or they that represent it) hath to punish, is not grounded on any concession, or gift of the subjects. But I have also showed formerly, that before the institution of commonwealth, every man had a right to every thing, and to do whatsoever he thought necessary to his own preservation; subduing, hurting, or killing any man in order thereunto. And this is the foundation of that right of punishing, [162] which is exercised in every commonwealth. For the subjects did not give the sovereign that right; but only in laying down theirs, strengthened him to use his own, as he should think fit, for the preservation of them all: so that it was not given, but left to him, and to him only; and (excepting the limits set him by natural law) as entire, as in the condition of mere nature, and of war of every one against his neighbour.

Private injuries, and revenges no punishments:

3. From the definition of punishment, I infer, first, that neither private revenges, nor injuries of private men, can properly be styled punishments; because they proceed not from public authority.

Nor denial of preferment:

4. Secondly, that to be neglected, and unpreferred by the public favour, is not a punishment; because no new evil is thereby on any man inflicted; he is only left in the estate he was in before.

Nor pain inflicted without public hearing:

5. Thirdly, that the evil inflicted by public authority, without precedent public condemnation, is not to be styled by the name of punishment; but of an hostile act; because the fact for which a man is punished, ought first to be judged by public authority, to be a transgression of the law.

Nor pain inflicted by usurped power:

6. Fourthly, that the evil inflicted by usurped power, and judges without authority from the sovereign, is not punishment; but an act of hostility; because the acts of power usurped, have not for author, the person condemned; and therefore are not acts of public authority.

Nor pain inflicted without respect to the future good.

7. Fifthly, that all evil which is inflicted without intention, or possibility of disposing the delinquent, or (by his example) other men, to obey the laws, is not punishment; but an act of hostility: because without such an end, no hurt done is contained under that name.

Natural evil consequences, no punishments.

8. Sixthly, whereas to certain actions, there be annexed by nature, divers hurtful consequences; as when a man in assaulting another, is himself slain, or wounded; or when he falleth into sickness by the doing of some unlawful act; such hurt, though in respect of God, who is the author of nature, it may be said to be inflicted, and therefore a punishment divine; yet it is not contained in the

name of punishment in respect of men, because it is not inflicted by the authority of man.

9. Seventhly, if the harm inflicted be less than the benefit, or contentment that naturally followeth the crime committed, that harm is not within the definition; and is rather the price, or redemption, than the punishment of a crime: because it is of the nature of punishment, to have for end, the disposing of men to obey the law; which end (if it be less than the benefit of the transgression) it attaineth not, but worketh a contrary effect.

Hurt inflicted, if less than the benefit of transgressing, is not punishment.

10. Eighthly, if a punishment be determined and prescribed in the law itself, and after the crime committed, there be a greater punishment inflicted, the excess is not punishment, but an act of hostility. For seeing the aim of punishment is not a revenge, but terror; and the terror of a great punishment unknown, is taken away by the declaration of a less, the unexpected addition is no part of the punishment. But where there is no punishment at all determined by the law, there whatsoever is inflicted, hath the nature of punishment. For he that goes about the violation of a law, wherein no penalty is determined, expecteth an indeterminate, that is to say, an arbitrary punishment.

Where the punishment is annexed to the law, a greater hurt is not punish· but h   '.
[163

11. Ninthly, harm inflicted for a fact done before there was a law that forbade it, is not punishment, but an act of hostility: for before the law, there is no transgression of the law: but punishment supposeth a fact judged, to have been a transgression of the law; therefore harm inflicted before the law made, is not punishment, but an act of hostility.

Hurt inflicted for a fact done before the law, no punishment.

12. Tenthly, hurt inflicted on the representative of the commonwealth, is not punishment, but an act of hostility: because it is of the nature of punishment, to be inflicted by public authority, which is the authority only of the representative itself.

The representative of the commonwealth unpunishable.

13. Lastly, harm inflicted upon one that is a declared enemy, falls not under the name of punishment: because seeing they were either never subject to the law, and therefore cannot transgress it; or having been subject to it, and professing to be no longer so, by consequence deny they can transgress it, all the harms that can be done them, must be taken as acts of hostility. But in declared hostility, all infliction of evil is lawful. From whence it followeth, that if a subject shall by fact, or word, wittingly, and deliberately deny the authority of the representative of the commonwealth, (whatsoever penalty hath been formerly ordained for treason,) he may lawfully

Hurt to revolted subjects is done by right of war, not by way of punishment.

be made to suffer whatsoever the representative will: for in denying subjection, he denies such punishment as by the law hath been ordained; and therefore suffers as an enemy of the commonwealth; that is, according to the will of the representative. For the punishments set down in the law, are to subjects, not to enemies; such as are they, that having been by their own acts subjects, deliberately revolting, deny the sovereign power.

14. The first, and most general distribution of punishments, is into *divine*, and *human*. Of the former I shall have occasion to speak, in a more convenient place hereafter.

15. *Human*, are those punishments that be inflicted by the commandment of man; and are either *corporal*, or *pecuniary*, or *ignominy*, or *imprisonment*, or *exile*, or mixed of these.

Punishments corporal.

16. *Corporal punishment* is that, which is inflicted on the body directly, and according to the intention of him that inflicteth it: such as are stripes, or wounds, or deprivation of such pleasures of the body, as were before lawfully enjoyed.

Capital.

17. And of these, some be *capital*, some *less* than *capital*. Capital, is the infliction of death; and that either simply, or with torment. Less than capital, are stripes, wounds, chains, and any other corporal pain, not in its own nature mortal. For if upon the infliction of a punishment death follow not in the intention of the inflictor, the punishment is not to be esteemed capital, though the harm prove mortal by an accident not to be foreseen; in which case death is not [164] inflicted, but hastened.

18. *Pecuniary punishment*, is that which consisteth not only in the deprivation of a sum of money, but also of lands, or any other goods which are usually bought and sold for money. And in case the law, that ordaineth such a punishment, be made with design to gather money, from such as shall transgress the same, it is not properly a punishment, but the price of privilege, and exemption from the law, which doth not absolutely forbid the fact, but only to those that are not able to pay the money: except where the law is natural, or part of religion; for in that case it is not an exemption from the law, but a transgression of it. As where a law exacteth a pecuniary mulct, of them that take the name of God in vain, the payment of the mulct, is not the price of a dispensation to swear, but the punishment of the transgression of a law indispensable. In like manner if the law impose a sum of money to be paid, to him that has been injured; this is

but a satisfaction for the hurt done him; and extinguisheth the accusation of the party injured, not the crime of the offender.

19. *Ignominy*, is the infliction of such evil, as is made dishonour- *Ignominy.* able; or the deprivation of such good, as is made honourable by the commonwealth. For there be some things honourable by nature; as the effects of courage, magnanimity, strength, wisdom, and other abilities of body and mind: others made honourable by the commonwealth; as badges, titles, offices, or any other singular mark of the sovereign's favour. The former, (though they may fail by nature, or accident,) cannot be taken away by a law; and therefore the loss of them is not punishment. But the latter, may be taken away by the public authority that made them honourable, and are properly punishments: such are degrading men condemned, of their badges, titles, and offices; or declaring them incapable of the like in time to come.

20. *Imprisonment*, is when a man is by public authority deprived *Imprisonment.* of liberty; and may happen from two divers ends; whereof one is the safe custody of a man accused; the other is the inflicting of pain on a man condemned. The former is not punishment; because no man is supposed to be punished, before he be judicially heard, and declared guilty. And therefore whatsoever hurt a man is made to suffer by bonds, or restraint, before his cause be heard, over and above that which is necessary to assure his custody, is against the law of nature. But the latter is punishment, because evil, and inflicted by public authority, for somewhat that has by the same authority been judged a transgression of the law. Under this word imprisonment, I comprehend all restraint of motion, caused by an external obstacle, be it a house, which is called by the general name of a prison; or an island, as when men are said to be confined to it; or a place where men are set to work, as in old time men have been condemned to quarries, and in these times to galleys; or be it a chain, or any other such impediment.

21. *Exile*, (banishment) is when a man is for a crime, condemned *Exile.* to depart out of the dominion of the commonwealth, or out of a [165] certain part thereof: and during a prefixed time, or for ever, not to return into it: and seemeth not in its own nature, without other circumstances, to be a punishment; but rather an escape, or a public commandment to avoid punishment by flight. And Cicero says,* there was never any such punishment ordained in the city of Rome;

but calls it a refuge of men in danger. For if a man banished, be nevertheless permitted to enjoy his goods, and the revenue of his lands, the mere change of air is no punishment; nor does it tend to that benefit of the commonwealth, for which all punishments are ordained, (that is to say, to the forming of men's wills to the observation of the law;) but many times to the damage of the commonwealth. For a banished man, is a lawful enemy of the commonwealth that banished him; as being no more a member of the same. But if he be withal deprived of his lands, or goods, then the punishment lieth not in the exile, but is to be reckoned amongst punishments pecuniary.

The punishment of innocent subjects is contrary to the law of nature.

22. All punishments of innocent subjects, be they great or little, are against the law of nature; for punishment is only for transgression of the law, and therefore there can be no punishment of the innocent. It is therefore a violation, first, of that law of nature, which forbiddeth all men, in their revenges, to look at any thing but some future good: for there can arrive no good to the commonwealth, by punishing the innocent. Secondly, of that, which forbiddeth ingratitude: for seeing all sovereign power, is originally given by the consent of every one of the subjects, to the end they should as long as they are obedient, be protected thereby; the punishment of the innocent, is a rendering of evil for good. And thirdly, of the law that commandeth equity; that is to say, an equal distribution of justice; which in punishing the innocent is not oberved.

But the harm done to innocents in war, not so.

23. But the infliction of what evil soever, on an innocent man, that is not a subject, if it be for the benefit of the commonwealth, and without violation of any former covenant, is no breach of the law of nature. For all men that are not subjects, are either enemies, or else thay have ceased from being so by some precedent covenants. But against enemies, whom the commonwealth judgeth capable to do them hurt, it is lawful by the original right of nature to make war; wherein the sword judgeth not, nor doth the victor make distinction of nocent [guilty], and innocent, as to the time past; nor has other respect of mercy, than as it conduceth to the good of his own people.

Nor that which is done to declared rebels.

And upon this ground it is, that also in subjects, who deliberately deny the authority of the commonwealth established, the vengeance is lawfully extended, not only to the fathers, but also to the third and fourth generation not yet in being, and consequently innocent of the fact, for which they are afflicted: because the nature of this offence, consisteth in the renouncing of subjection; which is a relapse into the condition of war, commonly called rebellion; and they that so offend, suffer not as subjects, but as enemies. For *rebellion*, is but [166] war renewed.

24. REWARD, is either of *gift*, or by *contract*. When by contract, it is called *salary*, and *wages*; which is benefit due for service performed, or promised. When of gift, it is benefit proceeding from the *grace* of them that bestow it, to encourage, or enable men to do them service. And therefore when the sovereign of a commonwealth appointeth a salary to any public office, he that receiveth it, is bound in justice to perform his office; otherwise, he is bound only in honour, to acknowledgment, and an endeavour of requital. For though men have no lawful remedy, when they be commanded to quit their private business, to serve the public, without reward, or salary; yet they are not bound thereto, by the law of nature, nor by the institution of the commonwealth, unless the service cannot otherwise be done; because it is supposed the sovereign may make use of all their means, insomuch as the most common soldier, may demand the wages of his warfare, as a debt.

Reward is either salary, or grace.

25. The benefits which a sovereign bestoweth on a subject, for fear of some power, and ability he hath to do hurt to the commonwealth, are not properly rewards; for they are not salaries; because there is in this case no contract supposed, every man being obliged already not to do the commonwealth disservice: nor are they graces; because they be extorted by fear, which ought not to be incident to the sovereign power: but are rather sacrifices, which the sovereign (considered in his natural person, and not in the person of the commonwealth) makes, for the appeasing the discontent of him he thinks more potent than himself; and encourage not to obedience, but on the contrary, to the continuance, and increasing of further extortion.

Benefits bestowed for fear, are not rewards.

26. And whereas some salaries are certain, and proceed from the public treasure; and others uncertain, and casual, proceeding from the execution of the office for which the salary is ordained; the latter is in some cases hurtful to the commonwealth; as in the case of judicature. For where the benefit of the judges, and ministers of a court of justice, ariseth from the multitude of causes that are brought to their cognizance, there must needs follow two inconveniences: one, is the nourishing of suits; for the more suits, the greater benefit: and another that depends on that, which is contention about jurisdiction; each court drawing to itself, as many causes

Salaries certain and casual.

as it can. But in offices of execution there are not those inconveniences; because their employment cannot be increased by any endeavour of their own. And thus much shall suffice for the nature of punishment and reward; which are, as it were, the nerves and tendons, that move the limbs and joints of a commonwealth.

27. Hitherto I have set forth the nature of man, (whose pride and other passions have compelled him to submit himself to government;) together with the great power of his governor, whom I compared to *Leviathan*, taking that comparison out of the two last verses of the one-and-fortieth of *Job*; where God having set forth the great power of *Leviathan*, calleth him King of the Proud. *There is nothing*, saith he, *on earth, to be compared with him. He is made so as* [167] *not to be afraid. He seeth every high thing below him; and is king of all the children of pride*. But because he is mortal, and subject to decay, as all other earthly creatures are; and because there is that in heaven, (though not on earth) that he should stand in fear of, and whose laws he ought to obey; I shall in the next following chapters speak of his diseases, and the causes of his mortality; and of what laws of nature he is bound to obey.

CHAPTER XXIX

OF THOSE THINGS THAT WEAKEN, OR TEND TO THE DISSOLUTION OF A COMMONWEALTH*

Dissolution of commonwealths proceedeth from their imperfect institution.

1. THOUGH nothing can be immortal, which mortals make; yet, if men had the use of reason they pretend to, their commonwealths might be secured, at least from perishing by internal diseases. For by the nature of their institution, they are designed to live, as long as mankind, or as the laws of nature, or as justice itself, which gives them life. Therefore when they come to be dissolved, not by external violence, but intestine disorder, the fault is not in men, as they are the *matter*; but as they are the *makers*, and orderers of them. For men, as they become at last weary of irregular jostling, and hewing one another, and desire with all their hearts, to conform themselves into one firm and lasting edifice; so for want, both of the art of making fit laws, to square their actions by, and also of humility, and patience, to suffer the rude and cumbersome points of their present

greatness to be taken off, they cannot without the help of a very able architect, be compiled, into any other than a crazy building, such as hardly lasting out their own time, must assuredly fall upon the heads of their posterity.

2. Amongst the *infirmities* therefore of a commonwealth, I will reckon in the first place, those that arise from an imperfect institution, and resemble the diseases of a natural body, which proceed from a defectuous procreation.

3. Of which, this is one, *that a man to obtain a kingdom, is sometimes content with less power, than to the peace, and defence of the commonwealth is necessarily required.* From whence it cometh to pass, that when the exercise of the power laid by, is for the public safety to be resumed, it hath the resemblance of an unjust act; which disposeth great numbers of men (when occasion is presented) to rebel; in the same manner as the bodies of children, gotten by diseased parents, are subject either to untimely death, or to purge the ill quality, derived from their vicious [vitiated] conception, by breaking out into biles and scabs. And when kings deny themselves some such necessary power, it is not always (though sometimes) out of ignorance of what is necessary to the office they undertake; but many times out of a hope to recover the same again at their pleasure: wherein they reason not well; because such as will hold them to their promises, shall be maintained against them by foreign commonwealths; who in order to the good of their own subjects let slip few occasions to *weaken* the estate of their neighbours. So was Thomas Becket, Archbishop of Canterbury, supported against Henry the Second, by the Pope; the subjection of ecclesiastics to the commonwealth, having been dispensed with by William the Conqueror at his reception, when he took an oath, not to infringe the liberty of the church. And so were the barons, whose power was by William Rufus (to have their help in transferring the succession from his elder brother, to himself) increased to a degree, inconsistent with the sovereign power, maintained in their rebellion against king John, by the French.

Want of absolute power.

[168]

4. Nor does this happen in monarchy only. For whereas the style of the ancient Roman commonwealth, was, *The Senate, and People of Rome*; neither senate, nor people pretended to the whole power; which first caused the seditions, of Tiberius Gracchus, Caius Gracchus, Lucius Saturninus, and others; and afterwards the wars between the senate and the people, under Marius and Sylla; and

again under Pompey and Caesar, to the extinction of their democracy, and the setting up of monarchy.

5. The people of Athens bound themselves but from one only action; which was, that no man on pain of death should propound the renewing of the war for the island of Salamis; and yet thereby, if Solon had not caused to be given out he was mad,* and afterwards in gesture and habit of a madman, and in verse, propounded it to the people that flocked about him, they had had an enemy perpetually in readiness, even at the gates of their city; such damage, or shifts, are all commonwealths forced to, that have their power never so little limited.

Private judgment of good and evil.

6.* In the second place, I observe the *diseases* of a commonwealth, that proceed from the poison of seditious doctrines, whereof one is, *That every private man is judge of good and evil actions.* This is true in the condition of mere nature, where there are no civil laws; and also under civil government, in such cases as are not determined by the law. But otherwise, it is manifest, that the measure of good and evil actions, is the civil law; and the judge the legislator, who is always the representative of the commonwealth. From this false doctrine, men are disposed to debate with themselves, and dispute the commands of the commonwealth; and afterwards to obey, or disobey them, as in their private judgments they shall think fit. Whereby the commonwealth is distracted and *weakened*.

Erroneous conscience.

7. Another doctrine repugnant to civil society, is, that *whatsoever a man does against his conscience, is sin*; and it dependeth on the presumption of making himself judge of good and evil. For a man's conscience, and his judgment is the same thing; and as the judgment, so also the conscience may be erroneous. Therefore,

[169] though he that is subject to no civil law, sinneth in all he does against his conscience, because he has no other rule to follow but his own reason; yet it is not so with him that lives in a commonwealth; because the law is the public conscience, by which he hath already undertaken to be guided. Otherwise in such diversity, as there is of private consciences, which are but private opinions, the commonwealth must needs be distracted, and no man dare to obey the sovereign power, further than it shall seem good in his own eyes.

Pretence of inspiration.

8. It hath been also commonly taught, *that faith and sanctity, are not to be attained by study and reason, but by supernatural inspiration, or infusion.* Which granted, I see not why any man should render a

reason of his faith; or why every Christian should not be also a prophet; or why any man should take the law of his country, rather than his own inspiration, for the rule of his action. And thus we fall again in the fault of taking upon us to judge of good and evil; or to make judges of it, such private men as pretend to be supernaturally inspired, to the dissolution of all civil government. Faith comes by hearing, and hearing by those accidents, which guide us into the presence of them that speak to us; which accidents are all contrived by God Almighty; and yet are not supernatural, but only, for the great number of them that concur to every effect, unobservable. Faith, and sanctity, are indeed not very frequent; but yet they are not miracles, but brought to pass by education, discipline, correction, and other natural ways, by which God worketh them in his elect, at such times as he thinketh fit. And these three opinions, pernicious to peace and government, have in this part of the world, proceeded chiefly from the tongues, and pens of unlearned divines; who joining the words of Holy Scripture together, otherwise than is agreeable to reason, do what they can, to make men think, that sanctity and natural reason, cannot stand together.

9. A fourth opinion, repugnant to the nature of a commonwealth, is this, *that he that hath the sovereign power is subject to the civil laws.** It is true, that sovereigns are all subject to the laws of nature; because such laws be divine, and cannot by any man, or commonwealth be abrogated. But to those laws which the sovereign himself, that is, which the commonwealth maketh, he is not subject. For to be subject to laws, is to be subject to the commonwealth, that is to the sovereign representative, that is to himself; which is not subjection, but freedom from the laws. Which error, because it setteth the laws above the sovereign, setteth also a judge above him, and a power to punish him; which is to make a new sovereign; and again for the same reason a third, to punish the second; and so continually without end, to the confusion, and dissolution of the commonwealth. *Subjecting the sovereign power to civil laws.*

10. A fifth doctrine, that tendeth to the dissolution of a commonwealth, is, *that every private man has an absolute propriety in his goods; such, as excludeth the right of the sovereign.* Every man has indeed a propriety that excludes the right of every other subject: and he has it only from the sovereign power; without the protection whereof, every other man should have equal right to the same. But if the right of the sovereign also be excluded, he cannot perform the office they *Attributing of absolute propriety to subjects.*

[170]

have put him into; which is, to defend them both from foreign enemies, and from the injuries of one another; and consequently there is no longer a commonwealth.

11. And if the propriety of subjects, exclude not the right of the sovereign representative to their goods; much less to their offices of judicature, or execution, in which they represent the sovereign himself.

Dividing of the sovereign power.

12. There is a sixth doctrine, plainly, and directly against the essence of a commonwealth; and 'tis this, *that the sovereign power may be divided*. For what is it to divide the power of a commonwealth, but to dissolve it? for powers divided mutually destroy each other. And for these doctrines, men are chiefly beholding to some of those, that making profession of the laws, endeavour to make them depend upon their own learning, and not upon the legislative power.

Imitation of neighbour nations.

13. And as false doctrine, so also oftentimes the example of different government in a neighbouring nation, disposeth men to alteration of the form already settled. So the people of the Jews were stirred up to reject God, and to call upon the prophet Samuel, for a king after the manner of the nations: so also the lesser cities of Greece, were continually disturbed, with seditions of the aristocratical, and democratical factions; one part of almost every commonwealth, desiring to imitate the Lacedemonians;* the other, the Athenians. And I doubt not, but many men have been contented to see the late troubles in England, out of an imitation of the Low Countries; supposing there needed no more to grow rich, than to change, as they had done, the form of their government. For the constitution of man's nature, is of itself subject to desire novelty: when therefore they are provoked to the same, by the neighbourhood also of those that have been enriched by it, it is almost impossible for them, not to be content with those that solicit them to change; and love the first beginnings, (though they be grieved with the continuance) of disorder; like hot bloods, that having gotten the itch, tear themselves with their own nails, till they can endure the smart no longer.

Imitation of the Greeks and Romans.

14. And as to rebellion in particular against monarchy; one of the most frequent causes of it, is the reading of the books of policy, and histories of the ancient Greeks, and Romans; from which, young men, and all others that are unprovided of the antidote of solid reason, receiving a strong, and delightful impression, of the great

exploits of war, achieved by the conductors of their armies, receive
withal a pleasing idea, of all they have done besides; and imagine
their great prosperity, not to have proceeded from the emulation of
particular men, but from the virtue of their popular form of government: not considering the frequent seditions, and civil wars, produced by the imperfection of their policy. From the reading, I say,
of such books, men have undertaken to kill their kings, because the
Greek and Latin writers, in their books, and discourses of policy, [171]
make it lawful, and laudable, for any man so to do; provided, before
he do it, he call him tyrant. For they say not *regicide*, that is, killing
a king, but *tyrannicide*, that is, killing of a tyrant is lawful. From the
same books, they that live under a monarch conceive an opinion,
that the subjects in a popular commonwealth enjoy liberty; but that
in a monarchy they are all slaves. I say, they that live under a
monarchy conceive such an opinion; not they that live under a
popular government: for they find no such matter. In sum, I cannot
imagine, how any thing can be more prejudicial to a monarchy, than
the allowing of such books to be publicly read, without present
applying such correctives of discreet masters, as are fit to take away
their venom: which venom I will not doubt to compare to the biting
of a mad dog, which is a disease the physicians call *hydrophobia*, or
fear of water. For as he that is so bitten, has a continual torment of
thirst, and yet abhorreth water; and is in such an estate, as if the
poison endeavoured to convert him into a dog: so when a monarchy
is once bitten to the quick, by those democratical writers, that
continually snarl at that estate; it wanteth nothing more
than a strong monarch, which nevertheless out of a certain
tyrannophobia, or fear of being strongly governed, when they have
him, they abhor.

15. As there have been doctors, that hold there be three souls in
a man; so there be also that think there may be more souls, (that is,
more sovereigns,) than one, in a commonwealth; and set up a *supremacy* against the *sovereignty*; *canons* against *laws*; and a *ghostly
authority* against the *civil*; working on men's minds, with words and
distinctions, that of themselves signify nothing, but bewray (by their
obscurity) that there walketh (as some think invisibly) another kingdom, as it were a kingdom of fairies, in the dark. Now seeing it is
manifest, that the civil power, and the power of the commonwealth
is the same thing; and that supremacy, and the power of making
canons, and granting faculties, implieth a commonwealth; it

followeth, that where one is sovereign, another supreme; where one can make laws, and another make canons; there must needs be two commonwealths, of one and the same subjects; which is a kingdom divided in itself, and cannot stand. For notwithstanding the insignificant distinction of *temporal*, and *ghostly*, they are still two kingdoms, and every subject is subject to two masters. For seeing the *ghostly* power challengeth the right to declare what is sin, it challengeth by consequence to declare what is law, (sin being nothing but the transgression of the law;) and again, the civil power challenging to declare what is law, every subject must obey two masters, who both will have their commands be observed as law; which is impossible. Or, if it be but one kingdom, either the *civil*, which is the power of the commonwealth, must be subordinate to the *ghostly*, and then there is no sovereignty but the *ghostly*; or the *ghostly* must be subordinate to the *temporal*, and then there is no *supremacy* but the *temporal*. When therefore these two powers oppose one another, the commonwealth cannot but be in great danger of civil war and dissolution. For the *civil* authority being more visible, and standing in the clearer light of natural reason, cannot choose but draw to it in all times a very considerable part of the people: and the *spiritual*, though it stand in the darkness of School distinctions, and hard words; yet because the fear of darkness, and ghosts, is greater than other fears, cannot want a party sufficient to trouble, and sometimes to destroy a commonwealth. And this is a disease which not unfitly may be compared to the epilepsy, or falling sickness (which the Jews took to be one kind of possession by spirits) in the body natural. For as in this disease, there is an unnatural spirit, or wind in the head that obstructeth the roots of the nerves, and moving them violently, taketh away the motion which naturally they should have from the power of the soul in the brain, and thereby causeth violent, and irregular motions (which men call convulsions) in the parts; insomuch as he that is seized therewith, falleth down sometimes into the water, and sometimes into the fire, as a man deprived of his senses; so also in the body politic, when the spiritual power, moveth the members of a commonwealth, by the terror of punishments, and hope of rewards* (which are the nerves of it,) otherwise than by the civil power (which is the soul of the commonwealth) they ought to be moved; and by strange, and hard words suffocates their understanding, it must needs thereby distract

[172]

218

the people, and either overwhelm the commonwealth with oppression, or cast it into the fire of a civil war.

16. Sometimes also in the merely civil government, there be *Mixed*
more than one soul; as when the power of levying money, (which is *government.*
the nutritive faculty,) has depended on a general assembly; the
power of conduct and command, (which is the motive faculty,) on
one man; and the power of making laws, (which is the rational
faculty,) on the accidental consent, not only of those two, but also of
a third;* this endangereth the commonwealth, sometimes for want
of consent to good laws; but most often for want of such nourishment, as is necessary to life, and motion. For although few perceive,
that such government, is not government, but division of the commonwealth into three factions, and call it mixed monarchy; yet the
truth is, that it is not one independent commonwealth, but three
independent factions; nor one representative person, but three. In
the kingdom of God, there may be three persons independent,
without breach of unity in God that reigneth; but where men reign,
that be subject to diversity of opinions, it cannot be so. And therefore if the king bear the person of the people, and the general
assembly bear also the person of the people, and another assembly
bear the person of a part of the people, they are not one person, nor
one sovereign, but three persons, and three sovereigns.

17. To what disease in the natural body of man, I may exactly
compare this irregularity of a commonwealth, I know not. But I have
seen a man, that had another man growing out of his side, with a
head, arms, breast, and stomach, of his own; if he had had another [173]
man growing out of his other side, the comparison might then have
been exact.

18. Hitherto, I have named such diseases of a commonwealth, as *Want of*
are of the greatest, and most present danger. There be other, not so *money.*
great; which nevertheless are not unfit to be observed. At first, the
difficulty of raising money, for the necessary uses of the commonwealth; especially in the approach of war. This difficulty ariseth
from the opinion, that every subject hath a propriety in his lands and
goods, exclusive of the sovereign's right to the use of the same.
From whence it cometh to pass, that the sovereign power, which
foreseeth the necessities and dangers of the commonwealth, (finding
the passage of money to the public treasury obstructed, by the
tenacity of the people,) whereas it ought to extend itself, to encoun-

ter, and prevent such dangers in their beginnings, contracteth itself as long as it can, and when it cannot longer, struggles with the people by stratagems of law, to obtain little sums, which not sufficing, he is fain at last violently to open the way for present supply, or perish; and being put often to these extremities, at last reduceth the people to their due temper; or else the commonwealth must perish. Insomuch as we may compare this distemper very aptly to an ague; wherein, the fleshy parts being congealed, or by venomous matter obstructed, the veins which by their natural course empty themselves into the heart, are not (as they ought to be) supplied from the arteries, whereby there succeedeth at first a cold contraction, and trembling of the limbs; and afterward a hot, and strong endeavour of the heart, to force a passage for the blood; and before it can do that, contenteth itself with the small refreshments of such things as cool for a time, till (if nature be strong enough) it break at last the contumacy of the parts obstructed, and dissipateth the venom into sweat; or (if nature be too weak) the patient dieth.

Monopolies, and abuses of publicans.

19. Again, there is sometimes in a commonwealth, a disease, which resembleth the pleurisy; and that is, when the treasure of the commonwealth, flowing out of its due course, is gathered together in too much abundance, in one, or a few private men, by monopolies, or by farms of the public revenues; in the same manner as the blood in a pleurisy, getting into the membrane of the breast, breedeth there an inflammation, accompanied with a fever, and painful stitches.

Popular men.

20. Also, the popularity of a potent subject, (unless the commonwealth have very good caution of his fidelity,) is a dangerous disease; because the people, (which should receive their motion from the authority of the sovereign,) by the flattery, and by the reputation of an ambitious man are drawn away from their obedience to the laws, to follow a man, of whose virtues, and designs they have no knowledge. And this is commonly of more danger in a popular government, than in a monarchy; because an army is of so great force, and multitude, as it may easily be made believe, they are the people. By [174] this means it was, that Julius Caesar, who was set up by the people against the senate, having won to himself the affections of his army, made himself master, both of senate and people. And this proceeding of popular, and ambitious men, is plain rebellion; and may be resembled to the effects of witchcraft.

21. Another infirmity of a commonwealth, is the immoderate greatness of a town, when it is able to furnish out of its own circuit, the number, and expense of a great army: as also the great number of corporations; which are as it were many lesser commonwealths in the bowels of a greater, like worms in the entrails of a natural man. To which may be added, the liberty of disputing against absolute power, by pretenders to political prudence; which though bred for the most part in the lees [dregs] of the people, yet animated by false doctrines, are perpetually meddling with the fundamental laws, to the molestation of the commonwealth; like the little worms, which physicians call *ascarides*.

Excessive greatness of a town, or multitude of corporations.

Liberty of disputing against sovereign power.

22. We may further add, the insatiable appetite, or βουλιμία, of enlarging dominion; with the incurable *wounds* thereby many times received from the enemy; and the *wens*, of ununited conquests, which are many times a burthen, and with less danger lost, than kept; as also the *lethargy* of ease, and *consumption* of riot and vain expense.

23. Lastly, when in a war (foreign or intestine,) the enemies get a final victory; so as (the forces of the commonwealth keeping the field no longer) there is no further protection of subjects in their loyalty; then is the commonwealth DISSOLVED, and every man at liberty to protect himself by such courses as his own discretion shall suggest unto him. For the sovereign, is the public soul, giving life and motion to the commonwealth; which expiring, the members are governed by it no more, than the carcase of a man, by his departed (though immortal) soul. For though the right of a sovereign monarch cannot be extinguished by the act of another; yet the obligation of the members may. For he that wants protection, may seek it anywhere; and when he hath it, is obliged (without fraudulent pretence of having submitted himself out of fear,) to protect his protection as long as he is able. But when the power of an assembly is once suppressed, the right of the same perisheth utterly; because the assembly itself is extinct; and consequently, there is no possibility for the sovereignty to re-enter.

Dissolution of the commonwealth.

CHAPTER XXX

OF THE OFFICE OF THE SOVEREIGN REPRESENTATIVE

The procuration of the good of the people.

1. THE OFFICE of the sovereign, (be it a monarch or an assembly,) consisteth in the end, for which he was trusted with the sovereign power, namely the procuration of *the safety of the people*; to which he is obliged by the law of nature, and to render an account thereof to God, the author of that law, and to none but him. But by safety here, is not meant a bare preservation, but also all other contentments of life, which every man by lawful industry, without danger, or hurt to the commonwealth, shall acquire to himself.

By instruction & laws.

2. And this is intended should be done, not by care applied to individuals, further than their protection from injuries, when they shall complain; but by a general providence, contained in public instruction, both of doctrine, and example; and in the making and executing of good laws, to which individual persons may apply their own cases.

Against the duty of a sovereign to relinquish any essential right of sovereignty:

3. And because, if the essential rights of sovereignty (specified before in the eighteenth chapter) be taken away, the commonwealth is thereby dissolved, and every man returneth into the condition, and calamity of a war with every other man, (which is the greatest evil that can happen in this life;) it is the office of the sovereign, to maintain those rights entire; and consequently against his duty, first, to transfer to another, or to lay from himself any of them. For he that deserteth the means, deserteth the ends; and he deserteth the means, that being the sovereign, acknowledgeth himself subject to the civil laws; and renounceth the power of supreme judicature; or of making war, or peace by his own authority; or of judging of the necessities of the commonwealth; or of levying money, and soldiers, when, and as much as in his own conscience he shall judge necessary; or of making officers, and ministers both of war, and peace; or of appointing teachers, and examining what doctrines are conformable, or contrary to the defence, peace, and good of the people.

Or not to see the people taught the grounds of them.

Secondly, it is against his duty, to let the people be ignorant, or misinformed of the grounds, and reasons of those his essential rights; because thereby men are easy to be seduced, and drawn to resist him, when the commonwealth shall require their use and exercise.

4. And the grounds of these rights, have the rather need to be diligently, and truly taught; because they cannot be maintained by any civil law, or terror of legal punishment. For a civil law, that shall forbid rebellion, (and such is all resistance to the essential rights of the sovereignty,) is not (as a civil law) any obligation, but by virtue [176] only of the law of nature, that forbiddeth the violation of faith; which natural obligation if men know not, they cannot know the right of any law the sovereign maketh. And for the punishment, they take it but for an act of hostility; which when they think they have strength enough, they will endeavour by acts of hostility, to avoid.

5. As I have heard some say, that justice is but a word, without substance; and that whatsoever a man can by force, or art, acquire to himself, (not only in the condition of war, but also in a commonwealth,) is his own, which I have already showed to be false: so there be also that maintain, that there are no grounds, nor principles of reason, to sustain those essential rights, which make sovereignty absolute. For if there were, they would have been found out in some place, or other; whereas we see, there has not hitherto been any commonwealth, where those rights have been acknowledged, or challenged. Wherein they argue as ill, as if the savage people of America, should deny there were any grounds, or principles of reason, so to build a house, as to last as long as the materials, because they never yet saw any so well built. Time, and industry, produce every day new knowledge. And as the art of well building, is derived from principles of reason, observed by industrious men, that had long studied the nature of materials, and the divers effects of figure, and proportion, long after mankind began (though poorly) to build: so, long time after men have begun to constitute commonwealths, imperfect, and apt to relapse into disorder, there may, principles of reason be found out, by industrious meditation, to make their constitution (excepting by external violence) everlasting. And such are those which I have in this discourse set forth: which whether they come not into the sight of those that have power to make use of them, or be neglected by them, or not, concerneth my particular interests, at this day, very little. But supposing that these of mine are not such principles of reason; yet I am sure they are principles from authority of Scripture; as I shall make it appear, when I shall come to speak of the kingdom of God, (administered by Moses,) over the Jews, his peculiar people by covenant.

Objection of those that say there are no principles of reason for absolute sovereignty.

Objection from the incapacity of the vulgar.

6. But they say again, that though the principles be right, yet common people are not of capacity enough to be made to understand them. I should be glad, that the rich and potent subjects of a kingdom, or those that are accounted the most learned, were no less incapable than they. But all men know, that the obstructions to this kind of doctrine, proceed not so much from the difficulty of the matter, as from the interest of them that are to learn. Potent men, digest hardly any thing that setteth up a power to bridle their affections; and learned men, any thing that discovereth their errors, and thereby lesseneth their authority: whereas the common people's minds, unless they be tainted with dependence on the potent, or scribbled over with the opinions of their doctors, are like clean paper, fit to receive whatsoever by public authority shall be im-

[177] printed in them. Shall whole nations be brought to *acquiesce* in the great mysteries of the Christian religion, which are above reason, and millions of men be made believe, that the same body may be in innumerable places, at one and the same time, which is against reason; and shall not men be able, by their teaching, and preaching, protected by the law, to make that received, which is so consonant to reason, that any unprejudicated man, needs no more to learn it, than to hear it? I conclude therefore, that in the instruction of the people in the essential rights (which are the natural, and fundamental laws) of sovereignty, there is no difficulty, (whilst a sovereign has his power entire,) but what proceeds from his own fault, or the fault of those whom he trusteth in the administration of the commonwealth; and consequently, it is his duty, to cause them so to be instructed; and not only his duty, but his benefit also, and security, against the danger that may arrive to himself in his natural person from rebellion.

Subjects are to be taught, not to affect change of government:

7. And (to descend to particulars) the people are to be taught, first, that they ought not to be in love with any form of government they see in their neighbour nations, more than with their own, nor (whatsoever present prosperity they behold in nations that are otherwise governed than they,) to desire change. For the prosperity of a people ruled by an aristocratical, or democratical assembly, cometh not from aristocracy, nor from democracy, but from the obedience, and concord of the subjects: nor do the people flourish in a monarchy, because one man has the right to rule them, but because they obey him. Take away in any kind of state, the obedience, (and consequently the concord of the people,) and they shall not only not

flourish, but in short time be dissolved. And they that go about by disobedience, to do no more than reform the commonwealth, shall find they do thereby destroy it; like the foolish daughters of Peleus, (in the fable;) which desiring to renew the youth of their decrepit father, did by the counsel of Medea, cut him in pieces, and boil him, together with strange herbs, but made not of him a new man.* This desire of change, is like the breach of the first of God's commandments: for there God says, *Non habebis Deos alienos*; Thou shalt not have the Gods of other nations; and in another place concerning *kings*, that they are *Gods*.*

8. Secondly, they are to be taught, that they ought not to be led *Nor adhere* with admiration of the virtue of any of their fellow-subjects, how *(against the* high soever he stand, or how conspicuously soever he shine in the *sovereign) to* commonwealth; nor of any assembly, (except the sovereign assem- *popular men:* bly,) so as to defer to them any obedience, or honour, appropriate to the sovereign only, whom (in their particular stations) they repre- sent; nor to receive any influence from them, but such as is conveyed by them from the sovereign authority. For that sovereign, cannot be imagined to love his people as he ought, that is not jealous of them, but suffers them by the flattery of popular men, to be seduced from their loyalty, as they have often been, not only secretly, but openly, so as to proclaim marriage with them *in facie ecclesiae* by preachers; and by publishing the same in the open streets: which may fitly [178] be compared to the violation of the second of the ten com- mandments.

9. Thirdly, in consequence to this, they ought to be informed, *Nor to* how great a fault it is, to speak evil of the sovereign representative, *dispute the* (whether one man, or an assembly of men;) or to argue and *sovereign* dispute his power; or any way to use his name irreverently, whereby *power:* he may be brought into contempt with his people, and their obedi- ence (in which the safety of the commonwealth consisteth) slack- ened. Which doctrine the third commandment by resemblance pointeth to.

10. Fourthly, seeing people cannot be taught this, nor when 'tis *And to have* taught, remember it, nor after one generation past, so much as know *days set apart* in whom the sovereign power is placed, without setting apart from *to learn their* their ordinary labour, some certain times, in which they may attend *duty:* those that are appointed to instruct them; it is necessary that some such times be determined, wherein they may assemble together, and (after prayers and praises given to God, the sovereign of sovereigns)

hear those their duties told them, and the positive laws, such as generally concern them all, read and expounded, and be put in mind of the authority that maketh them laws. To this end had the Jews every seventh day, a sabbath, in which the law was read and expounded; and in the solemnity whereof they were put in mind, that their king was God; that having created the world in six days, he rested the seventh day; and by their resting on it from their labour, that that God was their king, which redeemed them from their servile, and painful labour in Egypt, and gave them a time, after they had rejoiced in God, to take joy also in themselves, by lawful recreation. So that the first table of the commandments, is spent all, in setting down the sum of God's absolute power; not only as God, but as king by pact, (in peculiar) of the Jews; and may therefore give light, to those that have sovereign power conferred on them by the consent of men, to see what doctrine they ought to teach their subjects.

And to honour their parents.

11. And because the first instruction of children, dependeth on the care of their parents; it is necessary that they should be obedient to them, whilst they are under their tuition; and not only so, but that also afterwards (as gratitude requireth,) they acknowledge the benefit of their education, by external signs of honour. To which end they are to be taught, that originally the father of every man was also his sovereign lord, with power over him of life and death; and that the fathers of families, when by instituting a commonwealth, they resigned that absolute power, yet it was never intended, they should lose the honour due unto them for their education. For to relinquish such right, was not necessary to the institution of sovereign power; nor would there be any reason, why any man should desire to have children, or take the care to nourish and instruct them, if they were afterwards to have no other benefit from them, than from other men. And this accordeth with the fifth commandment.

[179]

And to avoid doing of injury:

12. Again, every sovereign ought to cause justice to be taught, which (consisting in taking from no man what is his) is as much as to say, to cause men to be taught not to deprive their neighbours, by violence, or fraud, of any thing which by the sovereign authority is theirs. Of things held in propriety, those that are dearest to a man are his own life, and limbs; and in the next degree, (in most men,) those that concern conjugal affection; and after them, riches and means of living. Therefore the people are to be taught, to abstain

226

from violence to one another's person, by private revenges; from violation of conjugal honour; and from forcible rapine, and fraudulent surreption of one another's goods. For which purpose also it is necessary they be showed the evil consequences of false judgment, by corruption either of judges or witnesses, whereby the distinction of propriety is taken away, and justice becomes of no effect: all which things are intimated in the sixth, seventh, eighth, and ninth commandments.

13. Lastly, they are to be taught, that not only the unjust facts, but the designs and intentions to do them, (though by accident hindered,) are injustice; which consisteth in the pravity [depravity] of the will, as well as in the irregularity of the act. And this is the intention of the tenth commandment, and the sum of the second table; which is reduced all to this one commandment of mutual charity, *thou shalt love thy neighbour as thyself*: as the sum of the first table is reduced to *the love of God*; whom they had then newly received as their king.

And to do all this sincerely from the heart.

14. As for the means, and conduits, by which the people may receive this instruction, we are to search, by what means so many opinions, contrary to the peace of mankind, upon weak and false principles, have nevertheless been so deeply rooted in them. I mean those, which I have in the precedent chapter specified: as that men shall judge of what is lawful and unlawful, not by the law itself, but by their own consciences; that is to say, by their own private judgments: that subjects sin in obeying the commands of the commonwealth, unless they themselves have first judged them to be lawful: that their propriety in their riches is such, as to exclude the dominion, which the commonwealth hath over the same: that it is lawful for subjects to kill such, as they call tyrants: that the sovereign power may be divided, and the like; which come to be instilled into the people by this means. They whom necessity, or covetousness keepeth attent on their trades, and labour; and they, on the other side, whom superfluity, or sloth carrieth after their sensual pleasures, (which two sorts of men take up the greatest part of mankind,) being diverted from the deep meditation, which the learning of truth, not only in the matter of natural justice, but also of all other sciences necessarily requireth, receive the notions of their duty, chiefly from divines in the pulpit, and partly from such of their neighbours or familiar acquaintance, as having the faculty of

The use of universities.

discoursing readily, and plausibly, seem wiser and better learned in cases of law, and conscience, than themselves. And the divines, and [180] such others as make show of learning, derive their knowledge from the universities, and from the schools of law, or from the books, which by men, eminent in those schools and universities, have been published. It is therefore manifest, that the instruction of the people, dependeth wholly, on the right teaching of youth in the universities. But are not (may some man say) the universities of England learned enough already to do that? or is it you, will undertake to teach the universities? Hard questions. Yet to the first, I doubt not to answer; that till towards the latter end of Henry the Eighth, the power of the Pope, was always upheld against the power of the commonwealth, principally by the universities; and that the doctrines maintained by so many preachers, against the sovereign power of the king, and by so many lawyers, and others, that had their education there, is a sufficient argument, that though the universities were not authors of those false doctrines, yet they knew not how to plant the true. For in such a contradiction of opinions, it is most certain, that they have not been sufficiently instructed; and 'tis no wonder, if they yet retain a relish of that subtle liquor, wherewith they were first seasoned, against the civil authority. But to the latter question, it is not fit, nor needful for me to say either aye, or no: for any man that sees what I am doing, may easily perceive what I think.

15. The safety of the people, requireth further, from him, or them that have the sovereign power, that justice be equally administered to all degrees of people; that is, that as well the rich, and mighty, as poor and obscure persons, may be righted of the injuries done them; so as the great, may have no greater hope of impunity, when they do violence, dishonour, or any injury to the meaner sort, than when one of these, does the like to one of them: for in this consisteth equity; to which, as being a precept of the law of nature, a sovereign is as much subject, as any of the meanest of his people. All breaches of the law, are offences against the commonwealth: but there be some, that are also against private persons. Those that concern the commonwealth only, may without breach of equity be pardoned; for every man may pardon what is done against himself, according to his own discretion. But an offence against a private man, cannot in equity be pardoned, without the consent of him that is injured; or reasonable satisfaction.

16. The inequality of subjects, proceedeth from the acts of sovereign power; and therefore has no more place in the presence of the sovereign; that is to say, in a court of justice, than the inequality between kings, and their subjects, in the presence of the King of kings. The honour of great persons, is to be valued for their beneficence, and the aids they give to men of inferior rank, or not at all. And the violences, oppressions, and injuries they do, are not extenuated, but aggravated by the greatness of their persons; because they have least need to commit them. The consequences of this partiality towards the great, proceed in this manner. Impunity maketh insolence; insolence, hatred; and hatred, an endeavour to pull down all oppressing and contumelious greatness, though with the ruin of the commonwealth.

17. To equal justice, appertaineth also the equal imposition of [181] taxes; the equality whereof dependeth not on the equality of riches, *Equal taxes.* but on the equality of the debt, that every man oweth to the commonwealth for his defence. It is not enough, for a man to labour for the maintenance of his life; but also to fight, (if need be,) for the securing of his labour. They must either do as the Jews did after their return from captivity, in re-edifying the temple, build with one hand, and hold the sword in the other; or else they must hire others to fight for them. For the impositions, that are laid on the people by the sovereign power, are nothing else but the wages, due to them that hold the public sword, to defend private men in the exercise of their several trades, and callings. Seeing then the benefit that every one receiveth thereby, is the enjoyment of life, which is equally dear to poor, and rich; the debt which a poor man oweth them that defend his life, is the same which a rich man oweth for the defence of his; saving that the rich, who have the service of the poor, may be debtors not only for their own persons, but for many more. Which considered, the equality of imposition, consisteth rather in the equality of that which is consumed, than of the riches of the persons that consume the same. For what reason is there, that he which laboureth much, and sparing the fruits of his labour, consumeth little, should be more charged, than he that living idly, getteth little, and spendeth all he gets; seeing the one hath no more protection from the commonwealth, than the other? But when the impositions, are laid upon those things which men consume, every man payeth equally for what he useth: nor is the commonwealth defrauded by the luxurious waste of private men.

*Public
charity.*

18. And whereas many men, by accident inevitable, become unable to maintain themselves by their labour; they ought not to be left to the charity of private persons; but to be provided for, (as far forth as the necessities of nature require,) by the laws of the commonwealth. For as it is uncharitableness in any man, to neglect the impotent; so it is in the sovereign of a commonwealth, to expose them to the hazard of such uncertain charity.

*Prevention of
idleness.*

19. But for such as have strong bodies, the case is otherwise: they are to be forced to work; and to avoid the excuse of not finding employment, there ought to be such laws, as may encourage all manner of arts; as navigation, agriculture, fishing, and all manner of manufacture that requires labour. The multitude of poor, and yet strong people still increasing, they are to be transplanted into countries not sufficiently inhabited: where nevertheless, they are not to exterminate those they find there; but constrain them to inhabit closer together, and not to range a great deal of ground, to snatch what they find; but to court each little plot with art and labour, to give them their sustenance in due season. And when all the world is overcharged with inhabitants, then the last remedy of all is war; which provideth for every man, by victory, or death.

*Good laws,
what.*

[182]

20. To the care of the sovereign, belongeth the making of good laws. But what is a good law? By a good law, I mean not a just law: for no law can be unjust. The law is made by the sovereign power, and all that is done by such power, is warranted, and owned by every one of the people; and that which every man will have so, no man can say is unjust. It is in the laws of a commonwealth, as in the laws of gaming: whatsoever the gamesters all agree on, is injustice to none of them. A good law is that, which is *needful*, for the *good of the people*, and withal *perspicuous*.

*Such as are
necessary.*

21. For the use of laws, (which are but rules authorized) is not to bind the people from all voluntary actions; but to direct and keep them in such a motion, as not to hurt themselves by their own impetuous desires, rashness or indiscretion; as hedges are set, not to stop travellers, but to keep them in their way. And therefore a law that is not needful, having not the true end of a law, is not good. A law may be conceived to be good, when it is for the benefit of the sovereign; though it be not necessary for the people; but it is not so. For the good of the sovereign and people, cannot be separated. It is a weak sovereign, that has weak subjects; and a weak people, whose sovereign wanteth power to rule them at his will. Unnecessary laws are not good laws; but traps for money: which where the right of sovereign power is acknowledged are superfluous; and where it is not acknowledged, unsufficient to defend the people.

22. The perspicuity, consisteth not so much in the words of the law itself, as in a declaration of the causes, and motives, for which it was made. That is it, that shows us the meaning of the legislator; and the meaning of the legislator known, the law is more easily understood by few, than many words. For all words, are subject to ambiguity; and therefore multiplication of words in the body of the law, is multiplication of ambiguity: besides it seems to imply, (by too much diligence,) that whosoever can evade the words, is without the compass of the law. And this is a cause of many unnecessary processes. For when I consider how short were the laws of ancient times; and how they grew by degrees still longer; methinks I see a contention between the penners, and pleaders of the law; the former seeking to circumscribe the latter; and the latter to evade their circumscriptions; and that the pleaders have got the victory. It belongeth therefore to the office of a legislator, (such as is in all commonwealths the supreme representative, be it one man, or an assembly,) to make the reason perspicuous, why the law was made; and the body of the law itself, as short, but in as proper, and significant terms, as may be. *Such as are perspicuous.*

23. It belongeth also to the office of the sovereign, to make a right application of punishments, and rewards. And seeing the end of punishing is not revenge, and discharge of choler; but correction, either of the offender, or of others by his example; the severest punishments are to be inflicted for those crimes, that are of most danger to the public; such as are those which proceed from malice to the government established; those that spring from contempt of justice; those that provoke indignation in the multitude; and those, which unpunished, seem authorized, as when they are committed by sons, servants, or favourites of men in authority: for indignation carrieth men, not only against the actors, and authors of injustice; but against all power that is likely to protect them; as in the case of Tarquin; when for the insolent act of one of his sons, he was driven out of Rome, and the monarchy itself dissolved. But crimes of infirmity; such as are those which proceed from great provocation, from great fear, great need, or from ignorance whether the fact be a great crime, or not, there is place many times for lenity, without prejudice to the commonwealth; and lenity, when there is such place *Punishments.* [183]

for it, is required by the law of nature. The punishment of the leaders and teachers in a commotion; not the poor seduced people, when they are punished, can profit the commonwealth by their example. To be severe to the people, is to punish that ignorance, which may in great part be imputed to the sovereign, whose fault it was, they were no better instructed.

Rewards.   24. In like manner it belongeth to the office, and duty of the sovereign, to apply his rewards always so, as there may arise from them benefit to the commonwealth: wherein consisteth their use, and end; and is then done, when they that have well served the commonwealth, are with as little expense of the common treasure, as is possible, so well recompensed, as others thereby may be encouraged, both to serve the same as faithfully as they can, and to study the arts by which they may be enabled to do it better. To buy with money, or preferment, from a popular ambitious subject, to be quiet, and desist from making ill impressions in the minds of the people, has nothing of the nature of reward; (which is ordained not for disservice, but for service past;) nor a sign of gratitude, but of fear: nor does it tend to the benefit, but to the damage of the public. It is a contention with ambition, like that of Hercules with the monster Hydra, which having many heads, for every one that was vanquished, there grew up three. For in like manner, when the stubbornness of one popular man, is overcome with reward, there arise many more (by the example) that do the same mischief, in hope of like benefit: and as all sorts of manufacture, so also malice increaseth by being vendible. And though sometimes a civil war, may be deferred, by such ways as that, yet the danger grows still the greater, and the public ruin more assured. It is therefore against the duty of the sovereign, to whom the public safety is committed, to reward those that aspire to greatness by disturbing the peace of their country, and not rather to oppose the beginnings of such men, with a little danger, than after a longer time with greater.

Counsellors.   25. Another business of the sovereign, is to choose good counsellors; I mean such, whose advice he is to take in the government of the commonwealth. For this word counsel, *consilium*, corrupted from *considium*, is of a large signification, and comprehendeth all assemblies of men that sit together, not only to deliberate what is to be done hereafter, but also to judge of facts past, and of law for the
[184]   present. I take it here in the first sense only: and in this sense, there is no choice of counsel, neither in a democracy, nor aristocracy;

because the persons counselling are members of the person counselled. The choice of counsellors therefore is proper to monarchy; in which, the sovereign that endeavoureth not to make choice of those, that in every kind are the most able, dischargeth not his office as he ought to do. The most able counsellors, are they that have least hope of benefit by giving evil counsel, and most knowledge of those things that conduce to the peace, and defence of the commonwealth. It is a hard matter to know who expecteth benefit from public troubles; but the signs that guide to a just suspicion, is the soothing of the people in their unreasonable, or irremediable grievances, by men whose estates are not sufficient to discharge their accustomed expenses, and may easily be observed by any one whom it concerns to know it. But to know, who has most knowledge of the public affairs, is yet harder; and they that know them, need them a great deal the less. For to know, who knows the rules almost of any art, is a great degree of the knowledge of the same art; because no man can be assured of the truth of another's rules, but he that is first taught to understand them. But the best signs of knowledge of any art, are, much conversing in it, and constant good effects of it. Good counsel comes not by lot, nor by inheritance; and therefore there is no more reason to expect good advice from the rich, or noble, in matter of state, than in delineating the dimensions of a fortress; unless we shall think there needs no method in the study of the politics, (as there does in the study of geometry,) but only to be lookers on; which is not so. For the politics is the harder study of the two. Whereas in these parts of Europe, it hath been taken for a right of certain persons, to have place in the highest council of state by inheritance; it is derived from the conquests of the ancient Germans; wherein many absolute lords joining together to conquer other nations, would not enter into the confederacy, without such privileges, as might be marks of difference in time following, between their posterity, and the posterity of their subjects; which privileges being inconsistent with the sovereign power, by the favour of the sovereign, they may seem to keep; but contending for them as their right, they must needs by degrees let them go, and have at last no further honour, than adhereth naturally to their abilities.

26. And how able soever be the counsellors in any affair, the benefit of their counsel is greater, when they give every one his advice, and the reasons of it apart, than when they do it in an

assembly, by way of orations; and when they have premeditated, than when they speak on the sudden; both because they have more time, to survey the consequences of action; and are less subject to be carried away to contradiction, though envy, emulation, or other passions arising from the difference of opinion.

27. The best counsel, in those things that concern not other [185] nations, but only the ease, and benefit the subjects may enjoy, by laws that look only inward, is to be taken from the general informations, and complaints of the people of each province, who are best acquainted with their own wants, and ought therefore, when they demand nothing in derogation of the essential rights of sovereignty, to be diligently taken notice of. For without those essential rights, (as I have often before said,) the commonwealth cannot at all subsist.

Commanders.   28. A commander of an army in chief, if he be not popular, shall not be beloved, nor feared as he ought to be by his army; and consequently, cannot perform that office with good success. He must therefore be industrious, valiant, affable, liberal and fortunate, that he may gain an opinion both of sufficiency, and of loving his soldiers. This is popularity, and breeds in the soldiers both desire, and courage, to recommend themselves to his favour; and protects the severity of the general, in punishing (when need is) the mutinous, or negligent soldiers. But this love of soldiers, (if caution be not given of the commander's fidelity,) is a dangerous thing to sovereign power; especially when it is in the hands of an assembly not popular. It belongeth therefore to the safety of the people, both that they be good conductors, and faithful subjects, to whom the sovereign commits his armies.

29. But when the sovereign himself is popular; that is, reverenced and beloved of his people, there is no danger at all from the popularity of a subject. For soldiers are never so generally unjust, as to side with their captain; though they love him, against their sovereign, when they love not only his person, but also his cause. And therefore those, who by violence have at any time suppressed the power of their lawful sovereign, before they could settle themselves in his place, have been always put to the trouble of contriving their titles, to save the people from the shame of receiving them. To have a known right to sovereign power, is so popular a quality, as he that has it needs no more, for his own part, to turn the hearts of his

subjects to him, but that they see him able absolutely to govern his own family: nor, on the part of his enemies, but a disbanding of their armies. For the greatest and most active part of mankind, has never hitherto been well contented with the present.

30. Concerning the offices of one sovereign to another, which are comprehended in that law, which is commonly called the *law of nations*, I need not say any thing in this place; because the law of nations, and the law of nature, is the same thing. And every sovereign hath the same right, in procuring the safety of his people, that any particular man can have, in procuring his own safety. And the same law, that dictateth to men that have no civil government, what they ought to do, and what to avoid in regard of one another, dictateth the same to commonwealths, that is, to the consciences of sovereign princes and sovereign assemblies; there being no court of natural justice, but in the conscience only; where not man, but God reigneth; whose laws, (such of them as oblige all mankind,) in respect of God, as he is the author of nature, are *natural*; and in respect [186] of the same God, as he is King of kings, are *laws*. But of the kingdom of God, as King of kings, and as King also of a peculiar people, I shall speak in the rest of this discourse.

CHAPTER XXXI

OF THE KINGDOM OF GOD BY NATURE

1. THAT the condition of mere nature, that is to say, of absolute liberty, such as is theirs, that neither are sovereigns, nor subjects, is anarchy, and the condition of war: that the precepts, by which men are guided to avoid that condition, are the laws of nature: that a commonwealth, without sovereign power, is but a word without substance, and cannot stand: that subjects owe to sovereigns, simple obedience, in all things, wherein their obedience is not repugnant to the laws of God, I have sufficiently proved, in that which I have already written. There wants only, for the entire knowledge of civil duty, to know what are those laws of God. For without that, a man knows not, when he is commanded any thing by the civil power, whether it be contrary to the law of God, or not: and so, either by too

The scope of the following chapters.

much civil obedience, offends the Divine Majesty, or through fear of offending God, transgresses the commandments of the commonwealth. To avoid both these rocks, it is necessary to know what are the laws divine. And seeing the knowledge of all law, dependeth on the knowledge of the sovereign power; I shall say something in that which followeth, of the KINGDOM OF GOD.

Who are subjects in the kingdom of God.

2. *God is king, let the earth rejoice*, saith the psalmist (97. 1). And again, (*Psalm* 99. 1) *God is king though the nations be angry; and he that sitteth on the cherubims, though the earth be moved.* Whether men will or not, they must be subject always to the divine power. By denying the existence, or providence of God, men may shake off their ease, but not their yoke. But to call this power of God, which extendeth itself not only to man, but also to beasts, and plants, and bodies inanimate, by the name of kingdom, is but a metaphorical use of the word. For he only is properly said to reign, that governs his subjects, by his word, and by promise of rewards to those that obey it, and by threatening them with punishment that obey it not. Subjects therefore in the kingdom of God, are not bodies inanimate, nor creatures irrational; because they understand no precepts as his: nor atheists; nor they that believe not that God has any care of the actions of mankind; because they acknowledge no word for his, nor have hope of his rewards or fear of his threatenings. They therefore that believe there is a God that governeth the world, and

[187] hath given precepts, and propounded rewards, and punishments to mankind, are God's subjects; all the rest, are to be understood as enemies.

A threefold word of God, reason, revelation, prophecy.

3. To rule by words, requires that such words be manifestly made known; for else they are no laws: for to the nature of laws belongeth a sufficient, and clear promulgation, such as may take away the excuse of ignorance; which in the laws of men is but of one only kind, and that is, proclamation, or promulgation by the voice of man. But God declareth his laws three ways; by the dictates of *natural reason*, by *revelation*, and by the *voice* of some *man*, to whom by the operation of miracles, he procureth credit with the rest. From hence there ariseth a triple word of God, *rational, sensible*, and *prophetic*: to which correspondeth a triple hearing; *right reason, sense supernatural*, and *faith*. As for sense supernatural, which consisteth in revelation, or inspiration, there have not been any universal laws so given, because God speaketh not in that manner, but to particular persons, and to divers men divers things.

4. From the difference between the other two kinds of God's word, *rational*, and *prophetic*, there may be attributed to God, a twofold kingdom, *natural*, and *prophetic*: natural, wherein he governeth as many of mankind as acknowledge his providence, by the natural dictates of right reason; and prophetic, wherein having chosen out one peculiar nation (the Jews) for his subjects, he governed them, and none but them, not only by natural reason, but by positive laws, which he gave them by the mouths of his holy prophets. Of the natural kingdom of God I intend to speak in this chapter.

A twofold kingdom of God, natural and prophetic.

5. The right of nature, whereby God reigneth over men, and punisheth those that break his laws, is to be derived, not from his creating them, as if he required obedience as of gratitude for his benefits; but from his *irresistible power*. I have formerly shown, how the sovereign right ariseth from pact: to show how the same right may arise from nature, requires no more, but to show in what case it is never taken away. Seeing all men by nature had right to all things, they had right every one to reign over all the rest. But because this right could not be obtained by force, it concerned the safety of every one, laying by that right, to set up men (with sovereign authority) by common consent, to rule and defend them: whereas if there had been any man of power irresistible; there had been no reason, why he should not by that power have ruled, and defended both himself, and them, according to his own discretion. To those therefore whose power is irresistible, the dominion of all men adhereth naturally by their excellence of power; and consequently it is from that power, that the kingdom over men, and the right of afflicting men at his pleasure, belongeth naturally to God Almighty; not as Creator, and gracious; but as omnipotent. And though punishment be due for sin only, because by that word is understood affliction for sin; yet the right of afflicting, is not always derived from men's sin, but from God's power.

The right of God's sovereignty is derived from his omnipotence.

[188]

6. This question, *why evil men often prosper, and good men suffer adversity*, has been much disputed by the ancient, and is the same with this of ours, *by what right God dispenseth the prosperities and adversities of this life*; and is of that difficulty, as it hath shaken the faith, not only of the vulgar, but of philosophers, and which is more, of the Saints, concerning the Divine Providence. *How good*, saith David, (*Psalm* 73. 1, 2, 3) *is the God of Israel to those that are upright in heart; and yet my feet were almost gone, my treadings had well-nigh*

Sin not the cause of all affliction.

slipt; for I was grieved at the wicked, when I saw the ungodly in such prosperity. And Job, how earnestly does he expostulate with God, for the many afflictions he suffered, notwithstanding his righteousness? This question in the case of Job, is decided by God himself, not by arguments derived from Job's sin, but his own power. For whereas the friends of Job drew their arguments from his affliction to his sin, and he defended himself by the conscience of his innocence, God himself taketh up the matter, and having justified the affliction by arguments drawn from his power, such as this, (*Job* 38. 4) *Where wast thou, when I laid the foundations of the earth?* and the like, both approved Job's innocence, and reproved the erroneous doctrine of his friends. Conformable to this doctrine is the sentence of our Saviour, concerning the man that was born blind, in these words, *Neither hath this man sinned, nor his fathers; but that the works of God might be made manifest in him.* And though it be said, *that death entered into the world by sin,* (by which is meant, that if Adam had never sinned, he had never died, that is, never suffered any separation of his soul from his body,) it follows not thence, that God could not justly have afflicted him, though he had not sinned, as well as he afflicteth other living creatures, that cannot sin.*

Divine laws.   7. Having spoken of the right of God's sovereignty, as grounded only on nature; we are to consider next, what are the Divine laws, or dictates of natural reason; which laws concern either the natural duties of one man to another, or the honour naturally due to our Divine Sovereign. The first are the same laws of nature, of which I have spoken already in the fourteenth and fifteenth chapters of this treatise; namely, equity, justice, mercy, humility, and the rest of the moral virtues. It remaineth therefore that we consider, what precepts are dictated to men, by their natural reason only, without other word of God, touching the honour and worship of the Divine Majesty.

Honour and worship what.   8. Honour consisteth in the inward thought, and opinion of the power, and goodness of another: and therefore to honour God, is to think as highly of his power and goodness, as is possible. And of that opinion, the external signs appearing in the words, and actions of men, are called *worship*; which is one part of that which the Latins understand by the word *cultus*. For *cultus* signifieth properly, and constantly, that labour which a man bestows on any thing, with a purpose to make benefit by it. Now those things whereof we make [189] benefit, are either subject to us, and the profit they yield, followeth the labour we bestow upon them, as a natural effect; or they are not subject to us, but answer our labour, according to their own wills. In the first sense the labour bestowed on the earth, is called *culture*; and the education of children, a *culture* of their minds. In the second sense, where men's wills are to be wrought to our purpose, not by force, but by complaisance, it signifieth as much as courting, that is, a winning of favour by good offices; as by praises, by acknowledging their power, and by whatsoever is pleasing to them from whom we look for any benefit. And this is properly *worship*: in which sense *Publicola*, is understood for a worshipper of the people; and *cultus Dei*, for the worship of God.

9. From internal honour, consisting in the opinion of power and goodness, arise three passions; *love*, which hath reference to goodness; and *hope*, and *fear*, that relate to power: and three parts of external worship; *praise*, *magnifying*, and *blessing*: the subject of praise, being goodness; the subject of magnifying and blessing, being power, and the effect thereof felicity. Praise, and magnifying are signified both by words, and actions: by words, when we say a man is good, or great: by actions, when we thank him for his bounty, and obey his power. The opinion of the happiness of another, can only be expressed by words. *Several signs of honour.*

10. There be some signs of honour, (both in attributes and actions,) that be naturally so; as amongst attributes, *good*, *just*, *liberal*, and the like; and amongst actions, *prayers*, *thanks*, and *obedience*. Others are so by institution, or custom of men; and in some times and places are honourable; in others, dishonourable; in others, indifferent: such as are the gestures in salutation, prayer, and thanksgiving, in different times and places, differently used. The former is *natural*; the latter *arbitrary* worship. *Worship natural and arbitrary.*

11. And of arbitrary worship, there be two differences: for sometimes it is a *commanded*, sometimes a *voluntary* worship: commanded, when it is such as he requireth, who is worshipped: free, when it is such as the worshipper thinks fit. When it is commanded, not the words, or gesture, but the obedience is the worship. But when free, the worship consists in the opinion of the beholders: for if to them the words, or actions by which we intend honour, seem ridiculous, and tending to contumely; they are no worship; because no signs of honour; and no signs of honour, because a sign is not a sign to him that giveth it, but to him to whom it is made; that is, to the spectator. *Worship commanded and free.*

Worship public and private.

12. Again, there is a *public*, and a *private* worship. Public, is the worship that a commonwealth performeth, as one person. Private, is that which a private person exhibiteth. Public, in respect of the whole commonwealth, is free; but in respect of particular men, it is not so. Private, is in secret free; but in the sight of the multitude, it is never without some restraint, either from the laws, or from the opinion of men; which is contrary to the nature of liberty.

The end of worship.

[190]

13. The end of worship amongst men, is power. For where a man seeth another worshipped, he supposeth him powerful, and is the readier to obey him; which makes his power greater. But God has no ends: the worship we do him, proceeds from our duty, and is directed according to our capacity, by those rules of honour, that reason dictateth to be done by the weak to the more potent men, in hope of benefit, for fear of damage, or in thankfulness for good already received from them.

Attributes of divine honour.

14. That we may know what worship of God is taught us by the light of nature, I will begin with his attributes. Where, first, it is manifest, we ought to attribute to him *existence*: for no man can have the will to honour that, which he thinks not to have any being.

15. Secondly, that those philosophers, who said the world, or the soul of the world was God, spake unworthily of him; and denied his existence: for by God, is understood the cause of the world; and to say the world is God, is to say there is no cause of it, that is, no God.

16. Thirdly, to say the world was not created, but eternal, (seeing that which is eternal has no cause,) is to deny there is a God.

17. Fourthly, that they who attributing (as they think) ease to God, take from him the care of mankind; take from him his honour: for it takes away men's love, and fear of him; which is the root of honour.*

18. Fifthly, in those things that signify greatness, and power; to say he is *finite*, is not to honour him: for it is not a sign of the will to honour God, to attribute to him less than we can; and finite, is less than we can; because to finite, it is easy to add more.

19. Therefore to attribute *figure* to him, is not honour; for all figure is finite:

20. Nor to say we conceive, and imagine, or have an *idea* of him, in our mind: for whatsoever we conceive is finite:

21. Nor to attribute to him *parts*, or *totality*; which are the attributes only of things finite:

22. Nor to say he is in this, or that *place*: for whatsoever is in place, is bounded, and finite:

23. Nor that he is *moved*, or *resteth*: for both these attributes ascribe to him place:

24. Nor that there be more Gods than one; because it implies them all finite: for there cannot be more than one infinite:

25. Nor to ascribe to him, (unless metaphorically, meaning not the passion but the effect,) passions that partake of grief; as *repentance, anger, mercy*: or of want; as *appetite, hope, desire*; or of any passive faculty: for passion, is power limited by somewhat else.

26. And therefore when we ascribe to God a *will*, it is not to be understood, as that of man, for a *rational appetite*; but as the power, by which he effecteth every thing.

27. Likewise when we attribute to him *sight*, and other acts of sense; as also *knowledge*, and *understanding*; which in us is nothing else, but a tumult of the mind, raised by external things that press the organical parts of man's body: for there is no such thing in God; and being things that depend on natural causes, cannot be attributed to him.

28. He that will attribute to God, nothing but what is warranted [191] by natural reason, must either use such negative attributes, as *infinite, eternal, incomprehensible*; or superlatives, as *most high, most great*, and the like; or indefinite, as *good, just, holy, creator*; and in such sense, as if he meant not to declare what he is, (for that were to circumscribe him within the limits of our fancy,) but how much we admire him, and how ready we would be to obey him; which is a sign of humility, and of a will to honour him as much as we can: for there is but one name to signify our conception of his nature, and that is, I AM: and but one name of his relation to us, and that is, *God*; in which is contained Father, King, and Lord.

29. Concerning the actions of divine worship, it is a most general precept of reason, that they be signs of the intention to honour God; such as are, first, *prayers*: for not the carvers, when they made images, were thought to make them gods; but the people that *prayed* to them. *Actions that are signs of divine honour.*

30. Secondly, *thanksgiving*; which differeth from prayer in divine worship, no otherwise, than that prayers precede, and thanks succeed the benefit; the end, both of the one and the other, being to acknowledge God, for author of all benefits, as well past, as future.

31. Thirdly, *gifts*; that is to say, *sacrifices* and *oblations*, (if they be of the best,) are signs of honour: for they are thanksgivings.

32. Fourthly, *not to swear by any but God*, is naturally a sign of honour: for it is a confession that God only knoweth the heart; and that no man's wit, or strength can protect a man against God's vengeance on the perjured.

33. Fifthly, it is a part of rational worship, to speak considerately of God; for it argues a fear of him, and fear, is a confession of his power. Hence followeth, that the name of God is not to be used rashly, and to no purpose; for that is as much, as in vain: and it is to no purpose, unless it be by way of oath, and by order of the commonwealth, no make judgments certain; or between commonwealths, to avoid war. And that disputing of God's nature is contrary to his honour: for it is supposed, that in this natural kingdom of God, there is no other way to know any thing, but by natural reason; that is, from the principles of natural science; which are so far from teaching us any thing of God's nature, as they cannot teach us our own nature, nor the nature of the smallest creature living. And therefore, when men out of the principles of natural reason, dispute of the attributes of God, they but dishonour him: for in the attributes which we give to God, we are not to consider the signification of philosophical truth; but the signification of pious intention, to do him the greatest honour we are able. From the want of which consideration, have proceeded the volumes of disputation about the nature of God, that tend not to his honour, but to the honour of our own wits, and learning; and are nothing else but inconsiderate, and vain abuses of his sacred name.

34. Sixthly, in *prayers*, *thanksgivings*, *offerings*, and *sacrifices*, it is a dictate of natural reason, that they be every one in his kind the [192] best, and most significant of honour. As for example, that prayers, and thanksgiving, be made in words and phrases, not sudden, nor light, nor plebeian; but beautiful, and well composed; for else we do not God as much honour as we can. And therefore the heathens did absurdly, to worship images for gods: but their doing it in verse, and with music, both of voice and instruments, was reasonable. Also that the beasts they offered in sacrifice, and the gifts they offered, and their actions in worshipping, were full of submission, and commemorative of benefits received, was according to reason, as proceeding from an intention to honour him.

35. Seventhly, reason directeth not only to worship God in secret; but also, and especially, in public, and in the sight of men: for without that, (that which in honour is most acceptable) the procuring others to honour him, is lost.

36. Lastly, obedience to his laws (that is, in this case to the laws of nature,) is the greatest worship of all. For as obedience is more acceptable to God than sacrifice; so also to set light by his commandments, is the greatest of all contumelies. And these are the laws of that divine worship, which natural reason dictateth to private men.

37. But seeing a commonwealth is but one person, it ought also to exhibit to God but one worship; which then it doth, when it commandeth it to be exhibited by private men, publicly. And this is public worship; the property whereof, is to be *uniform*: for those actions that are done differently, by different men, cannot be said to be a public worship. And therefore, where many sorts of worship be allowed, proceeding from the different religions of private men, it cannot be said there is any public worship, nor that the commonwealth is of any religion at all. *Public worship consisteth in uniformity.*

38. And because words (and consequently the attributes of God) have their signification by agreement, and constitution of men, those attributes are to be held significative of honour, that men intend shall so be; and whatsoever may be done by the wills of particular men, where there is no law but reason, may be done by the will of the commonwealth, by laws civil. And because a commonwealth hath no will, nor makes no laws, but those that are made by the will of him, or them that have the sovereign power; it followeth, that those attributes which the sovereign ordaineth, in the worship of God, for signs of honour, ought to be taken and used for such, by private men in their public worship. *All attributes depend on the laws civil.*

39. But because not all actions are signs by constitution; but some are naturally signs of honour, others of contumely, these latter (which are those that men are ashamed to do in the sight of them they reverence) cannot be made by human power a part of Divine worship; nor the former (such as are decent, modest, humble behaviour) ever be separated from it. But whereas there be an infinite number of actions, and gestures, of an indifferent nature; such of them as the commonwealth shall ordain to be publicly and universally in use, as signs of honour, and part of God's worship, are to be taken and used for such by the subjects. And that which is said in the *Not all actions.* [193]

Scripture, *It is better to obey God than man*, hath place in the kingdom of God by pact, and not by nature.

Natural punishments.

40. Having thus briefly spoken of the natural kingdom of God, and his natural laws, I will add only to this chapter a short declaration of his natural punishments. There is no action of man in this life, that is not the beginning of so long a chain of consequences, as no human's providence is high enough, to give a man a prospect to the end. And in this chain, there are linked together both pleasing and unpleasing events; in such manner, as he that will do any thing for his pleasure, must engage himself to suffer all the pains annexed to it; and these pains, are the natural punishments of those actions, which are the beginning of more harm than good. And hereby it comes to pass, that intemperance is naturally punished with diseases; rashness, with mischances; injustice, with the violence of enemies; pride, with ruin; cowardice, with oppression; negligent government of princes, with rebellion; and rebellion, with slaughter. For seeing punishments are consequent to the breach of laws; natural punishments must be naturally consequent to the breach of the laws of nature; and therefore follow them as their natural, not arbitrary effects.

The conclusion of the second part.

41. And thus far concerning the constitution, nature, and right of sovereigns; and concerning the duty of subjects, derived from the principles of natural reason. And now, considering how different this doctrine is, from the practice of the greatest part of the world, especially of these western parts, that have received their moral learning from Rome, and Athens; and how much depth of moral philosophy is required, in them that have the administration of the sovereign power; I am at the point of believing this my labour, as useless, as the commonwealth of Plato; for he also is of opinion that it is impossible for the disorders of state, and change of governments by civil war, ever to be taken away, till sovereigns be philosophers. But when I consider again, that the science of natural justice, is the only science necessary for sovereigns, and their principal ministers; and that they need not be charged with the sciences mathematical, (as by Plato they are,) farther, than by good laws to encourage men to the study of them; and that neither Plato, nor any other philosopher hitherto, hath put into order, and sufficiently, or probably proved all the theorems of moral doctrine, that men may learn thereby, both how to govern, and how to obey; I recover some hope, that one time or other, this writing of mine, may fall into the hands of a sovereign, who will consider it himself, (for it is short, and I think clear,*) without the help of any interested, or envious interpreter; and by the exercise of entire sovereignty, in protecting the public teaching of it, convert this truth of speculation, into the utility of practice.

OF A
CHRISTIAN COMMONWEALTH

CHAPTER XXXII

OF THE PRINCIPLES OF CHRISTIAN POLITICS

1. I HAVE derived the rights of sovereign power, and the duty of subjects hitherto, from the principles of nature only; such as experience has found true, or consent (concerning the use of words) has made so; that is to say, from the nature of men, known to us by experience, and from definitions (of such words as are essential to all political reasoning) universally agreed on. But in that I am next to handle, which is the nature and rights of a CHRISTIAN COMMONWEALTH, whereof there dependeth much upon supernatural revelations of the will of God; the ground of my discourse must be, not only the natural word of God, but also the prophetical.

The word of God delivered by prophets is the main principle of Christian politics.

2. Nevertheless, we are not to renounce our senses, and experience; nor (that which is the undoubted word of God) our natural reason. For they are the talents which he hath put into our hands to negotiate, till the coming again of our blessed Saviour; and therefore not to be folded up in the napkin of an implicit faith, but employed in the purchase of justice, peace, and true religion. For though there be many things in God's word above reason; that is to say, which cannot by natural reason be either demonstrated, or confuted; yet there is nothing contrary to it; but when it seemeth so, the fault is either in our unskilful interpretation, or erroneous ratiocination.

Yet is not natural reason to be renounced.

3. Therefore, when any thing therein written is too hard for our examination, we are bidden to captivate our understanding to the words; and not to labour in sifting out a philosophical truth by logic, of such mysteries as are not comprehensible, nor fall under any rule of natural science. For it is with the mysteries of our religion, as with wholesome pills for the sick; which swallowed whole, have the virtue to cure; but chewed, are for the most part cast up again without effect.

[196]

What it is to
captivate the
understanding.

4. But by the captivity of our understanding, is not meant a submission of the intellectual faculty to the opinion of any other man; but of the will to obedience, where obedience is due. For sense, memory, understanding, reason, and opinion are not in our power to change; but always, and necessarily such, as the things we see, hear, and consider suggest unto us; and therefore are not effects of our will, but our will of them. We then captivate our understanding and reason, when we forbear contradiction; when we so speak, as (by lawful authority) we are commanded; and when we live accordingly; which in sum, is trust, and faith reposed in him that speaketh, though the mind be incapable of any notion at all from the words spoken.

How God
speaketh to
men.

5. When God speaketh to man, it must be either immediately; or by mediation of another man, to whom he had formerly spoken by himself immediately. How God speaketh to a man immediately, may be understood by those well enough, to whom he hath so spoken; but how the same should be understood by another, is hard, if not impossible to know. For if a man pretend* to me, that God hath spoken to him supernaturally and immediately, and I make doubt of it, I cannot easily perceive what argument he can produce, to oblige me to believe it. It is true, that if he be my sovereign, he may oblige me to obedience, so, as not by act or word to declare I believe him not; but not to think any otherwise than my reason persuades me. But if one that hath not such authority over me, should pretend the same, there is nothing that exacteth either belief, or obedience.

6. For to say that God hath spoken to him in the Holy Scripture, is not to say God hath spoken to him immediately, but by mediation of the prophets, or of the apostles, or of the church, in such manner as he speaks to all other Christian men. To say he hath spoken to him in a dream, is no more than to say he dreamed that God spake to him;* which is not of force to win belief from any man, that knows dreams are for the most part natural, and may proceed from former thoughts; and such dreams as that, from self-conceit, and foolish arrogance, and false opinion of a man's own godliness, or other virtue, by which he thinks he hath merited the favour of extraordinary revelation. To say he hath seen a vision, or heard a voice, is to say, that he hath dreamed between sleeping and waking: for in such manner a man doth many times naturally take his dream for a vision, as not having well observed his own slumbering. To say he speaks by supernatural inspiration, is to say he finds an ardent desire to speak, or some strong opinion of himself, for which he can allege no natural and sufficient reason. So that though God Almighty can speak to a man by dreams, visions, voice, and inspiration; yet he obliges no man to believe he hath so done to him that pretends it; who (being a man) may err, and (which is more) may lie.

7. How then can he, to whom God hath never revealed his will immediately (saving by the way of natural reason) know when he is to obey, or not to obey his word, delivered by him, that says he is a prophet? Of four hundred prophets, of whom the king of Israel asked counsel, concerning the war he made against Ramoth Gilead, (1 *Kings* 22) only Micaiah was a true one. The prophet that was sent to prophesy against the altar set up by Jeroboam, (1 *Kings* 13) though a true prophet, and that by two miracles done in his presence appears to be a prophet sent from God, was yet deceived by another old prophet, that persuaded him as from the mouth of God, to eat and drink with him. If one prophet deceive another, what certainty is there of knowing the will of God, by other way than that of reason? To which I answer out of the Holy Scripture, that there be two marks, by which together, not asunder, a true prophet is to be known. One is the doing of miracles; the other is the not teaching any other religion than that which is already established. Asunder (I say) neither of these is sufficient. *If a prophet rise amongst you, or a dreamer of dreams, and shall pretend the doing of a miracle, and the miracle come to pass; if he say, Let us follow strange Gods, which thou hast not known, thou shalt not hearken to him, &c. But that prophet and dreamer of dreams shall be put to death, because he hath spoken to you to revolt from the Lord your God.* (*Deut.* 13. 1–5.) In which words two things are to be observed; first, that God will not have miracles alone serve for arguments, to approve the prophet's calling; but (as it is in the third verse) for an experiment of the constancy of our adherence to himself. For the works of the Egyptian sorcerers, though not so great as those of Moses, yet were great miracles. Secondly, that how great soever the miracle be, yet if it tend to stir up revolt against the king, or him that governeth by the king's authority, he that doth such miracle, is not to be considered otherwise than as sent to make trial of their allegiance. For these words, *revolt from the Lord your God*, are in this place equivalent to *revolt from your king*. For they had made God their king by pact at the foot of Mount Sinai; who

ruled them by Moses only; for he only spake with God, and from time to time declared God's commandments to the people. In like manner, after our Saviour Christ had made his disciples acknowledge him for the Messiah, (that is to say, for God's anointed, whom the nation of the Jews daily expected for their king, but refused when he came,) he omitted not to advertise them of the danger of miracles. *There shall arise,* saith he, *false Christs, and false prophets, and shall do great wonders and miracles, even to the seducing (if it were possible) of the very elect.* (*Matt.* 24. 24.) By which it appears, that false prophets may have the power of miracles; yet are we not to take their doctrine for God's word. St. Paul says further to the Galatians, (*Gal.* 1. 8) that *if himself, or an angel from heaven preach another gospel to them, than he had preached, let him be accursed.* That gospel was, that Christ was King; so that all preaching against the power of the king received, in consequence to these words, is by St. Paul accursed. For his speech is addressed to those, who by his preaching had already received Jesus for the Christ, that is to say, for King of the Jews.

The marks of a prophet in the old law, miracles, and doctrine [198] *conformable to the law.*

8. And as miracles, without preaching that doctrine which God hath established; so preaching the true doctrine, without the doing of miracles, is an unsufficient argument of immediate revelation. For if a man that teacheth not false doctrine, should pretend to be a prophet without showing any miracle, he is never the more to be regarded for his pretence, as is evident by *Deut.* 18. 21, 22, *If thou say in thy heart, How shall we know that the word* (of the prophet) *is not that which the Lord hath spoken? when the prophet shall have spoken in the name of the Lord, that which shall not come to pass, that is the word which the Lord hath not spoken, but the prophet has spoken it out of the pride of his own heart, fear him not.* But a man may here again ask, when the prophet hath foretold a thing, how shall we know whether it will come to pass or not? For he may foretell it as a thing to arrive after a certain long time, longer than the time of man's life; or indefinitely, that it will come to pass one time or other: in which case this mark of a prophet is unuseful; and therefore the miracles that oblige us to believe a prophet, ought to be confirmed by an immediate, or a not long deferred event. So that it is manifest, that the teaching of the religion which God hath established, and the showing of a present miracle, joined together, were the only marks whereby the Scripture would have a true prophet, that is to say, immediate revelation, to be acknowledged;

neither of them being singly sufficient to oblige any other man to regard what he saith.

9. Seeing therefore miracles now cease, we have no sign left, whereby to acknowledge the pretended revelations, or inspirations of any private man; nor obligation to give ear to any doctrine, farther than it is conformable to the Holy Scriptures, which since the time of our Saviour, supply the place, and sufficiently recompense the want of all other prophecy; and from which, by wise and learned interpretation, and careful ratiocination, all rules and precepts necessary to the knowledge of our duty both to God and man, without enthusiasm, or supernatural inspiration, may easily be deduced. And this Scripture is it, out of which I am to take the principles of my discourse, concerning the rights of those that are the supreme governors on earth, of Christian commonwealths; and of the duty of Christian subjects towards their sovereigns. And to that end, I shall speak in the next chapter, of the books, writers, scope, and authority of the Bible.

Miracles ceasing, prophets cease, and the Scripture supplies their place.

CHAPTER XXXIII [199]

OF THE NUMBER, ANTIQUITY, SCOPE, AUTHORITY, AND INTERPRETERS OF THE BOOKS OF HOLY SCRIPTURE

1. BY the Books of Holy SCRIPTURE, are understood those, which ought to be the *canon*, that is to say, the rules of Christian life. And because all rules of life, which men are in conscience bound to observe, are laws; the question of the Scripture, is the question of what is law throughout all Christendom, both natural and civil. For though it be not determined in Scripture, what laws every Christian king shall constitute in his own dominions; yet it is determined what laws he shall not constitute. Seeing therefore I have already proved, that sovereigns in their own dominions are the sole legislators; those books only are canonical, that is, law, in every nation, which are established for such by the sovereign authority. It is true, that God is the sovereign of all sovereigns; and therefore, when he speaks to any subject, he ought to be obeyed, whatsoever any earthly potentate command to the contrary. But the question is not of obedience to God, but of *when* and *what* God hath said; which to subjects that have no supernatural revelation, cannot be known, but by that natu-

Of the books of Holy Scripture.

ral reason, which guideth them, for the obtaining of peace and justice, to obey the authority of their several commonwealths; that is to say, of their lawful sovereigns. According to this obligation, I can acknowledge no other books of the Old Testament, to be Holy Scripture, but those which have been commanded to be acknowledged for such, by the authority of the Church of England. What books these are, is sufficiently known, without a catalogue of them here; and they are the same that are acknowledged by St. Jerome,* who holdeth the rest, namely, the *Wisdom of Solomon, Ecclesiasticus, Judith, Tobias,* the first and the second of *Maccabees,* (though he had seen the first in Hebrew) and the third and fourth of *Esdras,* for *Apocrypha.* Of the canonical, Josephus,* a learned Jew, that wrote in the time of the emperor Domitian, reckoneth *twenty-two,* making the number agree with the Hebrew alphabet. St. Jerome does the same, though they reckon them in different manner. For Josephus numbers *five* Books of *Moses, thirteen* of *Prophets,* that writ the history of their own times (which how it agrees with the prophets' writings contained in the Bible we shall see hereafter), and *four* of *hymns* and moral precepts. But St. Jerome reckons *five* books of *Moses, eight* of *Prophets,* and *nine* of other Holy Writ, which he calls of Hagiographa. The Septuagint, who were seventy learned men of the Jews, sent for by Ptolemy king of Egypt, to translate the Jewish law, out of the Hebrew into the Greek, have left us no other for Holy [200] Scripture in the Greek tongue, but the same that are received in the Church of England.

2. As for the Books of the New Testament, they are equally acknowledged for canon by all Christian churches, and by all sects of Christians, that admit any books at all for canonical.

Their antiquity.

3. Who were the original writers of the several Books of Holy Scripture, has not been made evident by any sufficient testimony of other history, (which is the only proof of matter of fact); nor can be by any arguments of natural reason: for reason serves only to convince the truth (not of fact, but) of consequence. The light therefore that must guide us in this question, must be that which is held out unto us from the books themselves: and this light, though it show us not the writer of every book, yet it is not unuseful to give us knowledge of the time, wherein they were written.

4. And first, for the *Pentateuch,* it is not argument enough that they were written by Moses, because they are called the five Books of *Moses*; no more than these titles, the Book of *Joshua,* the Book of

Judges, the Book of *Ruth*, and the Books of the *Kings*, are arguments
sufficient to prove, that they were written by *Joshua*, by the *Judges*,
by *Ruth*, and by the *Kings*. For in titles of books, the subject is
marked, as often as the writer. The history of Livy, denotes the
writer; but the history of Alexander, is denominated from the
subject. We read in the last chapter of *Deuteronomy*, verse 6,
concerning the sepulchre of Moses, *that no man knoweth of his
sepulchre to this day*, that is, to the day wherein those words were
written. It is therefore manifest, that those words were written after
his interment. For it were a strange interpretation, to say Moses
spake of his own sepulchre (though by prophecy), that it was not
found to that day, wherein he was yet living. But it may perhaps be
alleged, that the last chapter only, not the whole *Pentateuch*, was
written by some other man, but the rest not: let us therefore
consider that which we find in the book of *Genesis*, (12. 6) *And
Abraham passed through the land to the place of Sichem, unto the plain
of Moreh, and the Canaanite was then in the land*; which must needs
be the words of one that wrote when the Canaanite was not in the
land; and consequently, not of Moses, who died before he came into
it. Likewise *Numbers* 21. 14, the writer citeth another more ancient
book, entitled, *The Book of the Wars of the Lord*, wherein were
registered the acts of Moses, at the Red Sea, and at the brook of
Arnon. It is therefore sufficiently evident, that the five Books of
Moses were written after his time, though how long after it be not so
manifest.

The Pentateuch not written by Moses.

5. But though Moses did not compile those books entirely, and
in the form we have them; yet he wrote all that which he is there said
to have written: as for example, the Volume of the Law, which is
contained, as it seemeth, in the eleventh of *Deuteronomy*, and
the following chapters to the twenty-seventh which was also commanded to be written on stones, in their entry into the land of
Canaan. And this did Moses himself write, (*Deut.* 31. 9) and
deliver to the priests and elders of Israel, to be read every seventh [201]
year to all Israel, at their assembling in the Feast of Tabernacles.
And this is that law which God commanded, that their kings
(when they should have established that form of government)
should take a copy of from the priests and Levites; and which
Moses commanded the priests and Levites to lay in the side of the
ark, (*Deut.* 31. 26); and the same which having been lost, was long
time after found again by Hilkiah, and sent to king Josias (2 *Kings*

22. 8) who causing it to be read to the people, (2 *Kings* 23. 1, 2, 3) renewed the covenant between God and them.

The book of Joshua written after his time.

6. That the book of *Joshua* was also written long after the time of Joshua, may be gathered out of many places of the book itself. Joshua had set up twelve stones in the midst of Jordan, for a monument of their passage; of which the writer saith thus, *They are there unto this day* (*Josh*, 4. 9); for *unto this day*, is a phrase that signifieth a time past, beyond the memory of man. In like manner, upon the saying of the Lord, that he had rolled off from the people the reproach of Egypt, the writer saith, *The place is called Gilgal unto this day* (*Josh*. 5. 9); which to have said in the time of Joshua had been improper. So also the name of the valley of Achor, from the trouble that Achan raised in the camp, the writer saith, *remaineth unto this day* (*Josh*. 7. 26); which must needs be therefore long after the time of Joshua. Arguments of this kind there be many other; as *Josh*. 8. 29, 13. 13, 14. 14, 15. 63.

The books of Judges and Ruth written long after the captivity.

7. The same is manifest by like arguments of the book of *Judges*, chap. 1. 21, 26, 6. 24, 10. 4, 15. 19, 17. 6, and *Ruth* 1. 1; but especially *Judg*. 18. 30, where it is said, that *Jonathan and his sons were priests to the tribe of Dan, until the day of the captivity of the land.*

The like of the books of Samuel.

8. That the books of *Samuel* were also written after his own time, there are the like arguments, 1 *Sam*. 5. 5, 7. 13, 15; 27. 6, and 30. 25, where, after David had adjudged equal part of the spoils, to them that guarded the ammunition, with them that fought, the writer saith, *He made it a statute and an ordinance to Israel to this day.* Again, when David (displeased, that the Lord had slain Uzzah, for putting out his hand to sustain the ark,) called the place Perez-Uzzah, the writer saith, (2 *Sam*. 6. 4) it is called so *to this day*: the time therefore of the writing of that book, must be long after the time of the fact; that is, long after the time of David.

The books of the Kings, and the Chronicles.

9. As for the two books of the *Kings*, and the two books of the *Chronicles*, besides the places which mention such monuments, as the writer saith, remained till his own days; such as are 1 *Kings* 9. 13, 9. 21, 10. 12, 12. 19. 2 *Kings* 2. 22, 8. 22, 10. 27, 14. 7, 16. 6, 17. 23, 17. 34, 17. 41, and 1 *Chron*. 4. 41, 5. 26: it is argument sufficient they were written after the captivity in Babylon, that the history of them is continued till that time. For the facts registered are always more ancient than the register; and much more ancient than such books as make mention of, and quote the register; as these books do in divers

places, referring the reader to the Chronicles of the Kings of Judah, to the Chronicles of the Kings of Israel, to the Books of the prophet Samuel, of the prophet Nathan, of the prophet Ahijah; to the Vision of Jehdo, to the books of the prophet Serveiah, and of the prophet Addo.

10. The books of *Ezra* and *Nehemiah* were written certainly after their return from captivity; because their return, the re-edification of the walls and houses of Jerusalem, the renovation of the covenant, and ordination of their policy, are therein contained. [202] *Ezra and Nehemiah.*

11. The history of *Queen Esther* is of the time of the captivity; and therefore the writer must have been of the same time, or after it. *Esther.*

12. The book of *Job* hath no mark in it of the time wherein it was written; and though it appear sufficiently (*Ezekiel* 14. 14, and *James* 5. 11) that he was no feigned person; yet the book itself seemeth not to be a history, but a treatise concerning a question in ancient time much disputed, *why wicked men have often prospered in this world, and good men have been afflicted*; and this is the more probable, because from the beginning, to the third verse of the third chapter, where the complaint of Job beginneth, the Hebrew is (as St. Jerome testifies) in prose; and from thence to the sixth verse of the last chapter, in hexameter verses; and the rest of that chapter again in prose. So that the dispute is all in verse; and the prose is added, but as a preface in the beginning, and an epilogue in the end. But verse is no usual style of such, as either are themselves in great pain, as Job; or of such as come to comfort them, as his friends; but in philosophy, especially moral philosophy, in ancient time frequent. *Job.*

13. The *Psalms* were written the most part by David, for the use of the choir. To these are added some songs of Moses, and other holy men; and some of them after the return from the captivity, as the 137th and the 126th, whereby it is manifest that the Psalter was compiled, and put into the form it now hath, after the return of the Jews from Babylon. *The Psalter.*

14. The *Proverbs*, being a collection of wise and godly sayings, partly of Solomon, partly of Agur, the son of Jaketh, and partly of the mother of king Lemuel, cannot probably be thought to have been collected by Solomon, rather than by Agur, or the mother of Lemuel; and that, though the sentences be theirs, yet the collection or compiling them into this one book, was the work of some other godly man, that lived after them all. *The Proverbs.*

Ecclesiastes
and the
Canticles.

15. The books of *Ecclesiastes* and the *Canticles* [Song of Solomon] have nothing that was not Solomon's, except it be the titles, or inscriptions. For *The Words of the Preacher, the son of David, king in Jerusalem*; and, *The Song of Songs*, which is Solomon's, seem to have been made for distinction's sake, then, when the Books of Scripture were gathered into one body of the law; to the end, that not the doctrine only, but the authors also might be extant.

The
Prophets.

16. Of the prophets, the most ancient, are Zephaniah, Jonah, Amos, Hosea, Isaiah, and Micah, who lived in the time of Amaziah, and Azariah, otherwise Ozias, kings of Judah. But the book of *Jonah* is not properly a register of his prophecy, (for that is contained in these few words, *Forty days and Nineveh shall be destroyed,*) but a history or narration of his frowardness and disputing God's commandments; so that there is small probability he should be the author, seeing he is the subject of it. But the book of *Amos* is his prophecy.

[203]   17. Jeremiah, Obadiah, Nahum, and Habakkuk prophesied in the time of Josiah.

18. Ezekiel, Daniel, Haggai, and Zechariah, in the captivity.

19. When Joel and Malachi prophesied, is not evident by their writings. But considering the inscriptions, or titles of their books, it is manifest enough, that the whole Scripture of the Old Testament, was set forth in the form we have it, after the return of the Jews from their captivity in Babylon, and before the time of Ptolomaeus Philadelphus,* that caused it to be translated into Greek by seventy men, which were sent him out of Judea for that purpose. And if the books of Apocrypha (which are recommended to us by the Church, though not for canonical, yet for profitable books for our instruction) may in this point be credited, the Scripture was set forth in the form we have it in, by Esdras; as may appear by that which he himself saith, in the second book, (chapter 14. verse 21, 22, &c.) where speaking to God, he saith thus, *Thy law is burnt; therefore no man knoweth the things which thou hast done, or the works that are to begin. But if I have found grace before thee, send down the holy spirit into me, and I shall write all that hath been done in the world, since the beginning, which were written in thy law, that men may find thy path, and that they which will live in the latter day, may live.* And verse 45: *And it came to pass when the forty days were fulfilled, that the highest spake, saying, The first that thou hast written, publish openly, that the worthy and unworthy may read it; but keep the seventy last, that thou*

mayest deliver them only to such as be wise among the people. And thus much concerning the time of the writing of the books of the Old Testament.

20. The writers of the New Testament lived all in less than an *The New* age after Christ's ascension, and had all of them seen our Saviour, or *Testament.* been his disciples, except St. Paul, and St. Luke; and consequently whatsoever was written by them, is as ancient as the time of the apostles. But the time wherein the books of the New Testament were received, and acknowledged by the church to be of their writing, is not altogether so ancient. For, as the books of the Old Testament are derived to us, from no other time than that of Esdras, who by the direction of God's spirit retrieved them, when they were lost: those of the New Testament, of which the copies were not many, nor could easily be all in any one private man's hand, cannot be derived from a higher time, than that wherein the governors of the church collected, approved, and recommended them to us, as the writings of those apostles and disciples, under whose names they go. The first enumeration of all the books, both of the Old and New Testament, is in the canons of the apostles, supposed to be collected by Clement, the first (after St. Peter)* bishop of Rome. But because that is but supposed, and by many questioned, the Council of Laodicea is the first we know, that recommended the Bible to the then Christian churches, for the writings of the prophets and apostles: and this Council was held in the 364th year after Christ. After which time, though ambition had so far prevailed on some doctors of the church, as no more to esteem emperors, though Christian, for [204] the shepherds of the people, but for sheep; and emperors not Christian, for wolves; and endeavoured to pass their doctrine, not for counsel, and information, as preachers; but for laws, as absolute governors; and thought such frauds as tended to make the people the more obedient to Christian doctrine, to be pious; yet I am persuaded they did not therefore falsify the Scriptures, though the copies of the books of the New Testament, were in the hands only of the ecclesiastics; because if they had had an intention so to do, they would surely have made them more favourable to their power over Christian princes, and civil sovereignty, than they are. I see not therefore any reason to doubt, but that the Old, and New Testament, as we have them now, are the true registers of those things, which were done and said by the prophets, and apostles. And so perhaps are some of those books which are called apocrypha, and if

left out of the canon, not for inconformity of doctrine with the rest, but only because they are not found in the Hebrew. For after the conquest of Asia by Alexander the Great, there were few learned Jews, that were not perfect in the Greek tongue. For the seventy interpreters that converted the Bible into Greek, were all of them Hebrews; and we have extant the works of Philo* and Josephus, both Jews, written by them eloquently in Greek. But it is not the writer, but the authority of the church, that maketh the book ca-

Their scope. nonical. And although these books were written by divers men, yet it is manifest the writers were all endued with one and the same spirit, in that they conspire to one and the same end, which is setting forth of the rights of the Kingdom of God, the Father, Son, and Holy Ghost. For the book of *Genesis*, deriveth the genealogy of God's people, from the creation of the world, to the going into Egypt: the other four books of Moses, contain the election of God for their king, and the laws which he prescribed for their government: the books of *Joshua*, *Judges*, *Ruth*, and *Samuel*, to the time of Saul, describe the acts of God's people, till the time they cast off God's yoke, and called for a king, after the manner of their neighbour nations. The rest of the history of the Old Testament derives the succession of the line of David, to the captivity, out of which line was to spring the restorer of the Kingdom of God, even our blessed Saviour God the Son, whose coming was foretold in the books of the prophets, after whom the Evangelists wrote his life, and actions, and his claim to the kingdom, whilst he lived on earth: and lastly, the *Acts*, and *Epistles* of the Apostles, declare the coming of God the Holy Ghost, and the authority he left with them and their successors, for the direction of the Jews, and for the invitation of the Gentiles. In sum, the histories and the prophecies of the Old Testament, and the gospels and epistles of the New Testament, have had one and the same scope, to convert men to the obedience of God; I., in Moses, and the Priests; II., in the man Christ; and III., in the Apostles and the successors to apostolical power. For these three at several times did represent the person of God: Moses, and his

[205] successors the High Priests, and Kings of Judah, in the Old Testament: Christ himself, in the time he lived on earth: and the Apostles, and their successors, from the day of Pentecost (when the Holy Ghost descended on them) to this day.

21. It is a question much disputed between the divers sects of Christian religion, *from whence the Scriptures derive their authority*;

which question is also propounded sometimes in other terms, as, *how we know them to be the word of God*, or, *why we believe them to be so*: and the difficulty of resolving it, ariseth chiefly from the improperness of the words wherein the question itself is couched. For it is believed on all hands, that the first and original *author* of them is God; and consequently the question disputed, is not that. Again, it is manifest, that none can know they are God's word, (though all true Christians believe it,) but those to whom God himself hath revealed it supernaturally; and therefore the question is not rightly moved, of our *knowledge* of it. Lastly, when the question is propounded of our *belief*; because some are moved to believe for one, and others for other reasons, there can be rendered no one general answer for them all. The question truly stated is, *by what authority they are made law*.

The question of the authority of the Scriptures stated.

22. As far as they differ not from laws of nature, there is no doubt, but they are the law of God, and carry their authority with them, legible to all men that have the use of natural reason: but this is no other authority, than that of all other moral doctrine consonant to reason; the dictates whereof are laws, not *made*, but *eternal*.

Their authority and interpretation.

23. If they be made law by God himself, they are of the nature of written law, which are laws to them only to whom God hath so sufficiently published them, as no man can excuse himself, by saying, he knew not they were his.

24. He therefore, to whom God hath not supernaturally revealed that they are his, nor that those that published them, were sent by him, is not obliged to obey them, by any authority, but his, whose commands have already the force of laws; that is to say, by any other authority, than that of the commonwealth, residing in the sovereign, who only has the legislative power. Again, if it be not the legislative authority of the commonwealth, that giveth them the force of laws, it must be some other authority derived from God, either private, or public: if private, it obliges only him, to whom in particular God hath been pleased to reveal it. For if every man should be obliged, to take for God's law, what particular men, on pretence of private inspiration, or revelation, should obtrude upon him, (in such a number of men, that out of pride and ignorance, take their own dreams, and extravagant fancies, and madness, for testimonies of God's spirit; or out of ambition, pretend to such divine testimonies, falsely, and contrary to their own consciences,) it were impossible that any divine law should be acknowledged. If public, it is the

authority of the *commonwealth*, or of the *church*. But the church, if it be one person, is the same thing with a commonwealth of Christians; [206] called a *commonwealth*, because it consisteth of men united in one person, their sovereign; and a *church*, because it consisteth in Christian men, united in one Christian sovereign. But if the church be not one person, then it hath no authority at all; it can neither command, nor do any action at all; nor is capable of having any power, or right to any thing; nor has any will, reason, nor voice; for all these qualities are personal. Now if the whole number of Christians be not contained in one commonwealth, they are not one person; nor is there an universal church that hath any authority over them; and therefore the Scriptures are not made laws, by the universal church: or if it be one commonwealth, then all Christian monarchs, and states are private persons, and subject to be judged, deposed, and punished by an universal sovereign of all Christendom. So that the question of the authority of the Scriptures, is reduced to this, *whether Christian kings, and the sovereign assemblies in Christian commonwealths, be absolute in their own territories, immediately under God; or subject to one Vicar of Christ, constituted over the universal church; to be judged, condemned, deposed, and put to death, as he shall think expedient, or necessary for the common good.*

25. Which question cannot be resolved, without a more particular consideration of the Kingdom of God; from whence also, we are to judge of the authority of interpreting the Scripture. For, whosoever hath a lawful power over any writing, to make it law, hath the power also to approve, or disapprove the interpretation of the same.

[207]

CHAPTER XXXIV

OF THE SIGNIFICATION OF SPIRIT, ANGEL, AND INSPIRATION IN THE BOOKS OF HOLY SCRIPTURE

Body and spirit how taken in the Scripture.

1. SEEING the foundation of all true ratiocination, is the constant signification of words; which in the doctrine following, dependeth not (as in natural science) on the will of the writer, nor (as in common conversation) on vulgar use, but on the sense they carry in the Scripture; it is necessary, before I proceed any further, to determine, out of the Bible, the meaning of such words, as by their ambiguity, may render what I am to infer upon them, obscure, or

disputable. I will begin with the words BODY and SPIRIT, which in the language of the Schools are termed, *substances*, *corporeal*, and *incorporeal*.

2. The word *body*,* in the most general acceptation, signifieth that which filleth, or occupieth some certain room, or imagined place; and dependeth not on the imagination, but is a real part of that we call the *universe*. For the *universe*,* being the aggregate of all bodies, there is no real part thereof that is not also *body*; nor any thing properly a *body*, that is not also part of (that aggregate of all *bodies*) the *universe*. The same also, because bodies are subject to change, that is to say, to variety of appearance to the sense of living creatures, is called *substance*, that is to say, *subject*, to various accidents; as sometimes to be moved; sometimes to stand still; and to seem to our senses sometimes hot, sometimes cold, sometimes of one colour, smell, taste, or sound, sometimes of another. And this diversity of seeming, (produced by the diversity of the operation of bodies on the organs of our sense) we attribute to alterations of the bodies that operate, and call them *accidents* of those bodies. And according to this acceptation of the word, *substance* and *body* signify the same thing; and therefore *substance incorporeal* are words, which when they are joined together, destroy one another, as if a man should say, an *incorporeal body*.

3. But in the sense of common people, not all the universe is called body, but only such parts thereof as they can discern by the sense of feeling, to resist their force, or by the sense of their eyes, to hinder them from a farther prospect. Therefore in the common language of men, *air*, and *aërial substances*, use not to be taken for *bodies*, but (as often as men are sensible of their effects) are called *wind*, or *breath*, or (because the same are called in the Latin *spiritus*) *spirits*; as when they call that aërial substance, which in the body of any living creature, gives it life and motion, *vital* and *animal spirits*. But for those idols of the brain, which represent bodies to us, where they are not, as in a looking-glass, in a dream, or to a distempered brain waking, they are (as the apostle saith generally of all idols*) [208] nothing; nothing at all, I say, there where they seem to be; and in the brain itself, nothing but tumult, proceeding either from the action of the objects, or from the disorderly agitation of the organs of our sense. And men, that are otherwise employed, than to search into their causes, know not of themselves, what to call them; and may therefore easily be persuaded, by those whose knowledge they much

reverence, some to call them *bodies*, and think them made of air compacted by a power supernatural, because the sight judges them corporeal; and some to call them *spirits*, because the sense of touch discerneth nothing in the place where they appear, to resist their fingers: so that the proper signification of *spirit* in common speech, is either a subtle, fluid, and invisible body, or a ghost, or other idol or phantasm of the imagination. But for metaphorical significations, there be many: for sometimes it is taken for disposition or inclination of the mind; as when for the disposition to control the sayings of other men, we say, *a spirit of contradiction*; for *a disposition to uncleanness, an unclean spirit*; for *perverseness, a froward spirit*; for *sullenness, a dumb spirit*, and for *inclination to godliness, and God's service, the Spirit of God*: sometimes for any eminent ability, or extraordinary passion, or disease of the mind, as when *great wisdom* is called *the spirit of wisdom*; and *madmen* are said to be *possessed with a spirit*.

4. Other signification of *spirit* I find nowhere any; and where none of these can satisfy the sense of that word in Scripture, the place falleth not under human understanding; and our faith therein consisteth not in our opinion, but in our submission; as in all places where God is said to be a *Spirit*; or where by the *Spirit of God*, is meant God himself. For the nature of God is incomprehensible;* that is to say, we understand nothing of *what he is*, but only *that he is*; and therefore the attributes we give him, are not to tell one another, *what he is*, nor to signify our opinion of his nature, but our desire to honour him with such names as we conceive most honourable amongst ourselves.

The spirit of God taken in the Scripture sometimes for a wind, or breath.

5. *Gen.* 1. 2. *The Spirit of God moved upon the face of the waters.* Here if by the *Spirit of God* be meant God himself, then is *motion* attributed to God, and consequently *place*, which are intelligible only of bodies, and not of substances incorporeal; and so the place is above our understanding, that can conceive nothing moved that changes not place, or that has not dimension; and whatsoever has dimension, is body. But the meaning of those words is best understood by the like place, (*Gen.* 8. 1) where, when the earth was covered with waters, as in the beginning, God intending to abate them, and again to discover the dry land, useth the like words, *I will bring my Spirit upon the earth, and the waters shall be diminished*: in which place, by *Spirit* is understood a wind, (that is an air or *spirit*

moved,) which might be called, as in the former place, the *Spirit of God*, because it was God's work.

6. *Gen.* 41. 38, Pharaoh calleth the Wisdom of Joseph, the *Spirit of God*. For Joseph having advised him to look out a wise and discreet man, and to set him over the land of Egypt, he saith thus, *Can we find such a man as this is, in whom is the Spirit of God?* And *Exod.* 28. 3, *Thou shalt speak* (saith God) *to all the wise hearted, whom I have filled with the spirit of wisdom, to make Aaron garments, to consecrate him.* Where extraordinary understanding, though but in making garments, as being the *gift* of God, is called the *Spirit of God*. The same is found again, *Exod.* 31. 3, 4, 5, 6, *and* 35. 31. And *Isaiah* 11. 2, 3, the prophet speaking of the Messiah, saith, *the Spirit of the Lord shall abide upon him, the spirit of wisdom and understanding, the spirit of counsel, and fortitude, and the spirit of the fear of the Lord.* Where manifestly is meant, not so many ghosts, but so many eminent *graces* that God would give him.

[209]
Secondly, for extraordinary gifts of the understanding.

7. In the book of *Judges*, an extraordinary zeal and courage in the defence of God's people, is called the *Spirit* of God; as when it excited Othniel, Gideon, Jephtha, and Sampson to deliver them from servitude, *Judges* 3. 10, 6. 34, 11. 29, 13. 25, 14. 6, 19. And of Saul, upon the news of the insolence of the Ammonites towards the men of Jabesh Gilead, it is said, (1 *Sam.* 11. 6) that *the Spirit of God came upon Saul, and his anger,* (or, as it is in the Latin, *his fury*), *was kindled greatly.* Where it is not probable was meant a ghost, but an extraordinary *zeal* to punish the cruelty of the Ammonites. In like manner by the *Spirit* of God, that came upon Saul, when he was amongst the prophets that praised God in songs, and music, (1 *Sam.* 19. 20), is to be understood, not a ghost, but an unexpected and sudden *zeal* to join with them in their devotion.

Thirdly, for extraordinary affections.

8. The false prophet Zedekiah saith to Micaiah (1 *Kings* 22. 24), *which way went the Spirit of the Lord from me to speak to thee?* Which cannot be understood of a ghost; for Micaiah declared before the kings of Israel and Judah, the event of the battle, as from a *vision*, and not as from a *spirit* speaking in him.

Fourthly, for the gift of prediction by dreams and visions.

9. In the same manner it appeareth, in the books of the Prophets, that though they spake by the *spirit* of God, that is to say, by a special grace of prediction; yet their knowledge of the future, was not by a ghost within them, but by some supernatural *dream* or *vision*.

Fifthly, for life.

10. *Gen.* 2. 7, it is said, *God made man of the dust of the earth, and breathed into his nostrils* (spiraculum vitae) *the breath of life, and man was made a living soul.* There the *breath of life* inspired by God, signifies no more, but that God gave him life; and (*Job* 27. 3) *as long as the Spirit of God is in my nostrils,* is no more than to say, *as long as I live.* So in *Ezek.* 1. 20, *the spirit of life was in the wheels,* is equivalent to, *the wheels were alive.* And, (*Ezek.* 2. 30) *the Spirit entered into me, and set me on my feet,* that is, *I recovered my vital strength;* not that any ghost or incorporeal substance entered into, and possessed his body.

Sixthly, for a subordination to authority.

[210]

11. In the eleventh chap. of *Numbers,* verse 17, *I will take* (saith God) *of the Spirit, which is upon thee, and will put it upon them, and they shall bear the burthen of the people with thee;* that is, upon the seventy elders: whereupon two of the seventy are said to prophesy in the camp; of whom some complained, and Joshua desired Moses to forbid them; which Moses would not do. Whereby it appears; that Joshua knew not that they had received authority so to do, and prophesied according to the mind of Moses, that is to say, by a *spirit,* or *authority* subordinate to his own.

12. In the like sense we read, (*Deut.* 34. 9) that *Joshua was full of the spirit of wisdom, because Moses had laid his hands upon him*: that is, because he was *ordained* by Moses, to prosecute the work he had himself begun, (namely, the bringing of God's people into the promised land), but prevented by death, could not finish.

13. In the like sense it is said, (*Rom.* 8. 9) *If any man have not the Spirit of Christ, he is none of his*: not meaning thereby the *ghost* of Christ, but a *submission* to his doctrine. As also, (1 *John* 4. 2) *Hereby you shall know the Spirit of God; every spirit that confesseth that Jesus Christ is come in the flesh, is of God*; by which is meant the spirit of unfeigned Christianity, or *submission* to that main article of Christian faith, that Jesus is the Christ; which cannot be interpreted of a ghost.

14. Likewise these words, (*Luke* 4. 1) *And Jesus full of the Holy Ghost,* (that is, as it is expressed, *Matt.* 4. 1, and *Mark* 1. 12, *of the Holy Spirit,*) may be understood, for *zeal* to do the work for which he was sent by God the Father: but to interpret it of a ghost, is to say, that God himself (for so our Saviour was,) was filled with God; which is very unproper, and insignificant. How we came to translate *spirits,* by the word *ghosts,** which signifieth nothing, neither in heaven, nor earth, but the imaginary inhabitants of man's brain, I examine not: but this I say, the word *spirit* in the text signifieth no such thing; but either properly a real *substance,* or metaphorically, some extraordinary *ability* or *affection* of the mind, or of the body.

15. The disciples of Christ, seeing him walking upon the sea, *Seventhly, (Matt.* 14. 26, and *Mark* 6. 49) supposed him to be a *Spirit*, meaning *for aërial* thereby an aërial *body*, and not a phantasm: for it is said, they all saw *bodies.* him; which cannot be understood of the delusions of the brain, (which are not common to many at once, as visible bodies are; but singular, because of the differences of fancies), but of bodies only. In like manner, where he was taken for a *spirit*, by the same apostles, (*Luke* 24. 3, 7); so also (*Acts* 12. 15) when St. Peter was delivered out of prison, and it would not be believed; but when the maid said he was at the door, they said it was his *angel*; by which must be meant a corporeal substance, or we must say, the disciples themselves did follow the common opinion both of Jews and Gentiles, that such apparitions were not imaginary, but real; and such as needed not the fancy of man for their existence: these the Jews called *spirits*, and *angels*, good or bad; as the Greeks called the same by the name of *demons*. And some such apparitions may be real, and substantial; that is to say, subtle bodies, which God can form by the same power, [211] by which he formed all things, and make use of, as of ministers, and messengers (that is to say, angels) to declare his will, and execute the same when he pleaseth, in extraordinary and supernatural manner. But when he hath so formed them they are substances, endued with dimensions, and take up room, and can be moved from place to place, which is peculiar to bodies; and therefore are not ghosts *incorporeal*, that is to say, ghosts that are in *no place*; that is to say, that are *nowhere*; that is to say, that seeming to be *somewhat*, are *nothing*. But if corporeal be taken in the most vulgar manner, for such substances as are perceptible by our external senses; then is substance incorporeal, a thing not imaginary, but real; namely, a thin substance invisible, but that hath the same dimensions that are in grosser bodies.

16. By the name of ANGEL, is signified generally, a *messenger*; and *Angel, what.* most often, a *messenger of God*: and by a messenger of God, is signified, any thing that makes known his extraordinary presence; that is to say, the extraordinary manifestation of his power, especially by a dream, or vision.

17. Concerning the creation of *angels*, there is nothing delivered in the Scriptures. That they are spirits, is often repeated: but by the name of spirit, is signified both in Scripture, and vulgarly, both

amongst Jews and Gentiles, sometimes thin bodies; as the air, the wind, the spirits vital, and animal, of living creatures; and sometimes the images that rise in the fancy in dreams, and visions; which are not real substances, nor last any longer than the dream, or vision they appear in; which apparitions, though no real substances, but accidents of the brain; yet when God raiseth them supernaturally, to signify his will, they are not improperly termed God's messengers, that is to say, his *angels*.

18. And as the Gentiles did vulgarly conceive the imagery of the brain, for things really subsistent without them, and not dependent on the fancy; and out of them framed their opinions of *demons*, good and evil; which because they seemed to subsist really, they called *substances*; and because they could not feel them with their hands, *incorporeal*: so also the Jews upon the same ground, without any thing in the Old Testament that constrained them thereunto, had generally an opinion, (except the sect of the Sadducees,) that those apparitions (which it pleased God sometimes to produce in the fancy of men, for his own service, and therefore called them his *angels*) were substances, not dependent on the fancy, but permanent creatures of God; whereof those which they thought were good to them, they esteemed the *angels of God*, and those they thought would hurt them, they called *evil angels*, or evil spirits; such as was the spirit of Python, and the spirits of madmen, of lunatics and epileptics: for they esteemed such as were troubled with such diseases, *demoniacs*.

19. But if we consider the places of the Old Testament where angels are mentioned, we shall find, that in most of them, there can [212] nothing else be understood by the word *angel*, but some image raised (supernaturally) in the fancy, to signify the presence of God in the execution of some supernatural work; and therefore in the rest, where their nature is not expressed, it may be understood in the same manner.

20. For we read, (*Gen.* 16) that the same apparition is called, not only an *angel*, but *God*; where that which (verse 7) is called the *angel* of the Lord, in the tenth verse, saith to Agar, *I will multiply thy seed exceedingly*; that is, speaketh in the person of God. Neither was this apparition a fancy figured, but a voice. By which it is manifest, that *angel* signifieth there, nothing but *God* himself, that caused Agar supernaturally* to apprehend a voice from heaven; or rather, nothing else but a voice supernatural, testifying God's special pres-

ence there. Why therefore may not the angels that appeared to Lot, and are called (*Gen*. 19. 12) *men*; and to whom, though they were two, Lot speaketh (verse 18) as but to one, and that one, as God, (for the words are, *Lot said unto them, Oh not so my Lord*) be understood of images of men, supernaturally formed in the fancy; as well as before by *angel* was understood a fancied voice? When the angel called to Abraham out of heaven, to stay his hand (*Gen*. 22. 11) from slaying Isaac, there was no apparition, but a voice; which nevertheless was called properly enough a messenger or *angel* of God, because it declared God's will supernaturally, and saves the labour of supposing any permanent ghosts. The angels which Jacob saw on the ladder of Heaven, (*Gen*. 28. 12) were a vision of his sleep; therefore only fancy, and a dream; yet being supernatural, and signs of God's special presence, those apparitions are not improperly called *angels*. The same is to be understood, (*Gen*. 31. 11) where Jacob saith thus, *The Angel of the Lord appeared to me in my sleep*. For an apparition made to a man in his sleep, is that which all men call a dream, whether such dream be natural, or supernatural: and that which there Jacob calleth an *angel*, was God himself; for the same angel saith (verse 13) *I am the God of Bethel*.

21. Also (*Exod*. 14. 19) the angel that went before the army of Israel to the Red Sea, and then came behind it, is (verse 19) the Lord himself; and he appeared, not in the form of a beautiful man, but in form (by day) of a *pillar of cloud*, and (by night) in form of a *pillar of fire*; and yet this pillar was all the apparition, and *angel* promised to Moses, (*Exod*. 14. 9) for the army's guide: for this cloudy pillar, is said, to have descended, and stood at the door of the Tabernacle, and to have talked with Moses.

22. There you see motion, and speech, which are commonly attributed to angels, attributed to a cloud, because the cloud served as a sign of God's presence; and was no less an angel, than if it had had the form of a man, or child of never so great beauty; or with wings, as usually they are painted, for the false instruction of common people. For it is not the shape; but their use, that makes them angels. But their use is to be significations of God's presence in supernatural operations; as when Moses (*Exod*. 33. 14) had [213] desired God to go along with the camp, (as he had done always before the making of the golden calf,) God did not answer, *I will go*, nor *I will send an angel in my stead*; but thus, *My presence shall go with thee*:

267

23. To mention all the places of the Old Testament where the name of angel is found, would be too long. Therefore to comprehend them all at once, I say, there is no text in that part of the Old Testament, which the Church of England holdeth for canonical, from which we can conclude, there is, or hath been created, any permanent thing (understood by the name of *spirit* or *angel,*) that hath not quantity; and that may not be, by the understanding divided; that is to say, considered by parts; so as one part may be in one place, and the next part in the next place to it; and, in sum, which is not (taking body for that, which is somewhat, or somewhere) corporeal; but in every place, the sense will bear the interpretation of angel, for messenger; as John Baptist is called an angel, and Christ the Angel of the Covenant; and as (according to the same analogy) the dove, and the fiery tongues, in that they were signs of God's special presence, might also be called angels. Though we find in *Daniel* two names of angels, Gabriel, and Michael; yet it is clear out of the text itself, (*Dan.* 12. 1) that by Michael is meant Christ, not as an angel, but as a prince: and that Gabriel (as the like apparitions made to other holy men in their sleep) was nothing but a supernatural phantasm, by which it seemed to Daniel, in his dream, that two saints being in talk, one of them said to the other, *Gabriel, Let us make this man understand his vision*: for God needeth not, to distinguish his celestial servants by names, which are useful only to the short memories of mortals. Nor in the New Testament is there any place, out of which it can be proved, that angels (except when they are put for such men as God hath made the messengers, and ministers of his word, or works) are things permanent, and withal incorporeal. That they are permanent, may be gathered from the words of our Saviour himself, (*Matt.* 25. 41) where he saith, it shall be said to the wicked in the last day, *Go ye cursed into everlasting fire prepared for the Devil and his angels*: which place is manifest for the permanence of evil angels, (unless we might think the name of Devil and his angels may be understood of the Church's adversaries and their ministers;) but then it is repugnant to their immateriality; because everlasting fire is no punishment to impatible* substances, such as are all things incorporeal. Angels therefore are not thence proved to be incorporeal. In like manner where St. Paul says, (1 *Cor.* 6. 3) *Know ye not that we shall judge the angels?* and (2 *Pet.* 2. 4) *For if God spared not the angels that sinned, but cast them down into hell.* And

(*Jude* 1. 6) *And the angels that kept not their first estate, but left their own habitation, he hath reserved in everlasting chains under darkness unto the judgment of the last day*; though it prove the permanence of angelical nature, it confirmeth also their materiality. And (*Matt. 22.* 30) *In the resurrection men do neither marry, nor give in marriage,* [214] *but are as the angels of God in heaven*: but in the resurrection men shall be permanent, and not incorporeal; so therefore also are the angels.

24. There be divers other places out of which may be drawn the like conclusion. To men that understand the signification of these words, *substance*, and *incorporeal*; as *incorporeal* is taken, not for subtle body, but for *not body*; they imply a contradiction: insomuch as to say, an angel or spirit is (in that sense) an incorporeal substance, is to say in effect, there is no angel nor spirit at all. Considering therefore the signification of the word *angel* in the Old Testament, and the nature of dreams and visions that happen to men by the ordinary way of nature; I was inclined to this opinion, that angels were nothing but supernatural apparitions of the fancy, raised by the special and extraordinary operation of God, thereby to make his presence and commandments known to mankind, and chiefly to his own people. But the many places of the New Testament, and our Saviour's own words, and in such texts, wherein is no suspicion of corruption of the Scripture, have extorted from my feeble reason, an acknowledgment, and belief, that there be also angels substantial, and permanent. But to believe they be in no place, that is to say, nowhere, that is to say, nothing, as they (though indirectly) say, that will have them incorporeal, cannot by Scripture be evinced.

25. On the signification of the word *spirit*, dependeth that of the word INSPIRATION; which must either be taken properly; and then it is nothing but the blowing into a man some thin and subtle air, or wind, in such manner as a man filleth a bladder with his breath; or if spirits be not corporeal, but have their existence only in the fancy, then it is nothing but the blowing in of a phantasm; which is improper to say, and impossible; for phantasms are not, but only seem to be, somewhat. That word therefore is used in the Scripture metaphorically only: as (*Gen.* 2. 7) where it is said that God *inspired* into man the breath of life, no more is meant, than that God gave unto him vital motion. For we are not to think that God made first

Inspiration, what.

a living breath, and then blew it into Adam after he was made, whether that breath were real, or seeming; but only as it is (*Acts* 17. 25) *that he gave him life, and breath*; that is, made him a living creature. And where it is said, (2 *Tim*. 3. 16) *all Scripture is given by inspiration from God*, speaking there of the Scripture of the Old Testament, it is an easy metaphor, to signify, that God inclined the spirit or mind of those writers, to write that which should be useful, in teaching, reproving, correcting, and instructing men in the way of righteous living. But where St. Peter. (2 *Pet*. 1. 21) saith, that *Prophecy came not in old time by the will of man, but the holy men of God spake as they were moved by the Holy Spirit*, by the Holy Spirit, is meant the voice of God in a dream or vision supernatural, which is not *inspiration*. Nor when our Saviour breathing on his disciples, said, *Receive the Holy Spirit*, was that breath the Spirit, but a sign of the spiritual graces he gave unto them. And though it be said of many, and of our Saviour himself, that he was full of the Holy Spirit; yet that fullness is not to be understood for *infusion* of the substance of God, but for accumulation of his gifts, such as are the gift of sanctity of life, of tongues, and the like, whether attained supernaturally, or by study and industry; for in all cases they are the gifts of God. So likewise where God says (*Joel* 2. 28) *I will pour out my Spirit upon all flesh, and your sons and your daughters shall prophesy, your old men shall dream dreams, and your young men shall see visions*, we are not to understand it in the proper sense, as if his *Spirit* were like water, subject to effusion or infusion; but as if God had promised to give them prophetical dreams, and visions. For the proper use of the word *infused*, in speaking of the graces of God, is an abuse of it; for those graces are virtues, not bodies to be carried hither and thither, and to be poured into men as into barrels.

[215]

26. In the same manner, to take *inspiration* in the proper sense, or to say that good *spirits* entered into men to make them prophesy, or evil *spirits* into those that became phrenetic, lunatic, or epileptic, is not to take the word in the sense of the Scripture; for the Spirit there is taken for the power of God, working by causes to us unknown. As also (*Acts* 2. 2) the wind, that is there said to fill the house wherein the apostles were assembled on the day of Pentecost, is not to be understood for the *Holy Spirit*, which is the Deity itself; but for an external sign of God's special working on their hearts, to effect in them the internal graces, and holy virtues he thought requisite for the performance of their apostleship.

CHAPTER XXXV

OF THE SIGNIFICATION IN SCRIPTURE OF KINGDOM OF GOD, OF HOLY, SACRED, AND SACRAMENT

1. THE *Kingdom of God* in the writings of divines, and specially in sermons, and treatises of devotion, is taken most commonly for eternal felicity, after this life, in the highest heaven, which they also call the Kingdom of Glory; and sometimes (for the earnest of that felicity) sanctification, which they term the Kingdom of Grace; but never for the monarchy, that is to say, the sovereign power of God over any subjects acquired by their own consent, which is the proper signification of kingdom.

The kingdom of God taken by divines metaphorically, but in the Scriptures properly.

2. To the contrary, I find the KINGDOM OF GOD, to signify in most places of Scripture, a *kingdom properly so named*, constituted by the votes of the people of Israel in peculiar manner; wherein they chose God for their king by covenant made with him, upon God's promising them the possession of the land of Canaan; and but seldom metaphorically; and then it is taken for *dominion over sin*; (and only in the New Testament;) because such a dominion as that, every subject shall have in the kingdom of God, and without prejudice to the sovereign.

3. From the very creation, God not only reigned over all men *naturally* by his might; but also had *peculiar* subjects, whom he commanded by a voice, as one man speaketh to another. In which manner he *reigned* over Adam, and gave him commandment to abstain from the tree of cognizance of good and evil; which when he obeyed not, but tasting thereof, took upon him to be as God, judging between good and evil, not by his creator's commandment, but by his own sense, his punishment was a privation of the estate of eternal life, wherein God had at first created him: and afterwards God punished his posterity for their vices, all but eight persons, with an universal deluge; and in these eight did consist the then *kingdom of God*.

4. After this it pleased God to speak to Abraham, and (*Gen.* 17. 7, 8) to make a covenant with him in these words, *I will establish my covenant between me, and thee, and thy seed after thee in their generations, for an everlasting covenant, to be a God to thee, and to thy seed after thee; and I will give unto thee, and to thy seed after thee, the land*

The original of the kingdom of God.

wherein thou art a stranger, all the land of Canaan for an everlasting possession. In this covenant Abraham promiseth for himself and his posterity to obey as God, the Lord that spake to him: and God on his part promiseth to Abraham the land of Canaan for an everlasting [217] possession. And for a memorial, and a token of this covenant, he ordaineth (verse 11) the *sacrament of circumcision.* This is it which is called the *old covenant* or *testament*; and containeth a contract between God and Abraham; by which Abraham obligeth himself, and his posterity, in a peculiar manner to be subject to God's positive law; for to the law moral he was obliged before, as by an oath of allegiance. And though the name of *King* be not yet given to God, nor of *kingdom* to Abraham and his seed; yet the thing is the same; namely, an institution by pact, of God's peculiar sovereignty over the seed of Abraham; which in the renewing of the same covenant by Moses, at Mount Sinai, is expressly called a peculiar *kingdom of God* over the Jews: and it is of Abraham (not of Moses) St. Paul saith (*Rom.* 4. 11) that he is the *father of the faithful;* that is, of those that are loyal, and do not violate their allegiance sworn to God, then by circumcision, and afterwards in the *new covenant* by baptism.

That the kingdom of God is properly his civil sovereignty over a peculiar people by pact.

5. This covenant, at the foot of Mount Sinai, was renewed by Moses, (*Exod.* 19. 5) where the Lord commandeth Moses to speak to the people in this manner, *If you will obey my voice indeed, and keep my covenant, then ye shall be a peculiar people to me, for all the earth is mine; and ye shall be unto me a sacerdotal kingdom, and an holy nation.* For a *peculiar people*, the vulgar Latin hath *peculium de cunctis populis*: the English translation made in the beginning of the reign of King James, hath a *peculiar treasure unto me above all nations*; and the Geneva French, *the most precious jewel of all nations.* But the truest translation is the first, because it is confirmed by St. Paul himself (*Tit.* 2. 14) where he saith, alluding to that place, that our blessed Saviour *gave himself for us, that he might purify us to himself, a peculiar* (that is, an extraordinary) *people*: for the word is in the Greek περιούσιος, which is opposed commonly to the word ἐπιούσιος: and as this signifieth *ordinary, quotidian*, or (as in the Lord's Prayer) *of daily use*; so the other signifieth that which is *overplus*, and *stored up*, and *enjoyed in a special manner*; which the Latins call *peculium*: and this meaning of the place is confirmed by the reason God rendereth of it, which followeth immediately, in that he addeth, *For all the earth is mine*, as if he should say, *All the nations of the world are mine*; but it is not so that you are mine, but in a *special manner*: for

they are all mine, by reason of my power; but you shall be mine, by your own consent, and covenant; which is an addition to his ordinary title, to all nations.

6. The same is again confirmed in express words in the same text, *Ye shall be to me a sacerdotal kingdom, and an holy nation.* The vulgar Latin hath it, *regnum sacerdotale*, to which agreeth the translation of that place (1 *Pet.* 2. 9) *Sacerdotium regale, a regal priesthood*; as also the institution itself, by which no man might enter into the *Sanctum Sanctorum*, that is to say, no man might enquire God's will immediately of God himself, but only the high-priest. The English translation before mentioned, following that of Geneva, has, *a kingdom of priests*; which is either meant of the succession of one high-priest [218] after another, or else it accordeth not with St. Peter, nor with the exercise of the high-priesthood: for there was never any but the high-priest only, that was to inform the people of God's will; nor any convocation of priests ever allowed to enter into the *Sanctum Sanctorum*.

7. Again, the title of a *holy nation* confirms the same: for *holy* signifies, that which is God's by special, not by general right. All the earth (as is said in the text) is God's; but all the earth is not called *holy*, but that only which is set apart for his especial service, as was the nation of the Jews. It is therefore manifest enough by this one place, that by the *kingdom of God*, is properly meant a commonwealth, instituted (by the consent of those which were to be subject thereto) for their civil government, and the regulating of their behaviour, not only towards God their king, but also towards one another in point of justice, and towards other nations both in peace and war; which properly was a kingdom, wherein God was king, and the high-priest was to be (after the death of Moses) his sole viceroy or lieutenant.

8. But there be many other places that clearly prove the same. As first (1 *Samuel* 8. 7) when the Elders of Israel (grieved with the corruption of the sons of Samuel) demanded a king, Samuel displeased therewith, prayed unto the Lord; and the Lord answering said unto him, *Hearken unto the voice of the people, for they have not rejected thee, but they have rejected me, that I should not reign over them.* Out of which it is evident, that God himself was then their king; and Samuel did not command the people, but only delivered to them that which God from time to time appointed him.

9. Again, (1 *Sam.* 12. 12) where Samuel saith to the people, *When ye saw that Nahash, king of the children of Ammon, came against you, ye said unto me, Nay, but a king shall reign over us, when the Lord your God was your king.* It is manifest that God was their king, and governed the civil state of their commonwealth.

10. And after the Israelites had rejected God, the prophets did foretell his restitution; as (*Isaiah* 24. 23) *Then the moon shall be confounded, and the sun ashamed, when the Lord of hosts shall reign in Mount Zion, and in Jerusalem*; where he speaketh expressly of his reign in Zion and Jerusalem; that is, on earth. And (*Micah* 4. 7) *And the Lord shall reign over them in Mount Zion*: this Mount Zion is in Jerusalem upon the earth. And (*Ezek.* 20. 33) *As I live, saith the Lord God, surely with a mighty hand, and a stretched out arm, and with fury poured out, I will rule over you*; and (verse 37) *I will cause you to pass under the rod, and I will bring you into the bond of the covenant*; that is, I will reign over you, and make you to stand to that covenant which you made with me by Moses, and brake in your rebellion against me in the days of Samuel, and in your election of another king.

11. And in the New Testament, the angel Gabriel saith of our Saviour (*Luke* 1. 32, 33) *He shall be great, and be called the Son of the most High, and the Lord shall give unto him the throne of his father [219] David; and he shall reign over the house of Jacob for ever; and of his kingdom there shall be no end.* This is also a kingdom upon earth; for the claim whereof, as an enemy to Caesar, he was put to death; the title of his cross, was, *Jesus of Nazareth, King of the Jews*; he was crowned in scorn with a crown of thorns; and for the proclaiming of him, it is said of the disciples (*Acts* 17. 7) *That they did all of them contrary to the decrees of Caesar, saying there was another king, one Jesus.* The kingdom therefore of God, is a real, not a metaphorical kingdom; and so taken, not only in the Old Testament, but the New; when we say, *For thine is the kingdom, the power, and glory*, it is to be understood of God's kingdom, by force of our covenant, not by the right of God's power; for such a kingdom God always hath; so that it were superfluous to say in our prayer, *Thy kingdom come*, unless it be meant of the restoration of that kingdom of God by Christ, which by revolt of the Israelites had been interrupted in the election of Saul. Nor had it been proper to say, *The kingdom of heaven is at hand*; or to pray, *Thy kingdom come*, if it had still continued.

12. There be so many other places that confirm this interpretation, that it were a wonder there is no greater notice taken of it, but

that it gives too much light to Christian kings to see their right of ecclesiastical government. This they have observed, that instead of a *sacerdotal kingdom*, translate, *a kingdom of priests*: for they may as well translate a *royal priesthood*, (as it is in St. Peter) into a *priesthood of kings*. And whereas, for a *peculiar people*, they put a *precious jewel*, or *treasure*, a man might as well call the special regiment, or company of a general, the general's precious jewel, or his treasure.

13. In short, the kingdom of God is a civil kingdom; which consisted, first, in the obligation of the people of Israel to those laws, which Moses should bring unto them from Mount Sinai; and which afterwards the high-priest for the time being, should deliver to them from before the cherubims in the *sanctum sanctorum*; and which kingdom having been cast off, in the election of Saul, the prophets foretold, should be restored by Christ; and the restoration whereof we daily pray for, when we say in the Lord's Prayer, *Thy kingdom come*; and the right whereof we acknowledge, when we add, *For thine is the kingdom, the power, and glory, for ever and ever, Amen*; and the proclaiming whereof, was the preaching of the apostles; and to which men are prepared, by the teachers of the Gospel; to embrace which Gospel, (that is to say, to promise obedience to God's government) is, to be in the *kingdom of grace*, because God hath *gratis* given to such the power to be the subjects (that is, children) of God hereafter, when Christ shall come in majesty to judge the world, and actually to govern his own people, which is called *the kingdom of glory*. If the kingdom of God (called also the kingdom of heaven, from the gloriousness and admirable height of that throne) were not a kingdom which God by his lieutenants, or vicars, who deliver his [220] commandments to the people, did exercise on earth; there would not have been so much contention, and war, about who it is, by whom God speaketh to us; neither would many priests have troubled themselves with spiritual jurisdiction, nor any king have denied it them.

14. Out of this literal interpretation of the *kingdom of God*, *Holy, what.* ariseth also the true interpretation of the word HOLY. For it is a word, which in God's kingdom answereth to that, which men in their kingdoms use to call *public*, or the *king's*.

15. The king of any country is the *public* person, or representative of all his own subjects. And God the king of Israel was the *Holy One* of Israel. The nation which is subject to one earthly sovereign, is the nation of that sovereign, that is, of the public person. So the

275

Jews, who were God's nation, were called (*Exod.* 19. 6) *a holy nation.* For by *holy*, is always understood either God himself, or that which is God's in propriety; as by public, is always meant, either the person of the commonwealth itself, or something that is so the commonwealth's, as no private person can claim any propriety therein.

16. Therefore the Sabbath (God's day) is a *holy day*; the temple (God's house) *a holy house*; sacrifices, tithes, and offerings (God's tribute) *holy duties*; priests, prophets, and anointed kings, under Christ (God's ministers) *holy men*; the celestial ministering spirits (God's messengers) *holy angels*; and the like: and wheresoever the world *holy* is taken properly, there is still something signified of propriety, gotten by consent. In saying *Hallowed be thy name*, we do but pray to God for grace to keep the first commandment, of *having no other Gods but him.* Mankind is God's nation in propriety: but the Jews only were a *holy nation.* Why, but because they became his propriety by covenant?

17. And the word *profane*, is usually taken in the Scripture for the same with *common*; and consequently their contraries, *holy* and *proper*, in the kingdom of God, must be the same also. But figuratively, those men also are called *holy*, that led such godly lives, as if they had forsaken all worldly designs, and wholly devoted and given themselves to God. In the proper sense, that which is made *holy* by God's appropriating or separating it to his own use, is said to be *sanctified* by God, as the seventh day in the fourth commandment; and as the elect in the New Testament were said to be *sanctified*, when they were endued with the spirit of godliness. And that which is made *holy* by the dedication of men, and given to God, so

Sacred, what. as to be used only in his public service, is called also SACRED, and said to be consecrated, as temples, and other houses of public prayer, and their utensils, priests, and ministers, victims, offerings, and the external matter of sacraments.

Degrees of 18. Of *holiness* there be degrees: for of those things that are set
sanctity. apart for the service of God, there may be some set apart again, for a nearer and more especial service. The whole nation of the Israelites were a people holy to God; yet the tribe of Levi was amongst the
[221] Israelites a holy tribe; and amongst the Levites, the priests were yet more holy; and amongst the priests, the high-priest was the most holy. So the land of Judea was the Holy Land; but the holy city wherein God was to be worshipped, was more holy; and again the

Temple more holy than the city, and the *sanctum sanctorum* more
holy than the rest of the Temple.

19. A SACRAMENT, is a separation of some visible thing from   *Sacrament.*
common use; and a consecration of it to God's service, for a sign,
either of our admission into the kingdom of God, to be of the
number of his peculiar people, or for a commemoration of the same.
In the Old Testament, the sign of admission was *circumcision*; in the
New Testament, *baptism*. The commemoration of it in the Old
Testament, was the *eating* (at a certain time, which was anniversary)
of the *Paschal Lamb*; by which they were put in mind of the night
wherein they were delivered out of their bondage in Egypt; and in
the New Testament, the celebrating of the *Lord's Supper*; by which,
we are put in mind of our deliverance from the bondage of sin, by
our blessed Saviour's death upon the cross. The sacraments of
admission, are but once to be used, because there needs but one
admission; but because we have need of being often put in mind of
our deliverance, and of our allegiance, the sacraments of *commemoration** have need to be reiterated. And these are the principal sacraments, and as it were the solemn oaths we make of our allegiance.
There be also other consecrations, that may be called sacraments, as
the word implieth only consecration to God's service; but as it
implies an oath, or promise of allegiance to God, there were no other
in the Old Testament, but *circumcision*, and the *passover*; nor are
there any other in the New Testament, but *baptism* and the *Lord's
Supper*.

CHAPTER XXXVI   [222]

OF THE WORD OF GOD, AND OF PROPHETS

1. WHEN there is mention of the *word of God*, or of *man*, it doth not   *Word, what.*
signify a part of speech, such as grammarians call a noun, or a verb,
or any simple voice, without a contexture with other words to
make it significative; but a perfect speech or discourse, whereby
the speaker *affirmeth*, *denieth*, *commandeth*, *promiseth*, *threateneth*,
wisheth, or *interrogateth*. In which sense it is not *vocabulum*, that
signifies a *word*; but *sermo*, (in Greek λόγος) that is, some *speech*,
discourse, or *saying*.

The words spoken by God, and concerning God, both are called God's word in Scripture.

2. Again, if we say the *word of God*, or of *man*, it may be understood sometimes of the speaker, (as the words that God hath spoken) or that a man hath spoken: in which sense, when we say, the Gospel of St. Matthew, we understand St. Matthew to be the writer of it: and sometimes of the subject: in which sense, when we read in the Bible, *the words of the days of the kings of Israel, or Judah*, it is meant, that the acts that were done in those days, were the subject of those words; and in the Greek, which (in the Scripture) retaineth many Hebraisms, by the word of God is oftentimes meant, not that which is spoken by God, but concerning God, and his government; that is to say, the doctrine of religion: insomuch, as it is all one, to say λόγος Θεοῦ, and *theologia*; which is, that doctrine which we usually call *divinity*, as is manifest by the places following, (*Acts* 13. 46) *Then Paul and Barnabas waxed bold, and said, it was necessary that the word of God should first have been spoken to you, but seeing you put it from you, and judge yourselves unworthy of everlasting life, lo, we turn to the Gentiles.* That which is here called the word of God, was the doctrine of Christian religion; as it appears evidently by that which goes before. And (*Acts* 5. 20) where it is said to the apostles by an angel, *Go stand and speak in the Temple, all the words of this life*; by the words of this life, is meant, the doctrine of the Gospel; as is evident by what they did in the Temple, and is expressed in the last verse of the same chapter, *Daily in the Temple, and in every house they ceased not to teach and preach Christ Jesus*: in which place it is manifest, that Jesus Christ was the subject of this *word of life*; or (which is all one) the subject of the *words of this life eternal*, that our Saviour offered them. So (*Acts* 15. 7) the word of God, is called *the word of the Gospel*, because it containeth the doctrine of the kingdom of Christ; and the same word (*Rom.* 10. 8, 9) is called *the word of faith*; that is, as is there expressed, the doctrine of Christ come, and raised from [223] the dead. Also (*Matt.* 13. 19) *When any one heareth the word of the kingdom*; that is, the doctrine of the kingdom taught by Christ. Again, the same word, is said (*Acts* 12. 24) *to grow and to be multiplied*; which to understand of the evangelical doctrine is easy, but of the voice, or speech of God, hard and strange. In the same sense (1 *Tim.* 4. 1) the *doctrine of devils*, signifieth not the words of any devil, but the doctrine of heathen men concerning *demons*, and those phantasms which they worshipped as gods.

3. Considering these two significations of the WORD OF GOD, as it is taken in Scripture, it is manifest in this latter sense (where it is

taken for the doctrine of Christian religion,) that the whole Scripture is the word of God: but in the former sense not so. For example,
though these words, *I am the Lord thy God*, &c. to the end of the
Ten Commandments, were spoken by God to Moses; yet the preface, *God spake these words and said*, is to be understood for the words
of him that wrote the holy history. The *word of God*, as it is taken for *The word*
that which he hath spoken, is understood sometimes *properly*, some- *of God*
times *metaphorically*. *Properly*, as the words, he hath spoken to his *metaphorically*
prophets: *metaphorically*, for his wisdom, power, and eternal decree, *used, first, for*
in making the world; in which sense, those fiats, *Let there be light,* *the decrees*
Let there be a firmament, Let us make man, &c. (*Gen.* 1) are the word *God;*
of God. And in the same sense it is said (*John* 1. 3) *All things were* *and power of*
made by it, and without it was nothing made that was made: and (*Heb.*
1. 3) *He upholdeth all things by the word of his power*; that is, by the
power of his word; that is, by his power: and (*Heb.* 11. 3) *The worlds*
were framed by the word of God; and many other places to the same
sense: as also amongst the Latins, the name of *fate*, which signifieth
properly *the word spoken*, is taken in the same sense.

4. Secondly, for the effect of his word; that is to say, for the thing *Secondly, for*
itself, which by his word is affirmed, commanded, threatened, or *the effect of*
promised; as (*Psalm* 105. 19) where Joseph is said to have been kept *his word;*
in prison, *till his word was come*; that is, till that was come to pass
which he had foretold to Pharaoh's butler (*Gen.* 40. 13), concerning
his being restored to his office: for there by *his word was come*, is
meant, the thing itself was come to pass. So also (1 *Kings* 18. 36)
Elijah saith to God, *I have done all these thy words*, instead of *I have
done all these things at thy word*, or commandment; and (*Jer.* 17. 15)
Where is the word of the Lord, is put for, *Where is the evil he threatened*.
And (*Ezek.* 12. 28) *There shall none of my words be prolonged any
more*: by *words* are understood those *things*, which God promised to
his people. And in the New Testament (*Matt.* 24. 35) *heaven and
earth shall pass away, but my words shall not pass away*; that is, there
is nothing that I have promised or foretold, that shall not come to
pass. And in this sense it is, that St. John the Evangelist, and, I
think, St. John only, calleth our Saviour himself as in the flesh *the
word of God*, as (*John* 1. 14) *the word was made flesh*; that is to say, the
word, or promise that Christ should come into the world; *who in the
beginning was with God*; that is to say, it was in the purpose of God
the Father, to send God the Son into the world, to enlighten men in [224]
the way of eternal life; but it was not till then put in execution, and

actually incarnate; so that our Saviour is there called the *word*, not because he was the promise, but the thing promised. They that taking occasion from this place, do commonly call him the verb of God, do but render the text more obscure. They might as well term him the noun of God: for as by *noun*, so also by *verb*, men understand nothing but a part of speech, a voice, a sound, that neither affirms, nor denies, nor commands, nor promiseth, nor is any substance corporeal, or spiritual; and therefore it cannot be said to be either God, or man; whereas our Saviour is both. And this *word*, which St. John in his gospel saith was with God, is (in his *first Epistle*, verse 1) called the *word of life*; and (verse 2) *the eternal life, which was with the Father*. So that he can be in no other sense called the *word*, than in that, wherein he is called eternal life; that is, *he that hath procured us eternal life*, by his coming in the flesh. So also (*Apocalypse* 19. 13) the apostle speaking of Christ, clothed in a garment dipped in blood, saith; his name is *the word of God*; which is to be understood, as if he had said his name had been, *He that was come according to the purpose of God from the beginning, and according to his word and promises delivered by the prophets*. So that there is nothing here of the incarnation of a word, but of the incarnation of God the Son, therefore called *the word*, because his incarnation was the performance of the promise; in like manner as the Holy Ghost is called (*Acts* 1. 4; *Luke* 24. 49) *the promise*.

Thirdly, for the words of reason and equity.

5. There are also places of the Scripture, where, by the *word of God*, is signified such words as are consonant to reason, and equity, though spoken sometimes neither by prophet, nor by a holy man. For Pharaoh Necho was an idolater; yet his words to the good king Josiah, in which he advised him by messengers, not to oppose him in his march against Charchemish, are said to have proceeded from the mouth of God; and that Josiah not hearkening to them, was slain in the battle; as is to be read (2 *Chron.* 35. 21, 22, 23). It is true, that as the same history is related in the first book of Esdras, not Pharaoh, but Jeremiah, spake these words to Josiah, from the mouth of the Lord. But we are to give credit to the canonical Scripture, whatsoever be written in the Apocrypha.

6. The *word of God*, is then also to be taken for the dictates of reason, and equity, when the same is said in the Scriptures to be written in man's heart; as *Psalm* 36. 31; *Jer.* 31. 33; *Deut.* 30. 11, 14, and many other like places.

7. The name of PROPHET, signifieth in Scripture sometimes *pro-* *Divers*
locutor; that is, he that speaketh from God to man, or from man to *acceptions of*
God: and sometimes *predictor*, or a foreteller of things to come: and *the word*
sometimes one that speaketh incoherently, as men that are dis- *prophet.*
tracted. It is most frequently used in the sense of speaking from God
to the people. So Moses, Samuel, Elijah, Isaiah, Jeremiah, and
others were *prophets*. And in this sense the high-priest was a *prophet*,
for he only went into the *sanctum sanctorum*, to enquire of God; and   [225]
was to declare his answer to the people. And therefore when
Caiaphas said, it was expedient that one man should die for the
people, St. John saith (chapter 11. 51) that *He spake not this of
himself, but being high-priest that year, he prophesied that one man
should die for the nation*. Also they that in Christian congregations
taught the people, (1 *Cor.* 14. 3) are said to prophesy. In the like
sense it is, that God saith to Moses (*Exod.* 4. 16) concerning Aaron,
*He shall be thy spokesman to the people; and he shall be to thee a mouth,
and thou shalt be to him instead of God*: that which here is *spokesman*,
is (*Exod.* 7. 1) interpreted prophet; *See* (saith God) *I have made thee
a God to Pharaoh, and Aaron thy brother shall be thy prophet*. In the
sense of speaking from man to God, Abraham is called a prophet
(*Gen.* 20. 7) where God in a dream speaketh to Abimelech in this
manner, *Now therefore restore the man his wife, for he is a prophet, and
shall pray for thee*; whereby may be also gathered, that the name of
prophet may be given, not unproperly to them that in Christian
churches, have a calling to say public prayers for the congregation.
In the same sense, the prophets that came down from the high place
(or hill of God) with a psaltery, and a tabret, and a pipe, and a harp
(1 *Sam.* 10. 5, 6) and (verse 10) Saul amongst them, are said to
prophesy, in that they praised God in that manner publicly. In the
like sense, is Miriam (*Exod.* 15. 20) called a prophetess. So is it also
to be taken (1 *Cor.* 11. 4, 5) where St. Paul saith, *Every man that
prayeth or prophesieth with his head covered, &c., and every woman
that prayeth or prophesieth with her head uncovered*: for prophecy in
that place, signifieth no more, but praising God in psalms, and holy
songs; which women might do in the church, though it were not
lawful for them to speak to the congregation. And in this signification it is, that the poets of the heathen, that composed hymns and
other sorts of poems in the honour of their gods, were called *vates*
(prophets) as is well enough known by all that are versed in the

books of the Gentiles, and as is evident (*Tit.* 1. 12), where St. Paul saith of the Cretans, that a prophet of their own said, they were liars; not that St. Paul held their poets for prophets, but acknowledgeth that the word prophet was commonly used to signify them that celebrated the honour of God in verse.

Prediction of future contingents, not always prophecy.

8. When by prophecy is meant prediction, or foretelling of future contingents; not only they were prophets, who were God's spokesmen, and foretold those things to others, which God had foretold to them; but also all those impostors, that pretend, by help of familiar spirits, or by superstitious divination of events past, from false causes, to foretell the like events in time to come: of which (as I have declared already in the twelfth chapter of this discourse) there be many kinds, who gain in the opinion of the common sort of men, a greater reputation of prophecy, by one casual event that may be but wrested to their purpose, than can be lost again by never so many failings. Prophecy is not an art, nor (when it is taken for prediction) a constant vocation; but an extraordinary, and temporary employment from God, most often of good men, but sometimes also of the wicked. The woman of Endor, who is said to have had a familiar spirit, and thereby to have raised a phantasm of Samuel, and foretold Saul his death, was not therefore a prophetess; for neither had she any science, whereby she could raise such a phantasm; nor does it appear that God commanded the raising of it; but only guided that imposture to be a means of Saul's terror and discouragement; and by consequent, of the discomfiture, by which he fell. And for incoherent speech, it was amongst the Gentiles taken for one sort of prophecy, because the prophets of their oracles, intoxicated with a spirit, or vapour from the cave of the Pythian oracle at Delphi, were for the time really mad, and spake like madmen; of whose loose words a sense might be made to fit any event, in such sort, as all bodies are said to be made of *materia prima*. In Scripture I find it also so taken (1 *Sam.* 18. 10) in these words, *And the evil spirit came upon Saul, and he prophesied in the midst of the house.*

[226]

The manner how God hath spoken to the prophets.

9.* And although there be so many significations in Scripture of the word *prophet*; yet is that the most frequent, in which it is taken for him, to whom God speaketh immediately, that which the prophet is to say from him, to some other man, or to the people. And hereupon a question may be asked, in what manner God speaketh to such a prophet. Can it (may some say) be properly said, that God hath voice and language, when it cannot be properly said, he hath a tongue, or other organs, as a man? The prophet David argueth thus, (*Psalm* 94. 9) *Shall he that made the eye, not see? or he that made the ear, not hear?* But this may be spoken, not as usually, to signify God's nature, but to signify our intention to honour him. For to *see*, and *hear*, are honourable attributes, and may be given to God, to declare (as far as our capacity can conceive) his almighty power. But if it were to be taken in the strict, and proper sense, one might argue from his making of all other parts of man's body, that he had also the same use of them which we have; which would be many of them so uncomely, as it would be the greatest contumely in the world to ascribe them to him. Therefore we are to interpret God's speaking to men immediately, for that way (whatsoever it be) by which God makes them understand his will. And the ways whereby he doth this, are many; and to be sought only in the Holy Scripture: where though many times it be said, that God spake to this, and that person, without declaring in what manner; yet there be again many places, that deliver also the signs by which they were to acknowledge his presence, and commandment; and by these may be understood, how he spake to many of the rest.

10. In what manner God spake to Adam, and Eve, and Cain, and Noah, is not expressed; nor how he spake to Abraham, till such time as he came out of his own country to Sichem in the land of Canaan; and then (*Gen.* 12. 7) God is said to have *appeared* to him. So there is one way, whereby God made his presence manifest; that is, by an *apparition*, or *visi͡n*. And again, (*Gen.* 15. 1) *the word of the Lord came to Abraham in a vision*; that is to say, somewhat, as a sign of God's presence, appeared as God's messenger, to speak to him. Again, the Lord appeared to Abraham (*Gen.* 18. 1) by an apparition of three angels; and to Abimelech (*Gen.* 20. 3) in a dream: to Lot (*Gen.* 19. 1) by an apparition of two angels: and to Hagar (*Gen.* 21. 17) by the apparition of one angel: and to Abraham again (*Gen.* 22. 11) by the apparition of a voice from heaven: and (*Gen.* 26. 24) to Isaac in the night; (that is, in his sleep, or by dream): and to Jacob (*Gen.* 18. 12) in a dream; that is to say (as are the words of the text) *Jacob dreamed that he saw a ladder, &c.* And (*Gen.* 32. 1) in a vision of angels: and to Moses (*Exod.* 3. 2) in the apparition of a flame of fire out of the midst of a bush: and after the time of Moses, (where the manner how God spake immediately to man in the Old Testament, is expressed) he spake always by a vision, or by a dream; as to Gideon, Samuel, Eliah, Elisha, Isaiah, Ezekiel, and the rest of the

To the extraordinary prophets of the Old Testament he spake by dreams, or visions.

[227]

prophets; and often in the New Testament, as to Joseph, to St. Peter, to St. Paul, and to St. John the Evangelist in the Apocalypse.

11. Only to Moses he spake in a more extraordinary manner in Mount Sinai, and in the Tabernacle; and to the high-priest in the Tabernacle, and in the *sanctum sanctorum* of the Temple. But Moses, and after him the high-priests were prophets of a more eminent place and degree in God's favour; and God himself in express words declareth, that to other prophets he spake in dreams and visions, but to his servant Moses, in such manner as a man speaketh to his friend. The words are these (*Numb.* 12. 6, 7, 8) *If there be a prophet among you, I the Lord will make myself known to him in a vision, and will speak unto him in a dream. My servant Moses is not so, who is faithful in all my house; with him I will speak mouth to mouth, even apparently, not in dark speeches; and the similitude of the Lord shall he behold.* And (*Exod.* 33. 11) *The Lord spake to Moses face to face, as a man speaketh to his friend.* And yet this speaking of God to Moses, was by mediation of an angel, or angels, as appears expressly, *Acts* 7. 35 and 53, and *Gal.* 3. 19, and was therefore a vision, though a more clear vision than was given to other prophets. And conformable hereunto, where God saith (*Deut.* 13. 1) *If there arise amongst you a prophet, or dreamer of dreams,* the latter word is but the interpretation of the former. And (*Joel* 2. 28) *Your sons and your daughters shall prophesy; your old men shall dream dreams, and your young men shall see visions*: where again, the word *prophesy* is expounded by *dream*, and *vision.* And in the same manner it was, that God spake to Solomon, promising him wisdom, riches, and honour; for the text saith, (1 *Kings* 3. 15) *And Solomon awoke, and behold it was a dream*: so that generally the prophets extraordinary in the Old Testament took notice of the word of God no otherwise, than from their dreams, or visions; that is to say, from the imaginations which they had in their sleep, or in an extasy: which imaginations in every true prophet were supernatural; but in false prophets were either natural or feigned.

12. The same prophets were nevertheless said to speak by the [228] spirit; as (*Zech.* 7. 12) where the prophet speaking of the Jews, saith, *They made their hearts hard as adamant, lest they should hear the law, and the words which the Lord of Hosts hath sent in his Spirit by the former prophets.* By which it is manifest, that speaking by the *spirit*, or *inspiration*, was not a particular manner of God's speaking, differ-

ent from vision, when they that were said to speak by the Spirit, were extraordinary prophets, such as for every new message, were to have a peculiar commission, or (which is all one) a new dream, or vision.

13. Of prophets, that were so by a perpetual calling in the Old Testament, some were *supreme*, and some *subordinate*: supreme were first Moses; and after him the high-priests, every one for his time, as long as the priesthood was royal; and after the people of the Jews had rejected God, that he should no more reign over them, those kings which submitted themselves to God's government, were also his chief prophets; and the high-priest's office became ministerial. And when God was to be consulted, they put on the holy vestments, and enquired of the Lord, as the king commanded them, and were deprived of their office, when the king thought fit. For king Saul (1 *Sam.* 13. 9) commanded the burnt offering to be brought, and (1 *Sam.* 14. 18) he commands the priests to bring the ark near him; and (verse 19) again to let it alone, because he saw an advantage upon his enemies. And in the same chapter Saul asketh counsel of God. In like manner king David, after his being anointed, though before he had possession of the kingdom, is said to *enquire of the Lord* (1 *Sam.* 23. 2) whether he should fight against the Philistines at Keilah; and (verse 10) David commandeth the priest to bring him the ephod, to enquire whether he should stay in Keilah, or not. And king Solomon (1 *Kings* 2. 27) took the priesthood from Abiathar, and gave it (verse 35) to Zadok. Therefore Moses, and the high-priests, and the pious kings, who enquired of God on all extraordinary occasions, how they were to carry themselves, or what event they were to have, were all sovereign prophets. But in what manner God spake unto them, is not manifest. To say that when Moses went up to God in Mount Sinai, it was a dream, or vision, such as other prophets had, is contrary to that distinction which God made between Moses, and other prophets (*Numb.* 12. 6, 7, 8). To say God spake or appeared as he is in his own nature, is to deny his infiniteness, invisibility, incomprehensibility. To say he spake by inspiration, or infusion of the Holy Spirit, as the Holy Spirit signifieth the Deity, is to make Moses equal with Christ, in whom only the Godhead (as St. Paul speaketh, *Col.* 2. 9) dwelleth bodily. And lastly, to say he spake by the Holy Spirit, as it signifieth the graces, or gifts of the Holy Spirit, is to attribute nothing to him supernatural. For God disposeth men

To prophets of perpetual calling, and supreme, God spake in the Old Testament from the mercy-seat, in a manner not expressed in the Scripture.

to piety, justice, mercy, truth, faith, and all manner of virtue, both moral and intellectual, by doctrine, example, and by several occasions, natural and ordinary.

14. And as these ways cannot be applied to God in his speaking to Moses, at Mount Sinai; so also, they cannot be applied to him, in [229] his speaking to the high-priests, from the mercy-seat. Therefore in what manner God spake to those sovereign prophets of the Old Testament, whose office it was to enquire of him, as it is not declared, so also it is not intelligible, otherwise than by a voice.* In the time of the New Testament, there was no sovereign prophet, but our Saviour; who was both God that spake, and the prophet to whom he spake.

To prophets of perpetual calling, but subordinate, God spake by the spirit.

15. To subordinate prophets of perpetual calling, I find not any place that proveth God spake to them supernaturally; but only in such manner, as naturally he inclineth men to piety, to belief, to righteousness, and to other virtues all other Christian men. Which way, though it consist in constitution, instruction, education, and the occasions and invitements men have to Christian virtues; yet it is truly attributed to the operation of the Spirit of God, or Holy Spirit (which we in our language call the Holy Ghost): for there is no good inclination, that is not of the operation of God. But these operations are not always supernatural. When therefore a prophet is said to speak in the spirit, or by the spirit of God, we are to understand no more, but that he speaks according to God's will, declared by the supreme prophet. For the most common acceptation of the word spirit, is in the signification of a man's intention, mind, or disposition.

16. In the time of Moses, there were seventy men besides himself, that *prophesied* in the camp of the Israelites. In what manner God spake to them, is declared in *Numbers*, chap. 11, verse 25. *The Lord came down in a cloud, and spake unto Moses, and took of the spirit that was upon him, and gave it to the seventy elders. And it came to pass, when the spirit rested upon them, they prophesied and did not cease.* By which it is manifest, first, that their prophesying to the people was subservient, and subordinate to the prophesying of Moses; for that God took of the spirit of Moses, to put upon them; so that they prophesied as Moses would have them: otherwise they had not been suffered to prophesy at all. For there was (verse 27) a complaint made against them to Moses; and Joshua would have had Moses to forbid them; which he did not, but said to Joshua, *be not jealous in my*

behalf. Secondly, that the spirit of God in that place, signifieth nothing but the mind and disposition to obey, and assist Moses in the administration of the government. For if it were meant they had the substantial spirit of God; that is, the divine nature, inspired into them, then they had it in no less manner than Christ himself, in whom only the spirit of God dwelt bodily. It is meant therefore of the gift and grace of God, that guided them to co-operate with Moses; from whom their spirit was derived. And it appeareth (verse 16) that, they were such as Moses himself should appoint for elders and officers of the people: for the words are, *Gather unto me seventy men, whom thou knowest to be elders and officers of the people*: where, *thou knowest*, is the same with *thou appointest*, or *hast appointed to be such*. For we are told before (*Exod*. 18. 24) that Moses following the counsel of Jethro his father-in-law, did appoint judges, and officers over the people, such as feared God; and of these were those seventy, whom God, by putting upon them Moses' spirit, inclined to [230] aid Moses in the administration of the kingdom: and in this sense the spirit of God is said (1 *Sam*. 16. 13, 14) presently upon the anointing of David, to have come upon David, and left Saul; God giving his graces to him he chose to govern his people, and taking them away from him, he rejected. So that by the spirit is meant inclination to God's service; and not any supernatural revelation.

17. God spake also many times by the event of lots; which were ordered by such as he had put in authority over his people. So we read that God manifested by the lots which Saul caused to be drawn (1 *Sam*. 14. 43) the fault that Jonathan had committed, in eating a honey-comb, contrary to the oath taken by the people. And (*Josh*. 18. 10) God divided the land of Canaan amongst the Israelites, by the *lots that Joshua did cast before the Lord in Shiloh*. In the same manner it seemeth to be, that God discovered (*Josh*. 7. 16, &c.) the crime of Achan. And these are the ways whereby God declared his will in the Old Testament.

God sometimes also spake by lots.

18. All which ways he used also in the New Testament. To the Virgin Mary, by a vision of an angel: to Joseph in a dream: again, to Paul in the way to Damascus in a vision of our Saviour: and to Peter in the vision of a sheet let down from heaven, with divers sorts of flesh; of clean, and unclean beasts; and in prison, by vision of an angel: and to all the apostles, and writers of the New Testament, by the graces of his spirit; and to the apostles again (at the choosing of Matthias in the place of Judas Iscariot) by lot.

*Every man
ought to
examine the
probability of
a pretended
prophet's
calling.*

19. Seeing then all prophecy supposeth vision, or dream, (which two, when they be natural, are the same,) or some especial gift of God, so rarely observed in mankind, as to be admired where observed; and seeing as well such gifts, as the most extraordinary dreams, and visions, may proceed from God, not only by his supernatural, and immediate, but also by his natural operation, and by mediation of second causes; there is need of reason and judgment to discern between natural, and supernatural gifts, and between natural, and supernatural visions or dreams. And consequently men had need to be very circumspect, and wary, in obeying the voice of man, that pretending himself to be a prophet, requires us to obey God in that way, which he in God's name telleth us to be the way to happiness. For he that pretends to teach men the way of so great felicity, pretends to govern them; that is to say, to rule and reign over them; which is a thing, that all men naturally desire, and is therefore worthy to be suspected of ambition and imposture; and consequently, ought to be examined, and tried by every man, before he yield them obedience; unless he have yielded it them already, in the institution of a commonwealth; as when the prophet is the civil sovereign, or by the civil sovereign authorized. And if this examination of prophets, and spirits, were not allowed to every one of the people, it had been to no purpose, to set out the marks, by which every man might be able to distinguish between those, whom they ought, and those whom they ought not to follow. Seeing therefore such marks are set out (*Deut.* 13. 1, &c.) to know a prophet by; and (1 *John* 4. 1, &c.) to know a spirit by: and seeing there is so much prophesying in the Old Testament; and so much preaching in the New Testament against prophets; and so much greater a number ordinarily of false prophets, than of true; every one is to beware of obeying their directions, at their own peril. And first, that there were many more false than true prophets, appears by this, that when Ahab (1 *Kings* 12) consulted four hundred prophets, they were all false impostors, but only one Micaiah. And a little before the time of the captivity, the prophets were generally liars. *The prophets* (saith the Lord, by *Jeremiah*, chapter 14. 14) *prophesy lies in my name. I sent them not, neither have I commanded them, nor spake unto them; they prophesy to you a false vision, a thing of nought; and the deceit of their heart.* Insomuch as God commanded the people by the mouth of the prophet Jeremiah (chapter 23. 16) not to obey them. *Thus saith the Lord of hosts, hearken not unto the words of the prophets, that prophesy*

[231]

to you. They make you vain, they speak a vision of their own heart, and not out of the mouth of the Lord.

20. Seeing then there was in the time of the Old Testament, such quarrels amongst the visionary prophets, one contesting with another, and asking, when departed the Spirit from me, to go to thee? as between Micaiah, and the rest of the four hundred; and such giving of the lie to one another, (as in *Jer.* 14. 14) and such controversies in the New Testament at this day, amongst the spiritual prophets: every man then was, and now is bound to make use of his natural reason, to apply to all prophecy those rules which God hath given us, to discern the true from false. Of which rules, in the Old Testament, one was, conformable doctrine to that which Moses the sovereign prophet had taught them; and the other the miraculous power of foretelling what God would bring to pass, as I have already showed out of *Deut.* 13. 1, &c. And in the New Testament there was but one only mark; and that was the preaching of this doctrine, *that Jesus is the Christ,** that is, king of the Jews, promised in the Old Testament. Whosoever denied that article, he was a false prophet, whatsoever miracles he might seem to work; and he that taught it was a true prophet. For St. John (1 *John* 4. 2, &c.) speaking expressly of the means to examine spirits, whether they be of God, or not; after he had told them that there would arise false prophets, saith thus, *Hereby know ye the Spirit of God. Every spirit that confesseth that Jesus Christ is come in the flesh, is of God*; that is, is approved and allowed as a prophet of God: not that he is a godly man, or one of the elect, for this, that he confesseth, professeth, or preacheth Jesus to be the Christ; but for that he is a prophet avowed. For God sometimes speaketh by prophets, whose persons he hath not accepted; as he did by Balaam; and as he foretold Saul of his death, by the Witch of Endor. Again in the next verse, *Every spirit that confesseth not that Jesus Christ is come in the flesh, is not of Christ. And this is the spirit of Anti-Christ.* So that the rule is perfect on both [232] sides; that he is a true prophet, which preacheth the Messiah already come, in the person of Jesus; and he a false one that denieth him come, and looketh for him in some future impostor, that shall take upon him that honour falsely, whom the apostle there properly calleth Anti-Christ. Every man therefore ought to consider who is the sovereign prophet; that is to say, who it is, that is God's vicegerent on earth; and hath next under God, the authority of governing Christian men; and to observe for a rule, that doctrine, which in

All prophecy but of the sovereign prophet, is to be examined by every subject.

the name of God, he hath commanded to be taught; and thereby to examine and try out the truth of those doctrines, which pretended prophets with miracle, or without, shall at any time advance: and if they find it contrary to that rule, to do as they did, that came to Moses, and complained that there were some that prophesied in the camp, whose authority so to do they doubted of; and leave to the sovereign, as they did to Moses, to uphold, or to forbid them, as he should see cause; and if he disavow them, then no more to obey their voice; or if he approve them, then to obey them, as men to whom God hath given a part of the spirit of their sovereign. For when Christian men, take not their Christian sovereign, for God's prophet; they must either take their own dreams, for the prophecy they mean to be governed by, and the tumour of their own hearts for the Spirit of God; or they must suffer themselves to be led by some strange prince; or by some of their fellow-subjects, that can bewitch them, by slander of the government, into rebellion, without other miracle to confirm their calling, than sometimes an extraordinary success and impunity; and by this means destroying all laws, both divine, and human, reduce all order, government, and society, to the first chaos of violence, and civil war.

[233]

CHAPTER XXXVII

OF MIRACLES, AND THEIR USE

A miracle is a work that causeth admiration.

1. BY *miracles* are signified the admirable works of God: and therefore they are also called *wonders*. And because they are for the most part, done, for a signification of his commandment, in such occasions, as without them, men are apt to doubt, (following their private natural reasoning,) what he hath commanded, and what not, they are commonly in holy Scripture, called *signs*, in the same sense, as they are called by the Latins, *ostenta*, and *portenta*, from showing, and fore-signifying that, which the Almighty is about to bring to pass.

And must therefore be rare, and whereof there is no natural cause known.

2. To understand therefore what is a miracle, we must first understand what works they are, which men wonder at, and call admirable. And there be but two things which make men wonder at any event: the one is, if it be strange, that is to say, such, as the like of it hath never, or very rarely been produced: the other is, if when

it is produced, we cannot imagine it to have been done by natural means, but only by the immediate hand of God. But when we see some possible, natural cause of it, how rarely soever the like has been done; or if the like have been often done, how impossible soever it be to imagine a natural means thereof, we no more wonder, nor esteem it for a miracle.

3. Therefore, if a horse, or cow should speak, it were a miracle; because both the thing is strange, and the natural cause difficult to imagine: so also were it, to see a strange deviation of nature, in the production of some new shape of a living creature. But when a man, or other animal, engenders his like, though we know no more how this is done, than the other; yet because 'tis usual, it is no miracle. In like manner, if a man be metamorphosed into a stone, or into a pillar, it is a miracle; because strange: but if a piece of wood be so changed; because we see it often, it is no miracle: and yet we know no more, by what operation of God, the one is brought to pass, than the other.

4. The first rainbow that was seen in the world, was a miracle, because the first; and consequently strange; and served for a sign from God, placed in heaven, to assure his people, there should be no more any universal destruction of the world by water. But at this day, because they are frequent, they are not miracles, neither to them that know their natural causes, nor to them who know them not. Again, there be many rare works produced by the art of man: yet when we know they are so done; because thereby we know also the means how they are done, we count them not for miracles, because not wrought by the immediate hand of God, but by mediation of human industry. [234]

5. Furthermore, seeing admiration and wonder, consequent to the knowledge and experience, wherewith men are endued, some more, some less; it followeth, that the same thing, may be a miracle to one, and not to another. And thence it is, that ignorant, and superstitious men make great wonders of those works, which other men, knowing to proceed from nature, (which is not the immediate, but the ordinary work of God,) admire not at all: as when eclipses of the sun and moon have been taken for supernatural works, by the common people; when nevertheless, there were others, who could from their natural causes, have foretold the very hour they should arrive: or, as when a man, by confederacy and secret intelligence, getting knowledge of the private actions of an ignorant, unwary

That which seemeth a miracle to one man, may seem otherwise to another.

man, thereby tells him, what he has done in former time; it seems to him a miraculous thing; but amongst wise, and cautelous men, such miracles as those, cannot easily be done.

The end of miracles.

6. Again, it belongeth to the nature of a miracle, that it be wrought for the procuring of credit to God's messengers, ministers, and prophets, that thereby men may know, they are called, sent, and employed by God, and thereby be the better inclined to obey them. And therefore, though the creation of the world, and after that the destruction of all living creatures in the universal deluge, were admirable works; yet because they were not done to procure credit to any prophet, or other minister of God, they use not to be called miracles. For how admirable soever any work be, the admiration consisteth not in that it could be done, because men naturally believe the Almighty can do all things, but because he does it at the prayer, or word of a man. But the works of God in Egypt, by the hand of Moses, were properly miracles; because they were done with intention to make the people of Israel believe, that Moses came unto them, not out of any design of his own interest, but as sent from God. Therefore after God had commanded him to deliver the Israelites from the Egyptian bondage, when he said (*Exod.* 4. 1) *They will not believe me, but will say, the Lord hath not appeared unto me*, God gave him power, to turn the rod he had in his hand into a serpent, and again to return it into a rod; and by putting his hand into his bosom, to make it leprous; and again by pulling it out, to make it whole, to make the children of Israel believe (as it is verse 5) that the God of their fathers had appeared unto him: and if that were not enough, he gave him power to turn their waters into blood. And when he had done these miracles before the people, it is said (verse 41) that *they believed him*. Nevertheless, for fear of Pharaoh, they durst not yet obey him. Therefore the other works which were done to plague Pharaoh, and the Egyptians, tended all to make the Israelites believe in Moses, and were properly miracles. In like manner if we consider all the miracles done by the hand of Moses, and all the rest of the prophets, till the captivity; and those of our Saviour, and his apostles afterwards; we shall find, their end was always to beget or confirm belief, that they came not of their own

[235] motion, but were sent by God. We may further observe in Scripture, that the end of miracles, was to beget belief, not universally in all men, elect and reprobate; but in the elect only; that is to say, in such as God had determined should become his subjects. For those

miraculous plagues of Egypt, had not for their end, the conversion of Pharaoh; for God had told Moses before, that he would harden the heart of Pharaoh, that he should not let the people go: and when he let them go at last, not the miracles persuaded him, but the plagues forced him to it. So also of our Saviour, it is written (*Matt.* 13. 58), that he wrought not many miracles in his own country, because of their unbelief; and (in *Mark* 6. 5) instead of, *He wrought not many*, it is, *He could work none.* It was not because he wanted power; which to say, were blasphemy against God; nor that the end of miracles was not to convert incredulous men to Christ; for the end of all the miracles of Moses, of the prophets, of our Saviour, and of his apostles was to add men to the church; but it was, because the end of their miracles, was to add to the church (not all men, but) such as should be saved; that is to say, such as God had elected. Seeing therefore our Saviour was sent from his Father, he could not use his power in the conversion of those, whom his Father had rejected. They that expounding this place of *St. Mark*, say, that this word, *He could not*, is put for, *He would not*, do it without example in the Greek tongue, (where *would not*, is put sometimes for *could not*, in things inanimate, that have no will; but *could not*, for *would not*, never,) and thereby lay a stumbling block before weak Christians; as if Christ could do no miracles, but amongst the credulous.

7. From that which I have here set down, of the nature and use of a miracle, we may define it thus: A MIRACLE *is a work of God, (besides his operation by the way of nature, ordained in the creation,) done for the making manifest to his elect, the mission of an extraordinary minister for their salvation.* *The definition of a miracle.*

8. And from this definition, we may infer; first, that in all miracles, the work done, is not the effect of any virtue in the prophet; because it is the effect of the immediate hand of God; that is to say, God hath done it, without using the prophet therein, as a subordinate cause.

9. Secondly, that no devil, angel, or other created spirit, can do a miracle. For it must either be by virtue of some natural science, or by incantation, that is, by virtue of words. For if the enchanters do it by their own power independent, there is some power that proceedeth not from God; which all men deny: and if they do it by power given them, then is the work not from the immediate hand of God, but natural, and consequently no miracle.

10. There be some texts of Scripture, that seem to attribute the

power of working wonders (equal to some of those immediate miracles, wrought by God himself) to certain arts of magic, and incantation. As for example, when we read that after the rod of Moses [236] being cast on the ground became a serpent, (*Exod.* 7. 11) *the magicians of Egypt did the like by their enchantments*; and that after Moses had turned the waters of the Egyptian streams, rivers, ponds, and pools of water into blood, (*Exod.* 7. 22) *the magicians did so likewise, with their enchantments*; and that after Moses had by the power of God brought frogs upon the land, (*Exod.* 8. 7) *the magicians also did so with their enchantments, and brought up frogs upon the land of Egypt*; will not a man be apt to attribute miracles to enchantments; that is to say, to the efficacy of the sound of words; and think the same very well proved out of this, and other such places? And yet there is no place of Scripture, that telleth us what an enchantment is. If therefore enchantment be not, as many think it, a working of strange effects by spells, and words; but imposture, and delusion, wrought by ordinary means; and so far from supernatural, as the impostors need not the study so much as of natural causes, but the ordinary ignorance, stupidity, and superstition of mankind, to do them; those texts that seem to countenance the power of magic, witchcraft, and enchantment, must needs have another sense, than at first sight they seem to bear.

11. For it is evident enough, that words have no effect, but on those that understand them; and then they have no other, but to signify the intentions, or passions of them that speak; and thereby produce hope, fear, or other passions, or conceptions in the hearer. Therefore when a rod seemeth a serpent, or the waters blood, or any other miracle seemeth done by enchantment; if it be not to the edification of God's people, not the rod, nor the water, nor any other thing is enchanted; that is to say, wrought upon by the words, but the spectator. So that all the miracle consisteth in this, that the enchanter has deceived a man; which is no miracle, but a very easy matter to do.

That men are apt to be deceived by false miracles. 12. For such is the ignorance and aptitude to error generally of all men, but especially of them that have not much knowledge of natural causes, and of the nature, and interests of men; as by innumerable and easy tricks to be abused. What opinion of miraculous power, before it was known there was a science of the course of the stars, might a man have gained, that should have told the people, this hour or day the sun should be darkened? A juggler by the handling of his goblets, and other trinkets, if it were not now ordinarily practised, would be thought to do his wonders by the power at least of the devil. A man that hath practised to speak by drawing in of his breath, (which kind of men in ancient time were called *ventriloqui,*) and so make the weakness of his voice seem to proceed, not from the weak impulsion of the organs of speech, but from distance of place, is able to make very many men believe it is a voice from Heaven, whatsoever he please to tell them. And for a crafty man, that hath enquired into the secrets, and familiar confessions that one man ordinarily maketh to another of his actions and adventures past, to tell them him again is no hard matter; and yet there be many, that by such means as that, obtain the reputation of being conjurers. But it is too long a business, to reckon up the several sorts [237] of those men, which the Greeks called θαυματουργόι, that is to say, workers of things wonderful: and yet these do all they do, by their own single dexterity. But if we look upon the impostures wrought by confederacy, there is nothing how impossible soever to be done, that is impossible to be believed. For two men conspiring, one to seem lame, the other to cure him with a charm, will deceive many: but many conspiring, one to seem lame, another so to cure him, and all the rest to bear witness, will deceive many more.

13. In this aptitude of mankind, to give too hasty belief to pretended miracles, there can be no better, nor I think any other caution, than that which God hath prescribed, first by Moses, (as I have said before in the precedent chapter,) in the beginning of the thirteenth and end of the eighteenth of *Deuteronomy*; that we take not any for prophets, that teach any other religion, than that which God's lieutenant, (which at that time was Moses,) hath established; nor any, (though he teach the same religion,) whose prediction we do not see come to pass. Moses therefore in his time, and Aaron, and his successors in their times, and the sovereign governor of God's people, next under God himself, that is to say, the head of the Church in all times, are to be consulted, what doctrine he hath established, before we give credit to a pretended miracle, or prophet. And when that is done, the thing they pretend to be a miracle, we must both see it done, and use all means possible to consider, whether it be really done; and not only so, but whether it be such, as no man can do the like by his natural power, but that it

Cautions against the imposture of miracles.

requires the immediate hand of God.* And in this also we must have recourse to God's lieutenant, to whom in all doubtful cases, we have submitted our private judgments. For example; if a man pretend, after certain words spoken over a piece of bread, that presently God hath made it not bread, but a god, or a man, or both, and nevertheless it looketh still as like bread as ever it did; there is no reason for any man to think it really done; nor consequently to fear him, till he enquire of God, by his vicar, or lieutenant, whether it be done, or not. If he say not, then followeth that which Moses saith (*Deut.* 18. 22) *he hath spoken it presumptuously, thou shalt not fear him.* If he say, 'tis done, then he is not to contradict it. So also if we see not, but only hear tell of a miracle, we are to consult the lawful Church; that is to say, the lawful head thereof, how far we are to give credit to the relators of it. And this is chiefly the case of men, that in these days live under Christian sovereigns. For in these times, I do not know one man, that ever saw any such wondrous work, done by the charm, or at the word, or prayer of a man, that a man endued but with a mediocrity of reason, would think supernatural: and the question is no more, whether what we see done, be a miracle; whether the miracle we hear, or read of, were a real work, and not the act of a tongue, or pen; but in plain terms, whether the report be true, or a lie. In which question we are not every one, to make our own private reason, or conscience, but the public reason, that is, the reason of God's supreme lieutenant, judge; and indeed we have [238] made him judge already, if we have given him a sovereign power, to do all that is necessary for our peace and defence. A private man has always the liberty, (because thought is free,) to believe, or not believe in his heart, those acts that have been given out for miracles, according as he shall see, what benefit can accrue by men's belief, to those that pretend, or countenance them, and thereby conjecture, whether they be miracles, or lies. But when it comes to confession of that faith, the private reason must submit to the public; that is to say, to God's lieutenant. But who is this lieutenant of God, and head of the Church, shall be considered in its proper place hereafter.

CHAPTER XXXVIII

OF THE SIGNIFICATION IN SCRIPTURE OF ETERNAL LIFE, HELL, SALVATION, THE WORLD TO COME, AND REDEMPTION

1.* THE maintenance of civil society, depending on justice; and justice on the power of life and death, and other less rewards and punishments, residing in them that have the sovereignty of the commonwealth; it is impossible a commonwealth should stand, where any other than the sovereign, hath a power of giving greater rewards than life, and of inflicting greater punishments than death. Now seeing *eternal life* is a greater reward than the *life present*; and *eternal torment* a greater punishment than the *death of nature*; it is a thing worthy to be well considered, of all men that desire (by obeying authority) to avoid the calamities of confusion, and civil war, what is meant in Holy Scripture, by *life eternal*, and *torment eternal*; and for what offences, and against whom committed, men are to be *eternally tormented*; and for what actions, they are to obtain *eternal life*.

2. And first we find that Adam was created in such a condition of life, as had he not broken the commandment of God, he had enjoyed it in the paradise of Eden everlastingly. For there was the *tree of life*; whereof he was so long allowed to eat, as he should forbear to eat of the tree of knowledge of good and evil; which was not allowed him. And therefore as soon as he had eaten of it, God thrust him out of Paradise, (*Gen.* 3. 22) *lest he should put forth his hand, and take also of the tree of life, and live for ever.* By which it seemeth to me, (with submission nevertheless both in this, and in all questions whereof the determination dependeth on the Scriptures, to the interpretation of the Bible authorized by the commonwealth, whose subject I am,) that Adam if he had not sinned, had had an eternal life on earth: and that mortality entered upon himself, and his posterity, by his first sin. Not that actual death then entered; for Adam then could never have had children; whereas he lived long after, and saw a numerous posterity ere he died. But where it is said, *In the day that thou eatest thereof, thou shalt surely die*, it must needs be meant of his mortality, and certitude of death. Seeing then eternal life was lost by

The place of Adam's eternity, if he had not sinned, had been the terrestrial Paradise.

Adam's forfeiture, in committing sin, he that should cancel that
[239] forfeiture was to recover thereby, that life again. Now Jesus Christ
hath satisfied for the sins of all that believe in him; and therefore
recovered to all believers, that ETERNAL LIFE, which was lost by the
sin of Adam. And in this sense it is, that the comparison of St. Paul
holdeth, (*Rom.* 5. 18, 19) *As by the offence of one, judgment came upon
all men to condemnation, even so by the righteousness of one, the free gift
came upon all men to justification of life.* Which is again (1 *Cor.* 15. 21,
22) more perspicuously delivered in these words, *For since by man
came death, by man came also the resurrection of the dead. For as in
Adam all die, even so in Christ shall all be made alive.*

*Texts
concerning
the place of
life eternal,
for believers.*

3. Concerning the place wherein* men shall enjoy that eternal
life, which Christ hath obtained for them, the texts next before
alleged seem to make it on earth. For if as in Adam, all die, that is,
have forfeited paradise and eternal life on earth, even so in Christ all
shall be made alive; then all men shall be made to live on earth; for
else the comparison were not proper. Hereunto seemeth to agree
that of the psalmist (*Psalm* 133. 3) *upon Zion God commanded the
blessing, even life for evermore*: for Zion, is in Jerusalem, upon earth:
as also that of St. John (*Rev.* 2. 7) *To him that overcometh I will give
to eat of the tree of life, which is in the midst of the paradise of God.* This
was the tree of Adam's eternal life; but his life was to have been on
earth. The same seemeth to be confirmed again by St. John (*Rev.* 21.
2), where he saith, *I John saw the holy city, new Jerusalem, coming
down from God out of heaven, prepared as a bride adorned for her
husband*: and again (verse 10) to the same effect: as if he should say,
the new *Jerusalem*, the paradise of God, at the coming again of
Christ, should come down to God's people from heaven, and not
they go up to it from earth. And this differs nothing from that,
which the two men in white clothing (that is, the two angels) said to
the apostles, that were looking upon Christ ascending (*Acts.* 1. 11)
*This same Jesus, who is taken up from you into heaven, shall so come, as
you have seen him go up into heaven.* Which soundeth as if they had
said, he should come down to govern them under his Father, eternally here; and not take them up to govern them in heaven; and is
conformable to the restoration of the kingdom of God, instituted
under Moses; which was a political government of the Jews on earth.
Again, that saying of our Saviour (*Matt.* 22. 30) *that in the resurrection they neither marry, nor are given in marriage, but are as the angels
of God in heaven*, is a description of an eternal life, resembling that

which we lost in Adam in the point of marriage. For seeing Adam, and Eve, if they had not sinned, had lived on earth eternally, in their individual persons; it is manifest, they should not continually have procreated their kind. For if immortals should have generated, as mankind doth now; the earth in a small time, would not have been able to afford them place to stand on. The Jews that asked our Saviour the question, whose wife the woman that had married many brothers should be, in the resurrection, knew not what were the consequences of life eternal: and therefore our Saviour puts them in mind of this consequence of immortality; that there shall be no generation, and consequently no marriage, no more than there is marriage, or generation among the angels. The comparison between that eternal life which Adam lost, and our Saviour by his victory over death hath recovered, holdeth also in this, that as Adam [240] lost eternal life by his sin, and yet lived after it for a time, so the faithful Christian hath recovered eternal life by Christ's passion, though he die a natural death, and remain dead for a time; namely, till the resurrection. For as death is reckoned from the condemnation of Adam, not from the execution; so life is reckoned from the absolution, not from the resurrection of them that are elected in Christ.

4. That the place wherein men are to live eternally, after the resurrection, is the heavens, meaning by heaven, those parts of the world, which are the most remote from earth, as where the stars are, or above the stars, in another higher heaven, called *coelum empyreum*,* (whereof there is no mention in Scripture, nor ground in reason) is not easily to be drawn from any text that I can find. By the Kingdom of Heaven, is meant the kingdom of the King that dwelleth in heaven; and his kingdom was the people of Israel, whom he ruled on earth by the prophets his lieutenants, first Moses, and after him Eleazar, and the sovereign priests, till in the days of Samuel they rebelled, and would have a mortal man for their king, after the manner of other nations. And when our Saviour Christ, by the preaching of his ministers, shall have persuaded the Jews to return, and called the Gentiles to his obedience, then shall there be a new kingdom of heaven; because our king shall then be God, whose *throne* is heaven; without any necessity evident in the Scripture, that man shall ascend to his happiness any higher than God's *footstool* the earth. On the contrary, we find written (*John* 3. 13) that *no man hath ascended into heaven, but he that came down from*

Ascension into heaven.

heaven, even the son of man, that is in heaven. Where I observe by the way, that these words are not, as those which go immediately before, the words of our Saviour, but of St. John himself; for Christ was then not in heaven, but upon the earth. The like is said of David (*Acts* 2. 34) where St. Peter, to prove the ascension of Christ, using the words of the Psalmist (*Psalm* 16. 10), *Thou wilt not leave my soul in hell, nor suffer thine holy one to see corruption,* saith, they were spoken (not of David but) of Christ; and to prove it, addeth this reason, *For David is not ascended into heaven.* But to this a man may easily answer, and say, that though their bodies were not to ascend till the general day of judgment, yet their souls were in heaven as soon as they were departed from their bodies; which also seemeth to be confirmed by the words of our Saviour (*Luke* 20. 37, 38) who proving the resurrection out of the words of Moses, saith thus, *That the dead are raised, even Moses shewed, at the bush, when he calleth the Lord, the God of Abraham, and the God of Isaac, and the God of Jacob. For he is not a God of the dead, but of the living; for they all live to him.* But if these words be to be understood only of the immortality of the soul, they prove not at all that which our Saviour intended to prove, which was the resurrection of the body,* that is to say, the immortality of the man. Therefore our Saviour meaneth, that those patriarchs were immortal; not by a property consequent to the essence and nature of mankind; but by the will of God, that was pleased of his mere grace, to bestow *eternal life* upon the faithful. And though

[241] at that time the patriarchs and many other faithful men were *dead*, yet as it is in the text, they *lived to God*; that is, they were written in the Book of Life with them that were absolved of their sins, and ordained to life eternal at the resurrection. That the soul of man is in its own nature eternal, and a living creature independent on the body; or that any mere man is immortal, otherwise than by the resurrection in the last day, (except Enoch and Elias,) is a doctrine not apparent in Scripture. The whole of the fourteenth chapter of *Job*, which is the speech not of his friends, but of himself, is a complaint of this mortality of nature; and yet no contradiction of the immortality at the resurrection. *There is hope of a tree* (saith he verse 7) *if it be cast down. Though the root thereof wax old, and the stock thereof die in the ground, yet when it scenteth the water it will bud, and bring forth boughs like a plant. But man dieth, and wasteth away, yea, man giveth up the ghost, and where is he?* And (verse 12) *Man lieth down, and riseth not, till the heavens be no more.* But when is it, that

the heavens shall be no more? St. Peter tells us, that it is at the general resurrection. For in his 2nd *Epistle*, chap. 3, verse 7, he saith, that *the heavens and the earth that are now, are reserved unto fire against the day of judgment, and perdition of ungodly men*, and (verse 12) *looking for, and hasting to the coming of God, wherein the heavens shall be on fire and shall be dissolved, and the elements shall melt with fervent heat. Nevertheless, we according to the promise look for new heavens, and a new earth, wherein dwelleth righteousness*. Therefore where Job saith, *man riseth not till the heavens be no more*; it is all one, as if he had said, the immortal life (and soul and life in the Scripture, do usually signify the same thing) beginneth not in man, till the resurrection, and day of judgment; and hath for cause, not his specifical nature, and generation; but the promise. For St. Peter says, *We look for new heavens and a new earth*, (not from nature) but *from promise*.

5. Lastly, seeing it hath been already proved out of divers evident places of Scripture, in chap. 35 of this book, that the kingdom of God is a civil commonwealth, where God himself is sovereign, by virtue first of the *old*, and since of the *new* covenant, wherein he reigneth by his vicar, or lieutenant; the same places do therefore also prove, that after the coming again of our Saviour in his majesty, and glory, to reign actually, and eternally, the kingdom of God is to be on earth. But because this doctrine (though proved out of places of Scripture not few, nor obscure) will appear to most men a novelty; I do but propound it; maintaining nothing in this, or any other paradox of religion; but attending the end of that dispute of the sword, concerning the authority, (not yet amongst my countrymen decided,) by which all sorts of doctrine are to be approved, or rejected; and whose commands, both in speech and writing, (whatsoever be the opinions of private men) must by all men, that mean to be protected by their laws, be obeyed. For the points of doctrine concerning the kingdom of God, have so great influence on the kingdom of man, as not to be determined, but by them, that under God have the sovereign power.

6. As the kingdom of God, and eternal life, so also God's enemies, and their torments after judgment, appear by the Scripture, to have their place on earth. The name of the place, where all men remain till the resurrection, that were either buried, or swallowed up of the earth, is usually called in Scripture, by words that signify *under ground*; which the Latins read generally *infernus*, and *inferi*,

[242]
The place after judgment of those who were never in the kingdom of God, or having been in, are cast out.

and the Greek ᾅδης, that is to say, a place where men cannot see; and containeth as well the grave, as any other deeper place. But for the place of the damned after the resurrection, it is not determined, neither in the Old, nor New Testament, by any note of situation; but only by the company: as that it shall be, where such wicked men were, as God in former times, in extraordinary and miraculous manner, had destroyed from off the face of the earth: as for example, *Tartarus.* that they are *in Inferno*, in *Tartarus*, or in the bottomless pit; because Korah, Dathan, and Abiram, were swallowed up alive into the earth. Not that the writers of the Scripture would have us believe, there could be in the globe of the earth, which is not only finite, but also (compared to the height of the stars) of no considerable magnitude, a pit without a bottom; that is, a hole of infinite depth, such as the Greeks in their *demonology* (that is to say, in their doctrine concerning *demons*,) and after them the Romans called *Tartarus*; of which Virgil (*Aen.* VI. 578, 579) says,

> Bis patet in praeceps tantum, tenditque sub umbras,
> Quantus ad aetherium coeli suspectus Olympum:*

for that is a thing the proportion of earth to heaven cannot bear: but that we should believe them there, indefinitely, where those men are, on whom God inflicted that exemplary punishment.

The congregation of giants. 7. Again, because those mighty men of the earth, that lived in the time of Noah, before the flood, (which the Greeks call *heroes*, and the Scripture *giants*, and both say were begotten by copulation of the children of God, with the children of men,) were for their wicked life destroyed by the general deluge; the place of the damned, is therefore also sometimes marked out, by the company of those deceased giants; as *Proverbs* 21. 16, *The man that wandereth out of the way of understanding, shall remain in the congregation of the giants*, and *Job* 26. 5, *Behold the giants groan under water, and they that dwell with them.* Here the place of the damned, is under the water. And *Isaiah* 14. 9, *Hell is troubled how to meet thee* (that is, the King of Babylon) *and will displace the giants for thee*: and here again the place of the damned, (if the sense be literal,) is to be under water.

Lake of fire. 8. Thirdly, because the cities of Sodom, and Gomorrah, by the extraordinary wrath of God, were consumed for their wickedness with fire and brimstone, and together with them the country about made a stinking bituminous lake: the place of the damned is sometimes expressed by fire, and a fiery lake: as in the *Apocalypse*, 21. 8. *But the timorous, incredulous, and abominable, and murderers, and whoremongers, and sorcerers, and idolaters, and all liars, shall have their* [243] *part in the lake that burneth with fire, and brimstone; which is the second death*. So that it is manifest, that hell fire, which is here expressed by metaphor, from the real fire of Sodom, signifieth not any certain kind, or place of torment; but is to be taken indefinitely, for destruction, as it is in *Rev*. 20. 14, where it is said, that *death and hell were cast into the lake of fire*; that is to say, were abolished, and destroyed; as if after the second death, there shall be no more dying, nor no more going into hell; that is, no more going to *Hades* (from which word perhaps our word Hell is derived,) which is the same with no more dying.

9. Fourthly, from the plague of darkness inflicted on the Egyptians, of which it is written (*Exod*. 10. 23) *They saw not one another, neither rose any man from his place for three days; but all the children of Israel had light in their dwellings*; the place of the wicked after judgment, is called *utter darkness*, or (as it is in the original) *darkness without*. And so it is expressed (*Matt*. 22. 13) where the king commanded his servants, *to bind hand and foot the man that had not on his wedding garment, and to cast him out*, εἰς τὸ σκότος τὸ ἐξώτερον, *into external darkness*, or *darkness without*: which though translated *utter darkness*, does not signify *how great*, but *where* that darkness is to be; namely, *without the habitation* of God's elect. *Utter darkness.*

10. Lastly, whereas there was a place near Jerusalem, called the *Valley of the Children of Hinnon*; in a part whereof, called *Tophet*, the Jews had committed most grievous idolatry, sacrificing their children to the idol Moloch; and wherein also God had afflicted his enemies with most grievous punishments; and wherein Josiah had burned the priests of Moloch upon their own altars, as appeareth at large in the 2nd of *Kings*, chap. 23, the place served afterwards to receive the filth, and garbage which was carried thither, out of the city; and there used to be fires made from time to time, to purify the air, and take away the stench of carrion. From this abominable place, the Jews used ever after to call the place of the damned, by the name of *Gehenna*, or *Valley of Hinnon*. And this *Gehenna*, is that word, which is usually now translated HELL; and from the fires from time to time there burning, we have the notion of *everlasting* and *unquenchable fire*. *Gehenna, and Tophet.*

Of the literal sense of the Scripture concerning hell.

11. Seeing now there is none, that so interprets the Scripture, as that after the day of judgment, the wicked are all eternally to be punished in the Valley of Hinnon; or that they shall so rise again, as to be ever after under ground or under water; or that after the resurrection, they shall no more see one another, nor stir from one place to another: it followeth, methinks, very necessarily, that that which is thus said concerning hell fire, is spoken metaphorically; and that therefore there is a proper sense to be enquired after, (for of all metaphors there is some real ground, that may be expressed in proper words,) both of the *place* of *hell*, and the nature of *hellish torments*, and *tormenters*.

[244]

Satan, Devil, not proper names, but appellatives.

12. And first for the tormenters, we have their nature and properties, exactly and properly delivered by the names of, *the Enemy*, or *Satan; the Accuser*, or *Diabolus; the Destroyer*, or *Abaddon*. Which significant names, *Satan, Devil, Abaddon*, set not forth to us any individual person, as proper names use to do; but only an office, or quality; and are therefore appellatives; which ought not to have been left untranslated, as they are, in the Latin, and modern Bibles; because thereby they seem to be proper names of *demons*; and men are the more easily seduced to believe the doctrine of devils; which at that time was the religion of the Gentiles, and contrary to that of Moses and of Christ.

13. And because by the *Enemy*, the *Accuser*, and *Destroyer*, is meant the enemy of them that shall be in the kingdom of God; therefore if the kingdom of God after the resurrection, be upon the earth, (as in the former chapter I have shown by Scripture it seems to be,) the Enemy, and his kingdom must be on earth also. For so also was it, in the time before the Jews had deposed God. For God's kingdom was in Palestine; and the nations round about, were the kingdoms of the Enemy; and consequently by *Satan*, is meant any earthly enemy of the Church.

Torments of hell.

14. The torments of hell, are expressed sometimes, by *weeping*, and *gnashing of teeth*, as *Matt.* 8. 12. Sometimes, by *the worm of conscience*; as *Isaiah* 66. 24, and *Mark* 9. 44, 46, 48: sometimes, by fire, as in the place now quoted, *where the worm dieth not, and the fire is not quenched*, and many places beside: sometimes by *shame and contempt*, as *Dan.* 12. 2. *And many of them that sleep in the dust of the earth, shall awake; some to everlasting life; and some to shame, and everlasting contempt*. All which places design metaphorically a grief, and discontent of mind, from the sight of that eternal felicity in others, which they themselves through their own incredulity, and disobedience have lost. And because such felicity in others, is not sensible but by comparison with their own actual miseries; it followeth that they are to suffer such bodily pains, and calamities, as are incident to those, who not only live under evil and cruel governors, but have also for enemy, the eternal king of the saints, God Almighty. And amongst these bodily pains, is to be reckoned also to every one of the wicked a second death. For though the Scripture be clear for an universal resurrection; yet we do not read, that to any of the reprobate is promised an eternal life. For whereas St. Paul (1 *Cor.* 15. 42, 43) to the question concerning what bodies men shall rise with again, saith, that *The body is sown in corruption, and is raised in incorruption; it is sown in dishonour, it is raised in glory; it is sown in weakness, it is raised in power.* Glory and power cannot be applied to the bodies of the wicked: nor can the name of *second death,* be applied to those that can never die but once: and although in metaphorical speech, a calamitous life everlasting, may be called an everlasting death, yet it cannot well be understood of a *second death.* The fire prepared for the wicked, is an everlasting fire: that is to say, [245] the estate wherein no man can be without torture, both of body and mind, after the resurrection, shall endure as long as the world stands; and in that sense the fire shall be unquenchable, and the torments everlasting: but it cannot thence be inferred, that he who shall be cast into that fire, or be tormented with those torments, shall endure, and resist them so as to be eternally burnt, and tortured, and yet never be destroyed, nor die. And though there be many places that affirm everlasting fire, and torments (into which men may be cast successively one after another as long as the world lasts;*) yet I find none that affirm there shall be an eternal life therein of any individual person; but to the contrary, an everlasting death, which is the second death: (*Rev.* 20. 13, 14) *For after death, and the grave shall have delivered up the dead which were in them, and every man be judged according to his works; death and the grave shall also be cast into the lake of fire. This is the second death.* Whereby it is evident, that there is to be a second death of every one that shall be condemned at the day of judgment, after which he shall die no more.

15. The joys of life eternal, are in Scripture comprehended all under the name of SALVATION, or *being saved.* To be saved, is to be secured, either respectively, against special evils, or absolutely, against all evils, comprehending want, sickness, and death itself.

The joys of life eternal, and salvation, the same thing.

And because man was created in a condition immortal, not subject to corruption, and consequently to nothing that tendeth to the dissolution of his nature; and fell from that happiness by the sin of Adam; it followeth, that to be *saved* from sin, is to be saved from all the evil, and calamities that sin hath brought upon us. And therefore in the holy Scripture, remission of sin, and salvation from death and misery, is the same thing, as it appears by the words of our Saviour, who having cured a man sick of the palsy, by saying, (*Matt.* 9. 2) *Son be of good cheer, thy sins be forgiven thee*; and knowing that the Scribes took for blasphemy, that a man should pretend to forgive sins, asked them (verse 5) *whether it were easier to say, Thy sins be forgiven thee, or, Arise and walk*; signifying thereby, that it was all one, as to the saving of the sick, to say, *Thy sins are forgiven*, and *Arise and walk*; and that he used that form of speech, only to shew he had power to forgive sins. And it is besides evident in reason, that since death and misery, were the punishments of sin, the discharge of sin must also be a discharge of death and misery; that is to say, salvation absolute, such as the faithful are to enjoy after the day of judgment, by the power, and favour of Jesus Christ, who for that cause is called our SAVIOUR.

Salvation from sin, and from misery, all one.

16. Concerning particular salvations, such as are understood, (1 *Sam.* 14. 39) *as the Lord liveth that saveth Israel*, that is, from their temporary enemies, and (2 *Sam.* 22. 4) *Thou art my Saviour, thou savest me from violence*; and, (2 *Kings* 13. 5) *God gave the Israelites a Saviour, and so they were delivered from the hand of the Assyrians*, and the like, I need say nothing; there being neither difficulty, nor interest to corrupt the interpretation of texts of that kind.

[246]

17. But concerning the general salvation, because it must be in the kingdom of heaven, there is great difficulty concerning the place. On one side, by *kingdom* (which is an estate ordained by men for their perpetual security against enemies and want) it seemeth that this salvation should be on earth. For by salvation is set forth unto us, a glorious reign of our king, by conquest; not a safety by escape: and therefore there where we look for salvation, we must look also for triumph; and before triumph, for victory; and before victory, for battle; which cannot well be supposed, shall be in heaven. But how good soever this reason may be, I will not trust to it, without very evident places of Scripture. The state of salvation is described at large, *Isaiah* 33. 20, 21, 22, 23, 24:

The place of eternal salvation.

18. *Look upon Zion, the city of our solemnities; thine eyes shall see*

306

Jerusalem a quiet habitation, a tabernacle that shall not be taken down; not one of the stakes thereof shall ever be removed, neither shall any of the cords thereof be broken.

19. *But there the glorious Lord will be unto us a place of broad rivers, and streams; wherein shall go no galley with oars, neither shall gallant ship pass thereby.*

20. *For the Lord is our Judge, the Lord is our law-giver, the Lord is our king, he will save us.*

21. *Thy tacklings are loosed; they could not well strengthen their mast; they could not spread the sail: then is the prey of a great spoil divided; the lame take the prey:*

22. *And the inhabitant shall not say, I am sick; the people that shall dwell therein shall be forgiven their iniquity.*

23. In which words we have the place from whence salvation is to proceed, *Jerusalem, a quiet habitation*; the eternity of it, *a tabernacle that shall not be taken down, &c.* The Saviour of it, *the Lord, their judge, their law-giver, their king, he will save us*; the salvation, *the Lord shall be to them as a broad moat of swift waters, &c.* The condition of their enemies, *their tacklings are loose, their masts weak, the lame shall take the spoil of them.* The condition of the saved, *the inhabitant shall not say, I am sick*: and lastly, all this is comprehended in forgiveness of sin, *the people that dwell therein shall be forgiven their iniquity.* By which it is evident, that salvation shall be on earth, then, when God shall reign, (at the coming again of Christ) in Jerusalem; and from Jerusalem shall proceed the salvation of the Gentiles that shall be received into God's kingdom: as is also more expressly declared by the same prophet, (*Isaiah* 65. 20, 21), *And they* (that is, the Gentiles who had any Jew in bondage) *shall bring all your brethren, for an offering to the Lord, out of all nations, upon horses, and in chariots, and in litters, and upon mules, and upon swift beasts, to my holy mountain, Jerusalem, saith the Lord, as the children of Israel bring on offering in a clean vessel into the house of the Lord. And I will also take of them for priests and for Levites, saith the Lord.* Whereby it is manifest, that the chief seat of God's kingdom (which is the place, from whence the salvation of us that were Gentiles shall proceed) shall be Jerusalem: [247] and the same is also confirmed by our Saviour, in his discourse with the woman of Samaria, concerning the place of God's worship; to whom he saith (*John* 4. 22) that the Samaritans worshipped they knew not what, but the Jews worshipped what they knew, *for sal-vation is of the Jews* (*ex Judaeis*, that is, begins at the Jews): as if he

should say, you worship God, but know not by whom he will save you, as we do, that know it shall be by one of the tribe of Judah, a Jew, not a Samaritan. And therefore also the woman not impertinently answered him again, *We know the Messias shall come*. So that which our Saviour saith, *Salvation is from the Jews*, is the same that Paul says (*Rom.* 1. 16, 17) *The Gospel is the power of God to salvation to every one that believeth: to the Jew first, and also to the Greek. For therein is the righteousness of God revealed from faith to faith*; from the faith of the Jew to the faith of the Gentile. In the like sense the prophet Joel describing the day of Judgment, (chap. 2. 30, 31) that God would *shew wonders in heaven, and in earth, blood, and fire, and pillars of smoke. The sun shall be turned to darkness, and the moon into blood, before the great and terrible day of the Lord come*: he addeth, (verse 32) *and it shall come to pass, that whosoever shall call upon the name of the Lord, shall be saved. For in Mount Zion, and in Jerusalem shall be salvation*. And *Obadiah* (verse 17) saith the same, *Upon Mount Zion shall be deliverance; and there shall be holiness, and the house of Jacob shall possess their possessions*, that is, the possessions of the *heathen*, which *possessions*, he expresseth more particularly in the following verses, by the *mount of Esau*, the *Land of the Philistines*, the *fields of Ephraim*, of *Samaria*, *Gilead*, and the *cities of the south*, and concludes with these words, *the kingdom shall be the Lord's*. All these places are for salvation, and the kingdom of God (after the day of judgment) upon earth. On the other side, I have not found any text that can probably be drawn, to prove any ascension of the saints into heaven; that is to say, into any *coelum empyreum*, or other aetherial region; saving that it is called the kingdom of Heaven: which name it may have, because God, that was king of the Jews, governed them by his commands, sent to Moses by angels from heaven; and after the revolt, sent his Son from heaven to reduce them to their obedience; and shall send him thence again, to rule both them, and all other faithful men, from the day of judgment, everlastingly: or from that, that the throne of this our great king is in heaven; whereas the earth is but his footstool. But that the subjects of God should have any place as high as his throne, or higher than his footstool, it seemeth not suitable to the dignity of a king, nor can I find any evident text for it in Holy Scripture.

The world to come.   **24.** From this that hath been said of the kingdom of God, and of salvation, it is not hard to interpret what is meant by the WORLD TO COME. There are three worlds mentioned in Scripture, the *old world*, the *present world*, and the *world to come*. Of the first, St. Peter speaks, (2 *Pet.* 2. 5) *If God spared not the old world, but saved Noah the eighth person, a preacher of righteousness, bringing the flood upon the world of the ungodly, &c.* So the *first world*, was from Adam to the general [248] flood. Of the present world, our Saviour speaks (*John* 18. 36) *My kingdom is not of this world.* For he came only to teach men the way of salvation, and to renew the kingdom of his Father, by his doctrine. Of the world to come, St. Peter speaks (2 *Pet.* 3. 13) *Nevertheless we according to his promise look for new heavens, and a new earth.* This is that WORLD, wherein Christ coming down from heaven in the clouds, with great power, and glory, shall send his angels, and shall gather together his elect, from the four winds, and from the uttermost parts of the earth, and thenceforth reign over them, (under his Father) everlastingly.

25. *Salvation* of a sinner, supposeth a precedent REDEMPTION; for *Redemption.* he that is once guilty of sin, is obnoxious to the penalty of the same; and must pay (or some other for him) such ransom, as he that is offended, and has him in his power, shall require. And seeing the person offended, is Almighty God, in whose power are all things; such ransom is to be paid before salvation can be acquired, as God hath been pleased to require. By this ransom, is not intended a satisfaction for sin, equivalent to the offence; which no sinner for himself, nor righteous man can ever be able to make for another: the damage a man does to another, he may make amends for by restitution, or recompense; but sin cannot be taken away by recompense; for that were to make the liberty to sin, a thing vendible. But sins may be pardoned to the repentant, either *gratis*, or upon such penalty, as God is pleased to accept. That which God usually accepted in the Old Testament, was some sacrifice, or oblation. To forgive sin is not an act of injustice, though the punishment have been threatened. Even amongst men, though the promise of good, bind the promisers; yet threats, that is to say, promises of evil, bind them not; much less shall they bind God, who is infinitely more merciful than men. Our Saviour Christ therefore to *redeem* us, did not in that sense satisfy for the sins of men, as that his death, of its own virtue, could make it unjust in God to punish sinners with eternal death; but did make that sacrifice, and oblation of himself, at his first coming, which God was pleased to require, for the salvation at his second coming, of such as in the meantime should repent, and believe in him. And though this act of our *redemption*, be not always in

Scripture called a *sacrifice*, and *oblation*, but sometimes a *price*; yet by *price* we are not to understand any thing, by the value whereof, he could claim right to a pardon for us, from his offended Father; but that price which God the Father was pleased in mercy to demand.

[247]*

CHAPTER XXXIX

OF THE SIGNIFICATION IN SCRIPTURE OF
THE WORD CHURCH

Church the Lord's house.

1. THE word Church, (*Ecclesia*) signifieth in the books of Holy Scripture divers things. Sometimes (though not often) it is taken for *God's house*, that is to say, for a temple, wherein Christians assembled to perform holy duties publicly, as (1 *Cor.* 14. 34) *Let your women keep silence in the Churches*: but this is metaphorically put, for the congregation there assembled; and hath been since used for the edifice itself, to distinguish between the temples of Christians, and idolaters. The Temple of Jerusalem was *God's house*, and the house of prayer; and so is any edifice dedicated by Christians to the worship of Christ, *Christ's house*: and therefore the Greek fathers call it Κυριακή, *the Lord's house*: and thence, in our language it came to be called *kirk*, and *church*.

Ecclesia, properly what.

2. Church (when not taken for a house) signifieth the same that *ecclesia* signified in the Grecian commonwealths; that is to say, a congregation, or an assembly of citizens, called forth, to hear the magistrate speak unto them; and which in the commonwealth of Rome was called *concio*, as he that spake was called *ecclesiastes*, and *concionator*. And when they were called forth by lawful authority, (*Acts* 19. 39) it was *Ecclesia legitima*, a *lawful Church*, ἔννομος ἐκκλησία. But when they were excited by tumultuous, and seditious clamour, then it was a confused Church, ἐκκλησία συγκεχυμένη.

3. It is taken also sometimes for the men that have right to be of the congregation, though not actually assembled; that is to say, for the whole multitude of Christian men, how far soever they be dispersed: as (*Acts* 8. 3) where it is said, that *Saul made havoc of the Church*: and in this sense is Christ said to be the head of the Church. And sometimes for a certain part of Christians, as (*Col.* 4. 15) *Salute the Church that is in his house*. Sometimes also for the elect only; as

(Eph. 5. 27) *A glorious Church, without spot, or wrinkle, holy, and without blemish*; which is meant of the *Church triumphant*, or *Church to come*. Sometimes, for a congregation assembled of professors of Christianity, whether their profession be true, or counterfeit, as it is understood, *(Matt.* 18. 17) where it is said, *Tell it to the Church; and if he neglect to hear the Church, let him be to thee as a Gentile, or publican.*

4. And in this last sense only it is that the *Church* can be taken for one person; that is to say, that it can be said to have power to will, to pronounce, to command, to be obeyed, to make laws, or to do any other action whatsoever. For without authority from a lawful congregation, whatsoever act be done in a concourse of people, it is the particular act of every one of those that were present, and gave their aid to the performance of it; and not the act of them all in gross, as of one body; much less the act of them that were absent, or that being present, were not willing it should be done. According to this sense, I define a CHURCH to be, *a company of men professing Christian religion, united in the person of one sovereign, at whose command they ought to assemble, and without whose authority they ought not to assemble.* And because in all commonwealths, that assembly, which is without warrant from the civil sovereign, is unlawful; that Church also, which is assembled in any commonwealth, that hath forbidden them to assemble, is an unlawful assembly.

5. It followeth also, that there is on earth, no such universal Church, as all Christians are bound to obey; because there is no power on earth, to which all other commonwealths are subject: there are Christians, in the dominions of several princes and states; but every one of them is subject to that commonwealth, whereof he is himself a member; and consequently, cannot be subject to the commands of any other person. And therefore a Church, such a one as is capable to command, to judge, absolve, condemn, or do any other act, is the same thing with a civil commonwealth, consisting of Christian men; and is called a *civil state*, for that the subjects of it are *men*; and a *Church*, for that the subjects thereof are *Christians*. *Temporal* and *spiritual* government, are but two words brought into the world, to make men see double, and mistake their *lawful sovereign*. It is true, that the bodies of the faithful, after the resurrection, shall be not only spiritual, but eternal; but in this life they are gross, and corruptible. There is therefore no other government in this life, neither of state, nor religion, but temporal; nor teaching of any

In what sense the church is one person.

[248]

Church defined.

A Christian commonwealth and a church all one.

doctrine, lawful to any subject, which the governor both of the state, and of the religion, forbiddeth to be taught. And that governor must be one; or else there must needs follow faction and civil war in the commonwealth, between the *Church* and *State*; between *spiritualists* and *temporalists*; between the *sword of justice*, and the *shield of faith*: and (which is more) in every Christian man's own breast, between the *Christian*, and the *man*. The doctors of the Church, are called pastors; so also are civil sovereigns. But if pastors be not subordinate one to another, so as that there may be one chief pastor, men will be taught contrary doctrines, whereof both may be, and one must be false. Who that one chief pastor is, according to the law of nature, hath been already shown; namely, that it is the civil sovereign: and to whom the Scripture hath assigned that office, we shall see in the chapters following.

[249]

CHAPTER XL

OF THE RIGHTS OF THE KINGDOM OF GOD, IN ABRAHAM, MOSES, THE HIGH-PRIESTS, AND THE KINGS OF JUDAH*

The sovereign right of Abraham.

1. THE father of the faithful, and first in the kingdom of God by covenant, was Abraham. For with him was the covenant first made; wherein he obliged himself, and his seed after him, to acknowledge and obey the commands of God; not only such, as he could take notice of, (as moral laws) by the light of nature; but also such, as God should in special manner deliver to him by dreams and visions. For as to the moral law, they were already obliged, and needed not have been contracted withal, by promise of the land of Canaan. Nor was there any contract, that could add to, or strengthen the obligation, by which both they, and all men else were bound naturally to obey God Almighty: and therefore the covenant which Abraham made with God, was to take for the commandment of God, that which in the name of God was commanded him, in a dream, or vision; and to deliver it to his family, and cause them to observe the same.

2. In this contract of God with Abraham, we may observe three points of important consequence in the government of God's people. First, that at the making of this covenant, God spake only to Abraham; and therefore contracted not with any of his family, or seed, otherwise than as their wills (which make the essence of all

covenants) were before the contract involved in the will of Abraham; who was therefore supposed to have had a lawful power, to make them perform all that he covenanted for them. According whereunto (*Gen.* 18. 18, 19) God saith, *All the nations of the earth shall be blessed in him, for I know him that he will command his children and his household after him, and they shall keep the way of the Lord.* From whence may be concluded this first point, that they to whom God hath not spoken immediately, are to receive the positive commandments of God, from their sovereign; as the family and seed of Abraham did from Abraham their father, and Lord, and civil sovereign. And consequently in every commonwealth, they who have no supernatural revelation to the contrary, ought to obey the laws of their own sovereign, in the external acts and profession of religion. As for the inward *thought*, and *belief* of men, which human governors can take no notice of (for God only knoweth the heart) they are not voluntary, nor the effect of the laws, but of the unrevealed will and of the power of God; and consequently fall not under obligation. *Abraham had the sole power of ordering the religion of his own people.*

[250]

3. From whence proceedeth another point, that it was not unlawful for Abraham, when any of his subjects should pretend private vision, or spirit, or other revelation from God, for the countenancing of any doctrine which Abraham should forbid, or when they followed, or adhered to any such pretender, to punish them; and consequently that it is lawful now for the sovereign to punish any man that shall oppose his private spirit against the laws: for he hath the same place in the commonwealth, that Abraham had in his own family. *No pretence of private spirit against the religion of Abraham.*

4. There ariseth also from the same, a third point; that as none but Abraham in his family, so none but the sovereign in a Christian commonwealth, can take notice what is, or what is not the word of God. For God spake only to Abraham; and it was he only, that was able to know what God said, and to interpret the same to his family: and therefore also, they that have the place of Abraham in a commonwealth, are the only interpreters of what God hath spoken. *Abraham sole judge and interpreter of what God spake.*

5. The same covenant was renewed with Isaac; and afterwards with Jacob; but afterwards no more, till the Israelites were freed from the Egyptians, and arrived at the foot of Mount Sinai: and then it was renewed by Moses (as I have said before, chap. 35) in such manner, as they became from that time forward the peculiar kingdom of God; whose lieutenant was Moses, for his own time: and the *The authority of Moses, whereon grounded.*

succession to that office was settled upon Aaron, and his heirs after him, to be to God a sacerdotal kingdom for ever.

6. By this constitution, a kingdom is acquired to God. But seeing Moses had no authority to govern the Israelites, as a successor to the right of Abraham, because he could not claim it by inheritance; it appeareth not as yet, that the people were obliged to take him for God's lieutenant, longer than they believed that God spake unto him. And therefore his authority (notwithstanding the covenant they made with God) depended yet merely upon the opinion they had of his sanctity, and of the reality of his conferences with God, and the verity of his miracles; which opinion coming to change, they were no more obliged to take any thing for the law of God, which he propounded to them in God's name. We are therefore to consider, what other ground there was, of their obligation to obey him. For it could not be the commandment of God that could oblige them; because God spake not to them immediately, but by the mediation of Moses himself: and our Saviour saith of himself, (*John* 5. 31) *If I bear witness of myself, my witness is not true*; much less if Moses bear witness of himself, (especially in a claim of kingly power over God's people) ought his testimony to be received. His authority therefore, as the authority of all other princes, must be grounded on the consent of the people, and their promise to obey him. And so it was: for *the people* [251] *(Exod.* 20. 18) *when they saw the thunderings, and the lightnings, and the noise of the trumpet, and the mountain smoking, removed, and stood afar off. And they said unto Moses, speak thou with us, and we will hear, but let not God speak with us lest we die.* Here was their promise of obedience; and by this it was they obliged themselves to obey whatsoever he should deliver unto them for the commandment of God.

Moses was (under God) sovereign of the Jews all his own time, though Aaron had the priesthood.

7. And notwithstanding the covenant constituted a sacerdotal kingdom, that is to say, a kingdom hereditary to Aaron; yet that is to be understood of the succession, after Moses should be dead. For whosoever ordereth, and establisheth the policy, as first founder of a commonwealth (be it monarchy, aristocracy, or democracy) must needs have sovereign power over the people all the while he is doing of it. And that Moses had that power all his own time, is evidently affirmed in the Scripture. First, in the text last before cited, because the people promised obedience, not to Aaron, but to him. Secondly, *(Exod.* 24. 1, 2) *And God said unto Moses, Come up unto the Lord, thou and Aaron, Nadab and Abihu, and seventy of the Elders of Israel. And Moses alone shall come near the Lord, but they shall not come nigh,*

neither shall the people go up with him. By which it is plain, that Moses, who was alone called up to God, (and not Aaron, nor the other priests, nor the seventy elders, nor the people who were forbidden to come up) was alone he, that represented to the Israelites the person of God; that is to say, was their sole sovereign under God. And though afterwards it be said (verse 9) *Then went up Moses and Aaron, Nadab and Abihu, and seventy of the elders of Israel, and they saw the God of Israel, and there was under his feet, as it were a paved work of a sapphire stone, &c.* yet this was not till after Moses had been with God before, and had brought to the people the words which God had said to him. He only went for the business of the people; the others, as the nobles of his retinue, were admitted for honour to that special grace, which was not allowed to the people; which was (as in the verse after appeareth) to see God and live, *God laid not his hand upon them, they saw God and did eat and drink* (that is, did live), but did not carry any commandment from him to the people. Again, it is everywhere said, *the Lord spake unto Moses*, as in all other occasions of government, so also in the ordering of the ceremonies of religion, contained in chapters 25, 26, 27, 28, 29, 30, and 31 of *Exodus*, and throughout *Leviticus*: to Aaron seldom. The calf that Aaron made, Moses threw into the fire. Lastly, the question of the authority of Aaron, by occasion of his and Miriam's mutiny against Moses, was (*Numb.* 12) judged by God himself for Moses. So also in the question between Moses and the people, who had the right of governing the people, when Korah, Dathan, and Abiram, and two hundred and fifty princes of the assembly *gathered themselves together (Numb.* 16. 3) *against Moses, and against Aaron, and said unto them, ye take too much upon you, seeing all the congregation are holy, every one of them, and the Lord is amongst them, why lift you up yourselves above the congregation of the Lord?* God caused the earth to swallow Korah, Dathan, and Abiram, with their wives and children alive, and consumed those two hundred and fifty princes with [252] fire. Therefore neither Aaron, nor the people, nor any aristocracy of the chief princes of the people, but Moses alone had next under God the sovereignty over the Israelites: and that not only in causes of civil policy, but also of religion: for Moses only spake with God, and therefore only could tell the people, what it was that God required at their hands. No man upon pain of death might be so presumptuous as to approach the mountain where God talked with Moses. *Thou shalt set bounds* (saith the Lord, *Exod.* 19. 12) *to the people round about, and say, Take heed to yourselves that you go not up into the Mount, or touch the border of it; whosoever toucheth the Mount shall surely be put to death.* And again (verse 21) *Go down, charge the people, lest they break through unto the Lord to gaze.* Out of which we may conclude, that whosoever in a Christian commonwealth holdeth the place of Moses, is the sole messenger of God, and interpreter of his commandments. And according hereunto, no man ought in the interpretation of the Scripture to proceed further than the bounds which are set by their several sovereigns. For the Scriptures, since God now speaketh in them, are the Mount Sinai; the bounds whereof are the laws of them that represent God's person on earth. To look upon them, and therein to behold the wondrous works of God, and learn to fear him is allowed; but to interpret them; that is, to pry into what God saith to him whom he appointeth to govern under him, and make themselves judges whether he govern as God commandeth him, or not, is to transgress the bounds God hath set us, and to gaze upon God irreverently.

All spirits were subordinate to the spirit of Moses.

8. There was no prophet in the time of Moses, nor pretender to the spirit of God, but such as Moses had approved, and authorized. For there were in his time but seventy men, that are said to prophesy by the spirit of God, and these were all of Moses his election; concerning whom God said to Moses, (*Numb.* 11. 16) *Gather to me seventy of the elders of Israel, whom thou knowest to be the elders of the people.* To these God imparted his spirit; but it was not a different spirit from that of Moses; for it is said (verse 25) *God came down in a cloud, and took of the spirit that was upon Moses, and gave it to the seventy elders.* But as I have shown before (chap. 36) by *spirit*, is understood the *mind*; so that the sense of the place is no other than this, that God endued them with a mind conformable, and subordinate to that of Moses, that they might prophesy, that is to say, speak to the people in God's name, in such manner, as to set forward (as ministers of Moses, and by his authority) such doctrine as was agreeable to Moses his doctrine. For they were but ministers; and when two of them prophesied in the camp, it was thought a new and unlawful thing; and as it is in verses 27 and 28 of the same chapter, they were accused of it, and Joshua advised Moses to forbid them, as not knowing that it was by Moses his spirit that they prophesied. By which it is manifest, that no subject ought to pretend to prophesy, or [253] to the spirit, in opposition to the doctrine established by him, whom God hath set in the place of Moses.

316

9. Aaron being dead, and after him also Moses, the kingdom, as being a sacerdotal kingdom, descended by virtue of the covenant, to Aaron's son, Eleazar the high-priest: and God declared him (next under himself) for sovereign, at the same time that he appointed Joshua for the General of their army. For thus God saith expressly (*Numb.* 27. 21) concerning Joshua; *He shall stand before Eleazar the priest, who shall ask counsel for him, before the Lord, at his word shall they go out, and at his word they shall come in, both he, and all the children of Israel with him*: therefore the supreme power of making war and peace, was in the priest. The supreme power of judicature belonged also to the high-priest: for the book of the law was in their keeping; and the priests and Levites only, were the subordinate judges in causes civil, as appears in *Deut.* 17. 8, 9, 10. And for the manner of God's worship, there was never doubt made, but that the high-priest till the time of Saul, had the supreme authority. Therefore the civil and ecclesiastical power were both joined together in one and the same person, the high-priest; and ought to be so, in whosoever governeth by divine right; that is, by authority immediate from God.

After Moses the sovereignty was in the high priest.

10. After the death of Joshua, till the time of Saul, the time between is noted frequently in the Book of *Judges* by this, *that there was in those days no king in Israel*; and sometimes with this addition, that *every man did that which was right in his own eyes*. By which is to be understood, that where it is said, *there was no king*, is meant, *there was no sovereign power* in Israel. And so it was, if we consider the act, and exercise of such power. For after the death of Joshua and Eleazar, *there arose another generation* (*Judges* 2. 10, 11) *that knew not the Lord, nor the works which he had done for Israel, but did evil in the sight of the Lord, and served Baalim.* And the Jews had that quality which St. Paul noteth, *to look for a sign*, not only before they would submit themselves to the government of Moses, but also after they had obliged themselves by their submission. Whereas signs, and miracles had for end to procure faith, not to keep men from violating it, when they have once given it; for to that men are obliged by the law of nature. But if we consider not the exercise, but the right of governing, the sovereign power was still in the high-priest. Therefore whatsoever obedience was yielded to any of the Judges (who were men chosen by God extraordinarily, to save his rebellious subjects out of the hands of the enemy,) it cannot be drawn into argument against the right the high-priest had to the sovereign

Of the sovereign power between the time of Joshua and of Saul.

power, in all matters, both of policy and religion. And neither the Judges, nor Samuel himself had an ordinary, but an extraordinary calling to the government; and were obeyed by the Israelites, not out of duty, but out of reverence to their favour with God, appearing in their wisdom, courage, or felicity. Hitherto therefore the right of regulating both the policy, and the religion, were inseparable.

[254]

Of the rights of the kings of Israel.

11. To the Judges, succeeded kings: and whereas before, all authority, both in religion, and policy, was in the high-priest; so now it was all in the king. For the sovereignty over the people, which was before, not only by virtue of the divine power, but also by a particular pact of the Israelites in God, and next under him, in the high-priest, as his vice-gerent on earth, was cast off by the people, with the consent of God himself. For when they said to Samuel (1 *Sam.* 8. 5) *Make us a king to judge us, like all the nations*, they signified that they would no more be governed by the commands that should be laid upon them by the priest, in the name of God; but by one that should command them in the same manner that all other nations were commanded; and consequently in deposing the high-priest of royal authority, they deposed that peculiar government of God. And yet God consented to it, saying to Samuel (verse 7) *Hearken unto the voice of the people, in all that they shall say unto thee; for they have not rejected thee, but they have rejected me, that I should not reign over them.* Having therefore rejected God, in whose right the priests governed, there was no authority left to the priests, but such as the king was pleased to allow them; which was more, or less, according as the kings were good, or evil. And for the government of civil affairs, it is manifest, it was all in the hands of the king. For in the same chapter, (verse 20), they say *they will be like all the nations; that their king shall be their judge, and go before them, and fight their battles*; that is, he shall have the whole authority, both in peace and war. In which is contained also the ordering of religion: for there was no other word of God in that time, by which to regulate religion, but the law of Moses, which was their civil law. Besides, we read (1 *Kings* 2. 27) that *Solomon thrust out Abiathar from being priest before the Lord*: he had therefore authority over the high-priest, as over any other subject; which is a great mark of supremacy in religion. And we read also, (1 *Kings* 8) that he dedicated the Temple; that he blessed the people; and that he himself in person made that excellent prayer, used in the consecration of all churches, and houses of prayer; which is another great mark of supremacy in religion. Again, we read (2 *Kings* 22) that when

there was question concerning the Book of the Law found in the Temple, the same was not decided by the high-priest, but Josiah sent both him and others to enquire concerning it, of Huldah, the prophetess; which is another mark of supremacy in religion. Lastly, we read (1 *Chron.* 26. 30) that David made Hashabiah and his brethren, Hebronites, officers of Israel among them westward, *in all the business of the Lord, and in the service of the king.* Likewise (verse 32) that he made other Hebronites, *rulers over the Reubenites, the Gadites, and the half tribe of Manasseh* (these were the rest of Israel that dwelt beyond Jordan) *for every matter pertaining to God, and affairs of the king.* Is not this full power, both *temporal* and *spiritual*, as they call it, that would divide it? To conclude; from the first institution of God's kingdom, to the captivity, the supremacy of religion, was in the same hand with that of the civil sovereignty; and the priest's office after the election of Saul, was not magisterial, but ministerial. [255]

12. Notwithstanding the government both in policy and religion, were joined, first in the high-priests, and afterwards in the kings, so far forth as concerned the right; yet it appeareth by the same holy history, that the people understood it not; but there being amongst them a great part, and probably the greatest part, that no longer than they saw great miracles, or (what is equivalent to a miracle) great abilities, or great felicity in the enterprises of their governors, gave sufficient credit, either to the fame of Moses, or to the colloquies between God and the priests; they took occasion, as oft as their governors displeased them, by blaming sometimes the policy, sometimes the religion, to change the government, or revolt from their obedience at their pleasure: and from thence proceeded from time to time the civil troubles, divisions, and calamities of the nation. As for example, after the death of Eleazar and Joshua, the next generation which had not seen the wonders of God, but were left to their own weak reason, not knowing themselves obliged by the covenant of a sacerdotal kingdom, regarded no more the commandment of the priest, nor any law of Moses, but did every man that which was right in his own eyes; and obeyed in civil affairs, such men, as from time to time they thought able to deliver them from the neighbour nations that oppressed them; and consulted not with God (as they ought to do) but with such men, or women, as they guessed to be prophets by their predictions of things to come; and though they had an idol in their chapel, yet if they had a Levite for their chaplain, they made account they worshipped the God of Israel.

The practice of supremacy in religion was not, in the time of the kings, according to the right thereof.

13. And afterwards when they demanded a king, after the manner of the nations; yet it was not with a design to depart from the worship of God their king; but despairing of the justice of the sons of Samuel, they would have a king to judge them in civil actions; but not that they would allow their king to change the religion which they thought was recommended to them by Moses. So that they always kept in store a pretext, either of justice, or religion, to discharge themselves of their obedience, whensoever they had hope to prevail. Samuel was displeased with the people, for that they desired a king, (for God was their king already, and Samuel had but an authority under him); yet did Samuel, when Saul observed not his counsel, in destroying Agag as God had commanded, anoint another king, namely, David, to take the succession from his heirs. Rehoboam was no idolater; but when the people thought him an oppressor, that civil pretence carried from him ten tribes to Jeroboam an idolater. And generally through the whole history of the kings, as well of Judah, as of Israel, there were prophets that always controlled the kings, for transgressing the religion; and sometimes also for errors of state; as Jehosaphat was reproved (2 *Chron.* 19. 2) [256] by the prophet Jehu, for aiding the king of Israel against the Syrians; and Hezekiah, by Isaiah, for shewing his treasures to the ambassadors of Babylon. By all which it appeareth, that though the power both of state and religion were in the kings; yet none of them were uncontrolled in the use of it, but such as were gracious for their own natural abilities, or felicities. So that from the practice of those times, there can no argument be drawn, that the right of supremacy in religion was not in the kings, unless we place it in the prophets; and conclude, that because Hezekiah praying to the Lord before the cherubims, was not answered from thence, nor then, but afterwards by the prophet Isaiah, therefore Isaiah was supreme head of the church; or because Josiah consulted Huldah the prophetess, concerning the Book of the Law, that therefore neither he, nor the high-priest, but Huldah the prophetess had the supreme authority in matter of religion; which I think is not the opinion of any doctor.

After the captivity, the Jews had no settled commonwealth. 14. During the captivity, the Jews had no commonwealth at all. And after their return, though they renewed their covenant with God, yet there was no promise made of obedience, neither to Esdras, nor to any other: and presently after they became subjects to the Greeks (from whose customs, and demonology, and from the doctrine of the Cabalists, their religion became much corrupted): in such sort as nothing can be gathered from their confusion, both in state and religion, concerning the supremacy in either. And therefore so far forth as concerneth the Old Testament, we may conclude, that whosoever had the sovereignty of the commonwealth amongst the Jews, the same had also the supreme authority in matter of God's external worship, and represented God's person; that is, the person of God the Father; though he were not called by the name of Father, till such time as he sent into the world his son Jesus Christ, to redeem mankind from their sins, and bring them into his everlasting kingdom, to be saved for evermore. Of which we are to speak in the chapter following.

CHAPTER XLI

OF THE OFFICE OF OUR BLESSED SAVIOUR*

1. WE find in Holy Scripture three parts of the office of the Messiah: the first of a *Redeemer*, or *Saviour*: the second of a *pastor, counsellor*, or *teacher*, that is, of a prophet sent from God, to convert such as God hath elected to salvation: the third of a *king*, an *eternal king*, but under his Father, as Moses and the high-priests were in their several times. And to these three parts are correspondent three times. For our redemption he wrought it at his first coming, by the sacrifice, wherein he offered up himself for our sins upon the cross: our conversion he wrought partly then in his own person; and partly worketh now by his ministers; and will continue to work till his coming again. And after his coming again, shall begin that his glorious reign over his elect, which is to last eternally. *Three parts of the office of Christ.*

2. To the office of a Redeemer, that is, of one that payeth the ransom of sin, (which ransom is death,) it appertaineth, that he was sacrificed, and thereby bare upon his own head, and carried away from us our iniquities, in such sort as God had required. Not that the death of one man, though without sin, can satisfy for the offences of all men, in the rigour of justice, but in the mercy of God, that ordained such sacrifices for sin, as he was pleased in his mercy to accept. In the old law (as we may read, *Levit.* 16) the Lord required, that there should every year once, be made an atonement for the sins of all Israel, both priests and others; for the doing whereof, Aaron *His office as a Redeemer.*

alone was to sacrifice for himself and the priests a young bullock; and for the rest of the people, he was to receive from them two young goats, of which he was to *sacrifice* one; but as for the other, which was the *scape-goat*, he was to lay his hands on the head thereof, and by a confession of the iniquities of the people, to lay them all on that head, and then by some opportune man, to cause the goat to be led into the wilderness, and there to *escape*, and carry away with him the in- iquities of the people. As the sacrifice of the one goat was a sufficient (because an acceptable) price for the ransom of all Israel; so the death of the Messiah, is a sufficient price, for the sins of all mankind, because there was no more required. Our Saviour Christ's sufferings seem to be here figured, as clearly, as in the oblation of Isaac, or in any other type of him in the Old Testament: he was both the sacrificed goat, and the scape-goat; *he was oppressed, and he was afflicted* (*Isaiah* 53. 7); *he opened not his mouth; he is brought as a lamb*

[262]

to the slaughter, and as a sheep is dumb before the shearer, so he opened not his mouth: here he is the *sacrificed goat. He hath borne our griefs* (verse 4), *and carried our sorrows*: and again, (verse 6), *the Lord hath laid upon him the iniquities of us all*: and so he is the *scape-goat. He was cut off from the land of the living* (verse 8) *for the transgression of my people*: there again he is the *sacrificed goat*. And again, (verse 11) *he shall bear their sins*: he is the *scape-goat*. Thus is the lamb of God equivalent to both those goats; sacrificed, in that he died; and escap- ing, in his resurrection; being raised opportunely by his Father, and removed from the habitation of men in his ascension.

Christ's kingdom not of this world.

3. For as much therefore, as he that *redeemeth*, hath no title to the thing *redeemed*, before *the redemption*, and ransom paid; and this ransom was the death of the Redeemer; it is manifest, that our Saviour (as man) was not king of those that he redeemed, before he suffered death; that is, during that time he conversed bodily on the earth. I say, he was not then king in present, by virtue of the pact, which the faithful make with him in baptism. Nevertheless, by the renewing of their pact with God in baptism, they were obliged to obey him for king, (under his Father) whensoever he should be pleased to take the kingdom upon him. According whereunto, our Saviour himself expressly saith, (*John* 18. 36) *My kingdom is not of this world*. Now seeing the Scripture maketh mention but of two worlds since the flood; this that is now, and shall remain unto the day of judgment, (which is therefore also called, the *last day*;) and that which shall be after the day of judgment, when there shall be a new

heaven, and a new earth; the kingdom of Christ is not to begin till the general resurrection. And that is it which our Saviour saith, (*Matt.* 16. 27) *The Son of man shall come in the glory of his Father, with his angels; and then he shall reward every man according to his works.* To reward every man according to his works, is to execute the office of a king; and this is not to be till he come in the glory of his Father, with his angels. When our Saviour saith, (*Matt.* 23. 2) *The Scribes and Pharisees sit in Moses' seat; all therefore whatsoever they bid you do, that observe and do*; he declared plainly, that he ascribed kingly power, for that time, not to himself, but to them. And so he doth also, where he saith (*Luke* 12. 14) *Who made me a judge or divider over you?* And (*John* 12. 47) *I came not to judge the world, but to save the world.* And yet our Saviour came into this world that he might be a king, and a judge in the world to come: for he was the Messiah, that is, the Christ, that is, the anointed priest, and the sovereign prophet of God; that is to say, he was to have all the power that was in Moses the prophet, in the high-priests that succeeded Moses, and in the kings that succeeded the priests. And St. John says expressly (chap. 5, verse 22) *the Father judgeth no man, but hath committed all judgment to the Son.* And this is not repugnant to that other place, *I came not to judge the world*: for this is spoken of the world present, the other [263] of the world to come; as also where it is said, that at the second coming of Christ, (*Matt.* 19. 28) *Ye that have followed me in the regeneration, when the Son of Man shall sit in the throne of his glory, ye shall also sit on twelve thrones, judging the twelve tribes of Israel,* it is manifest his kingdom was not begun when he said it.*

4. If then Christ whilst he was on earth, had no kingdom in this world, to what end was his first coming? It was to restore unto God, by a new covenant, the kingdom, which being his by the old covenant, had been cut off by the rebellion of the Israelites in the election of Saul. Which to do, he was to preach unto them, that he was the *Messiah*, that is, the king promised to them by the prophets; and to offer himself in sacrifice for the sins of them that should by faith submit themselves thereto; and in case the nation generally should refuse him, to call to his obedience such as should believe in him amongst the Gentiles. So that there are two parts of our Saviour's office during his abode upon the earth: one to proclaim himself the Christ; and another by teaching, and by working of miracles, to persuade, and prepare men to live so, as to be worthy of the immortality believers were to enjoy, at such time as he should

The end of Christ's coming was to renew the covenant of the kingdom of God, and to persuade the elect to embrace it, which was the second part of his office.

come in majesty, to take possession of his Father's kingdom. And therefore it is, that the time of his preaching, is often by himself called the *regeneration*; which is not properly a kingdom, and thereby a warrant to deny obedience to the magistrates that then were; (for he commanded to obey those that sat then in Moses' chair, and to pay tribute to Caesar;) but only an earnest of the kingdom of God that was to come, to those to whom God had given the grace to be his disciples, and to believe in him; for which cause the godly are said to be already in the *kingdom of grace*, as naturalized in that heavenly kingdom.

The preaching of Christ not contrary to the then law of the Jews, nor of Caesar.

5. Hitherto therefore there is nothing done, or taught by Christ, that tendeth to the diminution of the civil right of the Jews, or of Caesar. For as touching the commonwealth which then was amongst the Jews, both they that bare rule amongst them, and they that were governed, did all expect the Messiah, and kingdom of God; which they could not have done, if their laws had forbidden him (when he came) to manifest, and declare himself. Seeing therefore he did nothing, but by preaching, and miracles go about to prove himself to be that Messiah, he did therein nothing against their laws. The kingdom he claimed was to be in another world: he taught all men to obey in the meantime them that sat in Moses' seat: he allowed them to give Caesar his tribute, and refused to take upon himself to be a judge. How then could his words, or actions be seditious, or tend to the overthrow of their then civil government? But God having determined his sacrifice, for the reduction of his elect to their former covenanted obedience, for the means, whereby he would bring the

[264]

same to effect, made use of their malice, and ingratitude. Nor was it contrary to the laws of Caesar. For though Pilate himself (to gratify the Jews) delivered him to be crucified; yet before he did so, he pronounced openly, that he found no fault in him: and put for title of his condemnation, not as the Jews required, *that he pretended to be king*; but simply, *that he was king of the Jews*; and notwithstanding their clamour, refused to alter it; saying, *What I have written, I have written.*

The third part of his office was to be king, under his Father, of the elect.

6. As for the third part of his office, which was to be *king*, I have already shewn that his kingdom was not to begin till the resurrection. But then he shall be king, not only as God, in which sense he is king already, and ever shall be, of all the earth, in virtue of his omnipotence; but also peculiarly of his own elect, by virtue of the pact they make with him in their baptism. And therefore it is, that

our Saviour saith (*Matt.* 19. 28) that his apostles should sit upon twelve thrones, judging the twelve tribes of Israel, *When the Son of Man shall sit in the throne of his glory*: whereby he signified that he should reign then in his human nature; and (*Matt.* 16. 27) *The Son of Man shall come in the glory of his Father, with his angels, and then he shall reward every man according to his works.* The same we may read, *Mark* 13. 26, and 14. 62, and more expressly for the time, *Luke* 22. 29, 30, *I appoint unto you a kingdom, as my Father hath appointed to me, that you may eat and drink at my table in my kingdom, and sit on thrones judging the twelve tribes of Israel.* By which it is manifest, that the kingdom of Christ appointed to him by his Father, is not to be before the Son of Man shall come in glory, and make his apostles judges of the twelve tribes of Israel. But a man may here ask, seeing there is no marriage in the kingdom of heaven, whether men shall then eat, and drink; what eating therefore is meant in this place? This is expounded by our Saviour (*John* 6. 27) where he saith, *Labour not for the meat which perisheth, but for that meat which endureth unto everlasting life, which the Son of Man shall give you.* So that by eating at Christ's table, is meant the eating of the tree of life; that is to say, the enjoying of immortality, in the kingdom of the Son of Man. By which places, and many more, it is evident, that our Saviour's kingdom is to be exercised by him in his human nature.

7. Again, he is to be king then, no otherwise than as subordinate, or vicegerent of God the Father, as Moses was in the wilderness; and as the high-priests were before the reign of Saul; and as the kings were after it. For it is one of the prophecies concerning Christ, that he should be like (in office) to Moses: *I will raise them up a prophet*, saith the Lord (*Deut.* 18. 18) *from amongst their brethren like unto thee, and will put my words into his mouth*, and this similitude with Moses, is also apparent in the actions of our Saviour himself, whilst he was conversant on earth. For as Moses chose twelve princes of the tribes, to govern under him; so did our Saviour choose twelve apostles, who shall sit on twelve thrones, and judge the twelve tribes of Israel. And as Moses authorized seventy elders, to [265] receive the Spirit of God, and to prophesy to the people, that is, (as I have said before,) to speak unto them in the name of God; so our Saviour also ordained seventy disciples, to preach his kingdom, and salvation to all nations. And as when a complaint was made to Moses, against those of the seventy that prophesied in the camp of Israel, he justified them in it, as being subservient therein to his

Christ's authority in the kingdom of God, subordinate to that of his Father.

government; so also our Saviour, when St. John complained to him of a certain man that cast our devils in his name, justified him therein, saying, (*Luke* 9. 50) *Forbid him not, for he that is not against us, is on our part.*

8. Again, our Saviour resembled Moses in the institution of *sacraments*, both of *admission* into the kingdom of God, and of *commemoration* of his deliverance of his elect from their miserable condition. As the children of Israel had for sacrament of their reception into the kingdom of God, before the time of Moses, the rite of *circumcision*, which rite having been omitted in the wilderness, was again restored as soon as they came into the Land of Promise; so also the Jews, before the coming of our Saviour, had a rite of *baptizing*, that is, of washing with water all those that being Gentiles, embraced the God of Israel. This rite St. John the Baptist used in the reception of all them that gave their names to the Christ, whom he preached to be already come into the world; and our Saviour instituted the same for a sacrament to be taken by all that believed in him. From what cause the rite of baptism first proceeded, is not expressed formally in the Scripture; but it may be probably thought to be an imitation of the law of Moses, concerning leprosy; wherein the leprous man was commanded to be kept out of the camp of Israel for a certain time; after which time being judged by the priest to be clean, he was admitted into the camp after a solemn washing. And this may therefore be a type of the washing in baptism; wherein such men as are cleansed of the leprosy of sin by faith, are received into the Church with the solemnity of baptism. There is another conjecture drawn from the ceremonies of the Gentiles, in a certain case that rarely happens; and that is, when a man that was thought dead, chanced to recover, other men made scruple to converse with him, as they would do to converse with a ghost, unless he were received again into the number of men, by washing, as children new-born were washed from the uncleanness of their nativity, which was a kind of new birth. This ceremony of the Greeks, in the time that Judea was under the dominion of Alexander, and the Greeks his successors, may probably enough have crept into the religion of the Jews. But seeing it is not likely our Saviour would countenance a heathen rite, it is most likely it proceeded from the legal ceremony of washing after leprosy. And for the other sacrament of eating the
[266]   *Paschal lamb*, it is manifestly imitated in the sacrament of the *Lord's Supper*; in which the breaking of the bread, and the pouring out of

the wine, do keep in memory our deliverance from the misery of sin, by Christ's passion, as the eating of the Paschal lamb, kept in memory the deliverance of the Jews out of the bondage of Egypt. Seeing therefore the authority of Moses was but subordinate, and he but a lieutenant of God; it followeth, that Christ, whose authority, as man, was to be like that of Moses, was no more but subordinate to the authority of his Father. The same is more expressly signified, by that that he teacheth us to pray, *Our Father, let thy kingdom come*; and, *For thine is the kingdom, the power and the glory*; and by that it is said, that *He shall come in the glory of his Father*; and by that which St. Paul saith, (1 *Cor.* 24) *then cometh the end, when he shall have delivered up the kingdom to God, even the Father*; and by many other most express places.

9. Our Saviour therefore, both in teaching, and reigning, representeth (as Moses did) the person of God; which God from that time forward, but not before, is called the Father; and being still one and the same substance, is one person as represented by Moses, and another person as represented by his son the Christ. For *person* being a relative to a *representer*, it is consequent to plurality of representers, that there be a plurality of persons, though of one and the same substance.

One and the same God is the person represented by Moses and Christ.

CHAPTER XLII

OF POWER ECCLESIASTICAL

1. FOR the understanding of POWER ECCLESIASTICAL, what, and in whom it is, we are to distinguish the time from the ascension of our Saviour, into two parts; one before the conversion of kings, and men endued with sovereign civil power; the other after their conversion. For it was long after the ascension, before any king, or civil sovereign embraced, and publicly allowed the teaching of Christian religion.

2. And for the time between, it is manifest, that the *power ecclesiastical*, was in the apostles; and after them in such as were by them ordained to preach the gospel, and to convert men to Christianity, and to direct them that were converted in the way of salvation; and after these, the power was delivered again to others by these ordained, and this was done by imposition of hands upon such as

Of the holy spirit that fell on the apostles.

327

were ordained; by which was signified the giving of the Holy Spirit, or Spirit of God, to those whom they ordained ministers of God, to advance his kingdom. So that imposition of hands was nothing else but the seal of their commission to preach Christ, and teach his doctrine; and the giving of the Holy Ghost by that ceremony of imposition of hands, was an imitation of that which Moses did. For Moses used the same ceremony to his minister Joshua, as we read (*Deut*. 34. 9) *And Joshua the son of Nun was full of the spirit of wisdom; for Moses had laid his hands upon him*. Our Saviour therefore between his resurrection, and ascension, gave his spirit to the apostles; first, by *breathing on them, and saying* (*John* 20. 22) *Receive ye the Holy Spirit*; and after his ascension (*Acts*. 2, 3) by sending down upon them, *a mighty wind, and cloven tongues of fire*; and not by imposition of hands; as neither did God lay his hands on Moses: and his apostles afterward, transmitted the same spirit by imposition of hands, as Moses did to Joshua. So that it is manifest hereby, in whom the power ecclesiastical continually remained, in those first times, where there was not any Christian commonwealth; namely, in them that received the same from the apostles, by successive laying on of hands.

Of the Trinity.

3. Here we have the person of God born now the third time. For as Moses, and the high-priests, were God's representative in the Old Testament; and our Saviour himself as man, during his abode on earth: so the Holy Ghost, that is to say the apostles, and their successors, in the office of preaching and teaching, that had received [268] the holy Spirit, have represented him ever since. But a person, (as I have shown before, chap. 13) is he that is represented, as often as he is represented; and therefore God, who has been represented (that is, personated) thrice, may properly enough be said to be three persons; though neither the word *Person*, nor *Trinity*, be ascribed to him in the Bible. *St. John*, indeed (1 *John* 5. 7) saith, *There be three that bear witness in heaven, the Father, the Word, and the Holy Spirit; and these three are One*. But this disagreeth not, but accordeth fitly with three persons in the proper signification of persons; which is, that which is represented by another. For so God the Father, as represented by Moses, is one person; and as represented by his Son, another person; and as represented by the apostles, and by the doctors that taught by authority from them derived, is a third person; and yet every person here, is the person of one and the same God. But a man may here ask, what it was whereof these three bear

328

witness. *St. John* therefore tells us (verse 11) that they bear witness, that *God hath given us eternal life in his Son*. Again, if it should be asked, wherein that testimony appeareth, the answer is easy; for he hath testified the same by the miracles he wrought, first by Moses; secondly, by his Son himself; and lastly by his apostles, that had received the Holy Spirit; all which in their times represented the person of God; and either prophesied or preached Jesus Christ. And as for the apostles, it was the character of the apostleship, in the twelve first and great apostles, to bear witness of his resurrection; as appeareth expressly (*Acts* 1. 21, 22), where St. Peter, when a new apostle was to be chosen in the place of Judas Iscariot, useth these words, *Of these men which have companied with us all the time that the Lord Jesus went in and out amongst us, beginning at the baptism of John, unto that same day that he was taken up from us, must one be ordained to be a witness with us of his resurrection*: which words interpret the *bearing of witness*, mentioned by St. John. There is in the same place mentioned another Trinity of witnesses in earth. For (1 *John* 5. 8) he saith, *there are three that bear witness in earth, the Spirit, and the water, and the blood, and these three agree in one*: that is to say, the graces of God's spirit, and the two sacraments, baptism, and the Lord's supper, which all agree in one testimony, to assure the consciences of believers, of eternal life; of which testimony he saith (verse 10) *He that believeth on the Son of man hath the witness in himself*. In this Trinity on earth, the unity is not of the thing; for the spirit, the water, and the blood, are not the same substance, though they give the same testimony: but in the Trinity of heaven, the persons are the persons of one and the same God, though represented in three different times and occasions. To conclude, the doctrine of the Trinity, as far as can be gathered directly from the Scripture, is in substance this; that God who is always one and the same, was the person represented by Moses; the person represented by his [269] Son incarnate; and the person represented by the apostles. As represented by the apostles, the Holy Spirit by which they spake, is God; as represented by his Son (that was God and man), the Son is that God; as represented by Moses, and the high-priests, the Father, that is to say, the Father of our Lord Jesus Christ, is that God: from whence we may gather the reason why those names *Father*, *Son*, and *Holy Spirit*, in the signification of the Godhead, are never used in the Old Testament: for they are persons, that is, they have their names from representing; which could not be, till divers men had represented God's person in ruling, or in directing under him.

4. Thus we see how the power ecclesiastical was left by our Saviour to the apostles; and how they were (to the end they might the better exercise that power,) endued with the Holy Spirit, which is therefore called sometimes in the New Testament *paracletus* which signifieth an *assister*, or one called to for help, though it be commonly translated a *comforter*. Let us now consider the power itself, what it was, and over whom.

The power ecclesiastical is but the power to teach.

5. Cardinal Bellarmine,* in his third general controversy, hath handled a great many questions concerning the ecclesiastical power of the pope of Rome; and begins with this, whether it ought to be monarchical, aristocratical, or democratical: all which sorts of power are sovereign, and coercive. If now it should appear, that there is no coercive power left them by our Saviour; but only a power to proclaim the kingdom of Christ, and to persuade men to submit themselves thereunto; and by precepts and good counsel, to teach them that have submitted, what they are to do, that they may be received into the kingdom of God when it comes; and that the apostles, and other ministers of the Gospel, are our schoolmasters, and not our commanders, and their precepts not laws, but wholesome counsels: then were all that dispute in vain.

An argument thereof, from the power of Christ himself.

6. I have shown already (in the last chapter,) that the kingdom of Christ is not of this world: therefore neither can his ministers (unless they be kings,) require obedience in his name. For if the supreme king have not his regal power in this world; by what authority can obedience be required of his officers? *As my Father sent me*, (so saith our Saviour) (*John* 20. 21) *I send you*. But our Saviour was sent to persuade the Jews to return to, and to invite the Gentiles, to receive the kingdom of his Father, and not to reign in majesty, no not, as his Father's lieutenant, till the day of judgment.

From the name of regeneration.

7. The time between the ascension and the general resurrection, is called, not a reigning, but a regeneration; that is, a preparation of men for the second and glorious coming of Christ, at the day of judgment; as appeareth by the words of our Saviour, (*Matt.* 19. 28). *You that have followed me in the regeneration, when the Son of man* [270] *shall sit in the throne of his glory, you shall also sit upon twelve thrones*; and of St. Paul (*Eph.* 6. 15) *Having your feet shod with the preparation of the gospel of peace.*

330

8. And is compared by our Saviour, to fishing; that is, to winning men to obedience, not by coercion, and punishing, but by persuasion: and therefore he said not to his apostles, he would make them so many Nimrods, *hunters of men; but fishers of men.* It is compared also to leaven; to sowing of seed, and to the multiplication of a grain of mustard-seed; by all which compulsion is excluded; and consequently there can in that time be no actual reigning. The work of Christ's ministers, is evangelization; that is, a proclamation of Christ, and a preparation for his second coming; as the evangelization of John the Baptist, was a preparation to his first coming.

From the comparison of it, with fishing, leaven, seed.

9. Again, the office of Christ's ministers in this world, is to make men believe, and have faith in Christ: but faith hath no relation to, nor dependence at all upon compulsion, or commandment; but only upon certainty, or probability of arguments drawn from reason, or from something men believe already. Therefore the ministers of Christ in this world, have no power by that title, to punish any man for not believing, or for contradicting what they say; they have I say no power by that title of Christ's ministers, to punish such: but if they have sovereign civil power, by politic institution, then they may indeed lawfully punish any contradiction to their laws whatsoever: and St. Paul, of himself and other the then preachers of the gospel, saith in express words (*2 Cor.* 1. 24), *We have no dominion over your faith, but are helpers of your joy.*

From the nature of faith.

10. Another argument, that the ministers of Christ in this present world have no right of commanding, may be drawn from the lawful authority which Christ hath left to all princes, as well Christians as infidels. St. Paul saith (*Col.* 3. 20) *Children obey your parents in all things; for this is well pleasing to the Lord*: and (verse 22) *Servants, obey in all things your masters according to the flesh; not with eye-service, as men-pleasers, but in singleness of heart, as fearing the Lord*; this is spoken to them whose masters were infidels; and yet they are bidden to obey them *in all things.* And again, concerning obedience to princes (*Rom.* 13 the first six verses) exhorting *to be subject to the higher powers*, he saith, *that all power is ordained of God*; and *that we ought to be subject to them, not only for fear of incurring their wrath, but also for conscience sake.* And St. Peter (1 *Pet.* 2. 13, 14, 15), *Submit yourselves to every ordinance of man, for the Lord's sake, whether it be to the king, as supreme, or unto governors, as to them that be sent by him for the punishment of evil doers, and for the praise of them that do well; for so is the will of God.* And again St. Paul (*Titus* 3. 1),

From the authority Christ hath left to civil princes.

Put men in mind to be subject to principalities and powers, and to obey magistrates. These princes, and powers, whereof St. Peter, and St. Paul here speak, were all infidels: much more therefore we are to [271] obey those Christians, whom God hath ordained to have sovereign power over us. How then can we be obliged to obey any minister of Christ, if he should command us to do any thing contrary to the command of the king, or other sovereign representant of the commonwealth, whereof we are members, and by whom we look to be protected? It is therefore manifest, that Christ hath not left to his ministers in this world, unless they be also endued with civil authority, any authority to command other men.

What Christians may do to avoid persecution.

11. But what (may some object) if a king, or a senate, or other sovereign person forbid us to believe in Christ? To this I answer, that such forbidding is of no effect; because belief, and unbelief never follow men's commands. Faith is a gift of God, which man can neither give, nor take away by promise of rewards, or menaces of torture. And if it be further asked, what if we be commanded by our lawful prince to say with our tongue, what we believe not; must we obey such command? Profession with the tongue is but an external thing, and no more than any other gesture whereby we signify our obedience; and wherein a Christian, holding firmly in his heart the faith of Christ, hath the same liberty which the prophet Elisha allowed to Naaman the Syrian. Naaman was converted in his heart to the God of Israel; for he saith (2 *Kings* 5. 17, 18) *Thy servant will henceforth offer neither burnt offering nor sacrifice unto other gods, but unto the Lord. In this thing the Lord pardon thy servant, that when my master goeth into the house of Rimmon to worship there, and he leaneth on my hand, and I bow myself in the house of Rimmon; when I bow down myself in the house of Rimmon, the Lord pardon thy servant in this thing.* This the prophet approved, and bid him *Go in peace.* Here Naaman believed in his heart; but by bowing before the idol Rimmon, he denied the true God in effect, as much as if he had done it with his lips. But then what shall we answer to our Saviour's saying, (*Matt.* 10. 33) *Whosoever denieth me before men, I will deny him before my Father which is in heaven?* This we may say, that whatsoever a subject, as Naaman was, is compelled to do in obedience to his sovereign, and doth it not in order to his own mind, but in order to the laws of his country, that action is not his, but his sovereign's; nor is it he that in this case denieth Christ before men, but his governor, and the law of his country. If any man shall accuse this doctrine, as

repugnant to true, and unfeigned Christianity; I ask him, in case there should be a subject in any Christian commonwealth, that should be inwardly in his heart of the Mahomedan religion, whether if his sovereign command him to be present at the divine service of the Christian church, and that on pain of death, he think that Mahomedan obliged in conscience to suffer death for that cause, rather than obey that command of his lawful prince. If he say, he ought rather to suffer death, then he authorizeth all private men, to disobey their princes in maintenance of their religion, true or false: if he say, he ought to be obedient, then he alloweth to himself, that [272] which he denieth to another, contrary to the words of our Saviour, (*Luke* 6. 31) *Whatsoever you would that men should do unto you, that do ye unto them*; and contrary to the law of nature, (which is the indubitable everlasting law of God) *Do not to another, that which thou wouldest not he should do unto thee.*

12. But what then shall we say of all those martyrs we read of in   *Of martyrs.* the history of the Church, that they have needlessly cast away their lives? For answer hereunto, we are to distinguish the persons that have been for that cause put to death; whereof some have received a calling to preach, and profess the kingdom of Christ openly; others have had no such calling, nor more has been required of them than their own faith. The former sort, if they have been put to death, for bearing witness to this point, that Jesus Christ is risen from the dead, were true martyrs; for a *martyr* is, (to give the true definition of the word) a witness of the resurrection of Jesus the Messiah; which none can be but those that conversed with him on earth, and saw him after he was risen: for a witness must have seen what he testifieth, or else his testimony is not good. And that none but such, can properly be called martyrs of Christ, is manifest out of the words of St. Peter, (*Acts* 1. 21, 22) *Wherefore of these men which have companied with us all the time that the Lord Jesus went in and out amongst us, beginning from the baptism of John unto that same day he was taken up from us, must one be ordained to be a martyr* (that is a witness) *with us of his resurrection*: where we may observe, that he which is to be a witness of the truth of the resurrection of Christ, that is to say, of the truth of this fundamental article of Christian religion, that Jesus was the Christ, must be some disciple that conversed with him, and saw him before, and after his resurrection; and consequently must be one of his original disciples: whereas they which were not so, can witness no more but that their antecessors

said it, and are therefore but witnesses of other men's testimony; and are but second martyrs, or martyrs of Christ's witnesses.

13. He, that to maintain every doctrine which he himself draweth out of the history of our Saviour's life, and of the Acts, or Epistles of the apostles; or which he believeth upon the authority of a private man, will oppose the laws and authority of the civil state, is very far from being a martyr of Christ, or a martyr of his martyrs. It is one article only, which to die for, meriteth so honourable a name; and that article is this, that *Jesus is the Christ*; that is to say, He that hath redeemed us, and shall come again to give us salvation, and eternal life in his glorious kingdom. To die for every tenet that serveth the ambition, or profit of the clergy, is not required; nor is it the death of the witness, but the testimony itself that makes the martyr: for the word signifieth nothing else, but the man that beareth witness, whether he be put to death for his testimony, or not.

[273]   14. Also he that is not sent to preach this fundamental article, but taketh it upon him of his private authority, though he be a witness, and consequently a martyr, either primary of Christ, or secondary of his apostles, disciples, or their successors; yet is he not obliged to suffer death for that cause; because being not called thereto, 'tis not required at his hands; nor ought he to complain, if he loseth the reward he expecteth from those that never set him on work. None therefore can be a martyr, neither of the first, nor second degree, that have not a warrant to preach Christ come in the flesh; that is to say, none, but such as are sent to the conversion of infidels. For no man is a witness to him that already believeth, and therefore needs no witness; but to them that deny, or doubt, or have not heard it. Christ sent his apostles, and his seventy disciples, with authority to preach; he sent not all that believed: and he sent them to unbelievers; *I send you* (saith he) *as sheep amongst wolves*; not as sheep to other sheep.

Argument from the points of their commission.

15. Lastly, the points of their commission, as they are expressly set down in the gospel, contain none of them any authority over the congregation.

To preach;

16. We have first (*Matt.* 10. 6, 7) that the twelve apostles were sent *to the lost sheep of the house of Israel*, and commanded to preach, *that the kingdom of God was at hand*. Now preaching in the original, is that act, which a crier, herald, or other officer useth to do publicly in proclaiming of a king. But a crier hath not right to command any

334

man. And (*Luke* 10. 2) the seventy disciples are sent out, as *Labourers, not as Lords of the harvest*; and are bidden (verse 9) to say, *The kingdom of God is come nigh unto you*; and by kingdom here is meant, not the kingdom of grace, but the kingdom of glory; for they are bidden (verses 11, 12) to denounce it to those cities which shall not receive them, as a threatening, *that it shall be more tolerable in that day for Sodom, than for such a city*. And (*Matt.* 20. 28) our Saviour telleth his disciples, that sought priority of place, their office was to minister, *even as the Son of Man came, not to be ministered unto, but to minister*. Preachers therefore have not magisterial, but ministerial power: *Be not called masters*, saith our Saviour, (*Matt.* 23. 10) *for one is your master, even Christ*.

17. Another point of their commission, is, to *Teach all nations*; as *And teach;* it is in *St. Matt.* 28. 19, or as in *St. Mark* 16. 15; *Go into all the world, and preach the gospel to every creature*. Teaching therefore, and preaching is the same thing. For they that proclaim the coming of a king, must withal make known by what right he cometh, if they mean men shall submit themselves unto him: as St. Paul did to the Jews of Thessalonica, when (*Acts* 17. 2, 3) *three Sabbath days he reasoned with them out of the Scriptures, opening, and alleging that Christ must needs have suffered, and risen again from the dead, and that this Jesus is Christ*. But to teach out of the Old Testament that Jesus was Christ, (that is to say, king,) and risen from the dead, is not to say, that men are bound, after they believe it, to obey those that tell them so, against the laws, and commands of their sovereigns; but that they shall do wisely, to expect the coming of Christ hereafter, in [274] patience, and faith, with obedience to their present magistrates.

18. Another point of their commission, is to *baptize, in the name* *To baptize;* *of the Father, and of the Son, and of the Holy Ghost*. What is baptism? Dipping into water. But what is it to dip a man into the water in the name of any thing? The meaning of these words of baptism is this. He that is baptized, is dipped or washed, as a sign of becoming a new man, and a loyal subject to that God, whose person was represented in old time by Moses, and the high-priests, when he reigned over the Jews; and to Jesus Christ, his Son, God, and Man, that hath redeemed us, and shall in his human nature represent his Father's person in his eternal kingdom after the resurrection; and to acknowledge the doctrine of the apostles, who, assisted by the spirit of the Father, and of the Son, were left for guides to bring us into that kingdom, to be the only, and assured way thereunto. This, being our

promise in baptism; and the authority of earthly sovereigns being not to be put down till the day of judgment; (for that is expressly affirmed by St. Paul (1 *Cor.* 15. 22, 23, 24) where he saith, *As in Adam all die, so in Christ all shall be made alive. But every man in his own order, Christ the first fruits, afterward they that are Christ's, at his coming; then cometh the end, when he shall have delivered up the kingdom to God, even the Father, when he shall have put down all rule, and all authority and power*) it is manifest, that we do not in baptism constitute over us another authority, by which our external actions are to be governed in this life; but promise to take the doctrine of the apostles for our direction in the way to life eternal.

And to forgive, and retain sins.

19. The power of *remission, and retention of sins*, called also the power of *loosing*, and *binding*, and sometimes the *keys of the kingdom of heaven*, is a consequence of the authority to baptize, or refuse to baptize. For baptism is the sacrament of allegiance, of them that are to be received into the kingdom of God; that is to say, into eternal life; that is to say, to remission of sin: for as eternal life was lost by the committing, so it is recovered by the remitting of men's sins. The end of baptism is remission of sins: and therefore St. Peter, when they that were converted by his sermon on the day of Pentecost, asked what they were to do, advised them (*Acts* 2. 38) to *repent, and be baptized in the name of Jesus, for the remission of sins*. And therefore seeing to baptize is to declare the reception of men into God's kingdom; and to refuse to baptize is to declare their exclusion; it followeth, that the power to declare them cast out, or retained in it, was given to the same apostles, and their substitutes, and successors. And therefore after our Saviour had breathed upon them, saying (*John* 20. 22) *Receive the Holy Ghost*, he addeth in the next verse, *Whosoever sins ye remit, they are remitted unto them; and whosoever sins ye retain, they are retained*. By which words, is not granted an authority to forgive, or retain sins, simply and absolutely, as God forgiveth or retaineth them, who knoweth the heart of man, and truth of his penitence and conversion; but conditionally, to the penitent: and this forgiveness, or absolution, in case the absolved have but a feigned repentance, is thereby without other act, or sentence of the absolved, made void, and hath no effect at all to salvation, but on the contrary to the aggravation of his sin. Therefore the apostles, and their successors, are to follow but the outward marks of repentance; which appearing, they have no authority to deny absolution; and if they appear not, they have no authority to

[275]

absolve. The same also is to be observed in baptism: for to a converted Jew, or Gentile, the apostles had not the power to deny baptism; nor to grant it to the unpenitent. But seeing no man is able to discern the truth of another man's repentance, further than by external marks, taken from his words and actions, which are subject to hypocrisy; another question will arise, who it is that is constituted judge of those marks? And this question is decided by our Saviour himself; *If thy brother* (saith he, *Matt.* 18. 15, 16, 17) *shall trespass against thee, go and tell him his fault between thee, and him alone; if he shall hear thee, thou hast gained thy brother. But if he will not hear thee, then take with thee one or two more. And if he shall neglect to hear them, tell it unto the Church; but if he neglect to hear the Church, let him be unto thee as an heathen man, and a publican.* By which it is manifest, that the judgment concerning the truth of repentance, belonged not to any one man, but to the Church, that is, to the assembly of the faithful, or to them that have authority to be their representant. But besides the judgment, there is necessary also the pronouncing of sentence: and this belonged always to the apostle, or some pastor of the Church, as prolocutor; and of this our Saviour speaketh in the 18th verse, *Whatsoever ye shall bind on earth, shall be bound in heaven; and whatsoever ye shall loose on earth, shall be loosed in heaven.* And conformable hereunto was the practice of St. Paul, (1 *Cor.* 5. 3, 4, 5) where he saith, *For I verily, as absent in body, but present in spirit, have determined already, as though I were present, concerning him that hath so done this deed; in the name of our Lord Jesus Christ, when ye are gathered together, and my spirit, with the power of our Lord Jesus Christ, to deliver such a one to Satan*; that is to say, to cast him out of the Church, as a man whose sins are not forgiven. St. Paul here pronounceth the sentence; but the assembly was first to hear the cause, (for St. Paul was absent;) and by consequence to condemn him. But in the same chapter (verses 11, 12) the judgment in such a case is more expressly attributed to the assembly: *But now I have written unto you, not to keep company, if any man that is called a brother be a fornicator, &c. with such a one, no not to eat. For what have I to do to judge them that are without? Do not ye judge them that are within?* The sentence therefore by which a man was put out of the Church, was pronounced by the apostle, or pastor; but the judgment concerning the merit of the cause, was in the Church; that is to say, (as the times were before the conversion of kings, and men that had sovereign authority in the commonwealth,) the assembly of

[276] the Christians dwelling in the same city: as in Corinth, in the assembly of the Christians of Corinth.

Of excommunication.

20. This part of the power of the keys, by which men were thrust out from the kingdom of God, is that which is called *excommunication*; and to *excommunicate*, is in the original, ἀποσυνάγωγον ποιεῖν, *to cast out of the synagogue*; that is, out of the place of divine service; a word drawn from the custom of the Jews, to cast out of their synagogues such as they thought in manners, or doctrine, contagious, as lepers were by the law of Moses separated from the congregation of Israel, till such time as they should be by the priest pronounced clean.

The use of excommunication without civil power.

21. The use and effect of excommunication, whilst it was not yet strengthened with the civil power, was no more, than that they, who were not excommunicate, were to avoid the company of them that were. It was not enough to repute them as heathen, that never had been Christians; for with such they might eat and drink; which with excommunicate persons they might not do; as appeareth by the words of St. Paul, (1 *Cor.* 5. 9, 10, &c.) where he telleth them, he had formerly forbidden them to *company with fornicators*; but (because that could not be without going out of the world,) he restraineth it to such fornicators, and otherwise vicious persons, as were of the brethren; *with such a one* (he saith) they ought not to keep company, *no not to eat*. And this is no more than our Saviour saith (*Matt.* 18. 17) *Let him be to thee as a heathen, and as a publican*. For publicans (which signifieth farmers, and receivers of the revenue of the commonwealth) were so hated, and detested by the Jews that were to pay it, as that *publican* and *sinner* were taken amongst them for the same thing: insomuch, as when our Saviour accepted the invitation of Zacchaeus a publican; though it were to convert him, yet it was objected to him as a crime. And therefore, when our Saviour, to *heathen*, added *publican*, he did forbid them to eat with a man excommunicate.

22. As for keeping them out of their synagogues, or places of assembly, they had no power to do it, but that of the owner of the place, whether he were Christian, or heathen. And because all places are by right, in the dominion of the commonwealth; as well he that was excommunicated, as he that never was baptized, might enter into them by commission from the civil magistrate; as Paul before his conversion entered into their synagogues at Damascus, (*Acts* 9. 2) to apprehend Christians, men and women,

and to carry them bound to Jerusalem, by commission from the high-priest.

23. By which it appears, that upon a Christian, that should become an apostate, in a place where the civil power did persecute, or not assist the Church, the effect of excommunication had nothing in it, neither of damage in this world, nor of terror: not of terror, because of their unbelief; nor of damage, because they returned thereby into the favour of the world; and in the world to come, were to be in no worse estate, than they which never had believed. The damage redounded rather to the Church, by provocation of them they cast out, to a freer execution of their malice. *Of no effect upon an apostate;* [277]

24. Excommunication therefore had its effect only upon those, that believed that Jesus Christ was to come again in glory, to reign over, and to judge both the quick, and the dead, and should therefore refuse entrance into his kingdom, to those whose sins were retained; that is, to those that were excommunicated by the Church. And thence it is that St. Paul calleth excommunication, a delivery of the excommunicate person to Satan. For without the kingdom of Christ, all other kingdoms after judgment, are comprehended in the kingdom of Satan. This is it that the faithful stood in fear of, as long as they stood excommunicate, that is to say, in an estate wherein their sins were not forgiven. Whereby we may understand, that excommunication in the time that Christian religion was not authorized by the civil power, was used only for a correction of manners, not of errors in opinion: for it is a punishment, whereof none could be sensible but such as believed, and expected the coming again of our Saviour to judge the world; and they who so believed, needed no other opinion, but only uprightness of life, to be saved. *But upon the faithful only.*

25. There lieth excommunication for injustice; as (*Matt.* 18) If thy brother offend thee, tell it him privately; then with witnesses; lastly, tell the Church; and then if he obey not, *Let him be to thee as an heathen man and a publican.* And there lieth excommunication for a scandalous life, as (1 *Cor.* 5. 11) *If any man that is called a brother, be a fornicator, or covetous, or an idolater, or a drunkard, or an extortioner, with such a one ye are not to eat.* But to excommunicate a man that held this foundation, that *Jesus was the Christ,* for difference of opinion in other points, by which that foundation was not destroyed, there appeareth no authority in the Scripture, nor example in the apostles. There is indeed in St. Paul (*Titus* 3. 10) a text that seemeth to be to the contrary. *A man that is an heretic, after the first and second* *For what fault lieth excommunication.*

admonition, reject. For an *heretic*, is he, that being a member of the Church, teacheth nevertheless some private opinion, which the Church has forbidden: and such a one, St. Paul adviseth Titus, after the first, and second admonition, to *reject*. But to *reject* (in this place) is not to *excommunicate* the man; but to *give over admonishing him, to let him alone, to set by disputing with him*, as one that is to be convinced only by himself. The same apostle saith (2 *Tim.* 2. 23) *Foolish and unlearned questions avoid*: the word *avoid* in this place, and *reject* in the former, is the same in the original, παραιτοῦ: but foolish questions may be set by without excommunication. And again, (*Titus* 3. 9) *Avoid foolish questions*, where the original περιΐστασο (*set them by*) is equivalent to the former word *reject*. There is no other place that can so much as colourably be drawn, to countenance the casting out of the Church faithful men, such as believed the foundation, only for a singular superstructure of their own, proceeding perhaps from a good and pious conscience. But on the contrary, all such places as [278] command avoiding such disputes, are written for a lesson to pastors, (such as Timothy and Titus were) not to make new articles of faith, by determining every small controversy, which oblige men to a needless burthen of conscience, or provoke them to break the union of the Church. Which lesson the apostles themselves observed well. St. Peter, and St. Paul, though their controversy were great, (as we may read in *Gal.* 2. 11) yet they did not cast one another out of the Church. Nevertheless, during the apostles' times, there were other pastors that observed it not; as Diotrephes (3 *John*, 9, &c.) who cast out of the Church, such as St. John himself thought fit to be received into it, out of a pride he took in pre-eminence; so early it was, that vainglory, and ambition had found entrance into the Church of Christ.

Of persons liable to excommuni-cation.

26. That a man be liable to excommunication, there be many conditions requisite; as first, that he be a member of some commonalty, that is to say, of some lawful assembly, that is to say, of some Christian Church, that hath power to judge of the cause for which he is to be excommunicated. For where there is no community, there can be no excommunication; nor where there is no power to judge, can there be any power to give sentence.

27. From hence it followeth, that one Church cannot be excommunicated by another: for either they have equal power to excommunicate each other, in which case excommunication is not discipline, nor an act of authority, but schism, and dissolution of

charity; or one is so subordinate to the other, as that they both have but one voice, and then they be but one Church; and the part excommunicated, is no more a Church, but a dissolute number of individual persons.

28. And because the sentence of excommunication, importeth an advice, not to keep company nor so much as to eat with him that is excommunicate, if a sovereign prince, or assembly be excommunicate, the sentence is of no effect. For all subjects are bound to be in the company and presence of their own sovereign (when he requireth it) by the law of nature; nor can they lawfully either expel him from any place of his own dominion, whether profane or holy; nor go out of his dominion, without his leave; much less (if he call them to that honour,) refuse to eat with him. And as to other princes and states, because they are not parts of one and the same congregation, they need not any other sentence to keep them from keeping company with the state excommunicate: for the very institution, as it uniteth many men into one community; so it dissociateth one community from another: so that excommunication is not needful for keeping kings and states asunder; nor has any further effect than is in the nature of policy itself; unless it be to instigate princes to war upon one another.

29. Nor is the excommunication of a Christian subject, that obeyeth the laws of his own sovereign, whether Christian, or heathen, of any effect. For if he believe that *Jesus is the Christ, he hath the Spirit of God*, (1 *John* 4. 1) *and God dwelleth in him, and he in God* (1 *John* 4. 15). But he that hath the spirit of God; he that dwelleth in God; he in whom God dwelleth, can receive no harm by the excommunication of men. Therefore, he that believeth Jesus to be the Christ, is free from all the dangers threatened to persons excommunicate. He that believeth it not, is no Christian. Therefore a true and unfeigned Christian is not liable to excommunication: nor he also that is a professed Christian, till his hypocrisy appear in his manners, that is, till his behaviour be contrary to the law of his sovereign, which is the rule of manners, and which Christ and his apostles have commanded us to be subject to. For the Church cannot judge of manners but by external actions, which actions can never be unlawful, but when they are against the law of the commonwealth. [279]

30. If a man's father, or mother, or master, be excommunicate, yet are not the children forbidden to keep them company, nor to eat with them; for that were (for the most part) to oblige them not to eat

at all, for want of means to get food; and to authorize them to disobey their parents, and masters, contrary to the precept of the apostles.

31. In sum, the power of excommunication cannot be extended further than to the end for which the apostles and pastors of the Church have their commission from our Saviour; which is not to rule by command and coercion, but by teaching and direction of men in the way of salvation in the world to come. And as a master in any science, may abandon his scholar, when he obstinately neglecteth the practice of his rules; but not accuse him of injustice, because he was never bound to obey him: so a teacher of Christian doctrine may abandon his disciples that obstinately continue in an unchristian life; but he cannot say, they do him wrong, because they are not obliged to obey him: for to a teacher that shall so complain, may be applied the answer of God to Samuel in the like place, (1 *Sam.* 8. 7) *They have not rejected thee, but me.* Excommunication therefore when it wanteth the assistance of the civil power, as it doth, when a Christian state, or prince is excommunicate by a foreign authority, is without effect; and consequently ought to be without terror. The name of *Fulmen excommunicationis* (that is, *the thunderbolt of excommunication*) proceeded from an imagination of the Bishop of Rome, which first used it, that he was king of kings, as the heathen made Jupiter king of the gods; and assigned him in their poems, and pictures, a thunderbolt, wherewith to subdue, and punish the giants, that should dare to deny his power: which imagination was grounded on two errors; one, that the kingdom of Christ is of this world, contrary to our Saviour's own words, (*John* 18. 36) *My kingdom is not of this world*; the other, that he is Christ's vicar, not only over his own subjects, but over all the Christians of the world; whereof there is no ground in Scripture, and the contrary [280] shall be proved in its due place.

Of the interpreter of the Scriptures, before civil sovereigns became Christians.

32. St. Paul coming to Thessalonica, where was a Synagogue of the Jews, (*Acts* 17. 2, 3) *as his manner was, went in unto them, and three Sabbath days reasoned with them out of the Scriptures, opening and alleging, that Christ must needs have suffered and risen again from the dead; and that this Jesus whom he preached was the Christ.* The Scriptures here mentioned were the Scriptures of the Jews, that is, the Old Testament. The men, to whom he was to prove that Jesus was the Christ, and risen again from the dead, were also Jews, and did believe already, that they were the word of God. Hereupon (as it is

342

in verse 4) some of them believed, and (as it is in verse 5) some
believed not. What was the reason, when they all believed the Scripture, that they did not all believe alike; but that some approved,
others disapproved the interpretation of St. Paul that cited them;
and every one interpreted them to himself? It was this; St. Paul came
to them without any legal commission, and in the manner of one that
would not command, but persuade; which he must needs do, either
by miracles, as Moses did to the Israelites in Egypt, that they might
see his authority in God's works; or by reasoning from the already
received Scripture, that they might see the truth of his doctrine in
God's word. But whosoever persuadeth by reasoning from principles written, maketh him to whom he speaketh judge, both of the
meaning of those principles, and also of the force of his inferences
upon them. If these Jews of Thessalonica were not, who else was the
judge of what St. Paul alleged out of Scripture? If St. Paul, what
needed he to quote any places to prove his doctrine? It had been
enough to have said, I find it so in Scripture, that is to say, in your
laws, of which I am interpreter, as sent by Christ. The interpreter
therefore of the Scripture, to whose interpretation the Jews of
Thessalonica were bound to stand, could be none: every one might
believe, or not believe, according as the allegation seemed to himself
to be agreeable, or not agreeable to the meaning of the places alleged.
And generally in all cases of the world, he that pretendeth any proof,
maketh judge of his proof him to whom he addresseth his speech.
And as to the case of the Jews in particular, they were bound by
express words (*Deut.* 17) to receive the determination of all hard
questions, from the priests and judges of Israel for the time being.
But this is to be understood of the Jews that were yet unconverted.

33. For the conversion of the Gentiles, there was no use of
alleging the Scriptures, which they believed not. The apostles therefore laboured by reason to confute their idolatry; and that done, to
persuade them to the faith of Christ, by their testimony of his life,
and resurrection. So that there could not yet be any controversy
concerning the authority to interpret Scripture; seeing no man was
obliged during his infidelity, to follow any man's interpretation of
any Scripture, except his sovereign's interpretation of the laws of his
country.

34. Let us now consider the conversion itself, and see what there [281]
was therein that could be cause of such an obligation. Men were
converted to no other thing than to the belief of that which the

apostles preached: and the apostles preached nothing, but that Jesus was the Christ, that is to say, the king that was to save them, and reign over them eternally in the world to come; and consequently that he was not dead, but risen again from the dead, and gone up into heaven, and should come again one day to judge the world, (which also should rise again to be judged,) and reward every man according to his works. None of them preached that himself, or any other apostle was such an interpreter of the Scripture, as all that became Christians, ought to take their interpretation for law. For to interpret the laws, is part of the administration of a present kingdom; which the apostles had not. They prayed then, and all other pastors ever since, *let thy kingdom come*; and exhorted their converts to obey their then ethnic princes. The New Testament was not yet published in one body. Every of the evangelists was interpreter of his own gospel; and every apostle of his own epistle; and of the Old Testament, our Saviour himself saith to the Jews (*John* 5. 39) *Search the Scriptures; for in them ye think to have eternal life, and they are they that testify of me*. If he had not meant they should interpret them, he would not have bidden them take thence the proof of his being the Christ: he would either have interpreted them himself, or referred them to the interpretation of the priests.

35.   When a difficulty arose, the apostles and elders of the Church assembled themselves together, and determined what should be preached, and taught, and how they should interpret the Scriptures to the people; but took not from the people the liberty to read, and interpret them to themselves. The apostles sent divers letters to the Churches, and other writings for their instruction; which had been in vain, if they had not allowed them to interpret, that is, to consider the meaning of them. And as it was in the apostles' time, so it must be till such time as there should be pastors, that could authorize an interpreter, whose interpretation should generally be stood to: but that could not be till kings were pastors, or pastors kings.

Of the power to make Scripture, law.

36.   There be two senses, wherein a writing may be said to be *canonical*; for *canon*, signifieth a *rule*; and a rule is a precept, by which a man is guided, and directed in any action whatsoever. Such precepts, though given by a teacher to his disciple, or a counsellor to his friend, without power to compel him to observe them, are nevertheless canons; because they are rules: but when they are given by one, whom he that receiveth them is bound to obey, then are those canons, not only rules, but laws. The question therefore here,

is of the power to make the Scriptures (which are the rules of Christian faith) laws.

37. That part of the Scripture, which was first law, was the Ten Commandments, written in two tables of stone, and delivered by God himself to Moses; and by Moses made known to the people. Before that time there was no written law of God, who as yet having not chosen any people to be his peculiar kingdom, had given no law to men, but the law of nature, that is to say, the precepts of natural reason, written in every man's own heart. Of these two tables, the first containeth the law of sovereignty; 1. That they should not obey, nor honour the gods of other nations, in these words, *Non habebis deos alienos coram me*, that is, *thou shalt not have for gods, the gods that other nations worship, but only me*: whereby they were forbidden to obey, or honour, as their king and governor, any other God, than him that spake unto them then by Moses, and afterwards by the high-priest. 2. That they *should not make any image to represent him*; that is to say, they were not to choose to themselves, neither in heaven, nor in earth, any representative of their own fancying, but obey Moses and Aaron, whom he had appointed to that office. 3. That *they should not take the name of God in vain*; that is, they should not speak rashly of their king, nor dispute his right, nor the commissions of Moses and Aaron, his lieutenants. 4. That *they should every seventh day abstain from their ordinary labour*, and employ that time in doing him public honour. The second table containeth the duty of one man towards another, as *to honour parents; not to kill; not to commit adultery; not to steal; not to corrupt judgment by false witness*; and finally, *not so much as to design in their heart the doing of any injury one to another*. The question now is, who it was that gave to these written tables the obligatory force of laws. There is no doubt but they were made laws by God himself: but because a law obliges not, nor is law to any, but to them that acknowledge it to be the act of the sovereign; how could the people of Israel that were forbidden to approach the mountain to hear what God said to Moses, be obliged to obedience to all those laws which Moses propounded to them? Some of them were indeed the laws of nature, as all the second table; and therefore to be acknowledged for God's laws; not to the Israelites alone, but to all people: but of those that were peculiar to the Israelites, as those of the first table, the question remains; saving that they had obliged themselves, presently after the propounding of them, to obey Moses, in these words (*Exod.* 20. 19), *Speak thou to us,*

and we will hear thee; but let not God speak to us, lest we die. It was therefore only Moses then, and after him the high-priest, whom (by Moses) God declared should administer this his peculiar kingdom, that had on earth, the power to make this short Scripture of the Decalogue to be law in the commonwealth of Israel. But Moses, and Aaron, and the succeeding high-priests, were the civil sovereigns. Therefore hitherto, the canonizing or making the Scripture law, belonged to the civil sovereign.

Of the judicial and Levitical law.

[283]

38. The judicial law, that is to say, the laws that God prescribed to the magistrates of Israel for the rule of their administration of justice, and of the sentences or judgments they should pronounce in pleas between man and man; and the Levitical law, that is to say, the rule that God prescribed touching the rites and ceremonies of the priests and Levites, were all delivered to them by Moses only; and therefore also became laws, by virtue of the same promise of obedience to Moses. Whether these laws were then written, or not written, but dictated to the people by Moses (after his being forty days with God in the Mount) by word of mouth, is not expressed in the text; but they were all positive laws, and equivalent to holy Scripture, and made canonical by Moses the civil sovereign.

The second law.

39. After the Israelites were come into the plains of Moab over against Jericho, and ready to enter into the land of promise, Moses to the former laws added divers others; which therefore are called *Deuteronomy*; that is, *second laws*. And are, (as it is written *Deut.* 29. 1) *the words of a covenant which the Lord commanded Moses to make with the children of Israel, besides the covenant which he made with them in Horeb.* For having explained those former laws, in the beginning of the book of *Deuteronomy*, he added others, that begin at the 12th chapter, and continue to the end of the 26th of the same book. This law (*Deut.* 27. 3) they were commanded to write upon great stones plastered over, at their passing over Jordan: this law also was written by Moses himself in a book; and delivered into the hands of the *priests, and to the elders of Israel* (*Deut.* 31. 9) and commanded (verse 26) *to be put in the side of the ark*; for in the ark itself was nothing but the *ten commandments*. This was the law, which Moses (*Deut.* 17. 18) commanded the kings of Israel should keep a copy of: and this is the law, which having been long time lost, was found again in the temple in the time of Josiah, and by his authority received for the law of God. But both Moses at the writing, and Josiah at the recovery thereof, had both of them the civil

sovereignty. Hitherto therefore the power of making Scripture canonical, was in the civil sovereign.

40. Besides this book of the law, there was no other book, from the time of Moses till after the Captivity, received amongst the Jews for the law of God. For the prophets (except a few) lived in the time of the Captivity itself; and the rest lived but a little before it; and were so far from having their prophecies generally received for laws, as that their persons were persecuted, partly by false prophets, and partly by the kings which were seduced by them. And this book itself, which was confirmed by Josiah for the law of God, and with it all the history of the works of God, was lost in the captivity, and sack of the city of Jerusalem, as appears by that of 2 *Esdras* 14. 21. *Thy law is burnt; therefore no man knoweth the things that are done of thee, or the works that shall begin.* And before the Captivity, between the time when the law was lost, (which is not mentioned in the Scripture, but may probably be thought to be the time of Rehoboam, when (1 *Kings* 14. 26) Shishak, king of Egypt, took the spoil of the temple,) and the time of Josiah, when it was found again, they had no written word of God, but ruled according to their own [284] discretion, or by the direction of such, as each of them esteemed prophets.

41. From hence we may infer, that the Scriptures of the Old Testament, which we have at this day, were not canonical, nor a law unto the Jews, till the renovation of their covenant with God at their return from the Captivity, and restoration of their commonwealth under Esdras. But from that time forward they were accounted the law of the Jews, and for such translated into Greek by seventy elders of Judea, and put into the library of Ptolemy at Alexandria,* and approved for the word of God. Now seeing Esdras was the high-priest, and the high-priest was their civil sovereign, it is manifest, that the Scriptures were never made laws, but by the sovereign civil power.

The Old Testament when made canonical.

42. By the writings of the Fathers that lived in the time before that the Christian religion was received, and authorized by Constantine the emperor,* we may find, that the books we now have of the New Testament were held by the Christians of that time (except a few, in respect of whose paucity the rest were called the Catholic Church, and others heretics) for the dictates of the Holy Ghost; and consequently for the canon, or rule of faith: such was the reverence and opinion they had of their teachers; as generally the

The New Testament began to be canonical under Christian sovereigns.

347

reverence that the disciples bear to their first masters, in all manner of doctrine they receive from them, is not small. Therefore there is no doubt, but when St. Paul wrote to the Churches he had converted; or any other apostle, or disciple of Christ, to those which had then embraced Christ, they received those their writings for the true Christian doctrine. But in that time, when not the power and authority of the teacher, but the faith of the hearer caused them to receive it, it was not the apostles that made their own writings canonical, but every convert made them so to himself.

43. But the question here, is not what any Christian made a law, or canon to himself, (which he might again reject by the same right he received it;) but what was so made a canon to them, as without injustice they could not do any thing contrary thereunto. That the New Testament should in this sense be canonical, that is to say, a law in any place where the law of the commonwealth had not made it so, is contrary to the nature of a law. For a law, (as has been already shown) is the commandment of that man, or assembly, to whom we have given sovereign authority, to make such rules for the direction of our actions as he shall think fit; and to punish us, when we do anything contrary to the same. When therefore any other man shall offer unto us any other rules, which the sovereign ruler hath not prescribed, they are but counsel, and advice; which, whether good, or bad, he that is counselled, may without injustice refuse to observe; and when contrary to the laws already established, without [285] injustice cannot observe, how good soever he conceiveth it to be. I say, he cannot in this case observe the same in his actions, nor in his discourse with other men; though he may without blame believe his private teachers, and wish he had the liberty to practise their advice; and that it were publicly received for law. For internal faith is in its own nature invisible, and consequently exempted from all human jurisdiction; whereas the words, and actions that proceed from it, as breaches of our civil obedience, are injustice both before God and man. Seeing then our Saviour hath denied his kingdom to be in this world, seeing he had said, he came not to judge, but to save the world, he hath not subjected us to other laws than those of the commonwealth; that is, the Jews to the law of Moses (which he saith (*Matt.* 5. 17) he came not to destroy, but to fulfil,) and other nations to the laws of their several sovereigns, and all men to the laws of nature; the observing whereof, both he himself, and his apostles have in their teaching recommended to us, as a necessary condition

of being admitted by him in the last day into his eternal kingdom, wherein shall be protection, and life everlasting. Seeing then our Saviour, and his apostles, left not new laws to oblige us in this world, but new doctrine to prepare us for the next; the books of the New Testament, which contain that doctrine, until obedience to them was commanded, by them that God had given power to on earth to be legislators, were not obligatory canons, that is, laws, but only good, and safe advice, for the direction of sinners in the way to salvation, which every man might take, and refuse at his own peril, without injustice.

44. Again, our Saviour Christ's commission to his apostles, and disciples, was to proclaim his kingdom (not present, but) to come; and to teach all nations; and to baptize them that should believe; and to enter into the houses of them that should receive them; and where they were not received, to shake off the dust of their feet against them; but not to call for fire from heaven to destroy them, nor to compel them to obedience by the sword. In all which there is nothing of power, but of persuasion. He sent them out as sheep unto wolves, not as kings to their subjects. They had not in commission to make laws; but to obey, and teach obedience to laws made; and consequently they could not make their writings obligatory canons, without the help of the sovereign civil power. And therefore the Scripture of the New Testament is there only law, where the lawful civil power hath made it so. And there also the king, or sovereign, maketh it a law to himself; by which he subjecteth himself, not to the doctor, or apostle that converted him, but to God himself, and his Son Jesus Christ, as immediately as did the apostles themselves.

45. That which may seem to give the New Testament, in respect of those that have embraced Christian doctrine, the force of laws, in the times, and places of persecution, is the decrees they made amongst themselves in their synod. For we read (*Acts* 15. 28) the style of the council of the apostles, the elders, and the whole Church, in this manner, *It seemed good to the Holy Ghost, and to us, to lay upon you no greater burthen than these necessary things, &c.* which is a style that signifieth a power to lay a burthen on them that had received their doctrine. Now *to lay a burthen on another*, seemeth the same as *to oblige*; and therefore the acts of that council were laws to the then Christians. Nevertheless, they were no more laws than are these other precepts, *Repent; be baptized; keep the*

Of the power of councils to make the Scriptures law.

[286]

349

commandments; believe the gospel; come unto me; sell all that thou hast; give it to the poor; and, *follow me;* which are not commands, but invitations, and callings of men to Christianity, like that of *Isaiah* 55. 1. *Ho, every man that thirsteth, come ye to the waters, come, and buy wine and milk without money.* For first, the apostles' power was no other than that of our Saviour, to invite men to embrace the kingdom of God; which they themselves acknowledged for a kingdom (not present, but) to come; and they that have no kingdom, can make no laws. And secondly, if their acts of council, were laws, they could not without sin be disobeyed. But we read not any where, that they who received not the doctrine of Christ, did therein sin; but that they died in their sins; that is, that their sins against the laws to which they owed obedience, were not pardoned. And those laws were the laws of nature, and the civil laws of the state, whereto every Christian man had by pact submitted himself. And therefore by the burthen, which the apostles might lay on such as they had converted, are not to be understood laws, but conditions proposed to those that sought salvation; which they might accept, or refuse at their own peril, without a new sin, though not without the hazard of being condemned, and excluded out of the kingdom of God for their sins past. And therefore of infidels, St. John saith not, the wrath of God shall *come* upon them, but (*John* 3. 36) *the wrath of God remaineth upon them;* and not that they shall be condemned, but that (*John* 3. 18) *they are condemned already.* Nor can it be conceived, that the benefit of faith, *is remission of sins,* unless we conceive withal, that the damage of infidelity, *is the retention of the same sins.*

46. But to what end is it (may some man ask) that the apostles, and other pastors of the Church, after their time, should meet together, to agree upon what doctrine should be taught, both for faith and manners, if no man were obliged to observe their decrees? To this may be answered, that the apostles, and elders of that council, were obliged even by their entrance into it, to teach the doctrine therein concluded, and decreed to be taught, so far forth, as no precedent law, to which they were obliged to yield obedience, was to the contrary; but not that all other Christians should be obliged to observe, what they taught. For though they might deliberate what each of them should teach; yet they could not deliberate what others should do, unless their assembly had had a legislative power; which none could have but civil sovereigns. For though God be the sovereign of all the world, we are not bound to take for his law, whatsoever

is propounded by every man in his name; nor anything contrary to [287]
the civil law, which God hath expressly commanded us to obey.

47. Seeing then the acts of council of the apostles, were then no
laws, but counsels; much less are laws the acts of any other doctors,
or council since, if assembled without the authority of the civil
sovereign. And consequently, the Books of the New Testament,
though most perfect rules of Christian doctrine, could not be made
laws by any other authority than that of kings or sovereign
assemblies.

48. The first council, that made the Scriptures we now have
canon, is not extant: for that collection of the canons of the apostles,
attributed to Clement, the first bishop of Rome after St. Peter, is
subject to question: for though the canonical books be there reckoned up; yet these words, *sint vobis omnibus clericis et laicis libri
venerandi, etc.** contain a distinction of clergy, and laity, that was not
in use so near St. Peter's time. The first council for settling the
canonical Scripture, that is extant, is that of Laodicea, (*Can.* 59)
which forbids the reading of other books than those in the churches;
which is a mandate that is not addressed to every Christian, but to
those only that had authority to read anything publicly in the
church; that is, to ecclesiastics only.

49. Of ecclesiastical officers in the time of the apostles, some *Of the*
were magisterial, some ministerial. Magisterial were the offices of *right of*
the preaching of the gospel of the kingdom of God to infidels; of *constituting*
administering the sacraments, and divine service; and of teaching *ecclesiastical*
the rules of faith and manners to those that were converted. Minis- *time of the*
terial was the office of deacons, that is, of them that were appointed *apostles.*
to the administration of the secular necessities of the church, at such
time as they lived upon a common stock of money, raised out of the
voluntary contributions of the faithful.

50. Amongst the officers magisterial, the first, and principal were
the apostles; whereof there were at first but twelve; and these were
chosen and constituted by our Saviour himself; and their office was
not only to preach, teach, and baptize, but also to be martyrs,
(witnesses of our Saviour's resurrection.) This testimony, was the
specifical and essential mark; whereby the apostleship was distinguished from other magistracy ecclesiastical; as being necessary
for an apostle, either to have seen our Saviour after his resurrection,
or to have conversed with him before, and seen his works, and other
arguments of his divinity, whereby they might be taken for

sufficient witnesses. And therefore at the election of a new apostle in the place of Judas Iscariot, St. Peter saith (*Acts* 1. 21, 22) *Of these men that have companied with us, all the time that the Lord Jesus went in and out amongst us, beginning from the baptism of John unto that same day that he was taken up from us*, must *one be ordained to be a witness with us of his resurrection*: where by this word *must*, is implied a necessary property of an apostle, to have companied with the first and prime apostles in the time that our Saviour manifested himself in the flesh.

[288]

Matthias made apostle by the congregation.

51. The first apostle, of those which were not constituted by Christ in the time he was upon the earth, was Matthias, chosen in this manner: there were assembled together in Jerusalem about one hundred and twenty Christians (*Acts* 1. 15). These (verse 23) appointed two, Joseph the Just, and Matthias, and caused lots to be drawn; *and* (verse 26) *the lot fell on Matthias, and he was numbered with the apostles*. So that here we see the ordination of this apostle, was the act of the congregation, and not of St. Peter, nor of the eleven, otherwise than as members of the assembly.

Paul and Barnabas made apostles by the Church of Antioch.

52. After him there was never any other apostle ordained, but Paul and Barnabas; which was done (as we read *Acts* 13. 1, 2, 3) in this manner. *There were in the Church that was at Antioch, certain prophets, and teachers; as Barnabas, and Simeon that was called Niger, and Lucius of Cyrene, and Manaen; which had been brought up with Herod the Tetrarch, and Saul. As they ministered unto the Lord, and fasted, the Holy Ghost said, Separate me Barnabas, and Saul for the work whereunto I have called them. And when they had fasted and prayed, and laid their hands on them, they sent them away.*

53. By which it is manifest, that though they were called by the Holy Ghost, their calling was declared unto them, and their mission authorized by the particular Church of Antioch. And that this their calling was to the apostleship, is apparent by that, that they are both called (*Acts* 14. 14) apostles: and that it was by virtue of this act of the Church of Antioch, that they were apostles, St. Paul declareth plainly (*Rom.* 1. 1) in that he useth the word, which the Holy Ghost used at his calling: for he styleth himself, *An apostle separated unto the gospel of God*; alluding to the words of the Holy Ghost, *Separate me Barnabas and Saul, &c.* But seeing the work of an apostle, was to be a witness of the resurrection of Christ, a man may here ask, how St. Paul, that conversed not with our Saviour before his passion, could know he was risen? To which is easily answered, that our

352

Saviour himself appeared to him in the way to Damascus, from heaven, after his ascension; *and chose him for a vessel to bear his name before the Gentiles, and kings, and children of Israel*; and consequently (having seen the Lord after his passion) he was a competent witness of his resurrection: and as for Barnabas, he was a disciple before the passion. It is therefore evident that Paul, and Barnabas were apostles; and yet chosen, and authorized (not by the first apostles alone, but) by the Church of Antioch; as Matthias was chosen, and authorized by the Church of Jerusalem.

54. *Bishop*, a word formed in our language out of the Greek *episcopus*, signifieth an overseer, or superintendent of any business, and particularly a pastor, or shepherd; and thence by metaphor was taken, not only amongst the Jews that were originally shepherds, but also amongst the heathen, to signify the office of a king, or any other rule, or guide of people, whether he ruled by laws, or doctrine. And so the apostles were the first Christian bishops, instituted by Christ himself: in which sense the apostleship of Judas is called (*Acts.* 1. 20) *his bishopric*. And afterwards, when there were constituted elders in the Christian Churches, with charge to guide Christ's flock by their doctrine, and advice; these elders were also called bishops. Timothy was an elder (which word *elder*, in the New Testament, is a name of office, as well as of age;) yet he was also a bishop. And bishops were then content with the title of elders. Nay St. John himself, the apostle beloved of our Lord, beginneth his second Epistle with these words, *The elder to the elect lady*. By which it is evident, that *bishop, pastor, elder, doctor*, that is to say, *teacher*, were but so many divers names of the same office in the time of the apostles. For there was then no government by coercion, but only by doctrine, and persuading. The kingdom of God was yet to come, in a new world; so that there could be no authority to compel in any Church, till the commonwealth had embraced the Christian faith; and consequently no diversity of authority, though there were diversity of employments.

55. Besides these magisterial employments in the Church; namely, apostles, bishops, elders, pastors, and doctors, whose calling was to proclaim Christ to the Jews, and infidels, and to direct, and to teach those that believed we read in the New Testament of no other. For by the names of *evangelists* and *prophets*, is not signified any office, but several gifts, by which several men were profitable to the Church: as evangelists, by writing the life and acts of our

What offices in the church are magisterial.
[289]

Saviour; such as were St. Matthew and St. John apostles, and St. Mark and St. Luke disciples, and whosoever else wrote of that subject, (as St. Thomas, and St. Barnabas are said to have done, though the Church have not received the books that have gone under their names:) and as prophets, by the gift of interpreting the Old Testament, and sometimes by declaring their special revelations to the Church. For neither these gifts, nor the gifts of languages, nor the gift of casting out devils, or of curing other diseases, nor any thing else, did make an officer in the Church, save only the due calling and election to the charge of teaching.

Ordination of teachers.

56. As the apostles, Matthias, Paul, and Barnabas, were not made by our Saviour himself, but were elected by the Church, that is, by the assembly of Christians; namely, Matthias by the Church of Jerusalem, and Paul, and Barnabas by the Church of Antioch; so were also the *presbyters*, and *pastors* in other cities, elected by the Churches of those cities. For proof whereof, let us consider, first, how St. Paul proceeded in the ordination of presbyters, in the cities where he had converted men to the Christian faith, immediately after he and Barnabas had received their apostleship. We read (*Acts* 14. 23) that *they ordained elders in every Church*; which at first sight

[290] may be taken for an argument, that they themselves chose, and gave them their authority: but if we consider the original text, it will be manifest, that they were authorized and chosen by the assembly of the Christians of each city. For the words there are, χειροτονή-σαντες αὐτοῖς πρεσβυτέρους κατ᾽ ἐκκλησίαν, that is, *when they had ordained them elders by the holding up of hands in every congregation.* Now it is well enough known, that in all those cities the manner of choosing magistrates, and officers, was by plurality of suffrages; and (because the ordinary way of distinguishing the affirmative votes from the negatives, was by holding up of hands) to ordain an officer in any of the cities, was no more but to bring the people together, to elect them by plurality of votes, whether it were by plurality of elevated hands, or by plurality of voices, or plurality of balls, or beans, or small stones, of which every man cast in one, into a vessel marked for the affirmative, or negative; for divers cities had divers customs in that point. It was therefore the assembly that elected their own elders: the apostles were only presidents of the assembly to call them together for such election, and to pronounce them elected, and to give them the benediction, which now is called consecration. And for this cause they that were presidents of the

assemblies, as (in the absence of the apostles) the elders were, were called προεστῶτες, and in Latin *antistites*; which words signify the principal person of the assembly, whose office was to number the votes, and to declare thereby who was chosen; and where the votes were equal, to decide the matter in question, by adding his own; which is the office of a president in council. And (because all the Churches had their presbyters ordained in the same manner,) where the word is *constitute*, (as *Titus* 1. 5) ἵνα καταστήσης κατά πόλιν πρεσβυτέρους, *For this cause left I thee in Crete, that thou shouldest constitute elders in every city*, we are to understand the same thing; namely, that he should call the faithful together, and ordain them presbyters by plurality of suffrages. It had been a strange thing, if in a town, where men perhaps had never seen any magistrate otherwise chosen than by an assembly, those of the town becoming Christians, should so much as have thought on any other way of election of their teachers, and guides, that is to say, of their presbyters, (otherwise called bishops) than this of plurality of suffrages, intimated by St. Paul (*Acts* 14. 23) in the word χειροτονήσαντες: nor was there ever any choosing of bishops, (before the emperors found it necessary to regulate them in order to the keeping of the peace amongst them,) but by the assemblies of the Christians in every several town.

57. The same is also confirmed by the continual practice even to this day, in the election of the bishops of Rome. For if the bishop of any place, had the right of choosing another, to the succession of the pastoral office, in any city, at such times as he went from thence, to plant the same in another place; much more had he had the right, to appoint his successors in that place, in which he last resided and died: and we find not, that ever any bishop of Rome appointed his [291] successor. For they were a long time chosen by the people, as we may see by the sedition raised about the election between *Damasus* and *Ursicinus*; which Ammianus Marcellinus* saith was so great, that *Juventius* the praefect, unable to keep the peace between them, was forced to go out of the city; and that there were above an hundred men found dead upon that occasion in the church itself. And though they afterwards were chosen, first, by the whole clergy of Rome, and afterwards by the cardinals; yet never any was appointed to the succession by his predecessor. If therefore they pretended no right to appoint their own successors, I think I may reasonably conclude, they had no right to appoint the successors of other bishops, without receiving some new power; which none

could take from the Church to bestow on them, but such as had a lawful authority, not only to teach, but to command the Church; which none could do, but the civil sovereign.

Ministers of the Church, what:

58. The word *minister*, in the original *Διάκονος*, signifieth one that voluntarily doth the business of another man; and differeth from a servant only in this, that servants are obliged by their condition, to do what is commanded them; whereas ministers are obliged only by their undertaking, and bound therefore to no more than that they have undertaken: so that both they that teach the word of God, and they that administer the secular affairs of the Church, are both ministers, but they are ministers of different persons. For the pastors of the Church, called (*Acts* 6. 4) *the ministers of the word*, are ministers of Christ, whose word it is: but the ministry of a deacon, which is called (verse 2 of the same chapter) *serving of tables*, is a service done to the Church or congregation: so that neither any one man, nor the whole church, could ever of their pastor say, he was their minister; but of a deacon, whether the charge he undertook were to serve tables, or distribute maintenance to the Christians, when they lived in each city on a common stock, or upon collections, as in the first times, or to take a care of the house of prayer, or of the revenue, or other worldly business of the Church, the whole congregation might properly call him their minister.

59. For their employment, as deacons, was to serve the congregation; though upon occasion they omitted not to preach the gospel, and maintain the doctrine of Christ, every one according to his gifts, as St. Stephen did: and both to preach, and baptize, as Philip did: for that Philip, which (*Acts* 8. 5) preached the gospel at Samaria, and (verse 38) baptized the Eunuch, was Philip the deacon, not Philip the apostle. For it is manifest (verse 1) that when Philip preached in Samaria, the apostles were at Jerusalem, and (verse 14) *when they heard that Samaria had received the word of God, sent Peter and John to them*; by imposition of whose hands, they that were baptized (verse 15), received (which before by the baptism of Philip they had

[292] not received) the Holy Ghost. For it was necessary for the conferring of the Holy Ghost, that their baptism should be administered, or confirmed by a minister of the word, not by a minister of the Church. And therefore to confirm the baptism of those that Philip the deacon had baptized, the apostles sent out of their own number from Jerusalem to Samaria, Peter and John; who conferred on them that before were but baptized, those graces that were signs

of the Holy Spirit, which at that time did accompany all true believers; which what they were may be understood by that which St. Mark saith (chap. 16. 17), *these signs follow them that believe in my name; they shall cast out devils; they shall speak with new tongues; they shall take up serpents; and if they drink any deadly thing, it shall not hurt them; they shall lay hands on the sick, and they shall recover.* This to do, was it that Philip could not give; but the apostles could, and (as appears by this place) effectually did to every man that truly believed, and was by a minister of Christ himself baptized: which power either Christ's ministers in this age cannot confer, or else there are very few true believers, or Christ hath very few ministers.

60. That the first deacons were chosen, not by the apostles, but by a congregation of the disciples; that is, of Christian men of all sorts, is manifest out of *Acts*, where we read that the *Twelve*, after the number of disciples was multiplied, called them together, and having told them, that it was not fit that the apostles should leave the word of God, and serve tables, said unto them, (verse 3) *Brethren, look you out among you seven men of honest report, full of the Holy Ghost, and of wisdom, whom we may appoint over this business.* Here it is manifest, that though the apostles declared them elected; yet the congregation chose them; which also (verse 5) is more expressly said, where it is written, that *the saying pleased the whole multitude, and they chose seven, &c.* *And how chosen.*

61. Under the Old Testament, the tribe of Levi were only capable of the priesthood, and other inferior offices of the Church. The land was divided amongst the other tribes (Levi excepted) which, by the subdivision of the tribe of Joseph, into Ephraim and Manasseh, were still twelve. To the tribe of Levi were assigned certain cities for their habitation, with the suburbs for their cattle: but for their portion, they were to have the tenth of the fruits of the land of their brethren. Again, the priests for their maintenance had the tenth of that tenth, together with part of the oblations [offerings], and sacrifices. For God had said to Aaron (*Numb.* 18. 20) *Thou shalt have no inheritance in their land, neither shalt thou have any part amongst them; I am thy part, and thine inheritance amongst the children of Israel.* For God being then king, and having constituted the tribe of Levi to be his public ministers, he allowed them for their maintenance, the public revenue, that is to say, the part that God had reserved to himself; which were tithes, and offerings: and that is it *Of ecclesiastical revenue, under the law of Moses.*

which is meant, where God saith, *I am thine inheritance*. And therefore to the Levites might not unfitly be attributed the name of *clergy*, [293] from *κλῆρος*, which signifieth lot or inheritance; not that they were heirs of the kingdom of God, more than other; but that God's inheritance, was their maintenance. Now seeing in this time God himself was their king, and Moses, Aaron, and the succeeding high-priests were his lieutenants; it is manifest, that the right of tithes, and offerings was constituted by the civil power.

62. After their rejection of God in the demanding of a king, they enjoyed still the same revenue; but the right thereof was derived from that, that the kings did never take it from them: for the public revenue was at the disposing of him that was the public person; and that (till the Captivity) was the king. And again, after the return from the Captivity, they paid their tithes as before to the priest. Hitherto therefore Church livings were determined by the civil sovereign.

In our Saviour's time, and after.

63. Of the maintenance of our Saviour, and his apostles, we read only they had a purse, (which was carried by Judas Iscariot;) and, that of the apostles, such as were fishermen, did sometimes use their trade; and that when our Saviour sent the twelve apostles to preach, he forbad them (*Matt.* 10. 9, 10) *to carry gold, and silver, and brass in their purses, for that the workman is worthy of his hire*: by which it is probable, their ordinary maintenance was not unsuitable to their employment; for their employment was (verse 8) *freely to give, because they had freely received*; and their maintenance was the *free gift* of those that believed the good tiding they carried about of the coming of the Messiah their Saviour. To which we may add, that which was contributed out of gratitude; by such as our Saviour had healed of diseases; of which are mentioned (*Luke* 8. 2, 3) *Certain women which had been healed of evil spirits and infirmities; Mary Magdalen, out of whom went seven devils; and Joanna the wife of Chuza, Herod's steward, and Susanna, and many others, which ministered unto him of their substance.*

64. After our Saviour's ascension, the Christians of every city lived in common (*Acts* 4. 34, 35) upon the money which was made of the sale of their lands and possessions, and laid down at the feet of the apostles, of good will, not of duty; for, *whilst the land remained* (saith St. Peter to Ananias, *Acts* 5. 4) *was it not thine? and after it was sold, was it not in thy power?* which sheweth he needed not have saved his land, nor his money by lying, as not being bound to contribute

any thing at all, unless he had pleased. And as in the time of the apostles, so also all the time downward, till after Constantine the Great, we shall find, that the maintenance of the bishops, and pastors of the Christian Church, was nothing but the voluntary contribution of them that had embraced their doctrine. There was yet no mention of tithes: but such was in the time of Constantine, and his sons, the affection of Christians to their pastors, as Ammianus Marcellinus saith (describing the sedition of Damasus and Ursicinus about the bishopric,) that it was worth their contention, in that the bishops of those times, by the liberality of their flock, and especially of matrons, lived splendidly, were carried in coaches, and [294] were sumptuous in their fare and apparel.

65. But here may some ask, whether the pastor were then bound to live upon voluntary contribution, as upon alms; *For who*, saith St. Paul (1 *Cor.* 9. 7) *goeth to war at his own charges? or who feedeth a flock, and eateth not of the milk of the flock?* And again, (verse 13) *Do ye not know that they which minister about holy things, live of the things of the temple; and they which wait at the altar, partake with the altar*; that is to say, have part of that which is offered at the altar for their maintenance? And then he concludeth, (verse 14) *Even so hath the Lord appointed, that they which preach the gospel should live of the gospel.* From which place may be inferred indeed, that the pastors of the Church ought to be maintained by their flocks; but not that the pastors were to determine, either the quantity, or the kind of their own allowance, and be (as it were) their own carvers. Their allowance must needs therefore be determined, either by the gratitude and liberality of every particular man of their flock, or by the whole congregation. By the whole congregation it could not be, because their acts were then no laws; therefore the maintenance of pastors, before emperors and civil sovereigns had made laws to settle it, was nothing but benevolence. They that served at the altar lived on what was offered. So may the pastors also take what is offered them by their flock; but not exact what is not offered. In what court should they sue for it, who had no tribunals? Or, if they had arbitrators amongst themselves, who should execute their judgments, when they had no power to arm their officers? It remaineth therefore, that there could be no certain maintenance assigned to any pastors of the Church, but by the whole congregation; and then only, when their decrees should have the force (not only of *canons*, but also) of *laws*; which laws could not be made, but by emperors, kings, or other civil

The ministers of the Gospel lived on the benevolence of their flocks.

sovereigns. The right of tithes in Moses' law, could not be applied to the then ministers of the gospel; because Moses and the high-priests were the civil sovereigns of the people under God, whose kingdom amongst the Jews was present; whereas the kingdom of God by Christ is yet to come.

66. Hitherto hath been shewn what the pastors of the Church are; what are the points of their commission (as that they were to preach, to teach, to baptize, to be presidents in their several congregations;) what is ecclesiastical censure, viz. excommunication, that is to say, in those places where Christianity was forbidden by the civil laws, a putting of themselves out of the company of the excommunicate, and where Christianity was by the civil law commanded, a putting the excommunicate out of the congregations of Christians; who elected the pastors and ministers of the Church (that it was, the congregation); who consecrated and blessed them, (that it was the pastor); what was their due revenue, (that it was none but their own possessions, and their own labour, and the voluntary contributions of devout and grateful Christians). We are to consider now, what office in the Church those persons have, who being civil sovereigns, have embraced also the Christian faith.

[295]

That the civil sovereign, being a Christian, hath the right of appointing pastors.

67. And first, we are to remember, that the right of judging what doctrines are fit for peace, and to be taught the subjects, is in all commonwealths inseparably annexed (as hath been already proved chapter 18), to the sovereign power civil, whether it be in one man, or in one assembly of men. For it is evident to the meanest capacity, that men's actions are derived from the opinions they have of the good, or evil, which from those actions redound unto themselves; and consequently, men that are once possessed of an opinion, that their obedience to the sovereign power, will be more hurtful to them, than their disobedience, will disobey the laws, and thereby overthrow the commonwealth, and introduce confusion, and civil war; for the avoiding whereof, all civil government was ordained. And therefore in all commonwealths of the heathen, the sovereigns have had the name of pastors of the people, because there was no subject that could lawfully teach the people, but by their permission and authority.

68. This right of the heathen kings, cannot be thought taken from them by their conversion to the faith of Christ; who never ordained, that kings, for believing in him, should be deposed, that is, subjected to any but himself, or (which is all one) be deprived of the

power necessary for the conservation of peace amongst their subjects, and for their defence against foreign enemies. And therefore
Christian kings are still the supreme pastors of their people, and
have power to ordain what pastors they please, to teach the Church,
that is, to teach the people committed to their charge.

69. Again, let the right of choosing them be (as before the conversion of kings) in the Church, for so it was in the time of the
apostles themselves (as hath been shown already in this chapter);
even so also the right will be in the civil sovereign, Christian. For in
that he is a Christian, he allows the teaching; and in that he is the
sovereign (which is as much as to say, the Church by representation,) the teachers he elects, are elected by the Church. And when an
assembly of Christians choose their pastor in a Christian commonwealth, it is the sovereign that electeth him, because 'tis done by his
authority; in the same manner, as when a town choose their mayor,
it is the act of him that hath the sovereign power: for every act done,
is the act of him, without whose consent it is invalid. And therefore
whatsoever examples may be drawn out of history, concerning the
election of pastors, by the people, or by the clergy, they are no
arguments against the right of any civil sovereign, because they that
elected them did it by his authority.

70. Seeing then in every Christian commonwealth, the civil sovereign is the supreme pastor, to whose charge the whole flock of his
subjects is committed, and consequently that it is by his authority, [296]
that all other pastors are made, and have power to teach, and perform all other pastoral offices; it followeth also, that it is from the
civil sovereign, that all other pastors derive their right of teaching,
preaching, and other functions pertaining to that office; and that
they are but his ministers; in the same manner as the magistrates of
towns, judges in courts of justice, and commanders of armies, are all
but ministers of him that is the magistrate of the whole commonwealth, judge of all causes, and commander of the whole militia,
which is always the civil sovereign. And the reason hereof, is not
because they that teach, but because they that are to learn, are his
subjects. For let it be supposed, that a Christian king commit the
authority of ordaining pastors in his dominions to another king (as
divers Christian kings allow that power to the Pope;) he doth not
thereby constitute a pastor over himself, nor a sovereign pastor over
his people; for that were to deprive himself of the civil power; which
depending on the opinion men have of their duty to him, and the

fear they have of punishment in another world, would depend also on the skill, and loyalty of doctors, who are no less subject, not only to ambition, but also to ignorance, than any other sort of men. So that where a stranger hath authority to appoint teachers, it is given him by the sovereign in whose dominions he teacheth. Christian doctors are our schoolmasters to Christianity; but kings are fathers of families, and may receive schoolmasters for their subjects from the recommendation of a stranger, but not from the command; especially when the ill teaching them shall redound to the great and manifest profit of him that recommends them: nor can they be obliged to retain them, longer than it is for the public good; the care of which they stand so long charged withal, as they retain any other essential right of the sovereignty.

The pastoral authority of sovereigns only is jure divino; *that of other pastors is* jure civili.

71. If a man therefore should ask a pastor, in the execution of his office, as the chief-priests and elders of the people (*Matt.* 21. 23) asked our Saviour, *By what authority doest thou these things, and who gave thee this authority*: he can make no other just answer, but that he doth it by the authority of the commonwealth, given him by the king, or assembly that representeth it. All pastors, except the supreme, execute their charges in the right, that is by the authority of the civil sovereign, that is, *jure civili*. But the king, and every other sovereign, executeth his office of supreme pastor, by immediate authority from God, that is to say, in *God's right*, or *jure divino*. And therefore none but kings can put into their titles (a mark of their submission to God only) *Dei gratia rex*, &c. Bishops ought to say in the beginning of their mandates, *By the favour of the King's Majesty, bishop of such a diocese*; or as civil ministers, *in His Majesty's name*. For in saying, *Divina providentia*, which is the same with *Dei gratia*, though disguised, they deny to have received their authority from the civil state; and slyly slip off the collar of their civil subjection, contrary to the unity and defence of the commonwealth.

[297]

Christian kings have power to execute all manner of pastoral function.

72. But if every Christian sovereign be the supreme pastor of his own subjects, it seemeth that he hath also the authority, not only to preach (which perhaps no man will deny;) but also to baptize, and to administer the sacrament of the Lord's Supper: and to consecrate both temples, and pastors to God's service; which most men deny; partly because they use not to do it; and partly because the administration of sacraments, and consecration of persons, and places to holy uses, requireth the imposition of such men's hands, as by the like imposition successively from the time of the apostles have been

ordained to the like ministry. For proof therefore that Christian kings have power to baptize, and to consecrate, I am to render a reason, both why they use not to do it, and how, without the ordinary ceremony of imposition of hands, they are made capable of doing it, when they will.

73. There is no doubt but any king, in case he were skilful in the sciences, might by the same right of his office, read lectures of them himself, by which he authorizeth others to read them in the universities. Nevertheless, because the care of the sum of the business of the commonwealth taketh up his whole time, it were not convenient for him to apply himself in person to that particular. A king may also if he please, sit in judgment, to hear and determine all manner of causes, as well as give others authority to do it in his name; but that the charge, that lieth upon him of command and government, constrain him to be continually at the helm, and to commit the ministerial offices to others under him. In the like manner our Saviour (who surely had power to baptize) baptized none (*John* 4. 2) himself, but sent his apostles and disciples to baptize. So also St. Paul, by the necessity of preaching in divers and far distant places, baptized few: amongst all the Corinthians he baptized only (1 *Cor.* 1. 14, 16) Crispus, Gaius, and Stephanas; and the reason was, (1 *Cor.* 1. 17) because his principal charge was to preach. Whereby it is manifest, that the greater charge, (such as is the government of the Church,) is a dispensation for the less. The reason therefore why Christian kings use not to baptize, is evident, and the same for which at this day there are few baptized by bishops, and by the Pope fewer.

74. And as concerning imposition of hands, whether it be needful, for the authorizing of a king to baptize, and consecrate, we may consider thus.

75. Imposition of hands, was a most ancient public ceremony amongst the Jews, by which was designed, and made certain, the person, or other thing intended in a man's prayer, blessing, sacrifice, consecration, condemnation, or other speech. So Jacob, in blessing the children of Joseph (*Gen.* 48. 14), *Laid his right hand on Ephraim the younger, and his left hand on Manasseh the first born*; and this he did *wittingly* (though they were so presented to him by Joseph, as he [298] was forced in doing it to stretch out his arms across) to design to whom he intended the greater blessing. So also in the sacrificing of the burnt offering, Aaron is commanded (*Exod.* 29. 10) *to lay his hands on the head of the bullock*; and (verse 15) *to lay his hand on the*

363

head of the ram. The same is also said again *Levit.* 1. 4, and 8. 14. Likewise Moses when he ordained Joshua to be captain of the Israelites, that is, consecrated him to God's service, (*Numb.* 27. 23) *Laid his hands upon him, and gave him his charge*, designing, and rendering certain, who it was they were to obey in war. And in the consecration of the Levites (*Numb.* 8. 10), God commanded that *the children of Israel should put their hands upon the Levites*. And in the condemnation of him that had blasphemed the Lord (*Levit.* 24. 14) God commanded that *all that heard him should lay their hands on his head, and that all the congregation should stone him*. And why should they only that heard him, lay their hands upon him, and not rather a priest, Levite, or other minister of justice, but that none else were able to design, and to demonstrate to the eyes of the congregation, who it was that had blasphemed, and ought to die? And to design a man, or any other thing, by the hand to the eye, is less subject to mistake, than when it is done to the ear by a name.

76. And so much was this ceremony observed, that in blessing the whole congregation at once, which cannot be done by laying on of hands, yet Aaron (*Levit.* 9. 22) *did lift up his hand toward the people when he blessed them*. And we read also of the like ceremony of consecration of temples amongst the heathen, as that the priest laid his hands on some post of the temple, all the while he was uttering the words of consecration. So natural it is to design any individual thing, rather by the hand, to assure the eyes, than by words to inform the ear, in matters of God's public service.

77. This ceremony was not therefore new in our Saviour's time. For Jairus (*Mark* 5. 23), whose daughter was sick, besought our Saviour (not to heal her) but *to lay his hands upon her that she might be healed*. And (*Matt.* 19. 13) *they brought unto him little children, that he should put his hands on them, and pray*.

78. According to this ancient rite, the apostles, and presbyters, and the presbytery itself, laid hands on them whom they ordained pastors, and withal prayed for them that they might receive the Holy Ghost; and that not only once, but sometimes oftener, when a new occasion was presented: but the end was still the same, namely a punctual, and religious designation of the person, ordained either to the pastoral charge in general, or to a particular mission: so (*Acts* 6. 6) *The apostles prayed, and laid their hands* on the seven deacons; which was done, not to give them the Holy Ghost, (for they were

full of the Holy Ghost before they were chosen, as appeareth immediately before, verse 3) but to design them to that office. And after   [299]
Philip the deacon had converted certain persons in Samaria, Peter
and John went down (*Acts* 8. 17) *and laid their hands on them, and
they received the Holy Ghost.* And not only an apostle, but a presbyter
had this power: for St. Paul adviseth Timothy (1 *Tim.* 5. 22) *Lay
hands suddenly on no man*; that is, design no man rashly to the office
of a pastor. The whole presbytery laid their hands on Timothy, as
we read 1 *Tim.* 4. 14, but this is to be understood, as that some did
it by the appointment of the presbytery, and most likely their
προεστὼς, or prolocutor, which it may be was St. Paul himself. For
in his second Epistle to *Timothy* (chap. 1. 6) he saith to him, *Stir up
the gift of God which is in thee, by the laying on of my hands*: where
note by the way, that by the Holy Ghost, is not meant the third
person in the Trinity, but the gifts necessary to the pastoral office.
We read also, that St. Paul had imposition of hands twice; once from
Ananias at Damascus, (*Acts* 9. 17, 18) at the time of his baptism; and
again (*Acts* 13. 3) at Antioch, when he was first sent out to preach.
The use then of this ceremony considered in the ordination of
pastors, was to design the person to whom they gave such power.
But if there had been then any Christian, that had had the power of
teaching before; the baptizing of him, that is, the making him a
Christian, had given him no new power, but had only caused him to
preach true doctrine, that is, to use his power aright; and therefore
the imposition of hands had been unnecessary; baptism itself had
been sufficient. But every sovereign, before Christianity, had the
power of teaching, and ordaining teachers; and therefore Christianity gave them no new right, but only directed them in the way of
teaching truth; and consequently they needed no imposition of
hands (besides that which is done in baptism) to authorize them to
exercise any part of the pastoral function, as namely, to baptize, and
consecrate. And in the Old Testament, though the priest only had
right to consecrate, during the time that the sovereignty was in the
high-priest; yet it was not so when the sovereignty was in the king:
for we read (1 *Kings* 8) that Solomon blessed the people, consecrated
the Temple, and pronounced that public prayer, which is the pattern now for consecration of all Christian churches, and chapels:
whereby it appears, he had not only the right of ecclesiastical government; but also of exercising ecclesiastical functions.

*The civil
sovereign, if a
Christian, is
head of the
Church in his
own
dominions.*

79. From this consolidation of the right politic, and ecclesiastic in Christian sovereigns, it is evident, they have all manner of power over their subjects, that can be given to man, for the government of men's external actions, both in policy, and religion; and may make such laws, as themselves shall judge fittest, for the government of their own subjects, both as they are the commonwealth, and as they are the Church: for both State, and Church are the same men.

[300]   80. If they please therefore, they may (as many Christian kings now do) commit the government of their subjects in matters of religion to the Pope; but then the Pope is in that point subordinate to them, and exerciseth that charge in another's dominion *jure civili*, in the right of the civil sovereign; not *jure divino*, in God's right; and may therefore be discharged of that office, when the sovereign, for the good of his subjects, shall think it necessary. They may also if they please, commit the care of religion to one supreme pastor, or to an assembly of pastors; and give them what power over the Church, or one over another, they think most convenient; and what titles of honour, as of archbishops, bishops, priests, or presbyters, they will; and make such laws for their maintenance, either by tithes, or otherwise, as they please, so they do it out of a sincere conscience, of which God only is the judge. It is the civil sovereign, that is to appoint judges, and interpreters of the canonical Scriptures; for it is he that maketh them laws. It is he also that giveth strength to excommunications; which but for such laws and punishments, as may humble obstinate libertines, and reduce them to union with the rest of the Church, would be contemned. In sum, he hath the supreme power in all causes, as well ecclesiastical, as civil, as far as concerneth actions, and words, for those only are known, and may be accused; and of that which cannot be accused, there is no judge at all, but God, that knoweth the heart. And these rights are incident to all sovereigns, whether monarchs, or assemblies: for they that are the representants of a Christian people, are representants of the Church: for a Church, and a commonwealth of Christian people, are the same thing.*

*Cardinal
Bellarmine's
books*, De
Summo
Pontifice
considered.

81. Though this that I have here said, and in other places of this book, seem clear enough for the asserting of the supreme ecclesiastical power to Christian sovereigns; yet because the Pope of Rome's challenge to that power universally, hath been maintained chiefly, and I think as strongly as is possible, by Cardinal Bellarmine, in his controversy *De Summo Pontifice*; I have thought it necessary, as

briefly as I can, to examine the grounds, and strength of his discourse.

82. Of five books he hath written of this subject, the first *The first* containeth three questions: one, which is simply the best govern- *book.* ment, *Monarchy, Aristocracy,* or *Democracy*; and concludeth for neither, but for a government mixed of all three: another, which of these is the best government of the Church; and concludeth for the mixed, but which should most participate of monarchy: the third, whether in this mixed monarchy, St. Peter had the place of monarch. Concerning his first conclusion, I have already sufficiently proved (chapter 18) that all governments which men are bound to obey, are simple, and absolute. In monarchy there is but one man supreme; and all other men that have any kind of power in the state, have it by his commission, during his pleasure; and execute it in his name: and in aristocracy, and democracy, but one supreme assembly, with the same power that in monarchy belongeth to the mon- [301] arch, which is not a mixed, but an absolute sovereignty. And of the three sorts, which is the best, is not to be disputed, where any one of them is already established; but the present ought always to be preferred, maintained, and accounted best; because it is against both the law of nature, and the divine positive law, to do any thing tending to the subversion thereof. Besides, it maketh nothing to the power of any pastor, (unless he have the civil sovereignty,) what kind of government is the best; because their calling is not to govern men by commandment, but to teach them, and persuade them by arguments, and leave it to them to consider, whether they shall embrace, or reject the doctrine taught. For monarchy, aristocracy, and democracy, do mark out unto us three sorts of sovereigns, not of pastors; or, as we may say, three sorts of masters of families, not three sorts of schoolmasters for their children.

83. And therefore the second conclusion, concerning the best form of government of the Church, is nothing to the question of the Pope's power without his own dominions: for in all other common-wealths his power (if he have any at all) is that of the schoolmaster only, and not of the master of the family.

84. For the third conclusion, which is, that St. Peter was monarch of the Church, he bringeth for his chief argument the place of St. Matthew (chap. 16. 18, 19) *Thou art Peter, and upon this rock I will build my Church, &c. And I will give thee the keys of heaven; whatso-ever thou shalt bind on earth, shall be bound in heaven, and whatsoever*

thou shalt loose on earth, shall be loosed in heaven. Which place well considered, proveth no more, but that the Church of Christ hath for foundation one only article; namely, that which Peter in the name of all the apostles professing, gave occasion to our Saviour to speak the words here cited; which that we may clearly understand, we are to consider, that our Saviour preached by himself, by John the Baptist, and by his apostles, nothing but this article of faith, *that he was the Christ*; all other articles requiring faith no otherwise, than as founded on that. John began first, (*Matt.* 3. 2) preaching only this, *the kingdom of God is at hand.* Then our Saviour himself (*Matt.* 4. 17) preached the same: and to his twelve apostles, when he gave them their commission, (*Matt.* 10. 7), there is no mention of preaching any other article but that. This was the fundamental article, that is the foundation of the Church's faith. Afterwards the apostles being returned to him, he (*Matt.* 16. 13) asketh them all, not Peter only, *who men said he was*; and they answered, that *some said he was John the Baptist, some Elias, and others Jeremiah, or one of the Prophets.* Then (verse 15) he asked them all again, (not Peter only) *whom say ye that I am?* Therefore St. Peter answered (for them all) *Thou art Christ, the Son of the living God*; which I said is the foundation of the faith of the whole Church; from which our Saviour takes the oc-
[302]   casion of saying, *upon this stone I will build my Church*: by which it is manifest, that by the foundation-stone of the Church, was meant the fundamental article of the Church's faith. But why then (will some object) doth our Saviour interpose these words, *thou art Peter?* If the original of this text had been rigidly translated, the reason would easily have appeared: we are therefore to consider, that the apostle Simon, was surnamed *Stone*, (which is the signification of the Syriac word *Cephas*, and of the Greek word Πετϱος). Our Saviour therefore after the confession of that fundamental article, alluding to his name, said (as if it were in English) thus, Thou art *Stone*, and upon this Stone I will build my Church: which is as much as to say, this article, that *I am the Christ*, is the foundation of all the faith I require in those that are to be members of my Church: neither is this allusion to a name, an unusual thing in common speech: but it had been a strange, and obscure speech, if our Saviour, intending to build his Church on the person of St. Peter, had said, *thou art a stone, and upon this stone I will build my Church*, when it was so obvious without ambiguity to have said, *I will build my Church on thee*; and yet there had been still the same allusion to his name.

85. And for the following words, *I will give thee the keys of heaven, &c.* it is no more than what our Saviour gave also to all the rest of his disciples, (*Matt.* 18. 18) *Whatsoever ye shall bind on earth, shall be bound in heaven. And whatsoever ye shall loose on earth, shall be loosed in heaven.* But howsoever this be interpreted, there is no doubt but the power here granted belongs to all supreme pastors; such as are all Christian civil sovereigns in their own dominions. In so much, as if St. Peter, or our Saviour himself had converted any of them to believe him, and to acknowledge his kingdom; yet because his kingdom is not of this world, he had left the supreme care of converting his subjects to none but him; or else he must have deprived him of the sovereignty, to which the right of teaching is inseparably annexed. And thus much in refutation of his first book, wherein he would prove St. Peter to have been the monarch universal of the Church, that is to say, of all the Christians in the world.

86. The second book hath two conclusions: one, that St. Peter *The second* was Bishop of Rome, and there died: the other, that the Popes of *book.* Rome are his successors. Both which have been disputed by others. But supposing them true; yet if by Bishop of Rome, be understood either the monarch of the Church, or the supreme pastor of it; not Silvester, but Constantine (who was the first Christian emperor) was that bishop; and as Constantine, so all other Christian emperors were of right supreme bishops of the Roman empire; I say of the Roman empire, not of all Christendom: for other Christian sovereigns had the same right in their several territories, as to an office essentially adherent to their sovereignty. Which shall serve for answer to his second book.

87. In the third book, he handleth the question whether the Pope [303] be Antichrist? For my part, I see no argument that proves he is so, *The third* in that sense the Scripture useth the name: nor will I take any *book.* argument from the quality of Antichrist, to contradict the authority he exerciseth, or hath heretofore exercised, in the dominions of any other prince, or state.

88. It is evident that the prophets of the Old Testament foretold, and the Jews expected a Messiah, that is, a Christ, that should re-establish amongst them the kingdom of God, which had been rejected by them in the time of Samuel, when they required a king after the manner of other nations. This expectation of theirs, made them obnoxious to the imposture of all such, as had both the ambition to attempt the attaining of the kingdom, and the art to deceive the people by counterfeit miracles, by hypocritical life, or by orations and doctrine plausible. Our Saviour therefore, and his apostles forewarned men of false prophets, and of false Christs. False Christs, are such as pretend to be the *Christ*, but are not, and are called properly *Antichrists*, in such sense, as when there happeneth a schism in the Church by the election of two Popes, the one calleth the other *Antipapa*, or the false Pope. And therefore Antichrist in the proper signification hath two essential marks; one, that he denieth Jesus to be Christ; and another that he professeth himself to be Christ. The first mark is set down by St. John in his first Epistle, 4. 3, *Every Spirit that confesseth not that Jesus Christ is come in the flesh, is not of God; and this is the spirit of Antichrist.* The other mark is expressed in the words of our Saviour, (*Matt.* 24. 5) *many shall come in my name, saying, I am Christ*; and again, (verse 23) *If any man shall say unto you, lo! here is Christ, there is Christ, believe it not.* And therefore Antichrist must be a false Christ, that is, some one of them that shall pretend themselves to be Christ. And out of these two marks, *to deny Jesus to be the Christ*, and *to affirm himself to be the Christ*, it followeth, that he must also be an *adversary of Jesus the true Christ*, which is another usual signification of the word Antichrist. But of these many Antichrists, there is one special one, ὁ Ἀντίχριστος, *the Antichrist*, or *Antichrist* definitely, as one certain person; not indefinitely *an Antichrist*. Now seeing the Pope of Rome neither pretendeth himself, nor denieth Jesus to be the Christ, I perceive not how he can be called Antichrist; by which word is not meant, one that falsely pretendeth to be *his* lieutenant, or vicar-general, but to be *He*. There is also some mark of the time of this special Antichrist, as (*Matt.* 24. 15), when that abominable destroyer, spoken of by Daniel (*Dan.* 9. 27) shall stand in the Holy place, and such tribulation as was not since the beginning of the world, nor ever shall be again, insomuch as if it were to last long, (*Matt.* 24. 22) *no flesh could be saved; but for the elect's sake those days shall be shortened* (made fewer). But that tribulation is not yet come; for it is to be followed immediately (verse 29) by a darkening of the sun and moon, a falling of the stars, a concussion of the heavens, and [304] the glorious coming again of our Saviour in the clouds. And therefore *the Antichrist* is not yet come; whereas, many Popes are both come and gone. It is true, the Pope in taking upon him to give laws to all Christian kings, and nations, usurpeth a kingdom in this world, which Christ took not on him: but he doth it not *as Christ*, but as *for Christ*, wherein there is nothing of *the Antichrist*.

89. In the fourth book, to prove the Pope to be the supreme judge in all questions of faith and manners, (*which is as much as to be the absolute monarch of all Christians in the world*,) he bringeth three propositions: the first, that his judgments are infallible:* the second, that he can make very laws, and punish those that observe them not: the third, that our Saviour conferred all jurisdiction ecclesiastical on the Pope of Rome. *Fourth book.*

90. For the infallibility of his judgments, he allegeth the Scriptures: and first, that of Luke 22. 31, 32: *Simon, Simon, Satan hath desired you that he may sift you as wheat; but I have prayed for thee, that thy faith fail not; and when thou art converted, strengthen thy brethren.* This, according to Bellarmine's exposition, is, that Christ gave here to Simon Peter two privileges: one, that neither his faith should fail, nor the faith of any of his successors: the other, that neither he, nor any of his successors, should ever define any point concerning faith, or manners erroneously, or contrary to the definition of a former Pope: which is a strange, and very much strained interpretation. But he that with attention readeth that chapter, shall find there *is* no place in the whole Scripture that maketh more against the Pope's authority, than this very place. The Priests and Scribes seeking to kill our Saviour at the Passover, and Judas possessed with a resolution to betray him, and the day of killing the Passover being come, our Saviour celebrated the same with his apostles, which he said, till the kingdom of God was come he would do no more; and withal told them, that one of them was to betray him: hereupon they questioned, which of them it should be; and withal (seeing the next Passover their master would celebrate should be when he was king) entered into a contention, who should then be the greatest man. Our Saviour therefore told them, that the kings of the nations had dominion over their subjects, and are called by a name (in Hebrew) that signifies bountiful; but I cannot be so to you, you must endeavour to serve one another; I ordain you a kingdom, but it is such as my Father hath ordained me; a kingdom that I am now to purchase with my blood, and not to possess till my second coming; then ye shall eat and drink at my table, and sit on thrones judging the twelve tribes of Israel: and then addressing himself to St. Peter, he saith; *Simon, Simon,* Satan seeks by suggesting a present domination, to weaken your faith of the future; but I have *Texts for the infallibility of the Pope's judgment in points of faith.*

371

prayed for thee, that thy faith shall not fail; thou therefore (note this,) being converted, and understanding my kingdom as of another world, confirm the same faith in thy brethren. To which St. Peter answered (as one that no more expected any authority in this world) *Lord, I am ready to go with thee, not only to prison, but to death.* [305] Whereby it is manifest, St. Peter had not only no jurisdiction given him in this world, but a charge to teach all the other apostles, that they also should have none. And for the infallibility of St. Peter's sentence definitive in matter of faith, there is no more to be attributed to it out of this text, than that Peter should continue in the belief of this point, namely, that Christ should come again, and possess the kingdom at the day of judgment; which was not given by this text to all his successors; for we see they claim it in the world that now is.

91. The second place is that of Matt. 16. 18, *Thou art Peter, and upon this rock I will build my Church, and the gates of hell shall not prevail against it.* By which (as I have already shown in this chapter) is proved no more, than that the gates of hell shall not prevail against the confession of Peter, which gave occasion to that speech; namely this, that *Jesus is Christ the Son of God.*

92. The third text is John 21. 16, 17: *Feed my sheep*; which contains no more but a commission of teaching: and if we grant the rest of the apostles to be contained in that name of *sheep*; then it is the supreme power of teaching: but it was only for the time that there were no Christian sovereigns already possessed of that supremacy. But I have already proved, that Christian sovereigns are in their own dominions the supreme pastors, and instituted thereto, by virtue of their being baptized, though without other imposition of hands. For such imposition being a ceremony of designing the person, is needless, when he is already designed to the power of teaching what doctrine he will, by his institution to an absolute power over his subjects. For as I have proved before, sovereigns are supreme teachers (in general) by their office; and therefore oblige themselves (by their baptism) to teach the doctrine of Christ: and when they suffer others to teach their people, they do it at the peril of their own souls; for it is at the hands of the heads of families that God will require the account of the instruction of his children and servants. It is of Abraham himself, not of a hireling, that God saith (*Gen.* 18. 19) *I know him that he will command his children, and his household after him, that they keep the way of the Lord, and do justice and judgment.*

93. The fourth place is that of *Exod.* 28. 30. *Thou shalt put in the breast-plate of judgment, the Urim and the Thummim*: which he saith is interpreted by the Septuagint δήλωσιν καὶ ἀλήθειαν, that is, *evidence* and *truth*: and thence concludeth, God hath given evidence, and truth, (which is almost infallibility,) to the high-priest. But be it evidence and truth itself that was given; or be it but admonition to the priest to endeavour to inform himself clearly, and give judgment uprightly; yet in that it was given to the high-priest, it was given to the civil sovereign: for such next under God was the high-priest in the commonwealth of Israel; and is an argument for evidence and [306] truth, that is, for the ecclesiastical supremacy of civil sovereigns over their own subjects, against the pretended power of the Pope. These are all the texts he bringeth for the infallibility of the judgment of the Pope, in point of faith.

94. For the infallibility of his judgment concerning manners, he bringeth one text, which is that of John 16. 13: *When the Spirit of truth is come, he will lead you into all truth*: where (saith he) by *all truth*, is meant, at least, *all truth necessary to salvation*. But with this mitigation, he attributeth no more infallibility to the Pope, than to any man that professeth Christianity, and is not to be damned: for if any man err in any point, wherein not to err is necessary to salvation, it is impossible he should be saved; for that only is necessary to salvation, without which to be saved is impossible. What points these are, I shall declare out of the Scripture in the chapter following. In this place I say no more, but that though it were granted, the Pope could not possibly teach any error at all, yet doth not this entitle him to any jurisdiction in the dominions of another prince; unless we shall also say, a man is obliged in conscience to set on work upon all occasions the best workman, even then also when he hath formerly promised his work to another. *Texts for the same, in point of manners.*

95. Besides the text, he argueth from reason, thus. If the Pope could err in necessaries, then Christ hath not sufficiently provided for the Church's salvation; because he hath commanded her to follow the Pope's directions. But this reason is invalid, unless he shew when, and where Christ commanded that, or took at all any notice of a Pope: nay granting whatsoever was given to St. Peter, was given to the Pope; yet seeing there is in the Scripture no command to any man to obey St. Peter, no man can be just, that obeyeth him, when his commands are contrary to those of his lawful sovereign.

96. Lastly, it hath not been declared by the Church, nor by the Pope himself, that he is the civil sovereign of all the Christians in the world; and therefore all Christians are not bound to acknowledge his jurisdiction in point of manners. For the civil sovereignty, and supreme judicature in controversies of manners, are the same thing: and the makers of civil laws, are not only declarers, but also makers of the justice and injustice of actions; there being nothing in men's manners that makes them righteous, or unrighteous, but their conformity with the law of the sovereign. And therefore when the Pope challengeth supremacy in controversies of manners, he teacheth men to disobey the civil sovereign; which is an erroneous doctrine, contrary to the many precepts of our Saviour and his apostles, delivered to us in the Scripture.

97. To prove the Pope has power to make laws, he allegeth many places; as first, (*Deut.* 17. 12) *The man that will do presumptuously, and will not hearken unto the priest, (that standeth to minister there* [307] *before the Lord thy God, or unto the judge,) even that man shall die; and thou shalt put away the evil from Israel.* For answer whereunto, we are to remember that the high-priest (next and immediately under God) was the civil sovereign; and all judges were to be constituted by him. The words alleged sound therefore thus. *The man that will presume to disobey the civil sovereign for the time being, or any of his officers in the execution of their places, that man shall die, &c.* which is clearly for the civil sovereignty, against the universal power of the Pope.

98. Secondly, he allegeth that of *Matt.* 16. 19 *Whatsoever ye shall bind, &c.* and interpreteth it for such *binding* as is attributed (*Matt.* 23. 4) to the Scribes and Pharisees, *They bind heavy burthens, and grievous to be borne, and lay them on men's shoulders*; by which is meant, (he says) making of laws; and concludes thence, that the Pope can make laws. But this also maketh only for the legislative power of civil sovereigns: for the Scribes, and Pharisees sat in Moses' chair, but Moses next under God was sovereign of the people of Israel: and therefore our Saviour commanded them to do all that they should say, but not all that they should do. That is, to obey their laws, but not follow their example.

99. The third place is *John* 21. 16 *Feed my sheep*; which is not a power to make laws, but a command to teach. Making laws belongs to the lord of the family; who by his own discretion chooseth his chaplain, as also a schoolmaster to teach his children.

100. The fourth place (*John* 20. 21) is against him. The words

are, *As my father sent me, so send I you.* But our Saviour was sent to redeem (by his death) such as should believe; and by his own, and his apostles' preaching to prepare them for their entrance into his kingdom; which he himself saith, is not of this world, and hath taught us to pray for the coming of it hereafter, though he refused (*Acts* 1. 6, 7) to tell his apostles when it should come; and in which, when it comes, the twelve apostles shall sit on twelve thrones (every one perhaps as high as that of St. Peter) to judge the twelve tribes of Israel. Seeing then God the Father sent not our Saviour to make laws in this present world, we may conclude from the text, that neither did our Saviour send St. Peter to make laws here, but to persuade men to expect his second coming with a steadfast faith; and in the meantime, if subjects, to obey their princes; and if princes, both to believe it themselves, and to do their best to make their subjects do the same; which is the office of a bishop. Therefore this place maketh most strongly for the joining of the ecclesiastical supremacy to the civil sovereignty, contrary to that which Cardinal Bellarmine allegeth it for.

101. The fifth place is *Acts* 15. 28, 29, *It hath seemed good to the Holy Spirit, and to us, to lay upon you no greater burthen, than these necessary things, that ye abstain from meats offered to idols, and from blood, and from things strangled, and from fornication.* Here he notes the word *laying of burthens* for the legislative power. But who is [308] there, that reading this text, can say, this style of the apostles may not as properly be used in giving counsel, as in making laws? The style of a law is, *we command*: but, *we think good*, is the ordinary style of them, that but give advice; and they lay a burthen that give advice, though it be conditional, that is, if they to whom they give it, will attain their ends: and such is the burthen, of abstaining from things strangled, and from blood; not absolute, but in case they will not err. I have shown before (chapter 25) that law is distinguished from counsel, in this, that the reason of a law is taken from the design, and benefit of him that prescribeth it; but the reason of a counsel, from the design and benefit of him, to whom the counsel is given. But here, the apostles aim only at the benefit of the converted Gentiles, namely their salvation; not at their own benefit; for having done their endeavour, they shall have their reward, whether they be obeyed, or not. And therefore the acts of this council, were not laws, but counsels.

102. The sixth place is that of *Rom.* 13. *Let every soul be subject to*

the higher powers, for there is no power but of God; which is meant, he saith, not only of secular, but also of ecclesiastical princes. To which I answer, first, that there are no ecclesiastical princes but those that are also civil sovereigns; and their principalities exceed not the compass of their civil sovereignty; without those bounds though they may be received for doctors, they cannot be acknowledged for princes. For if the apostle had meant, we should be subject both to our own princes, and also to the Pope, he had taught us a doctrine, which Christ himself hath told us is impossible, namely, *to serve two masters.* And though the apostle say in another place, (2 *Cor.* 13. 10) *I write these things being absent, lest being present I should use sharpness, according to the power which the Lord hath given me;* it is not, that he challenged a power either to put to death, imprison, banish, whip, or fine any of them, which are punishments; but only to excommunicate, which (without the civil power) is no more but a leaving of their company, and having no more to do with them, than with a heathen man, or a publican; which in many occasions might be a greater pain to the excommunicant, than to the excommunicate.

103. The seventh place is 1 *Cor.* 4. 21. *Shall I come unto you with a rod, or in love, and the spirit of lenity?* But here again, it is not the power of a magistrate to punish offenders, that is meant by a rod; but only the power of excommunication, which is not in its own nature a punishment, but only a denouncing of punishment, that Christ shall inflict, when he shall be in possession of his kingdom, at the day of judgment. Nor then also shall it be properly a punishment, as upon a subject that hath broken the law; but a revenge, as upon an enemy, or revolter, that denieth the right of our Saviour to the kingdom. And therefore this proveth not the legislative power of any bishop, that has not also the civil power.

[309]   104. The eighth place is 1 *Timothy* 3. 2. *A bishop must be the husband of but one wife, vigilant, sober, &c.* which he saith was a law. I thought that none could make a law in the Church, but the monarch of the Church, St. Peter. But suppose this precept made by the authority of St. Peter; yet I see no reason why to call it a law, rather than an advice, seeing Timothy was not a subject, but a disciple of St. Paul; nor the flock under the charge of Timothy, his subjects in the kingdom, but his scholars in the school of Christ: if all the precepts he giveth Timothy, be laws, why is not this also a law, (1 *Tim.* 5. 23) *Drink no longer water, but use a little wine for thy health's*

sake. And why are not also the precepts of good physicians, so many laws? But that it is not the imperative manner of speaking, but an absolute subjection to a person, that maketh his precepts laws?

105. In like manner, the ninth place, 1 *Tim.* 5. 19. *Against an elder receive not an accusation, but before two or three witnesses,* is a wise precept, but not a law.

106. The tenth place is *Luke* 10. 16. *He that heareth you, heareth me; and he that despiseth you, despiseth me.* And there is no doubt, but he that despiseth the counsel of those that are sent by Christ, despiseth the counsel of Christ himself. But who are those now that are sent by Christ, but such as are ordained pastors by lawful authority? And who are lawfully ordained, that are not ordained by the sovereign pastor? And who is ordained by the sovereign pastor in a Christian commonwealth, that is not ordained by the authority of the sovereign thereof? Out of this place therefore it followeth, that he which heareth his sovereign being a Christian, heareth Christ; and he that despiseth the doctrine which his king being a Christian, authorizeth, despiseth the doctrine of Christ (which is not that which Bellarmine intendeth here to prove, but the contrary). But all this is nothing to a law. Nay more, a Christian king, as a pastor, and teacher of his subjects, makes not thereby his doctrines laws. He cannot oblige men to believe; though as a civil sovereign he may make laws suitable to his doctrine, which may oblige men to certain actions, and sometimes to such as they would not otherwise do, and which he ought not to command; and yet when they are commanded, they are laws; and the external actions done in obedience to them, without the inward approbation, are the actions of the sovereign, and not of the subject, which is in that case but as an instrument, without any motion of his own at all; because God hath commanded to obey them.

107. The eleventh, is every place, where the apostle for counsel, putteth some word, by which men use to signify command; or calleth the following of his counsel by the name of obedience. And therefore they are alleged out of 1 *Cor.* 11. 2, *I commend you for keeping my precepts as I delivered them to you.* The Greek is, *I commend you for keeping those things I delivered to you, as I delivered them.* Which is far from signifying that they were laws, or any thing [310] else, but good counsel. And that of 1 *Thess.* 4. 2. *You know what commandments we gave you*: where the Greek word is παραγγελίας ἐδώκαμεν, equivalent to παρεδώκαμεν, *what we delivered to you,* as in the place next before alleged, which does not prove the traditions of the apostles, to be any more than counsels; though as is said in the 8th verse, *he that despiseth them, despiseth not man, but God*: for our Saviour himself came not to judge, that is, to be king in this world; but to sacrifice himself for sinners, and leave doctors in his Church, to lead, not to drive men to Christ, who never accepteth forced actions, (which is all the law produceth,) but the inward conversion of the heart; which is not the work of laws, but of counsel, and doctrine.

108.   And that of 2 *Thess*. 3. 14. *If any man obey not our word by this Epistle, note that man, and have no company with him, that he may be ashamed*: where from the word *obey*, he would infer, that this epistle was a law to the Thessalonians. The epistles of the emperors were indeed laws. If therefore the epistle of St. Paul were also a law, they were to obey two masters. But the word *obey*, as it is in the Greek ὑπακούει, signifieth *hearkening to*, or *putting in practice*, not only that which is commanded by him that has right to punish, but also that which is delivered in a way of counsel for our good; and therefore St. Paul does not bid kill him that disobeys; nor beat, nor imprison, nor amerce [fine] him, which legislators may all do; but avoid his company, that he may be ashamed: whereby it is evident, it was not the empire of an apostle, but his reputation amongst the faithful, which the Christians stood in awe of.

109.   The last place is that of *Heb*. 13. 17. *Obey your leaders, and submit yourselves to them, for they watch for your souls, as they that must give account*: and here also is intended by obedience, a following of their counsel: for the reason of our obedience, is not drawn from the will and command of our pastors, but from our own benefit, as being the salvation of our souls they watch for, and not for the exaltation of their own power, and authority. If it were meant here, that all they teach were laws, then not only the Pope, but every pastor in his parish should have legislative power. Again, they that are bound to obey, their pastors, have no power to examine their commands. What then shall we say to St. John, who bids us (1 *John* 4. 1) *Not to believe every spirit, but to try the spirits whether they are of God, because many false prophets are gone out into the world*? It is therefore manifest, that we may dispute the doctrine of our pastors; but no man can dispute a law. The commands of civil sovereigns are on all sides granted to be laws: if any else can make a law besides himself, all commonwealth, and consequently all peace and justice

must cease; which is contrary to all laws, both divine and human. Nothing therefore can be drawn from these, or any other places of Scripture, to prove the decrees of the Pope, where he has not also the civil sovereignty, to be laws.

110. The last point he would prove, is this, *That our Saviour Christ has committed ecclesiastical jurisdiction immediately to none but the Pope.* Wherein he handleth not the question of supremacy between the Pope and Christian kings, but between the Pope and other bishops. And first, he says it is agreed, that the jurisdiction of bishops, is at least in the general *de jure divino*, that is, in the right of God; for which he alleges St. Paul, *Eph.* 4. 11, where he says, that Christ after his ascension into heaven, *gave gifts to men, some apostles, some prophets, and some evangelists, and some pastors, and some teachers.* And thence infers, they have indeed their jurisdiction in God's right; but will not grant they have it immediately from God, but derived through the Pope. But if a man may be said to have his jurisdiction *de jure divino*, and yet not immediately; what lawful jurisdiction, though but civil, is there in a Christian commonwealth, that is not also *de juro divino*? For Christian kings have their civil power from God immediately; and the magistrates under him exercise their several charges in virtue of his commission; wherein that which they do, is no less *de jure divino mediato*, than that which the bishops do, in virtue of the Pope's ordination. All lawful power is of God, immediately in the Supreme Governor, and mediately in those that have authority under him: so that either he must grant every constable in the state, to hold his office in the right of God; or he must not hold that any bishop holds his so, besides the Pope himself.

111. But this whole dispute, whether Christ left the jurisdiction to the Pope only, or to other bishops also, if considered out of those places where the Pope has the civil sovereignty, is a contention *de lana caprina*:* for none of them (where they are not sovereigns) has any jurisdiction at all. For jurisdiction is the power of hearing and determining causes between man and man; and can belong to none, but him that hath the power to prescribe the rules of right and wrong; that is, to make laws; and with the sword of justice to compel men to obey his decisions, pronounced either by himself, or by the judges he ordaineth thereunto; which none can lawfully do but the civil sovereign.

112. Therefore when he allegeth out of chapter 6 of *Luke*, that

our Saviour called his disciples together, and chose twelve of them which he named apostles, he proveth that he elected them (all, except Matthias, Paul and Barnabas,) and gave them power and command to preach, but not to judge of causes between man and man: for that is a power which he refused to take upon himself, saying, *Who made me a judge, or a divider, amongst you?* and in another place, *My kingdom is not of this world.* But he that hath not the power to hear, and determine causes between man and man, cannot be said to have any jurisdiction at all. And yet this hinders not, but that our Saviour gave them power to preach and baptize in all parts of the world, supposing they were not by their own lawful sovereign forbidden: for to our own sovereigns Christ himself, and [312] his apostles, have in sundry places expressly commanded us in all things to be obedient.

113. The arguments by which he would prove, that bishops receive their jurisdiction from the Pope (seeing the Pope in the dominions of other princes hath no jurisdiction himself,) are all in vain. Yet because they prove, on the contrary, that all bishops receive jurisdiction when they have it from their civil sovereigns, I will not omit the recital of them.

114. The first is from chapter 11 of *Numbers*, where Moses not being able alone to undergo the whole burthen of administering the affairs of the people of Israel, God commanded him to choose seventy elders, and took part of the spirit of Moses, to put it upon those seventy elders: by which is understood, not that God weakened the spirit of Moses, for that had not eased him at all; but that they had all of them their authority from him; wherein he doth truly, and ingenuously interpret that place. But seeing Moses had the entire sovereignty in the commonwealth of the Jews, it is manifest, that it is thereby signified, that they had their authority from the civil sovereign: and therefore that place proveth, that bishops in every Christian commonwealth have their authority from the civil sovereign; and from the Pope in his own territories only, and not in the territories of any other state.

115. The second argument, is from the nature of monarchy; wherein all authority is in one man, and in others by derivation from him: but the government of the Church, he says, is monarchical. This also makes for Christian monarchs. For they are really monarchs of their own people; that is, of their own Church (for the Church is the same thing with a Christian people;) whereas the

power of the Pope, though he were St. Peter, is neither monarchy, nor hath any thing of *archical*, nor *cratical*, but only of *didactical*;* for God accepteth not a forced, but a willing obedience.

116. The third, is, from that the *see* of St. Peter is called by St. Cyprian, the *head*, the *source*, the *root*, the *sun*, from whence the authority of bishops is derived. But by the law of nature (which is a better principle of right and wrong, than the word of any doctor that is but a man) the civil sovereign in every commonwealth, is the *head*, the *source*, the *root*, and the *sun*, from which all jurisdiction is derived. And therefore the jurisdiction of bishops, is derived from the civil sovereign.

117. The fourth, is taken from the inequality of their jurisdictions: for if God (saith he) had given it them immediately, he had given as well equality of jurisdiction, as of order: but we see, some are bishops but of one town, some of a hundred towns, and some of many whole provinces; which differences were not determined by the command of God; their jurisdiction therefore is not of God, but of man; and one has a greater, another a less, as it pleaseth the Prince of the Church. Which argument, if he had proved before, that the Pope had an universal jurisdiction over all Christians, had been for his purpose. But seeing that hath not been proved, and that it is [313] notoriously known, the large jurisdiction of the Pope was given him by those that had it, that is, by the Emperors of Rome, (for the Patriarch of Constantinople, upon the same title, namely, of being bishop of the capital city of the empire, and seat of the emperor, claimed to be equal to him,) it followeth, that all other bishops have their jurisdiction from the sovereigns of the place wherein they exercise the same: and as for that cause they have not their authority *de jure divino*; so neither hath the Pope his *de jure divino*, except only where he is also the civil sovereign.

118. His fifth argument is this, *if bishops have their jurisdiction immediately from God, the Pope could not take it from them, for he can do nothing contrary to God's ordination*; and this consequence is good, and well proved. *But* (saith he) *the Pope can do this, and has done it.* This also is granted, so he do it in his own dominions, or in the dominions of any other prince that hath given him that power; but not universally, in right of the Popedom: for that power belongeth to every Christian sovereign, within the bounds of his own empire, and is inseparable from the sovereignty. Before the people of Israel had (by the commandment of God to Samuel) set over themselves a

king, after the manner of other nations, the high-priest had the civil government; and none but he could make, nor depose an inferior priest: but that power was afterwards in the king, as may be proved by this same argument of Bellarmine; for if the priest (be he the high-priest or any other) had his jurisdiction immediately from God, then the king could not take it from him; *for he could do nothing contrary to God's ordinance.* But it is certain that king Solomon (1 *Kings* 2. 26, 27) deprived Abiathar the high-priest of his office, and placed Zadok (verse 35) in his room. Kings therefore may in like manner ordain, and deprive bishops, as they shall think fit, for the well-governing of their subjects.

119. His sixth argument is this, if bishops have their jurisdiction *de jure divino* (that is, *immediately from God,*) they that maintain it, should bring some word of God to prove it: but they can bring none. The argument is good; I have therefore nothing to say against it. But it is an argument no less good, to prove the Pope himself to have no jurisdiction in the dominion of any other prince.

120. Lastly, he bringeth for argument, the testimony of two popes, Innocent and Leo; and I doubt not he might have alleged, with as good reason, the testimonies of all the popes almost since St. Peter: for considering the love of power naturally implanted in mankind, whosoever were made Pope, he would be tempted to uphold the same opinion. Nevertheless, they should therein but do, as Innocent, and Leo did, bear witness of themselves, and therefore their witness should not be good.

[314]
Of the Pope's temporal power.

121. In the fifth book he hath four conclusions. The first is, *that the Pope is not lord of all the world*: the second, *that the Pope is not the lord of all the Christian world*: the third, *that the Pope (without his own territory) has not any temporal jurisdiction* DIRECTLY. These three conclusions are easily granted. The fourth is, *that the Pope has (in the dominions of other princes) the supreme temporal power* INDIRECTLY: which is denied; unless he mean by *indirectly*, that he has gotten it by indirect means, then is that also granted. But I understand, that when he saith: he hath it *indirectly*, he means, that such temporal jurisdiction belongeth to him of right, but that this right is but a consequence of his pastoral authority, the which he could not exercise, unless he have the other with it: and therefore to the pastoral power (which he calls spiritual) the supreme power civil is necessarily annexed; and that thereby he hath a right to change kingdoms,

giving them to one, and taking them from another, when he shall think it conduces to the salvation of souls.

122. Before I come to consider the arguments by which he would prove this doctrine, it will not be amiss to lay open the consequences of it; that princes, and states, that have the civil sovereignty in their several commonwealths, may bethink themselves, whether it be convenient for them, and conducing to the good of their subjects, of whom they are to give an account at the day of judgment, to admit the same.

123. When it is said, the Pope hath not (in the territories of other states) the supreme civil power *directly*; we are to understand, he doth not challenge it, as other civil sovereigns do, from the original submission thereto of those that are to be governed. For it is evident, and has already been sufficiently in this treatise demonstrated, that the right of all sovereigns, is derived originally from the consent of every one of those that are to be governed; whether they that choose him, do it for their common defence against an enemy, as when they agree amongst themselves to appoint a man, or an assembly of men to protect them; or whether they do it, to save their lives, by submission to a conquering enemy. The Pope therefore, when he disclaimeth the supreme civil power over other states *directly*, denieth no more, but that his right cometh to him by that way; he ceaseth not for all that, to claim it another way; and that is, (without the consent of them that are to be governed) by a right given him by God, (which he calleth *indirectly*,) in his assumption to the papacy. But by what way soever he pretend, the power is the same; and he may (if it be granted to be his right) depose princes and states, as often as it is for the salvation of souls, that is, as often as he will; for he claimeth also the sole power to judge, whether it be to the salvation of men's souls, or not. And this is the doctrine, not only that Bellarmine here, and many other doctors, teach in their sermons and books, but also that some councils have decreed, and the Popes have accordingly, when the occasion hath served them, put in [315] practice. For the fourth council of Lateran,* held under Pope Innocent the Third, (in the third chapter De *Haereticis*,) hath this canon. *If a king, at the Pope's admonition, do not purge his kingdom of heretics, and being excommunicate for the same, make not satisfaction within a year, his subjects are absolved of their obedience.* And the practice hereof hath been seen on divers occasions; as in the deposing of

Childeric, king of France; in the translation of the Roman empire to Charlemagne; in the oppression of John king of England; in transferring the kingdom of Navarre; and of late years, in the League against Henry the Third of France, and in many more occurrences. I think there be few princes that consider not this as unjust, and inconvenient; but I wish they would all resolve to be kings, or subjects. Men cannot serve two masters: they ought therefore to ease them, either by holding the reins of government wholly in their own hands; or by wholly delivering them into the hands of the Pope; that such men as are willing to be obedient, may be protected in their obedience. For this distinction of temporal and spiritual power is but words. Power is as really divided, and as dangerously to all purposes, by sharing with another *indirect* power, as with a *direct* one. But to come now to his arguments.

124. The first is this, *The civil power is subject to the spiritual: therefore he that hath the supreme power spiritual, hath right to command temporal princes, and dispose of their temporals in order to the spiritual.* As for the distinction of temporal, and spiritual, let us consider in what sense it may be said intelligibly, that the temporal, or civil power is subject to the spiritual. There be but two ways that those words can be made sense. For when we say, one power is subject to another power, the meaning either is, that he which hath the one, is subject to him that hath the other; or that the one power is to the other, as the means to the end. For we cannot understand, that one power hath power over another power; or that one power can have right or command over another. For subjection, command, right, and power, are accidents, not of powers, but of persons: one power may be subordinate to another, as the art of a saddler, to the art of a rider. If then it be granted, that the civil government be ordained as a means to bring us to a spiritual felicity; yet it does not follow, that if a king have the civil power, and the Pope the spiritual, that therefore the king is bound to obey the Pope, more than every saddler is bound to obey every rider. Therefore as from subordination of an art, cannot be inferred the subjection of the professor; so from the subordination of a government, cannot be inferred the subjection of the governor. When therefore he saith, the civil power is subject to the spiritual, his meaning is, that the civil sovereign, is subject to the spiritual sovereign. And the argument stands thus, *The civil sovereign is subject to the spiritual; therefore the spiritual prince may command temporal princes.* Where the conclusion is the

same with the antecedent he should have proved. But to prove it, he [316] allegeth first, this reason, *kings and popes, clergy and laity, make but one commonwealth; that is to say, but one Church: and in all bodies the members depend one upon another: but things spiritual depend not of things temporal: therefore temporal depend on spiritual. And therefore are subject to them.* In which argumentation there be two gross errors: one is, that all Christian kings, popes, clergy, and all other Christian men, make but one commonwealth: for it is evident that France is one commonwealth, Spain another, and Venice a third, &c. And these consist of Christians; and therefore also are several bodies of Christians; that is to say, several Churches: and their several sovereigns represent them, whereby they are capable of commanding and obeying, of doing and suffering, as a natural man; which no general or universal Church is, till it have a representant; which it hath not on earth: for if it had, there is no doubt but that all Christendom were one commonwealth, whose sovereign were that representant, both in things spiritual and temporal: and the Pope, to make himself this representant, wanteth three things that our Saviour hath not given him, to *command*, and to *judge*, and to *punish*, otherwise than (by excommunication) to run from those that will not learn of him: for though the Pope were Christ's only vicar, yet he cannot exercise his government, till our Saviour's second coming: and then also it is not the Pope, but St. Peter himself, with the other apostles, that are to be judges of the world.

125. The other error in this his first argument is, that he says, the members of every commonwealth, as of a natural body, depend one of another: it is true, they cohere together; but they depend only on the sovereign, which is the soul of the commonwealth; which failing, the commonwealth is dissolved into a civil war, no one man so much as cohering to another, for want of a common dependence on a known sovereign; just as the members of the natural body dissolve into earth, for want of a soul to hold them together. Therefore there is nothing in this similitude, from whence to infer a dependence of the laity on the clergy, or of the temporal officers on the spiritual; but of both on the civil sovereign; which ought indeed to direct his civil commands to the salvation of souls; but is not therefore subject to any but to God himself. And thus you see the laboured fallacy of the first argument, to deceive such men as distinguish not between the subordination of actions in the way to the end; and the subjection of persons one to another in the administration of the means.

For to every end, the means are determined by nature, or by God himself supernaturally: but the power to make men use the means, is in every nation resigned (by the law of nature, which forbiddeth men to violate their faith given) to the civil sovereign.

[317]   126. His second argument is this, *every commonwealth, (because it is supposed to be perfect and sufficient in itself,) may command any other commonwealth, not subject to it, and force it to change the administration of the government; nay depose the prince, and set another in his room, if it cannot otherwise defend itself against the injuries he goes about to do them: much more may a spiritual commonwealth command a temporal one to change the administration of their government, and may depose princes, and institute others, when they cannot otherwise defend the spiritual good.*

127. That a commonwealth, to defend itself against injuries, may lawfully do all that he hath here said, is very true; and hath already in that which hath gone before been sufficiently demonstrated. And if it were also true, that there is now in this world a spiritual commonwealth, distinct from a civil commonwealth, then might the prince thereof, upon injury done him, or upon want of caution that injury be not done him in time to come, repair, and secure himself by war; which is in sum, deposing, killing, or subduing, or doing any act of hostility. But by the same reason, it would be no less lawful for a civil sovereign, upon the like injuries done, or feared, to make war upon the spiritual sovereign; which I believe is more than Cardinal Bellarmine would have inferred from his own proposition.

128. But spiritual commonwealth there is none in this world: for it is the same thing with the kingdom of Christ; which he himself saith, is not of this world; but shall be in the next world, at the resurrection, when they that have lived justly, and believed that he was the Christ, shall (though they died *natural* bodies) rise *spiritual* bodies; and then it is, that our Saviour shall judge the world, and conquer his adversaries, and make a spiritual commonwealth. In the meantime, seeing there are no men on earth, whose bodies are spiritual; there can be no spiritual commonwealth amongst men that are yet in the flesh; unless we call preachers, that have commission to teach, and prepare men for their reception into the kingdom of Christ at the resurrection, a commonwealth; which I have proved already to be none.

129. The third argument is this; *it is not lawful for Christians to tolerate an infidel, or heretical king, in case he endeavour to draw them*

to his heresy, or infidelity. But to judge whether a king draw his subjects
to heresy, or not, belongeth to the Pope. Therefore hath the Pope
right, to determine whether the prince be to be deposed, or not deposed.

130. To this I answer, that both these assertions are false. For
Christians, (or men of what religion soever,) if they tolerate not their
king, whatsoever law he maketh, though it be concerning religion,
do violate their faith, contrary to the divine law, both *natural* and
positive: nor is there any judge of heresy amongst subjects, but their
own civil sovereign: *for heresy is nothing else, but a private opinion,* [318]
obstinately maintained, contrary to the opinion which the public person
(that is to say, the representant of the commonwealth) *hath com-*
manded to be taught. By which it is manifest, that an opinion publicly
appointed to be taught, cannot be heresy; nor the sovereign princes
that authorize them, heretics. For heretics are none but private men,
that stubbornly defend some doctrine, prohibited by their lawful
sovereigns.

131. But to prove that Christians are not to tolerate infidel, or
heretical kings, he allegeth a place in *Deut.* 17 where God forbiddeth
the Jews, when they shall set a king over themselves, to choose a
stranger: and from thence inferreth, that it is unlawful for a Christian, to choose a king that is not a Christian. And 'tis true, that he
that is a Christian, that is, he that hath already obliged himself to
receive our Saviour when he shall come, for his king, shall tempt
God too much in choosing for king in this world, one that he
knoweth will endeavour, both by terror, and persuasion to make him
violate his faith. But it is (saith he) the same danger, to choose one
that is not a Christian, for king, and not to depose him, when he is
chosen. To this I say, the question is not of the danger of not
deposing; but of the justice of deposing him. To choose him, may in
some cases be unjust; but to depose him, when he is chosen, is in no
case just. For it is always a violation of faith, and consequently
against the law of nature, which is the eternal law of God. Nor do we
read, that any such doctrine was accounted Christian in the time of
the apostles; nor in the time of the Roman emperors, till the Popes
had the civil sovereignty of Rome. But to this he hath replied, that
the Christians of old, deposed not Nero, nor Diocletian, nor Julian,
nor Valens an Arian,* for this cause only, that they wanted temporal
forces. Perhaps so. But did our Saviour, who for calling for, might
have had twelve legions of immortal, invulnerable angels to assist
him, want forces to depose Caesar, or at least Pilate, that unjustly,

without finding fault in him, delivered him to the Jews to be crucified? Or if the apostles wanted temporal forces to depose Nero, was
it therefore necessary for them in their epistles to the new made
Christians, to teach them (as they did) to obey the powers constituted over them, (whereof Nero in that time was one,) and that they
ought to obey them, not for fear of their wrath, but for conscience
sake? Shall we say they did not only obey, but also teach what they
meant not, for want of strength? It is not therefore for want of
strength, but for conscience sake, that Christians are to tolerate their
heathen princes, or princes (for I cannot call any one whose doctrine
is the public doctrine, an heretic) that authorize the teaching of an
error. And whereas for the temporal power of the Pope, he allegeth
further, that St. Paul (1 *Cor.* 6) appointed judges under the heathen
princes of those times, such as were not ordained by those princes;
it is not true. For St. Paul does but advise them, to take some of their
[319] brethren to compound their differences, as arbitrators, rather than
to go to law one with another before the heathen judges; which is a
wholesome precept, and full of charity, fit to be practised also in the
best Christian commonwealths. And for the danger that may arise to
religion, by the subjects tolerating of a heathen, or an erring prince,
it is a point, of which a subject is no competent judge; or if he be, the
Pope's temporal subjects may judge also of the Pope's doctrine. For
every Christian prince, as I have formerly proved, is no less supreme
pastor of his own subjects, than the Pope of his.

132. The fourth argument, is taken from the baptism of kings;
wherein, that they may be made Christians they submit their scep-
tres to Christ; and promise to keep, and defend the Christian faith.
This is true; for Christian kings are no more but Christ's subjects:
but they may, for all that, be the Pope's fellows; for they are supreme
pastors of their own subjects; and the Pope is no more but king, and
pastor, even in Rome itself.

133. The fifth argument, is drawn from the words spoken by our
Saviour, *Feed my sheep*; by which was given all power necessary for
a pastor; as the power to chase away wolves, such as are heretics; the
power to shut up rams, if they be mad, or push at the other sheep
with their horns, such as are evil (though Christian) kings; and
power to give the flock convenient food: from whence he inferreth,
that St. Peter had these three powers given him by Christ. To which
I answer, that the last of these powers, is no more than the power, or
rather command to teach. For the first, which is to chase away

wolves, that is, heretics, the place he quoteth is (*Matt.* 7. 15) *Beware
of false prophets which come to you in sheep's clothing, but inwardly are
ravening wolves*. But neither are heretics false prophets, or at all
prophets: nor (admitting heretics for the wolves there meant,) were
the apostles commanded to kill them, or if they were kings, to
depose them; but to beware of, fly, and avoid them: nor was it to St.
Peter, nor to any of the apostles, but to the multitude of the Jews
that followed him into the mountain, men for the most part not yet
converted, that he gave this counsel, to beware of false prophets:
which therefore, if it confer a power of chasing away kings, was
given, not only to private men; but to men that were not at all
Christians. And as to the power of separating, and shutting up of
furious rams, (by which he meaneth Christian kings that refuse to
submit themselves to the Roman pastor,) our Saviour refused to
take upon him that power in this world himself, but advised to let
the corn and tares grow up together till the day of judgment: much
less did he give it to St. Peter, or can St. Peter give it to the Popes.
St. Peter, and all other pastors, are bidden to esteem those Christians that disobey the Church, that is, (that disobey the Christian
sovereign) as heathen men, and as publicans. Seeing then men [320]
challenge to the Pope no authority over heathen princes, they ought
to challenge none over those that are to be esteemed as heathen.

134. But from the power to teach only, he inferreth also a coercive power in the Pope, over kings. The pastor (saith he) must give
his flock convenient food: therefore the Pope may, and ought to
compel kings to do their duty. Out of which it followeth, that the
Pope, as pastor of Christian men, is king of kings: which all Christian kings ought indeed either to confess, or else they ought to take
upon themselves the supreme pastoral charge, every one in his own
dominion.

135. His sixth, and last argument, is from examples. To which I
answer, first, that examples prove nothing: secondly, that the examples he allegeth make not so much as a probability of right. The fact
of Jehoiada, in killing Athaliah, (2 *Kings* 11) was either by the
authority of king Joash, or it was a horrible crime in the high-priest,
which (ever after the election of king Saul) was a mere subject. The
fact of St. Ambrose, in excommunicating Theodosius the emperor,
(if it were true he did so,) was a capital crime. And for the Popes,
Gregory I, Gregory II, Zachary, and Leo III, their judgments are
void, as given in their own cause; and the acts done by them con-

formably to this doctrine, are the greatest crimes (especially that of Zachary) that are incident to human nature. And thus much of *Power Ecclesiastical*; wherein I had been more brief, forbearing to examine these arguments of Bellarmine, if they had been his, as a private man, and not as the champion of the Papacy against all other Christian Princes, and States.

[321]

CHAPTER XLIII

OF WHAT IS NECESSARY FOR A MAN'S RECEPTION INTO THE KINGDOM OF HEAVEN

The difficulty of obeying God and man both at once;

1. THE most frequent pretext of sedition, and civil war, in Christian commonwealths hath a long time proceeded from a difficulty, not yet sufficiently resolved, of obeying at once, both God and man, then when their commandments are one contrary to the other. It is manifest enough, that when a man receiveth two contrary commands, and knows that one of them is God's, he ought to obey that, and not the other, though it be the command even of his lawful sovereign (whether a monarch, or a sovereign assembly,) or the command of his father. The difficulty therefore consisteth in this, that men when they are commanded in the name of God, know not in divers cases, whether the command be from God, or whether he that commandeth, do but abuse God's name for some private ends of his own. For as there were in the Church of the Jews, many false prophets, that sought reputation with the people, by feigned dreams and visions; so there have been in all times in the Church of Christ, false teachers, that seek reputation with the people, by fantastical and false doctrines; and by such reputation (as is the nature of ambition,) to govern them for their private benefit.

Is none to them that distinguish between what is, and what is not necessary to salvation.

2. But this difficulty of obeying both God, and the civil sovereign on earth, to those that can distinguish between what is *necessary*, and what is not *necessary for their reception into the kingdom of God*, is of no moment. For if the command of the civil sovereign be such, as that it may be obeyed, without the forfeiture of life eternal; not to obey it is unjust; and the precept of the apostle takes place; *Servants obey your masters in all things*; and, *Children obey your parents in all things*; and the precept of our Saviour, *The Scribes and Pharisees sit in Moses' chair, all therefore they shall say, that observe, and do*. But if the

390

command be such, as cannot be obeyed, without being damned to eternal death, then it were madness to obey it, and the council of our Saviour takes place, (*Matt.* 10. 28) *Fear not those that kill the body, but cannot kill the soul.* All men therefore that would avoid, both the punishments that are to be in this world inflicted, for disobedience to their earthly sovereign, and those that shall be inflicted in the world to come for disobedience to God, have need be taught to distinguish well between what is, and what is not necessary to eternal salvation.

3. All that is NECESSARY *to salvation*, is contained in two virtues, *faith in Christ*, and *obedience to laws*. The latter of these, if it were perfect, were enough to us. But because we are all guilty of disobedience to God's law, not only originally in Adam, but also actually by our own transgressions, there is required at our hands now, not only *obedience* for the rest of our time, but also a *remission of sins* for the time past; which remission is the reward of our faith in Christ. That nothing else is necessarily required to salvation, is manifest from this, that the kingdom of heaven is shut to none but to sinners; that is to say, to the disobedient, or transgressors of the law; nor to them, in case they repent, and believe all the articles of Christian faith, necessary to salvation.

[322]
All that is necessary to salvation is contained in faith and obedience.

4. The obedience required at our hands by God, that accepteth in all our actions the will for the deed, is a serious endeavour to obey him; and is called also by all such names as signify that endeavour. And therefore obedience, is sometimes called by the names of *charity*, and *love*, because they imply a will to obey; and our Saviour himself maketh our love to God, and to one another, a fulfilling of the whole law: and sometimes by the name of *righteousness*; for righteousness is but the will to give to every one his own; that is to say, the will to obey the laws: and sometimes by the name of *repentance*; because to repent, implieth a turning away from sin, which is the same with the return of the will to obedience. Whosoever therefore unfeignedly desireth to fulfil the commandments of God, or repenteth him truly of his transgressions, or that loveth God with all his heart, and his neighbour as himself, hath all the obedience necessary to his reception into the kingdom of God: for if God should require perfect innocence, there could no flesh be saved.

What obedience is necessary;

5. But what commandments are those that God hath given us? Are all those laws which were given to the Jews by the hand of Moses, the commandments of God? If they be, why are not Chris-

And to what laws.

tians taught to obey them? If they be not, what others are so, besides the law of nature? For our Saviour Christ hath not given us new laws, but counsel to observe those we are subject to; that is to say, the laws of nature, and the laws of our several sovereigns: nor did he make any new law to the Jews in his sermon on the Mount, but only expounded the law of Moses, to which they were subject before. The laws of God therefore are none but the laws of nature, whereof the principal is, that we should not violate our faith, that is, a commandment to obey our civil sovereigns, which we constituted over us, by mutual pact one with another. And this law of God, that commandeth obedience to the law civil, commandeth by consequence obedience to all the precepts of the Bible; which (as I have proved in the precedent chapter) is there only law, where the civil sovereign hath made it so; and in other places, but counsel; which a man at his own peril may without injustice refuse to obey.

[323]

In the faith of a Christian, who is the person believed.

6. Knowing now what is the obedience necessary to salvation, and to whom it is due; we are to consider next concerning faith, whom, and why we believe; and what are the articles, or points necessary to be believed by them that shall be saved. And first, for the person whom we believe, because it is impossible to believe any person, before we know what he saith, it is necessary he be one that we have heard speak. The person therefore, whom Abraham, Isaac, Jacob, Moses, and the prophets, believed, was God himself, that spake unto them supernaturally: and the person, whom the apostles and disciples that conversed with Christ believed, was our Saviour himself. But of them, to whom neither God the Father, nor our Saviour ever spake, it cannot be said, that the person whom they believed, was God. They believed the apostles, and after them the pastors and doctors of the Church, that recommended to their faith the history of the Old and New Testament: so that the faith of Christians ever since our Saviour's time, hath had for foundation, first, the reputation of their pastors, and afterward, the authority of those that made the Old and New Testament to be received for the rule of faith; which none could do but Christian sovereigns; who are therefore the supreme pastors, and the only persons, whom Christians now hear speak from God; except such as God speaketh to, in these days supernaturally. But because there be many false prophets *gone out into the world*, men are to examine such spirits (as St. John adviseth us, 1 *John* 4. 1) *whether they be of God, or not.* And therefore, seeing the examination of doctrines belongeth to the supreme pas-

tor, the person which all they that have no special revelation are to believe, is (in every commonwealth) the supreme pastor, that is to say, the civil sovereign.

7. The causes why men believe any Christian doctrine, are various: for faith is the gift of God; and he worketh it in each several man, by such ways, as it seemeth good unto himself. The most ordinary immediate cause of our belief, concerning any point of Christian faith, is, that we believe the Bible to be the word of God. But why we believe the Bible to be the word of God, is much disputed, as all questions must needs be, that are not well stated. For they make not the question to be, *why we believe it*, but, *how we know it*; as if *believing* and *knowing* were all one. And thence while one side ground their knowledge upon the infallibility of the Church, and the other side, on the testimony of the private spirit, neither side concludeth what it pretends. For how shall a man know the infallibility of the Church, but by knowing first the infallibility of the Scripture? Or how shall a man know his own private spirit to be other than a belief, grounded upon the authority, and arguments of his teachers; or upon a presumption of his own gifts? Besides, there is nothing in the Scripture, from which can be inferred the infallibility of the Church; much less, of any particular Church; and least of all, the infallibility of any particular man.

8. It is manifest therefore, that Christian men do not know, but only believe the Scripture to be the word of God; and that the means of making them believe which God is pleased to afford men ordinarily, is according to the way of nature, that is to say, from their teachers. It is the doctrine of St. Paul concerning Christian faith in general (*Rom.* 10. 17), *faith cometh by hearing*, that is, by hearing our lawful pastors. He saith also, (verses 14, 15, of the same chapter) *how shall they believe in him of whom they have not heard? and how shall they hear without a preacher? and how shall they preach, except they be sent?* Whereby it is evident, that the ordinary cause of believing that the Scriptures are the word of God, is the same with the cause of the believing of all other articles of our faith, namely, the hearing of those that are by the law allowed and appointed to teach us, as our parents in their houses, and our pastors in the churches: which also is made more manifest by experience. For what other cause can there be assigned, why in Christian commonwealths all men either believe, or at least profess the Scripture to be the word of God, and in other commonwealths scarce any; but that in Christian common-

The causes of Christian faith.

[324]
Faith comes by hearing.

wealths they are taught it from their infancy; and in other places they are taught otherwise?

9. But if teaching be the cause of faith, why do not all believe? It is certain therefore that faith is the gift of God, and he giveth it to whom he will. Nevertheless, because to them to whom he giveth it, he giveth it by the means of teachers, the immediate cause of faith is hearing. In a school, where many are taught, and some profit, others profit not, the cause of learning in them that profit, is the master; yet it cannot be thence inferred, that learning is not the gift of God. All good things proceed from God; yet cannot all that have them, say they are inspired; for that implies a gift supernatural, and the immediate hand of God; which he that pretends to, pretends to be a prophet, and is subject to the examination of the Church.

10. But whether men *know*, or *believe*, or *grant* the Scriptures to be the word of God; if out of such places of them, as are without obscurity, I shall show what articles of faith are necessary, and only necessary for salvation, those men must needs *know*, *believe*, or *grant* the same.

The only necessary article of Christian faith;

11. The (*unum necessarium*) only article of faith, which the Scripture maketh simply necessary to salvation, is this, that JESUS IS THE CHRIST. By the name of *Christ*, is understood the king, which God had before promised by the prophets of the Old Testament, to send into the world, to reign (over the Jews, and over such of other nations as should believe in him) under himself eternally; and to give them that eternal life, which was lost by the sin of Adam. Which when I have proved out of Scripture, I will further show when, and in what sense some other articles may be also called *necessary*.

[325]

Proved from the scope of the Evangelists:

12. For proof that the belief of this article, *Jesus is the Christ*, is all the faith required to salvation, my first argument shall be from the scope of the Evangelists; which was by the description of the life of our Saviour, to establish that one article, *Jesus is the Christ*. The sum of St. Matthew's Gospel is this, that Jesus was of the stock of David; born of a Virgin; which are the marks of the true Christ: that the Magi came to worship him as King of the Jews: that Herod for the same cause sought to kill him: that John the Baptist proclaimed him: that he preached by himself, and his apostles that he was that king: that he taught the law, not as a scribe, but as a man of authority: that he cured diseases by his word only, and did many other miracles, which were foretold the Christ should do: that he was saluted king

when he entered into Jerusalem: that he forewarned them to beware of all others that should pretend to be Christ: that he was taken, accused, and put to death, for saying he was king: that the cause of his condemnation written on the cross was, JESUS OF NAZARETH, THE KING OF THE JEWS. All which tend to no other end than this, that men should believe, that *Jesus is the Christ.* Such therefore was the scope of St. Matthew's Gospel. But the scope of all the evangelists (as may appear by reading them) was the same. Therefore the scope of the whole Gospel, was the establishing of that only article. And St. John expressly makes it his conclusion (*John* 20. 31), *These things are written, that you may know that Jesus is the Christ, the Son of the living God.*

13. My second argument is taken from the subjects of the ser- *From the* mons of the apostles, both whilst our Saviour lived on earth, and *sermons of* after his ascension. The apostles in our Saviour's time, were sent, *the apostles:* (*Luke* 9. 2) *to preach the kingdom of God*: for neither there, nor *Matt.* 10. 7 giveth he any commission to them, other than this, *As ye go, preach, saying, the kingdom of heaven is at hand*; that is, that Jesus is the *Messiah*, the *Christ*, the *King* which was to come. That their preaching also after his ascension was the same, is manifest out of *Acts* 17. 6, 7, *They drew* (*saith* St. Luke) *Jason and certain brethren unto the rulers of the city, crying, these that have turned the world upside down are come hither also, whom Jason hath received. And these all do contrary to the decrees of Caesar, saying, that there is another king, one Jesus.* And out of the 2nd and 3rd verses of the same chapter, where it is said, that St. Paul, *as his manner was, went in unto them; and three sabbath days reasoned with them out of the Scriptures; opening and alleging, that Christ must needs have suffered, and risen again from the dead, and that this Jesus (whom he preached) is Christ.*

14. The third argument is from those places of Scripture, by *From the* which all the faith required to salvation is declared to be easy. For if *easiness of the* an inward assent of the mind to all the doctrines concerning Chris- *doctrine:* tian faith now taught, (whereof the greatest part are disputed,) were necessary to salvation, there would be nothing in the world so hard, as to be a Christian. The thief upon the cross though repenting, could not have been saved for saying, *Lord remember me when thou* [326] *comest into thy kingdom*; by which he testified no belief of any other article, but this, that *Jesus was the king.* Nor could it be said (as it is, *Matt.* 11. 30) that *Christ's yoke is easy, and his burthen light*: nor that *little children believe in him*, as it is *Matt.* 18. 6. Nor could St. Paul

have said (1 *Cor.* 1. 21) *It pleased God by the foolishness of preaching, to save them that believe.* Nor could St. Paul himself have been saved, much less have been so great a doctor of the Church so suddenly, that never perhaps thought of transubstantiation, nor purgatory, nor many other articles now obtruded.

From formal and clear texts.   15. The fourth argument is taken from places express, and such as receive no controversy of interpretation; as first, *John* 5. 39. *Search the Scriptures, for in them ye think ye have eternal life; and they are they that testify of me.* Our Saviour here speaketh of the Scriptures only of the Old Testament; for the Jews at that time could not search the Scriptures of the New Testament, which were not written. But the Old Testament hath nothing of Christ, but the marks by which men might know him when he came; as that he should descend from David; be born at Bethlehem, and of a Virgin; do great miracles, and the like. Therefore to believe that this Jesus was He, was sufficient to eternal life: but more than sufficient is not necessary; and consequently no other article is required. Again, (*John* 11. 26) *Whosoever liveth and believeth in me, shall not die eternally.* Therefore to believe in Christ, is faith sufficient to eternal life; and consequently no more faith than that is necessary, but to believe in Jesus, and to believe that Jesus is the Christ, is all one, as appeareth in the verses immediately following. For when our Saviour (verse 26) had said to Martha, *Believest thou this?* she answereth (verse 27) *Yea, Lord, I believe that thou art the Christ, the Son of God, which should come into the world*: therefore this article alone is faith sufficient to life eternal; and more than sufficient is not necessary. Thirdly, *John* 20. 31. *These things are written that ye might believe, that Jesus is the Christ, the Son of God, and that believing ye might have life through his name.* There, to believe that *Jesus is the Christ*, is faith sufficient to the obtaining of life; and therefore no other article is necessary. Fourthly, 1 *John* 4. 2: *Every spirit that confesseth that Jesus Christ is come in the flesh, is of God.* And 1 *John* 5. 1. *Whosoever believeth that Jesus is the Christ, is born of God.* And verse 5. *Who is he that overcometh the world, but he that believeth that Jesus is the Son of God?* Fifthly, *Acts* 8. 36, 37. *See*, saith the Eunuch, *here is water, what doth hinder me to be baptized? And Philip said, if thou believest with all thy heart, thou mayst. And he answered and said, I believe that Jesus Christ is the Son of God.* Therefore this article believed, *Jesus is the Christ*, is sufficient to baptism, that is to say, to our reception into the kingdom of God, and by consequence, only necessary. And generally in all places where our Saviour saith to any man, *Thy faith hath saved thee*, the cause he saith it, is some confession, which directly, or by consequence, implieth a belief, that *Jesus is the Christ*.

16. The last argument is from the places, where this article is made the foundation of faith: for he that holdeth the foundation, shall be saved. Which places are first, *Matt*. 24. 23, 24. *If any man shall say unto you, Lo here is Christ, or there, believe it not, for there shall arise false Christs, and false prophets, and shall shew great signs and wonders, &c.* Here we see, this article *Jesus is the Christ*, must be held, though he that shall teach the contrary should do great miracles. The second place is, *Gal*. 1. 8. *Though we, or an angel from heaven preach any other gospel unto you, than that we have preached unto you, let him be accursed.* But the gospel which Paul, and the other apostles, preached, was only this article, that *Jesus is the Christ*: therefore for the belief of this article, we are to reject the authority of an angel from heaven; much more of any mortal man, if he teach the contrary. This is therefore the fundamental article of Christian faith. A third place is, 1 *John* 4. 1, 2. *Beloved, believe not every spirit. Hereby ye shall know the Spirit of God; every spirit that confesseth that Jesus Christ is come in the flesh, is of God.* By which it is evident, that this article, is the measure, and rule, by which to estimate, and examine all other articles; and is therefore only fundamental. A fourth is, *Matt*. 16. 16, 18, where after St. Peter had professed this article, saying to our Saviour, *Thou art Christ the Son of the living God*, our Saviour answered, *Thou art Peter, and upon this rock I will build my Church*: from whence I infer, that this article is that, on which all other doctrines of the Church are built, as on their foundation. A fifth is (1 *Cor*. 3. 11, 12, &c.) *Other foundation can no man lay, than that which is laid, Jesus is the Christ. Now if any man build upon this foundation, gold, silver, precious stones, wood, hay, stubble; every man's work shall be made manifest; for the day shall declare it, because it shall be revealed by fire, and the fire shall try every man's work, of what sort it is. If any man's work abide, which he hath built thereupon, he shall receive a reward. If any man's work shall be burnt, he shall suffer loss; but he himself shall be saved, yet so as by fire.* Which words, being partly plain and easy to understand, and partly allegorical and difficult; out of that which is plain, may be inferred, that pastors that teach this foundation, that *Jesus is the Christ*, though they draw from it false consequences, (which all men are sometimes

From that it is the foundation of all other articles.

397

subject to,) they may nevertheless be saved; much more that they may be saved, who being no pastors, but hearers, believe that which is by their lawful pastors taught them. Therefore the belief of this article is sufficient; and by consequence, there is no other article of faith necessarily required to salvation.

[328]   17. Now for the part which is allegorical, as *that the fire shall try every man's work*, and that *they shall be saved, but so as by fire*, or *though fire*, (for the original is διὰ πυρὸς,) it maketh nothing against this conclusion which I have drawn from the other words, that are plain. Nevertheless, because upon this place there hath been an argument taken, to prove the fire of purgatory, I will also here offer you my conjecture concerning the meaning of this trial of doctrines, and saving of men as by fire. The apostle here seemeth to allude to the words of the prophet *Zechariah*, (13. 8, 9), who speaking of the restoration of the kingdom of God, saith thus, *Two parts therein shall be cut off, and die, but the third shall be left therein; and I will bring the third part through the fire, and will refine them as silver is refined, and will try them as gold is tried; they shall call on the name of the Lord, and I will hear them.* The day of judgment, is the day of the restoration of the kingdom of God; and at that day it is, that St. Peter tells us (2 *Pet.* 3. 7, 10, 12) shall be the conflagration of the world, wherein the wicked shall perish; but the remnant which God will save, shall pass through that fire, unhurt, and be therein (as silver and gold are refined by the fire from their dross) tried, and refined from their idolatry, and be made to call upon the name of the true God. Alluding whereto St. Paul here saith, that *the day* (that is, the day of judgment, the great day of our Saviour's coming to restore the kingdom of God in Israel) shall try every man's doctrine, by judging, which are gold, silver, precious stones, wood, hay, stubble; and then they that have built false consequences on the true foundation, shall see their doctrines condemned; nevertheless they themselves shall be saved, and pass unhurt through this universal fire, and live eternally, to call upon the name of the true and only God. In which sense there is nothing that accordeth not with the rest of Holy Scripture, or any glimpse of the fire of purgatory.

In what sense other articles may be called necessary.

18. But a man may here ask, whether it be not as necessary to salvation, to believe, that God is omnipotent; Creator of the world; that Jesus Christ is risen; and that all men else shall rise again from the dead at the last day; as to believe, that *Jesus is the Christ*. To which I answer, they are; and so are many more articles: but they are

such, as are contained in this one, and may be deduced from it, with more, or less difficulty. For who is there that does not see, that they who believe Jesus to be the Son of the God of Israel, and that the Israelites had for God the Omnipotent Creator of all things, do therein also believe, that God is the Omnipotent Creator of all things? Or how can a man believe, that Jesus is the king that shall reign eternally, unless he believe him also risen again from the dead? For a dead man cannot exercise the office of a king. In sum, he that holdeth this foundation, *Jesus is the Christ*, holdeth expressly all that he seeth rightly deduced from it, and implicitly all that is conse- [329] quent thereunto, though he have not skill enough to discern the consequence. And therefore it holdeth still good, that the belief of this one article is sufficient faith to obtain remission of sins to the *penitent*, and consequently to bring them into the kingdom of heaven.

19. Now that I have shown, that all the obedience required to salvation, consisteth in the will to obey the law of God, that is to say, in repentance; and all the faith required to the same, is compre- hended in the belief of this article, *Jesus is the Christ*; I will further allege those places of the Gospel, that prove, that all that is necessary to salvation is contained in both these joined together. The men to whom St. Peter preached on the day of Pentecost, next after the ascension of our Saviour, asked him, and the rest of the apostles, saying, (*Acts* 2. 37), *Men and brethren, what shall we do?* To whom St. Peter answered (in the next verse) *Repent, and be baptized every one of you, for the remission of sins, and ye shall receive the gift of the Holy Ghost.* Therefore repentance, and baptism, that is, believing that *Jesus is the Christ*, is all that is necessary to salvation. Again, our Saviour being asked by a certain ruler (*Luke* 18. 18), *What shall I do to inherit eternal life?* answered, (verse 20) *Thou knowest the com- mandments, do not commit adultery, do not kill, do not steal, do not bear false witness, honour thy father and thy mother*: which when he said he had observed, our Saviour added, (verse 22) *Sell all thou hast, give it to the poor, and come and follow me*: which was as much as to say, rely on me that am the king. Therefore to fulfil the law, and to believe that Jesus is the king, is all that is required to bring a man to eternal life. Thirdly, St. Paul saith (*Rom.* 1. 17), *The just shall live by faith*; not every one, but the *just*; therefore *faith* and *justice* (that is, the *will to be just*, or *repentance*) are all that is necessary to life eternal. And (*Mark* 1. 15) our Saviour preached, saying, *The time is fulfilled, and*

That faith and obedience are both of them necessary to salvation.

399

the kingdom of God is at hand, repent and believe the evangel, that is, the good news that the Christ was come. Therefore to repent, and to believe that Jesus is the Christ, is all that is required to salvation.

What each
of them
contributes
thereunto.

20. Seeing then it is necessary that faith, and obedience (implied in the word repentance) do both concur to our salvation; the question by which of the two we are justified, is impertinently disputed. Nevertheless, it will not be impertinent, to make manifest in what manner each of them contributes thereunto; and in what sense it is said, that we are to be justified by the one, and by the other. And first, if by righteousness be understood the justice of the works themselves, there is no man that can be saved; for there is none that hath not transgressed the law of God. And therefore when we are said to be justified by works, it is to be understood of the will, which God doth always accept for the work itself, as well in good, as in evil men. And in this sense only it is, that a man is called *just*, or *unjust*; and that his justice justifies him, that is, gives him the title, in God's acceptation, of *just*; and renders him capable of *living by his faith*, which before he was not. So that justice justifies in that sense, in which to *justify*, is the same as that to *denominate a man just*; and not in the signification of discharging the law; whereby the punishment of his sins should be unjust.

[330]

21. But a man is then also said to be justified, when his plea, though in itself insufficient, is accepted; as when we plead our will, our endeavour to fulfil the law, and repent us of our failings, and God accepteth it for the performance itself: and because God accepteth not the will for the deed, but only in the faithful; it is therefore faith that makes good our plea; and in this sense it is, that faith only justifies. So that *faith* and *obedience* are both necessary to salvation; yet in several senses each of them is said to justify.

Obedience to
God and to
the civil
sovereign not
inconsistent,
whether
Christian,

22.* Having thus shown what is necessary to salvation; it is not hard to reconcile our obedience to God, with our obedience to the civil sovereign; who is either Christian, or infidel. If he be a Christian, he alloweth the belief of this article, that *Jesus is the Christ*; and of all the articles that are contained in, or are by evident consequence deduced from it: which is all the faith necessary to salvation. And because he is a sovereign, he requireth obedience to all his own, that is, to all the civil laws; in which also are contained all the laws of nature, that is, all the laws of God: for besides the laws of nature, and the laws of the Church, which are part of the civil law, (for the Church that can make laws is the commonwealth,) there be no other laws divine. Whosoever therefore obeyeth his Christian sovereign, is not thereby hindered, neither from believing, nor from obeying God. But suppose that a Christian king should from this foundation *Jesus is the Christ*, draw some false consequences, that is to say, make some superstructions of hay, or stubble, and command the teaching of the same; yet seeing St. Paul says, he shall be saved; much more shall he be saved, that teacheth them by his command; and much more yet, he that teaches not, but only believes his lawful teacher. And in case a subject be forbidden by the civil sovereign to profess some of those his opinions, upon what just ground can he disobey? Christian kings may err in deducing a consequence, but who shall judge? Shall a private man judge, when the question is of his own obedience? Or shall any man judge but he that is appointed thereto by the Church, that is, by the civil sovereign that representeth it? Or if the pope, or an apostle judge, may he not err in deducing of a consequence? Did not one of the two, St. Peter, or St. Paul err in a superstructure, when St. Paul withstood St. Peter to his face? There can therefore be no contradiction between the laws of God, and the laws of a Christian commonwealth.

23.* And when the civil sovereign is an infidel, every one of his own subjects that resisteth him, sinneth against the laws of God (for such are the laws of nature,) and rejecteth the counsel of the apostles, that admonisheth all Christians to obey their princes, and all children and servants to obey their parents and masters in all things. And for their *faith*, it is internal, and invisible; they have the licence that Naaman had, and need not put themselves into danger for it. But if they do, they ought to expect their reward in heaven, and not complain of their lawful sovereign; much less make war upon him. For he that is not glad of any just occasion of martyrdom, has not the faith he professeth, but pretends it only, to set some colour upon his own contumacy. But what infidel king is so unreasonable, as knowing he has a subject, that waiteth for the second coming of Christ, after the present world shall be burnt, and intendeth then to obey him (which is the intent of believing that Jesus is the Christ,) and in the meantime thinketh himself bound to obey the laws of that infidel king, (which all Christians are obliged in conscience to do,) to put to death or to persecute such a subject? *Or infidel.*

[331]

24. And thus much shall suffice, concerning the kingdom of God, and policy ecclesiastical. Wherein I pretend not to advance any position of my own, but only to show what are the consequences that *Conclusion.*

seem to me deducible from the principles of Christian politics, (which are the holy Scriptures,) in confirmation of the power of civil sovereigns, and the duty of their subjects. And in the allegation of Scripture, I have endeavoured to avoid such texts as are of obscure, or controverted interpretation; and to allege none, but in such sense as is most plain, and agreeable to the harmony and scope of the whole Bible; which was written for the re-establishment of the kingdom of God in Christ. For it is not the bare words, but the scope of the writer, that giveth the true light, by which any writing is to be interpreted; and they that insist upon single texts, without considering the main design, can derive nothing from them clearly; but rather by casting atoms of Scripture, as dust before men's eyes, make everything more obscure than it is; an ordinary artifice of those that seek not the truth, but their own advantage.

OF THE KINGDOM OF DARKNESS

CHAPTER XLIV

OF SPIRITUAL DARKNESS, FROM MISINTERPRETATION OF SCRIPTURE

1. BESIDES these sovereign powers, *divine*, and *human*, of which I have hitherto discoursed, there is mention in Scripture of another power, namely, (*Eph.* 6. 12) that of *the rulers of the darkness of this world*; (*Matt.* 12. 26) *the kingdom of Satan*; and (*Matt.* 9. 34) *the principality of Beelzebub over demons*, that is to say, over phantasms that appear in the air: for which cause Satan is also called, (*Eph.* 2. 2) *the prince of the power of the air*; and (because he ruleth in the darkness of this world) *the prince of this world* (*John* 16. 11): and in consequence hereunto, they who are under his dominion, in opposition to the faithful (who are the *children of the light*) are called the *children of darkness*. For seeing Beelzebub is prince of phantasms, inhabitants of his dominion of air and darkness, the children of darkness, and these demons, phantasms, or spirits of illusion, signify allegorically the same thing. This considered, the kingdom of darkness, as it is set forth in these, and other places of the Scripture, is nothing else but a *confederacy of deceivers, that to obtain dominion over men in this present world, endeavour by dark, and erroneous doctrines, to extinguish in them the light, both of nature, and of the gospel; and so to disprepare them for the kingdom of God to come.*

The kingdom of Darkness, what.

2. As men that are utterly deprived from their nativity, of the light of the bodily eye, have no idea at all, of any such light; and no man conceives in his imagination any greater light, than he hath at some time, or other, perceived by his outward senses: so also is it of the light of the gospel, and of the light of the understanding, that no man can conceive there is any greater degree of it, than that which he hath already attained unto. And from hence it comes to pass, that men have no other means to acknowledge their own darkness, but only by reasoning from the unforeseen mischances, that befall them

[334]
The Church not yet fully freed of darkness.

in their ways. The darkest part of the kingdom of Satan, is that which is without the Church of God; that is to say, amongst them that believe not in Jesus Christ. But we cannot say, that therefore the Church enjoyeth (as the land of Goshen) all the light, which to the performance of the work enjoined us by God, is necessary. Whence comes it, that in Christendom there has been, almost from the time of the Apostles, such jostling of one another out of their places, both by foreign, and civil war; such stumbling at every little asperity of their own fortune, and every little eminence of that of other men; and such diversity of ways in running to the same mark, *felicity*, if it be not night amongst us, or at least a mist? We are therefore yet in the dark.

Four causes of spiritual darkness.*

3. The enemy has been here in the night of our natural ignorance, and sown the tares of spiritual errors; and that, first, by abusing, and putting out the light of the Scriptures: for we err, not knowing the Scriptures. Secondly, by introducing the demonology of the heathen poets, that is to say, their fabulous doctrine concerning demons, which are but idols, or phantasms of the brain, without any real nature of their own, distinct from human fancy; such as are dead men's ghosts, and fairies, and other matter of old wives' tales. Thirdly, by mixing with the Scripture divers relics of the religion, and much of the vain and erroneous philosophy of the Greeks, especially of Aristotle. Fourthly, by mingling with both these, false, or uncertain traditions, and feigned, or uncertain history. And so we come to err, *by giving heed to seducing spirits*, and the demonology of such *as speak lies in hypocrisy*, (or as it is in the original, (1 *Tim.* 4. 1, 2) *of those that play the part of liars*) *with a seared conscience*, that is, contrary to their own knowledge. Concerning the first of these, which is the seducing of men by abuse of Scripture, I intend to speak briefly in this chapter.

Errors from misinterpreting the Scriptures, concerning the kingdom of God:

4. The greatest and main abuse of Scripture, and to which almost all the rest are either consequent, or subservient, is the wresting of it, to prove that the kingdom of God, mentioned so often in the Scripture, is the present Church, or multitude of Christian men now living, or that being dead, are to rise again at the last day: whereas the kingdom of God was first instituted by the ministry of Moses, over the Jews only; who were therefore called his peculiar people; and ceased afterward, in the election of Saul, when they refused to be [335] governed by God any more, and demanded a king after the manner of the nations; which God himself consented unto, as I have more at

large proved before in the 35th chapter. After that time, there was no other kingdom of God in the world, by any pact, or otherwise, than he ever was, is, and shall be king, of all men, and of all creatures, as governing according to his will, by his infinite power. Nevertheless, he promised by his prophets to restore this his government to them again, when the time he hath in his secret counsel appointed for it shall be fully come, and when they shall turn unto him by repentance, and amendment of life: and not only so, but he invited the Gentiles to come in, and enjoy the happiness of his reign, on the same conditions of conversion and repentance; and he promised also to send his Son into the world, to expiate the sins of them all by his death, and to prepare them by his doctrine, to receive him at his second coming: which second coming not yet being, the kingdom of God is not yet come, and we are not now under any other kings by pact, but our civil sovereigns; saving only, that Christian men are already in the kingdom of grace, in as much as they have already the promise of being received at his coming again.

5. Consequent to this error, that the present Church is Christ's kingdom, there ought to be some one man, or assembly, by whose mouth our Saviour (now in heaven) speaketh, and giveth law, and which representeth his person to all Christians, or divers men, or divers assemblies that do the same to divers parts of Christendom. This power regal under Christ, being challenged, universally by the Pope, and in particular commonwealths by assemblies of the pastors of the place, (when the Scripture gives it to none but to civil sovereigns,) comes to be so passionately disputed, that it putteth out the light of nature, and causeth so great a darkness in men's understanding, that they see not who it is to whom they have engaged their obedience. *As that the kingdom of God is the present Church.*

6. Consequent to this claim of the Pope to be vicar-general of Christ in the present Church, (supposed to be that kingdom of his to which we are addressed in the gospel,) is the doctrine, that it is necessary for a Christian king, to receive his crown by a bishop; as if it were from that ceremony, that he derives the clause of *Dei gratia* in his title; and that then only he is made king by the favour of God, when he is crowned by the authority of God's universal vicegerent on earth; and that every bishop whosoever be his sovereign, taketh at his consecration an oath of absolute obedience to the Pope.* Consequent to the same, is the doctrine of the fourth Council of Lateran, held under Pope Innocent the Third, (chap. 3. *De* *And that the Pope is his vicar general:*

Hereticis), *that if a king at the Pope's admonition, do not purge his kingdom of heresies, and being excommunicate for the same, do not give satisfaction within a year, his subjects are absolved of the bond of their obedience.* Where, by heresies are understood all opinions which the Church of Rome hath forbidden to be maintained. And by this [336] means, as often as there is any repugnancy between the political designs of the Pope, and other Christian princes, as there is very often, there ariseth such a mist amongst their subjects, that they know not a stranger that thrusteth himself into the throne of their lawful prince, from him whom they had themselves placed there; and in this darkness of mind, are made to fight one against another, without discerning their enemies from their friends, under the conduct of another man's ambition.

And that the pastors are the clergy. 7. From the same opinion, that the present Church is the kingdom of God, it proceeds that pastors, deacons, and all other ministers of the Church, take the name to themselves of the *clergy*; giving to other Christians the name of *laity*, that is, simply *people*. For clergy signifies those, whose maintenance is that revenue, which God having reserved to himself during his reign over the Israelites, assigned to the tribe of Levi (who were to be his public ministers, and had no portion of land set them out to live on, as their brethren) to be their inheritance. The Pope therefore, (pretending the present Church to be, as the realm of Israel, the kingdom of God) challenging to himself and his subordinate ministers, the like revenue, as the inheritance of God, the name of clergy was suitable to that claim. And thence it is, that tithes, and other tributes paid to the Levites, as in God's right, amongst the Israelites, have a long time been demanded, and taken of Christians, by ecclesiastics, *jure divino*, that is, in God's right. By which means, the people everywhere were obliged to a double tribute; one to the state, another to the clergy; whereof, that to the clergy, being the tenth of their revenue, is double to that which a king of Athens (and esteemed a tyrant) exacted of his subjects for the defraying of all public charges: for he demanded no more but the twentieth part; and yet abundantly maintained therewith the commonwealth. And in the kingdom of the Jews, during the sacerdotal reign of God, the tithes and offerings were the whole public revenue.

8. From the same mistaking of the present Church for the kingdom of God, came in the distinction between the *civil* and the *canon* laws: the civil law being the acts of *sovereigns* in their own do-

minions, and the canon law being the acts of the *Pope* in the same dominon. Which canons, though they were but canons, that is, *rules propounded*, and but voluntarily received by Christian princes, till the translation of the empire to Charlemagne; yet afterwards, as the power of the Pope increased, became *rules commanded*, and the emperors themselves (to avoid greater mischiefs, which the people blinded might be led into) were forced to let them pass for laws.

9. From hence it is, that in all dominions, where the Pope's ecclesiastical power is entirely received, Jews, Turks, and Gentiles, are in the Roman Church tolerated in their religion, as far forth, as in the exercise and profession thereof they offend not against the civil power: whereas in a Christian, though a stranger, not to be of the Roman religion, is capital; because the Pope pretendeth, that all Christians, are his subjects. For otherwise it were as much against [337] the law of nations, to persecute a Christian stranger, for professing the religion of his own country, as an infidel; or rather more, in as much as they that are not against Christ, are with him.

10. From the same it is, that in every Christian state there are certain men, that are exempt, by ecclesiastical liberty, from the tributes, and from the tribunals of the civil state; for so are the secular clergy, besides monks and friars, which in many places, bear so great a proportion to the common people, as if need were, there might be raised out of them alone, an army, sufficient for any war the Church militant should employ them in, against their own, or other princes.

11. A second general abuse of Scripture, is the turning of conse-cration into conjuration, or enchantment. To *consecrate*, is in Scrip-ture, to offer, give, or dedicate, in pious and decent language and gesture, a man, or any other thing to God, by separating of it from common use; that is to say, to sanctify, or make it God's, and to be used only by those, whom God hath appointed to be his public ministers, (as I have already proved at large in the 35th chapter;) and thereby to change, not the thing consecrated, but only the use of it, from being profane and common, to be holy, and peculiar to God's service. But when by such words, the nature or quality of the thing itself, is pretended to be changed, it is not consecration, but either an extraordinary work of God, or a vain and impious conjuration. But (seeing for the frequency of pretending the change of nature in their consecrations, it cannot be esteemed a work extraordinary,) it

Error from mistaking consecration for conjuration.

407

is no other than a *conjuration* or *incantation*, whereby they would have men to believe an alteration of nature that is not, contrary to the testimony of man's sight, and of all the rest of his senses. As for example, when the priest, instead of consecrating bread and wine to God's peculiar service in the sacrament of the Lord's Supper, (which is but a separation of it from the common use, to signify, that is, to put men in mind of their redemption, by the passion of Christ, whose body was broken, and blood shed upon the cross for our transgressions,) pretends, that by saying of the words of our Saviour, *This is my body*, and *this is my blood*, the nature of bread is no more there, but his very body; notwithstanding there appeareth not to the sight, or other sense of the receiver, any thing that appeared not before the consecration. The Egyptian conjurers, that are said to have turned their rods to serpents, and the water into blood, are thought but to have deluded the senses of the spectators, by a false show of things, yet are esteemed enchanters. But what should we have thought of them, if there had appeared in their rods nothing like a serpent, and in the water enchanted, nothing like blood, nor like any thing else but water, but that they had faced down the king, that they were serpents that looked like rods, and that it was blood that seemed water? That had been both enchantment, and lying. And yet in this daily act of the priest, they do the very same, by turning the holy words into the manner of a charm, which produceth nothing new to the sense; but they face us down, that it hath turned the bread into a man; nay more, into a God; and require men to worship it, as if it were our Saviour himself present God and man, and thereby to commit most gross idolatry. For if it be enough to excuse it of idolatry, to say it is no more bread, but God; why should not the same excuse serve the Egyptians, in case they had the faces to say, the leeks, and onions they worshipped, were not very leeks, and onions, but a divinity under their *species*, or likeness. The words, *This is my body*, are equivalent to these, *this signifies*, or *represents my body*; and it is an ordinary figure of speech: but to take it literally, is an abuse; nor though so taken, can it extend any further, than to the bread which Christ himself with his own hands consecrated. For he never said, that of what bread soever, any priest whatsoever, should say, *This is my body*, or, *this is Christ's body*, the same should presently be transubstantiated. Nor did the Church of Rome ever establish this transubstantiation, till the time of Innocent the Third; which was not above 500 years ago, when the

[338]

power of popes was at the highest, and the darkness of the time grown so great, as men discerned not the bread that was given them to eat, especially when it was stamped with the figure of Christ upon the cross, as if they would have men believe it were transubstantiated, not only into the body of Christ, but also into the wood of his cross, and that they did eat both together in the sacrament.

12.* The like incantation, instead of consecration, is used also in the sacrament of baptism: where the abuse of God's name in each several person, and in the whole Trinity, with the sign of the cross at each name, maketh up the charm. As first, when they make the holy water, the priest saith, *I conjure* thee, thou creature of water, in the name of God the Father Almighty, and in the name of Jesus Christ his only Son our Lord, and in virtue of the Holy Ghost, that thou become conjured water, to drive away all the powers of the enemy, and to eradicate, and supplant the enemy, &c.* And the same in the benediction of the salt to be mingled with it: *That thou become conjured salt, that all phantasms, and knavery of the devil's fraud may fly and depart from the place wherein thou art sprinkled; and every unclean spirit be conjured by Him that shall come to judge the quick and the dead.* The same in the benediction of the oil; *That all the power of the enemy, all the host of the devil, all assaults and phantasms of Satan, may be driven away by this creature of oil.* And for the infant that is to be baptized, he is subject to many charms: first, at the church door the priest blows thrice in the child's face, and says: *Go out of him unclean spirit, and give place to the Holy Ghost the comforter.* As if all children, till blown on by the priest, were demoniacs. Again, before his entrance into the church, he saith as before, *I conjure thee, &c. to go out, and depart from this servant of God*: and again the same exorcism is repeated once more before he be baptized. These, and some other [339] incantations, are those that are used instead of benedictions, and consecrations, in administration of the sacraments of baptism, and the Lord's supper; wherein every thing that serveth to those holy uses (except the unhallowed spittle of the priest) hath some set form of exorcism.

Incantation in the ceremonies of baptism:

13. Nor are the other rites, as of marriage, of extreme unction, of visitation of the sick, of consecrating churches and churchyards, and the like, exempt from charms; inasmuch as there is in them the use of enchanted oil, and water, with the abuse of the cross, and of the holy word of David, *asperges me Domine hyssopo,** as things of efficacy to drive away phantasms, and imaginary spirits.

And in marriage, in visitation of the sick, and in consecration of places.

*Errors from
mistaking
eternal life,
and
everlasting
death:*

14. Another general error, is from the misinterpretation of the words *eternal life, everlasting death*, and the *second death*. For though we read plainly in Holy Scripture, that God created Adam in an estate of living for ever, which was conditional, that is to say, if he disobeyed not his commandment; which was not essential to human nature, but consequent to the virtue of the tree of life; whereof he had liberty to eat, as long as he had not sinned; and that he was thrust out of Paradise after he had sinned, lest he should eat thereof, and live for ever; and that Christ's Passion is a discharge of sin to all that believe on him; and by consequence, a restitution of eternal life, to all the faithful, and to them only: yet the doctrine is now, and hath been a long time far otherwise; namely, that every man hath eternity of life by nature, inasmuch as his soul is immortal: so that the flaming sword at the entrance of Paradise, though it hinder a man from coming to the tree of life, hinders him not from the immortality which God took from him for his sin; nor makes him to need the sacrificing of Christ, for the recovering of the same; and consequently, not only the faithful and righteous, but also the wicked and the heathen, shall enjoy eternal life, without any death at all; much less a second, and everlasting death. To salve this, it is said, that by second, and everlasting death, is meant a second, and everlasting life, but in torments; a figure never used but in this very case.

15. All which doctrine is founded only on some of the obscurer places of the New Testament; which nevertheless, the whole scope of the Scripture considered, are clear enough in a different sense, and is unnecessary to the Christian faith. For supposing that when a man dies, there remaineth nothing of him but his carcass; cannot God, that raised inanimated dust and clay into a living creature by his word, easily raise a dead carcass to life again, and continue him alive for ever, or make him die again, by another word? The *soul* in Scripture, signifieth always, either the life, or the living creature; [340]   and the body and soul jointly, the *body alive*. In the fifth day of the creation, God said, Let the waters produce *reptile animae viventis*,* the creeping thing that hath in it a living soul; the English translate it, *that hath life*. And again, God created whales, *et omnem animam viventem*; which in the English is, *every living creature*. And likewise of man, God made him of the dust of the earth, and breathed in his face the breath of life, *et factus est homo in animam viventem*, that is, *and man was made a living creature*. And after Noah came out of the ark, God saith, he will no more smite *omnem animam viventem*, that is, *every living creature*. And (*Deut*. 12. 23), *Eat not the blood, for the blood is the soul*; that is, *the life*. From which places, if by *soul* were meant a *substance incorporeal*, with an existence separated from the body, it might as well be inferred of any other living creature as of man. But that the souls of the faithful, are not of their own nature, but by God's special grace, to remain in their bodies, from the resurrection to all eternity, I have already I think sufficiently proved out of the Scriptures, in the 38th chapter. And for the places of the New Testament, where it is said that any man shall be cast body and soul into hell fire, it is no more than body and life; that is to say, they shall be cast alive into the perpetual fire of Gehenna.

16. This window it is, that gives entrance to the dark doctrine, first, of eternal torments; and afterwards of purgatory, and consequently of the walking abroad, especially in places consecrated, solitary, or dark, of the ghosts of men deceased; and thereby to the pretences of exorcism and conjuration of phantasms; as also of invocation of men dead; and to the doctrine of indulgences; that is to say, of exemption for a time, or for ever, from the fire of purgatory, wherein these incorporeal substances are pretended by burning to be cleansed, and made fit for heaven. For men being generally possessed before the time of our Saviour, by contagion of the demonology of the Greeks, of an opinion, that the souls of men were substances distinct from their bodies,* and therefore that when the body was dead, the soul of every man, whether godly, or wicked, must subsist somewhere by virtue of its own nature, without acknowledging therein any supernatural gift of God; the doctors of the Church doubted a long time, what was the place, which they were to abide in, till they should be reunited to their bodies in the resurrection; supposing for a while, they lay under the altars: but afterward the Church of Rome found it more profitable, to build for them this place of purgatory; which by some other Churches in this latter age has been demolished.

17. Let us now consider, what texts of Scripture seem most to confirm these three general errors, I have here touched. As for those which Cardinal Bellarmine hath alleged, for the present kingdom of God administered by the Pope, (than which there are none that make a better show of proof,) I have already answered them; and made it evident, that the kingdom of God, instituted by Moses, ended in the election of Saul: after which time the priest of his own authority never deposed any king. That which the high-priest did to

As the doctrine of purgatory, and exorcisms, and invocation of saints.

The texts alleged for the doctrines aforementioned have been [341] *answered before.*

Athaliah, was not done in his own right, but in the right of the young king Joash her son: but Solomon in his own right deposed the high-priest Abiathar, and set up another in his place. The most difficult place to answer, of all those that can be brought, to prove the kingdom of God by Christ is already in this world, is alleged, not by Bellarmine, nor any other of the Church of Rome; but by Beza;* that will have it to begin from the resurrection of Christ. But whether he intend thereby, to entitle the Presbytery to the supreme power ecclesiastical in the commonwealth of Geneva, (and consequently to every presbytery in every other commonwealth,) or to princes, and other civil sovereigns, I do not know. For the presbytery hath challenged the power to excommunicate their own kings, and to be the supreme moderators in religion, in the places where they have that form of Church-government, no less than the Pope challengeth it universally.

18. The words are (*Mark* 9. 1), *Verily I say unto you, that there be some of them that stand here, which shall not taste of death, till they have seen the kingdom of God come with power.* Which words, if taken grammatically, make it certain, that either some of those men that stood by Christ at that time, are yet alive; or else, that the kingdom of God must be now in this present world. And then there is another place more difficult: for when the apostles after our Saviour's resurrection, and immediately before his ascension, asked our Saviour, saying, (*Acts* 1. 6), *Wilt thou at this time restore again the kingdom to Israel?* he answered them, *It is not for you to know the times and the seasons, which the Father hath put in his own power; but ye shall receive power by the coming of the Holy Ghost upon you, and ye shall be my (martyrs) witnesses both in Jerusalem, and in all Judea, and in Samaria, and unto the uttermost part of the earth.* Which is as much as to say, My kingdom is not yet come, nor shall you foreknow when it shall come; for it shall come as a thief in the night; but I will send you the Holy Ghost, and by him you shall have power to bear witness to all the world (by your preaching) of my resurrection, and the works I have done, and the doctrine I have taught, that they may believe in me, and expect eternal life, at my coming again. How does this agree with the coming of Christ's kingdom at the resurrection? And that which St. Paul says (1 *Thess.* 1. 9, 10) *That they turned from idols, to serve the living and true God, and to wait for his Son from heaven*; where to wait for his Son from heaven, is to wait for his coming to be king in power; which were not necessary, if his kingdom had been then present.

Answer to the text on which Beza inferreth that the kingdom of Christ began at the resurrection.

Again, if the kingdom of God began, as Beza on that place (*Mark* 9. 1) would have it, at the resurrection; what reason is there for Christians ever since the resurrection to say in their prayers, *Let thy kingdom come*? It is therefore manifest, that the words of St. Mark are not so to be interpreted. There be some of them that stand here (saith   [342] our Saviour) that shall not taste of death till they have seen the kingdom of God come in power. If then this kingdom were to come at the resurrection of Christ, why is it said, *some of them*, rather than *all*? For they all lived till after Christ was risen.

19. But they that require an exact interpretation of this text, let them interpret first the like words of our Saviour to St. Peter, concerning St. John, (chap. 21. 22) *If I will that he tarry till I come, what is that to thee?* upon which was grounded a report that he should not die. Nevertheless the truth of that report was neither confirmed, as well grounded; nor refuted, as ill grounded on those words; but left as a saying not understood. The same difficulty is also in the place of *St. Mark.* And if it be lawful to conjecture at their meaning, by that which immediately follows, both here, and in *St. Luke*, where the same is again repeated, it is not improbable, to say they have relation to the Transfiguration, which is described in the verses immediately following; where it is said, that *after six days Jesus taketh with him Peter, and James, and John* (not all, but some of his disciples), *and leadeth them up into a high mountain apart by themselves, and was transfigured before them. And his raiment became shining, exceeding white as snow; so as no fuller on earth can white them. And there appeared unto them, Elias with Moses and they were talking with Jesus, &c.* So that they saw Christ in glory and majesty, as he is to come; insomuch as *they were sore afraid.* And thus the promise of our Saviour was accomplished by way of *vision*: for it was a vision, as may probably be inferred out of *St. Luke*, that reciteth the same story (chap. 9. 28) and saith, that Peter and they that were with him, were heavy with sleep: but most certainly out of *Matt.* 17. 9 (where the same is again related;) for our Saviour charged them, saying, *Tell no man the vision until the Son of Man be risen from the dead.* Howsoever it be, yet there can from thence be taken no argument, to prove that the kingdom of God taketh beginning till the day of judgment.

Explication of the place in Mark 9. 1.

20. As for some other texts, to prove the Pope's power over civil sovereigns (besides those of Bellarmine;) as that the two swords that Christ and his apostles had amongst them, were the spiritual and the temporal sword, which they say St. Peter had given him by Christ:

Abuse of some other texts in defence of the power of the Pope.

413

and, that of the two luminaries, the greater signifies the Pope, and the lesser the King; one might as well infer out of the first verse of the Bible, that by heaven is meant the Pope, and by earth the King: which is not arguing from Scripture, but a wanton insulting over princes, which came in fashion after the time the Popes were grown so secure of their greatness, as to contemn all Christian kings; and treading on the necks of emperors,* to mock both them and the Scripture, in the words of Psalm 91. 13, *Thou shalt tread upon the lion and the adder; the young lion and the dragon thou shalt trample under thy feet.*

The manner of consecrations in the Scripture, was without exorcisms.

[343]

21. As for the rites of consecration, though they depend for the most part upon the discretion and judgment of the governors of the Church, and not upon the Scriptures; yet those governors are obliged to such direction, as the nature of the action itself requireth; as that the ceremonies, words, and gestures, be both decent, and significant, or at least conformable to the action. When Moses consecrated the tabernacle, the altar, and the vessels belonging to them, (*Exod.* 40. 9) he anointed them with the oil which God had commanded to be made for that purpose; and they were holy: there was nothing exorcised, to drive away phantasms. The same Moses (the civil sovereign of Israel) when he consecrated Aaron (the high-priest) and his sons, did wash them with water, (not exorcised water,) put their garments upon them, and anointed them with oil; and they were sanctified, to minister unto the Lord in the priest's office; which was a simple and decent cleansing, and adorning them, before he presented them to God, to be his servants. When king Solomon, (the civil sovereign of Israel) consecrated the temple he had built, (1 *Kings* 8) he stood before all the congregation of Israel; and having blessed them, he gave thanks to God, for putting into the heart of his father, to build it; and for giving to himself the grace to accomplish the same; and then prayed unto him, first, to accept that house, though it were not suitable to his infinite greatness; and to hear the prayers of his servants that should pray therein, or (if they were absent,) towards it; and lastly, he offered a sacrifice of peace-offering, and the house was dedicated. Here was no procession; the king stood still in his first place; no exorcised water; no *Asperges me*, nor other impertinent application of words spoken upon another occasion; but a decent and rational speech, and such as in making to God a present of his new-built house, was most conformable to the occasion.

22. We read not that St. John did exorcise the water of Jordan; nor Philip the water of the river wherein he baptized the Eunuch; nor that any pastor in the time of the apostles, did take his spittle, and put it to the nose of the person to be baptized, and say, *in odorem suavitatis*, that is, *for a sweet savour unto the Lord*; wherein neither the ceremony of spittle, for the uncleanness; nor the application of that Scripture for the levity, can by any authority of man be justified.

23. To prove that the soul separated from the body, liveth eternally, not only the souls of the elect, by especial grace, and restoration of the eternal life which Adam lost by sin, and our Saviour restored (by the sacrifice of himself,) to the faithful; but also the souls of reprobates, as a property naturally consequent to the essence of mankind, without other grace of God, but that which is universally given to all mankind; there are divers places, which at the first sight seem sufficiently to serve the turn: but such, as when I compare them with that which I have before (chapter 38) alleged out of the fourteenth of *Job*, seem to me much more subject to a diverse interpretation, than the words of Job.

The immortality of man's soul, not proved by Scripture to be of nature, but of grace.

24. And first there are the words of Solomon (*Eccles.* 12. 7), *Then shall the dust return to dust, as it was, and the spirit shall return to God that gave it*. Which may bear well enough (if there be no other text directly against it) this interpretation, that God only knows, (but man not,) what becomes of a man's spirit, when he expireth; and the same Solomon, in the same book, (chapter 3. 20, 21) delivereth the same sentence in the same sense I have given it. His words are: *All go* (man and beast) *to the same place; all are of the dust, and all turn to dust again; who knoweth that the spirit of man goeth upward, and that the spirit of the beast goeth downward to the earth?* That is, none knows but God; nor is it an unusual phrase to say of things we understand not, *God knows what*, and, *God knows where*. That of (*Gen.* 5. 24) *Enoch walked with God, and he was not; for God took him*; which is expounded, (*Heb.* 11. 5), *He was translated, that he should not die; and was not found, because God had translated him. For before his translation, he had this testimony, that he pleased God*; making as much for the immortality of the body, as of the soul, proveth, that this his translation was peculiar to them that please God; not common to them with the wicked, and depending on grace, not on nature. But on the contrary, what interpretation shall we give besides the literal sense, of the words of Solomon (*Eccles.* 3. 19), *That which befalleth*

[344]

415

the sons of men, befalleth beasts; even one thing befalleth them; as the one dieth, so doth the other; yea, they have all one breath (one spirit), *so that a man hath no pre-eminence above a beast, for all is vanity.* By the literal sense, here is no natural immortality of the soul; nor yet any repugnancy with the life eternal, which the elect shall enjoy by grace. And (*Eccles.* chap. 4. 3) *Better is he that hath not yet been, than both they;* that is, than they that live, or have lived; which, if the soul of all them that have lived, were immortal, were a hard saying; for then to have an immortal soul, were worse than to have no soul at all. And again, (chapter 9. 5) *The living know they shall die, but the dead know not anything;* that is, naturally, and before the resurrection of the body.

25. Another place which seems to make for a natural immortality of the soul, is that, where our Saviour saith, that Abraham, Isaac, and Jacob are living: but this is spoken of the promise of God, and of their certitude to rise again, not of a life then actual; and in the same sense that God said to Adam, that on the day he should eat of the forbidden fruit, he should certainly die; from that time forward he was a dead man by sentence; but not by execution, till almost a thousand years after. So Abraham, Isaac, and Jacob were alive by promise, then, when Christ spake; but are not actually till the resurrection. And the history of Dives and Lazarus, makes nothing against this, if we take it, (as it is) for a parable.

26. But there be other places of the New Testament, where an immortality seemeth to be directly attributed to the wicked. For it is evident, that they shall all rise to judgment. And it is said besides in many places, that they shall go into *everlasting fire, everlasting tor-* [345] *ments, everlasting punishments; and that the worm of conscience never dieth;* and all this is comprehended in the word *everlasting death,* which is ordinarily interpreted *everlasting life in torments.* And yet I can find no where that any man shall live in torments everlastingly. Also, it seemeth hard, to say, that God who is the father of mercies, that doth in heaven and earth all that he will; that hath the hearts of all men in his disposing; that worketh in men both to do, and to will; and without whose free gift a man hath neither inclination to good, nor repentance of evil, should punish men's transgressions without any end of time, and with all the extremity of torture, that men can imagine, and more.* We are therefore to consider, what the meaning is, of *everlasting fire,* and other the like phrases of Scripture.

27. I have showed already, that the kingdom of God by Christ

beginneth at the day of judgment: that in that day, the faithful shall rise again, with glorious, and spiritual bodies, and be his subjects in that his kingdom, which shall be eternal: that they shall neither marry nor be given in marriage, nor eat and drink, as they did in their natural bodies; but live for ever in their individual persons, without the specifical eternity of generation: and that the reprobates also shall rise again, to receive punishments for their sins: as also, that those of the elect, which shall be alive in their earthly bodies at that day, shall have their bodies suddenly changed, and made spiritual and immortal. But that the bodies of the reprobate, who make the kingdom of Satan, shall also be glorious, or spiritual bodies, or that they shall be as the angels of God, neither eating, nor drinking, nor engendering; or that their life shall be eternal in their individual persons, as the life of every faithful man is, or as the life of Adam had been if he had not sinned, there is no place of Scripture to prove it; save only these places concerning eternal torments; which may otherwise be interpreted.

28. From whence may be inferred, that as the elect after the resurrection shall be restored to the estate, wherein Adam was before he had sinned; so the reprobate shall be in the estate, that Adam and his posterity were in after the sin committed; saving that God promised a Redeemer to Adam, and such of his seed as should trust in him, and repent; but not to them that should die in their sins, as do the reprobate.

29. These things considered, the texts that mention *eternal fire, eternal torments, or the worm that never dieth*, contradict not the doctrine of a second, and everlasting death, in the proper and natural sense of the word *death*. The fire, or torments prepared for the wicked in Gehenna, Tophet, or in what place soever, may continue for ever;* and there may never want wicked men to be tormented in them; though not every, nor any one eternally. For the wicked being left in the estate they were in after Adam's sin, may at the resurrection live as they did, marry, and give in marriage, and have gross and corruptible bodies, as all mankind now have; and consequently may engender perpetually, after the resurrection, as they did before: for [346] there is no place in Scripture to the contrary. For St. Paul, speaking of the resurrection (1 *Cor.* 15) understandeth it only of the resurrection to life eternal; and not the resurrection to punishment. And of the first, he saith that the body is *sown in corruption, raised in incorruption; sown in dishonour, raised in honour; sown in weakness,*

Eternal torments, what.

417

raised in power; sown a natural body, raised a spiritual body. There is no such thing can be said of the bodies of them that rise to punishment. So also our Saviour, when he speaketh of the nature of man after the resurrection, meaneth the resurrection to life eternal, not to punishment. The text is, *Luke* 20, verses 34, 35, 36, a fertile text. *The children of this world marry, and are given in marriage; but they that shall be counted worthy to obtain that world, and the resurrection from the dead, neither marry, nor are given in marriage: neither can they die any more; for they are equal to the angels, and are the children of God, being the children of the resurrection.* The children of this world, that are in the estate which Adam left them in, shall marry, and be given in marriage; that is, corrupt, and generate successively; which is an immortality of the kind, but not of the persons of men: they are not worthy to be counted amongst them that shall obtain the next world, and an absolute resurrection from the dead; but only a short time, as inmates of that world; and to the end only to receive condign [merited] punishment for their contumacy. The elect are the only children of the resurrection; that is to say, the sole heirs of eternal life: they only can die no more: it is they that are equal to the angels, and that are the children of God; and not the reprobate. To the reprobate there remaineth after the resurrection, a *second*, and *eternal* death: between which resurrection, and their second, and eternal death, is but a time of punishment and torment; and to last by succession of sinners thereunto, as long as the kind of man by propagation shall endure; which is eternally.

Answer of the texts alleged for purgatory.

30. Upon this doctrine of the natural eternity of separated souls, is founded (as I said) the doctrine of purgatory. For supposing eternal life by grace only, there is no life, but the life of the body; and no immortality till the resurrection. The texts for purgatory alleged by Bellarmine out of the canonical Scripture of the Old Testament, are first, the fasting of David for Saul and Jonathan, mentioned (2 *Sam.* 1. 12); and again, (2 *Sam.* 3. 35) for the death of Abner. This fasting of David, he saith, was for the obtaining of something for them at God's hands, after their death; because after he had fasted to procure the recovery of his own child, as soon as he knew it was dead, he called for meat. Seeing then the soul hath an existence separate from the body, and nothing can be obtained by men's fasting for the souls that are already either in heaven, or hell, it followeth that there be some souls of dead men, that are neither in heaven, nor in hell; and therefore they must be in some third place,

which must be purgatory. And thus with hard straining, he has wrested those places to the proof of a purgatory: whereas it is [347] manifest, that the ceremonies of mourning, and fasting, when they are used for the death of men, whose life was not profitable to the mourners, they are used for honour's sake to their persons; and when 'tis done for the death of them by whose life the mourners had benefit, it proceeds from their particular damage: and so David honoured Saul, and Abner, with his fasting; and in the death of his own child, recomforted himself, by receiving his ordinary food.

31. In the other places, which he allegeth out of the Old Testament, there is not so much as any show, or colour of proof. He brings in every text wherein there is the word *anger*, or *fire*, or *burning*, or *purging*, or *cleansing*, in case any of the fathers have but in a sermon rhetorically applied it to the doctrine of purgatory, already believed. The first verse of *Psalm*, 37. *O Lord, rebuke me not in thy wrath, nor chasten me in thy hot displeasure*: what were this to purgatory, if Augustine had not applied the *wrath* to the fire of hell, and the *displeasure* to that of purgatory? And what is it to purgatory, that of *Psalm* 66. 12. *We went through fire and water, and thou broughtest us to a moist place*; and other the like texts, (with which the doctors of those times intended to adorn, or extend their sermons, or commentaries) haled to their purposes by force of wit?

32. But he allegeth other places of the New Testament, that are not so easy to be answered. And first that of *Matt.* 12. 32: *Whosoever speaketh a word against the Son of man, it shall be forgiven him; but whosoever speaketh against the Holy Ghost, it shall not be forgiven him neither in this world, nor in the world to come*: where he will have purgatory to be the world to come, wherein some sins may be forgiven, which in this world were not forgiven: notwithstanding that it is manifest, there are but three worlds; one from the creation to the flood, which was destroyed by water, and is called in Scripture *the old world*; another from the flood, to the day of judgment, which is *the present world*, and shall be destroyed by fire; and the third, which shall be from the day of judgment forward, everlasting, which is called *the world to come*; and in which it is agreed by all, there shall be no purgatory: and therefore the world to come, and purgatory, are inconsistent. But what then can be the meaning of those our Saviour's words? I confess they are very hardly to be reconciled with all the doctrines now unanimously received: nor is it any shame, to confess the profoundness of the Scripture to be too great to be

Places of the New Testament for purgatory answered.

sounded by the shortness of human understanding. Nevertheless, I may propound such things to the consideration of more learned divines, as the text itself suggesteth. And first, seeing to speak against the Holy Ghost, as being the third person of the Trinity, is to speak against the Church, in which the Holy Ghost resideth; it seemeth the comparison is made, between the easiness of our Saviour, in bearing with offences done to him while he himself taught the world, that is, when he was on earth, and the severity of the pastors after him, against those which should deny their authority, which was from the Holy Ghost. As if he should say, you that deny [348] my power; nay you that shall crucify me, shall be pardoned by me, as often as you turn unto me by repentance: but if you deny the power of them that teach you hereafter, by virtue of the Holy Ghost, they shall be inexorable, and shall not forgive you, but persecute you in this world, and leave you without absolution, (though you turn to me, unless you turn also to them,) to the punishments (as much as lies in them) of the world to come: and so the words may be taken as a prophecy, or prediction concerning the times, as they have long been in the Christian Church. Or if this be not the meaning, (for I am not peremptory in such difficult places,) perhaps there may be places left after the resurrection for the repentance of some sinners: and there is also another place, that seemeth to agree therewith. For considering the words of St. Paul (1 *Cor.* 15. 29), *What shall they do which are baptized for the dead, if the dead rise not at all? why also are they baptized for the dead?* a man may probably infer, as some have done, that in St. Paul's time, there was a custom by receiving baptism for the dead, (as men that now believe, are sureties and undertakers for the faith of infants, that are not capable of believing,) to undertake for the persons of their deceased friends, that they should be ready to obey, and receive our Saviour for their king, at his coming again; and then the forgiveness of sins in the world to come, has no need of a purgatory. But in both these interpretations, there is so much of paradox, that I trust not to them; but propound them to those that are thoroughly versed in the Scripture, to inquire if there be no clearer place that contradicts them. Only of thus much, I see evident Scripture, to persuade me, that there is neither the word, nor the thing of purgatory, neither in this, nor any other text; nor anything that can prove a necessity of a place for the soul without the body; neither for the soul of Lazarus during the four days he was dead; nor for the souls of them which the Roman

Church pretend to be tormented now in purgatory. For God, that could give a life to a piece of clay, hath the same power to give life again to a dead man, and renew his inanimate, and rotten carcass, into a glorious, spiritual, and immortal body.

33. Another place is that of 1 *Cor.* 3, where it is said, that they which build stubble, hay, &c. on the true foundation, their work shall perish; but *they themselves shall be saved, but as through fire*: this fire, he will have to be the fire of purgatory. The words, as I have said before, are an allusion to those of *Zech.* 13. 9, where he saith, *I will bring the third part through the fire, and refine them as silver is refined, and will try them as gold is tried*: which is spoken of the coming of the Messiah in power and glory; that is, at the day of judgment, and conflagration of the present world; wherein the elect shall not be consumed, but be refined; that is, depose their erroneous doctrines, and traditions, and have them as it were singed off; and shall afterwards call upon the name of the true God. In like manner, the apostle saith of them, that holding this foundation, *Jesus is the Christ*, shall build thereon some other doctrines that be erroneous, that they shall not be consumed in that fire which [349] reneweth the world, but shall pass through it to salvation; but so, as to see, and relinquish their former errors. The builders, are the *pastors*; the foundation, that *Jesus is the Christ*; the stubble and hay, *false consequences drawn from it through ignorance, or frailty*; the gold, silver, and precious stones, are their *true doctrines*; and their refining or purging, the *relinquishing of their errors*. In all which there is no colour at all for the burning of incorporeal, that is to say, impatible souls.

34. A third place is that of 1 *Cor.* 15. 29 before mentioned, concerning baptism for the dead: out of which he concludeth, first, that prayers for the dead are not unprofitable; and out of that, that there is a fire of purgatory: but neither of them rightly. For of many interpretations of the word baptism, he approveth this in the first place, that by baptism is meant (metaphorically) a baptism of penance; and that men are in this sense baptized, when they fast, and pray, and give alms: and so, baptism for the dead, and prayer for the dead, is the same thing. But this is a metaphor, of which there is no example, neither in the Scripture, nor in any other use of language; and which is also discordant to the harmony, and scope of the Scripture. The word baptism is used (*Mark* 10. 38, and *Luke* 12. 50) for being dipped in one's own blood, as Christ was upon the cross,

Baptism for the dead, how understood.

421

and as most of the apostles were, for giving testimony of him. But it is hard to say, that prayer, fasting, and alms, have any similitude with dipping. The same is used also *Matt.* 3. 11 (which seemeth to make somewhat for purgatory) for a purging with fire. But it is evident the fire and purging here mentioned, is the same whereof the prophet Zechariah speaketh (chapter 13. 9) *I will bring the third part through the fire, and will refine them, &c.* And St. Peter after him (1 Epistle 1. 7) *That the trial of your faith, which is much more precious than of gold that perisheth, though it be tried with fire, might be found unto praise, and honour, and glory at the appearing of Jesus Christ*; and St. Paul (1 *Cor.* 3. 13) *The fire shall try every man's work of what sort it is.* But St. Peter, and St. Paul speak of the fire that shall be at the second appearing of Christ; and the prophet Zechariah of the day of judgment. And therefore this place of St. Matthew may be interpreted of the same; and then there will be no necessity of the fire of purgatory.

35. Another interpretation of baptism for the dead, is that which I have before mentioned, which he preferreth to the second place of probability: and thence also he inferreth the utility of prayer for the dead. For if after the resurrection, such as have not heard of Christ, or not believed in him, may be received into Christ's kingdom; it is not in vain, after their death, that their friends should pray for them, till they should be risen. But granting that God, at the prayers of the faithful, may convert unto him some of those that have not heard Christ preached, and consequently cannot have rejected Christ, and that the charity of men in that point, cannot be blamed; yet this [350] concludeth nothing for purgatory; because to rise from death to life, is one thing; to rise from purgatory to life is another; as being a rising from life to life, from a life in torments to a life in joy.

36. A fourth place is that of *Matt.* 5. 25, 26: *Agree with thine adversary quickly, whilst thou art in the way with him, lest at any time the adversary deliver thee to the judge, and the judge deliver thee to the officer, and thou be cast into prison: verily I say unto thee, thou shalt by no means come out thence, till thou hast paid the uttermost farthing.* In which allegory, the offender is the *sinner*; both the adversary and the judge is *God*; the way is this *life*; the prison is the *grave*; the officer, *death*; from which, the sinner shall not rise again to life eternal, but to a second death, till he have paid the utmost farthing, or Christ pay it for him by his passion, which is a full ransom for all manner of sin, as well lesser sins, as greater

crimes; both being made by the passion of Christ equally venial.

37. The fifth place, is that of *Matt.* 5. 22: *Whosoever is angry with his brother without a cause, shall be guilty in judgment. And whosoever shall say to his brother, Raca, shall be guilty in the council; but whosoever shall say, thou fool, shall be guilty to hell fire.* From which words he inferreth three sorts of sins, and three sorts of punishments; and that none of those sins, but the last, shall be punished with hell fire; and consequently, that after this life, there is punishment of lesser sins in purgatory. Of which inference, there is no colour in any interpretation that hath yet been given of them: shall there be a distinction after this life of courts of justice, as there was amongst the Jews in our Saviour's time, to hear, and determine divers sorts of crimes, as the judges, and the council? Shall not all judicature appertain to Christ, and his apostles? To understand therefore this text, we are not to consider it solitarily, but jointly with the words precedent, and subsequent. Our Saviour in this chapter interpreteth the law of Moses; which the Jews thought was then fulfilled, when they had not transgressed the grammatical sense thereof, howsoever they had transgressed against the sentence, or meaning of the legislator. Therefore whereas they thought the sixth commandment was not broken, but by killing a man; nor the seventh, but when a man lay with a woman, not his wife; our Saviour tells them the inward anger of a man against his brother, if it be without just cause, is homicide: you have heard (saith he) the Law of Moses, *Thou shalt not kill*, and that *Whosoever shall kill, shall be condemned before the judges*, or before the session of the Seventy: but I say unto you, to be angry with one's brother without cause, or to say unto him *Raca*, or *Fool*, is homicide, and shall be punished at the day of judgment, and session of Christ, and his apostles, with hell fire. So that those words were not used to distinguish between divers crimes, and divers courts of justice, and divers punishments; but to tax the distinction between sin, and sin, which the Jews drew not from the difference of the will in obeying God, but from the difference of their temporal courts of justice; and to show them that he that had the will to hurt [351] his brother, though the effect appear but in reviling, or not at all, shall be cast into hell fire, by the judges, and by the session, which shall be the same, not different, courts at the day of judgment. This considered, what can be drawn from this text, to maintain purgatory, I cannot imagine.

38. The sixth place is *Luke* 16. 9. *Make ye friends of the*

unrighteous Mammon; that when ye fail, they may receive you into everlasting tabernacles. This he alleges to prove invocation of saints departed. But the sense is plain, that we should make friends with our riches, of the poor; and thereby obtain their prayers whilst they live. *He that giveth to the poor, lendeth to the Lord.*

39. The seventh is *Luke* 23. 42: *Lord, remember me, when thou comest into thy kingdom.* Therefore, saith he, there is remission of sins after this life. But the consequence is not good. Our Saviour then forgave him; and at his coming again in glory, will remember to raise him again to life eternal.

40. The eighth is *Acts* 2. 24 where St. Peter saith of Christ, *that God had raised him up, and loosed the pains of death, because it was not possible he should be holden of it*: which he interprets to be a descent of Christ into purgatory, to loose some souls there from their torments: whereas it is manifest, that it was Christ that was loosed; it was he that could not be holden of death, or the grave; and not the souls in purgatory. But if that which Beza says, in his notes on this place be well observed, there is none that will not see, that instead of *pains*, it should be *bands*; and then there is no further cause to seek for purgatory in this text.

[352]

CHAPTER XLV

OF DEMONOLOGY, AND OTHER RELICS OF THE RELIGION OF THE GENTILES

The original of demonology.

1. THE impression made on the organs of sight, by lucid bodies, either in one direct line, or in many lines, reflected from opaque, or refracted in the passage through diaphanous bodies, produceth in living creatures, in whom God hath placed such organs, an imagination of the object, from whence the impression proceedeth; which imagination is called *sight*; and seemeth not to be a mere imagination, but the body itself without us; in the same manner, as when a man violently presseth his eye, there appears to him a light without, and before him, which no man perceiveth but himself; because there is indeed no such thing without him, but only a motion in the interior organs, pressing by resistance outward, that makes him think so. And the motion made by this pressure, continuing after the object which caused it is removed, is that we call *imagination*, and

memory, and (in sleep, and sometimes in great distemper of the organs by sickness, or violence) a *dream*: of which things I have already spoken briefly, in the second and third chapters.

2. This nature of sight having never been discovered by the ancient pretenders to natural knowledge; much less by those that consider not things so remote (as that knowledge is) from their present use; it was hard for men to conceive of those images in the fancy, and in the sense, otherwise, than of things really without us:* which some (because they vanish away, they know not whither, nor how) will have to be absolutely incorporeal, that is to say immaterial; forms without matter; colour and figure, without any coloured or figured body; and that they can put on airy bodies (as a garment) to make them visible when they will to our bodily eyes; and others say, are bodies and living creatures, but made of air, or other more subtle and ethereal matter, which is, (then, when they will be seen,) condensed. But both of them agree on one general appellation of them, DEMONS. As if the dead of whom they dreamed, were not inhabitants of their own brain, but of the air, or of heaven, or hell; not phantasms, but ghosts; with just as much reason, as if one should say, he saw his own ghost in a looking-glass, or the ghosts of the stars in a river; or call the ordinary apparition of the sun, of the quantity of about a foot, the *demon*, or ghost of that great sun that enlighteneth the whole visible world: and by that means have feared them, as things of an unknown, that is, of an unlimited power to do them good or harm; and consequently, given occasion to the governors of the heathen commonwealths to regulate this their fear, by [353] establishing that DEMONOLOGY (in which the poets, as principal priests of the heathen religion, were specially employed or reverenced) to the public peace, and to the obedience of subjects necessary thereunto; and to make some of them good *demons*, and others evil; the one as a spur to the observance, the other, as reins to withhold them from violation of the laws.

3. What kind of things they were, to whom they attributed the name of *demons*, appeareth partly in the genealogy of their gods, written by Hesiod,* one of the most ancient poets of the Grecians; and partly in other histories; of which I have observed some few before, in the 12th chapter of this discourse. *What were the demons of the ancients.*

4. The Grecians, by their colonies and conquests, communicated their language and writings into Asia, Egypt, and Italy; and therein, by necessary consequence their *demonology*, or (as St. Paul calls it) *How that doctrine was spread.*

425

their doctrines of devils: and by that means, the contagion was derived also to the Jews, both of Judea, and Alexandria, and other parts, whereinto they were dispersed. But the name of *demon* they did not (as the Grecians) attribute to spirits both good, and evil; but to the evil only: and to the good *demons* they gave the name of the spirit of God; and esteemed those into whose bodies they entered to be prophets. In sum, all singularity if good, they attributed to the spirit of God; and if evil, to some *demon*, but a *κακοδαίμων*, an evil *demon*, that is, a *devil*. And therefore, they called *demoniacs*, that is, *possessed by the devil*, such as we call madmen or lunatics; or such as had the falling sickness; or that spoke anything, which they for want of understanding, thought absurd: as also of an unclean person in a notorious degree, they used to say he had an unclean spirit; of a dumb man, that he had a dumb devil; and of John the Baptist (*Matt.* 11. 18), for the singularity of his fasting, that he had a devil; and of our Saviour, because he said, he that keepeth his sayings should not see death *in aeternum*, (*John* 8. 52), *Now we know thou hast a devil; Abraham is dead, and the prophets are dead*: and again, because he said (*John* 7. 20) *They went about to kill him*, the people answered, *Thou hast a devil, who goeth about to kill thee?* Whereby it is manifest, that the Jews had the same opinion with the Greeks concerning phantasms, namely, that they were not phantasms, that is, idols of the brain, but things real, and independent on the fancy.

5. Which doctrine if it be not true, why (may some say) did not our Saviour contradict it, and teach the contrary? Nay, why does he use on divers occasions such forms of speech as seem to confirm it? To this I answer, that first, where Christ saith, (*Luke* 24. 39) *A spirit hath not flesh and bone*, though he show that there be spirits, yet he denies not that they are bodies: and where St. Paul says, (1 *Cor.* 15. 44) *we shall rise spiritual bodies*, he acknowledgeth the nature of spirits, but that they are bodily spirits; which is not difficult to understand. For air and many other things are bodies, though not flesh and bone, or any other gross body to be discerned by the eye. But when our Saviour speaketh to the devil, and commandeth him to go out of a man, if by the devil, he meant a disease, as frenzy, or lunacy, or a corporeal spirit, is not the speech improper? Can diseases hear? Or can there be a corporeal spirit in a body of flesh and bone, full already of vital and animal spirits? Are there not therefore spirits, that neither have bodies, nor are mere imaginations? To the first I answer, that the addressing of our Saviour's command to the

How far received by the Jews.

Why our Saviour controlled it not.

[354]

426

madness, or lunacy he cureth, is no more improper than was his rebuking of the fever, or of the wind, and sea; for neither do these hear: or than was the command of God, to the light, to the firmament, to the sun, and stars, when he commanded them to be: for they could not hear before they had a being. But those speeches are not improper, because they signify the power of God's word: no more therefore is it improper, to command madness, or lunacy (under the appellation of devils, by which they were then commonly understood,) to depart out of a man's body. To the second, concerning their being incorporeal, I have not yet observed any place of Scripture, from whence it can be gathered, that any man was ever possessed with any other corporeal spirit, but that of his own, by which his body is naturally moved.

6. Our Saviour, immediately after the Holy Ghost descended upon him in the form of a dove, is said by St. Matthew (chapter 4. 1), to have been *led up by the Spirit into the wilderness*; and the same is recited (*Luke* 4. 1) in these words, *Jesus being full of the Holy Ghost, was led in the Spirit into the wilderness*: whereby it is evident that by *spirit* there, is meant the Holy Ghost. This cannot be interpreted for a possession: for Christ, and the Holy Ghost, are but one and the same substance; which is no possession of one substance, or body, by another. And whereas in the verses following, he is said *to have been taken up by the devil into the holy city, and set upon a pinnacle of the temple*, shall we conclude thence that he was possessed of the devil, or carried thither by violence? And again, *carried thence by the devil into an exceeding high mountain, who showed him thence all the kingdoms of the world*: wherein we are not to believe he was either possessed, or forced by the devil; nor that any mountain is high enough, (according to the literal sense,) to show him one whole hemisphere. What then can be the meaning of this place, other than that he went of himself into the wilderness; and that this carrying of him up and down, from the wilderness to the city, and from thence into a mountain, was a vision? Conformable whereunto, is also the phrase of St. Luke, that he was led into the wilderness, not *by*, but *in*, the Spirit: whereas concerning his being taken up into the mountain, and unto the pinnacle of the temple, he speaketh as St. Matthew doth. Which suiteth with the nature of a vision.

The Scriptures do not teach that spirits are incorporeal.

7. Again, where St. Luke (chap. 22. 3, 4) says of Judas Iscariot, that *Satan entered into him, and thereupon that he went and communed with the chief priests, and captains, how he might betray Christ unto*

[355] *them*: it may be answered, that by the entering of Satan (that is the *enemy*) into him, is meant, the hostile and traitorous intention of selling his Lord and Master. For as by the Holy Ghost, is frequently in Scripture understood, the graces and good inclinations given by the Holy Ghost; so by the entering of Satan, may be understood the wicked cogitations, and designs of the adversaries of Christ, and his disciples. For as it is hard to say, that the devil was entered into Judas, before he had any such hostile design; so it is impertinent to say, he was first Christ's enemy in his heart, and that the devil entered into him afterwards. Therefore the entering of Satan, and his wicked purpose, was one and the same thing.

8. But if there be no immaterial spirit, or any possession of men's bodies by any spirit corporeal, it may again be asked, why our Saviour and his apostles did not teach the people so; and in such clear words, as they might no more doubt thereof. But such questions as these, are more curious, than necessary for a Christian man's salvation. Men may as well ask, why Christ that could have given to all men faith, piety, and all manner of moral virtues, gave it to some only, and not to all: and why he left the search of natural causes, and sciences, to the natural reason and industry of men, and did not reveal it to all, or any man supernaturally; and many other such questions: of which nevertheless there may be alleged probable and pious reasons. For as God, when he brought the Israelites into the land of Promise, did not secure them therein, by subduing all the nations round about them; but left many of them, as thorns in their sides, to awaken from time to time their piety and industry: so our Saviour, in conducting us toward his heavenly kingdom, did not destroy all the difficulties of natural questions; but left them to exercise our industry, and reason; the scope of his preaching, being only to show us this plain and direct way to salvation, namely, the belief of this article, *that he was the Christ, the Son of the living God, sent into the world to sacrifice himself for our sins, and at his coming again, gloriously to reign over his elect, and to save them from their enemies eternally*: to which, the opinion of possession by spirits, or phantasms, is no impediment in the way; though it be to some an occasion of going out of the way, and to follow their own inventions. If we require of the Scripture an account of all questions, which may be raised to trouble us in the performance of God's commands; we may as well complain of Moses for not having set down the time of the creation of such spirits, as well as of the creation of the earth,

and sea, and of men, and beasts. To conclude, I find in Scripture that there be angels, and spirits, good and evil; but not that they are incorporeal, as are the apparitions men see in the dark, or in a dream, or vision; which the Latins call *spectra*, and took for *demons*. And I find that there are spirits corporeal, (though subtle and invisible;) but not that any man's body was possessed or inhabited by them; and that the bodies of the saints shall be such, namely, [356] spiritual bodies, as St. Paul calls them.

9. Nevertheless, the contrary doctrine, namely, that there be incorporeal spirits, hath hitherto so prevailed in the Church, that the use of exorcism, (that is to say, of ejection of devils by conjuration) is thereupon built; and (though rarely and faintly practised) is not yet totally given over. That there were many demoniacs in the primitive Church, and few madmen, and other such singular diseases; whereas in these times we hear of, and see many madmen, and few demoniacs, proceeds not from the change of nature, but of names. But how it comes to pass that whereas heretofore the apostles, and after them for a time, the pastors of the Church, did cure those singular diseases, which now they are not seen to do; as likewise, why it is not in the power of every true believer now, to do all that the faithful did then, that is to say, as we read (*Mark* 16. 17, 18), *in Christ's name to cast out devils, to speak with new tongues, to take up serpents, to drink deadly poison without harm-taking, and to cure the sick by the laying on of their hands*, and all this without other words, but *in the name of Jesus*, is another question. And it is probable, that those extraordinary gifts were given to the Church, for no longer a time, than men trusted wholly to Christ, and looked for their felicity only in his kingdom to come; and consequently, that when they sought authority, and riches, and trusted to their own subtlety for a kingdom of this world, these supernatural gifts of God were again taken from them.

The power of casting out devils, not the same it was in the primitive church.

10. Another relic of Gentilism, is the *worship of images*, neither instituted by Moses in the Old, nor by Christ in the New Testament; nor yet brought in from the Gentiles; but left amongst them, after they had given their names to Christ. Before our Saviour preached, it was the general religion of the Gentiles, to worship for gods, those appearances that remain in the brain from the impression of external bodies upon the organs of their senses, which are commonly called *ideas*, *idols*, *phantasms*, *conceits*, as being representations of those external bodies, which cause them, and have nothing

Another relic of Gentilism, worshipping of images, left in the Church, not brought into it.

in them of reality, no more than there is in the things that seem to stand before us in a dream: and this is the reason why St. Paul says, (1 *Cor.* 8. 4) *we know that an idol is nothing*: not that he thought that an image of metal, stone, or wood, was nothing; but that the thing which they honoured, or feared in the image, and held for a god, was a mere figment, without place, habitation, motion, or existence, but in the motions of the brain. And the worship of these with divine honour, is that which is in the Scripture called idolatry, and rebellion against God. For God being King of the Jews, and his lieutenant being first Moses, and afterwards the high-priest; if the people had been permitted to worship, and pray to images, (which are representations of their own fancies,) they had had no further dependence on the true God, of whom there can be no similitude; nor

[357]

on his prime-ministers, Moses and the high-priests; but every man had governed himself according to his own appetite, to the utter eversion [overturning] of the commonwealth, and their own destruction for want of union. And therefore the first law of God was, *they should not take for gods*, ALIENOS DEOS, that is, *the gods of other nations, but that only true God, who vouchsafed to commune with Moses, and by him to give them laws and directions, for their peace, and for their salvation from their enemies.* And the second was, that *they should not make to themselves any image to worship, of their own invention.* For it is the same deposing of a king, to submit to another king, whether he be set up by a neighbour nation, or by ourselves.

Answer to certain seeming texts for images.

11. The places of Scripture pretended to countenance the setting up of images, to worship them; or to set them up at all in the places where God is worshipped, are first, two examples; one of the cherubims over the ark of God; the other of the brazen serpent. Secondly, some texts whereby we are commanded to worship certain creatures for their relation to God; as to worship his footstool. And lastly, some other texts, by which is authorized a religious honouring of holy things. But before I examine the force of those places, to prove that which is pretended, I must first explain what is to be understood by *worshipping*, and what by *images*, and *idols*.

What is worship.

12. I have already shown in the 20th chapter of this discourse, that to honour, is to value highly the power of any person: and that such value is measured, by our comparing him with others. But because there is nothing to be compared with God in power; we

honour him not but dishonour him by any value less than infinite. And thus honour is properly of its own nature, secret, and internal in the heart. But the inward thoughts of men, which appear outwardly in their words and actions, are the signs of our honouring, and these go by the name of *worship*; in Latin, *cultus*. Therefore, to pray to, to swear by, to obey, to be diligent, and officious in serving: in sum, all words and actions that betoken fear to offend, or desire to please, is *worship*, whether those words and actions be sincere, or feigned: and because they appear as signs of honouring, are ordinarily also called *honour*.

13. The worship we exhibit to those we esteem to be but men, as to kings, and men in authority, is *civil worship*: but the worship we exhibit to that which we think to be God, whatsoever the words, ceremonies, gestures or other actions be, is *divine worship*. To fall prostrate before a king, in him that thinks him but a man, is but civil worship: and he that putteth off his hat in the church, for this cause, that he thinketh it the house of God, worshippeth with divine worship. They that seek the distinction of divine and civil worship, not in the intention of the worshipper, but in the words δουλεία, and λατρεία, deceive themselves. For whereas there be two sorts of servants; that sort, which is of those that are absolutely in the power of their masters, as slaves taken in war, and their issue, whose bodies are not in their own power, (their lives depending on the will of their masters, in such manner as to forfeit them upon the least disobedience,) and that are bought and sold as beasts, were called δοῦλοι, that is properly, slaves, and their service δουλεία: the other, which is of those that serve (for hire, or in hope of benefit from their masters) voluntarily; are called θῆτες; that is, domestic servants; to whose service the masters have no further right, than is contained in the covenants made betwixt them. These two kinds of servants have thus much common to them both, that their labour is appointed them by another: and the word λάτρις, is the general name of both, signifying him that worketh for another, whether, as a slave, or a voluntary servant. So that λατρεία signifieth generally all service; but δουλεία the service of bondmen only, and the condition of slavery: and both are used in Scripture (to signify our service of God) promiscuously. Δουλεία, because we are God's slaves; λατρεία, because we serve him: and in all kinds of service is contained, not only obedience, but also worship; that is, such actions, gestures, and words, as signify *honour*.

Distinction between divine and civil worship.

[358]

An image,
what.
Phantasms.

14. An *image* (in the most strict signification of the word) is the resemblance of something visible: in which sense the phantastical forms, apparitions, or seemings of visible bodies to the sight, are only *images*; such as are the show of a man, or other thing in the water, by reflection, or refraction; or of the sun, or stars by direct vision in the air; which are nothing real in the things seen, nor in the place where they seem to be; nor are their magnitudes and figures the same with that of the object; but changeable, by the variation of the organs of sight, or by glasses; and are present oftentimes in our imagination, and in our dreams, when the object is absent; or changed into other colours, and shapes, as things that depend only upon the fancy. And these are the *images* which are originally and most properly called *ideas*, and *idols*, and derived from the language of the Grecians, with whom the word εἴδω signifieth *to see*. They also are called PHANTASMS, which is in the same language, *apparitions*. And from these images it is, that one of the faculties of man's nature, is called the *imagination*. And from hence it is manifest, that there neither is, nor can be, any image made of a thing invisible.

15. It is also evident, that there can be no image of a thing infinite: for all the images, and phantasms that are made by the impression of things visible, are figured: but figure is a quantity every way determined. And therefore there can be no image of God; nor of the soul of man; nor of spirits; but only of bodies visible, that is, bodies that have light in themselves, or are by such enlightened.

Fictions.

[359]

Material
images.

16. And whereas a man can fancy shapes he never saw; making up a figure out of the parts of divers creatures; as the poets make their centaurs, chimeras, and other monsters never seen: so can he also give matter to those shapes, and make them in wood, clay, or metal. And these are also called images, not for the resemblance of any corporeal thing, but for the resemblance of some phantastical inhabitants of the brain of the maker. But in these idols, as they are originally in the brain, and as they are painted, carved, moulded, or moulten in matter, there is a similitude of the one to the other, for which the material body made by art, may be said to be the image of the fantastical idol made by nature.

17. But in a larger use of the word image, is contained also, any representation of one thing by another. So an earthly sovereign may be called the image of God: and an inferior magistrate the image of an earthly sovereign. And many times in the idolatry of the Gentiles there was little regard to the similitude of their material idol to the idol in their fancy, and yet it was called the image of it. For a stone unhewn has been set up for Neptune, and divers other shapes far different from the shapes they conceived of their gods. And at this day we see many images of the Virgin Mary, and other saints, unlike one another, and without correspondence to any one man's fancy; and yet serve well enough for the purpose they were erected for; which was no more but by the names only, to represent the persons mentioned in the history; to which every man applieth a mental image of his own making, or none at all. And thus an image in the largest sense, is either the resemblance, or the representation of some thing visible; or both together, as it happeneth for the most part.

18. But the name of idol is extended yet further in Scripture, to signify also the sun, or a star, or any other creature, visible or invisible, when they are worshipped for gods.

19. Having shown what is *worship*, and what an *image*; I will now put them together, and examine what that IDOLATRY is, which is forbidden in the second commandment, and other places of the Scripture. *Idolatry, what.*

20. To worship an image, is voluntarily to do those external acts, which are signs of honouring either the matter of the image, which is wood, stone, metal, or some other visible creature; or the phantasm of the brain, for the resemblance, or representation whereof, the matter was formed and figured; or both together, as one animate body, composed of the matter and the phantasm, as of a body and soul.

21. To be uncovered, before a man of power and authority, or before the throne of a prince, or in such other places as he ordaineth to that purpose in his absence, is to worship that man, or prince with civil worship; as being a sign, not of honouring the stool, or place, but the person; and is not idolatry. But if he that doth it, should suppose the soul of the prince to be in the stool, or should present a petition to the stool, it were divine worship, and idolatry.

22. To pray to a king for such things, as he is able to do for us, though we prostrate ourselves before him, is but civil worship; [360] because we acknowledge no other power in him, but human: but voluntarily to pray unto him for fair weather, or for any thing which God only can do for us, is divine worship, and idolatry. On the other side, if a king compel a man to it by the terror of death, or other great corporal punishment, it is not idolatry: for the worship which the

sovereign commandeth to be done unto himself by the terror of his laws, is not a sign that he that obeyeth him, does inwardly honour him as a God, but that he is desirous to save himself from death, or from a miserable life; and that which is not a sign of internal honour, is no worship; and therefore no idolatry. Neither can it be said, that he that does it, scandalizeth, or layeth any stumbling block before his brother; because how wise, or learned soever he be that worshippeth in that manner, another man cannot from thence argue, that he approveth it; but that he doth it for fear; and that it is not his act, but the act of his sovereign.

23. To worship God, in some peculiar place, or turning a man's face towards an image, or determinate place, is not to worship, or honour the place, or image; but to acknowledge it holy, that is to say, to acknowledge the image, or the place to be set apart from common use. For that is the meaning of the word *holy*; which implies no new quality in the place, or image; but only a new relation by appropriation to God; and therefore is not idolatry; no more than it was idolatry to worship God before the brazen serpent; or for the Jews, when they were out of their own country, to turn their faces (when they prayed) towards the temple of Jerusalem; or for Moses to put off his shoes when he was before the flaming bush, the ground appertaining to Mount Sinai, which place God had chosen to appear in, and to give his laws to the people of Israel, and was therefore holy ground, not by inherent sanctity, but by separation to God's use; or for Christians to worship in the churches, which are once solemnly dedicated to God for that purpose, by the authority of the king, or other true representant of the Church. But to worship God, as inanimating, or inhabiting such image, or place; that is to say, in infinite substance in a finite place, is idolatry: for such finite gods, are but idols of the brain, nothing real; and are commonly called in the Scripture by the names of *vanity*, and *lies*, and *nothing*. Also to worship God, not as inanimating, or present in the place, or image; but to the end to be put in mind of him, or of some works of his, in case the place, or image be dedicated, or set up by private authority, and not by the authority of them that are our sovereign pastors, is idolatry. For the commandment is, *thou shalt not make to thyself any graven image*. God commanded Moses to set up the brazen serpent; he did not make it to himself; it was not therefore against the commandment. But the making of the golden calf by Aaron, and

the people, as being done without authority from God, was idolatry; [361] not only because they held it for God, but also because they made it for a religious use, without warrant either from God their sovereign, or from Moses, that was his lieutenant.

24. The Gentiles worshipped for gods, Jupiter, and others; that living, were men perhaps that had done great and glorious acts; and for the children of God, divers men and women, supposing them gotten between an immortal deity, and a mortal man. This was idolatry, because they made them so to themselves, having no authority from God, neither in his eternal law of reason, nor in his positive and revealed will. But though our Saviour was a man, whom we also believe to be God immortal, and the Son of God; yet this is no idolatry; because we build not that belief upon our own fancy, or judgment, but upon the Word of God revealed in the Scriptures. And for the adoration of the Eucharist, if the words of Christ, *this is my body*, signify, *that he himself, and the seeming bread in his hand, and not only so, but that all the seeming morsels of bread that have ever since been, and any time hereafter shall be consecrated by priests, be so many Christ's bodies, and yet all of them but one body*, then is that no idolatry, because it is authorized by our Saviour: but if that text do not signify that, (for there is no other that can be alleged for it,) then, because it is a worship of human institution, it is idolatry. For it is not enough to say, God can transubstantiate the bread into Christ's body: for the Gentiles also held God to be omnipotent, and might upon that ground no less excuse their idolatry, by pretending, as well as others, a transubstantiation of their wood, and stone into God Almighty.

25. Whereas there be, that pretend divine inspiration to be the supernatural entering of the Holy Ghost into a man, and not an acquisition of God's graces, by doctrine, and study; I think they are in a very dangerous dilemma. For if they worship not the man whom they believe to be so inspired, they fall into impiety; as not adoring God's supernatural presence. And again, if they worship him, they commit idolatry; for the apostles would never permit themselves to be so worshipped. Therefore the safest way is to believe, that by the descending of the dove upon the apostles; and by Christ's breathing on them, when he gave them the Holy Ghost; and by the giving of it by imposition of hands, are understood the signs which God has been pleased to use, or ordain to be used, of his

promise to assist those persons in their study to preach his kingdom, and in their conversation, that it might not be scandalous, but edifying to others.

Scandalous worship of images.

26. Besides the idolatrous worship of images, there is also a scandalous worship of them; which is also a sin; but not idolatry. For *idolatry* is to worship by signs of an internal, and real honour: but *scandalous worship*, is but seeming worship, and may sometimes be

[362] joined with an inward, and hearty detestation, both of the image, and of the phantastical *demon*, or idol, to which it is dedicated; and proceed only from the fear of death, or other grievous punishment; and is nevertheless a sin in them that so worship, in case they be men whose actions are looked at by others, as lights to guide them by; because following their ways, they cannot but stumble, and fall in the way of religion: whereas the example of those we regard not, works not on us at all, but leaves us to our own diligence and caution; and consequently are no causes of our falling.

27. If therefore a pastor lawfully called to teach and direct others, or any other, of whose knowledge there is a great opinion, do external honour to an idol for fear; unless he make his fear, and unwillingness to it, as evident as the worship; he scandalizeth his brother, by seeming to approve idolatry. For his brother arguing from the action of his teacher, or of him whose knowledge he esteemeth great, concludes it to be lawful in itself. And this scandal, is sin, and a *scandal given*. But if one being no pastor, nor of eminent reputation for knowledge in Christian doctrine, do the same, and another follow him; this is no scandal given; for he had no cause to follow such example: but is a pretence of scandal which he taketh of himself for an excuse before men: for an unlearned man, that is in the power of an idolatrous king, or state, if commanded on pain of death to worship before an idol, he detesteth the idol in his heart, he doth well; though if he had the fortitude to suffer death, rather than worship it, he should do better. But if a pastor, who as Christ's messenger, has undertaken to teach Christ's doctrine to all nations, should do the same, it were not only a sinful scandal, in respect of other Christian men's consciences, but a perfidious forsaking of his charge.

28. The sum of that which I have said hitherto, concerning the worship of images, is this, that he that worshippeth in an image, or any creature, either the matter thereof, or any fancy of his own, which he thinketh to dwell in it; or both together; or believeth that

436

such things hear his prayers, or see his devotions, without ears, or eyes, committeth idolatry: and he that counterfeiteth such worship for fear of punishment, if he be a man whose example hath power amongst his brethren, committeth a sin. But he that worshippeth the Creator of the world before such an image, or in such a place as he hath not made, or chosen of himself, but taken from the commandment of God's word, as the Jews did in worshipping God before the cherubims, and before the brazen serpent for a time, and in, or towards the Temple of Jerusalem, which was also but for a time, committeth not idolatry.

29. Now for the worship of saints, and images, and relics, and other things at this day practised in the Church of Rome, I say they are not allowed by the Word of God, nor brought into the Church of Rome, from the doctrine there taught; but partly left in it at the [363] first conversion of the Gentiles; and afterwards countenanced, and confirmed, and augmented by the bishops of Rome.

30. As for the proofs alleged out of Scripture, namely, those examples of images appointed by God to be set up; they were not set up for the people, or any man to worship; but that they should worship God himself before them; as before the cherubims over the ark, and before the brazen serpent. For we read not, that the priest, or any other did worship the cherubims; but contrarily we read (2 *Kings* 18. 4) that Hezekiah brake in pieces the brazen serpent which Moses had set up, because the people burnt incense to it. Besides, those examples are not put for our imitation, that we also should set up images, under pretence of worshipping God before them; because the words of the second commandment, *thou shalt not make to thyself any graven image, &c.* distinguish between the images that God commanded to be set up, and those which we set up to ourselves. And therefore from the cherubims, or brazen serpent, to the images of man's devising; and from the worship commanded by God, to the will-worship of men, the argument is not good. This also is to be considered, that as Hezekiah brake in pieces the brazen serpent, because the Jews did worship it, to the end they should do so no more; so also Christian sovereigns ought to break down the images which their subjects have been accustomed to worship; that there be no more occasion of such idolatry. For at this day, the ignorant people, where images are worshipped, do really believe there is a divine power in the images; and are told by their pastors, that some of them have spoken; and have bled; and that miracles

Answer to the argument from the cherubims, and brazen serpent.

have been done by them; which they apprehend as done by the saint, which they think either is the image itself, or in it. The Israelites, when they worshipped the calf, did think they worshipped the God that brought them out of Egypt; and yet it was idolatry, because they thought the calf either was that God, or had him in his belly. And though some man may think it impossible for people to be so stupid, as to think the image to be God, or a saint; or to worship it in that notion; yet it is manifest in Scripture to the contrary; where when the golden calf was made, the people said, (*Exod.* 32. 4) *These are thy gods, O Israel*; and where the images of Laban (*Gen.* 31. 30) are called his gods. And we see daily by experience in all sorts of people, that such men as study nothing but their food and ease, are content to believe any absurdity, rather than to trouble themselves to examine it; holding their faith as it were by entail unalienable, except by an express and new law.

Painting of fancies no idolatry; but abusing them to religious worship is.

[364]

31.   But they infer from some other places, that it is lawful to paint angels, and also God himself: as from God's walking in the garden; from Jacob's seeing God at the top of the ladder; and from other visions, and dreams. But visions, and dreams, whether natural, or supernatural, are but phantasms: and he that painteth an image of any of them, maketh not an image of God, but of his own phantasm, which is, making of an idol. I say not, that to draw a picture after a fancy, is a sin; but when it is drawn, to hold it for a representation of God, is against the second commandment; and can be of no use, but to worship. And the same may be said of the images of angels, and of men dead; unless as monuments of friends, or of men worthy remembrance. For such use of an image, is not worship of the image; but a civil honouring of the person, not that is, but that was: but when it is done to the image which we make of a saint, for no other reason, but that we think he heareth our prayers, and is pleased with the honour we do him, when dead, and without sense, we attribute to him more than human power; and therefore it is idolatry.

32.   Seeing therefore there is no authority, neither in the law of Moses, nor in the Gospel, for the religious worship of images, or other representations of God, which men set up to themselves; or for the worship of the image of any creature in heaven, or earth, or under the earth: and whereas Christian kings, who are living representants of God, are not to be worshipped by their subjects, by any act, that signifieth a greater esteem of his power, than the nature of mortal man is capable of; it cannot be imagined, that the religious

worship now in use, was brought into the Church by misunderstanding of the Scripture. It resteth therefore, that it was left in it, by not destroying the images themselves, in the conversion of the Gentiles that worshipped them.

33. The cause whereof, was the immoderate esteem, and prices set upon the workmanship of them, which made the owners (though converted from worshipping them as they had done religiously for demons) to retain them still in their houses, upon pretence of doing it in the honour of Christ, of the Virgin Mary, and of the Apostles, and other the pastors of the primitive Church; as being easy, by giving them new names, to make that an image of the Virgin Mary, and of her son our Saviour, which before perhaps was called the image of Venus, and Cupid; and so of a Jupiter to make a Barnabas, and of Mercury a Paul, and the like. And as worldly ambition creeping by degrees into the pastors, drew them to an endeavour of pleasing the new-made Christians; and also to a liking of this kind of honour, which they also might hope for after their decease, as well as those that had already gained it: so the worshipping of the images of Christ and his apostles, grew more and more idolatrous; save that somewhat after the time of Constantine, divers emperors, and bishops, and general councils, observed, and opposed the unlawfulness thereof; but too late, or too weakly.

How idolatry was left in the Church.

34. The canonizing of saints, is another relic of Gentilism: it is neither a misunderstanding of Scripture, nor a new invention of the Roman Church, but a custom as ancient as the commonwealth of Rome itself. The first that ever was canonized at Rome, was Romulus, and that upon the narration of Julius Proculus, that swore before the senate, he spake with him after his death, and was assured by him, he dwelt in heaven, and was there called *Quirinus*, and would be propitious to the state of their new city: and thereupon the senate gave *public testimony* of his sanctity.* Julius Caesar, and other emperors after him, had the like *testimony*; that is, were canonized for saints; for by such testimony is CANONIZATION now defined; and is the same with the ἀποθέωσις of the heathen.

Canonizing of saints.

[365]

35. It is also from the Roman Heathen, that the Popes have received the name, and power of PONTIFEX MAXIMUS. This was the name of him that in the ancient commonwealth of Rome, had the supreme authority under the senate and people, of regulating all ceremonies, and doctrines concerning their religion: and when Augustus Caesar changed the state into a monarchy, he took to

The name of Pontifex.

himself no more but this office, and that of tribune of the people, (that is to say, the supreme power both in state, and religion;) and the succeeding emperors enjoyed the same. But when the emperor Constantine lived, who was the first that professed and authorized Christian religion, it was consonant to his profession, to cause religion to be regulated (under his authority) by the Bishop of Rome: though it do not appear they had so soon the name of Pontifex; but rather, that the succeeding bishops took it of themselves, to countenance the power they exercised over the bishops of the Roman provinces. For it is not any privilege of St. Peter, but the privilege of the city of Rome, which the emperors were always willing to uphold, that gave them such authority over other bishops; as may be evidently seen by that, that the bishop of Constantinople, when the emperor made that city the seat of the empire, pretended to be equal to the bishop of Rome; though at last, not without contention, the Pope carried it, and became the *Pontifex Maximus*; but in right only of the emperor; and not without the bounds of the empire; nor any where, after the emperor had lost his power in Rome; though it were the Pope himself that took his power from him. From whence we may by the way observe, that there is no place for the superiority of the Pope over other bishops, except in the territories whereof he is himself the civil sovereign; and where the emperor having sovereign power civil, hath expressly chosen the Pope for the chief pastor under himself, of his Christian subjects.

Procession of images.

36. The carrying about of images in *procession*, is another relic of the religion of the Greeks, and Romans. For they also carried their idols from place to place, in a kind of chariot, which was peculiarly dedicated to that use, which the Latins called *thensa*, and *vehiculum Deorum*; and the image was placed in a frame, or shrine, which they called *ferculum*: and that which they called *pompa*, is the same that now is named *procession*. According whereunto, amongst the divine honours which were given to Julius Caesar by the senate, this was one, that in the pomp (or procession) at the Circaean games, he should have *thensam et ferculum*, a sacred chariot, and a shrine; which was as much, as to be carried up and down as a god: just as at this day the Popes are carried by Switzers under a canopy.

[366]

Wax candles, and torches lighted.

37. To these processions also belonged the bearing of burning torches, and candles, before the images of the gods, both amongst the Greeks, and Romans. For afterwards the emperors of Rome received the same honour; as we read of Caligula,* that at his

reception to the empire, he was carried from Misenum to Rome, in the midst of a throng of people, the ways beset with altars, and beasts for sacrifice, and burning *torches*: and of Caracalla,* that was received into Alexandria with incense, and with casting of flowers, and δαδουχίαις, that is, with torches; for δαδοῦχοι were they that amongst the Greeks carried torches lighted in the processions of their gods. And in process of time, the devout, but ignorant people, did many times honour their bishops with the like pomp of wax candles, and the images of our Saviour, and the saints, constantly, in the church itself. And thus came in the use of wax candles; and was also established by some of the ancient Councils.

38. The heathens had also their *aqua lustralis*, that is to say, *holy water*. The Church of Rome imitates them also in their *holy days*. They had their *bacchanalia*; and we have our *wakes*, answering to them: they their *saturnalia*, and we our *carnivals*, and Shrove-Tuesday's liberty of servants: they their procession of *Priapus*; we our fetching in, erection, and dancing about *May-poles*; and dancing is one kind of worship: they had their procession called *Ambarvalia*; and we our procession about the fields in the *Rogation-week*. Nor do I think that these are all the ceremonies that have been left in the Church, from the first conversion of the Gentiles; but they are all that I can for the present call to mind; and if a man would well observe that which is delivered in the histories, concerning the religious rites of the Greeks and Romans, I doubt not but he might find many more of these old empty bottles of Gentilism, which the doctors of the Roman Church, either by negligence or ambition, have filled up again with the new wine of Christianity, that will not fail in time to break them.

CHAPTER XLVI   [367]

OF DARKNESS FROM VAIN PHILOSOPHY,
AND FABULOUS TRADITIONS

1. By Philosophy,* is understood *the knowledge acquired by reason-*   What
ing, from the manner of the generation of any thing, to the properties: or   philosophy is.
from the properties, to some possible way of generation of the same; to the
end to be able to produce, as far as matter, and human force permit, such
effects, as human life requireth. So the geometrician, from the con-

struction of figures, findeth out many properties thereof; and from the properties, new ways of their construction, by reasoning; to the end to be able to measure land, and water; and for infinite other uses. So the astronomer, from the rising, setting, and moving of the sun, and stars, in divers parts of the heavens, findeth out the causes of day, and night, and of the different seasons of the year; whereby he keepeth an account of time; and the like of other sciences.

Prudence no part of philosophy.

2. By which definition it is evident, that we are not to account as any part thereof, that original knowledge called experience, in which consisteth prudence: because it is not attained by reasoning, but found as well in brute beasts, as in man; and is but a memory of successions of events in times past, wherein the omission of every little circumstance altering the effect, frustrateth the expectation of the most prudent: whereas nothing is produced by reasoning aright, but general, eternal, and immutable truth.

No false doctrine is part of philosophy:

3. Nor are we therefore to give that name to any false conclusions: for he that reasoneth aright in words he understandeth, can never conclude an error:

No more is revelation supernatural:

4. Nor to that which any man knows by supernatural revelation; because it is not acquired by reasoning:

Nor learning taken upon credit of authors.

5. Nor that which is gotten by reasoning from the authority of books; because it is not by reasoning from the cause to the effect, nor from the effect to the cause; and is not knowledge, but faith.

Of the beginnings and progress of philosophy.

6. The faculty of reasoning being consequent to the use of speech, it was not possible, but that there should have been some general truths found out by reasoning, as ancient almost as language itself. The savages of America, are not without some good moral sentences; also they have a little arithmetic, to add, and divide in numbers not too great: but they are not, therefore, philosophers. For as there were plants of corn and wine in small quantity dispersed in the fields and woods, before men knew their virtue, or made use of them for their nourishment, or planted them apart in fields, and vineyards; in which time they fed on acorns, and drank water: so also there have been divers true, general, and profitable speculations from the beginning; as being the natural plants of human reason. But they were at first but few in number; men lived upon gross experience; there was no method; that is to say, no sowing, nor planting of knowledge by itself, apart from the weeds, and common plants of error and conjecture. And the cause of it being the want of leisure from procuring the necessities of life, and

[368]

defending themselves against their neighbours, it was impossible, till the erecting of great commonwealths, it should be otherwise. *Leisure* is the mother of *philosophy*; and *Commonwealth*, the mother of *peace* and *leisure*. Where first were great and flourishing *cities*, there was first the study of *philosophy*. The *Gymnosophists* of India, the *Magi* of Persia, and the *Priests* of Chaldea and Egypt, are counted the most ancient philosophers; and those countries were the most ancient of kingdoms. *Philosophy* was not risen to the Grecians, and other people of the west, whose *commonwealths* (no greater perhaps than Lucca, or Geneva) had never *peace*, but when their fears of one another were equal; nor the *leisure* to observe anything but one another. At length, when war had united many of these Grecian lesser cities, into fewer, and greater; then began *seven men*,* of several parts of Greece, to get the reputation of being *wise*; some of them for *moral* and *politic* sentences; and others for the learning of the Chaldeans and Egyptians, which was *astronomy*, and *geometry*. But we hear not yet of any *schools* of *philosophy*.

7. After the Athenians, by the overthrow of the Persian armies, had gotten the dominion of the sea; and thereby, of all the islands, and maritime cities of the Archipelago, as well of Asia as Europe; and were grown wealthy; they that had no employment, neither at home nor abroad, had little else to employ themselves in, but either (as St. Luke says, *Acts* 17. 21), *in telling and hearing news*, or in discoursing of *philosophy* publicly to the youth of the city. Every master took some place for that purpose. Plato in certain public walks called *Academia*, from one *Academus*: Aristotle in the walk of the temple of Pan, called *Lyceum*: others in the *Stoa*, or covered walk, wherein the merchants' goods were brought to land: others in other places; where they spent the time of their leisure, in teaching or in disputing of their opinions: and some in any place, where they could get the youth together to hear them talk. And this was it which Carneades* also did at Rome, when he was ambassador: which caused Cato to advise the senate to dispatch him quickly, for fear of corrupting the manners of the young men, that delighted to hear him speak (as they thought) fine things.

Of the schools of philosophy amongst the Athenians.

8. From this it was, that the place where any of them taught, and disputed, was called *schola*, which in their tongue signifieth *leisure*; and their disputations, *diatribae*, that is to say, *passing of the time*. Also the philosophers themselves had the name of their sects, [369] some of them from these their Schools: for they that followed

443

Plato's doctrine, were called *Academics*; the followers of Aristotle *Peripatetics*, from the walk he taught in; and those that Zeno taught, *Stoics*, from the *Stoa*: as if we should denominate men from *Moorfields*, from *Paul's Church*, and from the *Exchange*, because they meet there often, to prate and loiter.

9. Nevertheless, men were so much taken with this custom, that in time it spread itself over all Europe, and the best part of Africa; so as there were schools publicly erected, and maintained for lectures, and disputations, almost in every commonwealth.

Of the schools of the Jews.

10. There were also schools, anciently, both before, and after the time of our Saviour, amongst the Jews: but they were schools of their law. For though they were called *synagogues*, that is to say, congregations of the people; yet, inasmuch as the law was every sabbath-day read, expounded, and disputed in them, they differed not in nature, but in name only, from public schools; and were not only in Jerusalem, but in every city of the Gentiles, where the Jews inhabited. There was such a school at Damascus, whereinto Paul entered, to persecute. There were others at Antioch, Iconium, and Thessalonica, whereinto he entered, to dispute: and such was the synagogue of the *Libertines*, *Cyrenians*, *Alexandrians*, *Cilicians*, and those of Asia; that is to say, the school of *Libertines*, and of *Jews* that were strangers in Jerusalem: and of this school they were that disputed (*Acts* 6. 9) with St. Stephen.

The schools of the Grecians unprofitable.

11. But what has been the utility of those schools? What science is there at this day acquired by their readings and disputings? That we have of geometry, which is the mother of all natural science, we are not indebted for it to the schools. Plato that was the best philosopher of the Greeks, forbad entrance into his School, to all that were not already in some measure geometricians. There were many that studied that science to the great advantage of mankind: but there is no mention of their schools; nor was there any sect of geometricians; nor did they then pass under the name of philosophers. The natural philosophy of those schools, was rather a dream than science, and set forth in senseless and insignificant language; which cannot be avoided by those that will teach philosophy, without having first attained great knowledge in geometry: for nature worketh by motion; the ways and degrees whereof cannot be known, without the knowledge of the proportions and properties of lines, and figures. Their moral philosophy is but a description of their own passions. For the rule of manners, without civil government, is the law of

444

nature; and in it, the law civil, that determineth what is *honest* and *dishonest*; what is *just* and *unjust*; and generally what is *good* and *evil*. Whereas they make the rules of *good*, and *bad*, by their own *liking* and *disliking*: by which means, in so great diversity of tastes, there is nothing generally agreed on; but every one doth (as far as he dares) whatsoever seemeth good in his own eyes, to the subversion of commonwealth. Their *logic*, which should be the method of reasoning, is nothing else but captions [quibbles] of words, and inventions how to puzzle such as should go about to pose them. To conclude, there is nothing so absurd, that the old philosophers (as Cicero saith,* who was one of them) have not some of them maintained. And I believe that scarce anything can be more absurdly said in natural philosophy, than that which now is called *Aristotle's Metaphysics*; nor more repugnant to government, than much of that he hath said in his *Politics*; nor more ignorantly, than a great part of his *Ethics*. [370]

12. The school of the Jews, was originally a school of the law of Moses; who commanded (*Deut*. 31. 10) that at the end of every seventh year, at the Feast of the Tabernacles, it should be read to all the people, that they might hear, and learn it. Therefore the reading of the law (which was in use after the captivity) every Sabbath day, ought to have had no other end, but the acquainting of the people with the Commandments which they were to obey, and to expound unto them the writings of the prophets. But it is manifest, by the many reprehensions of them by our Saviour, that they corrupted the text of the law with their false commentaries, and vain traditions; and so little understood the prophets, that they did neither acknowledge Christ, nor the works he did; of which the prophets prophesied. So that by their lectures and disputations in their synagogues, they turned the doctrine of their law into a fantastical kind of philosophy, concerning the incomprehensible nature of God, and of spirits; which they compounded of the vain philosophy and theology of the Grecians, mingled with their own fancies, drawn from the obscurer places of the Scripture, and which might most easily be wrested to their purpose; and from the fabulous traditions of their ancestors. *The schools of the Jews unprofitable.*

13. That which is now called an *University*, is a joining together, and an incorporation under one government of many public schools, in one and the same town or city. In which, the principal schools were ordained for the three professions, that is to say, of the Roman *University, what it is.*

445

religion, of the Roman law, and of the art of medicine. And for the study of philosophy it hath no otherwise place, than as a handmaid to the Roman religion: and since the authority of Aristotle is only current there, that study is not properly philosophy, (the nature whereof dependeth not on authors,) but *Aristotelity*. And for geometry, till of very late times it had no place at all; as being subservient to nothing but rigid truth. And if any man by the ingenuity of his own nature, had attained to any degree of perfection therein, he was commonly thought a magician, and his art diabolical.

[371]

Errors brought into religion from Aristotle's metaphysics.

14. Now to descend to the particular tenets of vain philosophy, derived to the Universities, and thence into the Church, partly from Aristotle, partly from blindness of understanding; I shall first consider these principles. There is a certain *philosophia prima*, on which all other philosophy ought to depend; and consisteth principally, in right limiting of the significations of such appellations, or names, as are of all others the most universal; which limitations serve to avoid ambiguity and equivocation in reasoning; and are commonly called definitions:* such as are the definitions of body, time, place, matter, form, essence, subject, substance, accident, power, act, finite, infinite, quantity, quality, motion, action, passion, and divers others, necessary to the explaining of a man's conceptions concerning the nature and generation of bodies. The explication (that is, the settling of the meaning) of which, and the like terms, is commonly in the Schools called *metaphysics*; as being a part of the philosophy of Aristotle, which hath that for title: but it is in another sense; for there it signifieth as much as *books written or placed after his natural philosophy*: but the Schools take them for *books of supernatural philosophy*: for the word *metaphysics* will bear both these senses. And indeed that which is there written, is for the most part so far from the possibility of being understood, and so repugnant to natural reason, that whosoever thinketh there is anything to be understood by it, must needs think it supernatural.

Errors concerning abstract essences.

15.* From these metaphysics, which are mingled with the Scripture to make School divinity, we are told, there be in the world certain essences separated from bodies, which they call *abstract essences, and substantial forms*: for the interpreting of which jargon, there is need of somewhat more than ordinary attention in this place. Also I ask pardon of those that are not used to this kind of discourse, for applying myself to those that are. The world, (I mean not the earth only, that denominates the lovers of it *worldly men*, but the *universe*, that is, the whole mass of all things that are), is corporeal, that is to say, body; and hath the dimensions of magnitude, namely, length, breadth, and depth: also every part of body, is likewise body, and hath the like dimensions; and consequently every part of the universe, is body, and that which is not body, is no part of the universe: and because the universe is all, that which is no part of it, is *nothing*; and consequently *nowhere*. Nor does it follow from hence, that spirits are *nothing*: for they have dimensions, and are therefore really *bodies*; though that name in common speech be given to such bodies only, as are visible, or palpable; that is, that have some degree of opacity: but for spirits, they call them incorporeal; which is a name of more honour, and may therefore with more piety be attributed to God himself; in whom we consider not what attribute expresseth best his nature, which is incomprehensible; but what best expresseth our desire to honour Him.

16. To know now upon what grounds they say there be *essences* [372] *abstract*, or *substantial forms*, we are to consider what those words do properly signify. The use of words, is to register to ourselves, and make manifest to others the thoughts and conceptions of our minds. Of which words, some are the names of the things conceived; as the names of all sorts of bodies, that work upon the senses, and leave an impression in the imagination: others are the names of the imaginations themselves; that is to say, of those ideas, or mental images we have of all things we see, or remember: and others again are names of names; or of different sorts of speech: as *universal*, *plural*, *singular*, are the names of names; and *definition*, *affirmation*, *negation*, *true*, *false*, *syllogism*, *interrogation*, *promise*, *covenant*, are the names of certain forms of speech. Others serve to show the consequence, or repugnance of one name to another; as when one saith, *a man is a body*, he intendeth that the name of *body* is necessarily consequent to the name of *man*; as being but several names of the same thing, *man*; which consequence is signified by coupling them together with the word *is*. And as we use the verb *is*, so the Latins use their verb *est*, and the Greeks their *ἔστι* through all its declinations. Whether all other nations of the world have in their several languages a word that answereth to it, or not, I cannot tell; but I am sure they have not need of it. For the placing of two names in order may serve to signify their consequence, if it were the custom, (for custom is it, that gives words their force,) as well as the words *is*, or *be*, or *are*, and the like.

17. And if it were so, that there were a language without any verb

answerable to *est*, or *is*, or *be*; yet the men that used it would be not a jot the less capable of inferring, concluding, and of all kind of reasoning, than were the Greeks, and Latins. But what then would become of these terms, of *entity*, *essence*, *essential*, *essentiality*, that are derived from it, and of many more than depend on these, applied as most commonly they are? They are therefore no names of things; but signs, by which we make known, that we conceive the consequence of one name or attribute to another: as when we say, *a man, is, a living body*, we mean not that the *man* is one thing, the *living body* another, and the *is*, or *being* a third: but that the *man*, and the *living body*, is the same thing; because the consequence, *if he be a man, he is a living body*, is a true consequence, signified by that word *is*. Therefore, *to be a body, to walk, to be speaking, to live, to see*, and the like infinitives; also *corporeity, walking, speaking, life, sight*, and the like, that signify just the same, are the names of *nothing*; as I have elsewhere* more amply expressed.

18. But to what purpose (may some man say) is such subtlety in a work of this nature, where I pretend to nothing but what is necessary to the doctrine of government and obedience? It is to this [373] purpose, that men may no longer suffer themselves to be abused, by them, that by this doctrine of *separated essences*, built on the vain philosophy of Aristotle, would fright them from obeying the laws of their country, with empty names; as men fright birds from the corn with an empty doublet, a hat, and a crooked stick. For it is upon this ground, that when a man is dead and buried, they say his soul (that is his life) can walk separated from his body, and is seen by night amongst the graves. Upon the same ground they say, that the figure, and colour, and taste of a piece of bread, has a being, there, where they say there is no bread: and upon the same ground they say, that faith, and wisdom, and other virtues, are sometimes *poured* into a man, sometimes *blown* into him from Heaven; as if the virtuous and their virtues could be asunder; and a great many other things that serve to lessen the dependence of subjects on the sovereign power of their country. For who will endeavour to obey the laws, if he expect obedience to be poured or blown into him? Or who will not obey a priest, that can make God, rather than his sovereign; nay than God himself? Or who, that is in fear of ghosts, will not bear great respect to those that can make the holy water, that drives them from him? And this shall suffice for an example of the errors, which are brought into the Church, from the *entities* and *essences* of Aristotle: which it

may be he knew to be false philosophy; but writ it as a thing consonant to, and corroborative of their religion; and fearing the fate of Socrates.

19. Being once fallen into this error of *separated essences*, they are thereby necessarily involved in many other absurdities that follow it. For seeing they will have these forms to be real, they are obliged to assign them *some place*. But because they hold them incorporeal, without all dimension of quantity, and all men know that place is dimension, and not to be filled, but by that which is corporeal; they are driven to uphold their credit with a distinction, that they are not indeed anywhere *circumscriptive*, but *definitive*: which terms being mere words, and in this occasion insignificant, pass only in Latin, that the vanity of them may be concealed. For the circumscription of a thing, is nothing else but the determination, or defining of its place; and so both the terms of the distinction are the same. And in particular, of the essence of a man, which (they say) is his soul, they affirm it, to be all of it in his little finger, and all of it in every other part (how small soever) of his body; and yet no more soul in the whole body, than in any one of those parts.* Can any man think that God is served with such absurdities? And yet all this is necessary to believe, to those that will believe the existence of an incorporeal soul, separated from the body.

20. And when they come to give account how an incorporeal substance can be capable of pain, and be tormented in the fire of hell or purgatory, they have nothing at all to answer, but that it cannot be known how fire can burn souls.*

21. Again, whereas motion is change of place, and incorporeal [374] substances are not capable of place, they are troubled to make it seem possible, how a soul can go hence, without the body, to heaven, hell, or purgatory; and how the ghosts of men (and I may add of their clothes which they appear in) can walk by night in churches, churchyards, and other places of sepulture. To which I know not what they can answer, unless they will say, they walk *definitivè*, not *circumscriptivè*, or *spiritually*, not *temporally*: for such egregious distinctions are equally applicable to any difficulty whatsoever.

22. For the meaning of *eternity*, they will not have it to be an *Nunc-stans.* endless succession of time; for then they should not be able to render a reason how God's will, and pre-ordaining of things to come, should not be before his prescience of the same, as the efficient cause before the effect, or agent before the action; nor of

many other their bold opinions concerning the incomprehensible nature of God. But they will teach us, that eternity is the standing still of the present time, a *nunc-stans*, as the Schools call it; which neither they, nor any else understand, no more than they would a *hic-stans* for an infinite greatness of place.

One body in many places, and many bodies in one place at once.

23. And whereas men divide a body in their thought, by numbering parts of it, and, in numbering those parts, number also the parts of the place it filled; it cannot be, but in making many parts, we make also many places of those parts; whereby there cannot be conceived in the mind of any man, more, or fewer parts, than there are places for: yet they will have us believe, that by the Almighty power of God, one body may be at one and the same time in many places; and many bodies at one and the same time in one place: as if it were an acknowledgment of the Divine Power to say, that which is, is not; or that which has been, has not been. And these are but a small part of the incongruities they are forced to, from their disputing philosophically, instead of admiring, and adoring of the divine and incomprehensible nature;* whose attributes cannot signify what he is, but ought to signify our desire to honour him, with the best appellations we can think on. But they that venture to reason of his nature, from these attributes of honour, losing their understanding in the very first attempt, fall from one inconvenience into another, without end, and without number; in the same manner, as when a man ignorant of the ceremonies of court, coming into the presence of a greater person than he is used to speak to, and stumbling at his entrance, to save himself from falling, lets slip his cloak; to recover his cloak, lets fall his hat; and with one disorder after another, discovers his astonishment and rusticity.

Absurdities in natural philosophy, as gravity the cause of heaviness.

[375]

24. Then for *physics*, that is, the knowledge of the subordinate and secondary causes of natural events; they render none at all, but empty words. If you desire to know why some kind of bodies sink naturally downwards toward the earth, and others go naturally from it; the Schools will tell you out of Aristotle, that the bodies that sink downwards, are *heavy*; and that this heaviness is it that causes them to descend: but if you ask what they mean by *heaviness*, they will define it to be an endeavour to go to the centre of the earth: so that the cause why things sink downward, is an endeavour to be below: which is as much as to say, that bodies descend, or ascend, because they do. Or they will tell you the centre of the earth is the place of rest, and conservation for heavy things; and therefore they endeav-

our to be there: as if stones and metals had a desire, or could discern the place they would be at, as man does; or loved rest, as man does not; or that a piece of glass were less safe in the window, than falling into the street.

25. If we would know why the same body seems greater (without adding to it) one time, than another; they say, when it seems less, it is *condensed*; when greater, *rarefied*. What is that *condensed*, and *rarefied*? Condensed, is when there is in the very same matter, less quantity than before; and rarefied, when more. As if there could be matter, that had not some determined quantity; when quantity is nothing else but the determination of matter; that is to say, of body, by which we say one body is greater, or lesser than another, by thus, or thus much. Or as if a body were made without any quantity at all, and that afterwards more, or less were put into it, according as it is intended the body should be more, or less dense. *Quantity put into body already made.*

26. For the cause of the soul of man, they say, *creatur infundendo*, and *creando infunditur*: that is, *it is created by pouring it in*, and *poured in by creation*. *Pouring in of souls.*

27. For the cause of sense, an ubiquity of *species*; that is, of the *shows* or *apparitions* of objects; which when they be apparitions to the eye, is *sight*; when to the ear, *hearing*; to the palate, *taste*; to the nostril, *smelling*; and to the rest of the body, *feeling*. *Ubiquity of apparition.*

28. For cause of the will, to do any particular action, which is called *volitio*, they assign the faculty, that is to say, the capacity in general, that men have, to will sometimes one thing, sometimes another, which is called *voluntas*; making the *power* the cause of the *act*: as if one should assign for cause of the good or evil acts of men, their ability to do them. *Will, the cause of willing.*

29. And in many occasions they put for cause of natural events, their own ignorance; but disguised in other words: as when they say, fortune is the cause of things contingent; that is, of things whereof they know no cause: and as when they attribute many effects to *occult qualities*; that is, qualities not known to them; and therefore also (as they think) to no man else. And to *sympathy*, *antipathy*, *antiperistasis*, *specifical qualities*, and other like terms, which signify neither the agent that produceth them, nor the operation by which they are produced. *Sympathy, antipathy, and other occult qualities.*

30. If such *metaphysics*, and *physics* as this, be not *vain philosophy*, there was never any; nor needed St. Paul to give us warning to avoid it. [376]

451

*And that
one makes
the things
incongruent,
and another
the
incongruity.*

31. And for their moral, and civil philosophy, it hath the same, or greater absurdities. If a man do an action of injustice, that is to say, an action contrary to the law, God they say is the prime cause of the law, and also the prime cause of that, and all other actions; but no cause at all of the injustice; which is the inconformity of the action to the law. This is vain philosophy. A man might as well say, that one man maketh both a straight line, and a crooked, and another maketh their incongruity. And such is the philosophy of all men that resolve of their conclusions, before they know their premises; pretending to comprehend, that which is incomprehensible; and of attributes of honour to make attributes of nature; as this distinction was made to maintain the doctrine of free-will, that is, of a will of man, not subject to the will of God.

*And that
private
appetite the
rule of public
good and
evil.*

32.* Aristotle, and other heathen philosophers define good, and evil, by the appetite of men; and well enough, as long as we consider them governed every one by his own law: for in the condition of men that have no other law but their own appetites, there can be no general rule of good, and evil actions. But in a commonwealth this measure is false: not the appetite of private men, but the law, which is the will and appetite of the state is the measure. And yet is this doctrine still practised; and men judge the goodness, or wickedness of their own, and of other men's actions, and of the actions of the commonwealth itself, by their own passions; and no man calleth good or evil, but that which is so in his own eyes, without any regard at all to the public laws; except only monks, and friars, that are bound by vow to that simple obedience to their superior, to which every subject ought to think himself bound by the law of nature to the civil sovereign. And this private measure of good, is a doctrine, not only vain, but also pernicious to the public state.

*And that
lawful
marriage is
incontinence.*

33. It is also vain and false philosophy, to say the work of marriage is repugnant to chastity, or continence, and by consequence to make them moral vice; as they do, that pretend chastity, and continence, for the ground of denying marriage to the clergy. For they confess it is no more, but a constitution of the Church, that requireth in those holy orders that continually attend the altar, and administration of the eucharist, a continual abstinence from women, under the name of continual chastity, continence, and purity. Therefore they call the lawful use of wives, want of chastity, and continence; and so make marriage a sin, or at least a thing so impure, and unclean, as to render a man unfit for the altar. If the law were made because the use of wives is incontinence, and contrary to chastity, then all marriage is vice: if because it is a thing too impure, and unclean for a man consecrated to God; much more should other natural, necessary, and daily works which all men do, render men unworthy to be priests, because they are more unclean.   [377]

34. But the secret foundation of this prohibition of marriage of priests, is not likely to have been laid so slightly, as upon such errors in moral philosophy; nor yet upon the preference of single life, to the estate of matrimony; which proceeded from the wisdom of St. Paul, who perceived how inconvenient a thing it was, for those that in those times of persecution were preachers of the gospel, and forced to fly from one country to another, to be clogged with the care of wife and children; but upon the design of the Popes, and priests of after times, to make themselves the clergy, that is to say, sole heirs of the kingdom of God in this world; to which it was necessary to take from them the use of marriage, because our Saviour saith, that at the coming of his kingdom the children of God *shall neither marry, nor be given in marriage, but shall be as the angels in heaven*; that is to say, spiritual. Seeing then they had taken on them the name of spiritual, to have allowed themselves (when there was no need) the propriety of wives, had been an incongruity.

35. From Aristotle's civil philosophy, they have learned, to call all manner of commonwealths but the popular, (such as was at that time the state of Athens), *tyranny*. All kings they called tyrants; and the aristocracy of the thirty governors set up there by the Lacedemonians that subdued them, the thirty tyrants:* as also to call the condition of the people under the democracy, *liberty*. A *tyrant* originally signified no more simply, but a *monarch*: but when afterwards in most parts of Greece that kind of government was abolished, the name began to signify, not only the thing it did before, but with it, the hatred which the popular states bare towards it. As also the name of king became odious after the deposing of the kings in Rome, as being a thing natural to all men, to conceive some great fault to be signified in any attribute, that is given in despite, and to a great enemy. And when the same men shall be displeased with those that have the administration of the democracy, or aristocracy, they are not to seek for disgraceful names to express their anger in; but call readily the one *anarchy*, and the other, *oligarchy*, or the *tyranny of a few*. And that which offendeth the people, is no other thing, but that they are governed, not as every one of them

And that all government but popular is tyranny.

453

would himself, but as the public representant, be it one man, or an assembly of men thinks fit; that is, by an arbitrary government: for which they give evil names to their superiors; never knowing (till perhaps a little after a civil war) that without such arbitrary government, such war must be perpetual; and that it is men, and arms, not words and promises, that make the force and power of the laws.

That not men, but law governs.

[378]

36. And therefore this is another error of Aristotle's politics, that in a well-ordered commonwealth, not men should govern, but the laws. What man, that has his natural senses, though he can neither write nor read, does not find himself governed by them he fears, and believes can kill or hurt him when he obeyeth not? Or that believes the law can hurt him; that is, words, and paper, without the hands and swords of men? And this is of the number of pernicious errors: for they induce men, as oft as they like not their governors, to adhere to those that call them tyrants, and to think it lawful to raise war against them: and yet they are many times cherished from the pulpit, by the clergy.

Laws over the conscience.

37. There is another error in their civil philosophy (which they never learned of Aristotle, nor Cicero, nor any other of the heathen,) to extend the power of the law, which is the rule of actions only, to the very thoughts and consciences of men, by examination, and *inquisition* of what they hold, notwithstanding the conformity of their speech and actions: by which, men are either punished for answering the truth of their thoughts, or constrained to answer an untruth for fear of punishment. It is true, that the civil magistrate, intending to employ a minister in the charge of teaching, may enquire of him, if he be content to preach such, and such doctrines; and in case of refusal, may deny him the employment. But to force him to accuse himself of opinions, when his actions are not by law forbidden, is against the law of nature; and especially in them, who teach, that a man shall be damned to eternal and extreme torments, if he die in a false opinion concerning an article of the Christian faith. For who is there, that knowing there is so great danger in an error, whom the natural care of himself, compelleth not to hazard his soul upon his own judgment, rather than that of any other man that is unconcerned in his damnation?

That private men may interpret the law as they please.

38. For a private man, without the authority of the commonwealth, that is to say, without permission from the representant thereof, to interpret the law by his own spirit, is another error in the politics; but not drawn from Aristotle, nor from any other of the

454

heathen philosophers. For none of them deny, but that in the power of making laws, is comprehended also the power of explaining them when there is need. And are not the Scriptures, in all places where they are law, made law by the authority of the commonwealth, and consequently, a part of the civil law?

39. Of the same kind it is also, when any but the sovereign restraineth in any man that power which the commonwealth hath not restrained; as they do, that impropriate the preaching of the gospel to one certain order of men, where the laws have left it free. If the state give me leave to preach, or teach; that is, if it forbid me not, no man can forbid me. If I find myself amongst the idolaters of America, shall I that am a Christian, though not in orders, think it a sin to preach Jesus Christ, till I have received orders from Rome? Or when I have preached, shall not I answer their doubts, and expound the Scriptures to them; that is, shall I not teach? But for this may some say, as also for administering to them the sacraments, [379] the necessity shall be esteemed for a sufficient mission; which is true: but this is true also, that for whatsoever, a dispensation is due for the necessity, for the same there needs no dispensation, when there is no law that forbids it. Therefore to deny these functions to those, to whom the civil sovereign hath not denied them, is a taking away of a lawful liberty, which is contrary to the doctrine of civil government.

40. More examples of vain philosophy, brought into religion by the doctors of School divinity, might be produced; but other men may if they please observe them of themselves. I shall only add this, that the writings of School divines, are nothing else for the most part, but insignificant trains of strange and barbarous words, or words otherwise used, than in the common use of the Latin tongue; such as would pose Cicero, and Varro, and all the grammarians of ancient Rome. Which if any man would see proved, let him (as I have said once before) see whether he can translate any School divine into any of the modern tongues, as French, English, or any other copious language: for that which cannot in most of these be made intelligible, is not intelligible in the Latin. Which insignificancy of language, though I cannot note it for false philosophy; yet it hath a quality, not only to hide the truth, but also to make men think they have it, and desist from further search. *Language of School divines.*

41. Lastly, for the errors brought in from false, or uncertain history, what is all the legend of fictitious miracles, in the lives of the *Errors from tradition.*

saints; and all the histories of apparitions, and ghosts, alleged by the doctors of the Roman Church, to make good their doctrines of hell, and purgatory, the power of exorcism, and other doctrines which have no warrant, neither in reason, nor Scripture; as also all those traditions which they call the unwritten word of God; but old wives' fables? Whereof, though they find dispersed somewhat in the writings of the ancient fathers; yet those fathers were men, that might too easily believe false reports; and the producing of their opinions for testimony of the truth of what they believed, hath no other force with them that (according to the counsel of St. John, 1 *John* 4. 1) examine spirits, than in all things that concern the power of the Roman Church, (the abuse whereof either they suspected not, or had benefit by it,) to discredit their testimony, in respect of too rash belief of reports; which the most sincere men, without great knowledge of natural causes, (such as the fathers were) are commonly the most subject to. For naturally, the best men are the least suspicious of fraudulent purposes. Gregory the Pope, and St. Bernard have somewhat of apparitions of ghosts, that said they were in purgatory; and so has our Bede: but nowhere, I believe, but by report from others. But if they, or any other, relate any such stories of their own knowledge, they shall not thereby confirm the more such vain reports; but discover their own infirmity, or fraud.

[380]
Suppression
of reason.

42. With the introduction of false, we may join also the suppression of true philosophy, by such men, as neither by lawful authority, nor sufficient study, are competent judges of the truth. Our own navigations make manifest, and all men learned in human sciences, now acknowledge there are antipodes: and every day it appeareth more and more, that years, and days are determined by motions of the earth. Nevertheless, men* that have in their writings but supposed such doctrine, as an occasion to lay open the reasons for, and against it, have been punished for it by authority ecclesiastical. But what reason is there for it? Is it because such opinions are contrary to true religion? That cannot be, if they be true.* Let therefore the truth be first examined by competent judges, or confuted by them that pretend to know the contrary. Is it because they be contrary to the religion established? Let them be silenced by the laws of those, to whom the teachers of them are subject; that is, by the laws civil. For disobedience may lawfully be punished in them, that against the laws teach even true philosophy. Is it because they tend to disorder in government, as countenancing rebellion, or

sedition? Then let them be silenced, and the teachers punished by virtue of his power to whom the care of the public quiet is committed; which is the authority civil. For whatsoever power ecclesiastics take upon themselves (in any place where they are subject to the state) in their own right, though they call it God's right, is but usurpation.

CHAPTER XLVII   [381]

OF THE BENEFIT THAT PROCEEDETH FROM SUCH
DARKNESS, AND TO WHOM IT ACCRUETH

1. CICERO maketh honourable mention* of one of the Cassii, a severe judge amongst the Romans, for a custom he had, in criminal causes, (when the testimony of the witnesses was not sufficient,) to ask the accusers, *cui bono*; that is to say, what profit, honour, or other contentment, the accused obtained, or expected by the fact. For amongst presumptions, there is none that so evidently declareth the author, as doth the benefit of the action. By the same rule I intend in this place to examine, who they may be, that have possessed the people so long in this part of Christendom, with these doctrines, contrary to the peaceable societies of mankind. *He that receiveth benefit by a fact, is presumed to be the author.*

2. And first, to this error, *that the present Church now militant on earth, is the kingdom of God,* (that is, the kingdom of glory, or the land of promise; not the kingdom of grace, which is but a promise of the land), are annexed these worldly benefits; first, that the pastors, and teachers of the Church, are entitled thereby, as God's public ministers, to a right of governing the Church; and consequently (because the Church, and commonwealth are the same persons) to be rectors, and governors of the commonwealth. By this title it is, that the Pope prevailed with the subjects of all Christian princes, to believe, that to disobey him, was to disobey Christ himself; and in all differences between him and other princes, (charmed with the word *power spiritual*,) to abandon their lawful sovereigns; which is in effect an universal monarchy over all Christendom. For though they were first invested in the right of being supreme teachers of Christian doctrine, by and under Christian emperors, within the limits of the Roman empire (as is acknowledged by themselves) by the title of *Pontifex Maximus*, who was an officer subject to the civil state; yet *That the Church militant is the kingdom of God, was first taught by the Church of Rome:*

after the empire was divided, and dissolved, it was not hard to obtrude upon the people already subjected to them, another title, namely, the right of St. Peter; not only to save entire their pretended power; but also to extend the same over the same Christian provinces, though no more united in the empire of Rome. This benefit of an universal monarchy, (considering the desire of men to bear rule) is a sufficient presumption, that the Popes that pretended to it, and for a long time enjoyed it, were the authors of the doctrine, by which it was obtained; namely, that the Church now on earth, is the kingdom of Christ. For that granted, it must be understood, that Christ hath some lieutenant amongst us, by whom we are to be told what are his commandments.

[382]   3. After that certain Churches had renounced this universal power of the Pope, one would expect in reason, that the civil sovereigns in all those Churches, should have recovered so much of it, as (before they had unadvisedly let it go) was their own right, and in their own hands. And in England it was so in effect; saving that they, by whom the kings administered the government of religion, by maintaining their employment to be in God's right, seemed to usurp, if not a supremacy, yet an independency on the civil power: and they but seemed to usurp it, inasmuch as they acknowledged a right in the king, to deprive them of the exercise of their functions at his pleasure.

And maintained also by the Presbytery.   4. But in those places where the presbytery took that office, though many other doctrines of the Church of Rome were forbidden to be taught; yet this doctrine, that the kingdom of Christ is already come, and that it began at the resurrection of our Saviour, was still retained. But *cui bono?* What profit did they expect from it? The same which the Popes expected: to have a sovereign power over the people. For what is it for men to excommunicate their lawful king, but to keep him from all places of God's public service in his own kingdom? And with force to resist him, when he with force endeavoureth to correct them? Or what is it, without authority from the civil sovereign, to excommunicate any person, but to take from him his lawful liberty, that is, to usurp an unlawful power over their brethren? The authors therefore of this darkness in religion, are the Roman, and the presbyterian clergy.

Infallibility.   5. To this head, I refer also all those doctrines, that serve them to keep the possession of this spiritual sovereignty after it is gotten. As first, that the *Pope in his public capacity cannot err*. For who is there,

458

that believing this to be true, will not readily obey him in whatsoever he commands?

6. Secondly, that all other bishops, in what commonwealth soever, have not their right, neither immediately from God, nor mediately from their civil sovereigns, but from the Pope, is a doctrine, by which there comes to be in every Christian commonwealth many potent men, (for so are bishops,) that have their dependence on the Pope, and owe obedience to him, though he be a foreign prince; by which means he is able, (as he hath done many times) to raise a civil war against the state that submits not itself to be governed according to his pleasure and interest. *Subjection of bishops.*

7. Thirdly, the exemption of these, and of all other priests, and of all monks, and friars, from the power of the civil laws. For by this means, there is a great part of every commonwealth, that enjoy the benefit of the laws, and are protected by the power of the civil state, which nevertheless pay no part of the public expense; nor are liable to the penalties, as other subjects, due to their crimes; and consequently, stand not in fear of any man, but the Pope; and adhere to him only, to uphold his universal monarchy. *Exemptions of the clergy.*

8. Fourthly, the giving to their priests (which is no more in the New Testament but presbyters, that is, elders) the name of *sacerdotes*, that is, sacrificers, which was the title of the civil sovereign, and his public ministers, amongst the Jews, whilst God was their king. Also, the making the Lord's Supper a sacrifice, serveth to make the people believe the Pope hath the same power over all Christians, that Moses and Aaron had over the Jews; that is to say, all power, both civil and ecclesiastical, as the high-priest then had. *The names of sacerdotes, and sacrificers.* [383]

9. Fifthly, the teaching that matrimony is a sacrament, giveth to the clergy the judging of the lawfulness of marriages; and thereby, of what children are legitimate; and consequently, of the right of succession to hereditary kingdoms. *The sacramentation of marriage.*

10. Sixthly, the denial of marriage to priests, serveth to assure this power of the Pope over kings. For if a king be a priest, he cannot marry, and transmit his kingdom to his posterity; if he be not a priest, then the Pope pretendeth this authority ecclesiastical over him, and over his people. *The single life of priests.*

11. Seventhly, from auricular confession, they obtain, for the assurance of their power, better intelligence of the designs of princes, and great persons in the civil state, than these can have of the designs of the state ecclesiastical. *Auricular confession.*

Canonization of saints, and declaring of martyrs.

12. Eighthly, by the canonization of saints, and declaring who are martyrs, they assure their power, in that they induce simple men into an obstinacy against the laws and commands of their civil sovereigns even to death, if by the Pope's excommunication, they be declared heretics or enemies to the Church; that is, (as they interpret it,) to the Pope.

Transubstantiation, penance, absolution.

13. Ninthly, they assure the same, by the power they ascribe to every priest, of making Christ; and by the power of ordaining penance; and of remitting, and retaining of sins.

Purgatory, indulgences, external works.

14. Tenthly, by the doctrine of purgatory, of justification by external works, and of indulgences, the clergy is enriched.

Demonology and exorcism.

15. Eleventhly, by their demonology, and the use of exorcism, and other things appertaining thereto, they keep (or think they keep) the people more in awe of their power.

School divinity.

16. Lastly, the metaphysics, ethics, and politics of Aristotle, the frivolous distinctions, barbarous terms, and obscure language of the Schoolmen, taught in the universities, (which have been all erected and regulated by the Pope's authority,) serve them to keep these errors from being detected, and to make men mistake the *ignis fatuus* of vain philosophy, for the light of the Gospel.

The authors of spiritual darkness, who they be.

17. To these, if they sufficed not, might be added other of their dark doctrines, the profit whereof redoundeth manifestly, to the setting up of an unlawful power over the lawful sovereigns of Christian people; or for the sustaining of the same, when it is set up; or to the worldly riches, honour, and authority of those that sustain it. And therefore by the aforesaid rule, of *cui bono*, we may justly pronounce for the authors of all this spiritual darkness, the Pope, and Roman clergy, and all those besides that endeavour to settle in the minds of men this erroneous doctrine, that the Church now on earth, is that kingdom of God mentioned in the Old and New Testament.

[384]

18. But the emperors, and other Christian sovereigns, under whose government these errors, and the like encroachments of ecclesiastics upon their office, at first crept in, to the disturbance of their possessions, and of the tranquillity of their subjects, though they suffered the same for want of foresight of the sequel, and of insight into the designs of their teachers, may nevertheless be esteemed accessories to their own, and the public damage. For without their authority there could at first no seditious doctrine have been publicly preached. I say they might have hindered the same in

the beginning: but when the people were once possessed by those spiritual men, there was no human remedy to be applied, that any man could invent: and for the remedies that God should provide, who never faileth in his good time to destroy all the machinations of men against the truth, we are to attend his good pleasure, that suffereth many times the prosperity of his enemies, together with their ambition, to grow to such a height, as the violence thereof openeth the eyes, which the wariness of their predecessors had before sealed up, and makes men by too much grasping let go all, as Peter's net was broken, by the struggling of too great a multitude of fishes; whereas the impatience of those, that strive to resist such encroachment, before their subjects' eyes were opened, did but increase the power they resisted. I do not therefore blame the emperor Frederic for holding the stirrup to our countryman Pope Adrian;* for such was the disposition of his subjects then, as if he had not done it, he was not likely to have succeeded in the empire. But I blame those, that in the beginning, when their power was entire, by suffering such doctrines to be forged in the universities of their own dominions, have holden the stirrup to all the succeeding Popes, whilst they mounted into the thrones of all Christian sovereigns, to ride, and tire, both them, and their people at their pleasure.

19. But as the inventions of men are woven, so also are they ravelled out; the way is the same, but the order is inverted. The web begins at the first elements of power, which are wisdom, humility, sincerity, and other virtues of the Apostles, whom the people, converted, obeyed out of reverence, not by obligation: their consciences were free, and their words and actions subject to none but the civil power. Afterwards the presbyters (as the flocks of Christ increased) assembling to consider what they should teach, and thereby obliging themselves to teach nothing against the decrees of their assemblies, made it to be thought the people were thereby obliged to follow their doctrine, and when they refused, refused to keep them company, (that was then called excommunication,) not as being infidels, but as being disobedient: and this was the first knot upon their liberty. And the number of presbyters increasing, the presbyters of the chief city of a province, got themselves an authority over the parochial presbyters, and appropriated to themselves the names of bishops: and this was a second knot on Christian liberty. Lastly, the bishop of Rome, [385] in regard of the imperial city, took upon him an authority (partly by the wills of the emperors themselves, and by the title of *Pontifex*

461

Maximus, and at last when the emperors were grown weak, by the privileges of St. Peter) over all other bishops of the empire: which was the third and last knot, and the whole *synthesis* and *construction*, of the pontifical power.

20. And therefore the *analysis*, or *resolution*, is by the same way; but beginneth with the knot that was last tied; as we may see in the dissolution of the preterpolitical Church government in England. First, the power of the Popes was dissolved totally by Queen Elizabeth; and the bishops, who before exercised their functions in right of the Pope, did afterwards exercise the same in right of the Queen and her successors; though by retaining the phrase of *jure divino*, they were thought to demand it by immediate right from God: and so was untied the third knot. After this, the presbyterians lately in England obtained the putting down of episcopacy: and so was the second knot dissolved. And almost at the same time, the power was taken also from the presbyterians: and so we are reduced to the independency of the primitive Christians to follow Paul, or Cephas, or Apollos, every man as he liketh best: which, if it be without contention, and without measuring the doctrine of Christ, by our affection to the person of his minister, (the fault which the apostle reprehended in the Corinthians,) is perhaps the best. First, because there ought to be no power over the consciences of men, but of the Word itself, working faith in every one, not always according to the purpose of them that plant and water, but of God himself, that giveth the increase: and secondly, because it is unreasonable in them, who teach there is such danger in every little error, to require of a man endued with reason of his own, to follow the reason of any other man, or of the most voices of any other men; which is little better, than to venture his salvation at cross and pile.* Nor ought those teachers to be displeased with this loss of their ancient authority. For there is none should know better than they, that power is preserved by the same virtues by which it is acquired; that is to say, by wisdom, humility, clearness of doctrine, and sincerity of conversation; and not by suppression of the natural sciences, and of the morality of natural reason; nor by obscure language; nor by arrogating to themselves more knowledge than they make appear; nor by pious frauds; nor by such other faults, as in the pastors of God's Church are not only faults, but also scandals, apt to make men stumble one time or other upon the suppression of their authority.

21. But after this doctrine, *that the Church now militant, is the kingdom of God spoken of in the Old and New Testament*, was received in the world; the ambition, and canvassing for the offices that belong thereunto, and especially for that great office of being Christ's lieutenant, and the pomp of them that obtained therein the principal public charges, became by degrees so evident, that they lost the inward reverence due to the pastoral function: insomuch as the wisest men, of them that had any power in the civil state, needed nothing but the authority of their princes, to deny them any further obedience. For, from the time that the Bishop of Rome had gotten to be acknowledged for bishop universal, by pretence of succession to St. Peter, their whole hierarchy, or kingdom of darkness, may be compared not unfitly to the *kingdom of fairies*; that is, to the old wives' *fables* in England, concerning *ghosts* and *spirits*, and the feats they play in the night. And if a man consider the original of this great ecclesiastical dominion, he will easily perceive, that the Papacy, is no other than the *ghost* of the deceased *Roman empire*, sitting crowned upon the grave thereof: for so did the Papacy start up on a sudden out of the ruins of that heathen power.

22. The *language* also, which they use, both in the churches, and in their public acts, being *Latin*, which is not commonly used by any nation now in the world, what is it but the *ghost* of the old *Roman language*?

23. The *fairies* in what nation soever they converse, have but one universal king, which some poets of ours call King Oberon; but the Scripture calls Beelzebub, prince of *demons*. The *ecclesiastics* likewise, in whose dominions soever they be found, acknowledge but one universal king, the *Pope*.

24. The *ecclesiastics* are *spiritual* men, and *ghostly* fathers. The fairies are *spirits*, and *ghosts*. *Fairies* and *ghosts* inhabit darkness, solitudes and graves. The *ecclesiastics* walk in obscurity of doctrine, in monasteries, churches, and churchyards.

25. The *ecclesiastics* have their cathedral churches; which, in what town soever they be erected, by virtue of holy water, and certain charms called exorcisms, have the power to make those towns, cities, that is to say, seats of empire. The *fairies* also have their enchanted castles, and certain gigantic ghosts, that domineer over the regions round about them.

26. The *fairies* are not to be seized on; and brought to answer for

the hurt they do. So also the *ecclesiastics* vanish away from the tribunals of civil justice.

27. The *ecclesiastics* take from young men, the use of reason, by certain charms compounded of metaphysics, and miracles, and traditions, and abused Scripture, whereby they are good for nothing else, but to execute what they command them. The *fairies* likewise are said to take young children out of their cradles, and to change them into natural fools, which common people do therefore call *elves*, and are apt to mischief.

28. In what shop, or operatory the fairies make their enchantment, the old wives have not determined. But the operatories of the *clergy*, are well enough known to be the universities, that received their discipline from authority pontifical.

[387] 29. When the *fairies* are displeased with anybody, they are said to send their elves, to pinch them. The *ecclesiastics*, when they are displeased with any civil state, make also their elves, that is, superstitious, enchanted subjects, to pinch their princes, by preaching sedition; or one prince enchanted with promises, to pinch another.

30. The *fairies* marry not; but there be amongst them *incubi*, that have copulation with flesh and blood. The *priests* also marry not.

31. The *ecclesiastics* take the cream of the land, by donations of ignorant men, that stand in awe of them, and by tithes. So also it is in the fable of *fairies*, that they enter into the dairies, and feast upon the cream, which they skim from the milk.

32. What kind of money is current in the kingdom of *fairies*, is not recorded in the story. But the *ecclesiastics* in their receipts accept of the same money that we do; though when they are to make any payment, it is in canonizations, indulgences, and masses.

33. To this, and such like resemblances between the *papacy*, and the kingdom of *fairies*, may be added this, that as the *fairies* have no existence, but in the fancies of ignorant people, rising from the traditions of old wives, or old poets: so the spiritual power of the *Pope* (without the bounds of his own civil dominion) consisteth only in the fear that seduced people stand in, of their excommunication; upon hearing of false miracles, false traditions, and false interpretations of the Scripture.

34. It was not therefore a very difficult matter, for Henry VIII by his exorcism; nor for queen Elizabeth by hers, to cast them out. But who knows that this spirit of Rome, now gone out, and walking by missions through the dry places of China, Japan, and the Indies, that

yield him little fruit, may not return, or rather an assembly of spirits worse than he, enter, and inhabit this clean swept house, and make the end thereof worse than the beginning? For it is not the Roman clergy only, that pretends the kingdom of God to be of this world, and thereby to have a power therein, distinct from that of the civil state. And this is all I had a design to say, concerning the doctrine of the POLITICS. Which when I have reviewed, I shall willingly expose it to the censure of my country.

1. FROM the contrariety of some of the natural faculties of the mind, one to another, as also of one passion to another, and from their reference to conversation, there has been an argument taken, to infer an impossibility that any one man should be sufficiently disposed to all sorts of civil duty. The severity of judgment, they say, makes men censorious, and unapt to pardon the errors and infirmities of other men: and on the other side, celerity of fancy, makes the thoughts less steady than is necessary, to discern exactly between right and wrong. Again, in all deliberations, and in all pleadings, the faculty of solid reasoning is necessary: for without it, the resolutions of men are rash, and their sentences unjust: and yet if there be not powerful eloquence, which procureth attention and consent, the effect of reason will be little. But these are contrary faculties; the former being grounded upon principles of truth; the other upon opinions already received, true, or false; and upon the passions and interests of men, which are different, and mutable.

2. And amongst the passions, *courage*, (by which I mean the contempt of wounds, and violent death) inclineth men to private revenges, and sometimes to endeavour the unsettling of the public peace: and *timorousness*, many times disposeth to the desertion of the public defence. Both these they say cannot stand together in the same person.

3. And to consider the contrariety of men's opinions, and manners in general, it is they say, impossible to entertain a constant civil amity with all those, with whom the business of the world constrains us to converse: which business, consisteth almost in nothing else but a perpetual contention for honour, riches, and authority.

4. To which I answer, that these are indeed great difficulties, but not impossibilities: for by education, and discipline, they may be, and are sometimes reconciled. Judgment, and fancy may have place in the same man; but by turns; as the end which he aimeth at requireth. As the Israelites in Egypt, were sometimes fastened to their labour of making bricks, and other times were ranging abroad to gather straw: so also may the judgment sometimes be fixed upon one certain consideration, and the fancy at another time wandering about the world. So also reason, and eloquence, (though not perhaps

[390] in the natural sciences, yet in the moral) may stand very well together. For wheresoever there is place for adorning and preferring of error, there is much more place for adorning and preferring of truth, if they have it to adorn. Nor is there any repugnancy between fearing the laws, and not fearing a public enemy; nor between abstaining from injury, and pardoning it in others. There is therefore no such inconsistence of human nature, with civil duties, as some think. I have known clearness of judgment, and largeness of fancy; strength of reason, and graceful elocution; a courage for the war, and a fear for the laws, and all eminently in one man; and that was my most noble and honoured friend, Mr. Sidney Godolphin; who hating no man, nor hated of any, was unfortunately slain in the beginning of the late civil war, in the public quarrel, by an undiscerned and an undiscerning hand.

5. To the Laws of Nature, declared in Chapter 15, I would have this added, *that every man is bound by nature, as much as in him lieth, to protect in war, the authority, by which he is himself protected in time of peace.* For he that pretendeth a right of nature to preserve his own body, cannot pretend a right of nature to destroy him, by whose strength he is preserved: it is a manifest contradiction of himself. And though this law may be drawn by consequence, from some of those that are there already mentioned; yet the times require to have it inculcated, and remembered.

6. And because I find by divers English books lately printed,* that the civil wars have not yet sufficiently taught men, in what point of time it is, that a subject becomes obliged to the conqueror; nor what is conquest; nor how it comes about, that it obliges men to obey his laws: therefore for further satisfaction of men therein, I say, the point of time, wherein a man becomes subject to a conqueror, is that point, wherein having liberty to submit to him, he consenteth, either by express words, or by other sufficient sign, to be his subject. When it is that a man hath the liberty to submit, I have showed before in the end of Chapter 21; namely, that for him that hath no obligation to his former sovereign but that of an ordinary subject, it is then, when the means of his life are within the guards and garrisons of the enemy; for it is then, that he hath no longer protection from him, but is protected by the adverse party for his contribution. Seeing therefore such contribution is everywhere, as a thing inevitable, (notwithstanding it be an assistance to the enemy,) esteemed lawful; a total submission, which is but an assistance to the enemy, cannot

468

be esteemed unlawful. Besides, if a man consider that they who submit, assist the enemy but with part of their estates, whereas they that refuse, assist him with the whole, there is no reason to call their submission, or composition, an assistance; but rather a detriment to the enemy. But if a man, besides the obligation of a subject, hath taken upon him a new obligation of a soldier, then he hath not the liberty to submit to a new power, as long as the old one keeps the field, and giveth him means of subsistence, either in his armies, or garrisons: for in this case, he cannot complain of want of protection, and means to live as a soldier. But when that also fails, a soldier also [391] may seek his protection wheresoever he has most hope to have it; and may lawfully submit himself to his new master. And so much for the time when he may do it lawfully, if he will. If therefore he do it, he is undoubtedly bound to be a true subject: for a contract lawfully made, cannot lawfully be broken.

7. By this also a man may understand, when it is, that men may be said to be conquered; and in what the nature of conquest, and the right of a conqueror consisteth: for this submission is it that implieth them all. Conquest, is not the victory itself; but the acquisition by victory, of a right over the persons of men. He therefore that is slain, is overcome, but not conquered: he that is taken, and put into prison, or chains, is not conquered, though overcome; for he is still an enemy, and may save himself if he can: but he that upon promise of obedience, hath his life and liberty allowed him, is then conquered, and a subject; and not before. The Romans used to say, that their general had *pacified* such a *province*, that is to say, in English, *conquered* it; and that the country was *pacified* by victory, when the people of it had promised *imperata facere*, that is, *to do what the Roman people commanded them*: this was to be conquered. But this promise may be either express, or tacit: express, by promise: tacit, by other signs. As for example, a man that hath not been called to make such an express promise, (because he is one whose power perhaps is not considerable;) yet if he live under their protection openly, he is understood to submit himself to the government: but if he live there secretly, he is liable to anything that may be done to a spy, and enemy of the state. I say not, he does any injustice, (for acts of open hostility bear not that name); but that he may be justly put to death. Likewise, if a man, when his country is conquered, be out of it, he is not conquered, nor subject: but if at his return, he submit to the government, he is bound to obey it. So that *conquest*

(to define it) is the acquiring of the right of sovereignty by victory. Which right, is acquired, in the people's submission, by which they contract with the victor, promising obedience, for life and liberty.

8. In the 29th chapter, I have set down for one of the causes of the dissolutions of commonwealths, their imperfect generation, consisting in the want of an absolute and arbitrary legislative power; for want whereof, the civil sovereign is fain to handle the sword of justice unconstantly, and as if it were too hot for him to hold: one reason whereof (which I have not there mentioned) is this, that they will all of them justify the war, by which their power was at first gotten, and whereon (as they think) their right dependeth, and not on the possession. As if, for example, the right of the kings of England did depend on the goodness of the cause of William the Conqueror, and upon their lineal, and directest descent from him; by which means, there would perhaps be no tie of the subjects' [392] obedience to their sovereign at this day in all the world: wherein whilst they needlessly think to justify themselves, they justify all the successful rebellions that ambition shall at any time after raise against them, and their successors. Therefore I put down for one of the most effectual seeds of the death of any state, that the conquerors require not only a submission of men's actions to them for the future, but also an approbation of all their actions past; when there is scarce a commonwealth in the world, whose beginnings can in conscience be justified.

9. And because the name of tyranny, signifieth nothing more, nor less, than the name of sovereignty, be it in one, or many men, saving that they that use the former word, are understood to be angry with them they call tyrants; I think the toleration of a professed hatred of tyranny, is a toleration of hatred to commonwealth in general, and another evil seed, not differing much from the former. For to the justification of the cause of a conqueror, the reproach of the cause of the conquered, is for the most part necessary: but neither of them necessary for the obligation of the conquered. And thus much I have thought fit to say upon the review of the first and second part of this discourse.

10. In the 35th chapter, I have sufficiently declared out of the Scripture, that in the commonwealth of the Jews, God himself was made the sovereign, by pact with the people; who were therefore called his *peculiar people*, to distinguish them from the rest of the world, over whom God reigned not by their consent, but by his own

power: and that in this kingdom Moses was God's lieutenant on earth; and that it was he that told them what laws God appointed them to be ruled by. But I have omitted to set down who were the officers appointed to do execution; especially in capital punishments; not then thinking it a matter of so necessary consideration, as I find it since. We know that generally in all commonwealths, the execution of corporal punishments, was either put upon the guards, or other soldiers of the sovereign power; or given to those, in whom want of means, contempt of honour, and hardness of heart, concurred, to make them sue for such an office. But amongst the Israelites it was a positive law of God their sovereign, that he that was convicted of a capital crime, should be stoned to death by the people; and that the witnesses should cast the first stone, and after the witnesses, then the rest of the people. This was a law that designed who were to be the executioners; but not that any one should throw a stone at him before conviction and sentence, where the congregation was judge. The witnesses were nevertheless to be heard before they proceeded to execution, unless the fact were committed in the presence of the congregation itself, or in sight of the lawful judges; for then there needed no other witnesses but the judges themselves. Nevertheless, this manner of proceeding being not thoroughly understood, hath given occasion to a dangerous opinion, that any man may kill another, in some cases, by a right of zeal; as if the executions done upon offenders in the kingdom of God in old time, proceeded not from the sovereign command, but from [393] the authority of private zeal: which, if we consider the texts that seem to favour it, is quite contrary.

11. First, where the Levites fell upon the people, that had made and worshipped the Golden Calf, and slew three thousand of them; it was by the commandment of Moses, from the mouth of God; as is manifest, *Exod.* 32. 27. And when the son of a woman of Israel had blasphemed God, they that heard it, did not kill him, but brought him before Moses, who put him under custody, till God should give sentence against him; as appears, *Levit.* 25. 11, 12. Again, (*Numb.* 25. 6, 7) when Phinehas killed Zimri and Cozbi, it was not by right of private zeal: their crime was committed in the sight of the assembly; there needed no witness; the law was known, and he the heir-apparent to the sovereignty; and, which is the principal point, the lawfulness of his act depended wholly upon a subsequent ratification by Moses, whereof he had no cause to doubt. And this

presumption of a future ratification, is sometimes necessary to the safety of a commonwealth; as in a sudden rebellion, any man that can suppress it by his own power in the country where it begins, without express law or commission, may lawfully do it, and provide to have it ratified, or pardoned, whilst it is in doing, or after it is done. Also *Numb.* 35. 30 it is expressly said, *Whosoever shall kill the murderer, shall kill him upon the word of witnesses*: but witnesses suppose a formal judicature, and consequently condemn that pretence of *jus zelotarum*. The law of Moses concerning him that enticeth to idolatry, (that is to say, in the kingdom of God to a renouncing of his allegiance, *Deut.* 13. 8, 9) forbids to conceal him, and commands the accuser to cause him to be put to death, and to cast the first stone at him; but not to kill him before he be condemned. And (*Deut.* 17. 4, 5, 6, 7) the process against idolatry is exactly set down: for God there speaketh to the people, as judge, and commandeth them, when a man is accused of idolatry, to enquire diligently of the fact, and finding it true, then to stone him; but still the hand of the witness throweth the first stone. This is not private zeal, but public condemnation. In like manner when a father hath a rebellious son, the law is, (*Deut.* 21, 18–21), that he shall bring him before the judges of the town, and all the people of the town shall stone him. Lastly, by pretence of these laws it was, that St. Stephen was stoned, and not by pretence of private zeal: for before he was carried away to execution, he had pleaded his cause before the high-priest. There is nothing in all this, nor in any other part of the Bible, to countenance executions by private zeal; which being oftentimes but a conjunction of ignorance and passion, is against both the justice and the peace of a commonwealth.

12. In the 36th chapter, I have said, that it is not declared in what manner God spake supernaturally to Moses: nor that he spake not to him sometimes by dreams and visions, and by a supernatural voice, as to other prophets: for the manner how he spake unto him from the mercy-seat, is expressly set down, *Numb.* 7. 89, in these words, *From that time forward, when Moses entered into the Tabernacle of the congregation to speak with God, he heard a voice which spake unto him from over the mercy-seat, which is over the Ark of the testimony, from between the cherubims he spake unto him.* But it is not declared in what consisteth the pre-eminence of the manner of God's speaking to Moses, above that of his speaking to other prophets, as to Samuel, and to Abraham, to whom he also spake by a voice, (that is, by

[394]

vision) unless the difference consist in the clearness of the vision. For *face to face*, and *mouth to mouth*, cannot be literally understood of the infiniteness, and incomprehensibility of the Divine nature.

13. And as to the whole doctrine, I see not yet, but the principles of it are true and proper; and the ratiocination solid. For I ground the civil right of sovereigns, and both the duty and liberty of subjects, upon the known natural inclinations of mankind, and upon the articles of the law of nature; of which no man, that pretends but reason enough to govern his private family, ought to be ignorant. And for the power ecclesiastical of the same sovereigns, I ground it on such texts, as are both evident in themselves, and consonant to the scope of the whole Scripture. And therefore am persuaded, that he that shall read it with a purpose only to be informed, shall be informed by it. But for those that by writing, or public discourse, or by their eminent actions, have already engaged themselves to the maintaining of contrary opinions, they will not be so easily satisfied. For in such cases, it is natural for men, at one and the same time, both to proceed in reading, and to lose their attention, in the search of objections to that they had read before: of which, in a time wherein the interests of men are changed (seeing much of that doctrine, which serveth to the establishing of a new government, must needs be contrary to that which conduced to the dissolution of the old,) there cannot choose but be very many.

14. In that part which treateth of a Christian commonwealth, there are some new doctrines, which, it may be, in a state where the contrary were already fully determined, were a fault for a subject without leave to divulge, as being an usurpation of the place of a teacher. But in this time, that men call not only for peace, but also for truth, to offer such doctrine as I think true, and that manifestly tend to peace and loyalty, to the consideration of those that are yet in deliberation, is no more, but to offer new wine, to be put into new casks, that both may be preserved together. And I suppose, that then, when novelty can breed no trouble, nor disorder in a state, men are not generally so much inclined to the reverence of antiquity, as to prefer ancient errors, before new and well-proved truth.

15. There is nothing I distrust more than my elocution; which nevertheless I am confident (excepting the mischances of the press) is not obscure. That I have neglected the ornament of quoting ancient poets, orators, and philosophers, contrary to the custom of late time, (whether I have done well or ill in it,) proceedeth from my [395]

473

judgment, grounded on many reasons. For first, all truth of doctrine dependeth either upon *reason*, or upon *Scripture*; both which give credit to many, but never receive it from any writer. Secondly, the matters in question are not of *fact*, but of *right*, wherein there is no place for *witnesses*. There is scarce any of those old writers, that contradicteth not sometimes both himself, and others; which makes their testimonies insufficient. Fourthly, such opinions as are taken only upon credit of antiquity, are not intrinsically the judgment of those that cite them, but words that pass (like gaping) from mouth to mouth. Fifthly, it is many times with a fraudulent design that men stick their corrupt doctrine with the cloves of other men's wit. Sixthly, I find not that the ancients they cite, took it for an ornament, to do the like with those that wrote before them. Seventhly, it is an argument of indigestion, when Greek and Latin sentences unchewed come up again, as they use to do, unchanged. Lastly, though I reverence those men of ancient time, that either have written truth perspicuously, or set us in a better way to find it out ourselves; yet to the antiquity itself I think nothing due. For if we will reverence the age, the present is the oldest. If the antiquity of the writer, I am not sure, that generally they to whom such honour is given, were more ancient when they wrote, than I am that am writing: but if it be well considered, the praise of ancient authors, proceeds not from the reverence of the dead, but from the competition, and mutual envy of the living.

16. To conclude, there is nothing in this whole discourse, nor in that I writ before of the same subject in Latin,* as far as I can perceive, contrary either to the Word of God, or to good manners; or tending to the disturbance of the public tranquillity. Therefore I think it may be profitably printed, and more profitably taught in the Universities, in case they also think so, to whom the judgment of the same belongeth. For seeing the Universities are the fountains of civil, and moral doctrine, from whence the preachers, and the gentry, drawing such water as they find, use to sprinkle the same (both from the pulpit and in their conversation) upon the people, there ought certainly to be great care taken, to have it pure, both from the venom of heathen politicians, and from the incantation of deceiving spirits. And by that means the most men, knowing their duties, will be the less subject to serve the ambition of a few discontented persons, in their purposes against the state; and be the less grieved with the contributions necessary for their peace, and defence; and the governors themselves have the less cause, to maintain at the common charge any greater army, than is necessary to make good the public liberty, against the invasions and encroachments of foreign enemies.

17. And thus I have brought to an end my Discourse of Civil and Ecclesiastical Government, occasioned by the disorders of the present time, without partiality, without application, and without other design than to set before men's eyes the mutual relation between protection and obedience; of which the condition of human [396] nature, and the laws divine, (both natural and positive) require an inviolable observation. And though in the revolution of states, there can be no very good constellation for truths of this nature to be born under, (as having an angry aspect from the dissolvers of an old government, and seeing but the backs of them that erect a new;) yet I cannot think it will be condemned at this time, either by the public judge of doctrine, or by any that desires the continuance of public peace. And in this hope I return to my interrupted speculation* of bodies natural; wherein, (if God give me health to finish it,) I hope the novelty will as much please, as in the doctrine of this artificial body it useth to offend. For such truth, as opposeth no man's profit, nor pleasure, is to all men welcome.

FINIS

EXPLANATORY NOTES

3 *Sidney Godolphin*: 1610–43, Royalist member of the Long Parliament and poet, killed in a skirmish in 1643 to which Hobbes alludes in §4 of 'A Review and Conclusion' which ends *Leviathan*. In his will Godolphin left £200 to Hobbes. His brother Francis, 1605–67, to whom Hobbes's dedicatory letter is addressed, also a 'King's Man', was governor of the Scilly Isles during the first civil war.

7 *life is but a motion of limbs*: the significance of Hobbes's casually reductionist definition of life (cf. VI. 58) is easily overlooked. He is taking it that life, or 'the soul' in a human being (see, for example, XLIV. 15), just is the ability to move (cf. Plato, *The Laws*, x. 895–9). Thus in seven words Hobbes disposes of the whole Cartesian problem of *how* the soul moves the body. But it takes Hobbes in Part 4 of *Leviathan* much more than seven words to reconcile the reduction of souls to life, and life to movement, with traditional Christian views about life and resurrection.

Leviathan: Hobbes's celebrated title, which captures in a single word his comparison of the state to a vast living organism, is drawn from the book of Job, ch. 41, in particular the last two verses, which Hobbes renders in XXVIII. 27 as 'There is nothing on earth, to be compared with him. He is made so as not to be afraid. He seeth every high thing below him, and is king of all the children of pride.' Perhaps because of the tradition (visible, for example, in Aquinas's comments on Job) of associating Leviathan with the Devil, in XVII. 13 Hobbes remarks, 'This is the generation of that great LEVIATHAN, or rather (to speak more reverently) of that *Mortal God*, to which we owe under the *Immortal God*, our peace and defence.' The name 'Leviathan' used to refer to the state reappears several times, for example XXI. 5 and XXIII. 2.

not by reading of books: the saying is merely quoted here, but Hobbes's antipathy to Aristotle in particular, and the scholastic book-learning of universities in general, as opposed to the new sciences of mechanics and optics (based, as he would have it, on the paradigm of geometry), is frequently evident in *Leviathan* and fully developed in XLVI. His attitude was definitively anticipated by Galileo in his 'Third Letter on Sunspots' to Mark Welsher in December 1612. 'They wish never to raise their eyes from those pages—as if this great book of the universe had been written to be read by Aristotle alone, and his eyes had been destined to see for all posterity.'

9 *Of Sense*: this chapter will be better appreciated if read in conjunction with ch. II of Hobbes's first major original work, *The Elements of Law* (Part I, *Human Nature*; Part II, *De Corpore Politico*). *The Elements of Law* was circulated in a number of manuscript copies from 1640 onwards, and the two Parts were

477

printed separately, as if they were distinct works, in London in 1650, almost certainly without Hobbes's knowledge (see the World's Classics edition, Oxford, 1994). Indeed, Chs. I–V of *Leviathan* should each be studied in conjunction with the corresponding chapters, namely II–VI, of the *Elements*. Hobbes's *Thomas White's De Mundo Examined*, ch. XXX, also treats the same topics as the chapters of *Leviathan* down to about Ch. VII.

9 *I have elsewhere written*: see *Elements of Law (Human Nature)*, ch. II, and, on optics, the *Tractatus Opticus* in Marin Mersenne's *Universae Geometriae Synopsis* (1644).

endeavour: this is a key concept for Hobbes. In *De Corpore*, XV. 2 (first published in 1655) he defines endeavour (or *conatus*) as '*motion made in less space and time than can be given*; that is *less than can be determined or assigned by exposition or number*; that is, *motion made through the length of a point, and in an instant or point of time*'. See also *Elements of Law (Human Nature)*, VII. 1–2, *White's De Mundo Examined*, XIII. 2, and *Leviathan*, VI. 1–2. On the one hand Hobbes's concept is among the first stirrings of the idea that led Leibniz and Newton to the differential calculus. On the other hand, and in the context of the physiology and mechanistic psychology of *Leviathan*, it refers to motion too minute or too quick to be perceived: in modern terms something, for example, like the impulses along nerve fibres.

fancy: from the Greek *phantasía*; used by Hobbes to mean (as here) the percipient's internal experience of an external object or (as in II. 2) the percipient's imaginings. Succinct objections to Hobbes's account of perception can be found in D. D. Raphael, *Hobbes: Morals and Politics* (London, 1977), 63–4.

11 *That when a thing . . . assented to*: even closer to Newton's definitive formulation of the Law of Inertia is Hobbes's wording in *De Corpore*, VIII. 19: 'Whatsoever is at rest will always be at rest, unless there be some other body besides it, which by endeavouring to get into its place by motion, suffers it no longer to remain at rest. . . . In like manner, whatsoever is moved will always be moved, except there be some other body beside it . . .'.

13 *For my part . . . I think myself awake*: Hobbes is setting out his solution to an enduring philosophical problem—once a separation is effected between my internal idea X, and the external reality that supposedly causes me to have the idea X, a waking idea and a dream idea would appear to have the same status from within the percipient. Hobbes robustly pushes the whole issue aside by pointing to an asymmetry between dreaming and waking.

14 *commonly related by historians*: see the concluding paragraphs of Plutarch's 'Life of Julius Caesar', and chs. xxxvi and xlviii of his 'Life of Brutus'.

the religion of the Gentiles: any religion not of the Judaeo-Christian species, but in Hobbes's writings particularly the polytheistic religions (which he also calls 'the religion of the heathen') of Greece and Rome, later called 'paganism' from their long survival among *pagani* (villagers) and country districts. See also note to p. 404 and Ch. XLV as a whole.

ghostly: religious or ordained persons; but Hobbes is already using the old term with more than a trace of derisive irony. His extended comparison of the Roman Church with the Kingdom of Fairies is reserved for XLVII. 21–33.

15 *Of the Consequence . . . Imaginations*: consequence in the literal sense of following in order one after another. This chapter is considerably enhanced by a prior reading of *Elements of Law (Human Nature)*, IV.

Not every . . . indifferently: Hobbes is an early contributor to the subject which in later writers (particularly David Hartley, 1705–57, and David Hume, 1711–76) is investigated as 'the association of ideas'. The key question is why and how 'Not every thought to every thought succeeds indifferently'.

17 *the seven wise men*: sages of the sixth century BC. Lists of the seven were constructed by Plato (see *Protagoras*, 343a–b) and Plutarch (see *Moralia*, 'The Dinner of the Seven Wise Men') among others. The names were often associated with particular wise aphorisms. Both Plato's and Plutarch's lists include Chilon (*fl.* 590 BC), to whom is attributed the maxim 'Consider the end'.

a spaniel ranges the field: in the seventeenth century spaniels were still useful hunting dogs, not the unfortunate pets of modern invention with ears designed to collect mud, rather than noses to detect game.

19 *Whatsoever we imagine is finite*: this apparent afterthought to the chapter contains a potentially devastating argument against making God the subject of any comprehensible or coherent statement whatsoever. Hobbes returns to the matter several times in *Leviathan*, notably in XI. 25, XXXI. 13–33, XXXIV. 4, XLV. 14–15, and XLVI. 22–3. But it is in *Elements of Law (Human Nature)*, XI. 2–4, that he most clearly asserts that we have no possible understanding of the language by means of which we attempt to talk about God. In *White's De Mundo Examined*, XXX. 33, Hobbes remarks: 'the way in which God understands passes *our* understanding. Yet we must believe [that he understands] as faithfully as we believe that he exists.'

No man therefore . . . the same place at once: Hobbes's harmless and abstract assertion of what, on the face of things, look like universally agreed principles of common (and not so common) sense, is given specific content later on; for example in XLVI. 19–21, where he attacks Thomistic (and arguably orthodox) accounts of the soul.

22 *there being nothing . . . but names*: Hobbes is taking a decisive position in relation to the long-running philosophical debate about what universal names like '*man, horse, tree*' are names of. In the view Hobbes is rejecting (originally associated with Plato), universals do not name any one thing in our experience, but they do name, or are the proper names of, some real entity or 'form' existing in some world, although not the world accessible to sense. This

doctrine Hobbes will not have at any price. His most vigorous rejection of it is in *Elements of Law (Human Nature)*, V. 6. The reasons why he rejects it become evident later in *Leviathan*, e.g. XLVI. 16–17.

23 *a bird in lime twigs*: possibly a reference to Hobbes's own activities at Oxford in catching birds. See John Aubrey's 'Brief Life' in the World's Classics edition of *The Elements of Law*, 237.

  definitions: for an account of what Hobbes means by definition see my Introduction, pp. xxii–xxiv, and *De Corpore*, VI. 14.

24 *science*: for a clear discussion of Hobbes's apparently 'conventionalist' account of science, see T. Sorell, *Hobbes* (London and New York, 1986), in particular pp. 45–50. See also *Leviathan*, V. 17, VII. 4, and, for Hobbes's near identification of 'philosophy' with 'science', XLVI. 1, and note to p. 441.

  For words . . . if but a man: Hobbes is thinking of reasoning as a sort of addition and subtraction of conceptions from a given conception. See V. 1–2. 'Thomas' is St Thomas Aquinas, *c*.1225–74, leading philosopher of medieval Western Christianity and mentor of Roman orthodoxy.

26 *conception*: a term Hobbes uses to include (*a*) the contents of our minds when and however they are actually being caused by external objects acting through our senses, and (*b*) those contents as they can return to us in memories, dreams, imaginations, and the like, and (*c*) whatever it is we have when we understand a name (and do not have when we fail to understand a name). In senses (*a*) and (*b*) conceptions are often spoken of by Hobbes as 'fancy'. Sense (*c*), obviously, but none too precisely, related to (*a*) and (*b*), is the focus of Hobbes's remarks in this paragraph. A 'name', as Hobbes explained in *Elements of Law (Human Nature)*, V. 2, is 'the voice of a man, arbitrarily imposed, for a mark to bring to his mind some conception concerning the thing on which it is imposed'.

27 *for one man calleth . . . another stupidity, &c.*: Hobbes published a magnificent translation of Thucydides' *History of the Peloponnesian War* in 1629. In his later writings he often quotes from, alludes to, or uses the *History*, especially for the confusions it attributes to democracy. In the present case compare Hobbes's words with the *History*, iii. 82: 'The received value of names imposed for signification of things, was changed into arbitrary. For inconsiderate boldness, was counted true-hearted manliness: provident deliberation, a handsome fear . . .', etc.

29 *any free . . . by opposition*: Hobbes's earliest account of what constitutes a free or voluntary action (and why it makes no sense to argue about a free *will*) can be found in *Elements of Law (Human Nature)*, XII. 1–5. Its later continuation is in his controversy with Bishop Bramhall (see the Molesworth edition of Hobbes's *English Works* (1839), iv. 229–78 and vol. v). His position is that it is non-sense to talk about a free *will*. But it is significant to talk about a free *action* when the action proceeds from the passions which are the will (fear, anger,

love, and the like) and when the action itself is not constrained by external physical force. In *Leviathan* see VI. 53, XIV. 8, XXI. 1–4, *et al.*

30 *Cicero saith . . . of philosophers*: see *De Divinatione*, ii. 119 (Loeb, p. 505). The quotation is much to Hobbes's taste: see XLVI. 11.

31 *names that signify nothing*: the examples that follow are drawn from theology. Hobbes argues seriously about such insignificant names in a number of places in *Leviathan*, for example VIII. 27, XXXIV. 2, and XLVI. 16–30. One of the instances he has already given, 'incorporeal substance', IV. 21, is of major philosophical and religious interest and he returns to it frequently in his works, for example in *An Answer to Bishop Bramhall* (*English Works*, iv. 383–4).

32 *ignes fatui*: useless fires.

33 *§1*: paragraphs 1–3 of the chapter should be read in conjunction with *Elements of Law* (*Human Nature*), XII.

34 *endeavour*: see note to p. 9.

appetite of excretion, and exoneration: desire to rid the body of waste products, and to empty the bowels. 'Excretion' and 'exoneration' are nearly synonyms.

35 *§§6–7*: these two paragraphs are of the utmost importance in understanding Hobbes's moral philosophy. They assert, in the light of the preceding and succeeding physiological accounts of aversions and desires, that what each individual calls good and evil when he or she is not a member of a civil society relates *only* to that individual's personal aversions and desires. Such is the 'natural' condition of mankind. The matter had earlier been deployed in *Elements of Law* (*Human Nature*), VII. But it is not the end of the story since the 'natural' condition of mankind is, because of the formation of civil societies in which the individual is a citizen, not the *usual* condition. Summaries of Hobbes's completed thesis can be seen in XV. 40 and XLVI. 32.

as I have said before: see I. 4.

36 *onerations and exonerations*: loadings (as with food and drink) and unloading (of same) by the body.

§14: the passions defined in §§14–48 have a brilliant portrayal in *Elements of Law* (*Human Nature*), IX. 21, where Hobbes compares the life of man to a race: 'But this race we must suppose to have no other goal, nor no other garland, but being foremost. And in it.'

37 *Fear of . . . superstition*: this apparently out-of-place and sarcastic reference to religion has been used to illustrate Hobbes's estrangement from conventional views, an estrangement that might amount to concealed atheism. But see *Leviathan*, XI. 26, and my Introduction, pp. xxxvi–xl.

40 *commonly by the Schools*: see, for example, Aquinas, *Summa Theologiae*, 1a, quest. 59, a. 1.

42 *μακαρισμός*: 'a pronouncing happy'.

43 *conscience*: Hobbes will later be much concerned with threats to the integrity of the state resulting from individuals following their private conscience in defiance of the civil law. Hence his concern to downgrade conscience from the law of God written in men's hearts (of the sort St Paul, Romans 2: 15, appeals to: '[The Gentiles] show that what the law requires is written on their hearts, while their conscience also bears witness . . .') to the rather thin outcome in *Elements of Law* (*Human Nature*), VI. 8, that conscience is a man's opinion of the truth of his own evidence.

44 *If Livy say . . . but Livy*: note that the verb form Hobbes uses is subjunctive: 'if Livy were to say . . .'. Livy (Roman historian, 59 BC–AD 17) in fact did not say God made a cow speak, but merely 'That a cow had spoken—a thing which had found no credence the year before—was now believed' (iii. 10, Loeb, ii. 35) or 'Prodigies were reported that year . . . that in Campania a cow spoke' (xli. 13, Loeb, xii. 223).

is faith in men only: Hobbes is arguing in the light of experience of the political problems caused by belief in those who claimed divine authority for their subversive opinions. Thus he argues that to believe or doubt a preacher (or Livy) is to trust in (or not, as the case may be) a man, not to have evidence for or against the content of what the man asserts.

51 *There was once . . . by the tragedy*: the tragedy *Andromeda* was by Euripides. 'Accident' in Hobbes's retelling of this anecdote means an unforeseeable and non-necessary consequence. The anecdote can be found in Lucian's delightfully readable 'How to Write History' (Loeb, vi. 3).

the story: told by Aulus Gellius, *Attic Nights*, xv. 10 (Loeb, iii. 85) and by Plutarch in the *Moralia*, 'The Bravery of Women: The Women of Miletus' (Loeb, iii. 509).

demon: the Greek word δαίμων does not carry the sense of 'malignant supernatural being', but only of an indwelling spirit or minor divinity. See Hobbes's later discussion in XLV. 3–4.

52 *where it is said*: Hobbes's hundreds of citations from the Bible are, in common with other quotations, printed in italics in the Head edition, and I have retained this convention throughout the present text. One might expect Hobbes to quote from the Authorized Version (the King James Bible of 1611), but his wording often differs from it, and suggests that he is translating from an original text, probably (and sometimes explicitly in the case of the Old Testament) from the Vulgate, the standard Latin version undertaken by St Jerome (*c*.342–420).

near to direct atheism: near, because God and human souls are commonly spoken of as 'spirits'. For Hobbes, this is not to say what God is, but simply that he exists (see XXXIV. 4). In *Elements of Law* (*Human Nature*), XI. 4, Hobbes remarks: 'By the name of spirit we understand a body natural, but of such subtilty that it worketh not on the senses; but that filleth up the place which the image of a visible body might fill up.' This at least seems to offer some way past his emphatic denials that God or human souls can be intelligibly spoken of as 'incorporeal substances'. See *Leviathan*, VIII. 27, XII. 7, *et al.*

53 *leaving the world . . . natural reason*: Hobbes's unequivocal and now almost universally accepted claim that scripture is concerned with illuminating the Kingdom of God (however that may be understood), not with communicating the conclusions of natural science, was one of the points in contention between Galileo (whom Hobbes had met) and the Roman Church. See Galileo's 'Letter to the Grand Duchess Christina' (1615) in *Discoveries and Opinions of Galileo*, ed. Stillman Drake (New York, 1957), 181–3.

54 *Suarez' . . . of God*: Francisco de Suarez (1584–1617), Jesuit and 'modern' Aristotelian regarded as an authority by the Roman Church and by some Protestants.

Of the Several Subjects of Knowledge: Hobbes's 'knowledge of fact' is what we know immediately from present or past experience together with the 'register' or records of such experience. His 'science', the 'consequences of one affirmation to another', from the example given, might appear to be only geometry, arithmetic, formal logic, or other deductive systems. However, on examination, science turns out to be all claims to knowledge which result from, or form part of, any body of facts that can be structured deductively. But Hobbes's account of science is not easy to grasp. See note to p. 24.

61 *Mordecai*: a Jewish exile at the court of Xerxes who attained an important palace position. See Esther 6: 1–12.

62 *to be descended . . . is dishonourable*: Hobbes, a man of respectable but relatively obscure parentage, very honourably sets a spring to catch himself.

63 *a hymn of Homer*: the anecdote derives from *The Homeric Hymns*, iv, 'To Hermes' (Loeb, *Hesiod*, pp. 363–4).

histories: particularly Thucydides, *History of the Peloponnesian War*, i. 5–6: 'For the Grecians in old time, and such barbarians as in the continent lived near unto the sea, or else inhabited the islands, after once they began to cross over one to another in ships, became thieves . . .', etc. (Hobbes's translation).

64 *Constantine the Great*: see note to p. 347.

Selden's most excellent treatise: John Selden's *Titles of Honour* (1614). Hobbes sent Selden (1584–1654) a presentation copy of *Leviathan*, and they became firm friends.

65 *Nor can a man any more live*: cf. VIII. 16. It is one of Hobbes's most challenging assertions that man is a restless, unsatisfiable creature whose search for power (in the special sense defined in X. 1 and used in XI. 2) ends only at death. Note that if life is the movement (see note to p. 7) which is desires, senses, imagination, etc., it is at first difficult to understand what 'life' a soul could have apart from the body. Hobbes grasps the nettle in Ch. XXXVIII: the soul *is* life; resurrection is *of the body*.

483

67 *pleasure to the sense . . . the imagination*: this is literally true in view of Hobbes's earlier identification of imagination with decaying sense. See II. 2.

69 *strong*: the Bear edition has *old* here, which may make easier sense to the modern reader.

70 *publicans, that is to say, farmers*: tax-gatherers, that is to say those to whom such collecting is farmed out (who pay a fixed sum to the state and gather what they can).

§23: this little paragraph has all the ingredients for the sort of scepticism with regard to reported miracles that received such celebrated expression in sect. X of David Hume's *Enquiry concerning Human Understanding* (1748). But see XXX. 3 and XXXVII.

71 *yet not have an idea*: see note to p. 19.

72 *old poets said*: quite a lot of classical writers observed this, but among *poets* it is, I think, only developed at length in Lucretius, *On the Nature of the Universe*, for example i. 62–79. But Lucretius is far more concerned to resist the fear caused by religion than to analyse the fear which causes it. See also Statius, *Thebaid*, iii. 661, and Petronius, poem 3 (Loeb, p. 343).

74 *as the Athenians . . . another Scipio*: the first example is mentioned by Thucydides, iii. 7; the second is in Plutarch's *Lives*, 'Cato the Younger', 58 (Loeb, viii. 375). In both instances it was felt that better luck might result from the leadership of someone bearing a name particularly associated with success.

75 *accidents*: in philosophical terminology an accident was a property which a thing might or might not have without ceasing to be that thing. For example, a man could be healthy, or not, without ceasing to be a man.

76 *consecrated*: Hobbes's 'religion of the Gentiles'—the polytheistic religions of classical Greece and Rome—did not 'consecrate' things to gods in the sense in which Christianity 'consecrated' buildings or persons. The gods had places where they abode, and the natural world was full of hidden life, parts of it being intrinsically special to such life, and thus 'holy'. For Hobbes's remarks on Christian consecration, see XLIV. 11.

77 *Nostradamus*: Michel de Nostredame, 1503–66, French physician and astro-loger whose two collections of predictions, the *Centuries*, expressed in obscure (as usual) and ambiguous (as always) quatrains of verse, achieved great fame (which has endured even unto its apotheosis in a film of 1995).

Numa Pompilius: second king of Rome, supposedly 715–673 BC: see Livy, *History of Rome*, I. xix (Loeb, i. 69).

78 *and Mahomet . . . a dove*: it is actually claimed that Mahomet received his revelations directly from the Angel Gabriel. The story about the dove is wholly apocryphal; but Hobbes might have replied that a bird at least has a throat and other means of speech (as parrots prove), whereas the 'speech' of an angel is either a phantasm of the human brain, without external reality, or the

pretended 'speech' of a bodiless spirit that has no means of speech (concerning which the words of Jeremiah 5: 21 might be reversed to express the physical and perhaps conceptual impossibility: 'speech have they but tongues not; sight have they but eyes not').

the same things . . . by the laws: an early example of this can be seen in the speech recorded by Sextus Empiricus in *Against the Physicists*, i. 54 (Loeb, iii. 31–2) and attributed by him to the sophist politician Critias (*c*.460–400 BC). But of course the same view applies in Christian commonwealths when (as Hobbes is about to argue) natural laws or the laws of God, and particular formulations of these laws, are embodied in the civil law.

the anger of the gods: once again Hobbes is either deliberately or thoughtlessly attributing activities to pagans which attach as well, or better, to Christians, as he himself was to experience. In 1666, after the divine anger shown in the plague of 1665 and the fire of London in 1666, the *Journal of the Commons*, on 17 October, records the order 'that the Committee to which the Bill against Atheism and Profaneness is committed, be empowered to receive information touching such books as tend to atheism, blasphemy and profaneness, or against the essence and attributes of God, and in particular the book published in the name of one [Thomas] White, and the book of Mr Hobbes, called the 'Leviathan', and to report the matter with their opinion to the House'.

but that of the Jews: the Jewish religion *was* tolerated within the Roman Empire, and a prohibition by Hadrian of circumcision is the only known Roman act specifically against the religion as such, although there were other occasional moves against proselytizing Jews.

82 *and those not . . . of reformation*: the Reformation went furthest in Churches organized according to Calvinist principles, particularly the Presbyterian Church. These words are omitted in the written copy of *Leviathan*, where the sentence concludes: 'on whom when men by common frailty are carried to execute their anger. They bear down not only religion which they reduce to private fancy but also the civil government that would uphold it reducing it to the natural condition of private force.'

84 *§8*: this paragraph, and the one following (which concludes with the most quoted sentence in all English philosophy), is the central statement of the first move in Hobbes's political theory: that unrestricted individual freedom (i.e. the right of nature) means the war of each against every man; cf. XXI. 8.

Let him therefore consider: it is a bold or unworldly human being that cannot still recognize the fears Hobbes describes and the precautions he lists.

85 *there was never . . . of war as this*: Hobbes may well be right, although his account, as he says, depends not upon what ever was actual, but on what, given human nature as it really is, *would* be actual in the absence of an effective sovereign power, and almost is actual in civil wars, when civil society breaks down. But there is at least one ancient report, given by Sextus Empiricus

(second century AD). Having quoted Orpheus, 'a theologian', to the effect that 'There was a time when every man lived by devouring his fellows', Sextus continues with an account of how the state of war was deliberately contrived in the Persian Empire: 'the shrewd Persians have a law that on the death of their king they must practise lawlessness for the next five days . . . in order to learn by experience how great an evil lawlessness is . . . so that they may become more trusty guardians of their kings' (*Against the Professors*, ii. 33; Loeb, iv. 205–7). In more general terms the notion of a state of war, or something like it, where there is no law, is very ancient. See, for example, Cicero, *Pro Sexto*, i. 42.

87 *general rule of reason*: this fundamental law of nature, 'seek peace' (as Hobbes paraphrases it), together with the second, that we should not seek to maintain our rights to all things, are different in kind from those laws that Hobbes derives from them in Ch. XV. The two fundamental laws are the conditions that reason shows to be necessary for avoiding the state of war. In both *Elements of Law* (*Human Nature*), XIV. 14 and XV. 2, and *De Cive* (I. 15 and II. 1–3) Hobbes treats these two laws separately from the derived laws, although in both *De Cive*, II. 3, and *Leviathan*, XIV. 5, there is an assumption that the second law can be derived from the first, and need not be regarded as an independent condition for the avoidance of the state of war. In *De Cive* (II. 1) Hobbes explains that 'By right reason in the natural state of men, I understand not, as many do, an infallible faculty, but the act of reasoning, that is, the peculiar and true ratiocination of every man concerning those actions of his which may either rebound to the damage, or benefit of his neighbours.'

This is that law . . . ne feceris: for the 'Golden Rule', see Matthew 7: 12, or Luke 6: 31: 'And as ye would that men should do to you, do ye also to them likewise.' Hobbes sets this in a context in which others adopt towards me the same rule. The Gospels do not seem to expect such reciprocation, although turning the other cheek can certainly be associated with vaster benefits than merely avoiding a here-and-now state of war. The 'law of all men' that Hobbes cites in Latin is the converse of the Golden Rule. It is 'do not do to others what you would not wish to be done to you'. See also XXVI. 13.

88 *voluntary act*: from his accounts of human physiology Hobbes asserts the generalization that, as a matter of fact, whatever a man does voluntarily (or 'freely', see note to p. 29) will have as its object some good to himself. See *Elements of Law* (*Human Nature*), VII, XII, and particularly XVI. 6: 'For by necessity of nature every man doth in all his voluntary actions intend some good unto himself.' And again, *De Cive*, I. 7: 'every man is desirous of what is good for him, and shuns what is evil . . . and this he doth, by a certain impulsion of nature, no less than that whereby a stone moves downward.' This is the position sometimes called 'psychological egoism'. See *Leviathan*, XV. 16, and my Introduction, pp. xxviii–xxxi.

91 *meritum congrui, and meritum condigni*: the distinction can be found in Aquinas's *Summa Theologiae*, 1a2ae, quest. 114, a. 3. *Meritum congrui* is a benefit in keeping with or in proportion to one's deserving; *meritum condigni* is a benefit without limit granted by someone else, for example by God placing one in a state of eternal bliss.

92 *To make covenant with God*: for a discussion of covenants see *Elements of Law (Human Nature)*, XV. 9–14. For a seventeenth-century claim to covenant with God, see the Scottish National Covenant of 1638, which speaks of Christians 'who have renewed their Covenant with God' and calls upon God 'to witness' the declaration. Hobbes seems to have less difficulty with the Old Testament covenant between God and the Jews: see XXXV. 2.

93 *§29*: the paragraph is important when read in conjunction with §4 as it sets some limit to what a man grants to Leviathan, the state, when he agrees to restrict his freedom in order to avoid the state of war. See also XXVIII. 2.

96 *justice is . . . his own*: Hobbes returns to the phrase or its like in XXVI. 4, XXX. 12, *et al.* It is originally drawn from Plato, *Republic*, I. 331e and 332c, and the idea is developed in Aristotle, *Nicomachean Ethics*, v. 1. See also Aquinas, *Summa Theologiae*, 2a2ae, quest. 58, a. 1.

The fool hath said . . . justice: Hobbes alludes to Psalm 14: 'The fool hath said in his heart, there is no God' (repeated in Psalm 53: 1).

The kingdom of God . . . violence: Hobbes seems to be paraphrasing the somewhat enigmatic text of Matthew 11: 12: 'And from the days of John the Baptist until now the kingdom of heaven suffereth violence, and the violent take it by force.'

Coke's: Sir Edward Coke, 1552–1634, English lawyer. His *Institutes of Law*, published between 1628 and 1644, began with a commentary on a textbook on tenure by Sir Thomas Littlejohn. See also XXVI. 11 and 24.

98 *§6*: in §§6–8 Hobbes turns to what will be one of his primary concerns in the later Parts of *Leviathan*, namely, under what conditions, if any, can religious belief and concerns justify disobedience to a worldly sovereign power. Cf. §8 with Ch. XXXVIII.

99 *manners*: the sense here, and in most other contexts in *Leviathan*, is 'customary mode of behaviour, what is usually done or habitually practised'.

writers: possibly Aquinas, *Summa Theologiae*, 2a2ae, quest. 61, or, more generally, Aristotle, *Nicomachean Ethics*, v. 3–4.

103 *as acquired by lot*: the second-born in a family would not normally think of their sibling's primogeniture as just like tossing a coin to decide who inherits the family property: but that is what Hobbes says here, and more clearly in *Elements of Law (Human Nature)*, XVII. 3–5.

105 *in foro interno*: literally 'in the internal forum'. See my Introduction, p. xxxiv, for an account of the important distinction Hobbes makes in this paragraph.

106 *Of Persons . . . Personated*: this chapter may seem legalistic and relatively uninteresting. Hobbes is attempting to clarify concepts which will be of much significance in his later arguments.

107 *Cicero useth it*: *De Oratore*, ii. 102 (Loeb, p. 275).

and sometimes warrant: these words are added in the large-paper copies and represent one of the tiny handful of changes which might be regarded as adjusting the meaning, however slightly. For another, see note to p. 109.

108 *hoc dicit . . . dicit Dominus*: 'Moses says this . . . the Lord says this.'

109 *on the day of Pentecost*: words occurring only in large-paper copies. The last sentence in §12 seems to imply the heretical view that the three persons of the Trinity are not coeternal and coequal, for which Bishop Bramhall, referring primarily to XLII. 3, reproved Hobbes. See *The Catching of the Leviathan* (London, 1658), 'sent to the press . . . as an appendix to Bramhall's *Castigations of Mr Hobbes*' (London, 1657), 473–4.

111 *Of the Causes . . . Commonwealth*: cf. *De Cive*, V.

And in all places . . . honour: cf. Thucydides, *History*, i. 5, where Thucydides describes the plunder and piracy of ancient times—'it being a matter at that time nowhere in disgrace, but rather carrying with it something of glory'.

113 *by Aristotle numbered*: the reference is to the *Politics*, i. 2: 'Now the reason why man is more of a political animal than bees or any other gregarious animals . . . is speech . . . and . . . a sense of good and evil, of just and unjust; and the association of living beings who have this sense makes a family and a state.' See also Aristotle's *History of Animals*, i. 1 (488^a8–13) and cf. Hobbes's *De Cive*, V. 5, and *Elements of Law* (*Human Nature*), XIX. 5.

114 *conform*: the printed Head and Bear texts had 'perform', which makes bad sense. The Head's list of errata changes it to 'form'. The large-paper copies have 'conform'.

115 *Of the Rights . . . by Institution*: some of the material in this chapter is usefully augmented by reading *De Cive*, VI.

116 *a new covenant . . . with God*: see note to p. 92.

118 *who shall . . . be published*: Hobbes's defence of state censorship will make modern liberal democrats wince; yet those same liberal democrats will take Hobbes's view about when, where, and to whom 'opinions and doctrines' about race, sex, and, to a lesser extent, religion can be communicated if the opinions are judged by the liberal democrats to 'incite hatred', i.e. be 'repugnant to peace' in precisely Hobbes's sense.

119 *These rules . . . are the civil laws*: Hobbes's identification of moral laws with civil laws (and with law of nature) is a main theme of *Leviathan*: see XX. 16, XXVI, *et al.* See also *Elements of Law* (*De Corpore Politico*), XX. 10, and *De Cive*, VI. 9.

120 *These are the rights . . . sovereignty*: evidently these rights, if vested in a king, would resolve in the king's favour almost all that was disputed between Charles I and his subjects. Thus the future king, Charles II, reading his manuscript copy *Leviathan*, would have been quite gratified, but for the clause that follows: 'man, or assembly of men'. Hobbes's personal sympathy was almost certainly with monarchy, but he regularly writes of the 'man or assembly of men' in whom the sovereign power resides. His political theory is thus compatible with support for *any* established sovereign power that can stop the war of every man against every man. See also note to p. 468.

121 *a kingdom . . . cannot stand*: Mark 3: 24. See also Matthew 12: 25 and Luke 11: 17.

this civil war: this is Hobbes's first explicit reference to the civil wars that form the historical background to *Leviathan*. The first was between king and Parliament, 1642–6; the second between the Parliamentary army and Scottish, Irish, and Royalist groups. It ended with the battle of Worcester in 1651.

123 *Of the Several . . . Power*: cf. *Elements of Law* (*De Corpore Politico*), XXIV, and *De Cive*, VII and X.

monarchy . . . democracy . . . aristocracy: Hobbes is employing the influential classification set up by Aristotle in *Politics*, iii. 7. See also Polybius, *History*, VI. iii–ix (Loeb, iii. 271–91).

128 *Ephori*: ephors, the five or so senior magistrates elected annually by the citizens of Sparta to advise (and in effect control) the king.

133 *paternal*: for more on the rights of women and the relations between parents and children see *Elements of Law* (*De Corpore Politico*), XXIII, and *De Cive*, IX.

in history: see, for example, Quintus Curtius, *History of Alexander*, vi. 5 (Loeb, ii. 47).

134 *as when . . . subjects*: an example familiar to Hobbes would have been Mary Queen of Scots marrying the Earl of Bothwell in 1567.

136 *servants*: in context the Hebrew original (*ebed*) signifies something closer to 'slaves'. Samuel is warning the Jews *against* having a king.

139 *Liberty*: see note to p. 29.

140 *no liberty . . . inclination to do*: essentially the same account of liberty reappears in David Hume's *Enquiry concerning Human Understanding* (1748), sect. VIII, pt. I: 'By liberty, then, we can only mean *a power of acting or not acting, according to the determination of the will*; that is, if we choose to remain at rest, we may; if we choose to move, we also may.'

as when . . . should sink: the example is drawn from Aristotle's *Nicomachean Ethics*, iii. 1, although Aristotle is more cautious than Hobbes: 'But with regard to the things that are done from fear of greater evils . . . it may be debated whether such actions are involuntary or voluntary. Something of the sort

489

happens also with regard to the throwing of goods overboard in a storm; for in the abstract no one throws goods away voluntarily, but on condition of its securing the safety of himself and his crew any sensible man does so. Such actions then, are mixed, but are more like voluntary actions . . .' (W. D. Ross's translation).

140 *And therefore . . . nor less*: David Hume suggests (see note to p. 119) that such necessity and liberty is a reason for holding God morally responsible for man's actions.

142 *Jeptha*: see Judges 11: 29–40.

by David: see 2 Samuel 11.

Aristides . . . Hyperbolus: Aristides (died 468 BC) was an Athenian politician, banished between 485 and 482. Hyperbolus was another Athenian politician: 'a lewd fellow' according to Thucydides (*History*, viii. 73).

145 *otherwise there is*: this clause (and §§11–15 in general, together with §21) opens a wider scope for civil disobedience than a sovereign might approve.

150 *letters be patent*: 'letters patent' (elsewhere in Ch. XXII simply referred to as 'letters') are publicly available documents issued by a monarch or government in order to record a contract, authorize an action, or confer a right or privilege.

§9: the effect of this paragraph is to establish the important distinction between the real person of the sovereign (monarch or member of the sovereign assembly) and the artificial man or Leviathan whose head he or they represent. The former is subject to the law. The latter cannot be since it is the law. See XXIX. 9.

157 *by obligation*: copies of the Head and Bear editions that I have seen have 'not' in front of these words; large-paper copies omit it. The written copy also omits it.

justice . . . without money: Hobbes's realism seems to refer to the familiar high costs of legal representation, not to bribery.

158 *&c.*: the written copy omits '&c.' and reads 'Independents', i.e. the various fragmentary reformed sects that broke away from the Presbyterians.

161 *Dei gratia . . . voluntate regis*: 'by the grace of God and the king; or by the providence of God and the will of the king.'

if the plea were public: this phrase occurs only in the large-paper copies.

164 *Let the civil law . . . another man's*: Cicero, *Pro Caecina*, xxv. 73 and 70 respectively (Loeb, pp. 171 and 167).

165 *in another place*: it is not clear where this other place might be in *Leviathan*.

168 *whose veins receiving . . . the same*: apart from developing once again the concept of Leviathan as an artificial man (see Hobbes's Introduction), Hobbes is appealing to the new knowledge of circulation published by William Harvey (1578–1657) in *De Motu Cordis et Sanguinis* (1628). Harvey was an acquaint-

ance of Hobbes's, and he asks after Harvey in a letter of Sept./Oct. 1655. See Letter 74 in *The Correspondence of Thomas Hobbes*, ed. Noel Malcolm (Clarendon Press, Oxford, 1994).

counsels, and commands: see also *Elements of Law (De Corpore Politico)*, XXIX. 1–6, and *De Cive*, XIV. 1–2. Hobbes's distinction can be seen at work in, for example, *Leviathan*, XXV. 10, XXVI. 2, and XLIII. 5.

171 *§10*: Hobbes's distinction between Old Testament commands and New Testament counsels is dubious in view of the numerous benefits the Israelites were supposed to lose if they disobeyed God's commands.

172 *experience*: see II. 4 and III. 6–10.

175 *Of Civil Laws*: much of this chapter is of primary interest to jurists and constitutional lawyers, but note the identification of natural law with civil law, and the relation to divine law discussed in §§8, 13, 36–9.

179 *Sir Edward Coke*: see note to p. 96.

185 *a great lawyer*: again Coke. The quotation is from the *Institutes of Law*, Part I, paragraph 709.

188 *Justinian*: 482–565, Eastern Roman Emperor (at Constantinople) 527–65. In 529 the first *Codex Justinianus* was issued—a formulation of all valid imperial laws from Hadrian onwards. Other definitive codifications of law followed. In 533 his lawyers, acting on Justinian's instructions, produced a systematic elementary treatise of law, the *Institutions*.

189 *how can a man ... by the declarer?*: this is precisely the question answered with great confidence by Locke, Clarke, and many others after and before Hobbes by reference to the performance of miracles and the fulfilling of prophecy. But Hobbes is surprisingly cautious about giving their answer. See Chs. XXXII and XXXVIII.

193 *the first motions of the mind ... be sins*: cf. XIII. 10. Hobbes is presumably thinking of such precepts as Matthew 5: 28: 'whosoever looketh on a woman to lust after her hath committed adultery with her already in his heart', and the (conspicuously Calvinist) theology of sin in thought and feeling based upon such texts as this.

194 *alter the religion there*: Hobbes presumably accepts that the argument could be turned upon all Christian missionaries in states with an established non-Christian religion.

199 *as the Stoics ... maintained*: a cardinal (and paradoxical) teaching of the Stoics was that all crimes were equal. See, for example, Cicero, *De Finibus*, iv. 23 and 28 (Loeb, pp. 371, 385), *Stoic Paradoxes*, paradox iii, and Plutarch's *Moralia*, 'On Common Conceptions', for a general critique of the Stoic position.

209 *And Cicero says*: see *Pro Caecina*, xxxiv. 100 (Loeb, p. 199).

212 *Of those . . . a Commonwealth*: much of the chapter is in effect an analysis of the sources of the English civil war. *Behemoth*, Hobbes's full account of these and of related events, was written 1667–8 and officially published in 1682.

214 *Solon . . . was mad*: see Plutarch's *Lives*, 'Solon', viii (Loeb, i. 421).

§6: the argument in §§6–8, that private opinion of good and evil, private conscience, and private religious inspiration, are calculated to destroy the body politic, lays out the ground for much of what Hobbes is to discuss in Chs. XXX–XLIII.

215 *subject to the civil laws*: the logic of Hobbes's argument is impeccable, but it is not the direction in which the English constitution went, nor does it seem compatible with XXII. 9.

216 *Lacedemonians*: Spartans. Sparta was a kingdom (regulated by custom and advisers); Athens a democracy.

218 *punishments . . . rewards*: see XXXI. 1, and XXXVIII, where Hobbes directly confronts the issue.

219 *Sometimes . . . a third*: Hobbes is listing the conflicting forces which led to civil war in England.

225 *like the foolish . . . new man*: Hobbes also uses this tasty illustration of his argument in *Elements of Law* (*De Corpore Politico*), XXVII. 15. Pelias was responsible for sending his nephew Jason to fetch the Golden Fleece. The unfortunate rejuvenation was attempted by Pelias' daughters after Jason's return with Medea, and at her suggestion.

Non habebis . . . are Gods: presumably Hobbes quotes the Vulgate Latin to emphasize the force of the word *alienus*—'strange', 'other', 'alien'. 'Another place' is Psalm 82: 6.

238 *cannot sin*: the argument in the paragraph is left unresolved. The problem of suffering does deter the faith of both philosophers and 'the vulgar', and Job gives no real answer to it in affirming merely that God does these things in the mystery of his power.

240 *Fourthly . . . honour*: the best-known and most influential view of this kind is to be found in the writings of Epicurus (341–*c*.270 BC) and his faithful exponent Lucretius (*c*.95–*c*.54 BC), for both of whom the gods exist, but take no care of man. See John Gaskin (ed.), *The Epicurean Philosophers* (London and Vermont, 1995), Introduction and pp. 42–3, 234–5. Plato identifies such a view as one variety of atheism at the beginning of *Laws*, x.

245 *may fall into . . . clear*: the future Charles II, into whose hands Hobbes did indeed put a fine manuscript copy of *Leviathan*, may well have found the work clear, but he could scarcely have judged it short. Hobbes's hope was dashed by the 'interested' interpretation of Clarendon and other Royalists which resulted in December 1651 in Hobbes being forbidden to come to the exiled court in Paris.

247 *Part 3*: the material in these twelve chapters has no counterpart in the *Elements of Law* and does not systematically correspond with chs. XVI–XVIII of *De Cive*, although individual topics can be related (see Howard Warrender's marginalia in his text of the English version of *De Cive*, Clarendon Press, Oxford, 1983). Chapter XXXII sets out in brief Hobbes's main purposes, and XXXIII examines the validity of the biblical canon (why they, and no other books, can be taken as canonical). Later chapters examine and define, usually in a somewhat reductionist way but always with biblical justification, such key religious concepts as 'body', 'spirit' (XXXIV), 'kingdom of God' (XXXV), 'prophecy', 'word of God' (XXXVI), 'miracle' (XXXVII), 'hell', 'resurrection' (XXXVIII), and 'church' (XXXIX). The remaining four chapters develop in detail Hobbes's systematic reduction and regulation of the claims of Churches or religious beliefs to direct political power, or to provide occasions for the overthrow of sovereign power.

248 *pretend*: in Hobbes's usage something like 'present for consideration', but already with overtones of 'make it appear (deceptively) that . . .'.

To say . . . God spake to him: this much-quoted aphorism, together with another in §3, the definition of superstition etc. in VI. 36, *et al.* can readily be used to display Hobbes's distaste for many aspects of religion. But taken literally and in context they can always (just!) be squared with possible interpretation of biblical sources. Indeed, A. P. Martinich (*The Two Gods of Leviathan*, Cambridge, 1992) argues that Hobbes is a religious reformer, not a concealed atheist. See my Introduction, pp. xxiv–xxviii.

252 *St. Jerome*: *c.*342–420, author of the authoritative translation of the Bible into Latin known as the Vulgate. See note to p. 52.

Josephus: AD *c.*37–*c.*101, Jewish historian and writer on religion, governor of Galilee, and friend of Vespasian (even after the Jewish rebellion). For his views on the canon of the Old Testament see *Contra Apionem*, i. 39–41 (Loeb, i. 179).

256 *Ptolomaeus Philadelphus*: second Ptolemy to rule Egypt after the division of the empire of Alexander the Great on his death in 323 BC. Ptolemy II reigned from 285 to 246 BC. He extended the library at Alexandria and, it is believed, caused the Hebrew Bible to be put into Greek by seventy translators—'the Septuagint'.

257 *(after St. Peter)*: the large-paper copies do not print this parenthetical reference to the primacy of St Peter.

258 *Philo*: *c.*30 BC–AD 45, prolific author of works on philosophical religion in the Hellenistic-Jewish tradition.

261 *body*: cf. *De Corpore*, VIII. 1: 'that, which having no dependence upon our thought is coincident or coextended with some part of space'.

For the universe: cf. the definitive statement of what I have called one-world realism (see Introduction, p. xxi) in XLVI. 15. See also *White's De Mundo Examined*, XXVII. 6.

261 *idols*: Hobbes is deliberately overlapping the Greek philosophical and the Jewish–Christian use of this term. In the former sense it means a mental image or conception as opposed to a thing in external reality (whether such an idol is sometimes or always 'false', and in what sense 'false', is a major philosophical question). In the latter sense it means a physical image or representation of a false god used as an object of worship. For Hobbes's full discussion see XLV. 14–20.

262 *God is incomprehensible*: see note to p. 19.

264 *spirits, by the word ghosts*: the soundness of Hobbes's view was belatedly recognized by the late twentieth-century change in most litanies from speaking about the 'Holy Ghost' to speaking about the 'Holy Spirit'.

266 *supernaturally*: note Hobbes's tendency to use this word to bridge gaps in what may be intelligible in terms of his one-world realism. Cf. XXIX. 8.

268 *impatible*: incapable of experiencing suffering or injury. Here and in XLIV. 33 Hobbes is asserting the conclusion, obvious to all but theologians, that if an entity is to burn, it must in some way be corporeal.

277 *commemoration*: Hobbes's Protestant credentials (possibly for a time in question in the 1640s) are confirmed by incidental remarks which emphasize the Eucharist as an act of remembrance rather than of transubstantiation. His intensely argued and documented attack on papal claims is reserved for XLII, and Part 4 of *Leviathan*.

282 *§9*: the problem of how God should speak without the mechanism for so doing is a serious issue of biblical interpretation which spills over into crucial philosophical questions about how a bodiless entity could act at all in or upon a world in which all that is real, in Hobbes's now commonly used analysis, is space and moving bodies. Hobbes's usual let-out is that we say God 'speaks' in order to do him honour. But on examination this 'speaking' reduces to the way 'whatsoever it be' that God makes us understand his will. However, some of these ways are suspect, or not unique to whatsoever God's genuine communications are (see XXXII. 6). Hence (see §11 below), when God 'speaks' in dreams, visions, etc., these speakings must in every true prophet be 'supernatural'. But see note to p. 166, and observe that, at the end of §14 below, Hobbes seems to admit that the manner of God's speaking is 'unintelligible'. See my Introduction, p. xxii, for the relation between Hobbes's philosophical one-world realism, and his acceptance of apparently incompatible matters of faith.

286 *as it is . . . by a voice*: these words only appear in large-paper copies. In the Head edition they are replaced by just three words: 'is not intelligible'.

289 *Jesus is the Christ*: this is the central and minimum affirmation which Hobbes requires of the Christian for salvation. It is much in evidence in the later chapters of *Leviathan*, e.g. XLIII. 11–17, and had already been argued at

length in *Elements of Law* (*De Corpore Politico*), XXV. 6–7, and *De Cive*, XVIII. 5–9.

296 *And when . . . of God*: note the extremely tough criteria which a contemporary event would have to satisfy in order to be a miracle. In the eighteenth century, the biblical miracles were to be tested in a similar way.

297 *§1*: the opening paragraph (cf. XLIII. 2) makes abundantly clear Hobbes's political concerns in cutting down the influences which a supposed future life can exert upon what we do in this life. His discussion is arguably consistent with a possible interpretation of scripture but it diminishes the scale of the horror (see note to p. 416). Hell (§§11–14) is not hell-fire. Resurrection is on earth. The second death (for sinners) is not eternal torment, and so on.

298 *the place wherein*: cf. XLVI. 15, where it is strongly suggested that what is no-where (has no place) is nothing. Consistent with his one-world realism, and with his citation of biblical texts, Hobbes thus makes the unexpected claim that eternal life is something in or of *this* world, even, particularly, 'on earth'.

299 *coelum empyreum*: celestial space, the limitless sky thought of as the abode of God. See Aquinas, *Summa Theologiae*, 1a, quest. 61, a. 4, and quest. 66, a. 3.

300 *resurrection of the body*: Hobbes is strenuously concerned to emphasize what many believers do not seem to notice (although they affirm it regularly in the Apostles' Creed), namely, that the Christian belief is in resurrection of the human person as a *body* incorruptible. The orthodox belief is not in an immaterial I-know-not-what existing as a soul (where 'soul' is understood more as a ghost than as the life of the body that Hobbes refers to in, for example, XLIV. 15). Cf. 1 Corinthians 15: 35–54 and Augustine, *City of God*, xiii. 23.

302 *Bis patet . . . Olympum*: '[Then Tartarus itself] yawns sheer down stretching into the gloom twice as far as in yon sky's upward view to heavenly Olympus.'

305 *as long as the world lasts*: this, and the earlier phrase 'as long as the world stands', are the readings of the Bear and Ornaments editions. The Head edition and the written copy have 'for ever' in both places. I have here and here alone in the present text preferred the usually less reliable readings of the Bear and Ornaments since they have the sound of Hobbes's intentions: this world, whatever its eternity, is the place of a future life or second death. See note to p. 417 for a similar divergence of texts.

310 *[247]*, *[248]*: these page numbers are repeated in the Head edition.

312 *Of the Rights . . . of Judah*: Ch. XL is almost entirely biblical exegesis. Its significance in Hobbes's overall theory can be identified in §§13–14.

321 *[261]*: in the Head edition, page numbers 257–60 inclusive do not occur. Nothing appears to have been omitted either deliberately or accidentally from the text.

Of the Office . . . Saviour: Ch. XLI apparently contributes little to Hobbes's general philosophical and political argument. Its general thesis (see XLII. 6) is 'that the kingdom of Christ is not of this world: therefore neither can his ministers . . . require obedience in his name'.

323 *it is manifest . . . said it*: these words occur only in the large-paper copies.

330 *Cardinal Bellarmine*: Robert, 1542–1621. Although mentioned here, Hobbes returns to his published work at length in §§81–135 of the present chapter. Bellarmine entered the Jesuit order in 1560 and was made a cardinal in 1599. His magisterial defence of the Roman Church against the Protestant, *Disputationes de Controversiis Christianae Fidei Adversus Huius Temporis Haereticos*, appeared between 1581 and 1592. An opponent of James I of the United Kingdom, and of Galileo, he is Hobbes's main adversary in Part 3 of *Leviathan*. The structure of Hobbes's argument is clearly outlined in §§5–6.

347 *the library . . . Alexandria*: see note to p. 256.

Constantine the emperor: AD 285–337, known as 'the Great', gradually consolidated his power in the Roman Empire after 316, and from 324 reunited the whole Empire under his own hand. He caused Constantinople to be established in 326 and was baptized on his deathbed, having favoured Christianity from about 306 onwards.

351 *sint vobis . . . venerandi, etc.*: 'these books are to be venerated by all of you, clergy and laity'—words from the *Apostolic Constitutions*, supposedly by Clement (end of first century AD) but now thought to have been written about AD 350.

355 *Ammianus Marcellinus*: 330–95; his *History of Rome*, originally from AD 96, survives for the years after 353. Ammianus was a pagan, but without animosity to Christians. The reference is to the *History*, XXVII. iii. 12–15 (Loeb, iii. 19–21).

366 *for a Church . . . same thing*: this expresses the main conclusion of the chapter so far, and §81 could easily have marked the start of a separate chapter of intense criticism of the arguments of Bellarmine. These are opposed to the conclusion reached by Hobbes, and Hobbes is attacking his most formidable opponent in the continuation of this chapter.

371 *judgments are infallible*: the formal claim to and definition of *ex cathedra* infallibility was not made until 1870. It was disputed then as Hobbes disputed it, and remains a crucial point of disagreement between the Roman Church and virtually all other Christian denominations.

379 *de lana caprina*: 'concerning the fluff on a goat', i.e. concerning trivialities.

381 *archical . . . cratical . . . didactical*: leadership or essential seniority . . . rule by power (autocratical) . . . teaching.

383 *fourth council of Lateran*: see note to p. 405.

387 *Nero . . . an Arian*: a list of real or apparent anti-Christian emperors. Valens was Eastern Emperor 364–78, an ardent and intolerant Arian, who followed

Julian (Julianus), the highly educated Neoplatonist, who favoured the ancient rituals but sanctioned religious toleration.

400 *§22*: this paragraph draws the vital political and religious conclusion of Part 3: belief that Jesus is the Christ, and the salvation that results from it, cannot be destroyed by obeying even the wrong-headed religious directions of a Christian sovereign power, because for God the will to do right is as good as the right thing done. 'There can therefore be no contradiction between the laws of God, and the laws of a Christian commonwealth.'

401 *§23*: this paragraph argues in effect the same conclusion for the non-Christian sovereign, since belief is hidden and inviolate, and biblical directions indicate that the Christian should observe the laws of the secular state.

404 *Four causes of spiritual darkness*: these are successively examined in Chs. XLIV–XLVII. The second cause, 'the demonology of the heathen poets', shows a much more active fear and dislike of classical paganism than is likely to be encountered now.

405 *obedience to the Pope*: at this point the written copy of *Leviathan* has a reference in Hobbes's hand: '*Vide Pontific. Greg.* 13. *fol.*' Innocent II was Pope 1198–1216. He made serious and much resented (e.g. by King John of England) attempts to enforce papal superiority over most of the rulers of Western Europe, and presided over the fourth Lateran Council in 1215. Gregory IX was Pope 1227–41. He too believed in papal authority over secular rulers, and issued a declaration concerning heresy (made at the Lateran Council) in a number of decretals (papal decrees, which in collected form become part of the canon law) from which Hobbes here quotes. The right of an external power to invalidate the allegiance of citizens to the sovereign power of their commonwealth would evidently subvert the whole political theory of *Leviathan*.

409 *§12*: the quotations in this paragraph are Hobbes's translations from the Latin of the Roman form of service. The Tridentine and Salisbury baptismal rituals are very similar. The Anglican form avoided the exorcism and 'conjuring'.

conjure: change by the intervention of a supernatural power. The Latin has 'Exorcizo te, creatura aquae . . .', etc.

asperges . . . hyssopo: Psalm 51: 7 : 'Sprinkle me, Lord, with hyssop [and I shall be clean].'

410 *reptile animae viventis*: the Latin here and in the rest of the paragraph is from the Vulgate. The word *anima* is notoriously difficult to render into English. Although commonly rendered 'soul', the meaning is indeed usually nearer to 'life'. The Hebrew words in Genesis are *nephesh hayyah*, a living being. Hobbes's argument in this paragraph is in accord with modern scholarship.

411 *substances distinct from their bodies*: classical mythology does indeed seem to represent this view in a haphazard way, and the common conception of immortality (if there still is one) may well be represented by Hobbes's paraphrase of the Roman Church's view. Moreover, Descartes's *Discourse on Method* (and

other writings) gave serious philosophical voice to the notion of persons as thinking substances. In 1637, at the end of Part V of the *Discourse*, he comments on 'the reasons which go to prove that our soul is in its nature entirely independent of body, and in consequence that it is not liable to die with it'. See also the 'Third Set of Objections' (particularly Objection II) which Hobbes contributed to Descartes's *Meditations* and which were printed in the first edition in 1641 together with Descartes's somewhat frosty replies.

412 *Beza*: Theodore Beza, 1519–1605, converted to Calvinism in 1549, and became Calvin's principal academic associate at Geneva in 1559. The notes to his translation of the New Testament are referred to by Hobbes here and in XLIV. 40.

414 *treading on . . . emperors*: Hobbes alludes to the story that in 1177, when Barbarossa kneeled in submission before Pope Alexander III, the Pope put his foot on the Emperor's neck and spoke the words Hobbes quotes.

416 *Also, it seemeth hard . . . and more*: Hobbes is actively contributing here and elsewhere (see note to p. 297) to humanizing the terrible Hell of medieval Christianity. See D. W. Walker, *The Decline of Hell* (University of Chicago Press, 1964).

417 *for ever*: the Bear and Ornaments editions read 'to the end of this world'; cf. note to p. 305. The written copy has 'for ever'.

425 *those that consider . . . really without us*: the written copy replaces these words with the following: 'other men that busy in the pursuit of power, honor and the means to satisfy and secure, their animal appetites, have either no leisure, or no will to look after any so remote a cause of that they look for, as this of knowing the nature of their own fancy, is the cause that all nations have conceived that those images, which are made by sense, are things really existent without us.'

Hesiod: *fl. c.*700 BC. His *Theogony* deals with the origin and genealogies of the gods, and the genesis of earth, sea, sky, and other great beings of the world.

439 *the senate . . . sanctity*: see Livy's *History*, i. 16 (Loeb, i. 59).

440 *Caligula*: emperor AD 37–41. Hobbes's anecdote is in Suetonius, *Lives of the Caesars*, iv. 13 (Loeb, i. 421).

441 *Caracalla*: son of the emperor Septimius Severus, and emperor 211–17, distinguished only for giving rights of citizenship to all free inhabitants of the Roman Empire.

By Philosophy: in modern terms it will be clear that Hobbes is defining not philosophy but science. A further attempt at definition can be found in *De Corpore*, I. 2.

443 *seven men*: see note to p. 17.

Carneades: 214–129 BC, a very astute critical analytic philosopher sent to Rome on a political embassy in 155, when he spoke persuasively on successive days for and against justice between men and between states. See Cicero, *De Republica*, iii. 5–8 (Loeb, p. 193, and further references to Lactantius).

445 *as Cicero saith*: *De Divinatione*, ii. 119 (Loeb, p. 505).

446 *definitions*: definitions of the 'most universal' names, of the sort Hobbes proceeds to list, are mainly dealt with by Hobbes in the early chapters of *De Corpore*.

   §15: the importance of this paragraph as a statement of Hobbes's fundamental ontological principles can scarcely be overstated.

448 *elsewhere*: for example, IV.

449 *no more soul . . . those parts*: cf. Aquinas, *Summa Theologiae*, 1a, quest. 76, a. 8.

   how fire can burn souls: see note to p. 268. Aquinas attempts a solution to the problem in *Summa Theologiae*, Supp. quest. 70, a. 3.

450 *incomprehensible nature*: see note to p. 19.

452 *§32*: see note to p. 35.

453 *the thirty tyrants*: in 404 BC at the conclusion of the Peloponnesian War between Athens and Sparta, an administration of thirty anti-democrats subservient to Sparta ruled Athens for about eighteen months.

456 *men*: the man in particular to whom Hobbes is alluding is probably Galileo, but there were others: for example, Giordano Bruno was burned at the stake in 1600 for (among other heresies) championing Copernicus, and Lucilio Vanini had his tongue cut out (and suffered other tortures) before being burned in 1619 for similar and additional heretical views.

   if they be true: the argument is potentially ambiguous. It seems to assert merely the logical principle that no true proposition (including those in astronomy and physics) can be contrary to any other true proposition (including those in religion). But this could be meant to suggest that if a proposition in physics etc. is established as true, then a religion (or religious proposition) which is contrary to it cannot also be true.

457 *Cicero maketh honourable mention*: see *Pro Roscio Amerino*, xxxi (Loeb, p. 199).

461 *Frederic . . . Pope Adrian*: the Englishman Nicholas Breakspear became Pope Adrian IV in 1154. In 1155 the Emperor Frederick I held the Pope's stirrup as he mounted, thereby making himself the Pope's inferior.

462 *cross and pile*: heads and tails.

468 *books lately printed*: see the entry by Quintin Skinner in G. E. Aylmer (ed.), *The Interregnum: The Quest for Settlement, 1646–60* (London and Basingstoke, 1972). This essay also examines the problem of obedience to *de facto* sovereign powers (particularly the English Puritan Commonwealth), the problem which forms the background to much of Hobbes's political theory.

474 *that I writ before . . . in Latin*: namely *De Cive*, originally published in Latin in Paris in 1642, followed by two further Latin editions in 1647. The first English

version appeared in London in 1651, before *Leviathan*, and while Hobbes was still in Paris.

475 *my interrupted speculation*: *De Corpore* was first published in Latin in 1655. The English version appeared as *Elements of Philosophy, the First Section concerning Body*, in 1656. Hobbes had reached ch. XIII by mid-1645, and was working on it with difficulty in 1646: 'The reason why I am taking so long over the first section of my [*De Corpore*] is partly laziness, but mostly the fact that I find it difficult to explain my meanings to my own satisfaction . . . However, I do not doubt that I shall finish it before the end of the year, provided I live and am in good health' (*Letters*, p. 133). In the event he had become a tutor in mathematics to the future Charles II by October 1646, and in August 1647 became exceedingly ill with 'a very severe and continuous fever'.

INDEX OF SUBJECTS

Subjects very frequently mentioned in the text are indexed only for substantial entries. Hobbes's definitions of terms are indicated by 'Def' before the page number.

abstraction 25, 446, 447
absurdity 29, 30, 53–4, 81, 88, 438, 449
action 106–7, 118
actor 106–7, 129
ambition Def 37
anarchy Def 123, 235, 453
angels Def 265
    not incorporeal 429
anger 13, 36, 197
Antichrist 289, 369–71
apostles:
    not interpreters of scripture 344
    not lawmakers 349
    power of 334–7, 351–4, 368–9
aristocracy Def 123, 123–5, 127, 128–9, 367
arrogance 102
assembly 114–17, 120, 123–9, 173–5, 176, 178–9
atheism 240
authority 24, 44, Def 107, 108, 114, 144, 200
avarice 79
    see also covetousness

baptism 272, 277, 322, 326, 335–7, 362–3, 396, 409, 415, 421–2
belief, see faith
benefit 67, 80, 87, 95–7, 104, 169–70
    common 32, 113–14, 154
benevolence Def 37, 100
bible, see scripture

bishop 353, 355, 359, 362, 376, 379–82, 459, 461–2
body 26, 54, 73, Def 261–2, 265, 268, 282, 410–11, 446, 450
    spiritual 386, 417, 425–9

canonization Def 439, 460
cause 21, 35, 38, 70, 71–2, 73
    final 183
    natural 291, 428
certainty 28–9
charity Def 37, 230, 391
charter 192
Christ:
    duel nature 279–80, 287, 325–7
    false Christs 250, 370
    kingdom of, see kingdom
    second coming 330, 334, 335, 339, 344
    see also saviour
Christianity, articles of 333, 341, 344, 368, 394–8, 421
church 257–8, 260, 310–11, Def 311, 366, 404–5
    of England 268, 462
    government of 367, 412
    not universal 260, 311, 385
    of Rome 81, 411–12, 437, 439
civitas 7, 114
    see also commonwealth
command Def 169, 171
commandments, ten 181, 225–7, 276, 345

commonwealth Def 114, 129, 138,
    172, 175, 176, 217–21, 228, 386
  by acquisition Def 115, 132–9
  Christian 247, 251, 473
  dissolution of 221, 470
  by institution Def 115, 115–22
  see also aristocracy; civitas;
    democracy; monarchy
compassion Def 39
competition 66, 83, 113, 474
conceptions 26, 480
confederacy 82, 97, 157
confession 459
conquest 66, 134, 221, 469–70
conscience xxxvii, 42–3, 482
  fallible 214
  God reigns in 235
consecration 76, 276–7, 318, 362–5,
    407–9, 414
consent 114, 117, 144, 271, 273, 314,
    470
contempt Def 34, 35, 39, 101–2
contract Def 89, 89–90, 469
  see also covenant; promise
conversion 343–4, 378
corporeality, see body
counsel 120, 163, 168, Def 169,
    169–75
  counsels of scripture 344, 348–9,
    375, 377–8
courage Def 36, 467
covenant (pact) 79, Def 89, 90, 95–8,
    107, 111, 113, 141, 179, 193, 205
  to accuse oneself 93–4
  entered into from fear 92–3, 98
  of mutual trust 91, 95–7
  not to defend oneself void 93
  when invalid 91–4
  with Abraham 190, 271–2, 312–13
  with God 92, 116, 314, 320, 347
  with Moses 249–50, 272–5, 313–16
covetousness Def 37, 62, 197
cowardice 145, 244, 467
creation 237, 241, 265, 428–9

credulity 70, 291–3, 437–8
crime 182, Def 193, 195
  depends on civil law 193–4
  not equal 199, 200–1
  excusable 199–200
  types of 202–5
cruelty Def 39
curiosity Def 37, 70, 71
custom 69, 130–1, 177

death 67, 98, 198, 204, 297–9, 333,
    424, 433–4, 467
  everlasting 391, 410
  fear of 66, 84, 86, 132
  second 303, 305, 410, 418, 422
definition xxii–xxiv, 23–4, 30, 247, 446
deliberation Def 39, 40–1, 68
democracy Def 123, 123–5, 138
  dangers of 157, 214, 220
  like monarchy 117, 128, 143
demons 50–2, 265, 266, 302, 304,
    403–4, 409, 411, 425–6
desire Def 34–5, 65–7
Devil 15, 52, 268
  Beelzebub 52, 403, 463
  devils 51–2, 293, 354, 425–7, 429
  Satan 304, 339, 403, 409, 427–8
diffidence Def 37, 62, 83
dignity Def 59, 113
discourse 42–4
discretion Def 46
doctrine 118, 120
  erroneous 421
dominion 61, 85, Def 107, 108
  despotical 134–6
  paternal 133–4, 135–7
dreams Def 12, 13–15, 198, 438, 472
  God speaks in 248, 263, 267, 283,
    288
drunkenness 104
duty Def 88, 473

ecclesiastical power, see jurisdiction;
  power

education 225–8, 239, 244–5, 467
elect of God 292, 324, 415–16,
    417–18, 421
eloquence 58, 59, 68, 173–4, 467–8
endeavour xxiii, xxviii, 9, Def 34,
    478
enthusiasm 51, 77, 251
equality 82–3, 91, 102–3
    before sovereign 229
equity 100, 104, 228
    as a natural law Def 103, 182, 210
error Def 29, 31, 184, 196, 201, 339,
    404, 454, 473
essences:
    abstract 446–7
    separated 448–9
eternity 449
    afterlife 78, 98, 271, 424
    eternal life 297–301, 334, 336, 390,
        394, 397, 399, 410, 415
    eternal torments 297, 411, 417–18,
        454
    immortality 299, 300–1, 306, 325,
        410, 415–17
evil 105, 119, 137–8
    problem of 237–8, 255
    see also good
excommunication 336–42, 360, 366,
    376, 383–5, 406, 412, 458
excuse 194–5, Def 199, 199–200, 201
exorcism 409, 411, 414–15
experience Def 12, 17–18, 20, 34, 41,
    172, 291, 442

fairies 14, 404
    kingdom of 463–4
    see also ghosts; spirits
faith Def 43, 44, 79, 80–1, 89, 331,
    332, 339–40, 348, 371–2
    belief Def 43, 248–9, 250, 313,
        332, 342–3
    Christian 391–401
    not knowledge 442
family 111, 131, 136

fancy 11, 45–7
fear 13–14, Def 36, 38, 60, 67, 94,
    132, 140
    of God 242
    of power invisible 37–8, 71, 72, 94,
        120, 198
felicity Def 41–2, 52, 60
    eternal 98, 271, 304
fool 96, 108, 179, 199
form 449
fortune 71–2, 75
fraud 81, 85, 204, 221, 474
    pious 257, 462
free 139–40
    see also liberty; voluntary; will

gain (profit) 81, 83, 101, 198, 334,
    458, 460, 475
generosity 94, 198
gentiles, see religion
geometry xv, 23, 31, 70
ghost 14, 73, 74, 263–4, 411, 449, 456
    Holy Ghost 108, 264, 328–30, 347,
        412, 427, 435
    power of 218
gift Def 89, 91, 358, 394, 411, 415–16,
    418, 429
glory Def 38, 83, 94
    vain-glory Def 38, 49, 68, 101,
        196–7, 340
God xxiv–xxviii, 20, 73, 191, 259,
    277–80, 285, 390
    attributes 240–1, 242
    corporeality xxii, 262, 283
    existence 70–1, 236
    immediate cause 291, 293, 394
    incomprehensible xxv, 73, 262,
        285, 479
    kingdom of, see kingdom
    knowledge of 241
    law of 235–6, 259; written 345, 347
    power of 140, 226, 237, 270, 309
    speech of 248–9, 263, 282–3, 494
    spirit of 261–4

golden rule 104, 180, 194
good 105, 113, 452
  common 113, 119, 124, 174–5,
    230–1, 232
  good and evil, knowledge of 105,
    113, 126, 137–8, 214–15, 271, 297
  private 33, 81, 124, 157, 172
  works 400
government 453–4, 457
  change of 367
  mixed 367
  spiritual 311–12
  temporal 311–12
grace, *see* gift
gratitude 67, 100
gravity 450
greed, *see* avarice; covetousness
grief Def 38

hate Def 34, 67, 102, 197, 229
heaven 67, 91, 271, 275, 299–301,
    308, 411
hell 67, 301–5
heresy 69, Def 387
heretic Def 340–1, 383, 388–9
history 44, 46, 55, 456
Hobbes:
  death of xvii
  education xi–xii
  influences on xii–xvi
  philosophy in three parts xviii–xx,
    xix n.
  Behemoth xiv
  De Cive xi, xvi, xviii, xxxi
  De Corpore xvi, xix, xxvii, 500
  Elements of Law xvi, xviii, xx, xxiii,
    xxv, xxx, xxxiii
  Leviathan, see *Leviathan*
  Peloponnesian War xii
  White's De Mundo xii, xxv n.
holy 275–7
Holy Ghost, *see* ghost
honour 48, Def 59–60, 60–3, 121–2,
    209

laws of 111
signs of 238
titles of 64–5
hope Def 36, 37, 38, 62, 74, 196–7
human nature xxviii–xxxi

idolatry 108, 408, 429–39, 471–2
ignorance 24
  of causes 32, 69–71
  of the law 194
  of signification of words 69
image 10, 425, 429–30, Def 432–3
imagination Def 11, 19, 424
immortality, *see* eternity
incorporeality, *see* body
Independents 121, 158, 462
infidel 334, 350, 351, 353, 386–7,
    407
infinite 19, 241, 431, 432
inspiration 214–15, Def 269–70
interest, *see* good
interpretation:
  of law 183–6
  of scripture 313

judge 103, 104, 118, 137, 161, 179,
    182, 183–8, 371, 401
judgement Def 42, 371, 467
  good Def 45, 46–7
  private 201, 214–15
jurisdiction 138, 161, 275, 348, 371,
    374, 381–2
  ecclesiastical 327–30, 379–80
justice/injustice 85, Def 88, Def 95,
    96, 98–9, 223, 228–9, 342, 452
  distributive/commutative Def
    99–100, 103
justification 400, 460

kingdom:
  of Christ 322–5, 348–9, 405, 412
  of darkness Def 403, 404, 463
  elective 127–8
  of glory 271, 275

of God 236–7, Def 271, Def 273,
    274, 301; by covenant 249,
    271–5, 470; by nature 271
of grace 271, 275
of heaven 299; keys to 369
heretical 386–7
knowledge 24, 31, 37, 42–3, 54–7, 442

labour 163–4, 230
laughter Def 38
law 69–70, 85, 106, 164, 215
    canon 406–7
    civil 119, 141, Def 176, 175 *passim*,
        193–4, 392
    common 189–91, 238
    ex post facto 195, 207
    fundamental 87, 100–1, 103, 191–2,
        203
    good 230–1
    interpretation of 179, 183–7, 231,
        454–5
    letter of 186
    moral 312
    of Moses 318–19, 326, 423
    of nations 235
    positive 189–90
    unwritten 177–8, 180, 183, 185–6
    written 177, 182–3, 185–6, 259, 345
    see also jurisdiction; liberty; power
        ecclesiastical
laws of nature xx, xxxii–xxxiv, Def 86,
    86–8, 95–106, 177–8, 181, 182
lawyers 178–9
legislator 176–7, 179, 186
Leviathan xxxiv–xxxv, 7, 114, 262
Leviathan:
    composition of xvi–xvii
    editions of xliv–xlv
    influence of xl–xliii
    Latin version xlviii–xlix
    'one world realism of' xxi–xxii
    present edition xlvi–xlviii
    structure of xx
liberty Def 86, 123–4, Def 139,

139–48, 192, 209, 221, 468
corporeal 141, 147
of God 140
natural 139–40
true liberty of subjects 144
life 7, 147, 269–71
love Def 37, 239, 391
lust Def 37, 40, 85

madness Def 48–9, 49–54, 179,
    426–7
magic 294, 407–9
magnanimity Def 37
man, artificial 7, 213, *et seq.*
manners Def 65, 69, 341, 371–2
marriage 452–3, 459, 464
martyr 333–4, 351, 460
materia prima 282
memory Def 12, 248
merit 65, Def 90
Messiah, *see* saviour
metaphor 21, 27, 47, 186
metaphysics 446–7, 451
minister 159, 162–3, 200
    of God 328, 331–2, 356–7
miracle 215, 249–51, Def 293, 290–6
monarchy 116–17, 123–32, 213–14,
    217, 381
money 167
motion xxviii, 10–12, 13, 33–4, 35–6,
    41, 53, 139
multitude 109, 112, 129, 170–1

names 22–7, 29, 243, 447–8
necessity 101, 137, 140, 171, 195
number 23, 27

oath Def 94, 95
obedience 138, 148, 224–5, 288,
    390–1, 440–1, 456
    protection, end of 147, 475
obligation xxxiii, 67, Def 88, 95, 105,
    144, 145, 147, 192, 221, 469
oligarchy 123, 453

ontology (Hobbes's) xxi–xxii
opinion Def 43, 172, 248
oratory, see eloquence; rhetoric
ordination 352, 354, 363

pact, see covenant
paradise, see heaven
pardon Def 101, 228
passions 8, 33–42, 48–54, 86, 111,
    196, 201–2, 467
peace Def 84, 86, 87, 103, 118
person 58, Def 106, 107–10, 114, 121,
    124, 243, 328–30
  artificial 106–8
  natural 106, 124
phantasm 425, 429, Def 432
philosophy 53–4, Def 441, 442
  beginnings of 442–3
  civil 452, 453–4
  errors of 446–9
  moral 444–5, 452
  natural 444, 450–1
  philosophers 30, 55, 142–3
  schools of 443–5
pity Def 39
pope 81, 213, 354, 405–7, 439–40,
    453, 457–8
  infallibility of 371, 393, 458–9
  jurisdiction of 361, 366, 379, 459,
    460–1, 462, 463
  power of 228, 362, 367, 374, 380–1
possession:
  as a basis of right 103, 107, 130, 146
  by a spirit 51–3, 77, 427, 428–9
power Def 58, 58–9, 60–5
  absolute 136–7
  civil 217–18, 339, 349, 384, 459
  ecclesiastical 327 passim, 473
  divided 120–1, 123–4
  irresistible 237
  limitations 127, 138
  spiritual/temporal 79, 217–18,
    311–12, 318–19, 382–5, 413–14,
    464

prayer 421–2, 430–1
preaching 334–5, 455
precedent 69, 185
presbytery 354, 364–5, 412, 458, 459,
    461–2
pride Def 49, 102, 212
  see also glory
priests 81–2, 406, 463–4
  of Israel 273, 275, 285, 317, 357
  marriage of 453, 459
  see also bishop; jurisdiction;
    minister; pope; power
    ecclesiastical; presbytery
promise Def 89, 90, 94, 97
property 85, 96, 119, 164–5, 216,
    219–20
prophecy 51–2, 80, 236, 249–51,
    281–90, 353–4
  false 284, 288–90, 370, 378, 390
  see also dreams; miracle; revelation
protection 147, 221, 475
prudence 17–19, 31–3, Def 47, 48,
    58–9, 82
punishment 120, 162, 194–5, Def
    205, 205–12, 231–2, 297
  capital 208, 471–2
  natural 206–7, 244
purgatory 398, 411, 418–19, 421–4,
    456
pusillanimity Def 37, 38

quantity 451

reason Def 28, 27–33, 48, 195–6, 247,
    248, 280, 288, 467
  dictates of 86, 106, 180, 181,
    236–7, 238, 280
  right reason 14–15, 28
rebellion 98, 210–11, 216–17, 223,
    472
  see also war
redemption, see salvation
religion Def 37–8, 71–82, 301,
    319–21, 424–41, 448, 455–7

of the gentiles 75–7, 404, 424–6, 429–30, 439
mysteries of 247
seeds of 71, 74–5, 79
repentance, *see* salvation
representation 106–7, 109–10, 115, 123–4, 129, 149, 207, 328
reputation 58
resurrection xxvii, 269, 299–301, 305, 333, 386, 416, 495
revelation 44, 78, 79, 236, 259, 287, 392
private xxxviii–xxxix
see also dreams; miracle; prophecy
revenge 101, 198, 202, 206
reward 120, 133, 211–12, 236, 297
rhetoric 31, 46, 113, 126, 170
see also eloquence
riches 58, 124–5, 196, 204, 224, 229, 467
right 69, 85, 103–4, 115, 118, 134, 144, 192
of all to all 87, 119, 237
inalienable 88–9
jure civili/jure divino 362, 366, 379, 406
laying down Def 86–7
of nature Def 86, 87
righteousness 98–9, 374, 391, 400

sacrament Def 277, 407–9, 455
salvation 305–10, 321–7, 336–8, 390–1, 394–401, 405, 416–17, 419–22
saviour 279–80, 285, 297–301, 308–10, 321–7, 369, 375
see also Christ
science 23–4, Def 31, 31–3, 42–3, 59
scripture 52–3, 247, 344–6
abuse of 404–5, 407–10
authority of 258–60
authorship of 252–9
interpretation of 251, 260, 297–8, 314–16, 342–4

security (safety) 67, 83–4, 97, 114
of the people 213, Def 222, 228, 232, 235
self-love xxix, xl–xli, 104, 122, 183
sense Def 9, 10–13, 15–16, 19, 33–6, 247–8, 312, 451
shame Def 39
sign 18, 21
sin 192–4, 200, 214, 217–18, 237–8, 336–8, 349–50, 391, 436, 438, 460
sincerity 79–80, 462
sociability 100–1, 113
soldier 145, 160, 211, 469–70
soul xxii, xxvii, 73, 297 *passim*, 410–11, 418–21, 448–51, 495
not incorporeal 449
sovereign/sovereignty xxxiv–xxxvi, Def 114, 115, 117–18, 120–1, 130, 144, 146–8, 177–9, 183–5, 202, 215–19, 221, 227–8, 327 *passim*
Christian 360 *passim*, 400–1
infidel 331–2, 386–8, 400–1
by institution 115–22, 132, 135–6
suits against sovereign 146
speech 19, 20–7, 31–2
spirit 50–4, 73, 217–19, 261–2, 265–6, 316, 409, 426–9, 446–7
corporeal xxvi, 429–30
immaterial 428–9
private Def 50, 313, 393
substance Def 261, 265–6
corporeal 260–1, 265
incorporeal 260–2, 265–6, 268–9, 410–11, 449
substantial forms 446–7
succession 127–8, Def 129, 129–31, 355–6
summum bonum 65
supernatural xxii, 50, 51–2, 76–80, 98
superstition 13–15, Def 37, 71, 73–4, 76–7

taxation 70, 122, 165–6, 219, 229
teaching 8, 160–1, 196, 224–8, 335, 342, 361–2, 393–4
thought 8, 9, 15, 16–17, 19, 28, 43, 47, 193, 313, 450, 454
toleration 386–8, 407, 470
treason 97, 203, 207
Trinity, the 328–30, 409, 419–20
trust 100, 104
tyranny 123, 453, 470
tyrant 217, 277

understanding Def 15, 26, 194, 241, 247–8
universal 22
universe 261, Def 447
university 227, Def 445–6

vain-glory, see glory
value Def 59, 60, 65, 99–100
virtue 45–54, 106, 286
vision 199, 248–9, 284, 288, 427

voluntary 33, Def 40, 66, 88, 100, 140
see also will

war Def 84, 113, 230, 468
causes of 66, 83
civil 7, 122, 219, 385, 390, 404; in England 121, 131, 301, 468
state of xxxi–xxxii, xxxiv–xxxv, 84–7, 105, 485
will xxix, 40, 140, 181, 241, 451, 480
freewill 140, 452
see also action; voluntary
wisdom 7, 18, 32, 68
wit 18, 33, 45, 47, 48
witchcraft 14, 294
wonder 291
words, see names
worship 74, Def 238, 239–44, Def 430–1
civil/divine Def 431, 433–4
of images 76, 434, 436–9

THE WORLD'S CLASSICS

A Select List

HANS ANDERSEN: Fairy Tales
Translated by L. W. Kingsland
Introduction by Naomi Lewis
Illustrated by Vilhelm Pedersen and Lorenz Frølich

ARTHUR J. ARBERRY (Transl.): The Koran

LUDOVICO ARIOSTO: Orlando Furioso
Translated by Guido Waldman

✓ ARISTOTLE: The Nicomachean Ethics
Translated by David Ross

✓ JANE AUSTEN: Emma
Edited by James Kinsley and David Lodge

Mansfield Park
Edited by James Kinsley and John Lucas

Northanger Abbey, Lady Susan, The Watsons,
and Sanditon
Edited by John Davie

HONORÉ DE BALZAC: Père Goriot
Translated and Edited by A. J. Krailsheimer

CHARLES BAUDELAIRE: The Flowers of Evil
Translated by James McGowan
Introduction by Jonathan Culler

WILLIAM BECKFORD: Vathek
Edited by Roger Lonsdale

R. D. BLACKMORE: Lorna Doone
Edited by Sally Shuttleworth

KEITH BOSLEY (Transl.): The Kalevala

JAMES BOSWELL: Life of Johnson
The Hill/Powell edition, revised by David Fleeman
Introduction by Pat Rogers

MARY ELIZABETH BRADDON: Lady Audley's Secret
Edited by David Skilton

ANNE BRONTË: The Tenant of Wildfell Hall
Edited by Herbert Rosengarten and Margaret Smith

✓CHARLOTTE BRONTË: Jane Eyre
Edited by Margaret Smith

Shirley
Edited by Margaret Smith and Herbert Rosengarten

EMILY BRONTË: Wuthering Heights
Edited by Ian Jack

GEORG BÜCHNER:
Danton's Death, Leonce and Lena, Woyzeck
Translated by Victor Price

JOHN BUNYAN: The Pilgrim's Progress
Edited by N. H. Keeble

EDMUND BURKE: A Philosophical Enquiry into the
Origin of our Ideas of the Sublime and Beautiful
Edited by Adam Phillips

FANNY BURNEY: Camilla
Edited by Edward A. Bloom and Lilian D. Bloom

THOMAS CARLYLE: The French Revolution
Edited by K. J. Fielding and David Sorensen

LEWIS CARROLL: Alice's Adventures in Wonderland
and Through the Looking Glass
Edited by Roger Lancelyn Green
Illustrated by John Tenniel

CATULLUS: The Poems of Catullus
Edited by Guy Lee

MIGUEL DE CERVANTES: Don Quixote
Translated by Charles Jarvis
Edited by E. C. Riley

GEOFFREY CHAUCER: The Canterbury Tales
Translated by David Wright

ANTON CHEKHOV: The Russian Master and Other Stories
Translated by Ronald Hingley

Ward Number Six and Other Stories
Translated by Ronald Hingley

JOHN CLELAND:
Memoirs of a Woman of Pleasure (Fanny Hill)
Edited by Peter Sabor

WILKIE COLLINS: Armadale
Edited by Catherine Peters

The Moonstone
Edited by Anthea Trodd

JOSEPH CONRAD: Chance
Edited by Martin Ray

Typhoon and Other Tales
Edited by Cedric Watts

√ Youth, Heart of Darkness, The End of the Tether
Edited by Robert Kimbrough

JAMES FENIMORE COOPER: The Last of the Mohicans
Edited by John McWilliams

DANTE ALIGHIERI: The Divine Comedy
Translated by C. H. Sisson
Edited by David Higgins

DANIEL DEFOE: Robinson Crusoe
Edited by J. Donald Crowley

THOMAS DE QUINCEY:
The Confessions of an English Opium-Eater
Edited by Grevel Lindop

CHARLES DICKENS: Christmas Books
Edited by Ruth Glancy

David Copperfield
Edited by Nina Burgis

The Pickwick Papers
Edited by James Kinsley

FEDOR DOSTOEVSKY: Crime and Punishment
Translated by Jessie Coulson
Introduction by John Jones

The Idiot
Translated by Alan Myers
Introduction by W. J. Leatherbarrow

Memoirs from the House of the Dead
Translated by Jessie Coulson
Introduction by Ronald Hingley

ARTHUR CONAN DOYLE:
Sherlock Holmes: Selected Stories
Introduction by S. C. Roberts

ALEXANDRE DUMAS *père*:
The Three Musketeers
Edited by David Coward

ALEXANDRE DUMAS *fils*:
La Dame aux Camélias
Translated by David Coward

MARIA EDGEWORTH: Castle Rackrent
Edited by George Watson

GEORGE ELIOT: Daniel Deronda
Edited by Graham Handley

Felix Holt, The Radical
Edited by Fred C. Thompson

✓ Middlemarch
Edited by David Carroll

✓ HENRY FIELDING: Joseph Andrews *and* Shamela
Edited by Douglas Brooks-Davies

GUSTAVE FLAUBERT: Madame Bovary
Translated by Gerard Hopkins
Introduction by Terence Cave

A Sentimental Education
Translated by Douglas Parmée

FORD MADOX FORD: The Good Soldier
Edited by Thomas C. Moser

BENJAMIN FRANKLIN:
Autobiography and Other Writings
Edited by Ormond Seavey

ELIZABETH GASKELL: Cousin Phillis and Other Tales
Edited by Angus Easson

North and South
Edited by Angus Easson

GEORGE GISSING: The Private Papers of Henry Ryecroft
Edited by Mark Storey

WILLIAM GODWIN: Caleb Williams
Edited by David McCracken

J. W. VON GOETHE: Faust, Part One
Translated by David Luke

KENNETH GRAHAME: The Wind in the Willows
Edited by Peter Green

H. RIDER HAGGARD: King Solomon's Mines
Edited by Dennis Butts

THOMAS HARDY: A Pair of Blue Eyes
Edited by Alan Manford

Jude the Obscure
Edited by Patricia Ingham

Tess of the D'Urbervilles
Edited by Juliet Grindle and Simon Gatrell

NATHANIEL HAWTHORNE:
Young Goodman Brown and Other Tales
Edited by Brian Harding

HESIOD: Theogony *and* Works and Days
Translated by M. L. West

E. T. A. HOFFMANN:
The Golden Pot and Other Tales
Translated and Edited by Ritchie Robertson

HOMER: The Iliad
Translated by Robert Fitzgerald
Introduction by G. S. Kirk

The Odyssey
Translated by Walter Shewring
Introduction by G. S. Kirk

THOMAS HUGHES: Tom Brown's Schooldays
Edited by Andrew Sanders

HENRIK IBSEN: An Enemy of the People, The Wild Duck,
Rosmersholm
Edited and Translated by James McFarlane

Peer Gynt
Translated by Christopher Fry and Johan Fillinger
Introduction by James McFarlane

HENRY JAMES: The Ambassadors
Edited by Christopher Butler

A London Life *and* The Reverberator
Edited by Philip Horne

The Spoils of Poynton
Edited by Bernard Richards

RUDYARD KIPLING: The Jungle Books
Edited by W. W. Robson

Stalky & Co.
Edited by Isobel Quigly

MADAME DE LAFAYETTE: The Princesse de Clèves
Translated and Edited by Terence Cave

WILLIAM LANGLAND: Piers Plowman
Translated and Edited by A. V. C. Schmidt

J. SHERIDAN LE FANU: Uncle Silas
Edited by W. J. McCormack

CHARLOTTE LENNOX: The Female Quixote
Edited by Margaret Dalziel
Introduction by Margaret Anne Doody

LEONARDO DA VINCI: Notebooks
Edited by Irma A. Richter

MIKHAIL LERMONTOV: A Hero of our Time
Translated by Vladimir Nabokov with Dmitri Nabokov

MATTHEW LEWIS: The Monk
Edited by Howard Anderson

JACK LONDON:
The Call of the Wild, White Fang, and Other Stories
Edited by Earle Labor and Robert C. Leitz III

NICCOLÒ MACHIAVELLI: The Prince
Edited by Peter Bondanella and Mark Musa
Introduction by Peter Bondanella

KATHERINE MANSFIELD: Selected Stories
Edited by D. M. Davin

MARCUS AURELIUS:
The Meditations of Marcus Aurelius
Translated by A. S. L. Farquharson
Edited by R. B. Rutherford

KARL MARX AND FRIEDRICH ENGELS:
The Communist Manifesto
Edited by David McLellan

CHARLES MATURIN: Melmoth the Wanderer
Edited by Douglas Grant
Introduction by Chris Baldick

HERMAN MELVILLE: The Confidence-Man
Edited by Tony Tanner

Moby Dick
✓ *Edited by Tony Tanner*

PROSPER MÉRIMÉE: Carmen and Other Stories
Translated by Nicholas Jotcham

MICHELANGELO: Life, Letters, and Poetry
Translated by George Bull with Peter Porter

✓ JOHN STUART MILL: On Liberty and Other Essays
Edited by John Gray

MOLIÈRE: Don Juan and Other Plays
Translated by George Graveley and Ian Maclean

GEORGE MOORE: Esther Waters
Edited by David Skilton

MYTHS FROM MESOPOTAMIA
Translated and Edited by Stephanie Dalley

E. NESBIT: The Railway Children
Edited by Dennis Butts

ORIENTAL TALES
Edited by Robert L. Mack

OVID: Metamorphoses
Translated by A. D. Melville
Introduction and Notes by E. J. Kenney

FRANCESCO PETRARCH:
Selections from the Canzoniere and Other Works
Translated by Mark Musa

√ EDGAR ALLAN POE: Selected Tales
Edited by Julian Symons

JEAN RACINE: Britannicus, Phaedra, Athaliah
Translated by C. H. Sisson

ANN RADCLIFFE: The Italian
Edited by Frederick Garber

The Mysteries of Udolpho
Edited by Bonamy Dobrée

The Romance of the Forest
Edited by Chloe Chard

THE MARQUIS DE SADE:
The Misfortune of Virtue and Other Early Tales
Translated and Edited by David Coward

PAUL SALZMAN (Ed.):
An Anthology of Elizabethan Prose Fiction

OLIVE SCHREINER: The Story of an African Farm
Edited by Joseph Bristow

SIR WALTER SCOTT: The Heart of Midlothian
Edited by Claire Lamont

Waverley
Edited by Claire Lamont

ANNA SEWELL: Black Beauty
Edited by Peter Hollindale

√ MARY SHELLEY: Frankenstein
Edited by M. K. Joseph

TOBIAS SMOLLETT: The Expedition of Humphry Clinker
Edited by Lewis M. Knapp
Revised by Paul-Gabriel Boucé

STENDHAL: The Red and the Black
Translated by Catherine Slater

LAURENCE STERNE: A Sentimental Journey
Edited by Ian Jack

Tristram Shandy
Edited by Ian Campbell Ross

ROBERT LOUIS STEVENSON: Kidnapped and Catriona
Edited by Emma Letley

The Strange Case of Dr. Jekyll and Mr. Hyde
and Weir of Hermiston
Edited by Emma Letley

√ BRAM STOKER: Dracula
Edited by A. N. Wilson

JONATHAN SWIFT: Gulliver's Travels
Edited by Paul Turner

A Tale of a Tub and Other Works
Edited by Angus Ross and David Woolley

WILLIAM MAKEPEACE THACKERAY: Barry Lyndon
Edited by Andrew Sanders

Vanity Fair
Edited by John Sutherland

LEO TOLSTOY: Anna Karenina
Translated by Louise and Aylmer Maude
Introduction by John Bayley

War and Peace
Translated by Louise and Aylmer Maude
Edited by Henry Gifford

ANTHONY TROLLOPE: The American Senator
Edited by John Halperin

The Belton Estate
Edited by John Halperin

Cousin Henry
Edited by Julian Thompson

The Eustace Diamonds
Edited by W. J. McCormack

The Kellys and the O'Kellys
Edited by W. J. McCormack
Introduction by William Trevor

Orley Farm
Edited by David Skilton

Rachel Ray
Edited by P. D. Edwards

The Warden
Edited by David Skilton

IVAN TURGENEV: First Love and Other Stories
Translated by Richard Freeborn

MARK TWAIN: Pudd'nhead Wilson and Other Tales
Edited by R. D. Gooder

GIORGIO VASARI: The Lives of the Artists
Translated and Edited by Julia Conaway Bondanella and Peter Bondanella

JULES VERNE: Journey to the Centre of the Earth
Translated and Edited by William Butcher

VIRGIL: The Aeneid
Translated by C. Day Lewis
Edited by Jasper Griffin

The Eclogues and The Georgics
Translated by C. Day Lewis
Edited by R. O. A. M. Lyne

HORACE WALPOLE : The Castle of Otranto
Edited by W. S. Lewis

IZAAK WALTON and CHARLES COTTON:
The Compleat Angler
Edited by John Buxton
Introduction by John Buchan

OSCAR WILDE: Complete Shorter Fiction
Edited by Isobel Murray

The Picture of Dorian Gray
Edited by Isobel Murray

MARY WOLLSTONECRAFT:
Mary *and* The Wrongs of Woman
Edited by Gary Kelly

VIRGINIA WOOLF: Mrs Dalloway
Edited by Claire Tomalin

Orlando
Edited by Rachel Bowlby

ÉMILE ZOLA:
The Attack on the Mill and Other Stories
Translated by Douglas Parmée

Nana
Translated and Edited by Douglas Parmée